Bill Clements

Texian to His Toenails

By Carolyn Barta

EAKIN PRESS  AUSTIN, TEXAS

FIRST EDITION

Copyright © 1996
By Carolyn Barta

Published in the United States of America
By Eakin Press
An Imprint of Sunbelt Media, Inc.
P.O. Drawer 90159 ★ Austin, TX 78709-0159

ISBN 1-57168-090-X

2   3   4   5   6   7   8   9

Library of Congress Cataloging-in-Publication Data

Barta, Carolyn.
   Bill Clements, Texian to his toenails / by Carolyn Barta. — 1st ed.
      p.   cm.
   Includes bibliographical references and index.
   ISBN 1-57168-090-X
      1. Clements, William P., 1917–   . 2. Governors — Texas — Biography. 3. Petro-
   leum industry and trade — Texas — History. 4. Texas — Politics and government —
   1951–   I. Title.
   F391.4.C58B37   1996
   976.4'063'092—dc20
   [B]   96-2707
   CIP

Dedicated to my mother
Aletha Nalls Jenkins Roberts
(1914–1995)
for her life of inspiration
and influence.

Gov. Clements with his family at the mansion at the time of his 1987 inauguration. Standing, from left, are George Seay, George Seay, Jr., Gov. Clements, Gill Clements, Bill Clements III. Seated are Pauline Seay, Nancy Seay, Rita Clements, Gill's daughters Peg and Cathy, and Pat Clements, Gill's wife.

Contents

Clements spends a typical day in his office as governor in 1989, working through dozens of bills. (AP Wirephoto)

Gov. Clements holds up a Bible a reporter left near him after comments he made regarding the NCAA investigation of the SMU football program. (AP Wirephoto)

Foreword

In the spring of 1981, when the state of Texas was planning to celebrate the 150th anniversary of its freedom as a self-governing nation, I was busy working on various projects on the Eastern Shore of Maryland, not too far from Washington. One afternoon I received a mysterious phone call from a deep-voiced man who asked if I was Michener the writer. When I said, "Yes," he said: "You and I had better get together for an exploration," and he invited me to drive over the Bay Bridge and into the horse country of northern Virginia. There I found my way to Wexford, the handsome former country estate of Jack and Jacqueline Kennedy. They were long gone, of course, but the present owners met us at the door of their establishment, greeted us warmly, and sat us down on a veranda overlooking the hunting hills that Jackie had loved.

The husband quickly introduced himself as Bill Clements, governor of Texas.

After tea we moved indoors to a book-lined study, where our wives deposited us while they went about other matters. The governor got right to the point: "Jim, a few years from now the state of Texas is going to celebrate its 150th anniversary of a free nation and I am so impressed by your writing that I wonder if I could persuade you to move to Texas, study our state, and write a powerful novel about things Texan?"

"That's a massive undertaking."

"Let's be frank. What would you demand? I mean, what would it cost us to get you into Texas? Whether you wrote the book or not. We'd like to have you as a fellow citizen."

"Do you mean how much money?"

"I suppose that's what I meant."

After a long, reflective pause: "First, am I available? Have I the time to spend on a big deal like this? The answer is yes. Second, is Texas an inviting subject? You bet it is. Its wars with Mexico. Its existence as a free nation. Its great occupations of oil wells and cowboys. It's a natural that any writer would grab at. But money? Now that's a ticklish problem, because I've never taken a nickel from anybody. I may need physical assistance like an office to work in and access to library shelves, but cash in hand? Never. I write the manuscript. I try to find it a home in the general marketplace. If lucky it gets published and I let it sink or swim according to its merit. So far I've had good luck doing it my way, so if you and I agree that Texas is my next project, you nor your friends owe me not one penny."

"What *would* we owe you?"

"An introduction to the powers that run the University. An office on campus where I can work. Access to the library shelves. And two graduate students working for their Ph.D.s in history."

"Do they help you do the writing?"

"I write every sentence of the manuscript. Always have. They find me books in the library. They bring the most recent scholarship to my attention. They read what I've written and show me where the clinkers are. And if they do good work, when they finish with me it seems they always land some very good job at some other university."

"They sound like requirements that can be met. No, let me say it another way. I give you my word that they will be met."

We shook hands, the deal was completed, and under those conditions I began my intensive study of things Texan. A major reason why I accepted so quickly was that the study in which we were holding our discussion was lined with bookshelves containing only row after row of books on Texas. Bill Clements, the rough and tumble oil millionaire and governor of Texas, was a history buff. I felt secure in his hands.

The consequences of my visit to Wexford are quickly told. I did put aside other projects. I did move to Texas. The University did provide me with work space and two superb young scholars, Robert Wooster, whose mother and father were both teachers and who had taught their son what scholarship was, and Jesus F. de la Teja, a scintillating refugee from Cuba. They were impeccable nominations and I am proud to say that Wooster is now a professor in the history department at Texas A&M University-Corpus Christi, and de la Teja is a professor of history at Southwest Texas State University in San Marcos. Each has published widely and faces a brilliant future.

As to my relationship with Governor Clements, he kept every promise he made that evening in Virginia. Indeed, he provided more than I could have expected. His private plane was always available to whisk me wherever I needed to go in Texas. He introduced me to his fellow oilmen and cattle barons, who told me the secrets of their professions. And he and his gracious wife instructed me in the social graces of Dallas society, but also in the nitty-gritty of Texas industrial life. Of the seven multimillionaire Texas tycoons I met, and from whom I learned so much, I watched six go into voluntary Chapter 11, the preliminary stage to normal bankruptcy, and I saw four of them crash into real bankruptcy.

I found Bill Clements to be a thoroughly honorable man, a worker for the good of his state, a man capable of running a worldwide oil-drilling business, but also apt to stumble into situations of maximum embarrassment, like when he was a commanding member of the board of governors of Southern Methodist University and their splendid football program won several years of probation which began by their dropping football altogether. (Under a severe revision of the program minus the governor, they have snapped back to be competitors again.)

I was close to Bill when, in 1982, he lost reelection as governor to my friend Mark White, a Democrat, but I also watched in 1986 when he defeated White to win back the Governor's Mansion. He was a good sport in losing, a magnanimous man in victory.

One final word about this remarkable man. As a loyal Democrat I say: "Damn the guy! By the strength of his personality he helped convert a Democratic Texas into a Republican one in which the conversion seems to grow stronger year by year." But we don't talk about that.

JAMES A. MICHENER
Texas Center for Writers
30 November 1995

Gov. and Mrs. Clements walk through the raised sabers of Texas A&M's Ross Volunteers, followed by Lt. Gov. and Mrs. Bill Hobby at the 1978 inauguration.

Introduction

WILLIAM P. CLEMENTS, JR., was nearing the end of his second four-year term as governor of Texas when he agreed to let journalism scholarship funds be raised at his expense at the annual Press Club of Dallas "Roast" in 1989. He was the prototypical honoree — a solo headliner from business or politics who would be put on a spit, figuratively, and roasted until it could be said in true Texas tradition, "Stick a fork in him; he's done."

After more than an hour of ribbing by individuals on stage and on videotape, it appeared that Bill Clements was "done." He had endured endless jokes about his inexplicable taste for loud plaid sport coats, his irascible personality, his outspokenness, his sense of self. Paul Eggers, a friend and former unsuccessful Republican gubernatorial candidate, praised Clements for being able to go through life "without having humility as one of [his] stumbling blocks." Oilman Boone Pickens recalled Clements wearing a sport coat so garish that an aide to the governor was prompted to say, "There's probably a '57 Chevy somewhere in East Austin without its seat covers." This was the governor, Pickens reminded, who had termed the Ixtoc I oil spill in the Gulf of Mexico "much ado about nothing" and advised waiting for a hurricane to blow it out to sea. Jim Wright, the former Democratic majority leader and speaker of the U.S. House, called the former oil drilling contractor a "crochety old curmudgeon . . .

xi

the one for whom crude oil got its name." Wright teased that folks who know Clements call him "Sweet Old Bill . . . sometimes we just use the initials." But Wright ended his remarks with a scent of praise: "Darn your hide, Bill Clements, you're one hell of a man."

The governor took it all in good humor, including, after the rolling of the show's credits on a giant video screen, the parting shot: "Watch for the book . . . *Bill Clements: A Legend in His Own Mind* . . . at a bookstore near you."[1]

Was Bill Clements a legend in his own mind, or would he prove to be a pivotal figure in Texas history? Future scholars may ponder that question, and this book should serve to open the inquiry. Certainly, he is a Texan with a colorful life story, a man who achieved personal success in both business and in politics. From college dropout and oilfield roughneck, he became founder of the world's largest offshore and overseas oil drilling contracting firm, SEDCO, Inc., and a self-made millionaire. Then he carved out a career in public life — serving as deputy secretary of defense before his partisan breakthrough that ended more than 100 years of Democratic domination of the Texas governorship. "I'm what Texas is all about. I'm living proof that this state has been a land of opportunities," Clements told a newspaper reporter.[2]

As a result of his narrow and generally unexpected win over Democrat John Hill in 1978, Clements will be recognized in history for becoming the first Republican governor since Reconstruction and for paving the way for other Republicans to gain victories in the Texas electoral process.

Political scientists Clifton McCleskey et al have noted in their text on Texas politics and government: "Indeed what was a historic event for all Texans . . . was euphoric for the state's Republicans, who believed a great barrier in the way of Texas's progress toward two-party competition had been crossed by the party's capture of the governorship."[3]

Clements was the right candidate to cross that barrier. "Not that we changed history, but somebody's got to be first. He was well suited for that role," said Tom Reed, Clements' political adviser in 1978.[4] The partisan picture in Texas already was changing when Clements appeared, a condition for which he was not responsible. Yet, Clements' election proved timely and central to continued partisan realignment in the state. For Republicans, he was an important transition figure in the thirty-year period from 1964 to 1994. In

1964, Texas Republicans had one U.S. senator, no members of Congress, and elected only one state legislator that year; in 1994, Texas Republicans held both U.S. Senate seats, elected a governor, and were near parity with Democrats in statewide offices. Clements, coming along in the middle of the period, could be called the fulcrum of the era's political seesaw in the state, proving not only that a Republican governor could be elected but that he could function in the traditionally Democratic environment that was Texas state government.

"By getting in there and making appointments and governing, it opened up doors for people to follow," said former President George Bush, who, with Sen. John Tower, helped blaze the Republican trail in Texas. "Winning the governorship was an important step in terms of making Republicanism respectable [in Texas]," Bush said. It also helped to dispel the notion that winning the Democratic primary was tantamount to election. "That's all changing," Bush said, "and I think Clements will get proper credit for his role in the change."[5]

Clements was well suited to the role he played because of his total life experience — as a roughneck, a risk-taking entrepreneur, a corporate manager, and a ticket-splitter in the Texas tradition. Those experiences gave him populist tendencies, a conservative philosophy, management skills, a distinctive (even paradoxical) personality, the power of personal wealth, and political acceptance.

Clements took with him to Austin the character traits he had developed over a lifetime, including his ability to project with certitude what he thought and to express those opinions in a blunt manner. "Now, some people get turned off by that," said former President Bush. "Sometimes it comes across as being intolerant of somebody else's views. Sometimes he takes a bite out of people's neck. Some mistake that for being unkind. But for those of us who worked closely with him, that was his strength . . . . When you come in as the first Republican governor since Reconstruction, you've got to break a little china; you've got to call 'em as you see 'em."[6]

Such comportment was not without consequence. Clements was defeated in his bid for election in 1982; however, he came back four years later to win a second term, becoming the first governor to serve as many as eight years. Clements believed he was born to succeed, but he was never afraid to fail. After being defeated in his second campaign in 1982 by Democrat Mark White, Clements shrugged and said, "Hell, I've drilled dry holes before."[7]

Clements also would serve as a metaphor for Texas in transition. From the boom and bust of the oil industry to the political makeover of a predominantly Democratic state into a two-party state, he personified the changes that occurred both economically and politically during his lifetime. He began his career as part of the old Texas — of Lyndon B. Johnson and the Democrats, of an economy based on oil, cattle and agriculture, and of a government steeped in rural interests. He evolved into a Republican, leading the state's transition into two-party politics, the modern era of high technology, a diversified economy, and corporate-style government management.

It's unlikely that Texas will ever again experience the petroleum heyday that allowed the creation and success of Clements' company. When he first went to the oilfields, Texas held the largest known oil reserves in the world and was the center of oil technology. By the spring of 1994, Texas oil production had dipped below 1.5 million barrels a day — a fifty-year low. When Clements created his company in 1947, oil and gas revenues accounted for 34 percent of the total taxes of the state. As late as the early 1980s, oil and gas severance taxes remained a significant portion of Texas' revenue picture; in 1982, they brought in 17.7 percent of the state's total tax revenue. When Clements left office in 1990, however, that figure was down to 8 percent. In the 1994–95 biennium, oil and gas production and regulation taxes were expected to produce only 6 percent of the state's total tax revenues.[8]

When Clements assumed office in 1979, Texas provided one-third of America's petroleum supplies, but the Middle East was in the process of becoming the new center of the world's oil universe.

As Clements was building his drilling company, the Texas oil empire was world renowned. Even OPEC, the Organization of Petroleum Exporting Countries, wanted to simulate, in a larger universe, the way in which the Texas Railroad Commission set oil production rates to manage the oil market and preserve the price in Texas.[9] The global nature of the Texas oil empire made Texans who were in the oil business cosmopolitan, but it didn't necessarily make them city slickers. Bill Clements was, in fact, very cosmopolitan, a man who understood the value of knowledge and the use of power, but never was he city slick.

McCleskey et al wrote:

The accession of William (Bill) Clements to the governorship after the November 1978 elections contradicts in several ways our perceived notions about the office and the persons who fill it. For one thing, Bill Clements does not look like a governor, and many times he does not behave in the way we have come to expect of governors. He is a craggy-featured man who would seem more at ease on the floor of a drilling rig than attending white-tie dinners. Many of his public utterances smack more of the oil patch from which he came than from the more circumspect language of professional politics. His speech is the salty, straightforward talk of everyday Texans.[10]

Former State Republican Chairman George Strake, who served as Clements' first secretary of state, always thought of Clements as "a roughneck who lives in a big house."[11] That's precisely the kind of person who would be successful in breaking the Democratic hold on the Governor's Mansion, setting the state on a course of political realignment that is explored in the political chapters of this book, and becoming the bridge between the old and the new Texas politics. The passage of time and subsequent elections have done much to resolve the unanswered question of 1978: whether Clements' initial victory was an aberration or the birth of a new era in Texas politics. Election results today show an increase in Republican state officeholders. But Clements also provided a new role model for the governor's office — that of a technocrat-manager, a conservative who was able to meld with the traditional good old boys, though never with the liberals.

Clements' public and private lives were not without controversy — from lawsuits to conflict of interest charges to divorce, but mostly from flareups created by his own outspokenness. The Ixtoc I blowout, creating the Gulf oil spill in Governor Clements' first term, was drilled for Mexico's PEMEX using a rig leased from SEDCO, Inc., the company he founded. While SEDCO had nothing to do with the operation and Clements had nothing to do with SEDCO at the time, public discussion of the potential environmental problems brought out his sometimes abrasive nature and provided political ammunition for his enemies. Clements' second term was marred by a football recruitment scandal at Southern Methodist University for which he absorbed blame as chairman of the SMU Board of Governors. He would later admit that his response to the situation was the wrong one.

Clements was a man who enjoyed and used power. Yet, his life is one largely marked by integrity, loyalty and energy, with few breaks in the character pattern. There is a remarkable continuity and texture to his life story. The continuing threads include a devotion to work, roots, family, the Boy Scouts, SMU, old friends, his native state and its colorful history, and a commitment to give back to the state and his community in public service and philanthropy part of the fruits of his labors as a successful businessman. True to his paradoxical nature, he would brag that he would win an election or that he knew how to drill a hole in the ground, but he never bragged about the money he gave to the Boy Scouts or any other charity.

Reverting to the term used for early-day Texans, Clements liked to say that he was "Texian to his toenails."[12] The term "Texian" generally was used for early colonists, when Texas was part of Mexico, and for leaders of the Texas Revolution. It suggests what Texas writer J. Frank Dobie called "out of the old rock." The Texians came to be regarded as elder statesmen and, after annexation, the term "Texan" replaced "Texian" in general usage.[13]

Clements' favorite historical figure is Sam Houston, the president of the Republic of Texas who was also a U.S. senator and governor of Texas. Clements found Houston an extraordinary individual: "He had the strength of his convictions, he was a man of character who was independent, he was very straightforward. He was a man of constancy and a singleness of purpose." Clements shared many of the characteristics he admired in Sam Houston; like Houston, he was an original.

Clements' love of Texas and its unique history produced some remarkable gubernatorial legacies, among them major restorations of the Governor's Mansion and the State Capitol. It was Clements who persuaded James A. Michener to write his epic *Texas*, to celebrate the state's sesquicentennial.

In writing this business and political biography, I have benefited from lengthy interviews with the subject, his colleagues in business and politics, as well as access to the personal papers and gubernatorial files in the William P. Clements, Jr., Collection at Texas A&M University. Governor Clements donated his papers to Texas A&M in 1991, along with a million-dollar endowment to support studies in public leadership. Dr. Charles R. Schultz, professor and Clements archivist at the Sterling C. Evans Library, Texas A&M, was especially helpful in offering assistance during my research at Texas A&M. I am appreciative of the many people who offered their time, insights, and recollections in interviews and their personal files to the author, especially Spencer Taylor, who provided his invaluable SEDCO files; Dillard Hammett for SEDCO files and photographs; Dave McNeely for his political files; and Tom Reed for his 1978 campaign files. I am also grateful to Si Dunn, editor of the work in progress, who polished the manuscript and kept the author moving forward, and to others who read parts of the work and made critical suggestions, particularly Patrick Barta, David J. Weber, and Paul LaRocque. Finally, my thanks to William P. Clements, Jr., for his cooperation in the project and for providing a life worth chronicling.

CAROLYN BARTA
15 January 1996

Bill and Rita on the porch at Clemgil ranch in Forney.

Part I

Businessman

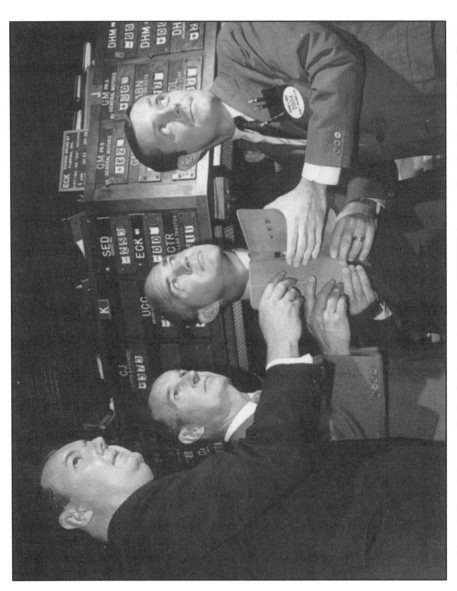

Clements, second from left, and Spencer Taylor, third from left, when SEDCO, Inc. went on the New York Stock Exchange in 1969.

Chapter 1

"Let's Do It"

The Decision to Run for Governor

ON THE BRISK FALL night of November 2, 1977, William P. Clements, Jr., drove to McFarlin Auditorium on the campus of Southern Methodist University in Dallas to moderate a panel on national energy policy. He was unaware that, before the evening was over, he would decide to run for governor of Texas, changing the course of his life and the face of Texas politics.

The nation's energy problems had long preyed on his mind, but particularly this year, the first year of President Jimmy Carter's administration. Bill Clements, a man who had made a fortune in the petroleum industry, had returned to Dallas in early 1977 after four years in the nerve center of the Pentagon as Richard Nixon's deputy secretary of defense. Clements was convinced that President Carter was surrounded by "inexperienced incompetents" in the energy area, including then Energy Secretary James Schlesinger.[1]

Not only did Clements have recent governmental experience at the Cabinet level, he also knew a thing or two about energy. He was frequently branded as a "Texas oilman," a term that caused him to bristle. "I'm not an oilman; I'm a drilling contractor," Clements would say. Finding oil, he believed, was not nearly as difficult as bringing it to the surface. One employed luck, the other expertise.

Clements had founded a little Texas-Mississippi-Louisiana oil drilling company with two rusty rigs in 1947. That venture thrived

3

and went on to become the international drilling company, SEDCO, Inc. His farflung company had drilled wells for almost every major oil company, from the Middle East to South America, from the Sahara Desert to the hostile waters of the North Sea, and it had pioneered the technology for semi-submersible offshore drilling rigs. Along the way, Bill Clements had become a wealthy man. Thirty years after founding his company on borrowed collateral, he returned to Dallas from Washington to resume his position as chairman of the board. On the night of the SMU conference, SEDCO had seventy-four offshore and land rigs performing work all over the world — property and equipment valued at $610.7 million. The company's earnings were $50.8 million on revenues of $355.5 million. But oil exploration and development was going through a difficult period, and this was much on his mind.

The picture for the oil industry had been far rosier at the beginning of 1973, when Clements relinquished his position as SEDCO's chief executive officer to accept President Nixon's appointment as general manager of the Pentagon. When Clements began his four-year stint in government service, those in the petroleum service industry, particularly offshore drillers, were enjoying an unprecedented worldwide demand for exploration services. The North Sea was booming. The future looked so bright that a classic case of speculative expansion occurred. The world's fleet of offshore rigs grew from 189 in 1973 to 335 in 1977. When the price of oil rose fourfold after the 1973 Arab oil embargo, many international concession agreements were judged to be too favorable to the oil companies. Properties were expropriated, taxes raised and agreements renegotiated, causing confusion and slowing the anticipated pace of exploration. The boom was over for nearly everyone whose business was related to international exploration.[2]

Not only was there anxiety in oil circles, but national security and consumer concerns were growing during the second wave oil crisis that occurred in the fall of 1977. Consumers feared gasoline rationing and the return of gas station lines. Instability in the Middle East produced continuing apprehension over adequate oil supplies and the need for greater domestic production.

Clements had recently ripped both Carter and Schlesinger in a newspaper interview, saying that President Carter couldn't have found a more "anti-business, anti-petroleum industry man" to bring into the administration than Schlesinger. Clements had claimed that neither Carter nor Schlesinger understood that the United States was firmly locked in a "petro culture."

"Right or wrong, our entire society is based upon petroleum and its products," he told a newspaper columnist. "Our lifestyle, our industry, our culture is built around energy. As we have grown, our energy requirements have grown. The availability of cheap petroleum has dictated our growth," he said. "But the day of abundance of cheap energy has passed. Now we must adjust, and it could be painful. Fundamentally, our government has not come to grips with the problem." Clements predicted in the interview that Carter's idea of conservation, without proper incentives to seek and discover new sources of energy, would eventually produce more unemployment, plus massive welfare needs.[3]

Interest was high in the program that Clements had agreed to moderate at SMU. More than 2,000 tickets had been distributed, and the audience overflow was diverted to the student center where the proceedings could be viewed on closed circuit TV. The panelists included Frank Ikard, president of the American Petroleum Institute; former Undersecretary of Commerce Edward O. Vetter; Robert Strauss, special ambassador for trade negotiations and former national Democratic Party chairman; and Harrison "Jack" Schmitt, a former astronaut who had become a Republican U.S. senator from New Mexico.

Schmitt, a geologist active in energy policy discussions before he went to Washington in 1976, was critical of the Carter administration's regulation and taxation of domestic energy sources. To halt the country's dependence on unstable foreign sources, he suggested looking for long-term alternatives to fossil fuels.[4]

Clements said President Carter was right about only one thing: the nation's energy crisis was the "moral equivalent of war." But he found the Carter administration wrong-headed in promoting policies of government intervention and controls rather than turning to the industry for its expertise in solving the crisis. "If you know anything about it [the oil industry]," Clements told the gathering at SMU, "they don't want you to have anything to do with it."[5]

After the program, Schmitt went with Bill and Rita Clements to their Highland Park home as their overnight house guest. The evening was still early, so Clements and his wife and Schmitt settled in the library for a nightcap, to rehash the program and talk politics. A member of the Republican National Committee from Texas when she and Clements had married in 1975, the former Rita Crocker Bass had been a GOP activist since the days when state Republicans complained that their numbers were so few they could hold their conventions in a phone booth. She remained vitally interested in politics, in Schmitt's election as a Republican from New Mexico, and in the future of Republicanism in Texas. Schmitt, who had made one of the Apollo moon trips, had won his Senate seat by defeating incumbent Sen. Joe Montoya, a seemingly entrenched New Mexico Democrat.

Schmitt had followed Texas politics and had wondered why no strong, well-financed Republican had come forward to win the governor's seat. He had noticed that most of the Texas Republican gubernatorial candidates over the past fifteen years had received 45 or 46 percent of the vote, but, because of a lack of adequate campaign financing or credibility, or both, all had been unable to take what seemed ripe for the plucking. The only Republican governor ever elected in the state was E. J. Davis, and he had been chosen during Reconstruction, when Texans who had supported the Confederacy could not vote.[6]

Rita and Bill Clements began to review the history of Texas Republican candidates and races. The only Republican who had ever won statewide election in the hundred-plus years since Reconstruction had been John Tower, a Wichita Falls government professor. Tower had won in a "fluke" special election in 1961 for the U.S. Senate seat vacated by Vice-President Lyndon Johnson. Afterward, he was able to build a following and retain his seat.

Texas, like the rest of the South, was home to what V. O. Key, an authority on Southern politics, called "a strange political schizophrenic, the Presidential Republican. He votes in Democratic primaries to have a voice in state and local matters, but when the Presidential election rolls around, he casts a ballot for the Republican presidential nominee. Locally, he is a Democrat; nationally, a Republican." While Republican presidential candidates didn't always win, they had been competitive (with the exception of the Lyndon Johnson-Barry Goldwater race in 1964) in Texas, starting with the elections of Dwight D. Eisenhower in the 1950s. Before Ike, the only Republican presidential nominee who had won in Texas was Herbert Hoover in 1928.[7] Ike's promise to return the tidelands to the state — oil — was part of the reason for his success, breaking the Democratic pattern and launching Texas on its "Presidential Republican" syndrome, which was interrupted only by the presence of a Southerner on the ticket in subsequent years.

Republicans had been much less competitive over the years in other elections in Texas. From 1877 to 1961, Texas Republicans were totally absent in the U.S. Senate, and had served a grand total of only fourteen terms in the U.S. House through 1962. Even after Texas' "Presidential Republicans" appeared willing to send a few Republicans to Washington, they remained uncomfortable with sending them to Austin. Republican successes at the local level after 1962 represented "but a small crack in an otherwise solid Democratic bulwark" and were nonexistent at the state executive level. Political scientists referred to Texas as a "one and two-thirds party state."[8]

As for Republican gubernatorial candidates, Jack Cox, a former state representative from Breckenridge and former Democrat, made the first "respectable" showing against Democrat John Connally in 1962. In the nightcap conversation with Schmitt, Clements later recalled, "We reviewed Cox versus Connally when Cox got 45 percent of the vote; Paul Eggers running against Preston Smith and getting 45.5 percent; and Eggers running again in 1970 against Smith and getting 46.6 percent of the vote. Then Hank Grover ran in '72 against [Dolph] Briscoe and got 47.5 percent of the vote."[9] The loss by Grover, a state senator from Houston, to Briscoe, a rancher from Uvalde, by less than 100,000 out of more than two million votes cast, was widely blamed on a shortage of funds and an underestimation by fellow Republicans and the press of his viability.

Rita's opinion was that Texas would never be a two-party state until it elected a Republican governor. Tower's election, while important, had failed to translate into significant gains for Republicans at the state and local level.

Schmitt and Bill and Rita Clements agreed in their conversation that the right candidate, a strong spokesman who was adequately funded and perhaps not too far removed from the Democratic traditions in the state, could win the race. But who would that candidate be? The word already was out in political circles that Texas Republican Party Chairman Ray Hutchison, a Dallas bond attorney who had served in the legislature, was lining up support for a race. Clements didn't believe Hutchison was the candidate who could break the Democratic hold. First of all, the traditional Republican money would be sucked up by Senator Tower's reelection bid, so Hutchison wouldn't have the necessary funding. Secondly, Hutchison was a big-city lawyer who didn't fit the mold for Texas governors.

Schmitt suggested that Clements himself might be the one who could make the breakthrough. Clements' presentation earlier in the evening at SMU had proved to Schmitt that the SEDCO CEO would be a strong spokesman on national issues that interested Texans — energy, defense and foreign policy — and he would be able to build on the already apparent dissatisfaction with the Democratic administration of President Carter in the state.

Clements dismissed the idea out-of-hand, but acknowledged that he had been approached by people for years to run for public office. The discussion continued until Bill and Rita retired to their upstairs bedroom. There, they continued to talk for another hour or so, and Clements grew increasingly receptive to the idea. "If Clements ever had any doubts about his abilities as a candidate or whether he had a chance to win, Mrs. Clements put them to rest," Ron Calhoun wrote in his *Dallas Times-Herald* column. When she finally declared, in the early morning hours, "Let's do it!" Clements replied, "Why not?"[10]

There was no overriding reason not to make the race. Despite problems in the oil industry worldwide, Clements had returned to Dallas from Washington to find his company well managed by a team headed by his son, B. Gill Clements, as president and chief operating officer. Bill Clements and his bride of just over two years had been on a round-the-world trip to survey SEDCO's extensive operations. Despite alarming market changes, Clements found no cracks had developed in the operations of SEDCO during his four-year hiatus. There were no special problems within the company that needed his personal and complete attention. While he had resumed his role as chief executive officer at SEDCO, he needed a new challenge. Rita was not only enthusiastic about the governor's race, she was well grounded in the Republican Party and possessed rare practical knowledge of Texas politics. In her, he had the perfect political partner. And it appeared he could make energy an issue focal point.

As far back as 1964, Clements had been approached about running for U.S. Senate. Peter O'Donnell, who was then Texas Republican chairman, had talked to Clements about running as the Republican candidate against U.S. Sen. Ralph Yarborough, a liberal Democrat who was an anathema to Texas' conservative business establishment. At the time, Clements, who was totally absorbed in his business, considered himself an independent. In 1968, when John Connally was governor, he tried to recruit Clements to run for governor as a Democrat.[11] According to one historian, O'Donnell also tried to draft Clements that same year to run as a Republican for governor.[12]

O'Donnell didn't know Clements when he first approached him to run in 1964 on the GOP ticket, but had heard about his financial success as a drilling contractor. Clements had recently completed the world's largest drilling contract — 1,000 wells in Argentina. When O'Donnell went to see him and made note of that fact, Clements responded that, yes, he had enjoyed some success. And, at age forty-six, he told O'Donnell, "I don't intend to just make money the rest of my life." He later would live up to that statement, but 1964 was not the year. The timing was not right; he couldn't abandon his business. But, he said, "I know a person I think would do it. His name is George Bush."[13]

Clements had been on a plane with Bush to the Middle East, where they were partners as drilling contractors for Shell Oil, working offshore Kuwait, and Bush indicated an interest in running for the Senate. O'Donnell previously had recruited Bush to be Harris County Republican chairman and was enthusiastic about the prospects of a Bush candidacy against Yarborough. Clements arranged a meeting in Houston of Bush, Clements, O'Donnell, and longtime Republican activist Albert Fay. Over lunch, Clements told Bush, "If you'll run, I'll raise the money."[14]

In time, Clements and O'Donnell became good friends. O'Donnell went back to the Clements trough in 1968, when Richard Nixon was seeking the Republican presidential nomination. The Republicans needed money for pre-convention work, and O'Donnell asked Clements to head up the Nixon fundraising effort in Dallas County. Clements was reluctant; he was for Nixon but was terribly busy with his business. "When do you have to have it?" he asked. "I'm only going to be in Dallas two days in the next six weeks." Then he looked at his appointments calendar, looked back at O'Donnell and said, "I can do it."[15]

Clements said later that Governor Connally, his Democratic friend, provided him with names of eighteen Texas "ticket-splitters" to tap for funds for Nixon. Connally wasn't active in that campaign until the final weeks, when he finally cranked up his own organization for Democrat Hubert Humphrey.[16] The presence of Alabama's governor, George Wallace, on the ballot that year caused a split that left Humphrey with a scant plurality in Texas over Nixon. Four years later, however, in the 1972 election, Nixon carried the state two-to-one over Democratic nominee George McGovern.[17]

A couple of days before the 1968 GOP convention started, Clements called O'Donnell in Miami Beach with the report: "I want you to know we've got the last of the money." Years later, O'Donnell said, "If he tells you, 'I can do it,' you can bank it. I can see his face right now when he looked at me and said, 'I can do it.'"[18]

The day after the late-night decision to run for governor was made in their bedroom at 4800 Preston Road, Bill and Rita Clements went to see O'Donnell; he was the first person they consulted. A Dallas investor, O'Donnell is credited with being one of the creators of the new Republican Party in Texas in the 1960s. He was Dallas County GOP chairman before becoming state chairman. He masterminded the "Draft Goldwater" movement nationally in 1964, helped engineer John Tower's reelection in 1966, and served on the Republican National Committee from 1969 to 1972.[19] Rita had begun her political involvement as a Dallas precinct chairman in the 1950s. She had worked in the trenches with O'Donnell — in campaigns, on the state Republican committee, as a delegate to state and national conventions, and she had followed him on the Republican National Committee in 1973. When it came to politics, Rita and Bill both had the utmost respect for O'Donnell.

"We're thinking about running. Do you think we can win?" Clements asked.

"Yes, I do. And if you run, I'll help you," O'Donnell responded.

O'Donnell had observed Clements as the leader of his own company and as deputy secretary of defense. He had already visualized what Clements would be like as governor. He believed Clements was a "born leader," organized, able to run a large organization and handle complex responsibilities.[20]

O'Donnell also knew that Clements had a wider appeal than most Republicans. Clements' grandfather had settled in Forney, where Clements owned and raised cattle on the Clemgil Farm. This was an important asset in a state grounded in rural values and ways. Clements had made his fortune in the state's most important natural resource, petroleum. He knew people in the oil business across the state. He had other networks to tap, including SMU and the Boy Scouts of America, institutions for which he had worked and which he had supported financially for years. He would appeal to the military because of the reputation he built as deputy secretary of defense. Bill Clements would never be mistaken for a "country club Republican," the elitist image that had stunted the Republican Party's growth in Texas and hurt George Bush in his unsuccessful statewide races for U.S. Senate in 1964 and 1970. While Clements had worked for Republican candidates, he had also supported Democrats. If properly used, O'Donnell knew these could be winning characteristics.

When the story surfaced that Clements intended to be a candidate, the Texas Federation of Republican Women (TFRW) was meeting in Brownsville. Hutchison, the expected nominee, was at the TFRW meeting to deliver a speech. Polly Sowell, state party vice-chairman, called Dallas. "Rita, what's going on?" she asked. Rita said that her hustand was going to run and, what's more, she said, he was going to win. "I must confess," Mrs. Sowell said later, "I told him he wouldn't win the Republican primary."[21]

Many questioned whether Clements had the right personality for politics. Former President George Bush, who was in the offshore drilling business before going to Congress in 1966, admitted later he was one of the doubters. "What I'd seen was this very domineering business ability — swashbuckling, strong — but not the warm and fuzzy side that sometimes you need in politics," Bush said. "When I first heard he was going to run, I was not sure he would adjust to it. Here was a guy making million-dollar decisions all the time, dealing in a tough environment in the offshore drilling business. It's extraordinarily tough. Difficult risk taking. Ups and downs. Victories and defeats. Calm weather and tropical storms. But he went after it [the election] with a vengeance and worked like the dickens."[22]

Exactly two weeks after the energy program at SMU and the conversation with Jack Schmitt, Bill Clements announced that he would be a candidate for the Republican nomination for governor — an act that would later earn him a place in Texas political history. Voters who had taken the first step toward the Republican Party in national elections, as "Presidential Republicans," would take the second step in state elections with Clements.

His decision to run may have been spontaneous, but it was not haphazard. Clements believed in trends and figures, and he calculated that Texas was ready to elect a Republican governor.

He also felt he was born to lead. His leadership talents had surfaced early, when he was a boy growing up in Dallas. Those growing-up years not only formed his character, but also provided personal relationships and human resources that would remain critically important to him throughout his business and political careers.

Chapter 2

Roots

Forney to Highland Park

IN 1871, WITH THE hostilities between the states still a bitter memory, America's westward expansion was under way. The Texas and Pacific Railroad was working its way west from Shreveport to El Paso. The railroad crew had reached the East Fork of the Trinity River, about twenty miles east of Dallas, when the winter of 1872 set in. Unable to proceed with building a bridge over the East Fork, hundreds of workers hunkered down in a tent city near the small community of Brooklyn, just inside the Kaufman County line. One of them was Oliver B. Clements, a muleskinner from Indiana who had hired out as a contractor for the railroad, using his teams of mules to clear right of way and prepare the roadbed.[1]

The rough-hewn Brooklyn of the early 1870s was a lively place, with more than one saloon to quench the thirst of railroad laborers and itinerant cowboys. But the community was also attracting a stable element. Permanent settlers found the area's blacklands fertile for farming and good grazing pasture for the fattening herds they drove to market in Shreveport. Land was selling for $1 an acre.[2] Drawn by the fertile land and friendly people, some of the workers decided to quit the railroad and put down roots in the community. Most were Irish immigrants, and they settled in a section that became known as Irish Ridge. "Ollie" B. Clements, who was Scotch-Irish, chose to stay and establish a livery stable.

13

He launched his new business at a pivotal time for Texas. In 1873 the final spike was driven in the East Texas section of the T&P Railroad. Now Dallas was connected to Shreveport and the southern states to the east. In November of that year, the tyranny and oppression that had been part of the Reconstruction tenure of Gov. Edmund J. Davis reached its end. Texans elected Richard B. Coke as governor. Davis refused to leave office and appealed to President Grant to send troops to the state. Grant twice declined to intercede and advised Davis to submit to the people's decision. The obstinate governor, however, armed ex-slaves and radicals and barricaded himself in his office, surrendering only when the Texas militia surrounded the Capitol. Governor Coke had to break down the door to get into his office. Davis would prove to be the state's last Republican governor for 105 years.[3]

Brooklyn grew with the railroad and, in 1874, its citizens decided their town was large enough for a post office but discovered there already was a Brooklyn post office in Shelby County. Their search for a new name settled on the construction superintendent who had brought the railroad, Col. John W. Forney, a former Union Army colonel and Philadelphia editor. Brooklyn became Forney, and by 1875, when the Forney post office was completed, the price of land in the area had soared from $1 to $15 to $20 an acre.[4]

In the 1870s and 1880s in Forney, a livery stable was big business. Everyone was transported by horses and wagons and buggies, and Ollie's livery stable covered a full block. The native prairie hay meadows had huge yields, which were baled and shipped out on the railroad. Ollie raised cotton, corn, and feed for his horses on a farm outside of town. By the mid-1880s, Forney had become the biggest hay market in the world, local residents would later boast in the hometown newspapers.

Ollie was also a horse and mule trader and sent boxcars loaded with horses and mules back to Indiana, where his father and brothers and sisters still lived. Ollie's family ancestry could be traced to Waynesboro, Virginia, the birthplace of John Clements in 1728.

John Clements, who was born on a farm outside of Waynesboro, died in North Carolina near the Cumberland Gap after being wounded in the last days of the American Revolution, fighting the British and Indians. He was buried in North Carolina. His wife's name was Elizabeth. They are well documented in Virginia and, according to family lore, John Clements' roots in Virginia go back to

Jamestown, where the first Clements was listed as one of the founders with his wife and children. There are, however, no records of the generation of John's mother and father.

John's son, Roger Clements (1762–1835), was married to Hannah Hathaway (1768–1846). Roger Clements was given a headright, a grant of land, in Kentucky for his service in the American Revolution. This land was located on the east side of the Kentucky River near Booneville, and he was one of the original settlers with Daniel Boone. Another area called Clements Bottom comes from his headright. Roger and three of his brothers were active in the American Revolution and fought in the last battle at Blue Lick, Kentucky, which occurred after the peace treaty was signed. One brother was killed in the battle; one was wounded and survived; and Roger was not hurt.

When the West began to open up, descendants of Roger Clements moved from Clements Bottom to Indiana. Ollie was born in Lebanon, Indiana, married, and was widowed. In Forney he met a young widow named Louise Corinne Hearin Norwood, who had come to Texas after the Civil War from Alabama. Ollie and Louise, who each had a daughter, married in 1880. They had one child, William Perry Clements, who was born in Forney on November 16, 1883.

Perry Clements grew up in town, in a one-story cottage. It had a porch that encircled the house, a cistern and well, and an outdoor privy. Ollie was a restless man, however, and when Perry was still a youngster, his father took off for greener pastures. He wound up in Arkansas, where he ran a lumber mill. After Ollie died in 1894 near Helena, Arkansas, Perry's mother became a schoolteacher in Forney.

In the summers, Perry worked on farms around Forney, baling hay and tending the farm animals for spending money. Perry loved the land and knew the area for miles around. Traveling salesmen, called drummers, would come into Forney on the railroad and hire a buggy to go to settlements in the area to sell their wares. Perry was happy to show the drummers the way to nearby communities such as Heath for fifty cents a day.[5]

All along the East Texas route, the railroad spawned prosperity. Communities flourished — Grand Saline, Wills Point, Terrell, all the way to Dallas. But Dallas flourished the most.

As Forney was becoming an agricultural center for hay and cotton, Dallas, in the adjoining county, was gaining a reputation as a major commercial and financial center. Dallas celebrated the arrival of its first train, the Houston & Texas Central Railway, in July 1872. The Texas & Pacific followed soon thereafter. By the late 1880s, Dallas had seven railroads and a population of 35,000. Opportunities appeared unlimited in Dallas, the distribution, manufacturing and retail center of the region. Early civic leader and lawyer Philip Lindsley wrote that by 1890, "people were now flying to Dallas like bees to a hive. They came on every train."[6]

Perry Clements was eighteen and a graduate of Forney High School when he decided, shortly after the turn of the century, to eschew farming and avail himself of the opportunities in nearby Dallas. The first job he found was with Fireman's Fund Insurance Co., selling insurance. Perry began socializing with other young people of similar station in Dallas, eventually meeting Miss Evelyn Cammack, a well-bred young lady with long, auburn hair, and blue-gray eyes, who had a job in a local office.

Willie Evelyn Cammack's ancestors also were Scotch-Irish, descendants of Warwick Cammack and his wife, Margaret Williams, the founders of the Cammack family in Virginia. Warwick Cammack was born in 1636 in Virginia and died in 1685. He owned considerable land in Virginia and lived near Front Royal on the Shenandoah River. His descendants subsequently moved to Kentucky, settling in Frankfort, where Christopher Cammack, his brother and sons established a furniture manufacturing shop on what was known as the Cammack Block which overlooked the Kentucky River. Christopher Cammack and his family are buried in the cemetery in Frankfort.

James Christopher Cammack, one of Christopher Cammack's sons, was sent to Natchitoches, Louisiana, at age eighteen to work with his uncle, Robert Burns Cammack, who had no children and owned plantations in Louisiana and Issaquena County, Mississippi. He raised cotton which he shipped from Cammack's Landing on the Mississippi River and on the Red River in Louisiana. James Christopher Cammack subsequently married Willie Ella Christmas, who was born in Issaquena County, Mississippi. James and Willie were the parents of Willie Evelyn Cammack.

An interesting root of the Cammack line is through Elizabeth Jones Poindexter, who was born in 1770 and was married to Christopher Cammack in Louisa County, Virginia. Elizabeth was a direct descendant of George Poindexter, born in 1627, Swan Farm, Isle of Jersey, who arrived in Virginia in 1657. George Poindexter established a plantation which subsequently was the location of Williamsburg, Virginia, and he was a senior warden of the Episcopal church built in Williamsburg in the 1670s. He also built a home in New Kent County, Virginia, in the 1680s, and it is now recognized as the oldest brick home in Virginia. Poindexter died in his Virginia home in 1690.

Willie Evelyn Cammack was nine years old when her father decided to move his family in 1891 from the Louisiana plantation to a place where his seven children could get a better education. After visiting several cities, he selected Dallas, then the largest city in Texas with a population of 38,000. It was there that Evelyn would meet Perry Clements. Remarkably, the Clements line and the Cammack line both settled in Virginia within 100 miles of each other, and then moved to Kentucky, again settling within 100 miles of each other. The family lines ultimately would be joined in Dallas.[7]

The fifth child of seven, Evelyn grew up in a large frame home at 3317 Colonial Street, near Ervay Street, south of downtown Dallas. It was an exciting time in Dallas. The magnificent Victorian Romanesque courthouse was under construction from 1890 to 1892 on John Neely Bryan's original courthouse square. There was an opera house, and 1893 saw the completion of Adolphus Busch's grandiose Oriental Hotel at Commerce and Akard (which would be the site of the Baker Hotel that Bill Clements would eventually purchase).[8]

Evelyn graduated in 1901 from the old Dallas High School on Bryan Street, in a class of twenty-one women and ten men. From 1901 to 1907, she watched the city undergo remarkable expansion. Dallas had some fifty factories — from meat packing to the manufacturing of hats to farm implements — the largest dry goods and clothing store in the Southwest, and the offices of twenty-seven railroad systems. By 1907, Dallas had a population of almost 100,000 and 450 businesses, along with churches, schools, hospitals, and beautiful homes.[9]

Evelyn's father died in 1907 and was buried in the Protestant or Greenwood Cemetery on Hall Street. Evelyn's mother lived until 1916; she also is buried in Greenwood Cemetery. Evelyn had several brothers and sisters who became active in Dallas business and community life. Two of her sisters were schoolteachers at the Cumberland Hill School, the Akard Street school built in 1881, which drew its pupils from the fine homes of families who lived on such fashionable thoroughfares as Ross, Thomas, McKinney and Maple avenues

north of downtown. It later became a melting pot of different nationalities.[10] And many years later, the early Dallas schoolhouse was
transformed into the corporate headquarters for the company
founded by Bill Clements. One of the Cammack sisters, Anna, married Charles Dealey, a brother of *Dallas Morning News* publisher
George B. Dealey. Sister Sadie married Charles Moore, who became
head of the Austin Road and Bridge Company. Evelyn's brother,
Robert B. Cammack, was a bookkeeper and cashier for the *Dallas
Morning News* for more than forty years. Dallas, with its confluence
of railroads, became the No. 1 distribution center in Texas for cotton buyers, and brother Chris Cammack worked at the Cotton Exchange Building.

At 5:30 on a warm June evening in 1912, Evelyn Cammack and
Perry Clements were married at the Cammack home on Colonial
Street. By then, Perry's interests had turned to oil.

The discovery of oil at Spindletop, around the salt domes near
Beaumont, on January 1, 1901, ushered Texas into the industrial age.
The Lucas discovery at Spindletop, the world's greatest gusher, produced a record 800,000 barrels of oil in its first nine days, literally
transforming the oil industry at the same time it launched Texas as
the industry's giant. By 1902, a year after the discovery at Spindletop, 130 wells were producing at Beaumont — more production
than in all the rest of the world.[11]

More Texas discoveries followed, and Perry Clements was
lured by discoveries in an oil-bearing formation geologists called the
Red River Uplift in the North Texas counties bordering on the Red
River. After the Gulf Coast fields, the next important area of discovery in Texas was the Red River Uplift. It included the Electra
field, discovered on the W. T. Waggoner Ranch in 1911 during the
drilling of artesian water wells, and the Burkburnett field, discovered in 1912, a dozen miles north of Wichita Falls and near the Red
River. Burkburnett was only a middling field for about five years,
until it hit its heyday in 1919 and became a boom town. Hundreds of
traders in oil stocks and leases invaded the area, and Wichita Falls —
fed by the Missouri-Kansas-Texas ("Katy") trains from Fort Worth
— became a headquarters for drilling, production, and supply companies.[12]

Perry Clements was following the activity in Electra and Burkburnett and saw opportunity in the fledgling North Texas oilfields.
Clements had an outgoing personality and was a natural-born sales-

man; he became a broker selling oil leases and participation in oil wells. He ran the Oil Exchange, listing new wells on a big board and selling interests in them.

Perry was also interested in a new residential development in Dallas — Highland Park. In the early days of Dallas, the main residential area was south of downtown, where Evelyn grew up. By the time Perry moved to town, East Dallas and Oak Cliff were developing as separate towns that would be annexed by Dallas. The North Dallas residential area was moving from Ross Avenue into Oak Lawn. As the automobile and electric streetcar provided easier access to the "suburbs," mansions were being built in Munger Place in East Dallas as well as the Cedar Springs area. But the development that interested Perry Clements was Highland Park, where the city's elite would be drawn to build their fine homes and mansions.

John Armstrong, the president of City National Bank and founder of Armstrong Packing Company, is credited with creating Highland Park. In 1906, using the money from the sale of his packing company to Swift & Company in Chicago, Armstrong bought 1,326 acres of land just outside of Dallas, which he and his family began developing as Highland Park in 1907. The land originally was owned by Dr. John Cole and his sons, granted to them by the Republic of Texas as colonists. After Armstrong purchased the land, he and his son-in-law, Hugh Prather, Sr., went to Los Angeles to engage the services of noted landscape architect Wilbur David Cook, who was designing Beverly Hills. Cook drew up the master plan for Highland Park.[13] When Armstrong died, his daughters inherited the property. One of Armstrong's daughters had married Edgar Flippen and the other married Hugh Prather. The two families became Flippen-Prather Realty Company, which marketed the lots in the original Highland Park addition. The Edgar Flippen home at 4800 Preston Road, a replica of Mount Vernon, was built in 1909 on 7.7 acres facing Exall Lake, as an example of the kind of fine homes that would be constructed in the addition.[14] It became the home of Bill and Rita Clements in 1977.

Perry Clements, in the early 1900s, enjoyed taking his bird dogs out to hunt quail on the Armstrong property. When development began, he knew he wanted to live in Highland Park. Perry and Evelyn Clements built their first house in 1912 on Harvard, near Hillcrest. They were living there when their first child, Betty, was born in 1913. That same year, the town of Highland Park was incorporated, and William Perry Clements, Sr., was listed as one of the incorporators.

After he achieved some financial success, Perry Clements built a larger home at Maplewood and Cambridge. It was there, in the house at 3633 Maplewood, that the second and last child was born to Perry and Evelyn Clements on April 13, 1917. His name was William Perry Clements, Jr.

"There is Highland Park and heaven," a Houston columnist has written, "although occasionally the locals get the two mixed up."[15] That appears to have been true for William P. Clements, Jr., who spent the first seventeen years of his life in this suburban Dallas enclave for the well-to-do. The Clements family was never as prosperous as most who lived there, but "Billy," as he was called growing up, was well-loved and enjoyed a normal childhood which became even idyllic in his memory.

Billy started kindergarten at Armstrong School, when his family lived on Maplewood. But Perry Clements' business career was marked by ups and downs. When his son was about seven years old, Perry Clements went broke for the first time; he was forced to sell the house on Maplewood to pay off his debts. The family moved to a small, two-bedroom, one-bath cottage at 3421 Normandy.

Somewhere along the way, the oil business had gone sour, and Perry sought other ways to make a living — working as a sales manager for the William Morris Buick Agency and selling advertising for the Walraven Book Cover Company until he eventually found his niche as a ranch manager and trading real estate. Business acumen would not prove to be the measure of Perry Clements. While he worked in several businesses, Perry always remained a farm boy from Forney at heart.

Highland Park, by the 1920s, was one of the most beautiful communities in the country. Lakeside Drive along Turtle Creek was laid out as the main thoroughfare, and 20 percent of the land was set aside for parks; there were tennis courts and croquet grounds and playgrounds for the children. The Dallas Country Club, the first country club in Texas, had moved to Highland Park. Alice Armstrong, the widow of the founder of Highland Park, donated the land for Armstrong School and 100 acres of land for the establishment of Southern Methodist University; Dallas Hall was built there in the middle of a prairie in 1915. One of Billy's favorite places to play was in the woods where Perkins School of Theology now stands.[16] The Clements' home was a block from Highland Park High School, and Billy was the high school football team's mascot as a youngster.

Clements credits his mother with having the greatest impact on his life. Friends and family members said she doted on her only son and, throughout his life, he adored her. She lived into her nineties and even when he lived in Washington and Austin, Clements tried to telephone her daily.

Clements said his mother ingrained in him the discipline of hard work. When he was a boy, she kept him busy doing chores. It was his responsibility to keep the chicken house clean. He had to look after the laying hens and the little chickens, and feed and water them. He made his spending money selling eggs in the neighborhood, and he had regular customers all the way over to the mansions on Beverly Drive.

One of his neighbors, a retired doctor, was an avid gardener who had fruit trees and raised vegetables. Billy also sold the doctor's fruit and vegetables (tomatoes, okra, and beans) from a basket on the back of his bicycle. The two split the profits, with the doctor carefully counting the money and doling out an equal share to Billy. This was Clements' introduction to business. He spent his profits on a BB gun.[17]

His mother was also his disciplinarian, a woman who brooked no nonsense — a characteristic that people would later attribute to Clements. Her primary interest was seeing that her mischievous young son behaved, which she insured through daily spankings and frequent raps on the knuckles with a spoon. Mrs. Clements was active in the Highland Park Methodist Church, where she organized the first young married women's Sunday school class. She made sure the Clements family was at church every Sunday, after which they often drove to Forney for a fried chicken dinner at the home of Perry's mother. "Nanny" was the only grandparent Bill Clements ever knew.

Close friends included members of the Francis family, who were pillars at Highland Park Methodist Church. Judge Francis was general counsel for the Magnolia Oil Company, and Mrs. Francis was Billy's Sunday school teacher. Judge Francis was the catcher and Perry Clements was the pitcher on the church baseball team. After games against other teams in the church league, the families would

gather for a picnic of fried chicken and potato salad. This constituted a big part of the family's social life. Billy often sat with the
Francis boys, Bill, Ed and Jim, at church. If they got out of line,
playing and not paying attention to the sermon, Judge Francis
would reach behind the pew and thump the offending boy on the
back of the neck, producing a throb that would be remembered.

For a special outing, Mrs. Clements and her son took the
streetcar downtown to buy his clothes at E. M. Kahn, across from
Sanger Bros. department store on Lamar Street, and then went to a
picture show at the Palace or the Majestic Theater on Elm Street.
Family members said Bill's mother was largely a homebody, who
had a strong sense of family and who loved to cook and sew and do
handiwork. She also had good taste, both in clothes and furnishings.
As one relative said, she loved "pretty things," and her son likely
acquired his taste for antiques and fine furnishings from his mother.

Bill's dad was more gregarious and known generally as a nice
man who liked to tell jokes and stories and was fun to be around. He
loved to hunt and fish and was one of the original members of the
Koon Kreek Klub, which was then a gentleman's fishing and hunting club near Athens. Perry Clements kept at least two bird dogs,
and another one of Bill's chores was to feed and water and bathe the
English setters. Perry was a fine field shot with a shotgun and taught
his son to hunt as a youngster. Bill got his first shotgun when he was
six years old (a 20-gauge L.C. Smith). His father often took him on
early morning trips with his adult friends to hunt quail and dove and
ducks. Perry kept live decoy ducks behind their house, and had
crates to carry them to hunting sites. Bill and his dad liked to work
the dogs on the Caruth homestead property. Hunting together, a
typically Texan activity, formed the basis of the relationship between father and son.

While at Armstrong School, Bill developed a lifelong interest in
the study of history. His favorite teacher was Miss Willie Shook, a
strict disciplinarian who taught Texas history and American history
to the sixth and seventh grades. Clements' love of Texas history
would manifest itself later in life when he collected some 8,000 volumes, largely books of Texana, in his personal library.

His mother also loved to read, a passion she passed along to her
son, giving him books as gifts when he was a child. She also owned a
complete set of RCA "Red Seal" recordings of opera and classical

music, but apparently failed to instill in Clements her taste for classical and operatic music.[18]

Family members say Clements derived the best of both parents. From his mother, he developed a sense of honor, strong work ethic, perseverance, reliability, appreciation for beauty, and love of history. From his father, he derived salesmanship, an outgoing and engaging personality, a feel for people, a love of land, a penchant for risk-taking, and a profound affection for hunting and fishing.

In 1929, Mr. Clements added an upstairs story of two bedrooms and a bath for Billy and his sister. Billy was twelve that year and an important stage of his life had begun. On April 13, 1929, his twelfth birthday, he joined the Boy Scouts.

For the next two and half years, Billy was totally immersed in scouting, which in those days provided the main extracurricular activity for boys. Troop 32 was housed in World War I barracks behind the Highland Park Methodist Church; the scoutmasters came from the men's Sunday school class. Clements later was a member of Troop 34 at the Episcopal Church of the Incarnation. Scouting gave Clements a sense of purpose as a youngster; it taught him the value of setting goals and experiencing the satisfaction of achieving goals.

In an interview sixty years later, he recalled setting a goal of reaching each rank in the minimum time allowed. "From the time you start out as a tenderfoot, if you do everything exactly on time, you can become an Eagle Scout in fourteen months. So, I did it."[19] He was awarded his Eagle in August 1930, at Camp Wisdom. At age thirteen, he made his first speech when he was selected to be the speaker representing the Eagle Scouts of Circle 10 Council at a dinner honoring the council's new Scout executive.[20]

Clements credited scouting with teaching him "management by objective," which became an integral part of his work ethic as an adult. "I had clearcut objectives I wanted to achieve, and I had a roadmap how to achieve them. It was my first experience with a disciplined approach to achieve an objective," he said. Scouting provided Clements with his first real experience with success (he also became senior patrol leader and a junior counselor at Camp Wisdom), and he wouldn't forget the feeling.

Also important to Clements were his years at Highland Park High School, where he established friendships and relationships that would last a lifetime, and where he exhibited early leadership traits. As one high school associate who later worked for Clements

recalled, he was "all-everything" in high school. "Everything he undertook, he succeeded in; in everything he got into, he rose to the
top," said Tom Rhodes.[21]

While Clements didn't identify it as such at the time, he was a
natural politician. He was elected president of his class for three
years — sophomore, junior, and senior years — and he was named
"most popular boy" his senior year. He was also editor of the 1934
yearbook, the *Highlander*, and was president of his high school fraternity.[22]

But his real passion was football. When Clements said he was
going out for football and wanted to play guard, Highland Park's
coach, Charlie Trigg, said: "You're kind of small for that." Clements
replied, "I'm pretty tough, too. I can handle that."[23] Although he
was only five feet eight inches tall and weighed 170 pounds,
Clements had drive and determination. He relished the fight and,
when the other boys had the jitters before the game, he was relaxed
and calm in the locker room. "We'd go in there and be nervous as
hell, and Clements would lie down on a table and go to sleep," recalled Rhodes, who also played on the football team.[24]

The Highland Park Scotties played schools from towns such as
Breckenridge, Royse City, Denison, Denton, Gainesville, McKinney, Sherman, Wichita Falls, Corsicana, and Greenville. Clements
got good coverage in the local newspapers.

Dallas newspaper columnist Bill McClanahan published a letter
from former Highland Park football player Johnny Blaine regarding
Clements' gridiron talents, which read: "He is stocky, fast and a
hard charger. He has not only been the main factor in Highland
Park's line, but on the whole team. He has never missed a quarter of
play to date. . . . Highland Park's greatest asset this season has been
its end runs, and Bill, with his great blocking, has been a factor in its
success, as he has been getting his man out of the play on every end
run. Among other qualifications, he is a born leader, a sure tackler, a
hard charger, plenty big and has plenty of fight."

Clements' football skills were acclaimed in the 1934 *Highlander*
report on the 19-0 win over Sherman; it called attention to the "inspired line play of Bill Clements" and blocks so vicious that "he left
some of their men in a near-crippled condition."[25]

Clements was quick, competitive, and he understood the game.
Trigg recognized his ability to read keys and assigned him to call
defensive signals. Clements also had an intense desire to win. The

team advanced farther than any previous Highland Park team, winning the district championship. And, in 1933, Clements became the first player from Highland Park ever named to the all-state football team.

Coach Trigg was an important factor in Clements' life in those years. In the summers, Trigg worked at Camp Stewart, a boys' camp at Hunt, Texas, and he took Clements as a junior counselor. Clements thought a lot of Trigg; he sought his advice for years after leaving Highland Park High School and kept up with Trigg even after he quit coaching and moved to West Texas.

Clements never made better than average grades while in high school. Football was a top priority, and he was involved in other high school activities. In his junior year, for example, he played the part of a "gentleman" in the school's Spring Follies of 1933 and Negro Minstrel.[26] It was true type-casting.

Clements' classmates recall there being two crowds at Highland Park High: the "hell-raisers" and the "straight arrows." The hell-raisers would steal liquor from their parents' liquor cabinets or go to a bootlegger in the Elm Thicket, a black neighborhood where they could buy nickel home-brew. While Clements was described by his high school friends as fun-loving, he was regarded as one of the "straight arrows." But he got along with those who ran in both crowds — an ability which perhaps presaged later political success.[27]

On Saturday nights, the teenagers went to the Dallas Country Club to dance to the music of big bands. Those whose parents weren't members were charged a dollar to get in by the guard at the club gate. The Clements family didn't belong to the country club, and Bill was one who didn't have the dollar to get in, so friends would sneak him in, either on the car floor or in the trunk. In the early 1930s during the Depression, even in Highland Park, some of the boys didn't have a nickel for a Coke date at Berry's Pharmacy, much less a dollar to get into the country club.[28]

Bill's best friend was Lindsley Waters. Lindsley belonged to a different Scout troop and they met at Camp Wisdom. Waters, called Buster or Bus, was business manager of the high school yearbook and a tackle on the football team. His family owned the Tennessee Dairy, which he managed as an adult. Other friends included Henry Beck, quarterback of the football team and vice-president of the senior class; and Philip Lindsley, who was president of a rival high school fraternity and associate editor of the school newspaper along with Jerry Cunningham. Jack Munger, another friend, lived in the old Flippen estate on Preston Road. After Saturday night dances at the country club, Clements and his friends would sometimes go to the Mungers' house to swim in their pool.

Bill established close friendships with some of the Highland Park girls, many of whom married classmates. His "best girl" was Mary Ann Thomasson (Todd), but he also went out with Mary Jane Chambers (Honea), who was assistant editor of the yearbook. When Clements was governor in 1988, he sent Mary Ann Thomasson Todd a letter with a photograph of her and Mary Jane Chambers (Honea) that was taken in 1933 in the backyard of his house on Normandy. They were decked out in their English riding habits for an outing at a public stable. Clements wrote in the letter: "You were a good looking girl as I remember and we had a lot of good times together. I have nothing but nostalgic and fond memories of our relationship, and I thought you would enjoy the photograph. I feel sure that your children and grandchildren would like to see how attractive you were as a high school girl in 1933. You were pretty special — I thought so then and I still do." The photo came from film he had discovered in his mother's mementos. He said in the letter that the two girls were probably at his house to visit his mother. Mary Ann said later, "He knew very well why we were over there — both of us — to see him." [29]

Betty Skillern (Baird), named the class' most popular girl in the 1934 yearbook, was Clements' date on graduation night. Her father owned Skillern's drug stores. She remembers Bill as being a gentleman but also spunky. He was driving his family car that night, with another couple in the back seat. "He was going too fast, and the police got after him," she recalled. "He said, 'I can outrun those guys.' We did, and we went into Elm Thicket and he turned off all the lights, and he said, 'Everybody crouch down.' The police came into Elm Thicket and were shining lights all around, and they never did see us." [30]

Bill got his inauguration with the "fast crowd" the day he went with a carload of friends to have his picture taken at *The Dallas Morning News* for being an all-state football selection. Tom Rose was driving the car, which contained his girlfriend and future wife, Helen Grayson, two other girls, and Clements. Rose suggested the event was cause for celebration. He knew where there was a bootlegger who sold homemade gin in half-pint bottles near the Trinity

River and the 16th green at Brook Hollow Golf Club. Bootleg gin was a whole new experience for Bill Clements; he didn't tolerate it well. When he got sick, rather than taking him home, his friends dropped him at the Thomasson house.[31] Clements spent a lot of time at the Thomassons' because of Mary Ann and her brother, William, who was also a good friend. They lived in a big house on Arcady, one block off Preston Road. Their father, Dr. A. R. Thomasson, was chief surgeon at Samuell Clinic and one of many Dallas professionals who had invested in the East Texas oilfield.

The development of the East Texas oilfield, discovered by C. M. "Dad" Joiner in 1930 with the eruption of the Daisy Bradford No. 3, coincided with Clements' high school years and made an impression on him. H. L. Hunt bought Dad Joiner's East Texas leases for $1.25 million and became a rich man. But he wasn't the only one to get rich from what proved to be, for twenty years, the world's largest oilfield — forty-two miles long and four to eight miles wide, covering 200 square miles.[32] Clements knew that there was East Texas oil money in Highland Park — local business and professional people who bought leases or shares and made fortunes.

W. L. Todd, Jr., and his brother, Harry Todd, were two of Bill's good friends. Their father, W. L. Todd, Sr., was head of Sims Oil Company and was involved in exploration and development of the East Texas field. It did not go unnoticed by Bill that the Todds were wealthy and that the East Texas oilfield was the source of their well-being. "They had a very nice home, lots of money to spend, two Packard automobiles, and I was impressed," Clements recalled.

Wanting to achieve and to make money became priorities for Clements while he was in high school. "Everybody aspired to be millionaires in those days," Philip Lindsley recalled. Yet, there was no stigma attached to going broke, because while East Texas oil was bringing overnight wealth to some, others were losing their fortunes to the Depression. Schoolmate Tom Rose believed Bill became a "driver" because his family wasn't as prosperous as those of many of his friends. A trait that he had in high school that would remain throughout his life, Rose said, was "drive, drive, drive." Philip Lindsley believed Clements was just "hatched out" that way. "He was that way from a little bitty kid; he had drive in the second grade," he said. Trigg remembered Clements as a young man "wanting to get ahead, to make money — because his family didn't have any. His parents were crazy about their children, they wanted them to have the best. But they were just ordinary, hard-working people."[33]

Clements was sentimental about leaving Highland Park and the friends he had gone to school with, many from the first grade. He felt a strong sense of loyalty to his high school friends, which became apparent later in life. But he was also excited about beginning the next stage of his life. He had offers to play football at several colleges. He thought he wanted to go to the U.S. Naval Academy at Annapolis, Maryland. But Ben Wiseman, the principal at Highland Park, and some of the Annapolis alumni suggested that Bill, who was barely seventeen, needed to mature before tackling the Naval Academy. They suggested he go to Kemper Military School for a year or two. That sounded like a good idea. Kemper was a popular spot for Highland Park boys, and Philip Lindsley was going to Kemper. He and Philip agreed to be roommates and secured their room reservation. At that point, Clements' life took an unexpected turn.

In April 1934, Perry Clements informed his son he had been wiped out by the Depression; he had exhausted his sources of making money and was flat broke. Not only would Bill not be going to college, but he was going to have to go to work and help support the family. It was a rude awakening for Bill, who had lived his life in the comfortable cocoon of Highland Park. He had no idea of the dire economic circumstances of his family. His sister was going to the College of Industrial Arts (C.I.A.) in Denton (which became Texas Woman's University). He never doubted that he would go to college. He was interested in engineering and had taken all the advanced math and science courses he could take at Highland Park High School. The idea of not going to college had never occurred to him.

Bill told his dad he thought he knew where he could get a job — from R. B. Whitehead, who was vice-president in charge of exploration for Atlantic Oil and Refining Company. Whitehead had a son at Highland Park, was president of the Highland Park Dads Club, and went to school football games. He had been a football player at the University of Chicago, and he'd been trying to recruit Bill to go to his alma mater, which at that time had an outstanding gridiron program. Bill paid a visit to Mr. Whitehead, who agreed to get him a job in the oilfields. It was a kindness Clements never forgot. When he became successful in business, he returned the favor many times for dozens of young people in need of a first opportunity — either to go to college or to get a job.

On June 1, 1934, William P. Clements, Jr., was one of 165 candidates for graduation in the Highland Park senior class. He listened as his pastor, Dr. Umphrey Lee, gave the commencement address at exercises held in McFarlin Auditorium on the SMU campus.[34] Afterward, with his high school diploma safely tucked away, Bill Clements headed for the South Texas oilfields and the beginning of the rest of his life.

Chapter 3

"Can't Do, Can't Stay"

Early Life in the Oilfields

Two DAYS AFTER HIS high school graduation, Bill Clements got off the bus in Sinton, Texas, just north of Corpus Christi in the coastal flatlands, where he was to go to work on a geophysical crew. Geophysics had been introduced in the Gulf Coast in 1922; by 1934, when Clements arrived in the South Texas oilfields, the torsion balance and seismograph were widely used to help determine locations for drilling.[1]

It was Bill's first taste of life in the Texas oilfields, and his first experience with supporting not just himself but also his family. On a salary of $150 a month, he could send home $100 a month and live on $50. Most of the oilfield workers rented rooms in private homes and had their meals in a local cafe. Clements rented a room from a family, at a cost of $10 a month, and he boarded at a small cafe in town for $1 a day or $30 a month. For that amount, he got breakfast and supper at the cafe and a sack lunch to take to the field. It was a different life, outside of the protected society of Highland Park, during difficult economic times, but Clements took to it.

The center of interest in the summer was the Sinton baseball team, which played teams from nearby towns such as Robstown and Corpus Christi and Gregory. Clements enjoyed baseball and had been recruited to play for his high school team, but he had chosen to concentrate on football. In Sinton, he played third base on the local

30

ball team. Sinton had a lighted field, and the team played at night, so Bill could play after work. Before long, he knew everybody in town and they knew him. He met the sons and daughters of South Texas ranchers and the local townspeople and was treated like a native son.

During the day, Clements worked on the geophysical crew. He learned to operate the torsion balance and seismograph equipment, which reduced the guesswork in determining favorable geophysical structures for finding oil. The geophysical lines would run for miles across the big South Texas ranches where the crew worked. Bill learned to survey, to read the instruments, and plot the data. The crew traveled all over South Texas, moving from Sinton to Victoria to McAllen.[2] Bill wasn't actually working on rigs, but he was around them. He knew then what he wanted to do: He wanted to get on one of those drilling rigs.

After he had been in the field a year, his dad got a job — as ranch manager for Eugene B. Smith's ranch east of Dallas, on the East Fork of the Trinity River. It would take his dad until the early 1940s to pay off his debts, but Bill would be able to go to college.

When Bill returned from the oilfields, he found that Coach Trigg had become Coach Matty Bell's assistant at Southern Methodist. Trigg wanted Clements to play for the Mustangs. Primarily because of Trigg, Clements decided to go to SMU, enroll in the engineering program, and play football. But shortly before he was scheduled to enroll for the fall semester, Bill had an attack of appendicitis and had to have his appendix removed. That ruled out football for the fall, but he was able to participate in spring training and made the traveling squad in the spring. There was only one hitch — Bill Clements and Matty Bell, the head coach, didn't hit it off. Clements didn't care for Matty Bell, and it appeared the feeling was mutual. Meantime, there was a coach at the University of Texas who had been a star player at Notre Dame under Knute Rockne. The Longhorns were using a Notre Dame-style system, similar to the one Clements had played under at Highland Park. He and Coach Trigg talked it over, and Clements decided that since he hadn't played yet for SMU and he still had his eligibility, he would transfer to the University of Texas. Trigg helped to arrange it.[3]

But Bill's year at SMU had not been wasted. He took as many course hours as he could, 20 to 22 hours each semester, loading up on math and science courses, and he went to summer school, accumulating almost enough hours to be classified as a junior.[4] He pledged a fraternity, Kappa Alpha, and renewed old Highland Park acquaintances. Among his fraternity brothers at SMU were his high school friends Lindsley Waters, Harry Todd, Robert Ritchie, and Randolph McCall. Bill was full of devilment around the fraternity house, which had repercussions for his fellow pledge brothers. As McCall told it: "Bill was anything but docile. We'd have certain things we were supposed to do. When anybody did something out of line, everybody had to line up and bend over to get paddled. Clements had a lead butt. Nothing hurt him. It didn't hurt him at all, and it didn't bother him that everybody else hurt."[5]

In the fall of 1936, Bill Clements transferred to the University of Texas. He lived in the KA house, and he worked for the athletic department at the football stadium, cutting weeds and doing other odd jobs to pay for his football scholarship. His fraternity socialized with the top sororities on campus, and in the course of these activities, Bill Clements met an attractive coed from Terrell named Pauline Allen Gill. Pauline had gone to the Hockaday School in Dallas, and then to the University of Texas, where she pledged Pi Beta Phi. Pauline ran in the same social strata as many of the Highland Park young people, and she and Bill had some mutual acquaintances. They began dating.[6]

Bill was attracted to Pauline, and he also appreciated her family background. Pauline came from an old and prestigious banking family in Terrell. Her father, Ben Gill, Jr., was vice-president of the American National Bank in Terrell when she and Bill were dating. Through her mother, Pauline was a descendant of Matthew Cartwright, Sr., of San Augustine, who was reputed to be the largest landowner in Texas in the 1850s. Cartwright had owned land all over the state, including in Kaufman County, where his family developed farming and ranching interests.[7] Pauline's mother died when she was eight, and she was raised by her father, and her maternal grandparents, Walter Payne Allen and America Cartwright Allen, in the Allens' home. Allen was president and chief executive officer of the bank, and Ben Gill, Jr., later became bank president. Pauline's paternal grandparents, banker Ben Gill, Sr. (who had spent thirteen years as a vice-president of the Seaboard National Bank in New York City and later was state insurance commissioner in Texas) and Mrs. Gill, lived just down the street.[8]

While Bill Clements found his love interest at the University of Texas, his football career was not flourishing. The coach had decided that, even though Clements then weighed 198 pounds, he ought to play in the backfield instead of guard. By the end of the year, Clements had lost interest in football and was tired of college life. Graduate engineers were making $110 a month in entry-level jobs after a five-year scholastic program, and Clements knew that he could go back to the oilfields and immediately get a job making $180 a month. So he left Austin and the University of Texas and went to San Antonio, where he was hired as a roughneck by Trinity Drilling Company.

"Oil was a fascinating business; it represented a challenge — a romance, if you will — that other businesses just didn't have for young people in their teens and early twenties at that time," Clements later told a magazine writer. "It was a frontier and it was glamorous . . . and this was a way to get rich quickly — at least in many people's minds."[9]

Getting a job as a roughneck in those days wasn't that difficult. The work, however, was. According to oil industry historians, it required strength, stamina, and coordination between mind and muscle in greater measure than most other oilfield jobs. And that suited Clements. He would later say that going to the oilfields instead of finishing college was "like getting a Ph.D. in life."[10]

Clements was sent to Edna, a little town outside Victoria in South Texas, into an area where more than 100 rigs were working. He found a room to rent and a cafe to feed him and began his life as a roughneck, working on rigs and making $180 a month. The rigs ran twenty-four hours a day, seven days a week. Most rigs had three crews; each worked an eight-hour shift, called a "tour" but pronounced "tower."[11] According to oilfield legend, the mispronunciation resulted from an uneducated oldtime driller who saw the word on a drilling report for the first time, and not knowing how to pronounce it, reasoned that it was spelled like "sour" and ought to be pronounced the same way.[12] There was a daylight tour from 8:00 A.M. to 4:00 P.M., an evening tour from 4:00 P.M. to midnight, and the morning tour or graveyard shift from midnight to 8:00 A.M. There were five-man crews, a driller and four assistants, and if one man didn't show up, somebody else got to work a double shift.

Bill worked for a driller named Z. A. "Boliver" Sloan. The No. 1 hand on the crew was Bruce Shanklin. They were drilling wells on the Keeran Ranch outside of Edna that were about 8,000 feet deep, using diesel rigs. Sloan and Shanklin taught Clements how to operate a drilling rig — how to work on the floor and work up in the derrick. One roughneck worked the lead tongs, one worked the spinning chain, one was up in the derrick. One worked on the engines if it was a power rig, or looked after the boilers if it was a steam rig, and did all the cat head work, while tripping the pipe in and out of the hole. It was skilled work, whether it was racking the pipe and keeping the machinery going, throwing the chain and tripping the pipe in and out of the hole, or working in the derrick ninety feet off of the floor racking the thribles (a stand of three joints of pipe) and looking after the mud system.

The crew Clements worked on would drill for a while at one location and then the rig would move and spud in somewhere else, and the crew would find another boardinghouse situation. In that manner, Clements moved around southwest Texas for about eighteen months.

The tool pusher generally supervised two or three rigs. He answered to the contractor or to the drilling superintendent over that geographical area. The tool pushers were looked upon as resourceful, tough, practical, skillful men — the men who made the oilfields go. Bill Clements developed an immediate respect for his tool pusher, a man named Pat Patterson. Behind his back, the hands called him "Screamin' Pat" because he was forever screaming at the hands to do something or other. He had the power to hire or fire a hand — in a minute.

Years later, Clements liked to tell the story of his encounter with "Screamin' Pat." The crew was replacing the liners on the rig's Abercrombie pump. The liners were made of metal and weighed 200 to 250 pounds, and they needed to be taken to a machine shop in town for maintenance. The crew had gotten the liners out and on the ground when Patterson told Clements matter-of-factly to put a liner in the back of his truck, which was about fifty yards away. Clements looked at the heavy piece of equipment and told the tool pusher, "I can't pick up that liner." Screamin' Pat, as the story goes, looked at Clements for a minute, and then very slowly and quietly, he said, "Can't *dooooooooo,* can't *staaaaaay."* Somehow, Clements picked up the liner, got it on his shoulders, and hauled it over to the truck. Screamin' Pat had made it real simple when he said, "Can't do, can't stay."

Clements definitely wanted to stay. He loved everything about being on an oil rig — the men, the machinery, the work. He loved the technology of drilling the wells and the various complications and problems that had to be solved — the fishing problems that arose when there was trouble down the hole. "There really wasn't anything about it I didn't like, even how dirty and how cold and how wet you would get," he said.

"A lot of times the next crew, regardless of which tour I was working, would come out short a hand. One of those crew members had left and just said goodbye and thank-you-very-much and I'm not going out anymore, or he was sick, or he went off drunk somewhere, so instead of the driller coming out with four hands he'd come out with three. And sure enough it's time to pull the bit, which means make a trip. So you have to pull all that pipe out of the hole, and you have seven or eight thousand feet of pipe in the hole and you have to put on a new bit and go back into the hole, and you're short a hand. And so he'd come out and say, 'I'm short a hand, who wants to make a double?' And every time he'd say that, I'd say, 'Me.' So instead of working eight hours a day, I'd work sixteen."

Although most of the work was routine, there was enough excitement to it for Clements. There were dangerous situations when the well would threaten to blow out, or there would be a coring situation in a pay zone when the crew would be anxious to see whether the well was going to be a success or whether it was going to be a dry hole.

Clements enjoyed his association with the men in the fields who had been raised in small towns and had gone to country schools. Most were high school graduates but came from a background totally different from his. Some had married their high school sweethearts, and the girls were living the itinerant life of an oilfield worker's wife. When the rig was shut down between moves, Bill would sometimes go with Bruce Shanklin or Boliver Sloan to their family home places. Sloan was from a farm in Smiley in South Texas; Shanklin's family lived in an oilfield camp in Luling, where his father worked on the pipeline.

Most of the oilfield hands were products of changing times in the state — economically displaced agricultural or small-town workers who gravitated to the expanding petroleum industry as their traditional source of livelihood was drying up. Often called "oilfield trash," according to oilfield historian Bobby Weaver, they developed a reputation for hard work, hard play, and good pay. As hard-working farm and ranch boys, they were used to going to town to celebrate on Saturday night. "When they left the farm for the oil patch," Weaver wrote, "the work wasn't a bit harder and they had plenty of money in their pockets. Thus every night became Saturday night."[13]

Clements, however, claimed a different experience. His recollections of his early days in the oilfields, perhaps romanticized somewhat in later life, revealed something about his own philosophy. The people he worked closely with came from hard-working farm backgrounds, and he remembered them as solid, church-going, dependable people who had a strong sense of right and wrong.

"You could depend on 'em. You could damn sure depend on 'em. And you didn't have to worry where they were. When you needed them, all you had to do was reach around in back and pat and there they were. They were right there with you," he said.

According to Clements, the work was too hard to be at the honky-tonk every night. "You've got that tool pusher looking down your throat . . . . And I'm making $180 a month and by God they expect me to earn $180, and you couldn't earn it in some beer hall . . . . I was ready to not make eight hours, but I was ready to be completely satisfactory as a top hand for sixteen hours 'cause I wanted the money. And you're not doing that and piddlin' around in some beer joint, I'll guarantee you. The two don't go together," Clements said.

"Now don't misunderstand me. There were some characters floating around in the oilfield that were hard-drinking, they were hard-playing, they were interested in honky tonks and they were what we termed floaters. They would come work for Trinity Drilling Co. for three or four or five days and fill in for someone who was sick or something like that, draw a check, go to town, get drunk, raise hell, get in jail, and then they would do it all over again. So, sure, there were those people. But they're everywhere," he said.

Clements maintained contact for years with Sloan and Shanklin. More than twenty years later, Sloan worked for Clements in Argentina. Shanklin went on to Peru for Standard of New Jersey, where he worked as a general superintendent. When Clements was campaigning for governor, Shanklin showed up at one of his rallies and, in his second term, Clements appointed Shanklin's daughter to a state commission. Clements also knew Sloan's son, Z. A. Sloan, Jr., who earned his doctorate in physics at the University of Texas, was on the faculty, and did research for the Defense Department on weapons design.

Clements valued these friendships. "I really think that that's what life is all about, to have and enjoy those kinds of relationships — because it is a reciprocating situation, I mean to have friends, you've got to be a friend," he said.[14]

Clements was fascinated by the technology of drilling and wanted to learn more about it and the machinery. He determined while working in the field for Trinity Drilling Company that he wanted to be part of the heavy equipment end of the drilling industry; he was not particularly interested in the production side. So he went to see the father of a high school classmate and fraternity brother, a man named John Shimer. Shimer was vice-president in charge of engineering for the Oil Well Supply Company, a wholly owned subsidiary of United States Steel, headquartered at 2001 N. Lamar in Dallas. Clements knew that Oil Well Supply was the largest manufacturer of drilling equipment in the world, and he had experience working on Oil Well equipment — from pumps to rotary tables to swivels. Shimer told Clements that Oil Well wasn't hiring, but offered to introduce him to Bill Whitican, who was vice-president and general manager working directly under Oil Well's president, Fred Murray. Clements made his pitch to Whitican, offering to work for nothing on a six-month trial basis. Whitican said Clements couldn't work for free, but agreed to hire him at a salary of $100 a month.[15]

Oil Well Supply sent Clements, at age twenty-two, to Houston to work in the central warehouse that distributed equipment to the Gulf Coast of Texas and Louisiana. He spent most of his time in a pickup truck, calling on drilling rigs within a fifty-mile radius of Houston. Clements went to the rigs, talked to the drillers and the tool pushers, took orders for supplies, and then delivered the material. He could talk their talk and walk their walk, and he got along very well in his new job. So well that Ralph Christy, the manager for the Gulf Coast for Oil Well Supply Company, took notice of Bill's energy and abilities. Oil Well Supply needed a sales engineer at Jennings, Louisiana, and Christy told Clements he had the job.

It was a nice promotion, and Clements moved to Jennings. He got a room, ate in a local cafe, and drove his Plymouth coupe around to the drilling rigs and production facilities in the area, selling, delivering, and working on oilfield equipment. If the crew on the rig needed help in repairing a pump or putting in a new piston or crank shaft, Clements would put on his overalls, which he carried in the car, and show them how to do it.

One of Oil Well's customers in Jennings was Orville Fisher, superintendent for Continental Oil Company (Conoco) in South Louisiana. Fisher took a liking to Bill Clements and enjoyed taking him on his rounds to visit contractor rigs. He had seventeen rigs under his supervision with different drilling contractors, and because he was such a good Oil Well customer, he could drive up to the Oil Well store and tell the store manager he wanted to take Bill with him for the day. Sometimes Fisher would pick up Bill at 6:30 A.M. and they wouldn't get back until after midnight. The wells being drilled in South Louisiana were deep and expensive and dangerous and, as they were driving around, Clements would ask questions and learn from Fisher. "They might be running a drill stem test, or they might be coring or doing those kind of things to find out what progress they were making at 12,000 or 13,000 feet," Clements said. While they waited for the results, Fisher and Clements went into the dog house (tool house) with some of the technicians and played cards. Clements learned how to play "Pitch" from Fisher, the best "Pitch" player he ever met. He also learned a lot about drilling and developed what turned out to be a lifelong friendship.

One day, Bill got a call to report to Dallas to see K. B. Winstead, sales manager for Oil Well Supply. Winstead was responsible for overseeing the Oil Well stores all over the country. Winstead told Clements there had been a discovery in Mississippi at a place outside of Yazoo City called Tinsley that Oil Well believed was going to be a boom area. Oil Well had no representative in Mississippi and wanted Clements to go to Jackson. He would live in the Heidelberg Hotel, where the drilling contractors and oil operators were living, get to know them, eat with them in the hotel dining room, and find out what was going on. He would visit the field and keep the home office in Dallas posted on who the operators and drilling contractors were and the progress of the field. This proved to be the beginning of a long and close relationship for him with K. B. Winstead and his wife, Dorothy, who had no children of their own. As a young man, Clements was good at cultivating mentors. Like Coach Charlie Trigg, K. B. Winstead became a mentor and lifelong friend.

Since leaving the University of Texas and going to the oilfields, Clements had continued to conduct a long distance romance with Pauline Gill. Clements not only had fallen in love with drilling rigs, he also had fallen in love with Pauline. And he had already asked

Pauline's father, Ben Gill, Jr., for his daughter's hand in marriage — even before he asked Pauline. Gill insisted that Pauline get her college degree first.

On April 6, 1940, nine months after Pauline graduated and one week before Bill's twenty-third birthday, Pauline Gill and Bill Clements were married in a big wedding in Terrell, Texas. Bill's groomsmen included his old Highland Park school chums, William "Billy Bob" Thomasson, Harry Todd (who by then was married to Mary Ann Thomasson, Bill's high school sweetheart), Delaney Lingo, and Manson Harris. Lindsley Waters was best man.[16]

Bill Clements couldn't imagine a better life. He was living in the Heidelberg Hotel in Jackson, hobnobbing with oil operators and drilling contractors, and had married his college sweetheart.

One of the people he met at the hotel was I. P. "Ike" LaRue. Ike, Sr., was in the land lease business, representing several major oil companies. He was buying thousands of acres of leases for these companies, and his son, Ike, Jr., worked for him. Bill Clements developed a friendship with both father and son. Pauline had known Ike, Jr., and his wife, Martha, at the University of Texas, and the two young couples became friends. Bill and Pauline and Ike, Jr., and Martha moved into a house with two apartments — an upper and a lower. Each small apartment had one bedroom, a bath, a living room, and a kitchenette.

During that period, "Big Ike," as he was called, went to Clements seeking help. Magnolia had asked him to put together a block of oil and gas leases of 35,000 to 40,000 acres north and east of Yazoo City, but part of the obligation included drilling a 5,000-foot well to validate the lease. Big Ike didn't know the first thing about a drilling rig or how to make a drilling contract, but knew Clements had some experience on a drilling rig. Clements told him there was "a hell of a difference" between working on the floor of a rig and making a drilling contract; he advised LaRue to get a lawyer. LaRue persisted, however, asking Clements to find a drilling contractor who would drill the well to validate the leases.

Among other tasks, Oil Well Supply Company had asked Clements to try to collect a bad debt of several years' standing — $250 for a used rotary table — from a fellow named "Peanuts" Love. Peanuts, in Clements' words, was a "hardly able" or "poor-boy" drilling contractor, but he provided Clements with the justification for helping Big Ike. Clements told Love he could get him a drilling contract, if he would agree to pledge the first $250 he made on the contract to Oil Well Supply to pay his debt. Love agreed, and Clements went to a lawyer and had a contract drawn up. That was Clements' first business deal with Big Ike LaRue. It would not be his last.

Bill left Jackson, Mississippi, but for several years thereafter, he would occasionally get a phone call from Big Ike, who would say, "Let's go into the drilling business." The conversation was always the same. Clements would say, "You know that is exactly what I want to do. I'm in love with drilling rigs and have been ever since I went to the field. But I don't have any money, and you don't have any money. How are we going to do this?" Ike would just laugh and hang up.

When Bill and Pauline left Jackson, they embarked on a decade of moves that would carry them beyond the end of World War II. In the first ten years of their marriage, they moved thirteen times.[17] The first move was from Jackson to Dallas, where Clements worked in Oil Well's engineering department. Their son, Ben Gill Clements, was born on October 13, 1941, in Dallas. The next move was to Tulsa, Oklahoma, where Clements learned how Oil Well financed drilling contractors, extended credit, and sold them machinery.

Bill worked in Tulsa until he got a call from Winstead to move to Pampa, Texas, to become store manager. Bill had no experience overseeing the vast inventory that managing a store entailed, and the Panhandle would be a completely new working environment. Winstead told him the work in the Panhandle had little to do with drilling activity because it was already "drilled up." The business had to do with production — pumper wells. It would provide Clements with a good opportunity to learn about pumping equipment — bottom hole pumps, sucker rods, geared powers — that was needed to produce oil rather than drilling for it with a drilling rig. So Bill and Pauline moved to Pampa, where Clements was in charge of a big tin building with a warehouse yard in the back full of pipe and sucker rods and other equipment needed for pumpers. They lived with baby Gill upstairs, over the store.

By then, the United States was fully engaged in World War II. But Clements, against his own wishes, never served in the armed forces. He was unaware of the fact that Oil Well Supply, as part of a national security industry, was granted six deferments; the company assigned one of them to Clements. He had been called up by his draft board to take his physical and had been reclassified. Instead of being drafted into the army, however, Clements was planning to join the navy by signing up with his former coach, Charlie Trigg, who was in charge of the navy's recruiting office in New Orleans.

When Clements informed Winstead of his plans, he was told about the deferment. He was also told that his salary would be frozen in place and he was prohibited from joining another company. Clements was upset, but there was nothing he could do about it. Winstead intended to organize a war division of Oil Well Supply Company, and he wanted Clements to be his assistant. Under the auspices of a war division, Winstead would convert plants and equipment manufactured by Oil Well for use in the war effort.[18]

Bill Clements undertook his first effort on behalf of Oil Well's war division while he was in Pampa. A huge air base was being built in Amarillo. Clements went to Amarillo, introduced himself to the captain in charge of the Army Engineers who were building the base, and asked to meet with the general contractor, C. S. Lambe of Amarillo, and with the army's construction engineer to see how Oil Well Supply might fit in.

Clements figured he could help build heating facilities and power plants for the base, using oilfield equipment. The base had to have heating facilities for the hospital area, a power center for electricity, and a smokestack. He convinced Lambe, who was old enough to be his grandfather, that he knew enough about feedwater heater pumps and boilers that he could produce all the steam that would be needed for the camp. Lambe told Clements to go ahead. Clements did the only thing he knew to do. He went out into the oilfields and recruited a bunch of roughnecks and drillers, and he put a crew together. They were paid by Oil Well Supply, working for Clements.

In a matter of months, the war division of Oil Well Supply Company was conducting sixteen major construction jobs, over which Clements had direct supervision. The projects were in Texas, Oklahoma, Colorado, and New Mexico and included work at prisoner-of-war camps in the Texas Panhandle, a Japanese relocation center in Colorado, heating facilities at an air base between Midland and Odessa, and expansion of the helium plant at Amarillo. All of the work had to do with heating systems and power plants, involving feedwater heater pumps and heating systems related to oilfield boilers, and required adapting oilfield equipment in a way no one had ever dreamed. Oil Well performed the work as a subcontractor for the general contractor that was working for the U.S. Army Corps of Engineers.

Clements moved back to Dallas for this work. He and Pauline moved into a two-bedroom, one-bath cottage on Caruth, but Clements was traveling most of the time and was rarely home. On December 30, 1942, Nancy Clements was born in Dallas.

During that period, domestic oilfields were practically shut down. Little effort was going into drilling new wells, which required a lot of pipe and steel, but rather into producing oil already found. There were still enormous reserves, so with all-out production effort, the country would not feel pinched for oil. In those days the U.S. was an exporter, not an importer, of oil. Fifty years later, the U.S. would be importing half the oil used in the country.

But there was a big oilfield being developed in Canada, and it would be the next stop for the Clements family. Wartime Oils, Ltd., a Canadian government company, was engaged in a joint U.S.-Canadian project that included developing a field called Turner Valley in Alberta. Oil Well Supply was the only source for all the materials needed to drill more wells and to develop maximum production out of Turner Valley, which was part of a war effort master plan involving Canada and Alaska. The plan also included developing a shallow field, Norman Wells, in the Yukon, dismantling a Corpus Christi refinery to be rebuilt in Alaska, and building a pipeline to the refinery. The whole effort was designed to supply oil products to a large force of the armed services in Alaska because military leaders believed the Japanese were going to invade America's northern territory.

In 1943 Bill and Pauline loaded up their two babies and their belongings and headed off to a little Alberta town of about 180 residents called Okotoks, which was an Indian name meaning Rocky Crossing. The Oil Well Supply store was located in Okotoks, the closest town to the Turner Valley oilfield. Again, Bill and Pauline lived over the store, this time with two children under age two. Bill had an office in Calgary, about thirty-five miles away, and spent most of his time there or in the field, making sure the inventory was available for the drilling and production work. In 1944 Clements got his next assignment: San Antonio.

Oil Well Supply had eleven stores operating in southwest Texas, under the jurisdiction of the San Antonio office. The war effort needed the maximum amount of oil to be produced out of South Texas, where some new fields had been discovered, including one on the King Ranch, and these efforts required equipment from Oil Well Supply. The company made Clements district manager in charge of southwest Texas, and the Clements family lived in San Antonio. Bill spent a lot of time on the road. He was in the Rio Grande Valley — in McAllen, Mission, Rio Grande City, Corpus Christi, and Victoria — visiting the stores and making sure they had adequate inventories of pipe and equipment required in the southwest Texas fields.

At age twenty-nine, Bill Clements was well on his way to a promising career with Oil Well Supply Company; he had a number of people working for him and a vast inventory to oversee. One associate at Oil Well described Clements as "someone who knew where he wanted to go and he was not going to let anything get in his way. He was a very pleasant, affable person, but he always had his objectives, pulling and directing him."[19]

When World War II ended, Bill Clements was on his way up the company ladder. But in the back of his mind, he still harbored the dream that one day he would own his own drilling rigs and become a millionaire.

Chapter 4

Betting on the Jockey

The Birth of SEDCO

T HE PHONE CALL CAME one November day in 1946. "Let's go into the drilling business," Ike LaRue said.

It was the standard opening for a conversation LaRue had initiated many times with Bill Clements. But he had picked a good time to make his pitch. The war had ended and the country was optimistic about business prospects for the future. Still, Clements, then district manager for Oil Well Supply in San Antonio, answered LaRue with the same response he had before.

"Ike, you haven't got any money, and I don't either. How are we going to go in the drilling business?"

"You're absolutely right," LaRue said. "I don't have any money, and I know that you have got very little. But I know a friend who has lots of money. So, let's go into the drilling business," LaRue said.

"Who's this friend?" asked Clements.

"It's Toddie Lee Wynne," LaRue said.

"Well, I know (of) Mr. Wynne, and I know his family. And you're right. He's got plenty of money," Clements said. "But why in the world would he want to go into the drilling business?"

"Because I want to," LaRue responded.

"Have you talked to him about it?" asked Clements.

"No. But he is my friend, and if I ask him to do it, he will do it," LaRue said. "He'll either put up the money or the credit. You will

44

run it, and I'll have a third, and you'll have a third, and he'll have a third."

Clements agreed to sleep on the idea, and when LaRue called him back the next day, the idea had taken hold. "I think it can work," Clements told LaRue, "if it's all as you represent." LaRue told Clements to meet him for breakfast at 7:00 A.M. the following day at the Adolphus Hotel in Dallas. After breakfast, they would go see Toddie Lee Wynne.[1]

Toddie Lee Wynne had been born in 1896 in Wills Point (East Texas). He had graduated from the University of Texas Law School, then gone to work negotiating oil leases. His father had told him when he was a young man, "Inch by inch and step by step, climb the ladder until you reach the top, where you can sit quietly by and look down on those who are struggling far beneath you."[2]

Toddie Lee had all the attributes to do exactly as he had been told. He had brains and business sense; he was handsome, and he was very well connected. The Wynnes were a prominent Wills Point family, and Toddie Lee was acquainted with other families of standing in East Texas, including the Murchisons of Athens. Clint Murchison, Sr., had hired Toddie Lee to be his lawyer for American Liberty Oil Company and had given him 10 percent interest in the company.

The fortunes of Clint Murchison and Toddie Lee Wynne grew out of the East Texas oilfields of the early 1930s. Clint Murchison had bought leases and constructed a pipeline and refinery in Tyler, with credit from Oil Well Supply. By the spring of 1931, the East Texas field was flowing at a half million barrels a day. The supply of oil dumped on the market far exceeded the demand, and as more wells were drilled, oil prices began to slide.

Because of the glut of oil and declining prices, the Texas Railroad Commission was given the authority to limit, or prorate, production in the field. Only so much oil could be produced per day from each well. It was common practice in East Texas, however, for oilmen to ignore the law and exceed the daily allowable, running illegal oil that became known as "hot oil." Murchison's company was known for running "hot oil." In fact, it was said that the American Liberty pipeline was "so hot you could fry an egg on it."[3]

Toddie Lee and Clint also developed other joint interests. Among them was the ownership of a million dollars' worth of racehorses, which were trained and raced on a track at Murchison's

Bluebird Farms in the Trinity River bottom just south of downtown Dallas. Both men liked to bet on the horses.

Wynne eventually became chief executive as well as chief counsel and a 50-50 partner with Murchison in American Liberty Oil. But he and Murchison had a falling out, and their partnership was dissolved beginning in 1944. Wynne ended up getting the exploration division of American Liberty Oil and part of Matagorda Island, with its club-house and guest quarters, in a difficult separation that took years to untangle. But Wynne became a millionaire many times over.

Ike LaRue was also from Athens, and a good friend of both Murchison and Wynne; Ike had been best man in Toddie Lee Wynne's wedding. When Ike LaRue and Bill Clements paid their call on Toddie Lee Wynne that November day in 1946, the bitter separation between Wynne and Murchison had already transpired. But Toddie Lee and Ike were still on good terms.

Clements always enjoyed telling the story of his first encounter with Toddie Lee Wynne. He and Ike went to Wynne's big pink house, which faced Turtle Creek on Lakeside Drive in Highland Park, and were met at the door by Toddie Lee's wife. After greetings, LaRue asked if Toddie Lee was ready to see them. She said, yes, Toddie Lee was upstairs. Clements thought that meant Wynne was waiting for them in an upstairs study or library. As he recalled later, "Damned if we don't go up and there Toddie Lee is in bed, all propped up with pillows behind him. And it turns out he's had a heart attack, and here he is in bed, and Ike doesn't seem to think anything of this."[4]

Ike introduced Clements to Toddie Lee, and proceeded to explain the reason for the visit — to create a drilling contracting company bankrolled by Toddie Lee in which each of the three would have one-third interest. But Toddie Lee wouldn't actually have to put up any of his own money. The idea was that Toddie Lee would guarantee $100,000 with Oil Well Supply Company, which would be used to buy two used rigs. That would cover a $25,000 down payment for each drilling rig and $25,000 for supplies for each. Then he would guarantee $100,000 at First National Bank, where he was a director, for working capital for the two rigs. Ike told Toddie Lee all about Clements and his knowledge of drilling rigs, recounting his career in the oilfields and his work for Oil Well Supply Company. Meanwhile, Clements said, "I'm sitting over there like a knot on a log, not saying anything, not being asked anything."

Toddie Lee listened to Big Ike's proposal and finally said, "You know, Ike, I've known you an awful long time. And I've known you to bet on the horses before. But I've never known you to bet on the jockey."

The comment was etched in Clements' memory.

Just as LaRue had predicted, however, Wynne agreed to the plan. Each man would own one-third interest, and Clements would be the "jockey," running the company. The credit with Oil Well and the bank was arranged, and Wynne guaranteed the accounts as agreed.

Pauline had misgivings about Bill leaving a promising career with Oil Well. While Bill had some nostalgia about it, he had known from the first day he walked on the floor of a drilling rig that he wanted to be a drilling contractor. His dream was about to come true. According to Clements, Oil Well Supply offered him a vice-presidency and a salary raise to stay with the company. When he appeared determined to pursue his dream, however, Oil Well adopted the attitude that instead of being a valued employee, he would be a potentially valued customer.

Clements found two diesel-powered rigs and arranged to buy them through Oil Well for $210,000. Later, as Clements worked the rigs, he would pay off the debt with Oil Well. And, over time, he would become the best customer Oil Well ever had, doing hundreds of millions of dollars' worth of business with them, with rigs all over the world.

Once the two rigs were secured, Clements went to LaRue and said, "Now, what we need is work." LaRue said he would handle that. He would call Sam Gladney, who was the general agent of Sun Oil Company in Dallas, in charge of the southwest region. Gladney was from Terrell, and he and LaRue were old friends from the East Texas network.

Gladney agreed to see them. He knew Ike, and having been reared in Terrell, he knew the family of Pauline Gill Clements. But letting drilling contracts was not his responsibility; John Ritter was in charge of production. Known by Sun Oil production employees as "King John," Ritter ruled the production department with an iron hand. Gladney took LaRue and Clements in to meet Ritter and told him to give the aspiring drilling contractors some work for their two rigs, and promptly left the room.

Clements remembers Ritter being visibly upset; his face turned red and it was clear he didn't appreciate the boss walking in with two strangers and ordering him to give them a couple of drilling contracts. To Clements, it was a rocky start. But Ritter recovered and began talking about some exploration and development work in Mississippi. Clements, who had worked in Mississippi for Oil Well, thought to himself, "How lucky can you get? I know Mississippi. I worked there." Sun Oil was drilling some gas wells at a place called Guinnville and participating in a wildcat well at a little town called Hazelhurst. Ritter gave the untested drilling contractors some of the Mississippi work, and that was the beginning of a thirty-five-year relationship between Clements' company and Sun Oil.

On January 1, 1947, the company that would later become SEDCO, Inc., was started as Southeastern Drilling Company, with what Clements called "two rusty rigs." Clements had the rigs trucked over to Mississippi and began hiring people to work on the crews. He served as the office manager, the contract solicitor, and the drilling superintendent.[5]

The first two wells were make-or-break jobs, because the drilling contrator's obligation was to complete the wells to total depth. On the deeper wildcat well at Hazelhurst, there were a couple of fishing jobs that gave Clements some sleepless nights. He lost the bit in the hole at 8,300 feet. Fishing a drilling bit out of a deep hole is costly, time consuming, and it doesn't always work. Years later, recounting the story to a reporter when he was running for governor, Clements admitted, "I thought my house of cards had collapsed before we got started." The infant company was strung out on credit, and his contract said he wouldn't get paid unless he drilled to 10,000 feet. But Clements retrieved the bit and completed the job.[6] The wildcat well at Hazelhurst eventually went a little below 11,000 feet, and the one at Guinnville went to about 6,300 feet.

Completing those first two wells was a milestone. If the wells hadn't been completed, Southeastern Drilling couldn't have stayed in business. From that point forward, Southeastern Drilling was able to get other contracts. One of the rigs was moved to Baxterville to drill wells for Gulf Oil and the other to Brookhaven to drill for Continental Oil.

Then Clements remembered another old friend, Orville Fisher, the superintendent who had driven Clements around from rig to rig and played cards with him in the dog houses near Jennings, Louisiana. Fisher had moved up to production manager for Conoco in

Houston. Clements went to see Fisher and told him how much he had learned from him. Then, with the brashness that was becoming part of his nature, Clements said, "Now I want a drilling contract from you."

Fisher gave one to him. The Continental Oil Company (Conoco) contract was just outside Palestine at Tennessee Colony in East Texas. But Clements didn't have another rig. So he went back to Oil Well Supply and asked for more credit. He figured he could do the job with an old, used steam rig, which was cheaper than a diesel rig. There already was a discovery well at Tennessee Colony that could supply the gas for the boilers, and there was plenty of water. With available water and fuel, a steam rig would do just fine, and it would only cost about $50,000. Oil Well agreed. The old steam rig paid for itself and more, drilling many wells there in East Texas, working for Continental Oil.

Southeastern Drilling Company's office was now in Jackson, Mississippi. The first two diesel-powered rigs were still working in Mississippi and the steam rig was working in Tennessee Colony in East Texas. Clements had one person working for him in the office, keeping the books. He was the general superintendent, which meant he would get up at 5:00 A.M., visit the rigs and work in the office, pay bills, and get home about midnight.

With the creation of the company, Bill and Pauline had moved with their two young children to Jackson, at first living in an apartment over a flower shop. As business progressed, they were able to buy some acreage, build their first house and, it seemed, to settle down. They had developed a circle of friends in Jackson. The children went to a private Episcopal school and had plenty of room to roam and play. With several acres, they could keep horses and chickens and dogs, and there was a lake on the property next door. The first Christmas after they moved into the house, in 1948, Perry and Evelyn Clements brought the grandchildren a pony and a pony cart. The children named the mare, a little paint, Velvet. When she had a colt, they called it Velveteen. Their dad had a corral and a shelter built for the horses.[7]

Bill had hardly been in business two years when he got a phone call in Jackson from R. L. "Pop" Warner, general production manager for Forest Oil Company. This was an oldline Pennsylvania company dating back to the birth of the American petroleum industry with Col. Edwin L. Drake's Pennsylvania discovery. Clements had known Warner when he was district manager for Oil Well in San Antonio. Warner told Clements his company had a discovery in West Texas, near McCamey and the Pecos River, that looked good. He was confident his company would drill twenty or twenty-five wells there and offered Clements some of the work. McCamey is located in Upton County, just south of Ector and Midland counties; the field was about seven miles south of McCamey on the north bank of the Pecos.

Clements had no extra rigs and knew nothing about drilling in West Texas, but he agreed to think about it. He called Big Ike and told him about the deal. It involved a serious decision, because there was no way Clements could supervise work in West Texas from Mississippi; he would have to move back to Texas if they took the work. Ike told Clements it was his call.

Clements didn't want to make that call. Southeastern Drilling was just getting established. He and Pauline had put down their roots, and she was not anxious to uproot and move again. They had their own place, the three-bedroom cottage with the acreage. The kids had their ponies. Everything was going just fine in Jackson, Mississippi.

But he couldn't resist. Clements paid a visit to Fred Goetzinger, treasurer of Oil Well Supply, and asked Oil Well to back him in buying his first new drilling rig.

Oil Well had a store at McCamey which serviced the shallow production work going on in the area. The wells on the Pecos River for Forest Oil Company, however, would be deep wells. Clements needed a new, jackknife rig, capable of drilling 7,500 to 8,000 feet. It had to be highly portable because he intended to move it from one well to the next, drilling more than one well. Clements thought he could put the rig together for about $200,000, but had no money to invest. He proposed to sign a note paying it off, monthly, over the next two years. Goetzinger agreed, and Southeastern Drilling Company was on its way to being a four-rig operation.

Clements went to work putting his rig together in McCamey, which wasn't much of a town. It had been an oilfield boomtown in the 1920s, until the Depression and the "black giant" East Texas field of the 1930s decimated the West Texas oil industry.[8] But the oilfields around McCamey had several revivals.

Clements spent his first few nights in McCamey in the Oil Well Supply Company warehouse, sleeping on a cot. He brought in some oilfield hands from Mississippi and Louisiana, including Howard Scallorn, who would be the tool pusher. The driller was E. A. "Crooked Hole" Spoon, and the roughnecks included K. D. "Kowdod" Reynolds, Johnny Clower, and an old character known as "Smokestack Shorty." Otis Conatser was working for Oil Well in McCamey when Clements put together the rig that would drill its first well on the Tippett Ranch. He remembered Clements as being "tough, but fair. If he spent a dollar, he wanted his money's worth." Clements also was a "straight-shooting guy. If he told you something, you could believe it," Conatser said.[9]

After about two years in business, Clements had four drilling rigs and a big debt. He had been able to make his payments to Oil Well, but otherwise was barely surviving.[10] Yet, Clements' memories of those days would be fond ones. He lived for a while in a trailer by the drilling rig on the Tippett Ranch and went dove hunting in his spare time.

In 1950, Southeastern Drilling established an office in the Employers Insurance Building on South Akard Street. The house in Jackson was sold and Bill and Pauline moved back to Dallas, where they rented a two-story frame house in University Park and enrolled Gill and Nancy in University Park Elementary School.

And then, opportunity knocked.

K. B. Winstead of Oil Well Supply Company invited Clements to lunch with him and Lloyd Tracy, vice-president and general sales manager for Oil Well, and Fred Goetzinger, Oil Well treasurer. The topic: eight additional rigs.

Oil Well Supply had sold eight of the biggest and best rigs it manufactured to Creole Petroleum, a wholly owned subsidiary of Standard of New Jersey. Creole's sole operation was in Venezuela; it was the biggest producer in the country and the crown jewel of Standard of New Jersey. Creole had ordered eight rigs for a massive new drilling program in Venezuela, but only three had been uncrated and used; the other five were still in a Venezuelan warehouse. The Venezuelan government had taken an adverse position against all the oil companies in the country, and Creole wanted to sell the rigs and get them out of the country in order to send a strong message to the government. Creole asked Oil Well to sell the Oil Well "96" rigs, which were as big and fine as any on the market, each valued at about $600,000 and with a capacity to drill to 17,000 or 18,000 feet.

Oil Well had gone to several drilling contractors but had been unable to unload the rigs, and this presented a dilemma to the Oil Well executives. They wanted to respond to Creole's owner, Standard of New Jersey, an important customer, but they had no buyer. They asked Clements to buy the rigs.

Clements thought they had to be joking; there was no way he could finance those rigs. But the Oil Well representatives offered to sell him the rigs on credit, if he would buy his spare parts and supplies from them. Clements, who had outfitted and manned four rigs, knew it would be a giant undertaking to do the same for eight more — all at the same time. He would need working capital to hire crews, get warehousing, move equipment, and increase headquarters personnel. But the Oil Well people had already talked to the First National Bank, and the bank was willing to handle Clements' receivables and extend him a $25,000 line of credit on each rig. All he had to do was sign on the dotted line.

Oil Well told Clements to go to Venezuela, inventory the rigs and equipment, and negotiate the trade with Creole Petroleum; Oil Well would stand good for whatever deal he made. So Clements went to Caracas, spent six weeks doing the inventory, and finally bought the eight rigs, plus all sorts of supplies to support and repair the rigs, for about twenty cents on the dollar. When Clements cabled Oil Well the price, Oil Well paid Standard of New Jersey, and arrangements were made to transport all the equipment back to Texas.

In the meantime, Clements had hired Sam Gladney's brother, Don Gladney, who had retired as vice-president in charge of Mobil's pipeline division, to prepare for the arrival of the rigs. Gladney went to West Texas and found a ten-acre warehouse site on Highway 80 between Midland and Odessa close to the airport. Southeastern Drilling filled up the ten acres with drilling equipment, but had no work. So Clements contacted Orville Fisher, who came through with a Conoco contract. Then he went to other big companies soliciting work. Sinclair and Gulf came through with some jobs. Magnolia (Mobil) eventually became Southeastern's biggest customer for the Oil Well "96" rigs. Six of the eight rigs were put to work in West Texas, one in East Texas, and one in Louisiana. Crews had to be hired for each one. The detail associated with getting the contracts, transporting and equipping the rigs, and obtaining and maintaining the manpower was enormous.[11] Still headquartered in Dallas, Bill, once again, was working night and day.

During that period, Toddie Lee Wynne decided he wanted out

of the drilling contracting business. Clements was beginning to expand beyond his expectations, and Wynne had no interest in the business. He asked Clements to figure out what his interest was worth. Clements finally came up with a figure of $83,000. Wynne asked for a note for that amount, but specified no set time for paying it off. He asked Clements to pay when he could. At Clements' request, he agreed to leave his guarantees in place at the bank and with Oil Well. Two years later, Clements paid him off.[12]

From the beginning of the company, Clements put a lot of stock in hiring quality workers. He wanted men who could do the job, who would stick with him, and who could advance with the company.

Among the first people hired was roughneck Bobby Lynch, who rigged up and spudded Rig 1 in April 1947, in Hazelhurst, Mississippi. Bill Carlton was hired as a roughneck in April 1947, in Columbia, Mississippi, to work on Rig 2.[13] Twenty-five years later, both men were still with the company and had moved into demanding foreign assignments.[14]

A man who would become a key employee in later years also came in on the ground floor. Spencer Taylor started working for Southeastern Drilling as a roughneck in the summer of 1947, while he was in college. Taylor's home was in Jackson, Mississippi, and he was a good friend of Fred LaRue, the youngest son of Big Ike LaRue. In subsequent summers, Taylor worked as a roughneck in West Texas, while finishing his engineering degree.[15] Clements enjoyed taking his dad and young son Gill dove hunting in West Texas, and it was on a rig site at McCamey where eight-year-old Gill Clements first met Spencer Taylor.[16]

Clements demanded loyalty from his workers. When Taylor came to Clements with a petroleum engineering degree from Oklahoma University in January 1950, asking for a permanent job, Clements wanted to make sure Taylor would make a long-term commitment. Taylor had an outstanding academic record, was president of his fraternity, and was being recruited by the major oil companies. Before Clements would hire Taylor, he wanted him to interview with those other companies and consider their offers first. If Clements hired him, he didn't want Taylor looking around later for a better opportunity or wishing he had pursued other offers. Clements' philosophy was: "If you are going to go to work for me, you are going to go to work for me." Taylor interviewed with the big companies and then went back to Clements, who told him he would have to learn the business from the ground up — working on rigs in West Texas and learning about materials in the warehouse. Clements told him, "Based on your performance, over time, you can come up the ladder." Taylor did, eventually becoming president of the company.[17]

W. G. Cox, meanwhile, wound up in Harlingen after a tour with the Marine Corps and was looking for a job when one fell into his lap. So began his long career in the oil industry. Cox was in a beer joint, drinking a beer, when he was approached by a man who said, "I've got a drilling job out here, and I've got a man off sick. I need someone. Can you work tonight?"

Cox said he could.

"What's your name?" the stranger asked.

"William Grant Cox," Cox replied.

"Mind if I just call you 'Bobby'?" the man said.

That man was Walter Etherington, and W. G. Cox became Bobby Cox for the rest of his career. In 1948 Clements went to Harlingen and hired Etherington, Cox, and Howard Archer. The three reported in July 1948 to work in the Yellow Creek field near Waynesboro, Mississippi, on a U15 with jackknife derrick and Caterpillar engines. All three had long careers with SEDCO, working for the company until their retirement.[18]

Cox noted later that "Clements, when he formed the company, had some pretty junky old equipment, but he had the attitude that you can have the finest equipment in the world, but if you have a bunch of lousy people, then you are going to be a mediocre performer. But if you have the junkiest equipment in the world and you have good people, they are going to make it work and you will excel."[19]

Clements paid wages in line with other contractors and, according to Cox, "he expected you to produce. He was of the opinion he hired a man to do a job and he didn't stand over him and look down his shirt collar." Those who produced got an opportunity to move up in the company.[20]

In 1949 Clements hired W. E. "Bill" Armentrout as office manager in Jackson, Mississippi. Armentrout was office manager when the company moved to Dallas. He had been four years ahead of Clements at Highland Park High School and SMU. He worked for Oil Well Supply, and when Clements offered him a job, Armentrout mentioned it to an associate at Oil Well. "He said if he was offered a job by Bill Clements, he'd take it the next day. That was the No. 2

man in the Oil Well Supply Co. credit department. That was good enough for me," said Armentrout.[21]

Clements also hired Bill McAfee, a graduate of East Texas State University, to work as a roughneck in Jackson, Mississippi, in 1950. McAfee was transferred to the main office in Dallas, where he became purchasing agent and later set up the company's purchasing department.[22]

During the early days in Dallas, the company was living on the edge; money was tight. Bobby Cox remembered hearing McAfee say that when the bills came in from Oil Well Supply, he would scrutinize them so that if he found a five-cent mistake, he could send them back for adjustment and delay payment.

Other early and important hires included Bill Gray, Howard Scallorn, and John Rhea, Jr., Clements had known Bill Gray when he worked for Oil Well in Pampa and had hired him to work on the first project for Oil Well's war division at the air base in Amarillo. Gray became the top operational man for Southeastern Drilling during the early days in Mississippi.

When Southeastern Drilling started work in Mississippi, John Rhea was a petroleum engineer and graduate of Louisiana State University who was working in Mississippi as a field drilling engineer for a subsidiary of Standard of California. He previously had worked for Standard of New Jersey in South America. Like Clements, Rhea was exempted from the draft because he was working in an essential industry. He spent most of the war in Colombia, working as a field production engineer and superintendent. In Mississippi, Rhea and Gray had become friends; Gray wanted Rhea to go to work for Southeastern Drilling. Clements met Rhea but, at the time, he couldn't afford to hire an engineer. He promised Rhea that when the day came that he could hire an engineer, he would call him.

In 1951, Clements called Rhea, who had moved to Colorado as a district engineer for Standard of California. Rhea had worked five years with Standard of California and five with Standard of New Jersey in South America. Within weeks, Rhea was in Dallas as Southeastern's first drilling engineer.

When Rhea joined the company, Clements had bought the Creole Petroleum rigs, which were operating in West Texas and New Mexico. Gray was the superintendent of the West Texas-New Mexico area. Six months later, Gray dropped dead of a heart attack at age thirty-six on the rig floor. His replacement in West Texas was

Walter Etherington. There were half a dozen men working in the office, along with stenographers and bookkeepers, when Rhea joined the company. "Bill Clements was the president, the big boss, and he stayed that way, too," Rhea said. By that time, Southeastern Drilling was working for Magnolia, Sinclair, Gulf, Shell, and had drilled for independents, including Bunker Hunt, and looking for more work.[23] The company was active in East Texas, West Texas, New Mexico, Oklahoma, Louisiana, and Mississippi. The West Texas division grew to sixteen rigs, making Southeastern Drilling the biggest contractor out there. Then, in 1952, Clements made another important decision — to move into offshore drilling.

John Ritter of Sun Oil, who had given the "two rusty rigs" their first drilling contracts in Mississippi, contacted Clements about a discovery in Copano Bay, near Aransas Pass, Texas. There was work to be done in shallow water off the Texas Gulf Coast from barge rigs. Clements didn't have any barge rigs and had never worked in the water, but that was no deterrent. He visited some barge rigs and determined he could build one. Clements located two barges that had been used to haul oil on the Mississippi River. He rented a slip off the Houston Ship Channel for the two barges and moved two of his Oil Well "96" rigs from West Texas onto the oil carrier barges. Two tugboats were hired to take the two barge rigs down the intercoastal canal to Copano Bay.

The trip required moving the barges through a drawbridge at Copano Bay. Clements was there to personally supervise the move through the drawbridge, along with the superintendent, tool pusher, and members of the rig crew who were on board. As the barge was approaching the bridge, Clements began to sense a problem. The bridge was opened and traffic was backed up on each side when it became apparent that the barge, with its 136-foot-high derrick, was not going to go through. The bridge operator called the highway department, and the highway department district manager from Corpus Christi appeared on the scene, as traffic continued to stack up. "And it ain't gonna go. You can see that," Clements said. One solution was to dismantle the derrick, take the barge through without the derrick and then erect the derrick again. This would have taken days.

The barge was huge, about 50 feet wide by 150 feet long and 12 feet deep. On top of it were the crew's quarters, which couldn't be dismantled. The barge contained a hydraulic system of pumps, used to flood some of the compartments so that the barge could sink in the shallow water and sit on the bottom to drill. When it became apparent it wasn't going to make it, panic began to set in — on the barge and off. Clements recalled the incident: "We are all stopped, and we are all looking at this little puzzle that we've got, and traffic is backed up . . . . All of these experts — whether they're the highway engineers, superintendents, or tool pushers or engineers or these boat captains — they are all about to pull their hair out. And I said, 'No, it ain't as bad as you think.'"

Clements suggested flooding some of the compartments of the barge to sink one side, causing the derrick to tilt away from the side where the bridge was lifted at an angle. The highway department people feared the worst — that the barge would get stuck and it would be weeks before the highway would be open again. Others were afraid the derrick would topple over. Neither happened. The water was pumped into the compartments, the barge began to tilt, and the derrick slipped through the drawbridge with about half of an inch to spare.[24]

Clements would have other crises — from sunken rigs to blowouts — but this was his first real test. His reaction became predictable. Don't blink. Solve the problem, and move on.

In 1952, Southeastern Drilling Company started drilling operations with its two shallow water marsh barges. The marsh operation was expanded from South Texas into the coastal areas of Louisiana, and further increased in scope when another drilling contracting firm, Cotton Dixon of Houston, which owned nine rigs, was bought and merged into Southeastern. According to Rhea, Clements recognized that land drilling was becoming too competitive, and he thought barge drilling offered more opportunity.

By this time, Southeastern Drilling was working for all the major oil companies. Texaco was a good customer, and Texaco in New York, on recommendation from their South Louisiana office, contacted Clements to build a barge and take it to drill offshore Trinidad. The job required drilling in sixteen feet of water on a very soft bottom. The conventional marsh barge worked in only six or eight feet of water, so Southeastern engineered and built an innovative new barge which had six-foot posts on top of the hull, with the rig built on top of the posts to enable drilling in the deeper water.

Rig 21 was built in 1955 in Beaumont, Texas; the posts that were added for extra height created a twenty-foot-high, post-type swamp barge. This was the industry's first post-type barge, and it became a design that was copied all over the world.[25] The job in Trinidad was Southeastern's first international work.

As the years went by, Clements reverted to his roots in many ways, including bringing into his business old Highland Park school acquaintances. One was Jerry Cunningham. Their paths had crossed again in 1951, when Cunningham was working in West Texas, managing an oil field service company called Drilling Mud Services. When Clements moved the Creole Petroleum rigs into West Texas, it was big news in the oil industry, and Cunningham called Clements to solicit some mud business.

Cunningham, the son of the president of Standard of Texas, had grown up in the oil industry and in a prosperous Highland Park family. As a student at the University of Colorado, he was a cheerleader and a hell-raiser. He had worked in the oilfields as a roughneck, drilling superintendent, and tool pusher. Then he had joined Milwhite Mud Sales (later Milchem) and had become vice-president in charge of the West Texas region of the company that sold mud and chemicals for drilling oil wells. Mud was big business. Used to lubricate the hole and the bit, it was an essential in drilling oil and gas wells.

Cunningham wanted to make a change. He had developed a drinking problem which was affecting his work habits and his family life. He contacted Clements in Dallas about going to work for Southeastern Drilling. The company was then big enough and so spread out that Clements needed someone with Cunningham's background and experience to help with customer relations. Cunningham went to Dallas for a discussion with Clements.

As was his habit, when Clements ran across a subject he didn't know much about, he studied it. Clements became an overnight expert on alcoholism, Cunningham said, and he found out that an alcoholic could never take another drink. He brought that fact to Cunningham's attention and said, "If you ever take another drink, I'll have to fire you."

Cunningham's response was: "That's way too much pressure."

"What can we do about it?" asked Clements.

"Just give me one drunk," Cunningham said.

Clements agreed. "I will give you one mistake, but the second mistake and you're gone."

Cunningham never had the first one. He joined Southeastern

Drilling Company in 1955 as a vice-president. He was soon moved to work with Howard Scallorn, one of the original hires, who was superintendent in New Orleans. Cunningham would be with the company for more than thirty years, including serving as president of SEDCO's Drilling Division. In 1989, Governor Clements would appoint him chairman of the Texas Commission on Alcohol and Drug Abuse, and Cunningham would be reappointed by Democratic Gov. Ann Richards.[26]

Although Clements was sometimes hard to work for, Cunningham said, "I'd be an absolute nothing if Bill Clements hadn't picked me up and given me this opportunity." An acquaintance from Oil Well said Clements "did a great job of rehabilitating people."[27]

Clements' employees knew what was expected of them. He had standards for both company and personal behavior, and employees either met those requirements or they were gone. "The best way to get a final paycheck was to get a divorce. He disapproved of philandering husbands and of divorce," Cox said.[28] Clements was known to personally retrieve straying husbands or an employee off on a binge. Company employees who got divorced were ostracized. For that reason, Clements' own divorce years later came as a shock to his business associates.

He also let employees know when they didn't measure up to expectations or made a mistake. "He could reprimand you in the strongest manner," Cunningham said. "When the discussion was over, it was over. He would never tolerate, 'I could have told you this' or 'I wish we would've done that.' Second guessing was not our mode."[29]

Some of his customers and suppliers found Clements intimidating. "He was very aggressive," said a former Oil Well employee. "He would never agree with you. He'd just look you in the eye and say, 'I don't know what you're talking about.' He would intimidate you if you let him, then he'd buy dinner and make up. But he'd scare people."[30] It was a manner that worked for Clements and enabled him to increase his business and make money.

Clements established the rules for ethical behavior. Shortly after Cunningham joined the company, he was working in Houston and invited two prime customers and their wives to the Rice-Louisiana State University football game. "When John Rhea, who had been promoted to executive vice-president, got wind of it, he and Bill upbraided me for doing business in an unethical manner,"

Cunningham said. "I'd been used to doing this as a usual way of obtaining business in the sales end of the oil spectrum — entertaining people, picking up all the bills, putting them on an airplane and taking them places. That was not the way they did business."

Clements also believed in giving the men he hired the responsibility to do the job and, as time went on, providing them the best equipment available to do the job. "From an operational standpoint, Bill believed in absolute perfection in the quality of the rigs, and the quality of the men who worked on them," Cunningham said.[31]

That didn't mean the company was trouble-free. There was always an element of danger to oil drilling; it was a backdrop for the work, day-by-day. When something goes wrong on an oil drilling rig, it can result in disaster or personal tragedy, and Clements encountered his share of crises.

One involved Rig 22. As the company moved into offshore work in the mid-1950s, it continued to upgrade its rigs. Rig 22, which could work in twenty-five feet of water, was built in 1956, to fulfill a drilling contract with the California Company. It was equipped with columns to give it extra height to drill in the Gulf of Mexico. A forerunner of later, more sophisticated offshore rigs, Rig 22 employed pistons which touched the ocean floor, allowing the rig to move down the hydraulic posts to a specific depth and anchor itself.[32]

Rig 22 was built at the Avondale shipyard, across the Mississippi River from New Orleans. The shipyard was loading drill pipe on the top deck when the barge began listing. As engineers tried to correct the problem, the bottom platform of the rig got caught under the dock and the rig turned over. Some forty-five men were working on the top of the rig, and nine were lost when it overturned. Clements went to New Orleans, where he used the district office of Oil Well Supply to negotiate the insurance claims.[33]

By 1955, eight years after it was founded, Southeastern Drilling Company's operations included sixteen land rigs, eight inland barges, three offshore fixed platform rigs, one offshore tender with rig, and one small offshore submersible barge. From this peak of twenty-nine rigs in 1955, the company began to reduce its U.S. operations, shifting to foreign work.[34]

As Armentrout explained, "Bill Clements had a lot of foresight. When things got tough in one phase of the business, he got into a phase that was making money. We went from land drilling in Mississippi to West Texas, where it got so competitive that if you had one twist-off, you lost your profit. He had a chance to get into shallow water on the Texas and Louisiana coast, where they were making money. From that, we got to go to Trinidad for the Texas Company, which was our first foreign job."[35]

Drilling in the Permian Basin was drying up, and Clements had decided that the company, to realize its potential, had to go further afield than offshore U.S. He wanted to go overseas and offshore. Ike LaRue had other ideas. LaRue had formed Larco Drilling and was interested in putting together land deals and drilling wildcat wells. When Southeastern Drilling got the contract from Texaco to go to Trinidad, Ike approached Clements about buying out his interest in the company. LaRue wanted to concentrate with his two sons, Fred (Bubba) and Ike, Jr., on land drilling in Mississippi, Alabama, and Florida. So, in 1955, Clements bought out LaRue for $1.2 million, paying him off in two years.[36]

The two partners had a friendly parting of the ways, with Clements remaining forever indebted to Ike LaRue. Clements recognized that he never would have gone into the drilling business had it not been for LaRue. Spencer Taylor, meanwhile, had been loaned to LaRue to drill wells in southern Alabama and Florida for a couple of years. He wanted to return to work for Clements, but Clements said, "I'll tell you when to come back." In June of 1955, he was called by Clements to come back.

"We were fixin' to go into the Middle East," Taylor recalled.[37]

Chapter 5

Growing a Company

"Bill, Bill, Bill . . . drill, drill, drill"

IN EIGHT YEARS UNDER Bill Clements' guidance, Southeastern Drilling Company had grown from a small, land-based drilling
contractor to a large land and offshore operation of twenty-nine rigs
covering a five-state area. But the opportunity that came along in
1955 enabled Clements to expand the horizons of his company beyond even his wildest imagination. It involved risk, but calculated
risk didn't bother Clements. Some thought his venturesome nature
was an outgrowth of his experiences as a youth — he had been without and he wasn't afraid to be without again.[1] Perhaps more than
that, Clements never *expected* to be without again. He had supreme
confidence in his own ability, and in his company's ability to perform. Whatever the reason, Clements had the essential characteristics for a successful entrepreneur: a high tolerance for risk, a sense of
what had to be done, and the confidence to do it.

Clements could see by the mid-1950s that the oil world was
changing. In 1955 the domestic oil industry was in a depression, the
first of three that would hit in a thirty-year period. (Another would
come in the early 1970s, before the OPEC embargo, and another
around 1982, lasting through the rest of the decade.) Oil was about
$3 a barrel, where it had been for several years. This slump would
reach its bottom in 1956, when the Hughes rotary rig count would
sink to its lowest level in several decades. The major oil companies

62

were slowing down their activity in the United States and had begun producing new fields in Saudi Arabia and other countries.[2]

Opportunities were emerging abroad and, with the change in the direction of the industry, Clements saw the opportunity to set a new goal — that of becoming a worldwide drilling contractor. Ironically, his chance to go global came along because of a small world known as the Texas oil patch. Clements had developed in the oil patch an acquaintance from Corpus Christi named Paul Turnbull. When Clements was unexpectedly contacted by Turnbull to take a look at an overseas drilling program, his aggressive nature kicked into high gear. He began refocusing Southeastern Drilling into an international drilling contracting company that would outgrow its original name and eventually become known worldwide by the acronym "SEDCO."

Paul Turnbull had been division engineer in charge of drilling and production activities in South Texas for Humble Oil and Refining Company, a Standard of New Jersey company, before establishing a small drilling company with his partner, Frank Zoch, called Turnbull and Zoch. Turnbull and Clements had become acquainted through the drilling business in South Texas and, coincidentally, Turnbull was married to Margaret "Tootsie" Rose, the sister of Clements' Highland Park schoolmate, Tom Rose.

Paul Turnbull had gotten a call one day from a buddy in New York with Standard Vacuum Oil Company about a Stanvac exploration program in India, West Pakistan and East Pakistan (now Bangladesh). Turnbull's friend was Tom Conger; the two men had worked together in the oilfields of East Texas. Conger said that Stanvac — a large and prestigious company jointly owned by Standard of New Jersey (now Exxon) and Socony Vacuum (now Mobil) — was looking for a drilling contractor for a program in India and East and West Pakistan. Turnbull had no experience overseas or with big rigs, and he knew such a job was beyond the capability of his small company. But he knew a fellow who might be interested. Turnbull called Clements.

At the time, Southeastern Drilling was active in Texas, New Mexico, Oklahoma, Louisiana, and Mississippi, working both on land and offshore, and it had one rig working overseas, offshore Trinidad. Southeastern Drilling had more balls in the air than a three-armed juggler, but Clements wasn't afraid to pitch one more. He and Turnbull went to New York to talk to the Stanvac people.

Clements was challenged and excited about the prospect of going overseas, but he had never been to India or to Pakistan. "You
could be talking about going to the moon, as far as I am concerned,"
he told the Stanvac representatives. "I want to see it. I want to go
over there." Clements wanted to meet with the Stanvac people
abroad, see the drilling sites, look at the bridges and the highways,
and see what the transportation problems were. Stanvac agreed to
foot the bill of $25,000 that would send Clements and Turnbull to
India and Pakistan for a month for their on-site inspection. They
met Conger in Calcutta, where he was assigned as the manager of
the program. In the course of the trip, Clements also met Cecil
Green, one of the founders in 1930 of Geophysical Service, Inc., an
industry giant in geophysical exploration. Green was in charge of
GSI's geophysical work for Stanvac; it was Green's job to determine
where to drill the wells.

After appraising the situation, Clements and Turnbull returned
to New York and made a proposal. They got the contract; it was a
partnership deal between SEDCO and Turnbull and Zoch, and they
called the subsidiary company Southeastern Asia Drilling Company. Thus, SEDCO's entry into worldwide drilling began with a
three-rig operation for Stanvac in India and East and West Pakistan.[3]

Walter Etherington, drilling superintendent in West Texas, was
selected to supervise the company's first major foreign operation.
He moved to Karachi, West Pakistan, in early 1956. There, he set up
the first rig in an agricultural area, which required the construction
of a dam to keep out irrigation water. The problems were immense.
On one occasion the fields were flooded, and the crew had to kill
more than 100 cobras and vipers that came over the dam. Et.hering-
ton started the second rig outside Calcutta, India, and the third in
Dhaka, East Pakistan.[4] The operation grew when a fourth rig was
added in what was then British Somaliland, in East Africa. Southeastern provided everything: the drilling rigs, trucking facilities,
transportation equipment, camps, and all auxiliary equipment. The
work would last several years and prove very profitable. Southeastern sent over enough expatriates with experience to get the job
done, but hired the bulk of the workforce locally, for economic and
political reasons. From that point forward, Turnbull and Zoch
joined Southeastern Drilling on a 50-50 basis on all foreign work.[5]

Once SEDCO got its start in foreign drilling with the Stanvac
deal, it moved into Iran in 1958 and then into other countries in the

Middle East. The opportunities came again from contacts in the industry, and Clements' aggressiveness. Through Oil Well Supply's agent in London, Clements became acquainted with George Heseldin, an Englishman who had been managing director for Iraq Petroleum Company, a subsidiary of British Petroleum. Heseldin had lived in Baghdad and worked in Iraq before he retired and moved back to London, where he was the chief consultant for the Beirut-based Contracting and Trading Co. (CAT Co.) in the Persian Gulf area. Heseldin knew that drilling opportunities were about to open up in Iran.[6]

Iran had been taken out of the world oil market when Mohammed Mossadegh, the prime minister, nationalized the oil industry in Iran in 1951 and canceled the British Petroleum concession which had been in operation since the early 1900s. By August 1953, however, Mossadegh had been ousted and the Shah of Iran, Reza Pahlavi, had been restored to his throne. With the Shah again in power, the stage was set to bring Iranian oil back into production and onto the world market.

In October 1954, oil production in southern Iran was put in the hands of a new consortium of Western companies which included BP, the four Aramco (the Arabian-American Oil Company) partners — Jersey, Socony, Texaco, and Standard of California — Gulf, Shell, and the French company, CFP. The establishment of this consortium marked one of the great turning points for the oil industry. Instead of allowing foreigners to own the oil concession, Iran's National Iranian Oil Company would own the country's oil resources, and the consortium would manage the industry and buy all the output, with each company in the consortium disposing of its share of the oil through its own independent marketing system.[7]

George Heseldin knew Baghar Mostoffi, who had been asked by the Shah to head the National Iranian Oil Company (NIOC). Baghar Mostoffi had been educated in England and was part of a family that had been in government in Iran for hundreds of years. His family was so influential that for seven generations it had been the keeper of the crown jewels of Iran. Heseldin knew that Mostoffi and National Iranian Oil were not happy with the consortium arrangement, and NIOC wanted to drill some wells in northern Iran.

Clements got a tip from his friends at Oil Well Supply that he ought to make a trip to London to see Heseldin. He met Heseldin at London's Hyde Park Hotel, where he also was introduced to Emile

Bustani, a Lebanese who had been educated at Massachusetts Institute of Technology and headed the CAT Co. From London, Clements went on alone to Tehran for a meeting with Baghar Mostoffi, which had been arranged by Heseldin. The result of that trip was a contract for two rigs, which were taken to Iran in early 1958.

Clements called the move into Iran from the neighboring countries of Pakistan and India a natural step because the petroleum industry was such a small, closed society. SEDCO had achieved vital prestige within that society with the Stanvac contract; the credibility that resulted had paved the way for the work in Iran.

One of the company's West Texas rigs was moved outside Qum, south of Tehran in northern Iran, to a huge surface structure about five or six miles long. Mostoffi pointed to a throw on the geological fault line and gave the order to make it the location for the first well. The site turned out to be a huge gas distillate field which Clements described as "the most dangerous, volatile situation you could have." Sure enough, Clements got a cable that the Qum well was blowing. He flew to Iran to find one of the scariest sights of his career. All along the fault line at the crest of the geological structure were little geysers of gas and water blowing up from the ground. "If anyone had struck a match or if some piece of metal had hit a piece of rock and sparked that thing, the whole country would have been on fire," Clements later recounted. The blowout finally was killed, and the field turned out to be a huge discovery, a continuing source of gas for Tehran into the 1990s.[8]

Rhea recalled that the company was really trying to expand in 1958. Etherington had moved to Beirut as the general manager overseeing operations in the Middle and Near East. And Etherington had learned that Japan's Arabian Oil Company, Ltd., which had won the offshore concession in the Neutral Zone between Saudi Arabia and Kuwait in 1957, was dissatisfied with its drilling contractor there. The Japanese company was looking for a new contractor to work in the Neutral Zone. Clements sent Rhea to Japan to try to get the job. He stayed in Tokyo six weeks, returning on New Year's Eve, 1958, with a contract which would last for several years. The company would drill offshore in the Neutral Zone using a fixed-platform unit.[9]

In 1959, Southeastern Drilling also went to work for the Iranian Oil Exploration & Producing Company (IOEPC), the consortium of the world's largest oil-producing companies. Under the direction of Jack Berlin, who was on loan from Standard of California, the consortium had been trying to operate old British Petroleum rigs with personnel pulled in from its eight companies. The situation was confusing and disorderly, and the consortium finally decided that, instead of trying to mesh personnel from eight different companies, it needed one good contractor. Aware of Southeastern's operation in northern Iran for NIOC, the consortium offered Southeastern a drilling contract.

Spencer Taylor went to Bandar Abbas for the beach landing and to help set up the rigs in southern Iran. "This was an isolated operation," he recalled. "Everything had to be shipped or flown in." The consortium had tried to employ Iranians, but when SEDCO appeared on the scene, most of the Iranian workers were standing around and watching. "We insisted they be trained," Taylor said, and eventually all of SEDCO's drillers in Iran were Iranians.[10] SEDCO was so successful that by 1965, it was the sole drilling contractor for the consortium, providing five land rigs. The company also had considerable construction equipment in Iran for building airstrips, jetties, roads, and camps.[11]

The heat was intense in the Iranian oilfields, with temperatures sometimes climbing to 120 or 125 degrees. However, most of the expatriated oilfield workers were from Texas and able to withstand the heat; camps were completely air-conditioned.[12] Clements was particularly proud of the SEDCO camps — totally self-contained mini-cities that began with these early foreign ventures and evolved over the years in different countries into sophisticated operations. "We could distill our own water. We had our own power, our own lights. We had our own laundry. We were totally self-sufficient," he said. "We had our own shower house, our own plumbing system and sewage system. We had our dining facility. We had our recreation hall. We had our radio communications. We had our own trucks, and when we got through drilling one well, we would pick everything up and move it to the next location. No one else had ever done it. We had a tool pusher that was in charge of the whole thing. And these men came right out of our organization, in West Texas or in Louisiana or the Texas Gulf Coast." Supplies were often brought in by airplane to airstrips built adjacent to the camps. "It was a hell of an operation," Clements said.[13]

Taylor had expected to live and work in the Middle East but got so involved in the company's expansion program that he never went overseas to stay. He assembled and ordered equipment, had it rigged up in the yards, ordered the camps and the trucks and other vehicles and had them shipped overseas. He became assistant to the president and, in 1962, vice-president of foreign operations, with primary responsibility for the work in Iran. Seasoned SEDCO people who went to Iran in the early stages included Etherington and Bobby Cox.

"Clements always visited the drilling sites," Cox recalled. "If he looked at a drilling rig, he knew how it ought to be functioning. He knew what he was talking about." If it wasn't functioning properly, Cox said, Clements would "read the Riot Act" to someone. "He could do it like no one else — other than a top sergeant in the U.S. Marine Corps. He could be rough on you. But you always knew where you stood with him." Cox recalled an incident that occurred in the Tehran office when Walter Etherington was in charge. Etherington was high on an accountant in the office whom Clements didn't think much of (his doubts were later justified). Etherington was defending the accountant. Clements cut him off, short. "Walter, be quiet. You wouldn't know a good accountant if he jumped up and bit you in the ass."[14] Clements operated according to the philosophy of "We've got a job to do, so put all the hogwash and talk aside and get on and do it," Cox said. "He had tenacity."

Over time, SEDCO had ten large land rigs and two offshore rigs in Iran, including a shipyard repair facility at Bushire, a big trucking operation, a training school at Ahwaz to teach Iranians English and drilling operations, a large central warehouse, and machine and electrical shop facilities. The company had its main office in Tehran, Iran's capital city in northern Iran, but some employees and families lived in Ahwaz in southwestern Iran.

While Iran was its biggest operation, the company was growing throughout the Middle East. Some of the early work in the Middle East was undertaken through a joint venture with the Lebanese men from CAT Co. — Emile Bustani, Shukri Shammas, and Abdullah Khoury. The joint venture company was called SEACAT, which stood for Southeast Asian Drilling Co. and CAT Co.[15] One Middle East operation involved a partnership with Zapata, the drilling company owned by George Bush. The partnership, SEACAT-Zapata, operated a drilling tender in Tunisia and also offshore Kuwait.

In 1965, SEDCO was still drilling for Arabian Oil Company, Ltd., offshore the Saudi Arabia-Kuwait Neutral Zone. It also worked offshore Iran for Pan American International Oil Company

(Standard of Indiana), and completed a contract with Dubai Petroleum Company (Conoco) to drill wells on land and offshore in Dubai. With the exception of Iraq, SEDCO would work in almost every country in the Middle East, including Qatar, Saudi Arabia, Sharjah, Oman, and Abu Dhabi.[16]

By 1972, SEDCO's activities in the Middle East included thirteen land rigs, three offshore rigs, and a fleet of boats all under long-term contract. In the company's office in Tehran, one might hear Persian, Armenian, English, Pakistani, Greek, Indian, or Arabic spoken. Although eventually SEDCO became known as an offshore company, Iran continued as its largest land operation, and work in the Middle East for many years constituted 30 to 40 percent of its revenues.[17] SEDCO continued to work in Iran until the Ayatollah Khomeini took over in 1979, forcing SEDCO to abandon the country.

In the summer of 1958, as the Iranian work was getting under way, Paul Turnbull and Frank Zoch learned of a potentially huge drilling job in Argentina, through a contact from a landman in Corpus Christi who brokered oil deals. William N. "Bill" Dillin of Corpus Christi had heard from a lawyer friend in Washington, D.C., Charles F. O'Neall, that Argentina, under the direction of a new president, had a great need for crude oil. O'Neall believed he could obtain a hearing with the government oil company, Yacimientos Petroliferos Fiscales (Y.P.F.), through an associate in Argentina, Antonio Angel Diaz, if he and Dillin could put together a deal with a drilling contractor. Dillin called Turnbull and Zoch, who informed Clements of the opportunity and told him that Dillin and O'Neall wanted a finder's fee if they were successful in putting together the deal. In July 1958, there was a meeting in Dallas of Dillin, O'Neall, Turnbull, Clements, and Taylor, who was then a vice-president.[18] The Southeastern officials decided to pursue the work.

Rhea, Southeastern's executive vice-president, knew South America from his World War II days working for Standard of New Jersey in Colombia; he spoke reasonably good Spanish. So in October 1958, Clements dispatched Rhea to Argentina to survey the situation. Rhea visited the Y.P.F. field operation in the Comodoro Rivadavia area in southern Argentina and, in his preliminary investigation, found the situation promising. He called Clements, who joined him in Argentina to formulate a bid and to meet Y.P.F. officials. On October 29, 1958, a proposal was drafted by Clements,

Rhea and Dr. Oscar Elkin, an Argentine attorney, and submitted to Y.P.F. However, in December, Y.P.F. announced that it would seek bids through an international public tender, and Southeastern ended up competing with several international drilling companies for the work.

Clements personally traveled to Comodoro Rivadavia in southern Argentina, where Y.P.F. rigs were working. He discovered Y.P.F. was spending a minimum of thirteen days and an average of sixteen days to drill wells to an average depth of 5,500 feet. Clements figured he could drill 1,000 wells on an average of nine days a well. How could he beat the best effort of Y.P.F. by four days? "Well, I wasn't a drilling contractor for nothing. Hell, I know how to drill a hole in the ground," Clements said, in telling the Argentina story decades later.[19]

In March 1959, the bid of Southeastern Argentina to drill 1,000 wells was accepted by Y.P.F. and contract negotiations began ironing out the details.[20] Kerr-McGee and an Italian drilling company also got contracts for 500 wells each and, according to the historian for Delta Drilling Company, Clements got the work because he had "close connections with powerful men in the Argentine government."[21] Throughout the negotiations, Southeastern was aided by a group of entrepreneurs known as the Houston brothers — Douglas, Robin, and Ted Houston — Argentines who had gone to school in the United States. They served as local liaisons with Y.P.F.

The Argentina deal brought another Clements friend from Highland Park days into the firm, Tom Rhodes. Clements and Rhodes had gone to elementary school and high school together. Rhodes later graduated Phi Beta Kappa from Stanford and from the University of Texas Law School and was practicing law in a small firm in Dallas when he was contacted by Clements for some legal help in 1958 and 1959. Rhodes joined Clements, Rhea and Dr. Oscar Elkin, the Argentine lawyer, in Buenos Aires to help draw up the contract for the Argentina deal, after SEDCO had been designated successful bidder.[22]

The contract awarded Southeastern Drilling Company of Argentina was to drill and complete 1,000 wells on land in the southern tip of Argentina. It was the largest drilling contract ever awarded, anywhere. By this time, Clements was negotiating contracts with major oil companies for work in India, Pakistan, Iran and Canada, as well as domestically, and he needed a lawyer to travel with him and be at his side as the contracts were negotiated. In 1960, Rhodes joined SEDCO as its general counsel.[23] Negotiating tough contracts became a trademark of the Clements-run company. Over the years, Rhodes would negotiate the fine print of the contracts, protecting the company from various kinds of liability and insuring that the company would get its money out of a deal. He became one of Clements' most trusted employees.

The work in Argentina began in 1960 and concluded in September of 1963. It was a turnkey job. "We would do all the work, putting in roads, water lines, digging the pits, all those things that an oil company normally would do," said Rhea, the company's officer reponsible for South America. "We had four years to do this; we did it in three and a half years." Rhea spent about half of his time in Argentina, living either in the field or in a hotel. The company's managing director in Buenos Aires was geologist Bruce Scrafford; Howard Archer was the field superintendent; and Edwin J. "Jack" Smith, Jr., was administrative manager.

Smith had been working in the Foreign Service for the State Department, including a three-year stint in Quito, Equador, when he learned of Clements' interest in Argentina from contacts at the First National Bank in Dallas. He had degrees from SMU in finance and economics and had taught Spanish while doing graduate work. He was perfect for the administrative and accounting job in Argentina except that he knew nothing about the drilling business. Clements told Smith that if he was willing to take a "short course" in drilling, he would hire him. Smith agreed and was dispatched to Louisiana to be a roustabout for five months on Rig 7 in the Gulf of Mexico. He was given these instructions by Clements: "Don't let anybody know you have a business degree and a master's degree from SMU and that you worked for the Foreign Service." Smith called his "short course" requirement typical of Clements' management style, but added that "it was very beneficial to me. When somebody started talking about a rotary table or a traveling block, I knew what it was." Smith was hired in 1959 and spent twenty-nine years with the company, eventually becoming insurance manager. He was one of the first employees in and the last to leave Argentina. "There's never been a contract even close to it — 1,000 wells was just unheard of then, or since then," Smith said.[24]

The rigs used in Argentina were smaller rigs, operating to a depth of 5,800 to 6,000 feet. The formations were relatively tight, which meant more wells were needed. SEDCO had a mass production operation. There was one large base camp for some 600 workers, approximately 100 Americans and the rest Argentine and Chilean. The workers were transported to the rigs to work twelve-hour shifts. They worked every day for two weeks and then had a week off; during time off, the workers were transported to their homes or to Buenos Aires. In the field camp, workers lived in bunk houses constructed in Houston — two rooms on a skid, with one person to a room. There were a few family homes at the camp site. All of the workers were fed in the camp. Some twenty rigs were used in the operation and they were moved frequently; some were on skids, others were truck mounted. It was an efficient operation, and by the end of the three and a half years, Rhea said, "we could drill one of those wells in three days." There was only a seven- or eight-hour interval between the time one well was plugged, or completed, and the rig was skidded and a new well spudded.[25]

The base camp was built in the pampas of Patagonia, with the closest town seventy or eighty miles away. The support activities, including the purchasing of all the food served in the camp, and the billing, collecting and accounting, were provided by the home office in Buenos Aires, which was staffed by ten or twelve people. The country underwent several nonviolent revolutions, and even with a tough contract, the company occasionally had difficulty collecting its money. When that occurred, Clements and Rhea would show up and, according to Smith, "throw a little weight around." If there was one thing for which Bill Clements would not stand, it was not being paid.

During the fulfilling of the contract, Clements visited Argentina several times a year, for several days on each visit. Rhodes said that Clements worked extremely hard during the Argentine period. In Buenos Aires, company officials would sometimes go out to dinner or to watch polo matches, but Clements was totally focused on business. Some Argentine associates wanted to entertain the company officials. "They'd even try to line up women for us. That was the last thing we wanted, but it was their idea of entertaining. We would go to these parties and Clements would talk business," Rhodes said. One Argentine playboy, a polo player and a friend of some of the Argentine associates, tried his best to get Clements to lighten up. "The last thing this polo player wanted to do was talk business. He wanted to bring in the dancing girls," Rhodes recalled.

The playboy, bored with Clements, would just shake his head and say, in mock derision, "Bill, Bill, Bill . . . drill, drill, drill."

"He wasn't too far off with that, because Bill was all business the whole time he was down there. We might go out for a drink and a steak, but he was still talking business most of the time," Rhodes said.[26]

Besides being hard-driving, Clements was also generous to people in the company. He wanted the officers of the company to have a stock interest, to share in the company's success. A separate subsidiary corporation, Southeastern Argentina, was set up for the work in Argentina. "When this job was over and done, we all participated in the profits, individually," said Rhea. The project was even more profitable because, at the conclusion, all of the rigs were sold to Y.P.F.

As the key men came on board, Clements promised them a piece of the action. Before the Argentine deal, several of the men were offered stock options. They signed notes for the stock, and when the job was finished, each one had enough to pay off his note. Rhea said Clements "let us in on the ownership of the company at a very low price. As the company grew, expanded and profited, our investment grew in geometric proportions." Among those who had ownership and enjoyed the $17 million profits from Argentina were John Rhea, Tom Rhodes, Spencer Taylor, Jerry Cunningham, Walter Etherington, Bill Armentrout, Howard Archer, and Howard Scallorn.[27]

However, the "finders" of the Argentine deal — Dillin, O'Neall and Diaz — weren't satisfied with their share. They had received a letter of agreement stating Dillin and O'Neall would split 10 percent of the profit, and Diaz and the Houston brothers would split another 10 percent. According to Clements, they were told their share of the profits would amount to about $3 million, split four ways. The Houston brothers remained longtime friends of Clements, but Diaz, Dillin and O'Neall sued, claiming Southeastern Argentina hid some of its profits. Dillin and O'Neall, meanwhile, had fled the country to evade paying income taxes, and both had federal tax liens against them. Rhodes called it a trumped-up lawsuit, but it nonetheless would cause Clements some embarrassment when he got into public life. A federal court in Arlington, Virginia, eventually decided in SEDCO's favor, and Dillin fled back to the Caribbean.[28]

The Argentina deal was SEDCO's first really big success.

"That's what made SEDCO," assessed the head of Delta Gulf, a drilling company which bid but didn't get an Argentina contract.[29]

Soon after moving back to Dallas, in 1951, Bill and Pauline bought some acreage in Preston Hollow, where they built a home at 4622 Meadowood. They had enjoyed the lifestyle in Jackson, Mississippi, where the children had room for their ponies and other animals, and there was still plenty of available land in North Dallas. The children kept their ponies, Velvet and Velveteen (another was later born, named Corduroy), and added Dalmatians and all kinds of pets. A creek ran behind the house, and Gill and Nancy spent countless hours "exploring." The children went to public school (Walnut Hill Elementary), where Gill started in the fifth grade and Nancy in the fourth. Most of their memories begin with this time period.

"We were a low-key, private family," Nancy Clements Seay recalled. "Dad was business-oriented and family-oriented. He would come home at night with a bunch of papers and read. We always had family dinner on time." Her mother and dad, she said, "weren't real social. They were at home nights . . . . Dad traveled a lot with his job. He was gone three or four weeks at a time. Mother traveled some with Dad, but by the time we were in school, they wanted us to have a stable, regular supportive home life, and they decided Mother was needed at home."[30]

Mrs. Clements enjoyed and remained close to her family in Terrell. Many Saturdays, when Nancy and Gill were youngsters, she would drive them to Terrell to spend time with their great-grandmother, grandfather, aunts, uncles, and cousins. There were big family group gatherings for lunch. The children were also close to their paternal grandparents. Evelyn Clements, who was an expert in handiwork and quilting, made exquisite doll clothes for Nancy, from ice skating and square dance and Valentine costumes to tiny quilted bathrobes and raincoats.

Even though Clements was traveling a lot, visiting the rigs in West Texas and the offshore locations in the early '50s and then India, East and West Pakistan, and Iran in the mid-to-late '50s, he managed to carve out time for his family.

Gill remembered going to West Texas when he was seven or eight with his father and grandfather ("Pops") Clements. After the day's business was done, they would find a stock tank and hunt doves. "Other than making some trips to West Texas to visit rigs, I don't remember much about that period," he said. Once the family settled on Meadowood, however, Clements became very active in his son's life. "From the time I was eleven to fourteen, I got an enormous amount of Dad's time," Gill recalled. Much of that activity revolved around the Boy Scouts, which had been so important in Clements' own development.

Gill and his father went one night to visit the Scout troop at Walnut Hill School. What they found was a mediocre Scout program of about fifteen boys; the troop had never produced an Eagle Scout. The troop obviously needed some leadership. Clements became the scoutmaster, devoting the equivalent of a day a week to the troop. The troop, under Clements' direction, took a weekend camping trip once a month and a two-week camping trip in the summer. "Somehow, he made the time," Gill said. In less than two years, before his thirteenth birthday, Gill was an Eagle Scout. When Clements finally resigned as scoutmaster, Troop 100 had divided into three troops with 140 boys and had several Eagle Scouts. "It was unique in the Dallas area; nobody had a program like Troop 100," Gill said.[31]

In 1953, through his friend and business associate Ike LaRue, Bill Clements became a member of the Koon Kreek Klub near Athens. It offered exclusive hunting and fishing privileges for its wealthy members, many of whom were from Dallas. When the club was organized in 1900, men would ride the train out from Dallas and then go by wagon from Athens to the private hunting and fishing lodge. Later, members were allowed to build houses. Clements took Gill hunting and fishing at Koon Kreek, and then on more ambitious trips to Canada and Africa. On some of the pack trips, they would ride horses for a week to get to the hunting site, sometimes being gone for three or four weeks.

Clements loved the "outdoorsy stuff. That was his parenting activity," said Nancy. She occasionally went along, though she wasn't inclined toward fishing and hunting. "They tried to include me — like when we were at Koon Kreek, I remember getting up in the middle of the night with Dad and him showing me how to bait a trot line with blood bait. It wasn't my favorite thing to do, but I enjoyed being with Dad." Nancy had her own activities, and her mother was as involved with her as Clements was with Gill. Where Gill had the Boy Scouts, Nancy went to Camp Waldemar in the Texas Hill Country for six weeks every summer from the time she was nine to sixteen years old. There she developed her own leadership skills.

To provide a special time together for the whole family, Clements liked to take long family car trips in the summer. They would be gone three weeks, sometimes longer — and this was before cars were air-conditioned. "We didn't go to Europe until I was in college, but we saw all forty-eight states," Nancy said. They took one trip up through middle America and the West, one to the Northeast which included New York, Maine and Canada, one through the Southeast, and one up the West Coast. On one trip they stayed five days in a log cabin in the Tetons, and on another, they ended up in Minnesota on a houseboat with the family of a former SEDCO employee. But usually, they were on the move, up and traveling before first light.

"Dad would say, 'I want to get an early start in the morning because I want to cover at least 200 miles before breakfast, before it gets hot,'" Nancy remembered. "At the end of the day, his great satisfaction was in saying we covered so many miles and we have pictures of everybody in front of three state capitols!"[32]

The family was usually joined by Pauline's father, Ben Gill, on these trips. Grandfather Gill and Clements liked to stop by the side of the road and look at the fields.

As a father, Clements was an authority figure who occasionally seemed to be trying to repeat some of the lessons of his own childhood, when he had to keep the chicken coop clean. For example, on a Saturday morning when Nancy and Gill were in high school, Nancy was awakened by her father and told, "Today, we're going to clean up the stables." Clements would lead the way. Or, on another Saturday, it might be the attic. "He taught us to work, to get grubby. He taught us how to do a good job and feel satisfied after we did it," Nancy said.

Gill and Nancy stayed in the Dallas public schools, attending Thomas Jefferson High School, where they were involved in various activities. Both were cheerleaders. Bill and Pauline were involved parents, serving as chaperones and parent sponsors for events. Nancy also ran for treasurer of the student council, which meant she had to make a speech before the student body at assembly. One night after dinner, she asked her father if he had any ideas for the speech. Clements thought for about a minute and said, "Yeah, I'll tell you exactly what to say. You stand up there and say, 'I'm Nancy Clements. I want to be your treasurer. When you pick your treasurer, you need someone good with figures. And I've got a good figure.'" Nancy's mother overheard and called out, "You're not really going to say that, are you?"

Nancy used the line and she won. "I was the only one who said anything funny," she said. "The whole auditorium was just rolling with laughter. You could hear them in the cafeteria talking about it. I give Dad the credit. He gave me the confidence to do this sort of thing."

While Clements had been reared a Methodist, Pauline was Episcopalian. They became active members of St. Michael and All Angels Episcopal Church in Dallas. Nancy grew up singing in the choir; Clements served on the vestry and through the years was a generous contributor to the church.

Business was not a big topic of conversation in the Clements household during those years of childhood. "I truly didn't know what he did until I got in college," Gill said. On school forms, when asked his father's occupation, he always put "petroleum engineer." Nor did he know his father's net worth. "Our lifestyle was somewhat above my friends. But I was in SMU before we had a swimming pool. We drove Chevrolets and Buicks. I didn't feel like we were a wealthy family," Gill said.[33]

"We were always very comfortable. We didn't want for anything. But we were never extravagant," Nancy said. "Money wasn't spent just for the sake of spending money. Home was a priority; clothes were not a priority. A lot of friends had a lot less than we did; we were on the high end, that was very clear. But we fit in well as a family to our environment," she said.

When the Clements family moved back to Dallas, they were invited to join the Dallas Country Club, Brook Hollow Golf Club, and Northwood Country Club. Pauline liked Northwood, so the family became members there. Many of their close friends were from the company, and when they socialized, it was usually with business associates. Clements was also active in the Petroleum Club.[34] Pauline was devoted to her family, and to creating a lovely home environment. She was interested in gardening, in antiques and furnishings, and served on the boards of the Dallas Woman's Club and the Dallas Garden Club. "She was home-focused, and he was business-focused. So they fit together very well," Nancy recalled. "He didn't allow a lot of frills like social life to take up his time."

She remembers her mother and father both as being very opinionated. She knew they were the ultimate authorities, that they had sovereignty over their children, but she and Gill also knew they could disagree. When she had a divergent opinion, Nancy would call it her "free choice." She explained it was a "teenage way of saying we could be different." Nancy was very close to her mother and, like her mother, was more value-oriented, where her father was more practical and pragmatic. "We thought differently about things. He had a different slant on things. He usually saw the big picture," Nancy said. She learned to value and trust his advice, she said, because it usually panned out. But knowing that they could have "free choice" on some things also helped her deal with differences she and her father had later in life, particularly over her parents' divorce. "Later on, there were some choices he made that I disagreed with, and that freed me up from thinking he was right about all things."[35]

Gill graduated from Thomas Jefferson in 1959, and went to SMU, where he became a member of Phi Delta Theta fraternity and met his future bride, Patricia Lindall. The Clements home was open to his college friends; they were welcome at the family dinner table, and Pauline was regarded by some as an away-from-home mom.[36] When Gill was in college, he and his father talked about a potential career, and Clements advised his son to study engineering if he was interested in going into the drilling contracting business. Gill, however, wanted to go to business school, and he chose to major in finance. When he graduated, his father told him there could be another opportunity to join the company if he would go to law school. Instead, Gill went to work for the First National Bank in a training program.[37] On October 26, 1963, Gill Clements married Pat Lindall. They would have three children: Catherine, born January 20, 1965; William Perry "Bill" Clements III, born January 14, 1967; and Margaret, born January 16, 1969. While their children were growing up, Gill and Pat Clements lived in Highland Park. They later moved to Forney and built a Texas Hill Country-style stone home, fashioned after an early Texas fort, on Clements land.

Nancy graduated from high school in 1960 and went to SMU for her freshman and sophomore years. Then she started dating George Seay, a Dallasite who attended the University of Texas. Nancy was ready to spread her wings; she wanted the expansiveness, the scope of the University of Texas, so she transferred for her junior year. Halfway into that year, she became "pinned" to George Seay. Like her mother, she was a member of Pi Beta Phi sorority. Like her father, she set goals for herself. One was to graduate magna cum laude, which she did. Nancy received her degree from the University of Texas, majoring in English and history. When Seay graduated, he went into the air force. They married on February 13, 1965, following her graduation, and George went to SMU Law School.[38] The Seays settled in Dallas and had two children: George Edward Seay III, born June 1, 1967, and Pauline Allen Seay, born October 14, 1969.

Clements spent the 1950s growing a company and a family. As his offspring spread their wings into adulthood, his business also was moving into its prime. In the early 1960s, SEDCO began forming long-range plans and goals to drill in the deep oceans of the world. To fulfill those goals would require Bill Clements' vision, and his commitment to develop the requisite technology. In the next decade, those two factors would guide SEDCO into its position as a worldwide leader in the offshore drilling industry.

Chapter 6

Offshore and Overseas

SEDCO in the '60s and Early '70s

BILL CLEMENTS WAS CONVINCED that the future of oil exploration and development was offshore, in deep water. To capitalize on that future required envisioning the needs of the oil industry and pushing the edge of drilling technology. Tom Rhodes, general counsel of SEDCO, felt Clements' success in business came from his ability to "anticipate moves, where the industry was going. His foresight was really unusual."[1]

Offshore drilling was still relatively young. The first successful well in the Gulf of Mexico had been spudded in 1937 one mile offshore Louisiana, resulting in the discovery of the Creole Field. In 1938, Standard Oil Company of Texas completed Texas' first offshore well in Galveston Bay. Fixed platforms were used, and exploration grew steadily farther from shore. In 1947, Kerr-McGee, an Oklahoma independent, put together the technology to strike oil ten and a half miles off the Louisiana coast. It was the first successful well drilled in the Gulf out of sight of land. Offshore drilling at that time posed a unique set of challenges. Besides the unknowns of building a platform, getting it into place and drilling in the ocean floor, essential knowledge about weather, tides, and currents was either rudimentary or almost nonexistent. While the Gulf was the focus of marine drilling in the U.S. following World War II, the period 1947-1953 was clouded by the dispute between the federal government and the states over ownership of submerged lands. When the issue was resolved in 1953 by congressional passage of the tidelands legislation, work escalated in the Gulf.[2]

Technology and equipment had been evolving since Southeastern Drilling got into offshore drilling in the 1950s in shallow water with the flat-bottom inland barges and then the post-type barge. Those rigs were followed by: the jackup (the legs of the unit penetrated the sea bed and the drilling rig was "jacked up" over the water), which was used in water depths up to 350 feet; the drillship (a highly mobile, ocean-going vessel used in deep water, far from land); and the semi-submersible. The submersible, used in relatively shallow water, is towed to a site, where its hulls are flooded so they come to rest on bottom. The semi-submersible was designed so that the hulls, when flooded, sink only a little below the surface of the water.[3] It was in the development of the semi-submersibles that SEDCO made its mark in offshore drilling equipment.

Peter O'Donnell, the Dallas investor and Republican Party guru, bought stock in SEDCO when the company went public in 1965, partly because of the semi-submersible rigs the company had developed. One day O'Donnell was having lunch with Clements at the Petroleum Club. There was a big globe in the club, which indicated land and water and measured water depth.

"Can you drill in that depth of water?" O'Donnell asked, referring to 1,000 fathoms (6,000 feet). Clements replied that he could. "Well there's as much of that as there is land," O'Donnell remarked.

"Yeah, and the geology under it is the same," Clements said.

"That's going to greatly expand the area where you can drill a well," O'Donnell said.

"Right," Clements responded.[4]

As the Argentina work was winding down, SEDCO was on its way to the development in the mid-to-late 1960s of the SEDCO 135 series — the most sophisticated semi-submersible units built at the time. The SEDCO 135 was set on giant tripods and was so named because it could drill sitting on sea bottom at a maximum water depth of 135 feet. Or, it could drill from a floating position in depths of up to 600 feet. From the keel to the top of the drilling derrick, it was as tall as a 30-story office building, and had the capacity to drill wells on the ocean floor to a depth of 25,000 feet.[5]

The christening in April 1965, in Pascagoula, Mississippi, of the first SEDCO 135 marked the beginning of a new era for the company — specialization in deep water drilling.[6] Key people were invited to the christening and to have dinner in New Orleans. The initial SEDCO 135 drilled its first deep well offshore Louisiana in the Gulf of Mexico, where it later survived Hurricane Betsy.

From 1964 through 1968, seven 135s were built and put into operation. Much of the technology was developed in partnership with the Royal Dutch Shell Group, which, with British Petroleum, owned two of the rigs that were operated by SEDCO. The other five rigs were owned and operated by SEDCO. The company, by then, was operating according to a conservative philosophy: It would not build any unit unless it had a contract for its use. By 1973, twelve of these units would be built, each more advanced and capable of operating in more severe ocean environments.

The first 135 series rigs cost from $6.5 million to $8.8 million each and were financed by the First National Bank in Dallas and U.S. Steel. They brought in about $8,000 a day in revenues. Large amounts of capital were needed to build this sophisticated equipment and expand the company, so the decision was made to take the company public. In May 1965, after operating as a privately owned company for eighteen years, Southeastern Drilling became publicly owned with the sale of 315,000 of its shares, representing about 18 percent of the total shares outstanding. In July 1965, the company's stock was qualified for listing in the national over-the-counter market.[7]

The year it went public, SEDCO drilled forty wells at a total footage of 393,484. The company had 1,075 employees, gross income of $15.4 million, and a net income of $3.4 million, which amounted to $2.12 per share. The officers were William P. Clements, Jr., president and director; Paul R. Turnbull, vice-president and director; John W. Rhea, Jr., vice-president and director; Spencer L. Taylor, vice-president and director; Jerry P. Cunningham, vice-president and director; Tom B. Rhodes, vice-president, general counsel and director; Frank P. Zoch, Jr., director; Shukri Shammas, director; W. C. McAfee, secretary; and Irving E. Davis, treasurer.

The future direction of SEDCO — offshore and overseas — was set by the time the company went public. Taylor believed Clements' vision was critical to the company's success. "If he hadn't wanted to go offshore and overseas, we would have been just another drilling contractor. He thought that's where the opportunities were." Over time, when anybody thought of deep-water drilling, they thought of SEDCO, he said.[8]

SEDCO reports began to read like exotic travelogues. In 1970 the SEDCO 135 left the Gulf of Mexico for West Africa — a move that was particularly notable because it ended SEDCO's drilling activities in the United States.[9]

The 135A, the second in the series, was towed to the island of Borneo, southwest of the Philippines, for a two-year contract for Brunei Shell Petroleum Company, Ltd. During the tow from Japan, the unit encountered two typhoons but survived to complete its first well in the waters offshore Sarawak. It eventually would work for eighteen years for Shell in Borneo, the longest offshore contract ever.

Disaster struck, however, on the third unit. The 135B was built in Japan for Shell to operate in Brunei in the South China Sea. As it was being towed from Japan to Brunei, the rig broke up just opposite the southern end of the Philippines. Thirteen lives were lost; there was only one survivor. The rig sank in several thousand feet of water and was never found. "Bill was convinced we ran over a floating mine from World War II. I thought it was a structural design problem," Taylor said.[10]

Clements flew to the Philippines, where he met Shell representatives from The Hague. They called in experts and questioned the survivor and witnesses on the tug. The investigation failed to come up with a conclusive cause for the loss. Clements thought it had hit a mine because of the description of the incident by witnesses on the tug. "They said they were going along nicely, there was no heavy sea and no big waves, and all of a sudden there was an explosion that sounded like a huge bomb going off. And in less than two minutes, the whole structure was gone. We are not talking about something that is little. It's longer than a football field and as high as a thirty-five-story building. And in two minutes, it was gone," Clements said in an interview years later.[11]

SEDCO employed Earl and Wright, a San Francisco engineering firm, to analyze the loss. Earl and Wright's chief engineer and vice-president, Bill Martinovich, gathered technical data and concluded that the tubular joint intersections on the rig had high stress concentrations which precipitated a low cycle fatigue failure. Technically, the World War II mine theory was possible, Martinovich said, but mathematically, his explanation was the logical one. Martinovich recommended some design changes in the 135, beginning a long-term relationship between Earl and Wright and SEDCO.[12]

Three more 135 units, costing an average of $10 million each, began work in 1966. The SEDCO 135D was completed in Rotterdam and towed to the west coast of Africa for a long-term contract with Shell BP in Nigeria. It was shut down in 1967 by the Biafra-Nigeria conflict but eventually worked seven years in West African waters, drilling wells offshore Nigeria, Togo, Ghana, and the Cameroons. The SEDCO 135E was constructed at Hiroshima by Mitsubishi Heavy Industries, and began work in southeast Australia for Shell.[13]

SEDCO's major involvement in Canada began with the SEDCO 135F, which was constructed in Victoria, British Columbia, the first offshore rig built in Canada. When SEDCO got a two-year contract from Shell in 1965 to drill up the coast of Western Canada, there were no semi-submersibles working in either Eastern or Western Canada.

Shell drilled a half-dozen exploratory wells with the 135F under the worst weather conditions ever recorded at that time. A 1968 Shell Canada report said the unit "remained on location throughout the winter in the face of storm winds gusting to 92 MPH and seas of up to fifty-eight feet. Drilling operations have been conducted in 72 MPH winds and thirty to forty feet seas." Jerry Cunningham, who supervised SEDCO's Canadian activity, said, "Several times, we experienced waves of ninety-five feet. In a week's time, we might experience the 100-year storm prediction more than once. It gave our equipment great credibility." From Canada, the 135F went to New Plymouth, New Zealand, where it made the Maui gas discovery, and then, under contract with Amoco U.K., it undertook the longest tow perhaps ever for a semi-submersible — six months and 16,000 miles — to the North Sea.[14]

Four sister vessels to the 135s were built from 1969 to 1973: the SEDCO H, I, J and K. The "135" designation was left off because the unit was no longer designed to rest on the bottom seabed in 135 feet of water but rather to operate principally in a floating position in 800 feet of water. The first three units were built at the same time at Halifax Shipyard. By the time the "H" series was completed, these rigs were costing upwards of $25 million each.

During the early 1970s, SEDCO had the H, I and J working off Nova Scotia, as far as 200 miles to the east of Newfoundland, in dreadful sea conditions with the constant threat of icebergs.

SEDCO's equipment and operating personnel had developed such a record that major oil companies wanted SEDCO for exploration and development programs in the North Sea.[15]

Even as SEDCO was increasing its activity in Canada, new joint ventures were getting under way in Europe and northern Africa. In 1966 two joint venture companies were formed: SEDNETH with Dutch partners and ALFOR with the Algerian government. The two joint ventures demonstrated the diversity of conditions under which SEDCO was able to work — SEDNETH offshore in the North Sea and ALFOR on land in the Sahara Desert.

The 1956 discovery of oil beneath the towering Saharan sand dunes provided a new frontier for world oil. France, which had controlled Algeria since the nineteenth century, took the lead in exploring it. But Algeria was caught up in a bloody war for independence, which it finally won in 1962. In 1966, ALFOR became the first drilling company to break the French drilling monopoly in the northern Africa country. It started with three land rigs and was operating eleven land rigs by 1972.[16]

The home office of ALFOR was in a suburb of Algiers on the Mediterranean coast. The drilling, however, was done in 125-degree temperatures in the Sahara Desert, anywhere from 20 to 300 miles from the village of Hassi Messaoud, where ALFOR maintained its desert base. The base included a warehouse, mechanical workshop, electrical workshop, and transportation shop. Transportation formed a big part of the operation, because all essentials had to be trucked into the drilling site, often over poor roads and long distances.

Algeria was also one of the most difficult places for expatriates to live because of the political climate. "Algeria had not been independent that long, and the Algerians had strong resentment against the French; they transferred that to other expatriates," said Bobby Cox, who was the general manager in Algeria. Most of the expatriates lived in Oran on the northern coast and were flown the 1,200 miles to the desert base for two weeks on the job and then back home for a week off. Each rig was equipped with a camp for about fifty people.[17]

Before going into any area, Clements would talk to people in the industry and others familiar with that region of the world and analyze the area from both an economic and political standpoint. In

Algeria, for example, he recognized an opportunity which could be fraught with problems, said Rhodes, who traveled with Clements on contract negotitions. Algeria was a socialistic country, and its leaders demanded 51 percent of the stock and directors' control. "We agreed each of us would have two directors and they would run the company. We insisted on arbitration clauses, which they rejected," Rhodes said. Clements wouldn't give in on that point, however, because he recognized the danger of doing business with the Algerian government. After threatening to walk out, Clements and Rhodes finally got the arbitration clauses. It would prove to be a wise demand. After drilling for almost fifteen years in the desert and paying off debt on the rigs, SEDCO wanted to take profit out of the country. The Algerians balked and tried to confiscate the rigs. The dispute went to Swiss arbitration, and ultimately was decided in SEDCO's favor.[18]

The joint venture called SEDNETH, for Sea Drilling Netherlands Company, came about because SEDCO and Netherlands Offshore Company (OFFNETH) were both interested in drilling in the Dutch territory of the North Sea, the newest oil province. A 50-50 partnership, SEDNETH was headquartered in The Hague, Netherlands.[19]

The waters of the North Sea, between Norway and Britain, were about to become the biggest new play for the world oil industry. Major natural gas deposits had been found in the relatively shallow southern reaches of the sea and were being produced when Phillips Petroleum of Bartlesville, Oklahoma, made a major oil find in 1969 on the Norwegian side. British Petroleum made a discovery toward the end of 1970 in the Forties field, on the British side, and other major strikes followed — including Shell and Exxon's discovery of the huge Brent field.

The North Sea rush was on, and SEDCO was well positioned to be a major player. Even before SEDNETH, SEDCO had gotten a contract to operate a platform rig, Rig 75, in the North Sea; it was only the second rig to venture into the North Sea.[20] The SEDNETH joint venture resulted in the construction of a semi-submersible known as the SEDNETH I, completed in 1967 to operate, like the 135s, in a water depth of 600 feet. The SEDNETH II, a five-legged pentagonal jackup, was completed in 1968 to work in waters of up to 200 feet in depth.

Bill Martinovich recalled meetings when SEDNETH was building the SEDNETH I in a Dutch shipyard for a drilling contract for Royal Dutch Shell. He had recommended some radical changes in the original design, including raising the deck so waves wouldn't smash into it. Royal Dutch Shell was opposed to the changes, saying they would increase costs. Martinovich recalled Clements, peering over his half glasses, telling Royal Dutch Shell how the rig was going to be built. "Bear in mind," Martinovich said, "Royal Dutch Shell is buying and SEDNETH is selling. And here's Clements telling the client how it's going to be." It was only one of many meetings in which Clements called the shots and backed down the client. "It was like going in to buy a brown suit, and the salesman says you don't want a brown suit, you want a gray suit. And Clements would sell them a gray suit," Martinovich said.[21]

In 1971-72, when work started booming in the North Sea, the 135F was towed from New Zealand to begin work for Amoco. Bobby Cox recalled that "a lot of companies were building rigs and bringing them in there — Santa Fe and Odeco were in there — but SEDCO was so far ahead of the other contractors in the design of their drilling equipment that there was minimum competition. We were absolutely the best. This had come from Bill Clements; he wanted to be the best. As the fortunes of the company got better, the equipment we had was the finest there was."[22]

To supervise its activities in the North Sea when the 135F moved there, Elmer Adkins opened a SEDCO office in Aberdeen, Scotland. The fishing and farming village of Aberdeen would be tranformed into a hub of oil industry activity as SEDCO operations grew, and a large training center was built there. With the harsh conditions of the North Sea and the rapid influx of SEDCO rigs into the area, there was no time for new recruits to master the complexities of rig work once they were on the job. The school opened on November 6, 1972, with eight roustabout trainees and a waiting list of more than 100. Within a year, 250 men would complete the program directed by Tommy Bicknell, who had been the University of Texas' coordinator of the School of Drilling Technology in Odessa. Recruits trained from seven weeks to three months, spending one week in the classroom, two weeks on a rig and one week off, until they were permanently placed on a rig.[23]

"The company spent a tremendous amount of money in training schools. The managers, tool pushers and drillers, in the beginning, were all expatriates. As the Scots were trained, they gradually moved upward, and we eventually moved the Scots all over the world," Cox said. Major oil companies and other drilling contractors soon began sending their workers to SEDCO's schools.

Cox eventually managed nine rigs in the North Sea. With other rigs offshore Norway, SEDCO had twelve rigs operating in English, Dutch and Norwegian waters, under the supervision of Etherington in London.[24]

From the building of the first 135s, Clements described the company as being in a "constant state of expansion." From 1965 to 1967, SEDCO doubled its gross income to $33.9 million; its net income grew by $2 million to $5.4 million. A two-for-one stock split was distributed on June 28, 1967. And, in 1967, the company completed acquisition of the Baylor Company of Houston, which designed and manufactured sophisticated electrical apparatus for use in offshore drilling, from oceanographic instrumentation to underwater television and underwater blow-out preventer stacks. Baylor had worked with Shell Oil, beginning in 1960, to pioneer a new concept for obtaining core samples from offshore locations in deep water. Shell thought it could position a vessel in deep water, hold it in place without anchors, and obtain cores while using thrusters, or propellers that operated like huge outboard motors, to overcome the forces of wind, waves, and ocean currents. Baylor Company became a major contributor to the project, which resulted in the world's first dynamically positioned vessel.[25]

Clements believed the dynamic positioning (DP) technology was vital to deep water drilling, so he approached W. B. Baylor, founder of the Baylor Company, about doing some experimental DP work for SEDCO. Ultimately, SEDCO bought the company. Bill Baylor took a seat on the SEDCO board of directors, and Duke Zinkgraf, who had guided Baylor's work in dynamic positioning, became president of Baylor. It became a wholly owned SEDCO subsidiary with ninety employees and continued its operations in Houston.[26]

Clements was captivated by the idea of dynamically positioned rigs. SEDCO already employed an engineering staff which ranged from forty to sixty engineers, working under chief engineer William L. McDonald, who would later become vice-president of engineering. But Clements felt the company needed even greater engineering and design capability to accomplish his dream — to construct a dy-namically positioned ocean unit that would work in any weather en-vironment and in any water depth. Martinovich, by then, was heavily involved in SEDCO work. When he told Clements that several companies had made overtures to buy Earl and Wright, Clem-ents' response was, "Hell, I'll buy you guys."[27] He invited the firm's owner, J. G. "Buzz" Wright, to come to Dallas with Martinovich to talk about a merger.

Earl and Wright had expertise in maritime and waterfront structures, and harbor and jetty installations. It was particularly well known for offshore drilling platforms, having designed nine of the thirteen platforms in use at the time in the ice-laden waters of Cook Inlet, Alaska. The California-based firm had designed the first fixed platform offshore California for Chevron and, in late 1963, the first one for Cook Inlet, Alaska. Dillard Hammett, who had been hired to manage construction and engineering for SEDCO, was one of two Shell engineers monitoring Earl and Wright's work on that first fixed platform for Cook Inlet. Hammett explained that Earl and Wright had moved from building bridges to applying civil engineer-ing priciples to the design of offshore structures. These structures were therefore sounder, lighter, and more efficient than naval archi-tects' designs.[28]

In August 1968, SEDCO acquired Earl and Wright, which con-tinued to operate with its seventy engineers in San Francisco.

SEDCO didn't buy Earl and Wright to get the added revenue, Martinovich said. "It was to enhance their greater agenda," which was mobile drilling, semi-submersibles, and dynamic positioning. "With us designing their semi-submersibles, it gave their design more credibility than those [companies] that had in-house designs," Martinovich said.[29]

Clements' message to shareholders in SEDCO's 1968 annual report stated: "SEDCO's long-term objective is to offer a broad range of deep water capabilities which can be packaged to provide a turnkey job for our customers in the exploration and exploitation of minerals from and under the ocean. We already possess many of the capabilities necessary for this integration as a result of the acquisi-tion of Baylor Company and Earl and Wright. These two firms pro-vide us with additional engineering skills and electronic capabilities which are particularly suited to the ocean environment and our ocean engineering concept."[30]

In 1968, B. Gill Clements joined the company. He had been with First National Bank for five years and was working in the loan department when he decided he didn't want to be a banker. About that time, SEDCO was growing at a fast pace; it had gone public in 1965, and the financial end of the business was expanding. There was a place for him at SEDCO. Gill recalled: "When Dad hired me, he said, 'Engineering is the core of our business. The finance area is a small but important part. You can help us in that regard, but I don't want any misunderstanding. You will not be in line to be president of the company.' I said I didn't expect that," Gill said.[31]

In 1969, SEDCO announced the proposed acquisition of Houston Contracting Company of Houston, the largest cross-country pipeline contractor in the United States. SEDCO's objective was to take the pipeline company international, thus enhancing SEDCO's position as a complete-service offshore contractor. One of Houston Contracting's biggest projects would be as joint venture partner constructing a 48-inch, 333-mile segment of the Petroline pipeline in Saudi Arabia. The Petroline, with a total length of 750 miles, connected the Saudi Arabian fields near Abqaiq on the eastern coast with a new port at Yanbu on the Red Sea.[32]

The acquisitions positioned SEDCO for entry into public trading on the New York Stock Exchange in 1969. At the beginning of that year, management decided to officially change the name of the company to SEDCO, Inc., from Southeastern Drilling, Inc. SEDCO had been the company's trademark for many years, and the name had been used informally in recent years; it was well known by that time in the international petroleum industry. Clements was elected chairman of the board and Spencer Taylor was named president of SEDCO, Inc., an arrangement that would last only a year because of the company's growing diversification and confusion on the outside as to who really ran the company. Several officers went to New York with Clements and Taylor on June 17, 1969, to observe the first trade in the company's stock on the New York Stock Exchange. Taylor recalled that he was mistaken as SEDCO's top man, which piqued Clements. Inside the company, there never was any doubt who ran the show.

That year, revenues were $41 million, of which $30 million was generated from operations offshore. Since becoming a public company in 1965, SEDCO's earnings had increased from $3.4 million to $7.1 million.[33] When SEDCO went on the "big board," its officers and key employees, whom Clements had offered an interest in the company, became millionaires overnight.

The company suffered its first decline in earnings in five years in fiscal 1970, due in part to a blowout and fire causing $4 million damage to the SEDCO 135G working offshore northern Australia. The SEDCO HELEN, a combination tug-workboat, was lost in January 1970, along with six crewmen.[34] The company, however, had broadened its capabilities with the acquisition of the pipeline company and the formation of TerraMar Consultants, which could provide independent analyses in geology, engineering, and management. Major oil companies were looking for a single contractor to develop their offshore concessions, and SEDCO was able to offer total services — from feasibility studies to exploration and development drilling, pipeline and platform construction work, loading facilities and production management.

The acquisitions and diversification of SEDCO, Inc., brought about a restructuring in 1970. The business was split into five operating divisions — Drilling, Construction, Manufacturing, Engineering and Consulting — with SEDCO, Inc., as the parent company providing support in the areas of policy and finance. William P. Clements, Jr., was chairman of the board and chief executive officer of SEDCO, Inc.; Tom B. Rhodes was senior vice-president; B. Gill Clements, treasurer; Carl F. Thorne, secretary; and Irving E. Davis, Jr., controller. Spencer L. Taylor became president of SEDCO Drilling Division, with Jerry P. Cunningham, senior vice-president of the Drilling Division. Other vice-presidents of the Drilling Division were B. R. Jones, R. Warren Sexton, Walter H. Etherington, and William L. McDonald.

John W. Rhea, who had been working as a consultant, came back to the SEDCO fold as chairman of the board of TerraMar Consultants. The other divisions were: Baylor Company, W. B. Baylor, board chairman; Houston Contracting Co., Harold J. Muckley, president; and Earl and Wright, J. G. Wright president.[35]

SEDCO's greatest achievement in 1970 was the receipt of a two-year contract for the design and operation of a dynamically positioned, self-propelled drill ship, expected to cost $15 million. The contract, awarded by Royal Dutch Shell, was the result of three years of research. It launched the company's construction of a second generation of ocean equipment. That year, 1970, SEDCO was the world's largest operator of semi-submersible equipment.[36]

By the late 1960s, Clements had become totally committed to ocean drilling and to developing the technology it required. A company brochure designed to attract engineers noted that the oceans of the world enveloped more than 70 percent of the earth's surface and beneath that vast cover of water lay 19 percent of the free world's oil reserves, some sixty billion barrels. And yet, only seven percent of the world's continental shelves had been geologically surveyed. "New approaches to sub-sea drilling and production, now on the drawing boards, clearly outdo even Buck Rogers' most fantastic dreams in many aspects, creating ever-changing and challenging opportunities," the company publication stated.[37]

The importance of the offshore industry was growing. In his 1971 message to shareholders, Clements quoted from a government report appraising the industry's future. Whereas in 1961, there were only three or four nations and about five companies with major offshore petroleum interests, by 1971, hundreds of companies were involved in sub-sea oil and gas exploration and development around the world. By 1971, production was under way or about to begin off the coasts of twenty-eight countries, and exploratory surveys were being carried out on the continental shelves of another fifty. "Offshore petroleum deposits are responsible for 16 percent of the oil and six percent of the natural gas produced by the free world, and projections are that by 1980 a third of the oil production — four times the present output of 6.5 million barrels per day — would come from beneath the ocean," the report said.[38]

It was a time of tremendous opportunity, with technology moving forward at a rapid rate. SEDCO would contribute to the evolving technology of ocean engineering in three areas: a dynamically stationed drill ship, a new generation of rectangular semi-submersibles to replace the triangular 135s, and a semi-submersible construction barge. Dillard Hammett, an engineering graduate of Oklahoma University, had been working for Shell in Alaska when he was hired by Clements in 1967 to spearhead the development of this new generation of offshore equipment. Clements had recently returned from Europe, where he had spent six weeks with Shell discussing the idea of a dynamically stationed ship. Design of that equipment was his next goal.

"Clements' philosophy on designing was to take a year — whatever you could accomplish in a year — then go build one. Instead of spending five years in engineering design on the first one, you would learn by building, and improve on the second and third and fourth one," Hammett said.

"Clements set the objectives and goals. Jerry Cunningham and I went out to the industry. Earl and Wright did the designs. Bill Mc-Donald worked with the shipyards. Spencer Taylor was the direct line to Clements." According to Hammett, that was the way the company worked in the late '60s and early '70s when this new equipment was coming on line. The results were the dynamically stationed SEDCO 445 drilling ship, the rectangular-shaped SEDCO 700 semi-submersible, and the SEDCO 400 semi-submersible drilling barge.[39]

The SEDCO 445 was the first full-scale oil exploration drilling ship equipped for dynamic stationing, substituting computer-controlled thrusters for anchors in deep water. It was equipped with a system of computerized sensors that fed orders to eleven thrusters positioned beneath the ship. Constructed by Mitsui Shipbuilding and Engineering Company in Japan for use in 1971 by Royal Dutch Shell, the 445 drilled its first well utilizing dynamic positioning in 1,300 feet of water offshore Brunei in 1972. Shell formed Shell Deepwater Drilling Company, Ltd. (Deepshell) in 1971 specifically for the SEDCO 445 to carry out a worldwide exploration program. SEDCO had a long-term contract with Deepshell that contracted work from any Shell company which had a deep-water location — from Borneo to Australia. This caused the crew to refer to the 445 as the "South Sea Island Cruise Ship." All SEDCO and Deepshell employees on board the 445 worked a schedule of twenty-eight days on and twenty-eight days off, flying to their homes — in the U.S., New Zealand, Canada, or wherever home might be — for their days off. After more than two years in operation, the 445 drillship went to West Africa, where it set a record for deep-water drilling, spudding in a well in 2,150 feet of water on May 1, 1974. "That is the deepest water that anybody, anywhere, anytime, has attempted to drill a well," wrote ship manager Charles Purbaugh, at the time.[40]

Hammett recalled that when the first dynamically stationed ship was being designed, some members of the SEDCO management group wanted to spend extra money to install a "black box," similar to those on airplanes, to determine cause in case of an accident. Clements rejected the idea the first time it was proposed, but accepted it later. "He was a good listener — the second time," Hammett said. "The first time you went in there with an idea or to give a report, he would tear you from one side to the other, asking all kinds of questions. If you made your case right, he would approve it. If you didn't make your case, he'd say 'no,'" Hammett said. "If you knew you were right and went in for a second audience, he was the best listener in the world. I guess he felt if you had the guts to come back the second time on something, it must be a good idea."[41]

Clements' business philosophy was to determine industry's needs and then design equipment to meet the needs. The SEDCO people discovered in their discussions with industry that it took too long to tow the triangular 135 around the world to new locations. So when SEDCO began design on the second generation of semi-submersibles, the SEDCO 700, it wanted a more mobile unit, as well as one that could work in extremely hostile environments. The oil discovery in the North Sea in 1969 provided much of the impetus to build the rectangular-shaped units in the 700 series.

SEDCO also was in the middle of a patent lawsuit with Kerr-McGee over the triangular 135. Kerr-McGee claimed it had a patent on the design and sued SEDCO for patent infringement. "We gave them the drawings for the triangle design. We wanted to go to a rectangular design anyway," Rhodes said. "They dropped the lawsuit, and we didn't build any more triangular-designed rigs. We traded them a dead horse to cut off the [legal] meter," he said.[42]

Earl and Wright's Bill Martinovich spearheaded the development of the second generation of semi-submersibles, along with the Baylor group that designed the huge mechanical propellers or thrusters, led by Duke Zinkgraf. The 700s added ship-shaped pontoons that looked like huge cigars, and propulsion, more than quadrupling the speed from two to over eight knots. The 700s also used gigantic thrusters or propellers to provide for dynamic stationing over the hole. The rig was designed to float freely so that there was minimum resistance to the wave action. The 1,800-horsepower thrusters on the first 700s assisted in moving and in supplementing the mooring system to keep the unit floating over location. The most sophisticated units that came along later — the 709 and 710 — could operate in deep water without anchors, totally dynamically positioned, utilizing computers to determine the thrust needed against waves and ocean currents. With the dynamic positioning, Tom Rhodes explained, the rig could be off center several hundred feet, but the pipe "was like a piece of spaghetti down there, still drilling."[43]

By December 1971, SEDCO had long-term drilling contracts

Oliver B. Clements and Louise Corrine Hearin Norwood were photographed in 1880, when they were married in Forney. W. Perry Clements was born to them in 1883 in Forney.

James Christopher Cammack, father of Evelyn Cammack, is pictured with his first wife, who died. He later married her sister, Willie Ellie Christmas, the mother of Evelyn Cammack.

Evelyn Cammack, top center, was in the 1901 graduating class of Dallas High School.

Evelyn Cammack, 29 years old, in 1911, a year before she married W. Perry Clements.

W. Perry Clements, at about 30 years old, in Dallas, near the time he married Evelyn Cammack.

The Cammack brothers and sisters in Dallas in 1916 include (from left) John Poindexter Cammack, James Christopher Cammack and Robert Burns Cammack, first row; Bessie Cammack Burr, Evelyn Cammack Clements and Anna Cammack Dealey, second row; and Sadie Cammack Moore, top.

W.P. (Bill) Clements, Jr., celebrates his third birthday at home on Maplewood.

Evelyn Clements with Bill, age 3, and his sister, Betty.

Bill, 3, fishes with his father, Perry Clements, from the bridge at Koon Kreek Klub in East Texas.

Evelyn Cammack had a big influence on her son, Bill, pictured here at age 10, with his sister, Betty, 14.

Bill Clements, in a high school yearbook photo, was president of his class for three years at Highland Park High School.

The Highland Park Scots won their first Class A football championship in 1933. Bill Clements was No. 13.

Bill Clements was Highland Park's first All-State football player, playing guard, in 1933.

Bill Clements, around 1960.

In 1938, by the age of 21, Bill Clements had left college and was working as a roughneck in the oilfields south of Edna, Texas. Clements is in the center with Bruce Shanklin second from left and the driller, Boliver Sloan, at far right.

Perry and Evelyn Clements brought their grandchildren, Gill and Nancy, a pony cart for Christmas when they lived in Jackson, Mississippi. Their father, Bill, who had founded Southeastern Drilling Co., is at left.

Clements, tool pusher Edgar Williams, and superintendent Walter Etherington take a break in front of a pump in 1952 in West Texas.

Bill Clements' parents, Evelyn and Perry, and his sister, Betty, in 1955 in Dallas.

Southeastern Drilling Company's first offshore mobile rig, a shallow water marsh rig, drilled in South Louisiana in 1952.

Clements, right, and workers in front of Southeastern Drilling Company's first rig in Mississippi.

Clements, far right, with associates in front of a rig in Argentina in the early 1960s.

Clements is pictured in front of a SEDCO triangular 135 rig in 1969.

Gov. Clements entertains old associates from SEDCO at the mansion during his second administration. They are, front row, from left, Gill Glements, Jack Fitch, Jerry Cunningham, Clements, Bill Bruyere, Walter Etherington; second row, Tom Rhodes, Harold Muckley, Dillard Hammett, Carl Thorne, Spencer Taylor, and John Rhea.

Peter O'Donnell, Clements' best friend and longtime political adviser, with Clements' old friend John Rhea from SEDCO, at the Governor's Mansion.

Clements was good friends with Margot and Ross Perot and Anne Armstrong, counselor to President Nixon, during the time he was in Washington, D.C.

SEDCO developed a reputation for building high-technology drilling rigs such as Rig 708, christened in 1977 to work in the Gulf of Alaska.

Clements' old friend from DOD days in Washington, Henry Kissinger, visits Texas in 1981.

The 1982 campaign included a whistlestop tour on July 4. Eddie Chiles, left, joins Clements and Dallas Cowboys coach Tom Landry and his wife, Alicia, inside the train. Standing are Temple Mayor John Sammons and barbecue chef Clem Mikeska.

Clements' favorite photo with his son, Gill, taken on safari in Kenya after Clements left office.

with major international oil companies (Royal Dutch Shell, Texaco-Ranger, Continental, British Petroleum, and Mobil) for five SEDCO 700 units to work in the North Sea. The units, scheduled for delivery in 1973 and 1974, cost from $27 million to $30 million each.[44]

Eventually, SEDCO would build thirteen units in the 700 series, with the last units costing more than $100 million each. To reduce the company's financial exposure, SEDCO would engage a major oil company as a 50-50 partner on a four-year contract for construction and operation of the giant rigs. At the end of the four years, the rig was paid off, with SEDCO owning half and the participating oil company owning half — a concept Clements developed for financing the expensive drilling rigs.[45]

By 1971, the search for oil and gas had moved into many deep, rough-water areas, such as the upper North Sea and offshore eastern Canada. Operating conventional construction equipment in such hostile areas was inefficient and costly, and weather conditions limited the construction season to three or four months a year. The SEDCO 400, a semi-submersible pipelay-derrick barge, was designed to construct facilities in those hostile areas. Martinovich recalled a SEDCO 400 design meeting in San Francisco with Clements. Martinovich brought up the cost factor. "This is ridiculous," he said. "It's going to cost way too much money." Clements, he recalled, "peers at me over those split glasses and he says, 'I appreciate your opinion on that. When you give me engineering opinions, on a scale of one to 100, I'll weigh them at 95. But when you talk to me about economics, I'll weigh that at about 20 points."

The demand for engineers was so great by SEDCO's customers in 1971 that Earl and Wright opened offices in Anchorage, Alaska, and in London, to be closer to customers developing the Alaska and North Sea oil reserves.

Designing offshore equipment in those days, according to Martinovich, was exciting and fun, because the rules hadn't been written. "If you go to build a hotel or a bridge, there are building codes. There was no book on offshore structures, either fixed or floating, when the business started. That made it more fun professionally. It was what [the engineer] and the client thought was all right. You didn't have to go to city hall or to a regulatory body to get approval; you were making the rules up as you went along."[46]

The 135 and the 700 series earned SEDCO's reputation as an

industry leader. Clements "was always just a step ahead of the rest of the industry in being forward-thinking," said Edwin L. Cox, a Dallas oil and gas producer. But it wasn't just the equipment that built the company's reputation. Drilling contracts were not always given to the lowest bidder, because oil-field operators place as much weight on a driller's integrity as they do on price.[47]

SEDCO was successful because Clements insisted on performance, both in equipment and personnel, on negotiating the toughest and most profitable contracts possible, and on maintaining good personal relationships with the customer. Companies, in fact, paid a premium for SEDCO to be their contractor. "SEDCO got the work because they delivered. These major oil companies loved SEDCO because they knew they could depend on them," Cox said.[48]

All companies have a company character, and SEDCO had its character — all business, no foolishness. After one trip abroad, Clements and Spencer Taylor called Dillard Hammett in and suggested his appearance wasn't professional enough. He liked to take his clothes in a carry-on bag, but Clements told him to get a suitcase so his clothes wouldn't look rumpled. "Everybody knows you're from Texas, so stop wearing those cowboy boots," Clements told him. "And stop smoking those cigars."[49]

Clements developed a close relationship with the top people at Shell, which was one of SEDCO's biggest customers, cultivating the people in charge of their drilling operation. "He was sincere, he wasn't fawning or anything like that. But he gained their respect and friendship. He always insisted on very honest relations with these people — no lavish gifts. He kept the relationship on a very business-like basis," attorney Rhodes said. Shell was SEDCO's biggest customer in the North Sea and also a long-term customer offshore Borneo and in Nigeria.

"Santa Fe and Odeco (owned by Southern Natural Gas) were probably our biggest competitors in the water. Eddie Chiles (Great Western Company) had a few rigs. Zapata had some rigs. George Bush joint-ventured some deals with us in the Persian Gulf. But SEDCO was probably the largest in offshore drilling," Rhodes said.

Rhodes believed SEDCO was successful because Clements "dedicated his business career to making a successful company. He was simple-minded in that resolve. Every night he took work home with him. I have never seen him leave and not take home work in his briefcase. Plus, he had foresight to anticipate where the industry was going. He didn't go down blind alleys. He had a sense of Iraq being a bad place to work and never got involved in Libya. He anticipated these problem countries."[50]

(Bunker Hunt discovered one of the world's largest oilfields in Libya. He owned billions of barrels of reserves, making him richer than his father, H. L. Hunt, until Col. Muammar Gaddafi overthrew the Libyan monarchy in 1969 and nationalized the Hunt holdings there.)[51]

Clements told a reporter who was assessing his business career during his first gubernatorial campaign, "There is no substitute for hard work. But judgment becomes an important factor. In Venezuela, Egypt, Indonesia, and Libya, for example, I had to decide whether to go in or not. I said, 'no deal.' And in every one of those places, as it turned out, I dodged lightning."[52]

Clements also was a strong advocate of moving employees up in the organization and giving them responsibility commensurate with their performance. Bill Armentrout said Clements was a good judge of personnel, from the time he went into business. "He hired good people, and he knew how to treat them so they stayed with him. The success of our foreign operation stemmed from these same people, who had worked for us in Mississippi and West Texas and on the Gulf Coast. These were people who knew what they were doing. They kept the oil companies happy. That was one of his very strong points," Armentrout said. Most of Clements' initial hires stayed with the company throughout their careers. "The people in SEDCO had a lot of loyalty; I think that was the inspiration of Bill," Rhodes said.[53]

In the late 1960s, Clements also began bringing on board second-generation management people who were younger and better educated. Some of the early hires — such as Bobby Cox, Etherington and Archer — were high school graduates who had climbed the SEDCO ladder. But Bobby Cox, who eventually became vice-president of operations, said, "Clements had the vision that the industry was going to change, and we added more engineers and started bringing on younger, smarter people."[54]

Among these were Hammett, Carl Thorne, and Steve Mahood. Carl Thorne joined SEDCO in 1968, a petroleum engineering graduate from the University of Texas fresh out of Baylor Law School. Thorne had been raised in a Mobil Oil camp and had worked as a roughneck and roustabout before going to law school. Rhodes, who was SEDCO's only lawyer, called and invited him to come to Dallas to interview with SEDCO. After looking at SEDCO's prospectus, Thorne determined the officers of the company were all millionaires, by virtue of their stock holdings. But, more important, he said, after going to dinner with the officers and their wives at the Petroleum Club, he determined they were down-to-earth people, committed to what they were doing. Thorne became assistant general counsel to Rhodes and was named secretary the same day Gill Clements was made treasurer. In early 1971, he was assigned to Iran, where he later became president of SEDCO International.

"There were really only two companies in the business, when you talk about semi-submersible rigs in the early days. It was SEDCO and Odeco, then Penrod [a Hunt company] built some semi-submersibles, and other people started building. But the 135 was the Cadillac of the whole industry. The 135 was far superior to anything, and then the first 700 unit was built; it is acknowledged today as one of the finest floaters ever built," Thorne said in 1995. Beyond the equipment, there was an atmosphere at SEDCO which fostered minimal politics. "You didn't have to worry about looking back over your shoulder. If you spend half your time looking over your shoulder, that was time you couldn't spend looking forward and trying to do something constructive." At SEDCO, he said, "People were allowed to seek their own level, cream was allowed to float to the top. It was a small company and very diverse in the personalities involved. It worked because of the strength of the people and their ability to allow people to fill their own volume."[55]

Steve Mahood, a graduate of SMU Law School, joined SEDCO in 1971 after being a supervisor of field operations with Houston Contracting. He was working on a pipeline job in Nigeria when he heard that Rhodes was looking for lawyers. Mahood knew the Clements family. He and Gill had been fraternity brothers in SMU undergraduate school, and he had often been in the Clements home. Mahood joined SEDCO as secretary and general counsel of the Drilling Division. He later became vice-president, secretary, and general counsel of SEDCO, Inc., when Rhodes retired.

Mahood sensed in 1971-72, after he came on board, that Clements was beginning to phase himself out of the day-to-day operations. Clements' philosophy, he said, was to "let the young people get involved and run with it." Clements was becoming interested in other challenges, such as civic work — and politics.[56]

On New Year's Day, 1972, Paul Turnbull, who was responsible for the company obtaining those first foreign contracts in India and Pakistan, died of a heart attack.[57] It was SEDCO's twenty-fifth anniversary in business, and SEDCO's farflung operations were scattered across the world. SEDCO's partnership with Turnbull and Zoch was dissolved after Turnbull's death.

In the time that Clements had been in business, the increase in free world crude oil production was staggering. It had gone from 8.7 million barrels per day in 1948 to 42 million barrels per day in 1972. But America's share of total world production had slipped from 64 percent to 22 percent. The number of drilling rigs in the U.S. had been declining steadily and in 1971 was a little more than a third the level of the mid-1950s.[58] SEDCO was firmly positioned in the new center of gravity of the oil industry, and was making money. Its gross sales, in 1972, were $130 million, with a net profit of $13.4 million. Massive new rigs were under construction, and SEDCO was poised for an expansion explosion. Drilling units under construction in 1972 included seven semi-submersibles, the SEDCO J and K and five 700s, and three land rigs at a total construction cost of more than $177 million.

Clements wrote in the 1972 annual report: "In our worldwide operations we find people generally have the same aspirations and goals for themselves and their families. This common thread is the basis of all our internal relationships with our multi-national employees. Everyone wants to be treated with dignity and integrity with full opportunity to fulfill his ambitions. We have these principles as our foundation for all SEDCO employee policies. The very fiber of SEDCO is dependent on the motivation, performance and high morale of our employees."[59]

Clements was chairman of the board and chief executive officer in 1972. His closest associates remained: Tom B. Rhodes, senior vice-president and general counsel of SEDCO, Inc.; John W. Rhea, Jr., vice-president of SEDCO, Inc.; Spencer L. Taylor, president of SEDCO Drilling Division; and Jerry P. Cunningham, senior vice-president of SEDCO Drilling Division. The next generation of workers also was getting into place with B. Gill Clements, treasurer, Stephen C. Mahood, secretary, and Dillard Hammett, vice-president-technical, SEDCO, Inc.; and Amos L. Carter, president of SEDCO International in the Drilling Division.

In 1972 the company had thirteen offshore units — including nine semi-submersibles, a dynamically positioned drill ship, a jackup drilling unit, fixed platform and jackup barge — working in South Africa, Borneo, Western Africa, the North Sea, Australia, Eastern Canada, Qatar, the Arabian Gulf, and Persian Gulf. It had seven semi-submersibles under construction, and it had eighteen land rigs working in Iran, Abu Dhabi, Oman, and Algeria. The Drilling Division in Dallas coordinated operations, construction, purchasing, and personnel for all of the drilling activities in the world. SEDCO's world was divided into three operational areas: Far East and North America, Europe and Africa, and the Middle East.[60]

SEDCO's customers that year included Standard of California, Shell-Brunei, Occidental, Amoco-Shell U.K., Atlantic Richfield, Shell-Canada, Amoco Canada, Mobil Oil, British Petroleum, Shell-SIPM, Texaco-Ranger, Continental, Qatar Oil Company, Dubai Petroleum, Iran Pan Am, the Iran Consortium, Abu Dhabi Petroleum Company, Shell Oman, Inpeco, and the Association Cooperative in Algeria.

As far as Clements was concerned, SEDCO was at the top of its game.

Spencer Taylor agreed. "When we started out," Taylor said, "there were other companies that had the opportunities to do the same thing we did. I don't know if they were complacent or what, but they just didn't take the opportunity to expand like we did. We kind of left them standing still."[61]

Chapter 7

Boss Talk

Becoming a Player in Different Areas

BILL CLEMENTS TRAVELED extensively in the 1960s and early 1970s. He made many business trips to Europe, the Middle East, and Pakistan; some years, he visited the Middle East three or four times. Shelma Ahrens, Clements' personal secretary from 1963 to 1973, kept his daily calendar. The pages from the 1960s bear repeated notations: "WPC in the Hague," "WPC in London," "WPC in Algiers."

"He visited all the countries they were working in — not just once a year, but constantly," Mrs. Ahrens said. "He knew what was going on in SEDCO in every country, all over the world," she said.[1]

In July 1969, President Nixon and Secretary of Defense Melvin Laird appointed a Blue Ribbon Defense Panel of fifteen businessmen from across the country to study the Department of Defense and report on improvements it needed. Clements was one of the appointees. To obtain the security clearance he needed to serve on the panel, Clements was required to list all foreign travel. It wasn't easy, according to Mrs. Ahrens. He didn't have just one passport; he had a box full of passports.

For 1963, he listed Iran, the Netherlands, United Kingdom, India, Greece, various countries in the Middle East, Hong Kong, France, West Germany, Norway, and Denmark. In 1965 he visited the Netherlands, Ireland, the U.K., Sweden, India, Pakistan, Thailand, Malaysia, Borneo, various Middle Eastern countries, Japan, and the Philippines. In 1967, besides repeat visits to other countries, he added Algeria, and in 1968, Spain and Portugal, to the list.[2]

"Every time he went into a new country, he had me go to the public library and get history books on that country," Mrs. Ahrens said. It was his way of preparing for the trip. He read and studied, she said, and was curious about anything he didn't know.

Clements liked to participate in the customs of the country. It once took him several years to buy a Persian rug, because he was buying like the Persians. That meant negotiating over extended time. He would drink tea, talk about how the rug was made, think about it. The next year, he'd go back, drink tea and talk some more. It took him four or five years to buy the rug, a particularly fine Nain, which he kept in his office. It was the rug on which employees stood when they said they were "called on the carpet."

He had a great affinity for the Middle East, where he developed the ability to establish rapport with influential people. "Bill can be severe, but he can also charm the birds out of the tree when he wants to be charming. They'd pull out their worry beads, he'd pull out his worry beads. That was typical of how Bill would engrain his way into these people. He would sense what they liked. He never worried in his life, but he'd get out these beads and thumb 'em," said Rhodes.[3]

Despite being frequently out of town and absorbed with business and professional activities (he was active in the American Association of Oilwell Drilling Contractors and served as its president in 1962), Clements became a player in Dallas civic leadership circles. He fit in with the Dallas business establishment; he was conservative, he had money, he had connections, and he could get the job done. In 1960 he became a director of the Dallas Citizens Council,[4] the small group of business executives that ran the affairs of the city from behind the scenes and became known as the Dallas "oligarchy."

Rule by oligarchy began under R. L. "Uncle Bob" Thornton, Sr., the self-made banker who in the 1930s had proposed to Dallas' two major bankers at the time, Nathan Adams of the First National Bank and Fred Florence of Republic National Bank, the creation of a civic ruling class of presidents and board chairmen of the city's largest businesses. He called them the "yes and no men." As Thornton said: "We didn't have time for no proxy people — what we needed was men who could give you boss talk."[5] When these men said "yes" to a course of action they felt was in Dallas' best interests, they could back up the decision with the resources — both money and manpower — of their individual companies. J. Erik Jonsson, head of Texas Instruments and a Dallas mayor, led the Citizens Council during some years of Clements' involvement.

Clements was as good as any at giving the "boss talk." He had a strong banking relationship with the First National Bank, which dated to Toddie Lee Wynne's original guarantees there for Clements' company. The banking connection was important in Dallas because the trunk of the power tree in those days was the big downtown banks: Republic and First National. "The chief executives of the big banks sit at the Big Table regardless. So do the newspaper publishers, the heads of the major utilities . . . and the bosses of the major insurance companies and retail stores," reported a magazine in the early 1970s.[6] Other leaders owned or ran businesses and rose through sheer force of their personalities.

In his early days on the Dallas Citizens Council, Clements was asked to chair a committee to recommend a course of action for the financially strapped Dallas Symphony Orchestra. "Well, you ought to know I've never been to a symphony," Clements said. "What's more, I really have no intention of going." Clements was told, "Under those circumstances, you can undoubtedly give us an objective opinion." Clements chaired the committee, and it reported that the symphony was a vital part of the community that absolutely had to be continued.[7]

In Dallas corporate life, leaders either lined up with the First National Bank or Republic National Bank. Because of the circumstances of his company's creation, Clements lined up with First National (which later became First International Bancshares). It was a relationship which would last over time, with Clements eventually going on the bank's board.

Through the bank, Clements became acquainted in the mid-1950s with Robert H. "Bobby" Stewart III, an SMU graduate who was working in the bank's oil department. At that time, oil was a huge part of the bank's business, and the oil business was a major factor in the success of Dallas. (According to Stewart, oilman H. L. Hunt, presumed to be the richest man in the country by the late 1940s, moved from Tyler to Dallas in 1938 to be closer to Dallas banks.)

First National Bank in Dallas was the first bank to purchase oil payments, financing drilling for payment after the well came in. Others followed suit, and oil became a bankable commodity. By the

1950s, bankers had their own geologists and petroleum engineers who would estimate the value of an oilman's reserves before making a loan.[8]

Stewart's grandfather had been chairman and his father on the board of First National, and he quickly climbed the ladder. In 1960 Stewart became president and CEO, the youngest bank president in the country, and in 1965, chairman of the board and CEO. By the 1960s, Stewart estimated that oil-related business constituted some 30 percent of the bank's business, whereas three decades later, in the 1990s, it had been reduced to a very small percentage. Clements was a good customer, and Stewart and Clements became fast friends. "Drilling contractors had big cash flows in those days," Stewart said. Clements was a good depositor, and his loans were always good. First National dealt not only with Clements but with the company's other top people — Spencer Taylor, Tom Rhodes, Gill Clements, and Jerry Cunningham. "You just didn't see anybody around Bill who wasn't able," Stewart said. By the early 1970s, Clements was serving on the board of the bank, and Stewart learned to pay attention if Clements said, "Bobby, I don't like that officer; I don't think he's competent." Stewart said Clements was right more often than wrong. "He was probably the most forthright, candid and wise person I've ever known," Stewart said. "He would tell you exactly what he thinks."[9]

When Stewart was CEO, Dewey Pressley was president of the bank. First National's board in the early 1970s also included oil and gas producer Edwin L. Cox, John Murchison of Murchison Brothers, and Charles Sharp of Fidelity Union Life.[10] These were important associations for Clements, in both business and civic life. Dewey Pressley was SEDCO's principal contact at the bank over the years. Even when the company borrowed money in New York, it went through Pressley at First National. Pressley, in turn, served on SEDCO's board. Clements also served on the board of Fidelity Union Life. Clements, Stewart, and Cox became heavily involved at Southern Methodist University, and Clements convinced Murchison to become a worker in the Boy Scouts.

In 1963 the First National Bank was building a new skyscraper — fifty stories of glass and steel with vertical stripes of outside lighting. It was to be the tallest building in Dallas at the time and headquarters of the biggest bank in Texas. SEDCO was one of the first companies to move into the bank, occupying lovely quarters on the forty-fourth floor. It was the place to be and, in 1965, even H. L. Hunt moved Hunt Oil Company to the new bank building.[11] The Dallas Petroleum Club also moved from the Baker Hotel to the top floor of the new bank building; Clements was chairman of the club's house committee for several years during that period. Both the SEDCO offices and the new Petroleum Club, under Clements' guidance, were beautifully decorated. "He likes to give the impression of a good old country boy, but he had impeccable taste," said his secretary Shelma Ahrens, particularly in furnishings and accessories. He showed less style when it came to his own dress. He would typically go to the Dreyfuss men's store downtown, buy three suits and wear them for a year or two, or until he thought they appeared worn. Then he would go back and replace them with three more. He had an affinity for short-sleeve shirts, even in winter.[12]

The Petroleum Club was a power club for Dallas' business establishment in the 1960s and 1970s, a place where business was conducted and a fair amount of politics played. The club provided the site for an important Clements management tool — the Friday Lunch. Every Friday, the SEDCO management group met in the Brick Room for lunch. Each member of the management team was expected to report on his area of activity and be prepared for a quiz by Clements. "Clements expected everybody to communicate, and they'd better know what they were talking about. I've seen some bloodletting if you went in unprepared," said Carl Thorne, who joined the management team in the late 1960s.[13]

Power in Dallas was defined in the 1960s by being rich, serving as head of a business, and being willing to "run through the chairs," or serve as chairman of certain civic concerns. Clements, however, was not well known as a power broker in Dallas, because he didn't piddle in city politics, and he didn't "run through the chairs." He picked his civic and political work very carefully and, outside of some circles, he was relatively unknown in Dallas.

"A lot of folks do a lot of things and none of them well. He picked a few, and did them well," said Stewart.[14] Clements' favorite charities were the Boy Scouts of America and Southern Methodist University. These two entities got the bulk of his time and, over the years, his money.

After becoming scoutmaster of the troop at Walnut Hill School, Clements became immersed in the Circle 10 Council, which oversaw scouting activities in eleven counties of North Texas. He helped hire Jim Tarr as scout executive for Circle 10 in 1964. They developed a friendship which went past 1979, when Tarr became chief scout executive for Boy Scouts of America.

In 1967 and 1968, Clements served as president of Circle 10 Council after heading Circle 10's camping committee. During that period, he helped to locate and arrange for the purchase of what eventually would be 2,000 acres for a Scout camp in East Texas. Some of the land adjoined Koon Kreek Klub in Henderson County. He made the first gift — $50,000 — to a capital fund campaign to acquire and improve the property, and then talked John Murchison of the Murchison brothers into heading the $1.3 million fund drive. With their oil holdings and other investments, the Murchisons were among the wealthiest families in Dallas, but John Murchison had never "carried a card" in any kind of civic campaign before Clements recruited him to work for the Boy Scouts. The East Texas camp, which was established in 1968, was named the Camp Clements Scout Reservation in honor of the Clements family.[15]

Clements later gave more than $100,000 to build the camp's Natural History Museum, which came about because Bill Perryman, an oilman and district Boy Scout chairman in Henderson County, had a giant beaver he wanted to give to the Boy Scouts. Ernest Waymon Peavy came up with the idea of a museum which would contain a collection of representative birds and animals of East Texas. Peavy agreed to collect and furnish the specimens, and Clements agreed to pay for the building. The specimens were put into place by the Dallas Museum of Natural History, and on April 14, 1973, the museum was dedicated.[16]

In 1969, Tarr read an article about Electronic Data Systems founder Ross Perot donating money for a new Girl Scout camp. The article mentioned that Perot had been an Eagle Scout. Tarr figured that made Perot a prime prospect to donate to the Boy Scouts. Tarr went to see Perot and asked him for $45,000 to fund one Scout staff member for three years. Perot wasn't challenged by that, and Tarr realized he'd made a big mistake; he'd gone too low. So he asked Clements, who had never met Perot, to go back with him to ask Perot for $1 million for the Circle 10 Foundation, the interest on which could be used to employ three staff members. Perot agreed; Clements and Perot became friends, and Clements later went on the EDS board of directors.

About the time of Perot's gift, Clements told Tarr he had to decide what his own major gift would be to the Boy Scouts. Tarr made a suggestion, which Clements liked. He agreed to fund the building of a second camp at the Clements Scout Reservation and any future capital improvements to the reservation, which amounted to more than $1 million over a three-year period.[17]

Clements was an effective arm-twister and used personal relationships in charity work just as he did in business. He had annual luncheons at SEDCO, where business associates were asked to be camp sponsors for low-income boys. He encouraged other businessmen, including those in his own company, to give money and time to the Boy Scouts. One of his recruits was John Harbin, who became chairman of Halliburton Oil Company and chairman of the trustees of the Circle 10 Council.

In 1968, Clements spent a week at Philmont Scout Ranch in New Mexico getting his Wood Badge. The program brought together men from various walks of life, from welders and builders to business executives, and taught them how to use the skills of others. Clements was so impressed with the training that he wanted Dillard Hammett of SEDCO, an Eagle Scout and scoutmaster, to go. "Dillard, you're a scouter. You need to go up there and get your Wood Badge. I'll give you a week off to go up there," he said. He also had printed a wallet-sized card for SEDCO employees, which said, on one side: "The skills common to leadership roles are adopted from a Wood Badge training program at the Philmont Scout Ranch. I have found this list to be an important and helpful reference for guiding my own actions in both my private and business life. I hope you will too." On the other side of the card were listed eleven "Skills Common to All Leadership Roles," which included planning, identifying and using resources, getting and giving information, sharing leadership, and setting an example.[18]

Clements was elected to the National Executive Board of the Boy Scouts of America in 1971, and later served as national finance chairman. He also served as first president of the five-state South Central region, and then talked Perot into succeeding him in that job. The height of his Boy Scout involvement occurred while he was most active with business, although he was involved in later years. He initiated a program giving thirty $3,000 scholarships a year to Eagle Scouts entering their freshman year in college. Over a period of years, Clements gave more than $1 million for these Eagle Scout scholarships. Hammett was the scholarship trustee. Tarr estimated that Clements gave more than $3 million to the Boy Scouts over time.[19]

Clements' contributions were recognized with the top four awards in scouting, the Silver Beaver (1964), the Silver Antelope (1970), the Distinguished Eagle Scout (1970), and the Silver Buffalo awards (1980). He was the first from Circle 10 Council to be named by the National Court of Honor to the rank of Distinguished Eagle Scout.[20]

Clements' other civic passion was Southern Methodist University. His first involvement started when Gill was in SMU in the late 1950s. Clements began work to improve the business school. He became chairman of SMU's board of development, general chairman of its master plan campaign, and served on the board of trustees. He was an extremely effective fundraiser, whatever the cause, but particularly for SMU. In 1965 he was head of the fund campaign to raise $37 million to complete the master plan. Clements could raise money because he was a good convincer. "He really knew how to convince people of the various causes he was talking about," said Edwin L. Cox, a Dallas oil and gas producer who was persuaded by Clements to get involved in SMU in the late 1950s. Clements knew the university and could talk about it in great detail.[21]

In 1962 Clements became a member of SMU's board of governors, and its chairman in 1965. He was the recipient of the Distinguished Alumnus Award in 1966.[22]

Early in his involvement at SMU, Clements recognized the need for the university to strengthen its endowment. He helped to organize an investment committee, headed by Peter O'Donnell, but Clements was a strong solicitor and was active in the management of the fund. The endowment grew from a sum of $12 million when the investment committee was formed in 1965 to a market value of $186.5 million in 1984.[23] (Over thirty years, the endowment would grow to more than $400 million.) And, in 1967, SEDCO began funding engineering scholarships at SMU.[24]

One mark Clements left on SMU was the campus' return to the Williamsburg style of architecture, stopping a trend toward a hodge-podge of architectural design. Several buildings constructed a few years before Clements accepted the board chairmanship deviated from the school's traditional look, which annoyed Clements. He felt the university should maintain a consistency in its architecture. In a showdown over the design of the Underwood Law Library,

Clements fought faculty and fellow board members in an effort to restore the strict Williamsburg architectural policy. Clements won, making architects redraw the library's preliminary plans several times until they conformed with the Williamsburg style.[25]

When Clements was chairman of the board of governors in the late 1960s, Adkins Hall, an old dormitory, needed extensive remodeling to be converted into a general-purpose lecture hall. Clements donated the money for the remodeling, and today the building is called Clements Hall.[26]

One of Clements' pet projects was the development of SMU's Fort Burgwin Research Center near Taos, New Mexico, beginning in about 1965. Dr. Fred Wendorf of SMU's Department of Anthropology had proposed that SMU get involved in restoring some Indian ruins and a frontier cavalry post ten miles south of Taos as an archeological research center. Wendorf, the former state archeologist in New Mexico, persuaded Clements and Dr. Willis Tate, chancellor of SMU, to go to Ranchos de Taos to look at the property. It included the ruins of the Pot Creek Pueblo and Fort Burgwin, which had been used to guard the road between Taos and Santa Fe between 1852 and 1860 and was abandoned during the Civil War.

The ruins were under the auspices of the local Rounds Foundation, named after Ralph Rounds, an avid amateur archeologist and Wichita, Kansas, lumber company owner who owned land around the fort. Wendorf had made a survey of the site in the 1950s and, under the sponsorship of Rounds and later the National Science Foundation, had begun restoring the fort. The Fort Burgwin Research Center functioned as a nonprofit entity, administered by its local board, until Dr. Wendorf approached SMU. The foundation wanted to make an affiliation with a university to provide a financial base and continuity for further research.[27]

Clements and Tate saw the fort's main building, which had been reconstructed according to old drawings from the Department of the Army, and relics discovered at the nearby Pot Creek Pueblo. They realized the potential of the area and began three-year negotiations with the foundation for SMU to acquire the property. SMU was represented by Dallas lawyer Robert Ritchie, an old Highland Park friend of Clements and his fraternity brother at SMU. The agreement that was finally signed in 1968 required SMU to make a twenty-year commitment before the property would actually be deeded to the university.[28]

Clements thought that an adjunct to the main SMU campus, far different and removed from University Park, in a camp-like atmosphere steeped in the history of the Southwest, would open up new educational opportunities for students. The pattern for such centers had been established by other prestigious universities. "His goal was to try to create a university with a national reputation," Edwin L. Cox said. And the concept of the Fort Burgwin Research Center fit right into that goal.[29] Because of his own study of geological formations, Clements knew that geology students could cover more years and varieties of structures in that area of northern New Mexico than anywhere in the United States. He envisioned a repository for the pots, implements, and tools that would be excavated at the pueblo by students of archeology and anthropology. SMU at Fort Burgwin also could offer a variety of courses in the summer, allowing for a cross-fertilization of different disciplines in an atmosphere conducive to intellectual inquiry.

By 1974, summer credit courses were being offered at Fort Burgwin in the humanities, history, archeology, geology, biology, anthropology, botany, linguistics, and creative writing. Adult non-credit courses also were offered in such topics as art history, history of the Southwest, and North American Indians. The first group of ten *casitas* were built to house students and faculty, along with a dining and meeting hall. Clements provided the funds, nearly $1 million, for the expansion.[30]

SMU agreed to lease to Clements a parcel of land adjoining Fort Burgwin. He built his own *casa* there in the early 1970s and eventually bought the land from SMU.

Over a forty-year period, beginning in the 1950s, Clements gave more than $5 million to academic programs at SMU. His gifts included $1 million to establish the Betty Clements Professorship in Applied Mathematics, in honor of his sister who died in 1973. Betty had earned her bachelor's degree from SMU and her master's degree from the University of California at Berkeley; she had been a public school math teacher. His financial support ranged from the School of Engineering and Applied Science to Perkins School of Theology, where he was a major donor to the W.J.A. Power Professorship in Biblical Hebrew and Old Testament Interpretation. Later in life, however, he would double his earlier contributions with a one-time $10 million major gift to the History Department, to launch a Ph.D.

program that would emphasize regional history and operate a Center for Southwest Studies.[31]

Besides the Boy Scouts and SMU, Clements' other avocations included building a personal library, historical preservation, building and stocking his farm property, and hunting.

In the late 1960s, while driving down Akard Street in downtown Dallas, Clements noticed that the Dallas Independent School District had a "For Sale" sign on the old Cumberland Hill School building. It was the oldest public school in the city and the oldest brick building in downtown Dallas, having replaced the original wooden school built by the Cumberland sect of the Presbyterian church. SEDCO corporate headquarters had spread over three floors at the First National Bank and was running out of room. Why not buy the school building, Clements asked himself, restore it to its nineteenth-century Victorian splendor, and use it as a corporate headquarters?[32]

Clements and son Gill stayed up the night before bids were opened, trying to figure out what the old school building was worth. They settled on $1,362,667. The only other bidder who showed up at the school district offices represented Republic National Bank. Republic's bid was $1,356,000. SEDCO won by $6,000.[33] The morning after the bids were opened, Clements received a call from James Aston, chief executive officer at Republic National Bank, who offered him a $500,000 profit for the building. Aston indicated an interest in building a forty-five-story building on the property. Clements replied that it wasn't for sale.[34]

As the story goes, Clements took his renovation idea to his company's board of directors, explaining that SEDCO could spend a million or so remodeling the old school building or spend about the same amount constructing a nice headquarters elsewhere. Members of the board, to a man, liked the idea of going elsewhere. "Fine," Clements said, "we'll remodel the school."[35]

When Clements purchased the school building, many assumed the wrecking bar wouldn't be far behind, that the Victorian edifice would be razed and replaced by another glass and concrete building. That would have been normal procedure for Dallas, but Clements was nostalgic about the old school. Two of his mother's sisters had taught there, and his mother had told him stories of the school in its heyday. Pauline's great-grandfather, Charles A. Gill, had been president of the Dallas School Board when the school was completed in

1889. And Clements felt Dallas already had destroyed too much of its early architecture. "I just didn't want to see it torn down," he said in 1970. "It has beauty, and Dallas has too few old buildings. In San Antonio, San Augustine, other places in Texas — there are restored old buildings that are beautiful and interesting." He believed the Victorian structure, restored and decorated with antiques and reproductions, would give SEDCO a unique corporate identity. "SEDCO will identify with this building as we could never do with just another modern glass-walled building. Everyone in town will be aware of this building, and know it's the SEDCO building. That is a corporate 'plus,'" Clements said. "We think this will be the most elegant and charming building in downtown Dallas," he said.[36]

In 1971 the building had been restored and remodeled, the interior decorated with antiques or suitable reproductions, and 120 employees of the SEDCO home office moved in. Shelma Ahrens recalled that "many people were upset when he bought the Cumberland Hill School and we had to move. Of course, it turned out beautifully."[37]

The Friday luncheons, a fixture at the Petroleum Club, continued in the new quarters. There was a dining room in the basement of the school building, and the luncheons were catered by SEDCO's next-door neighbor, the Fairmont Hotel. While on a trip to London, Clements had personally purchased the china to be used in the new SEDCO dining room. The management luncheons grew over the years because the number of department and division heads grew. All the managers wanted to go, to make and hear the reports. The Friday luncheons helped to maintain the family atmosphere at SEDCO as it grew to be a larger company and, as such, were great for morale. They also continued to function as a critical management tool.

Clements liked officing in the school building, and it provided a place to house his personal "li-berry," as he called it. A great pastime of Clements was reading and collecting books. Part of his fortune had been spent acquiring books, a habit he had begun when he first started drawing a paycheck in the oilfields. His grade-school history teacher, Miss Willie Shook, had sparked his interest in Texas history. And his mother gave him books for birthdays and Christmas, adventure books by quality authors, such as Robert Louis Stevenson's *Treasure Island* and James Fenimore Cooper's *The Last of the Mohicans* and *The Deerslayer*. As an adult, he frequently read three or four books at the same time. His favorite books were histories, biographies, and books about Texas and the Southwest. Clements became a serious book collector and enjoyed buying rare books from catalogs.[38] In fact, he was an inveterate catalog shopper.

As a collector, Clements developed an impressive library, largely of Texana, which contained more than 8,000 volumes. He added more than 2,000 volumes when he bought the Western library accumulated by M. S. Cook of Corsicana about the time SEDCO moved to the Cumberland School. He sent Shelma Ahrens to Corsicana to card every book. When SEDCO moved into the school building, Clements had bookshelves built to properly house his library which, in the early 1970s, was valued at more than $1 million.[39]

In the 1950s and 1960s, Clements also was buying property near Forney, where he developed a ranch operation concentrating on Brangus cattle. His father, Perry Clements, found the first piece of property, the 165-acre Carter farm, owned by a couple he had gone to school with in the 1890s. The elder Clements became manager of the Clemgil Farm property and continued to recommend property acquisition over the years.

For relaxation, Clements went on hunting trips, including to Africa on safari. On one safari, he went to Mozambique. Another, in 1971, was to Kenya and Tanzania with his hunting friends Lloyd Birdwell, Jack Harbin, Bill Johns, and son Gill. The hunters shot buffalo, zebra, bush pig, crocodile, elephant, lion, roan, and hippos. The 1971 safari was eighteen months in the planning. Clements and his group didn't just call a travel agent and say, "Book us a safari." They made the arrangements with the guide, including shipping the firearms, ordering the food and ammunition for the camp, and getting the trophies returned. Planning such a trip involved a lot of reading and notes and memos back and forth between the hunters and the guide, plus the exchanging of newspaper articles and information on the locale. For Clements and his companions, making the preparations contributed to the enjoyment of the hunt.[40]

Clements was able to spend time pursuing his avocations because he believed in delegating responsibility. He had strong people working for him and let them carry the ball. "He was in charge, he ran the company," said Shelma Ahrens, "but the president and vice-presidents did the work." Clements, she said, kept a spotless desk. There was a drawer for her, and he had a "to-do" drawer. "He would route his mail and they would handle it," she said, of the officers.

Clements took a briefcase of work home at night and returned the next day with the work ready to be distributed. This freed him up during the day for other activities. When he hired Mrs. Ahrens in 1963, she was to be his personal secretary. She did almost no SEDCO work, but worked on his other activities. Clements, however, always insisted on handling two tasks himself. He wrote his own thank-you notes, and he personally selected gifts for his close friends and business associates — always looking for something unusual. One year, having discovered that piñon made good firewood, he ordered a truckload and had one of his ranch hands deliver and unload the wood at his friends' homes for Christmas.

Clements was just getting involved in politics when he hired Mrs. Ahrens in the fall of 1963. He told her that her main job was to get George Bush elected senator over Ralph Yarborough in 1964. Clements was Bush's finance chairman. Mrs. Ahrens went to work organizing luncheons and fundraising activities for the Senate campaign.[41]

The Bush campaign provided Clements with his first taste of Republican politics. At the time, he considered himself a "Texas ticket-splitter," or an independent. Like most Texas businessmen of means, Clements was conservative, but usually supported conservative Democrats because that's where the power was. And there were few Republican candidates. In most races, Clements noted, "you either supported conservative Democrats or you didn't support anybody."[42] At the time, the Democratic Party was sharply divided into two camps — conservative and liberal. There was almost no need for the Republican Party, because divergent philosophies were contained within the Democratic Party.

Like many Texans, however, Clements had supported Republican Dwight D. Eisenhower for president in 1952 and 1956, because Ike was strong on national security and, in the 1952 campaign, favored giving back Texas' tidelands. Several states including Texas were making claims to oil deposits submerged off their coasts, a position opposed by Democrat Adlai Stevenson. Billions of dollars hung in the balance if the offshore lands could be shifted from federal to state jurisdiction. Texas Democrats, called "Shivercrats" because they were led by Democratic Gov. Allan Shivers, defected to Eisenhower. Democrat Price Daniel, who promised in the 1952 U.S. Senate campaign to fight Texas' tidelands battles in Washington, was supported by Clements. (Shivers and Daniel both had opposition in the Democratic primary in 1952 but in a peculiarity of Texas politics, they were "cross-filed" in both the Democrat and Republican columns in the general election.) Daniel was elected and helped pass a law signed by President Eisenhower recognizing state ownership to three leagues offshore in the Gulf of Mexico (four million acres). When Daniel returned to Texas to win the governorship in 1956, he had Clements' support again.[43]

In the 1950s, Republicans in Texas were able to muster only a few primaries in selected areas — such as Midland. George and Barbara Bush held the first GOP primary there in 1952. "There were three people who voted in our precinct, me, Barbara and some Democrat who staggered into the wrong place," the former president remembered four decades later.[44]

The party had begun a surge in Dallas County, where Republican Congressman Bruce Alger had been in office since 1954. In 1960, Dallas gave Richard Nixon the largest vote margin over John Kennedy of any city in the country. Still, when Republican John Tower was elected to the U.S. Senate in the 1961 special election, Republicans held no seats in the Texas legislature. That was rectified in 1962, when Dallas County sent six Republican legislators to Austin. Peter O'Donnell was largely credited with the rise of Republicanism in Dallas, aided by a group of women who assumed leadership roles as volunteers. One of them was Rita Bass.[45] O'Donnell had been a committed Republican from the 1950s and was chairman of Dallas County — Texas' most successful Republican county organization — before becoming state chairman.[46]

At the time, the Dallas political climate was dominated by mainstream conservatives, but extremist conservatives were attracting attention. As described in a newspaper retrospective on the times, "In Dallas politics of the early '60s, conservatives were in control and ultraconservatives were out of control." Dallas had been marked by two incidents. Days before the 1960 election, vice-presidential candidate Lyndon Johnson and his wife were jostled by placard-carrying hecklers in downtown Dallas, after which Johnson claimed they were spat upon. "I only hope the day never comes when a man cannot walk his lady across the street in Dallas," Johnson remarked. In October 1963, United Nations Ambassador Adlai Stevenson, in Dallas to speak at a UN Day program, was struck on the head with a sign carried by a woman picketer. Meanwhile, the John Birch Society, a militant ad hoc anti-Communist organization, was active. And H. L. Hunt sought to spread his own brand of ultra-conservatism through his nationwide *Facts Forum* and *Lifeline* radio programs.[47] Clements occasionally bumped into Hunt distributing his right-wing pamphlets in the First National Bank parking garage.

Clements' political philosophy was simple: He was in favor of less government and a strong national security, and he was against communism. His position on the political spectrum was in the mainstream in Dallas and in the state's business circles at the time.

Clements, however, was no fan of President John F. Kennedy, and at the time Kennedy was assassinated in Dallas on November 22, 1963, Clements was having lunch at the Petroleum Club. Many members of Dallas' business establishment disregarded their own political feelings in a show of civic unity and went to the Trade Mart for the lunch that was planned that day for the president. Not Clements. "I would not have been at any occasion with Mr. Kennedy," he said.[48]

Clements was a strong supporter of then-Democrat John Connally, having met Connally and his wife, Nellie, when they were all students at the University of Texas. In 1964 he broke with his friend Peter O'Donnell, who had launched the national Draft Goldwater campaign, by voting for Texan Lyndon Johnson. (When he later became a Republican candidate for governor, Clements explained that he thought 1964 would be his only opportunity to help vote a Texan into the presidency.)

Texas was so emotionally and politically traumatized by the Kennedy assassination, and Lyndon Johnson's personal power was so strong, that virtually all of the gains of the Republican Party in the state were wiped out in the 1964 election. Both Republican congressmen lost; ten of the eleven Republican seats in the 150-member Texas House of Representatives were lost, and there were no state senators.[49] George Bush lost his U.S. Senate election. "We all got buried in the Johnson landslide," Bush said. Two years later, however, Bush sold his stock in the oil business and became one of two Republican congressmen elected from Texas.[50]

O'Donnell understood the political environment in the '60s in Texas and recognized that Clements was an independent, but he stayed after him to work for Republican causes. In 1968, O'Donnell got Clements involved in raising funds for Richard Nixon's presidential campaign. By then, Clements had demonstrated his abilities as a fundraiser for the Boy Scouts and SMU as well as in the 1964 Bush campaign. Several Texas Nixon backers that year (including Clements) tried to convince Governor Connally to support Nixon, or at least to "go fishing" and not be involved in the presidential campaign.[51]

As a result of the 1968 campaign, Clements was invited to the White House for dinner. He accepted, but at the last minute, SEDCO developed a problem which Clements felt demanded his attention. In the middle of a meeting with company officers, Clements told Mrs. Ahrens to call the White House and cancel him for dinner. "Mr. Clements, I don't think you can cancel a dinner at the White House," she said. He looked at her hard and said, "I think you can. And I think you should."[52]

Business still came first, but Clements was getting more involved in Republican politics. He was chairman of a fundraising dinner honoring Sen. John G. Tower for a "Decade of Service" on May 27, 1971, at Dallas' Fairmont Hotel, which a local political writer called the most successful fundraiser for a Republican in Texas history.[53]

In 1972, the Nixon reelection effort was floundering in Texas, and some of the national campaign people who had met Clements in 1968 wanted him to take charge of the state's Committee to Re-Elect the President. Clements signed on as state co-chairman, with Erik Jonsson, in the summer of 1972. Then he called O'Donnell and asked, "What do I do now?"[54]

In an August 16, 1972, statement which he gave to a press officer who was preparing a news release announcing his appointment, Clements wrote: "The main reason I'm taking this job is because the President asked me to . . . and further, I think it is of the utmost urgency if we want to continue our way of life that we re-elect President Nixon. The Democratic nominee [George McGovern] is advocating a philosophical revolution which is just another word for socialism, and I am violently opposed to this type of government. . . . The two reasons I took this responsibility: 1) I was asked to and I just couldn't refuse, and second, I think it is damned important."[55] An Eisenhower quotation was printed in the volunteer manual for Nixon's reelection effort: "Politics ought to be the part-time profession of every citizen." Clements' interest in politics and public service was picking up.

Clements didn't become co-chairman in name only. He helped set up the organization and went to work. There was a state office in Austin; he set up a smaller office in Dallas. O'Donnell recalled attending a workshop session with Jonsson and Clements during which Clements, at one point, turned to Jonsson, who was head of the mammoth Texas Instruments, and said, "In my company, when we make a decision, we take action." That statement made an impression on O'Donnell. "When he [Clements] decides something, something begins to happen — immediately," O'Donnell said.[56]

The Dallas office of the Texas Committee to Re-Elect the President was located in the Baker Hotel, which Clements had acquired the preceding year. In the summer of 1971, Clemgil Realty had purchased the entire downtown Dallas block bounded by Commerce, Akard, Jackson, and Browder. The block contained the Baker Hotel, which had opened in 1925 as the successor to Dallas' famed Oriental Hotel. Clemgil Realty was incorporated by Clements, his wife Pauline, and son Gill; Clements was president, and his father, W. P. Clements, Sr., was chairman of the board, which included Nancy Clements Seay.

The Texas CREP took over several rooms in the Baker Hotel. O'Donnell, an adviser to the campaign, officed there, with his secretary. Jonsson and Clements both had offices, and Clements was there whenever something was going on. Mrs. Ahrens worked there for the duration of the campaign. Tom Pauken (who twenty-three years later would be state Republican chairman) headed up voter blocs. Rita Bass, a longtime Republican activist who was married to Dick Bass, was in charge of voter registration and the get-out-the-vote effort and had an office at the Baker. It was during that 1972 campaign that Clements and Rita Bass became friends. James A. Baker of Houston (later President Ronald Reagan's chief of staff and President George Bush's secretary of state) was state party finance chairman and a regional chairman for the committee in the Houston area. Ed Vetter was county chairman for Dallas. Scott Caven was staff director in Dallas, and Nancy Brataas, in Washington, was in charge of telephone operations for Texas. Linda Montgomery, who had been a Dallas newspaper reporter, was hired to handle press relations in the Dallas office.[57]

Mrs. Montgomery's impression of Clements was that he was an optimistic man who always looked on the bright side and never thought there was anything he couldn't do. He didn't, however, trust reporters, and he always asked Mrs. Montgomery what to expect when he was going to be interviewed. "He had no knowledge of the press and how it worked. I felt like we were learning together. I wanted him not to make a fool of himself because it would make me look foolish. And I liked him," she said. "But it made me flinch when he would say stupid things. He didn't have any social manners, he just shot his mouth off. He would just walk up and say what he thought."[58] He told one reporter to go back to her publisher and tell him to put more photos of Richard Nixon on page one and use fewer stories on George McGovern. "He had the impression everybody could do the things he could do," Mrs. Montgomery said, including picking up the phone and calling newspaper publishers. "He got attention when he phoned."[59] His modus operandi as a political operative was similar to the way he worked in business. He would gather people together, listen to their advice, act on their advice and disperse the work. He found a little intimidation would go a long way, and he would crack heads, as necessary.

Tom Pauken had recently returned to Dallas from working in the White House counsel's office and serving as associate director of the White House Fellows Program when he volunteered to work for the Committee to Re-Elect the President, organizing voter blocs (youths, Hispanics, blacks, veterans, etc.). He recognized Clements as a "guy who was new to the process, but he would get things done. He would size up people in this new arena; if he felt that you knew what you were doing, he would let you run with the ball," Pauken said. Pauken, who had seen the height of insecurity among personnel in the Nixon administration, found Clements to be a "very secure guy." In Washington, he found, "Guys would rise high, but they were pretty insecure human beings, so they were nervous about making decisions and appeared to put on a front. Clements was never that way."[60]

Scott Caven was hired to run the Dallas office because he worked for Goldman Sachs in Dallas and, as a young law school graduate, had worked for Gov. John Connally. Goldman Sachs was SEDCO's investment banker, and Caven's boss, Tom Walker, who had handled SEDCO's first public stock offering, gave Caven a three-month leave of absence to work for the campaign. "I had been a lifelong Democrat, as had everyone in Texas in 1972," said Caven, who thought Clements was going to head a Democrats for Nixon organization in the state. "It was not until I went over there that I found out it was a Republican organization." With that election, Caven became a Republican.

Caven found Clements to be a "very hard-charging individual. Some people find him abrasive; I find him effective. He's not a classic politician. There's no equivocation about anything he says or does. He rubs people the wrong way, but he's a man of principle and sticks by his principles. I won't say he's easy to work for, but we worked well together." Caven and Clements had breakfast several times a week to discuss what needed to be done, and then Clements gave him free rein to execute the plan. "I've rarely met a man more able to get things done. He was a very determined man, and very organized," Caven said.[61]

George McGovern was clearly unpopular in Texas. Texas conservative Democrats were dispirited after McGovern's nomination at the national convention in Miami and allowed liberals to take control of the party and the campaign. (A young lawyer from Arkansas named Bill Clinton came to Texas to be the field man for the national Democratic campaign.) Democratic officeholders in Texas distanced themselves from the national ticket, but didn't defect openly as top state officials had in 1952 and 1956. However, John Connally (still a Democrat until his party switch in 1973) campaigned hard for Nixon, organizing Democrats for Nixon and hosting a reception for the president at his Picosa Ranch near Floresville.[62]

Tom Reed, a Californian who was a regional CREP chairman in charge of several states including Texas, later said, "We could have run Daffy Duck that year and won in a landslide."[63] But Clements was taking no chances; he worked hard in the campaign. He wove a scenario for reporters of how Richard Nixon could lose the state of Texas — if newly registered Democrats turned out in higher numbers than newly registered Republicans. The big registration gains were in predominantly black precincts and in the suburbs, and Clements wanted to "make it damn clear to the guy in suburbia, that if you sit on your duff and don't vote, we're liable to go down the drain." In the final weeks of the campaign, Clements repeatedly preached to potential Nixon voters who might think the election was "in the bag" that Nixon needed their vote.[64]

Nixon won in Texas by a two-to-one margin, 2,147,970 to 1,091,808; the Democratic ticket carried only Massachusetts and the District of Columbia. It was a runaway, with Nixon getting almost 67 percent of the vote in Texas, compared to the national Republican margin of almost 61 percent. There were a few coattails at the state level, but the Republicans didn't have many candidates on the ballot. Besides John Tower for Senate and Hank Grover for governor, the Republicans had only two other candidates running statewide, one for state treasurer and one for Texas railroad commissioner; of that field only Tower won. While fielding candidates in only half of the legislative districts (thirteen state senate and seventy-three state representative candidates), Republicans increased their representation in the Texas House from ten to seventeen of 150 members and from two to three state senators out of thirty-one. While seventeen state house members didn't sound too impressive, the state's two most populous counties — Harris and Dallas — made major gains. Dallas picked up six seats and Harris five. Those gains were attributed as much to the new single-member legislative districts as to the Nixon landslide.

Bill Clements, meanwhile, got an excellent evaluation on his performance as co-chair of the Texas Committee to Re-Elect the President. The evaluation form said he was the "right man in the right place at the right time," that he brought "great management skill" to the campaign, and through his ability to "recruit good people, decisiveness, and hard work, he inspired confidence in the campaign." [65]

And he had been bitten by the political bug. He would soon be given a political appointment in Washington that would change his life.

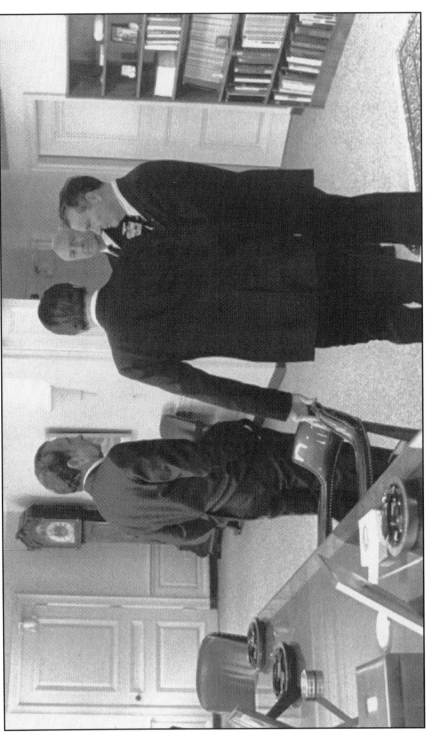

Deputy Secretary of Defense Clements meets with President Nixon, Defense Secretary Elliot Richardson and Adm. Thomas Moorer.

Part II

Deputy Secretary of Defense

William P. Clements, Jr., is sworn in as deputy secretary of defense by Defense Secretary Elliot Richardson in January 1973. Holding the Bible is Adm. Thomas Moorer, chairman, Joint Chiefs of Staff. (AP Wirephoto)

Chapter 8

DOD 1

A Texan Goes to Washington

THE NAME OF WILLIAM P. Clements, Jr., first cracked the public consciousness on December 12, 1972, when he was nominated by President Richard Nixon to be deputy secretary of defense. If confirmed, Clements would act as general manager of the Department of Defense, overseeing DOD's $80 billion budget, its 3.4 million employees, and the procurement of 116 major weapons systems costing over $150 billion.[1] Clements had been involved in the upper echelons of politics and in the higher levels of Dallas business and civic circles. His name was a familiar one in the oil industry. But he was far from well known, either at home or nationally. Who was this man, and why had President Nixon selected him to be the No. 2 man at the Pentagon?

What the news media discovered was that Clements had a reputation among his peers as a strong, positive person who had infinite faith in the rightness of his own opinions. "He doesn't deny somebody else the right to their opinion, but he tends to believe his is right," one Clements friend said. Another acquaintance pictured him as a hard-driving, demanding individual who "runs everything that I've seen him in."

Some acquaintances called him direct and forthright; others called him tactless and arrogant. "When he has something to say, he just lays it right out there without giving too much of a damn who's listening," one Republican said. A "high-ranking Democrat" was quoted in one news story as saying, "He may be the toughest sonofabitch you know. He makes gut decisions and doesn't back off." The Democratic official described Clements as being philosophically to the right of Barry Goldwater. "But if you want tanks made, he'll make them for you quicker and better than anybody else."[2]

Clements wasn't chosen because of his long-time service to the Republican Party. When asked at a press conference about his politics, Clements described himself as an "independent." But his leadership of the president's reelection campaign in Texas had brought him to the attention of key figures in the administration. And John Connally, Nixon's secretary of the treasury who had organized Democrats for Nixon in 1972, had pushed Clements' appointment at the White House.

Connally and Clements shared a common character trait: cocky self-assurance. Clements was actually more an intimate of Connally than he was of Republican Sen. John Tower, although Tower, a member of the Senate Armed Services Committee, strongly supported Clements for the deputy secretary's job. Clements had contributed to Tower's campaign and worked with him on the SMU board of trustees.

But the two key factors in Clements' appointment were his reputation as a hard-nosed business manager and his work on the Blue Ribbon Defense Panel that had studied the functioning of the Department of Defense and the Armed Services in 1969 and 1970. There was no question that his service as one of fifteen businessmen on the Blue Ribbon Panel was instrumental. Nixon said Clements would bring "strong management and executive talents as well as wide knowledge of defense and national security matters" to the Pentagon.[3]

Though Clements had long been interested in international relations as a result of SEDCO's extensive foreign business, much of his knowledge of defense and security matters had been gained on the Blue Ribbon Defense Panel. The panel had made a thorough examination of the organization and management of the Defense Department, including the Joint Chiefs of Staff, the defense agencies, and the military services. It also had examined procurement policies and practices and research and development efforts. The panel's report had been made to the president on July 1, 1970, and half of its 100 recommendations already had been put into effect. Clements was reported to have been one of the hardest-working members of the panel.[4]

He was also one of the most independent. Members of the panel had reserved the right to submit supplemental statements on areas not addressed by the commission's report. Clements and Lewis F. Powell, Jr., a Virginia lawyer who was later appointed to the U.S. Supreme Court by President Nixon, decided to write one, and five other panel members signed the minority report after it was written. The supplemental statement dealt with the shifting of the balance of strategic military power against the United States and disquieting trends which threatened to turn the U.S. into a second-rate power. The report maintained that Russia was quickly closing on the United States in weapons strength and was moving toward a first-strike nuclear capability. It suggested that the world order over which the U.S. had presided since World War II was in danger of being lost to a new Soviet-dominated world order.

In examining the general world posture, the report noted that the strategic significance of the Middle East was profound, with the petroleum resources there being vital to the economic well being of much of the free world. Effective control of those resources was cited as an "obvious Soviet strategic objective." As Clements explained years later, "Lewis and I were convinced if we had problems with Russia of a major nature, it would not be in Germany, it would be in the Persian Gulf," where the Soviets already were supplying armaments and personnel to Syria, Egypt, and Iraq.[5]

The supplemental report also expressed concern over public hostility toward the military, which was largely an outgrowth of the war in Southeast Asia. Promulgated on college campuses, the hostility had become broadbased; what had become known as the "military-industrial complex" was under attack. According to the minority report: "Few are willing to speak out in defense of the military, and even fewer in support of increased defense funding . . . . One has to go back to the days of McCarthyism to find such intolerance and repression of rational discussion of issues of the gravest national import."[6]

At the press conference following his nomination, Clements said that rebuilding the image of and public support for the Department of Defense would be his No. 1 goal. "I think that most everyone would agree that the DOD has sort of been everybody's whipping boy here for the last few years, and the public image of the department — you know, it just needs to undergo a radical change."[7]

Before selecting Clements, Nixon announced he was moving Elliot L. Richardson from his post as secretary of Health, Education and Welfare to secretary of defense, succeeding Melvin Laird. Nixon knew the war in Vietnam would soon be over, and he wanted a new team in place to redirect the Department of Defense. His selection of Clements to be deputy secretary produced something of an "odd couple" situation. Where Richardson was a Boston Brahmin, proper but liberal by Republican standards, Clements was a tough-minded, conservative Texan out of the rough-and-tumble oil industry, an obvious hawk on defense matters.

Syndicated columnists Evans and Novak tried to analyze the unusual match. "The message to hard-liners on Capitol Hill is unmistakable: don't worry too much about Richardson and the bright-eyed young liberal aides he brings over to the Pentagon from the Department of HEW; if he goes wrong, Bill Clements will be there to set him right." Clements' strong national defense posture was expected to balance the "more dovish Richardson."[8]

At the time of Clements' nomination, the country was awaiting the signing of a peace agreement to end the Vietnam War. Presidential adviser Henry Kissinger had negotiated a draft peace settlement with the North Vietnamese in October 1972, pronouncing before the election that "peace is at hand." However, Kissinger had been unable to get the North Vietnamese to accept changes that the South Vietnamese insisted on. Over the 1972 Christmas holidays, Nixon resumed B-52 raids on the North to pressure Hanoi into resuming negotiations that would result in the signing of the peace settlement.[9]

The Department of Defense in the coming days would be charged with the reorganization of defense policies that had been heavily weighted toward Vietnam at the expense of Europe and other parts of the world. Spending priorities would have to be reordered, and public support for the armed services, which had suffered declining esteem and morale, would have to grow.

Clements was familiar with the problems of the department after spending eighteen months on the Blue Ribbon Panel; he wasn't about to step into such a difficult situation without a clear mandate as to his responsibilities and his authority. Called initially about the DOD job by National Security Adviser Henry Kissinger,

Clements had said he was not inclined to take it, but changed his mind and agreed to meet with Nixon. He flew to Washington, where he was shuttled by helicopter to Camp David to meet with the president-elect and his chief of staff, Bob Haldeman, on November 22, 1972.

In his own eleven-page memo of the hour-long meeting at Camp David, Clements wrote that the visit with the president was "unbelievable for me in the frankness of the discussion and in the firm convictions expressed by the President to me of things that he wanted done . . . . It was astounding to me that the President would delegate such responsibility to me." Clements further wrote, "John Connally has now called me and confirmed to me the general thoughts of the President and that these responsibilities are to be mine. Connally told me that he understood that I had received a tremendous 'charge' from the President, and he hoped that I wasn't overwhelmed with such responsibilities."[10]

The memo, written by Clements on November 30, 1972, said that the president had started off by stating "that I was to be his 'hawk' and that I was to never forget that this was my role," and that Elliot Richardson would be the dove, "although he is not as dovish as most people think." Clements responded that he could play the role of hawk "beautifully." Nixon then warned Clements that he might have problems with "dovish" newspapers such as *The New York Times* and the *Washington Post*. Clements also noted that Nixon twice discussed at some length that he should "stand up" to Kissinger and suggested that if he reached an impasse with Kissinger, he should come directly to the president.

President Nixon told Clements he was not pleased with the job Secretary Melvin Laird had done. He thought Laird was too political. The president wanted a "new pattern, new strength, new toughness for the next fifteen year period. There is great danger, and we must turn the DOD around in the interest of our own national security," Clements wrote in his notes.

Nixon had talked about the appointment with Connally at Connally's ranch, and Connally had assured him that Clements wanted the deputy's job rather than the job of secretary. As such, Clements would be the chief operating officer of the Pentagon, which Nixon considered the sixth most important job in Washington, behind the president, vice-president, and the secretaries of state, treasury and defense.

Nixon told Clements, "You are working for me, not Elliot Richardson." He also told Clements that he would be the senior Texan in the administration, and the president would consult with him in that spirit.[11]

At Camp David, Clements hammered out his special charter with the president, which included authorization to select his own team, rather than having to rely on political appointees. Clements would select the three service secretaries — army, air force and navy — the undersecretaries, and all of the assistant secretaries. Nixon agreed to give him a free hand to make the selections. Clements would be invited to all Cabinet meetings, whether or not the secretary of defense was there. By law, the deputy secretary of defense, unlike his counterpart in any other department, is vested with the same powers as the secretary and, in the absence of the secretary, could authorize any action.[12]

According to Clements' notes on the Camp David meeting, the president charged him to "stand up" to the Joint Chiefs of Staff and to the services generally, to reorganize the services and make them lean and tough. Nixon wanted better hardware and better judgment exercised "to get more for our money."

The president spoke at length at the Camp David meeting about the fact that the U.S. had not been developing good weapons systems. As an example, he said, the Shah of Iran "didn't want our tanks because the Shah considered them inferior to the Russian tanks." The president, according to Clements' minutes of the meeting, said, "Isn't that a helluva note!" The president also said that U.S. tanks couldn't stand up to the big Russian tanks in Vietnam and that this was a "horrible indictment of the DOD."

Clements and Nixon also talked about personal matters. Nixon said he understood Clements' wife, Pauline, did not want to move to Washington but, he said, the wives of his official family were close, and he felt sure Pauline would enjoy the association.[13]

Not only did Pauline not want to move to Washington, she also did not share her husband's new interest in politics. Clements later admitted that their marriage was strained when he went to Washington.

After the meeting at Camp David, Clements met with Elliot Richardson, who assured him that their different backgrounds would complement each other. Richardson told Clements that he knew the political and civil service side and he would depend on

Clements for operations. Clements wrote that Richardson seemed to be "a very nice person, intelligent, well organized, quiet."[14]

Clements' Senate confirmation was not without controversy. The first dustup came with the revelation of the civil suit that had been filed against Southeastern Drilling, Clements, and three others by Buenos Aires businessman Antonio A. Diaz in 1966. Diaz charged conspiracy to hide millions in alleged profits from the company's Argentine oil deal, claiming there was no proper accounting of millions of dollars Southeastern charged off to expenses and deducted from profits.[15]

The New York Times reported that the Argentine contract to drill 1,000 wells helped propel Southeastern "from a relatively small wildcat outfit to a worldwide operation that last year grossed $130 million. Mr. Clements and members of his family invested only $310 in the Argentine deal, court records show. The contract was so successful that within five years this investment was worth at least $4.2 million to them." *The Times* reported that SEDCO destroyed many of its records of the Argentine operation in 1964, shortly after drilling was completed, and the subsidiaries handling the operation were dissolved.[16]

Clements responded that published reports were unfair and misleading. "We had a complete clean bill of health from the IRS. We have nothing to hide," he said. "It would be naive of anyone to think it wasn't all thoroughly investigated years ago."[17]

Clements was introduced to the Senate Armed Services Committee by his fellow Texan, Sen. John Tower, and received vigorous support from such stalwart members as Strom Thurmond, Harry Byrd, Scoop Jackson, Barry Goldwater, and Stuart Symington. Chairman John Stennis, D-Miss., praised him for "what we in Mississippi call gumption." Clements also was endorsed by Texas' Democratic senator, Lloyd Bentsen, who said: "Bill Clements has a record of service to his community and accomplishments in his professional life that mark him as a man of excellence who has given his best to every undertaking of his life." Clements never forgot the support given him by Senator Bentsen then and throughout his DOD service, and he remained a political friend of the Democrat in later years.

Clements pledged to resign from the board of governors of SMU, which was a defense contractor in the field of research, and to give up his membership on the National Petroleum Council, as well as his directorships of the International Association of Drilling Contractors and Independent Petroleum Association. The board of SEDCO had resolved that neither SEDCO nor its subsidiaries would perform any Defense Department work. At the time of the appointment, SEDCO had thirty-eight rigs under contract in Iran, Abu Dhabi, Oman, Algeria, the North Sea, and the Arabian Gulf, and offshore Canada, Australia, Borneo, and Africa. Clements was president of the Boy Scouts of America's South Central Region and on the BSA national executive board. He also was on the executive committee of the Dallas Citizens Council.[18]

According to reports filed with the Securities and Exchange Commission, Clements was the owner of 1.6 million shares of SEDCO, a little more than 17 percent of the shares outstanding, worth around $102 million. His salary as chairman and CEO was $81,100 plus $11,363 from SEDCO's profit-sharing plan. But he was giving up his stock in Keebler Company, because it sold cookies, crackers and biscuits to the armed services. He also was giving up his directorships of First National Bank and Fidelity Union Life Insurance.

Clements told *Business Week* that money was no longer important to him. "Beyond a certain point, it loses its significance. There was a time for my business endeavors, and now there is a time to serve my country. My motive in taking this job is patriotism," he said, explaining that his overall goal was to "reverse the trend toward Soviet superiority."[19]

The Armed Services Committee forwarded Clements' name to the full Senate with no negative votes, reporting that the nominee demonstrated in hearings "a thorough grasp of the many problems associated with the management of the defense establishment . . . a keen awareness of the weapons acquisition process and the need for reform in the field of procurement practices and procedures." The report also stated, "The committee believes that Mr. Clements is a man of highest integrity, ability and character."[20]

Chairman Stennis emphasized that the No. 2 job at the Department of Defense was not just another office but one that "carries tremendous power and responsibility . . . . He will be acting Secretary of Defense in the absence of the secretary and at meetings to which the secretary cannot go." Senator Stennis said the committee had found nothing derogatory in the lawsuit filed against Clements, and he expressed confidence that Clements would solve some of the problems of the Defense Department through better management and better procurement.

Senator Tower, in his testimony, described Clements as an able, self-made man, who had contributed to the economic growth of the country, but who also was public spirited. He called attention to the time, energy and resources Clements had given to furthering privately supported higher education, and quoted SMU's president on Clements' departure from that institution's board of governors. "He said simply, 'He will be irreplaceable.' It is that kind of irreplaceable man who should fill positions in the government of the United States," Tower said.[21]

Sen. Harold Hughes, D-Iowa, led the opposition to Clements' confirmation. He said Clements failed to tell the Armed Services Committee that the bank on whose board he sat had extended $7.8 million in credit to LTV Aerospace Corp., maker of the A7 Corsair attack plane, for which it hoped to get a government contract. Clements had 3,420 shares of the bank's stock, valued at $171,000, but had agreed to sell his stock and resign his directorship. Hughes also expressed misgivings about Clements' philosophy of defense, saying it was tougher than the president's.

Clements was confirmed by a vote of 74 to 11 in the Senate. The opposing votes came from the Senate's most outspoken antiwar bloc — all Democrats. Voting with Hughes were Senators James Abourezk, Robert C. Byrd, Frank Church, J. William Fulbright, Mike Gravel, William D. Hathaway, Mike Mansfield, Walter Mondale, Gaylord Nelson, and William Proxmire.[22]

The week that Clements was confirmed was a week of momentous events. On January 20, 1973, President Nixon was inaugurated for his second term. Two days later, Lyndon B. Johnson died at his ranch in Texas. On January 23, 1973, the day the Senate confirmed Bill Clements as deputy secretary of defense, the Vietnam peace settlement was signed in Paris. On the night of January 23, President Nixon announced in a broadcast to the nation that the peace agreement had been reached and the ceasefire in Southeast Asia would begin on January 27, 1973, ending a decade of U.S. military involvement in a conflict that had split the nation.[23]

The next day, Clements was briefed by Adm. Thomas Moorer, chairman of the Joint Chiefs of Staff, on the ceasefire, the withdrawal of 145,000 troops, and the release of the prisoners of war on approximately February 6, 1973.[24]

Clements was sworn in by Admiral Moorer on January 31, 1973, and then flew to Dallas to make his exit from SEDCO. On February 2, 1973, the SEDCO board of directors accepted his resignation as chairman and announced the realignment in SEDCO's management structure. Edwin L. Cox, a director, was elevated to the post of chairman of the board. Tom B. Rhodes, senior vice-president and general counsel, would be vice-chairman of the board. Spencer L. Taylor, president of the Drilling Division, was elected chairman of the executive committee. B. Gill Clements, treasurer, was promoted to president and CEO of SEDCO, Inc. Dillard Hammett and John W. Rhea, Jr., joined the board as new directors.[25]

Clements had left it up to his top management to select his successor. There were two natural choices — Spencer Taylor and John Rhea — but the selection of either created problems by leaving out the other one. B. Gill Clements, who was thirty-one and had been with the company only five years, became the compromise choice. Clements later said he was as surprised as anyone that they selected his son, Gill. Others, however, said it was Bill Clements who planted the seed. The more seasoned company leaders rallied around Gill to make sure he succeeded, and he quickly grew into the job.

In a message he wrote to employees in a company magazine, Gill Clements took note of his father's favorite passage of Scripture, in the third chapter of Ecclesiastes: "To everything there is a season, and a time to every purpose under the heaven . . . a time to break down and a time to build up . . . a time to reap, and a time to sow . . . a time to keep silent, and a time to speak." This, said Gill Clements, was his father's "season to serve." The younger Clements wrote in his message to employees, "William P. Clements Jr. is a teacher, a builder, a leader of men, and the greatest father a son could have. Our future success may well be measured by what we do to carry on SEDCO's traditions of being first and best."[26]

Clements also resigned from the vestry at St. Michael and All Angels Church in Dallas and from various civic boards. In a letter to SMU Chancellor Willis Tate, he wrote, "I have told you many times how much my association with you and SMU has meant to me. There is no way for me to properly express my sense of regret. I especially cherish the years you and I have spent together working in the interest of SMU."[27]

One of the congratulatory letters Clements received was from his Argentine associate, David Oscar Elkin. "Your country," Elkin wrote, "will have the services and devotion of an outstanding citizen, and will benefit from the formidable talent, drive, leadership and strength of purpose that are a part indivisible from you; all of which personal virtues I witnessed during the fruitful years of our relationship in the past.

"I well realize that accepting Mr. Nixon's designation, you have taken a capital decision with great influence in your private and business life," Elkin wrote.[28]

Little did Elkin know how prophetic his statement would be — how great the influence would be on Bill Clements, particularly on his private life and on setting the direction for his remaining years.

Clements quickly became totally engrossed in his work at the Pentagon. The war was ending, and the POWs were coming home. The challenges of rebuilding and modernizing the military and restoring American power and prestige were great. Clements had built army camps and power installations and supplied oilfields during World War II, but he had never worn a uniform. Now he was rubbing elbows with generals and admirals and service secretaries and security officials and ambassadors. He had been frustrated by his inability to go on active duty in World War II, which was one reason he wanted to serve in the Department of Defense.[29] Once there, he was immediately thrust into the vortex of power in Washington. The job was an important one, and Clements was stimulated by it.

His first full day in the Pentagon began with a meeting with National Security Adviser Henry Kissinger at the White House. It didn't end until late in the evening, after he and Mrs. Clements had returned to the White House for a black tie dinner with President and Mrs. Nixon in honor of King Hussein I of Jordan and Queen Alia. In between were numerous phone calls, briefings, and other meetings at the Pentagon.

He met or talked daily with such associates as Adm. Thomas Moorer, chairman of the Joint Chiefs of Staff; Navy Secretary John Warner; Adm. Elmo Zumwalt, chief of naval operations; Gen. Creighton Abrams, army chief of staff; Gen. Brent Scowcroft, National Security Council deputy; Gen. Alexander Haig, vice chief of staff of the army; Gen. George S. Brown, commander of Air Force Systems Command; and Lawrence Eagleburger, a foreign service employee serving DOD as a deputy assistant secretary.[30]

A Kissinger protégé, Eagleburger became assistant secretary of state for Internal Affairs, or general manager of the State Department, six months after Clements assumed office. Clements, Kissinger, and Eagleburger became confidants and friends, and Eagleburger years later would be named to the SEDCO board of directors. Clements also counted Admiral Moorer and General Scowcroft among his good friends and political allies in Washington; their relationships continued after he left the nation's capital.

Clements' biggest job in those first few months was to recruit the forty-two people to serve in the various high-level positions in the Pentagon — the assistants and undersecretaries and secretaries of the services — according to the authority delegated to him by President Nixon. Nixon told his chief of staff and the White House personnel office not to interfere. "I never had to worry about the phone ringing and somebody at the White House saying, 'I have a longtime buddy over here who needs to be made assistant secretary,'" Clements said. He recruited his own team, selecting the members for their managerial ability and technical expertise and without regard for political background. Clements felt the single most important thing he did at DOD was recruiting the defense team.[31] Peter O'Donnell from Dallas was an important part of that process, from the time Clements accepted the appointment. O'Donnell spent four months in Washington, living in the same hotel-apartment building as Clements. The two went to work together and often had lunch or dinner together. They talked about recruiting into the night.[32]

Clements believed what former business executive and White House adviser Frederic V. Malek had written in a 1972 *Harvard Business Review* article: that a major challenge to any administration was to find and attract men and women who possessed extra dimensions.

Malek wrote about the difficulties of transferring success from the private to the public sector. Public scrutiny, rigid controls, and the short time span to achieve results were among the problems faced by business leaders who accepted government posts, Malek wrote in "Mr. Executive goes to Washington." They had to be able to inform, persuade, and gain the confidence of members of Congress. They had to learn rapidly, take hold quickly and exert forceful leadership, because the average Cabinet or sub-Cabinet level appointee remained in office just twenty-two months.

Malek listed the most critical personal characteristics needed to succeed as a businessman in government: the ability to communicate and to create a feeling of purposiveness within a department, mental toughness, flexibility and managerial ability. "Part of the ability to communicate is charismatic, inspirational leadership which can earn essential congressional or public support for departmental programs and initiatives. It serves as a catalyst, mobilizing the force of a vast and unwieldy bureaucracy and moving it toward the administration's goals," he wrote.[33]

Clements was determined to get the most qualified managers from the world of business into the Pentagon. In the first six weeks after assuming his position, he was interviewing people from such companies as Boeing Aircraft, RCA, U.S. Steel, PepsiCo, and Xerox. He personally appealed to bosses in industry to recommend and release the best people in their organization for service at DOD. Clements told them, "If you don't like the way this Defense Department is running, you've got to get me good people to help run it."[34]

One personnel recruitment meeting that included cocktails and dinner at the Pentagon with Secretary Richardson and service personnel drew the top officers of such corporations as Martin Marietta, Cutler-Hammer, Inc., Todd Shipyards, Bath Iron Works, United Aircraft, Halliburton Company, Hughes Aircraft, PepsiCo, Inc., General Dynamics, Sperry Rand, Menasco Manufacturing, DuPont Companies, Raytheon Company, Texas Instruments, Fairchild Industries, and Sears, Roebuck & Company.[35]

Among Clements' top recruits were Dr. Malcomb Currie, an applied physicist who became the Pentagon's director of Defense Research and Engineering; and Howard "Bo" Callaway, a West Point graduate and Georgia's first Republican congressman since Reconstruction, who became secretary of the army. Norm Augustine of LTV became assistant secretary of the army for research and development. Clements brought in top people from companies such as Boeing and Hughes Aircraft. He was proud of the fact that of the forty-two people he recruited, eighteen later became presidents or CEOs of major corporations. They included Mal Currie, who became chairman and CEO of Hughes, and Augustine, who headed Martin Marietta.

The deputy secretary of defense, called the DepSec in military jargon, was the nuts and bolts chief of the Pentagon, while the secretary of defense, called the SecDef, handled the protocol. The DepSec was "Mr. Inside" and the SecDef was "Mr. Outside."

The DepSec had three active-duty officers who served as his military aides. Clements selected as his top two military assistants Army Col. John Jones and Navy Capt. Kenneth Carr. Each got their first star while working for Clements. Jones eventually retired with the two-star rank of major general; Carr retired with three stars, as a vice-admiral.

"One thing he made clear with the people he picked for his staff was that he insisted on straightforward answers," Jones said. "His expression was: 'If you've got an opinion, don't lay behind the log. Tell me what your honest opinion is.' He wanted people to be absolutely frank, honest, forthright with him, and he would be also with them."

Clements brought Carr on board because he anticipated the development of the Trident submarine on his watch and he wanted someone with experience in nuclear submarines. Carr's assignment at the time was chief of staff to the Commander Submarine Force, U.S. Atlantic Fleet, and he would later command that force after he left the Pentagon. Clements thought it was a disgrace that the last successful major weapon system developed by the U.S. was the Polaris submarine, which was being upgraded to the Poseidon system. While he regarded the Polaris-Poseidon as the most important deterrent to Russia, Clements was committed to the development of the more advanced Trident submarine system, which would require several billion dollars and eight years of concentrated effort. About the time Carr came on board, Clements signed a letter to the navy about the Trident, with a handwritten note, "Get on with it."[36]

Carr got a good idea about Clements' personality when he observed him at his first press conference responding to a reporter's question. After hearing Clements' answer, the reporter replied, "What you meant to say was . . ." and he paraphrased Clements. "Clements looked him in the eye and said, 'What I meant to say is exactly what I said,'" Carr recalled.[37]

A military assistant sat in on all interviews Clements conducted to fill in the staff, taking notes for the record. According to Jones, "One of his real strengths was just an uncanny ability to interview and size up people. He focused on their track record, what they had done, how large an organization they had managed, how successful they had been." Jones said Clements also had the ability to separate the talkers from the workers. "One of his great contributions to the Pentagon was just the outstanding group of people he put in the key positions," Jones said.

One active-duty assistant went in at 6:30 A.M. to organize the day and worked until about 6:30 P.M. The other went in later and worked until Clements left the Pentagon, often at 8:00 or 9:00 P.M. "His personal energy allowed him to see a tremendous number of people. He was always in early and stayed late, and worked on Saturday, almost like a normal work day. His basic psyche was to work hard. He'd always worked hard. It was just his personality," Jones said. "He was willing to work whatever hours he felt necesary to get the job done. Everything that came into his 'in box' he liked to deal with it that day. If he didn't, he'd take it home with him at night, even if he left at 8:30 or nine o'clock," Jones said. And Clements understood that the art of running any large organization depended heavily on two-way communication. "The relations between civilian and military hierarchy were not always smooth. But there was an unusual degree of open, straightforward communication between military and civilian leadership in the Pentagon," Jones said.[38]

Carr recalled that Clements "had a memory like a steel trap. The detail, conversations, commitments were right in his head. It never ceased to amaze me how much he was capable of absorbing."

To hire his personal secretary, Clements asked for a list of the five secretaries with the highest civil service ratings in the Pentagon to interview. He wasn't going to have a secretary assigned to him, regardless of whose secretary he swiped. He selected Janie Harris, a career civil servant of twenty-one years, nine of them in the Pentagon. When Clements hired her, Ms. Harris told him, "If I'm ever doing anything you don't like, I want you to tell me, not say it behind my back." Clements responded, "I want you to know you work for me and me alone. You don't work for anyone else." Ms. Harris said later, "We shook hands on the deal and never had any problems."[39]

Ms. Harris, in fact, moved to Dallas at the end of Clements' tenure in Washington, becoming his secretary at SEDCO and later in Austin, after he became governor.

When Peter O'Donnell was ready to go home after four months in Washington, Clements brought in Jack Hammack, a Dallas acquaintance who had been president of the Dallas Petroleum Club. Hammack picked up where O'Donnell left off, acting as a modified headhunter for the Defense Department.

"Bill Clements had, innately and through acquired skills, tremendous intangible leadership. He always surrounded himself with outstanding people, strong people. Most leaders surround themselves with yes men; he didn't. He wanted their opinions even if they were different from his," Hammack said. Clements was sometimes harsh in his dealings with Pentagon associates. "But he was able to command tremendous respect from people who worked for him," Hammack said, even if they disagreed.[40]

When he hired his team, Clements made an effort to get four-year commitments. He was the first deputy secretary who completed the full four years.

Clements loved the trappings of his position, as well as the work. He had a huge office on the third floor of the Pentagon which featured a bank of windows. From the windows, he could see the National Monument and the Jefferson Memorial. There was a clear view of the Pentagon parade grounds, where the armed services appeared in full dress for ceremonies and parades. Clements was impressed with the ceremonial aspects of the military, and liked being in the company of military leaders, present and past. He loved to walk to his office down the Eisenhower corridor, where portraits of the former secretaries and deputy secretaries were hung along with Medal of Honor winners.

Clements carefully decorated his office, selecting a desk that had been used by Gen. U.S. Grant. A picture of his Texian hero, Sam Houston, was hung under a seal of the State of Texas. A clock gave the time in various parts of the world. Decorative items included sculptures by a favorite artist, Charles Russell.

Clements kept a busy schedule, often receiving courtesy calls from industry leaders, defense contractors, top service personnel, and foreign ambassadors. On a typical day he might attend a verification panel meeting in the situation room at the White House regarding the Strategic Arms Limitation Treaty (SALT), followed by a briefing on a specific foreign situation. In his first few months, Clements attended many meetings on SALT and the all-volunteer army. Occasionally he would have lunch in the office with a friend from home, but his conversations with anyone from SEDCO were rare. There are frequent entries in his diary that he had lunch in his office alone.

The evenings often included receptions and black tie dinners with top service personnel or members of the diplomatic corps and foreign visitors. Or he and Mrs. Clements might have dinner at a Washington restaurant with visitors from home or with other displaced Texans, though there were periods when Mrs. Clements was not in Washington. George Bush was then chairman of the Republican National Committee. Anne Armstrong, a GOP leader married to South Texas rancher Tobin Armstrong, was a special counselor to the president. The Bushes and the Armstrongs, in particular, extended the hand of friendship to help Clements make the adjustment to his new world. In his first year in Washington, Clements and his wife, Pauline, had Thanksgiving dinner with the Bushes.

His path crossed with other Texans, such as Senators Tower and Bentsen, and Jim Collins, Republican congressman from Dallas. Clements' friendship with Supreme Court Justice Lewis Powell, his acquaintance from the Blue Ribbon Panel, grew. Clements talked frequently with John Connally back in Texas. Once Peter O'Donnell returned to Dallas, he also talked often with him by phone. Later, Ed Vetter, who worked for Texas Instruments and had been Dallas County chairman in the Nixon campaign, went to Washington as undersecretary of commerce, replacing Texan James A. Baker. "We had a little Texas mafia there," Vetter said.[41]

Clements was required to testify occasionally before committees on Capitol Hill. Ken Carr recalled that after Clements presented his prepared testimony on one occasion, congressional committee members left the room, and only the hired staff remained to question him. Clements was offended; he wasn't going to sit there and talk to staffers. He was a top-guy to top-guy person. He and Carr abruptly left.[42]

When Clements got involved in foreign affairs, he often dealt with Lawrence Eagleburger, who had been a career foreign service officer in the State Department before he became deputy assistant secretary of defense. Eagleburger recalled his first contact with Clements shortly after the new deputy secretary arrived at DOD. A group of British parliamentarians was at the Pentagon to be briefed by Clements. Eagleburger thought, "Oh, my God, here we've got this Texas cowboy who's going to try to talk to these sophisticated Britishers, and he's going to botch it up." Eagleburger couldn't have been more surprised with the meeting. Clements, he said, "was absolutely superb. He knew what he was talking about and he was able to deal with them at a level well above their own knowledge. It surprised the hell out of me. It was the first time I ran into him, so I remember it," he said later.

"Because of the Blue Ribbon commission, he'd had some experience in what the Pentagon was about. He didn't come in totally uneducated. But I thought we were going to be getting a guy who'd show up in cowboy boots and spurs and every third word would be a cuss word. And I couldn't have been more wrong," said Eagleburger.[43]

Little did he know that Clements never wore cowboy boots because they made his feet hot.

Eagleburger later moved on to the White House as deputy assistant to the president for national security operations and subsequently followed Henry Kissinger to the State Department as his executive assistant after Kissinger became secretary of state.[44] But he went away an admirer of Bill Clements, partly because he hadn't expected a lot. "Everything he did that I was involved with, I found him smart as hell and prepared to listen and a really tough fighter when it became necessary to fight," he said.

Early in his tenure, Clements was involved in plans for the return of the prisoners of war from Southeast Asia. The Paris agreement beginning the ceasefire on January 27, 1973, had specified a sixty-day deadline for all troop withdrawals. On March 27, 1973, the U.S. began a three-day airlift of the last 5,236 American troops from Vietnam, as the North Vietnamese released the remaining prisoners from Hanoi, completing the repatriation of 587 American POWs.[45] Clements had many telephone conversations on the return of the POWs with his old friend from Dallas, Ross Perot. Perot had long worked as a private citizen for the release of the POWs. Through an organization he set up called United We Stand, Perot had spent more than a million dollars advertising the plight of the prisoners and trying to deliver mail, clothing, and food to the POWs.

On April 12 and 13, 1973, Clements returned to Texas on his first official trip to speak to the Houston Rotary Club and to the Dallas Council on World Affairs, which attracted an overflow crowd at Dallas' Statler Hilton Hotel.

In his speeches, Clements emphasized the challenges of the Cold War. He warned that with the technological gains of the Soviet Union, the United States could not afford to "let down" militarily. The Russians, he said, had developed a submarine with a missile range of 4,000 miles, and their missiles were targeted against American cities and military installations. Clements cautioned against complacency with the end of war in Vietnam. He also predicted that some Texas military bases would be among those closed by the Pentagon. "I'm from Texas. I'm a Texan to my toenails, but you must remember we are going to have to take our share of the reductions, and you should be prepared for this," he said. The speech was played at the top of page one in *The Dallas Morning News*. A photo of Clements was captioned, "William P. Clements ... 'Texan to my toenails.'"[46] (When he got into politics, Clements preferred to call himself "Texian," an older term, but used "Texan" as well.)

In Houston, Clements noted that he had been called a hard-line hawk. "I want to get this straight right now. I am not a dove, certainly, and neither am I a hawk. If anything, I'm an American eagle." Like his friend, Perot, Clements had a fondness for the winged symbol of America and liked reproductions and objets d'art of the mighty eagle.

He also elaborated on his philosophy of arms reductions. "We are now negotiating for mutual and balanced reductions in deployments in Europe, but it would be ridiculous to reduce our levels while negotiations are going on. As the President said: 'There is one unbreakable rule of international diplomacy. You can't get something in a negotiation unless you have something to give.' If we cut our defense before negotiations begin, any incentive for other nations to cut theirs will go right out the window."[47]

While the U.S. was reducing its defense spending, Russia was stepping up its expenditures for defense and research and development. "It is increasingly clear to me that we must take vigorous action to maintain our superiority," he said. "Let us never send the President of the United States to the conference table as the head of the second strongest nation in the world."

Clements also spoke out against amnesty for those who did not serve in Vietnam. "Those who served were right, and those who bugged out were wrong. Our nation cannot tolerate a permissiveness under which every citizen would be permitted to decide which laws he will obey and which laws he will defy. More than two and one-half million Americans obeyed the law and served in Southeast Asia. It would be an insult to them to grant total forgiveness to a few thousand who abandoned America," he said.

Clements talked further about the importance of the Persian Gulf-Arabian Sea area to oil and gas supplies for the United States, which could not meet its needs with domestic production. Some 70 percent of the free world's petroleum reserves were in the area surrounding the Persian Gulf where it met the Arabian Sea, and he predicted that by 1985, the U.S. would be drawing a quarter of its petroleum supplies from that troubled region. The Gulf area already was providing more than 90 percent of Japan's petroleum and 60 percent of Europe's.

He gave a short lesson in geopolitics related to the energy problem, noting that the U.S. had good relations with the two countries that provided stability in the area — Iran and Saudi Arabia. Clements pointed out that Iraq had not been stable for many years and the present regime, which had cozied up to Russia, was not friendly to the U.S. Iraq recently had created an incident with Kuwait over a border situation and threatened to take two islands from Kuwait. "The relationship between Iraq and Iran has been shaky for years, with many border incidents. I suggest that you keep your eye on Iraq," he said.[48]

Later events would prove Clements' fears to be well founded.

On June 2, 1973, Clements was in Dallas for a big welcome home celebration for the POWs, the Dallas Salute to Vietnam Veterans at the Cotton Bowl. The event was preceded by an informal buffet dinner at the Dallas Convention Center for the men and their families.

The festivities at the Cotton Bowl honored 450 POW returnees and their families who were seated on the field. Clements was the senior civilian government and Defense Department official at the event. He believed nothing had given the country so much of a lift in recent years as the return of the POWs. In his tribute to the Americans who served in Southeast Asia, he noted how the nation was moved by the returning POWs, who stepped off their planes at Clark Air Force Base and said, "God Bless America." He welcomed the POWs home, on behalf of the 2.2 million military and civilian personnel in the DOD.[49]

In press remarks the day after the salute, Clements talked about the emotional issue of the men still missing in action in Southeast Asia, calling it insensitive and cruel to offer false hope to their families. "There is not a shred of evidence that would give us hope that there are survivors among the MIAs," Clements said. "The MIAs are on my mind, on everybody's mind, but it serves no purpose to allow families of the men of whom we can find no trace at all to be tormented by rumors."

"The cruelest thing going on," he said, "is the profit making on bracelets and bumper stickers and fund raising that uses the sadness of the families of these men and the sympathies of their countrymen for profit. The rumor-mongering by charlatans makes my blood boil." Clements was acting secretary of defense and was speaking the DOD position when he said, "We have not one hard piece of evidence that any MIA is alive in Southeast Asia."[50]

Clements was acting secretary because Elliot Richardson was being moved by President Nixon from the secretary's post to be attorney general. Nixon had given Richardson the charge of "getting to the bottom" of the Watergate scandal, in which agents of Nixon's reelection committee had attempted to tap telephone lines at Democratic headquarters. In an April 30, 1973, broadcast to the nation, Nixon announced that Richardson would have "absolute authority to make all decisions bearing upon the Watergate case and related matters." To obtain Richardson's confirmation, the president had to agree to the appointment of an independent special prosecutor to handle the Watergate investigation. Richardson selected Harvard Professor Archibald Cox as special prosecutor.[51] In May 1973, Sen. Sam Ervin's Special Watergate Committee began its hearings.

James Schlesinger, who was director of the Central Intelligence Agency, was nominated to succeed Richardson as secretary of defense but had not been confirmed. Clements, therefore, had assumed increased responsibilities. But Clements never wanted to be secretary of defense. He wanted to be the operational manager. He reported to four committee chairmen on Capitol Hill, besides the president. Rep. George Mahon of Texas was chairman of House Appropriations, and Eddie Hebert of Louisiana was chairman of House Armed Services. In the Senate, John McClellan of Arkansas was chairman of the Budget Committee and Sen. John Stennis of Mississippi was chairman of the Armed Services Committee. They were all Democrats, and all were older than Clements, who was fifty-six. They had years of seniority on Capitol Hill. Clements respected the chairmen, got along well with them, and considered his relationship with them a source of strength in his position.

According to Clements in an interview years later, "When Elliot was moved to the attorney general's office by Nixon, these four guys, plus Tower, called me on the phone and said, 'Don't you want to be Secretary of Defense?' I said, 'No. I know what this job is. I've recruited all these people; I have an obligation to them. This job is the one I came up here to do and what I'm going to do until I go back to Dallas.'"⁵²

Clements made hundreds of speeches during his four years at the Pentagon. He most frequently addressed military groups, although he also appeared before civic clubs and at educational institutions. Besides being a strong advocate for the nation's defense, Clements often was historian and teacher.

In August 1973, for example, Clements was asked to deliver the speech at the keel laying of the nuclear-powered guided missile frigate *Texas*. He used the occasion to impart a little Texas history. One could sense his great affection for what he called "one of the legendary states of this great American republic" — a state that had joined the Union in 1845 and, at the time of the speech, ranked first in the nation's production of oil, natural gas, cotton, and cattle.

Texas had something of a naval tradition. One of the first acts of the provisional government in independent Texas had been to establish a publicly owned and operated navy. "Mexican forces operating in Texas were eventually defeated by their failure to receive support by sea," Clements said. "In fact, without Texan control of the sea in the Gulf of Mexico through the crucial spring of 1836, the decisive victory at San Jacinto could not have been achieved." At the height of Texas' nine years as an independent republic, the Texas Navy had thirteen men-of-war in its fleet, he noted.

"Much has changed since the days when the newly purchased and commissioned ships of the Texas Navy, the *Independence* and the *Brutus*, set sail from New Orleans to take up patrol off Galveston Bay," Clements said. "Today we are entering a hopeful but complex and uncertain international environment in which lasting peace seems to be a possibility for the very first time. But this chance for peace carries with it a challenge: the challenge that our defense establishment remain strong enough, and the American people remain concerned enough with the security of our great nation to demand that that strength be maintained."⁵³

Clements always spoke out for maintaining peace through strength. During his first year, he issued an order that no speech would go out of the Pentagon without mentioning the new volunteer army. But in November, after several months on the job, Clements was not happy with his speechwriters. "I want to quit voicing platitudes," he said at a daily staff meeting. "There's no one around here writing like I'm talking," he complained. The speech-writers, of course, would never write exactly like Clements talked. He referred to the Pentagon, for example, as the "Pentygon" and frequently mangled names. But he thought the speeches could be more to the point. Clements wanted to "shoot it straight," he told his staff. "We lost our ass on SALT I, and we're fumbling the ball on SALT II," he said. Clements felt the only way to build support for DOD was through full communications with the American people.[54]

Chapter 9

DOD 2

A Whole New Life

THE AUTUMN OF 1973 WAS a difficult time in Washington. Not only were the Watergate investigations under way, but the Justice Department had been looking into allegations of bribery, extortion, and tax fraud against Vice President Spiro T. Agnew. On October 10, 1973, Vice President Agnew resigned.

But there were other worries for the deputy secretary of defense. On October 6, 1973, war broke out in the Middle East as Syria and Egypt attacked the territories occupied by Israel since 1967. The hostilities took both Israel and Washington by surprise. The sixteen days of fighting became known as the Yom Kippur War because the attack came on the holiest day of the Jewish year. Adm. Thomas Moorer recalled that "the Russians had given the Egyptians some equipment to cross the [Suez] canal. The Egyptians would run up to the canal and stop, run up to the canal and stop. On Yom Kippur, when they knew the Israelis were in religious services, they kept coming."[1]

When the October War of 1973 started, Clements was taking his first vacation from Washington. The Pentagon's intelligence was that there was no likelihood of war in the immediate future. Washington was completely caught off guard. Nixon was in Key Biscayne trying to decide how to deal with Watergate-related legal demands that he surrender tapes of White House conversations. Clements and his wife, Pauline, had joined their good friends, the Ed Coxes, at John Gardner's Tennis Ranch in the mountains outside of Scottsdale, Arizona, for a tennis weekend. In the predawn hours, Clements was awakened by Ken Carr and told that war had broken out. His bags were packed, and a plane was dispatched to return him to Washington. Thus began two weeks of daily meetings at the White House of the Washington Special Action Group (WSAG), the National Security Council's crisis committee.

Israel made an emergency request for military supplies and, for the next week, the critical debate was to what extent should the U.S. resupply Israel. After four days of intense fighting, the Israelis had suffered heavy losses to their aircraft and tanks. Without resupply, they were doomed. Nixon told Kissinger, who had been appointed secretary of state a few weeks earlier, to replace their losses. Instead of allowing American planes to transport the supplies, however, Kissinger decided that Israel should hire private charter companies to do it. The logistics were complicated. U.S. airlines and charter companies refused to make their aircraft available for fear of Arab reprisals, nor did they want to risk their planes in a war zone. Access to the international air space around Israel was difficult. "None of the NATO nations would let us land an airplane in their country because they were afraid the Arabs would boycott their oil," Admiral Moorer said. England and France were highly dependent on Arab oil, as was most of Europe.

Admiral Moorer came up with a proposal to deploy three C-5A aircraft, the largest transport planes in the American arsenal, on resupply missions. Though the jet transports could fly sixty to eighty tons of supplies directly to Israel, it was considered a minimal response borne out of fear that a larger number of American planes would alienate the Arabs and the Soviets. The roles played by Kissinger, Schlesinger, and Clements in the resupply effort have been debated in dozens of books and articles.[2] Various reports said Schlesinger was dragging his heels in following the White House order to resupply Israel, while some blamed Clements for delays, saying he had pro-Arab sympathies. Other accounts accused Kissinger of playing a devious game, holding back supplies from Israel to create a climate ripe for diplomacy and unfairly blaming the Pentagon for the delays. Clements has said he was unaware of a problem with the charter planes and denied any foot-dragging. To the contrary, he said he followed White House orders during the crisis.

Finally, on October 13, 1973, Nixon ordered a full-scale airlift, with unlimited use of U.S. Air Force transport aircraft if charters were a problem. Later that day, the first thirty USAF C-130s were airborne to Lod airport, near Tel Aviv. Over the next thirty-two days, 566 air force missions would be flown, outstripping the Soviet resupply airlift to the Arabs.[3]

According to Clements, "Our problem was a presidential problem. Only one person could make the decision on what to do and when to do it. What we were doing at DOD, we were waiting for Nixon's decision — a presidential directive," he said. "There was no dissension, no contrary opinions. But until Nixon made that decision, nothing happened."[4]

In all that he did, Clements left a paper trail — notebooks, diaries, letters, and news clippings. He signified that he had read a document with the initial "C," underlined, usually in red pen. He also underlined important passages in documents and news clippings, sometimes writing "agree" or "yes" or "nuts!" in the margin.

Beside a passage in one news report that said, "Almost from the start, the DOD had maintained that there was no practical solution other than a full-scale airlift," Clements wrote, "True."

One report said that Clements could not have challenged Kissinger's recognized primacy in foreign policy unless he had Nixon's support. Clements wrote "Right" in the margin.[5]

According to Eagleburger, "During the 1973 war, when Henry [Kissinger] was trying to crank up support for the Israelis, Schlesinger was less than cooperative." Schlesinger and Kissinger didn't get along, and Eagleburger's view was that orders would be issued and Schlesinger would take a long time to carry them out.

Eagleburger felt Clements' "intellectual prejudices" were more pro-Arab and less enthusiastically supportive of the Israelis. "But when push came to shove on the war, and on support for the Israelis thereafter, he was thoroughly cooperative. And when decisions were made, he carried them out — which was a unique experience, if you had been dealing with Schlesinger."[6]

On October 25, 1973, American military forces were put on a worldwide nuclear alert in reaction to the possibility of Soviet troop movement into the war between Israel and Egypt. Clements was called into the Pentagon at 1:00 A.M., and stayed until 5:00 A.M. and then was back in the office at 8:20 A.M.[7] Within hours, the situation was eased; the fighting in the Middle East stopped, and a cease-fire went into effect. There was some suspicion later that the alert was a political ploy by President Nixon to deflect the heat from Watergate, but Clements felt that suspicion was never borne out.

While involved with the Mideast war, Clements also was continuing with his normal daily activities, which included budget matters, weapons procurement, and personnel decisions. Washington, meanwhile, was consumed with the choice of a new vice-president and with Watergate. For vice-president, Nixon wanted Connally, who had joined the Republican Party in May of that year. But Connally was too controversial in Washington; he likely would have had a difficult confirmation fight. Nixon settled for Congressman Gerald Ford, whose confirmation was assured. On October 12, 1973, the president nominated Ford as vice-president.[8]

During the course of the October War, the world experienced the first of numerous oil shocks. On October 16, 1973, OPEC abandoned the creeping increase of oil prices in favor of a dramatic rise. Six Gulf states raised the price of oil by 70 percent from $3.01 to $5.12. The Arab members of OPEC, meeting in Kuwait, agreed to cut their oil production by five percent and to continue reducing it by five percent every month until Israel withdrew from all occupied Arab territories. On October 19, President Nixon asked the Congress for a $2.2 billion package of assistance to Israel to pay for the military equipment sent by the airlift. The next day, Saudi Arabia declared a total embargo on oil exports to the United States.

Kissinger wrote that those three actions — the October 16 OPEC decision on price, the October 17 Kuwait decision on Arab production cutbacks, and the October 20 Arab embargo — revolutionized the world oil market. The OPEC ministers in Tehran boosted the oil price from $5.12 a barrel to $11.65 a barrel on December 22-23, 1973 — a hike of 128 percent, on top of the 70 percent increase in October, and the Arab oil embargo was not lifted until March 1974.[9]

While recruiting his DOD team, Clements had approached Californian Tom Reed, whom he had met during the 1972 Nixon campaign, to come to work at the Pentagon as a special assistant. In between occasional stints in politics, Reed was chairman of a company that developed ski resorts and vineyards. He had been a Republican national committeeman from California and was campaign coordinator for the Southwestern states in the 1972 campaign. The beginning of Reed's service at DOD coincided with the outbreak of the Middle East war, and his immediate assignment was to work on some intelligence projects related to the Middle East. One was to talk to the production vice-presidents with the "Seven Sisters" — Exxon, Mobil, Chevron, Texaco, Gulf, Royal Dutch/Shell and British Petroleum — to find out what was really going on in the Middle East regarding price increases and the embargo. Reed said he generated "a very clear picture of the pending crisis that was going to strike us that the intelligence community did not even remotely appreciate." During the Mideast crisis, Reed said, Clements' understanding of the Persian Gulf was of inestimable benefit to the U.S.[10]

Amid the oil crisis, Clements participated in meetings with several visitors from the Middle East, including Moshe Dayan and Golda Meir of Israel, Anwar Sadat of Egypt, and the Shah of Iran. Because of his operations in the Middle East, he was familiar with and liked their part of the world. "He liked them, and they liked him," recalled his secretary, Janie Harris.[11]

Kenneth Carr recalled a meeting between Clements and the sultan of Oman. The British were scheduled to pull out of Oman, leaving an airport there. Clements had received his briefing papers on the meeting but went beyond them, asking the sultan, "When the British pull out, how about letting us use this airfield?" The sultan agreed. According to Carr, Clements sometimes "went beyond the agenda prepared for him. He had ideas, and he knew what he wanted to do."[12]

Clements did not hesitate to freelance in meetings with foreign dignitaries. He was seated on one side of the sultan of Oman at a State Department dinner when the sultan expressed fear of being invaded by Russian-armed South Yemen. "We can take care of that," Clements told him. "We have a tow missile which is the most sophisticated, accurate anti-tank missile in the world," Clements said. How could Oman get the missiles? asked the sultan. "We'll put them on an airplane and send them to you with people to teach your people how to operate them," Clements promised. The missiles were sent, enabling Oman to turn back South Yemen's Russian tanks when the invasion occurred.[13]

Clements' interest in the Middle East and in energy policy, however, came under fire. Congressman Les Aspin, the Wisconsin Democrat and critic of Pentagon policies, wanted Clements to dispose of more than 1.6 million shares of SEDCO stock or place it in trust. Aspin contended Clements' holdings, valued at about $98 million, constituted an obvious and potentially dangerous conflict of interest, because Clements had become involved in shaping the government's energy policy. Clements was DOD's representative on the Cabinet-level Emergency Energy Action Group, which advised Nixon on special steps to be taken to deal with the fuel crisis. Clements also played a prominent role in the Pentagon's own fuel-allocation and conservation program.

Questions also were raised about Clements' relationship with the Shah of Iran and its possible impact on arms sales to that Persian Gulf area. Clements was uninvolved in any direct requests for military hardware by the government of Iran to the U.S. government. After Clements left SEDCO for Washington, however, SEDCO got involved in a joint venture in Iran. The U.S. Export-Import Bank authorized a direct loan of more than $11 million to SED-IRAN, an Iranian corporation 50 percent owned by SEDCO and 50 percent by Iranian interests, to help finance the sale of eight land-based drilling rigs.[14]

Clements believed he should be active in Mideast affairs and energy matters, because he had experience in those areas. Secretary Schlesinger thought differently. Schlesinger wanted to exclude Clements from Middle East and energy policy work precisely because of his oil interests. By December 1973, questions were being raised by the press about whether Clements had been removed from any energy policy role or whether he had divested himself of his SEDCO stock. Clements had several conversations with Sen. John Stennis, Armed Services Committee chairman. Stennis agreed that while Clements had expertise in energy and the Middle East, he increased his own political vulnerability by remaining active in those areas. Stennis suggested to Clements that his portfolio of responsibilities was full without his being involved in energy policy. In January 1974, Clements agreed to remove himself from energy policy, both in the DOD and in the executive branch — a decision that pleased Schlesinger but did not help the growing discord between the two men.[15]

It was at the height of the Middle East war that the famous "Saturday Night Massacre" occurred, beginning the demise of the Nixon presidency. On October 20, 1973, President Nixon ordered Atty. Gen. Elliot Richardson to fire Archibald Cox, the special prosecutor. The Court of Appeals had ordered the president to obey

Cox's subpoena to hand over nine of the White House tapes related to Watergate. Richardson refused to fire Cox. The result was that, on a Saturday night, the White House announced that Cox had been fired as special prosecutor and that Richardson and his deputy, William Ruckelshaus, had resigned.

From that point on, President Nixon was on an inexorable slide toward resignation. Watergate dominated the news, and almost paralyzed Washington in the coming months of 1974. On March 12, 1974, Clements wrote a letter to his friend Robert C. Hill, who was U.S. ambassador in Buenos Aires, Argentina. "I wish I could send you good news in regard to the President, but I see no improvement in his situation at this time. He continues to be harassed by both the press and certain elements in the Congress, and it certainly is not clear to me just where it will all end. There is still a strong feeling that the President does have sufficient votes in the Congress to turn back any vote on impeachment, but how long that support will remain, and further how long it will be before it comes to a vote, is highly problematical."[16]

It was July before the whole affair came to a head. The Supreme Court ruled that Nixon had to turn over sixty-four White House tapes sought by Leon Jaworski, the special prosecutor who followed Archibald Cox, and the House Judiciary Committee passed articles of impeachment. Nixon announced in a televised address to the nation on August 8, 1974, that he would resign, which he did the next day.[17] In the last days of the Nixon presidency, *The New York Times* reported that the Pentagon kept close watch to guard against any possibility of orders going directly to military units from the White House. It was reported that Schlesinger, in consultation with Air Force Gen. George S. Brown, chairman of the Joint Chiefs of Staff, made the decision to monitor all orders to insure that nobody in the White House ordered a military move against Congress, and that no one in Congress ordered a coup d'etat against the president. The concern was that while Nixon faced impeachment and was considering resignation, he still retained full authority as commander in chief of the armed services. And he had close ties to men influential in the services, including Gen. Alexander M. Haig, his White House chief of staff.[18]

Clements considered these reports "pure bunk." On several press accounts retained in his files, he wrote in the margin, "No," and "not true" and "awful." In an October appearance at Duke Uni-

versity, General Brown said he was "utterly amazed" when he read
the account that he had joined Schlesinger in issuing such orders.
Schlesinger, he said, brought up the question in conversation during
the third week in July about whether the White House could issue
some military order without the JCS chairman knowing about it.
General Brown, who had just replaced the retiring Admiral Moorer
in July as JCS chairman, said "absolutely, no." No orders were issued, and no instructions were sent out to unified commands.

Brown confirmed, however, that he did send out a signal to senior American commanders around the world at the time of the
presidential change, "kind of telling everybody to lean forward in
their foxholes a little bit, keep their powder dry sort of thing."
Brown said it wasn't a concern for a domestic problem or U.S.
troops misbehaving. "It was that some foreign power might do
something foolish with the feeling that we were without leadership." He described it as a normal precautionary measure. Clements
wrote in red pen in the margin of the General Brown transcript, "I
asked him to do this and all agreed w/H.K."[19]

As the Watergate affair escalated and the president withdrew
more from day-to-day activities, Clements was determined to keep
the Defense Department removed, as best he could, from the in-
trigue and surrealistic atmosphere that enveloped Washington.
Throughout the period when the White House appeared to be under
siege from Watergate, his attitude was to maintain stability at the
Pentagon.

"Every day, it was put the left foot here and the right foot there
and procure hardware and worry about [Secretary General Leonid]
Breznev and worry about the Mideast war, with all the crisis backdrop of a White House under siege and a President not fully capable
of paying attention to what was going on," said Tom Reed. Clements, according to Reed, "was determined to be very careful. His
reaction to Watergate was to tend to your knitting and see to it that
the Pentagon is stable and strong and not give anybody alarm."[20]

On Friday, August 9, 1974, the day Nixon bid adieu to his
White House staff and Gerald Ford was sworn in as president,
Clements was at the White House for a Cabinet meeting. He had
known Ford when the latter was a congressman from Michigan and
liked him. Clements and Ford, in fact, had a mutual regard for each
other. Ford proposed no changes in Clements' role at the Pentagon.

Clements admitted that he watched Nixon leave with real regret. He regretted it not only from the standpoint of Nixon as a person, but from the standpoint of the country. "It wasn't good for the country. The country was all torn up. People were taking sides. There was a real dichotomy between Washington and the American public." At the same time, Clements had no personal or social relationship with Nixon. "He was my boss. I worked for him. But he put me over there at DOD and then left me alone," Clements said. "I'd go to Cabinet meetings, we'd shake hands, and he'd ask, 'How is it going,' and I'd say 'terrific,' and he'd say, 'Wonderful, wonderful,'" Clements recounted.[21]

When Ford took office as president, he had no vice-president. On August 13, 1974, Clements submitted a letter to Ford recommending George Bush for consideration as vice-president. "George is a person of absolute integrity, high energy, attractive, articulate, of great moral character, and he has a marvelous family. He is a terrific blend of the best in the East and Texas. We, in Texas, consider George a complete 'Texian,'" Clements wrote. Utilization of the old term suggested that Bush embodied the characteristics attributed to the state's early colonists, that he was independent, steadfast, and bold.

"As I have heard you speak of the 'glue' that the country needs to bind us together; cohesiveness and moving forward together to solve our problems; the great need to put salve on our wounds; etc., it is my judgment that George is the partner you need to help you move the country in these directions." Clements also wrote that George Bush would make "an enormous contribution to your winning team in '76."[22]

The choice actually narrowed to Bush or Nelson Rockefeller, the former four-term governor of New York. On the heels of Watergate, Ford decided that Bush, as national GOP chairman, was too partisan, and that Rockefeller was more seasoned and better prepared to step in as president. He named Rockefeller. Ford later selected Bush as U.S. representative to the People's Republic of China and then to be director of the Central Intelligence Agency.[23]

In September 1974, not long after taking office, President Ford showed his confidence in Clements by sending the deputy secretary to Saigon. Clements was the highest-ranking American official to visit Vietnam since the signing of the Paris cease-fire agreements almost two years before, and he went bearing reassurance that the administration would continue to try to get more military aid from Congress for Vietnam in the defense appropriations bill.[24]

Those were heady days for Bill Clements, being a part of Cabinet meetings and national security briefings, testifying before committees on Capitol Hill, making decisions that had far-reaching consequences for the future of the country, representing the U.S. government to foreign governments. The work was consequential. He took it seriously, and he thoroughly enjoyed it. But Mrs. Clements was not getting the same satisfaction from being in Washington. She loved her home in Dallas and being close to her two children and five grandchildren. In the first few months in Washington, she had little to do other than sit in their hotel apartment while Clements was working twelve-hour days. She spent considerable time back in Dallas.

The Clementses lived in a fifth-floor apartment in the Sheraton Park hotel, a stately old red-brick building in northwest Washington — one of the two or three top apartment complexes where Washington's wealthy and powerful resided. It was the same apartment John and Nellie Connally had occupied during Connally's tenure as secretary of the treasury. In a rare newspaper interview published in January 1974, Pauline Clements confided that it had taken her about a year to get acclimated to the Washington environment. She had traded tennis matches on the family court at home and her Dallas Garden Club time for teas at the Pentagon, luncheons at the White House, and foreign embassy receptions. The couple averaged three nights out a week fulfilling Clements' social obligations as deputy secretary.

"It's worse than being a doctor. You learn to treasure just a day or two off," she said. "Everyone thinks we lead such a glamorous life, but you soon get used to socializing with ambassadors, senators or the First Lady," Mrs. Clements said.[25]

Mrs. Clements related that each night, her husband brought home in his briefcase — which she called his "Pandora's box" — a list of his activities and invitations so that she could update her own calendar. She sometimes traveled with Clements when he was making an out-of-town speech.

Clements' hours in the Pentagon were long and erratic, which left little time for relaxation and made personal planning practically impossible. There was not much time for private life. He worked in some informal dinners with friends at the 1789 Restaurant, a favorite, and occasionally spent weekends in the Virginia countryside with his wife or took weekend trips to Dallas. Only rarely were the two able to visit Pauline's favorite vacation spots, the Eldorado Country Club in Palm Desert, California, or her favorite summer spot in Harbor Springs, Michigan.

Mrs. Clements admitted that she had been against moving to Washington. "We had moved thirteen times in our first ten years of marriage," she said, before they settled in Dallas and built their home in 1951. But, she said, "You have to learn to roll with the punches, and it's not bad."

In February 1974, they moved to a house in northwest Washington, a block from their good friends, Republican National Chairman George Bush and his wife, Barbara. Mrs. Clements busied herself with decorating the new house and selecting furniture. For a while after the Clementses moved into their new home, Mrs. Clements spent more time in Washington.

But the marriage was in trouble. Clements had found a whole new life, and Pauline hadn't. "He and Pauline were not comfortable. She did not want to come to Washington. It was equally obvious he was tired of drilling holes in the ground," said one of Clements' friends in Washington. "He had a wife who didn't share his goals and objectives in life — as often happens later in life."

On June 2, 1974, Bill and Pauline separated; she returned to Dallas to stay. They had talked about divorce several months before, but the children convinced them not to break up the family. So he bought the house in Washington and tried to make a go of it. It didn't work out. On July 12, 1974, he filed for divorce. Clements' close associates at the Pentagon were surprised; he had been circumspect about his marital problems.

The next day he went to Horseman's Hut in Middleburg, Virginia, for the weekend. A few days later he flew to Santa Fe to attend the convocation and dedication of SMU's Fort Burgwin campus in Taos on July 27, 1974. Clements, who had not graduated, was awarded an honorary doctor of humane letters from SMU. He was cited for "his perceptive valuation of the Southwest that has made possible SMU at Fort Burgwin." While there, Clements announced that he was building a home in northern New Mexico adjacent to the SMU campus.[26]

On July 28, 1974, a tiny item appeared in the *Dallas Morning News* "Weathervane," a political gossip column. "Sources both in and out of the Republican party say one of the primary reasons William P. Clements, Jr., deputy secretary of defense, wants a divorce is Republican National Committeewoman Rita Bass of Dallas. The recently-divorced Mrs. Bass denied, however, that she and the former Dallas oilman are dating or contemplating marriage." [27]

Rita Bass and Bill Clements had become friends during the 1972 Nixon campaign, when he was state chairman of the Committee to Re-Elect the President and she served as a volunteer chairman, and both had offices at the campaign headquarters at the old Baker Hotel. After Clements moved to Washington, their friendship grew. He occasionally received telephone calls and correspondence from Mrs. Bass, who was then a national Republican committeewoman from Texas. A June 7, 1973, letter to Clements at the Pentagon asked for money for the state party operation.

"There is no question that the Republican Party has been financially hurt by Watergate. Some people have used it as an easy excuse to refrain from contributing to the party. Of course, we Republicans deplore the Watergate affair. However, as we express our deep concern, we must also keep in mind that the Republican party was not involved and should not be condemned for the foolish acts of politically inexperienced amateurs, who were employed by the CREP," she wrote. Texas Republicans, she said, "must not let Watergate sidetrack us from our realizable goal of making this a two-party state." She noted that, with John Connally's conversion, a coalition of conservatives guided by a viable Republican organization could win some important statewide races in 1974.

She asked Clements to contribute $1,000 or more to the Texas GOP, and promised to call in the next few days to "follow up on this appeal." The letter was signed, "Cordially, Rita." [28]

In June 1973, Rita and her husband, Richard D. "Dick" Bass, were taking their four teenage children on an American history/college reconnaissance tour of several weeks. The road trip included a look at eleven colleges in the South and then a stop in Washington, D.C., before the family visited thirteen colleges in the East. The itinerary included Dick's alma mater, Yale, and Rita's, Wellesley. Rita sent an itinerary to Clements with the notation beside June 28, 1973, "lunch with you!"

The day the Basses were in Washington, Clements, joined by Pauline and Tobin Armstrong, hosted them for lunch in the secretary of defense dining room. Clements gave them a tour of the Pentagon. Several days later, Clements received postcards from each of the Bass children, Barbara, Jimmy, Bonnie, and Dan, thanking him for lunch and the Pentagon tour, and thank-yous from Rita and Dick. Dick Bass wrote: "Having lunch in that rarified atmosphere of top responsibility and authority and visiting the communications nerve center of our global armed forces was a rare privilege and pleasure. I thoroughly enjoyed becoming better acquainted with Pauline and hope we can see more of you two in the future, particularly to share our mutual interest in paintings and antiques — to say nothing of good government." [29]

Clements received several short notes from Rita on personalized memo paper later in the summer and fall of 1973, usually enclosing articles or political information, and they exchanged several telephone calls. One note included an Austin research report on the question of whether George Bush should consider running in the 1974 elections for governor of Texas. The report concluded that despite the "Watergate attitude," Bush could defeat incumbent Democratic Gov. Dolph Briscoe. (Bush did not run for governor. Watergate heavily impacted the 1974 elections, and Briscoe was easily reelected.) [30]

Rita Crocker had gotten involved in politics ringing doorbells for Eisenhower's presidential campaign while she was attending the University of Texas. She recalled one man coming to the door who had never heard of Eisenhower. "Here I was, a young college student, thinking about it day and night, excited about it, and I thought everybody knew who was running for President. I was utterly disillusioned," she said. But she went on to the next doorbell — and to many more doorbells thereafter.

At the age of twenty, she married Richard D. Bass, who was serving in the navy. He had been in his father's oil exploration business. Bass was dashing, rich, and good-looking. Rita finished college at UT while Dick completed his navy tour. The Basses joined the Dallas social whirl, often retreating to the Bass family ranch near Waco. They had four children, Dan, born in 1955, twins Bonnie and Barbara in 1957 and Jim in 1959. Rita went into volunteer work, becoming chairman of the Crystal Charity Ball and then president of the Junior League. In 1958 she became Republican precinct chairman, and politics became an increasingly important part of her life. She worked in a succession of campaigns: John Tower and George Bush for senator, Barry Goldwater and Richard Nixon for president. She became acquainted with

Peter O'Donnell, Dallas' leading Republican. O'Donnell, who was Dallas County GOP chairman and then state GOP chairman and national chairman of Draft Goldwater, recalled that "sometimes, she would get all the kids in bed and she'd work all night long."[31]

Rita was smart and a natural-born organizer. She rose in the Republican ranks and, in 1973, was named to the Republican National Committee. She had a hard time convincing her husband to let her take the national committee job because of the time it required in Washington.

On November 1, 1973, several months after the summer "college reconnaissance" tour, Rita filed for divorce from Bass. They had separated in August, only weeks after the conclusion of the tour. An adventurer whose passions were skiing and mountain-climbing, Bass shared family oil interests with his brother and was a major stockholder in Vail Associates. He also was a risk-taking entrepreneur. In the early to mid-1970s, he was the developer of Snowbird ski resort in Utah. Rita was also a ski enthusiast; she and Dick had founded the Dallas Ski Club. Dick didn't share her passion for politics, but there were other problems. Their divorce was final on May 17, 1974, ending twenty-two years of marriage.

"I guess, from my standpoint, I was not allowed to be the person I wanted to be, to be an individual and to be able to really express myself," she later explained. "But really, more than that even, I think sometimes love just dies. And when it dies, it dies."[32]

The divorces of Clements and Rita were hard on their respective families. Gill Clements acted as an intermediary between his father and mother to help negotiate the divorce settlement. It was a difficult time for his mother, Gill recalled. "And when your mother is hurting, you are hurting," he said.[33] Clements' relationship with his children was strained — particularly with his daughter, Nancy, for several years. It was also difficult for Clements' business family at SEDCO, because Pauline had been part of company life. SEDCO officers, such as Spencer Taylor, Jerry Cunningham, Tom Rhodes and John Rhea, and their wives, were friends of Pauline, too. They had socialized and traveled together as couples. Clements' associates at SEDCO all described Pauline Clements as a "lovely lady."

In the final divorce decree of February 5, 1975, Pauline Clements received half of the couple's vast assets. Her settlement included 805,535 shares of SEDCO stock, which was selling that day for $23 a share, 339.5 shares of common stock in Fidelity Union Life

Insurance Company, the Baker Hotel property at Main and Akard in downtown Dallas, the residence at 4622 Meadowood and all the contents, including art objects, fur, silver, and china. She was a millionaire many times over. Clements got equal amounts of SEDCO and Fidelity Union stock, the Clemgil cattle operation in Forney, cattle and ranch equipment, residences in Washington, D.C., and Taos, his collection of Texas books and Charles M. Russell paintings and bronzes.

Both agreed to will all property owned at the time of their deaths to children and grandchildren or to charitable foundations, except that either could bequeath up to five percent of their estate to other blood relatives.[34] Rita would therefore not be entitled to any property acquired by Clements before his divorce.

Clements was smitten by Rita, and she obviously was interested in him. By the fall of 1974, they were spending more time together. They were planning to marry by Christmas of that year when they went to the Crocker Ranch in Brady, where Clements met Mason and Florabel Crocker, Rita's parents. On Christmas Eve, they attended the Episcopal church and enjoyed turkey and eggnog with the Crockers' friends. After returning to Washington, Clements wrote the Crockers that he was grateful for their understanding in a "somewhat difficult" situation. He added, "I hope both of you could see how very much I love Rita, and I am sure that we will be happy together."

On March 5, 1975, Clements wrote to his cousin, the Rev. James C. Cammack of Fayetteville, North Carolina, regarding a Washington, D.C., trip planned by Cammack. After exchanging some family news, including that his mother was ninety-three years old and getting along well, Clements wrote, "No doubt by now, via the grapevine, you have heard that Pauline and I are divorced . . . . For the past several years we have had some difficulties, as you might imagine, all of which reached a climax when I moved to Washington." Clements informed his cousin of his impending marriage to Rita Crocker Bass. "She has four children and is forty-three years old," he wrote. "She is most attractive and capable — in fact, she is beautiful, and I am sure we will be extremely happy."[35]

Bill Clements, who was fifty-seven, and Rita Crocker Bass were married on March 8, 1975, at 11:00 A.M. in the Navy Chapel at the Naval Security Station in Washington by a navy chaplain. Rita wore a yellow wool dress. Clements asked his top military aides, Adm.

Kenneth Carr and Brig. Gen. John Jones, to serve as ushers at the wedding. They had not met Rita before the wedding.

After the ceremony, there was a champagne brunch at the Chevy Chase Country Club in Chevy Chase, Maryland. A small group of close friends and family and Pentagon hierarchy attended the ceremony. Rita's daughters attended, along with her mother and father and her brother, the Rev. Byron Crocker, and his wife. Dallas friends attending included Ed and Ann Cox, Paul and Virginia Eggers, Peter and Edith O'Donnell, and Duncan and Elizabeth Boeckman. Most of the military and civilian hierarchy from the Pentagon attended. However, none of Clements' immediate family was there, and the only SEDCO friends who attended were John Rhea, Jr., and his wife, Rosemary.[36]

The night before the wedding, the Coxes and O'Donnells, along with Bob Stewart who was unable to attend, hosted an informal dinner at the Metropolitan Club in Washington. Peter and Edith O'Donnell, recognizing that there was little in the way of a material gift appropriate to give the newlyweds, gave them a different kind of wedding gift. In a handwritten note to Bill and Rita, they recognized Rita's conscientious and continuous service on the board of the O'Donnell Foundation since its organization in November 1957, as well as Bill's great interest in SMU, the campus at Taos, and his interest in anthropology and archeology. "And it recognizes that you both will be spending time in the years ahead at your lovely home at Fort Burgwin." The gift was a contribution of securities to SMU whose income would be sufficient to establish the Bill and Rita Clements visiting professorships at Fort Burgwin, which would draw distinguished professors in the anthropological sciences to the Fort Burgwin campus during summer sessions.[37]

Clements and his bride settled in Washington, but spent weekends at "Wexford," the estate built by President John F. Kennedy and his wife, Jacqueline, in the Virginia hunt country. Clements bought the property, which included forty-five acres, near Middleburg, Virginia, for $380,000 from William H. Perry in February 1975. Over time, the original purchase was expanded to 168 acres. One hour from Washington, the retreat was built on Rattlesnake Mountain looking west to the Blue Ridge Mountains. The estate included a stable, a guest house, and a four-bedroom colonial style cottage, which Rita decorated with English and American eighteenth-century antiques and reproductions.[38]

Six months after marrying Bill, Rita resigned her post as Republican national committeewoman. She didn't want to jeopardize Clements' nonpartisan job. President Ford agreed that it was a good idea, but it was her decision. From that point on, Rita's political know-how was channeled into Bill's career. But Clements always encouraged her to be her own person.

"Maybe on the surface, we don't seem like we're very much alike. And maybe regarding surface personality, we're not. But as far as the way we feel about things, our values, our beliefs and our approach of absolute utter respect for each other, the two of us are very much alike," Rita said in an interview several years later. "Bill is the kind of person who would never say, 'you can't do that' or 'you have to do this.' He says, 'You be your own person,' and 'I want to encourage you.'"[39]

From the standpoint of the families, it was not an easy time. (Pauline Clements would later remarry.) But, despite those problems, Bill and Rita found themselves to be very well suited to each other, and to the political life that would follow.

Chapter 10

DOD 3

Father of the Cruise Missile

As DEPUTY SECRETARY of defense from 1973 through 1976, Clements served under two presidents, Nixon and Ford, and with three secretaries of defense — Elliot Richardson, James Schlesinger, and Donald Rumsfeld. While the secretary's job was vacant, and as the nominees awaited confirmation, Clements was acting secretary of defense. Of the three secretaries, Clements worked with Schlesinger for the longest period.

Clements and Schlesinger didn't get along. But according to Clements, Schlesinger didn't get along with anybody. Schlesinger clearly didn't get along with Henry Kissinger, who was wearing two hats — as secretary of state and national security adviser — for most of Schlesinger's tenure. Over the more than two years that Clements and Schlesinger worked together, their distaste for one another became well known. And yet there was remarkable accomplishment during that period.

Tom Reed, who worked in the Pentagon for both Clements and Schlesinger, called them the "best pair of secretary and deputy secretary of defense the country has had in recent times. Having said that, they couldn't stand each other. But neither could Gilbert and Sullivan, who made some of the greatest music in our history."[1]

If Clements and Elliot Richardson were considered an odd couple, Schlesinger and Clements were even odder. They were about as different as two people could be. Where Clements was practical-minded, Schlesinger was intellectual. Where Clements was frank and aboveboard, Schlesinger was shrewd and devious. Born and reared in New York, Schlesinger had earned a doctorate in economics and had taught at Harvard and the University of Virginia. He was Rand Corporation's director of strategic studies in California when he went to Washington in 1969 as assistant director of the Bureau of the Budget. There he developed a reputation as a bureaucracy-trimmer and budget-cutter, paring $6 billion from the Department of Defense's operating costs and overseeing a study of U.S. intelligence services. The scholarly Schlesinger served a stint as head of the Atomic Energy Commission and was director of the Central Intelligence Agency when Nixon moved him to DOD. At forty-four, he was the youngest civilian to take over top reins at the Pentagon. He was a birdwatcher, and he enjoyed drinking bourbon. Clements thought Schlesinger "drank to excess, which was an absolute taboo" in such a security-sensitive job. Schlesinger's friends, of whom there reportedly were not many, according to newspaper reports, said his favorite pastime was arguing — usually about strategic questions. He was a man who enjoyed holding the floor at length.[2]

Clements' military aide, John Jones, described Schlesinger as "somewhat aloof, a brilliant individual, a real intellectual, but he didn't relate well to people. Mr. Clements was a very outgoing individual. Dr. Schlesinger came up through the academic world, think tanks. They had very different lives, career progressions, personalities."[3]

Clements didn't trust Schlesinger because he felt Schlesinger was less than forthright. Clements' other military aide, Ken Carr, recalled an illustrative incident when Clements suggested that the secretary talk to Rep. Eddie Hebert, chairman of the House Armed Services Committee, before proceeding on a particular course of action. As Schlesinger proceeded, Clements asked if he had talked to Hebert. Schlesinger replied, "Yes." Clements subsequently discovered that Hebert had advised against the action. Carr related that Schlesinger "said he had checked it out with Hebert, but he didn't say Hebert told him not to do it."

Schlesinger also enjoyed being in combat with Kissinger. "Most of his time, he was worried about headlines and whether Kissinger was getting ahead of him. He was a big philosopher. Clements liked to get the job done; he didn't like to just sit around and talk about it," Carr said.[4]

Brent Scowcroft, who was deputy national security adviser, said Clements and Schlesinger had a "very difficult relationship. First of all, Clements didn't like Schlesinger." Schlesinger's efforts to limit Clements' realm of responsibility, by excluding him from Middle East affairs and energy policy, became an additional bone of contention.[5]

Scowcroft thought Clements was good for morale in the Pentagon. "He was well liked. He was accessible and he was organized. And Secretary Schlesinger was none of those things. He was a very unpredictable individual, who tended to keep the building in kind of a turmoil with his habits. Bill became a stabilizing, calming influence. He would regularize the way things happened," Scowcroft said.

In contrast, Clements and Kissinger got along very well. "Kissinger respected Clements, though I don't think it started out that way," Carr said.[6]

Admiral Moorer confirmed that one of the first times he and Clements met together with Kissinger, Clements "used a little salty language." The meeting concerned the growing oil shortage in 1973. Clements told Kissinger he'd "better get off his ass" and do something about the situation. "Henry looked at him kind of sideways. He was not accustomed to that. But they got along fine," Moorer said.[7]

Eagleburger, who left the Pentagon to work with Kissinger on the NSC staff at the White House, recalled that "Kissinger often went to Bill Clements because Schlesinger was so impossible. That put Bill in a very tough spot, but he didn't seem to mind. Clements made up for what I thought was a less-than-adequate performance by the secretary. It was tough for him to do it in the No. 2 position, but he did it."[8]

Kissinger acknowledged that his relations with Schlesinger were strained "most of the time." Without Clements, he said, "we would never have gotten a lot of the things done." Kissinger found Clements to be "outspoken and to the point, a man who gets things done — both initially and over a period of time. He also was very opinionated. I soon learned that if you stood up to him, he was very objective. You just couldn't let him blow you away." One might think it would be the other way around, with Kissinger being the intimidator. But Kissinger said, "Nobody's going to blow Bill Clements away." Kissinger would later joke that he and Clements got along because "we both speak with an accent." Kissinger liked Clements. He thought the Texan was a patriot whose strong opinions were not directed at promoting himself but at getting a job done. "He had run big organizations before, so he knew at which point conversations had to stop and you had to move to action," Kissinger said in an interview years later.[9]

Clements' aide, John Jones, said that Clements and Schlesinger, despite their differences, maintained a businesslike, professional relationship. "Mr. Clements didn't always agree with what Dr. Schlesinger did or thought, but he would go in and tell him, and they usually would reach an accommodation," Jones said. Clements had the authority to make any decision within the Pentagon. "He could sign a piece of paper and make the final decision. But if it was a controversial decision, he would normally go over and talk to Dr. Schlesinger before he signed the paper," Jones said.[10]

According to Tom Reed, who became director of the telecommunications system in the Pentagon and worked under the secretary, Schlesinger "was not an outstanding manager. He would wander off into all sorts of musings about the meaning of history. Bill, on the other hand, could not conceive of all of the circuitousness that Jim engaged in; he was not a circuitous person. Schlesinger could not abide Bill's hard-driving, hard-nosed, tell-everybody-what-you-think-of-them way of doing business. But they totally agreed on the objective. The Soviets were the enemy, no doubt about it. But they had to think through how we were going to win, and not just throw money all over the place. They saw eye-to-eye about it. Schlesinger would have great lengthy seminars on the meaning of civilization, while Bill Clements had five minutes for every meeting. The net result was one of the best combinations running the Pentagon I have seen."[11]

But the working relationship, nonetheless, was not an easy one. Nor were the issues faced by the Defense Department leadership in those years. Among them were the new all-volunteer army; military base closures following the end of the Vietnam War; and admitting women to the service academies.

Shortly after he appeared at the Pentagon, and even before he was confirmed, Clements recalled that outgoing Secretary Mel Laird came into his office with an aide carrying a three-foot stack of reports and documents. "We've been saving these for you," Laird told him. They were reports on recommended base closures; the outgoing administration had delayed making the politically sensitive decisions. Clements wanted to avoid a lot of discussion and second-guessing on the closures by Congress, so he was determined to make a "statement" with the first announcement. He asked which would be the most politically sensitive bases to close and then picked one — the Boston Navy Yard, in the home state of Massachusetts Democrat Sen. Edward M. Kennedy. The decision to close the Boston Navy Yard, Clements said, sent Kennedy "up the wall," but it was done. To show that he was serious about not wanting a long, drawn-out debate over the closures, Clements also announced at the same time the closure of a Texas base. In due time, several more bases were closed, including others in Texas.[12]

The elimination of the draft and the move to all-volunteer military services was a Nixon initiative that had started under Secretary Laird. But the transition was difficult for the army. Clements, along with Secretary of the Army Howard "Bo" Callaway, inherited the problem.

The air force had always been fairly successful at recruiting, as was the navy. But the army was having a tough time attracting qualified soldiers. With the draft, it wasn't necessary to recruit. That draft mentality lingered, with the army continuing to place a low priority on recruiting activities and its recruiting staff. Clements felt that attitude had to change if the volunteer army was to be successful. He met with Gen. Creighton Abrams, the army chief of staff, about the need to put top-grade young officers in charge of the recruiting effort. Finally, Abrams just said, "We're going to do it."

Clements said, "We took our best captains and lieutenants out of company infantry units and put them in recruiting. That made it work. We got the top guys coming out of West Point, who knew our mission was to get top people for the Army."[13]

The army recognized it needed to draw a higher percentage of high school graduates, who made good scores on their qualifications tests. In 1964 the army had 67 percent high school graduates. That figure was down to 52 percent in December of 1973. During Clements' tenure, the army "pulled itself up by its bootstraps and got a much higher quality soldier," John Jones said. He cited the period of time when Clements was in the Pentagon as the key to the volunteer army, and Clements "definitely contributed to the success of it," Jones said.[14]

In December 1973, the Senate, responding to public pressure, included as part of a military pay bill a provision that women would be admitted to the service academies — West Point, the Naval Academy, and the Air Force Academy. Clements was opposed to the admission of women in the academies, as was House Armed Services Committee Chairman Hebert, a seventy-two-year-old Southerner who had represented Louisiana for more than three decades. At a meeting in January 1974, Hebert advised Clements and Schlesinger, "Drop it into my lap. I can say things you can't. Those bastards are just playing for votes back home," he said, referring to the senators. He promised not to let the issue get out of the House.[15]

Clements had numerous telephone calls and meetings with Anne Armstrong, counselor to the president, on the subject of women in the service academies. It was one battle he finally lost.

Secretary Callaway told him during a meeting in March 1974, "I'm about to give in on women at West Point. I'm not going to lobby." Clements responded, "This is your call, Bo. I'm not going to go and lobby myself, but I'm not going to tell you not to, either." Clements predicted, "We're going to be victims of demagoguery." Callaway detailed what the standards would be for women, and Clements replied: "Well, the world won't end. I'm just sorry to be any part of this thing . . . . I'm committed to Hebert, and I'm unalterably opposed to it. If it comes about, we're going to do it in a manner which will hurt us the least."[16]

Aligned with Clements, Callaway, and Hebert was Gen. George S. Brown, air force chief of staff who would succeed Adm. Thomas Moorer as chairman of the Joint Chiefs in July 1974. In a meeting with Clements in May 1974, General Brown favored opposing the admission of women "all the way . . . until the point that the decision is made, then we should accept gracefully. But we want a reasonable program."[17]

Texas Congressman O. C. Fisher, who was also opposed to the admission of women, headed a House subcommittee which held hearings on the issue; the full House Armed Services Committee held hearings in June 1974. A related question debated at the time was whether, if women were admitted to the academies, laws excluding women from combat should also be repealed. By the spring of 1975, it became apparent that the question was not whether women would be admitted, but when. The House voted on May 20, 1975, to admit women to the three service academies as part of a military hardware authorization bill. The question of women in combat was not addressed.[18]

Clements also was worried about the military academies becoming too much like regular universities. He thought they should have a core curriculum to train military people for military careers. Lt. Col. Pete Dawkins, a White House fellow who had come over to the Pentagon as a military assistant to the deputy secretary, was charged with studying the core curriculum and helping Clements get it shifted back to basic engineering and military courses. In recognition of that initiative, Ross Perot, a graduate of the U.S. Naval Academy, funded an endowment at each of the military academies for an annual award to be made in Clements' name to a distinguished military professor.[19]

Clements was appalled at the archaic telecommunications system the Pentagon employed in the early 1970s. Communications security was nonexistent. There was no network between the various armed forces; each service had its own communications system, and the systems wouldn't interconnect. Officers in field command in the different services couldn't talk to one another. Tom Reed, an engineer by training who had gone to Washington to work on Clements' staff, took the job of modernizing the Defense Department's telecommunications system. In January 1974, he took charge of the Worldwide Military Command Control Systems (WWMCCS) under the Office of the Secretary of Defense. Reed held that job until he was appointed secretary of the air force in the autumn of 1975. The modernization of the communications system continued for several years thereafter and, according to Reed, by the time of Operation Desert Storm in 1991, "The Navy and Army were in a seamless web of communication."[20]

Clements had primary responsibility at DOD for the development of major weapons systems programs. He was involved in decisions on the F-14, F-15 and F-16 jet fighters, a new heavy-lift helicopter, the fleet ballistic missile submarines, the Poseidon and Trident submarines, the Main Battle Tank, and the cruise missile.[21]

Clements' military aide, Ken Carr, was impressed with his boss' ability to make a decision on these major weapons systems when others were reluctant to do so in the second-guessing atmosphere at the Pentagon. He was also impressed with Clements' willingness to correct a mistake. After initially approving development of a new heavy-lift helicopter by the army, for example, Clements later reversed himself and authorized development by the Marine Corps, when he found out that the marines were farther along in development and could have the helicopter operating sooner. More than twenty years later, the CH-53E, the marine chopper, was still the workhorse helicopter in the field. "He was willing to listen," Carr said. "If you could show him he was wrong, he'd reverse his decision. He didn't waste a lot of time making decisions." [22]

The F-14 jet fighter, in production when Clements appeared on the scene, was designed as an interceptor to protect navy ships from enemy aircraft. At $17.9 million each, it was then the world's most expensive fighter, and it was also the most advanced. The swing-wing F-14 Tomcat was equipped with a thirteen-foot Phoenix air-to-air missile. Originally supposed to cost $11.5 million a plane, the program was plagued by overruns. The contract with Grumman Aerospace Corp. was a continuing problem for the Pentagon. Shaken by enormous losses in the program in 1972, before Clements arrived at the Pentagon, Grumman had its line of credit cut off by U.S. banks. The credit was later restored, but Grumman was in debt to the navy for advances and had to go to Congress seeking more funding. Clements, Navy Secretary John Warner, and Adm. Elmo Zumwalt, chief of naval operations, were responsible for renegotiating the contract in 1974. [23]

Meanwhile, the F-15 was on its way to becoming the mainstay fighter plane of the air force. The $12.3 million jet went into production in 1973 and was to be ready for combat by July 1975. McDonnell Douglas Corp. was building the F-15. The Shah of Iran was interested in buying some F-14s or F-15s and, after observing both in an air show, decided on a contract for the navy's more expensive F-14.

Clements was hard-nosed about spending government money. Jack Hammack recalled one incident in which McDonnell Corp. wanted to increase the cost of 300 F-15s by some $2 million a plane. The decision was bumped to Clements. A McDonnell representative paid a call on Clements and explained the problem and why it would require a cost increase. Clements said, "That's agreeable. We'll do that." The company representative jumped up and shook his hand, pleased that Clements had agreed so readily. Then Clements delivered the postscript. "But I will tell you that as long as I'm here in the Defense Department, McDonnell will never get another defense contract." The McDonnell representative responded, "Mr. Secretary, let me come back to see you tomorrow." The McDonnell representatives changed their minds and built the planes at the earlier agreed-on cost.[24]

Also on Clements' watch, the Pentagon continued developing AWACS, the Airborne Warning and Control System aircraft equipped to spot low-flying enemy aircraft and direct friendly interceptors. Clements was focused on developing a post-Vietnam generation of aircraft, and that included a new, low-cost fighter for the air force. Clements wanted the low-cost fighter bought on a competitive basis, which led to a "flyoff" between General Dynamics' F-16 and the Northrop Corporation's F-17 for the air force contract. The F-16 was the winner, and Clements signed the contract to put it into joint production in the United States and NATO countries. In the 1990s, the F-16 was the standard fighter for the air force and NATO. By increasing the horsepower of its jet engines by 30 percent, the F-17 was upgraded into the F-18, making it the finest and most expensive fighter plane in the skies twenty years later.[25]

But the development of the cruise missile was regarded as Clements' greatest accomplishment in the area of weapons systems. "He was the daddy of the cruise missile, no doubt about it," Carr said.[26]

The Department of Defense had developed in the various services the components for a cruise missile but had not put them together. By 1973, after many years of technical advances, the U.S. had developed a nuclear device which was much smaller than the nuclear bombs that were dropped on Japan during World War II. When Clements arrived at the Pentagon, a bomb the size of a basketball had been put in the silo-based Minuteman. The army also had developed a small jet engine to be used in unmanned reconnaissance drones. Concurrently, the air force had developed a small terrain guidance system for the F-111 airplane that would keep it at a level of 100 feet above whatever the terrain might be.

"All three of these components — the weapon, the engine and the guidance system — were now in miniature form," Clements said. "By taking the already existing technology and pulling it together, we could develop what was later known as a cruise missile."[27]

Clements said in a January 1977 magazine interview that the

go-ahead to develop the cruise missiles came during a discussion with Henry Kissinger at a National Security Council meeting. "I raised this issue as being something that was a possibility; that we did have the technology, we could do things now we couldn't do ten years ago when we dropped other missile programs in being at that time. During this ten-year period, our technology had moved forward in guidance, propulsion and, more particularly, electronics. These advances meant we could now bring forward systems in a way we couldn't do heretofore. This had a lot of appeal to Henry, who was then the National Security Advisor to the President. He approved my idea of going forward with cruise missiles," Clements said.[28]

The cruise missile was a radical departure from any weapon system the DOD had in its arsenal in 1973 and generated enormous resistance from the armed services. "The Air Force didn't want it because it supposedly was a threat to their bomber force. The Navy didn't want it because it was a threat to their aircraft carrier strike force. The Army didn't want it because it was a threat to their artillery," Clements explained.

Clements worked with Dr. Mal Currie, director of Defense Research and Engineering, and his staff to develop the program, and then led efforts to overcome congressional resistance, especially in the Senate Armed Services Committee, and fought a prolonged battle with the services to keep the program going. Clements testified before Congress that it would be possible to "put this thing [the cruise missile] into a pickle barrel from 600 miles away."

The project started with the Submarine Launched Cruise Missile (SLCM) for the navy, to be launched through torpedo tubes. The SLCM was then adapted for the army, using a surface launcher, and became known as the Ground Launched Cruise Missile (GLCM). For the air force, the missile was termed the Air Launched Cruise Missile (ALCM). The army, locked into an artillery mentality, fought the GLCM from the beginning and eventually turned it over to the air force. The navy perfected the SLCM and later adapted it to the surface fleet to be launched from the deck of ships. Ultimately, the navy became enthusiastic about the cruise missile, although it took some years to get to that point, Clements said.[29]

According to a 1994 U.S. Naval War College research report, the ALCM and SLCM would not have gone into full production had it not been for intervention from the highest civilian levels. Segments of the military services did not want cruise missiles because they threatened their missions and doctrine and competed for scarce funding, the report said. There was also a "not invented here" rationale within the services that was almost insurmountable. Clements was credited with kicking the program into high gear. According to Dr. Currie, the U.S. "wouldn't have had a cruise missile without Bill Clements grasping, conceptually, the idea and pushing the hell out of it."[30]

A news magazine explained that the missile could steer itself just over the treetops at 600 miles an hour and find a target with only a thirty-foot error after a 2,000-mile flight. "They are called cruise missiles because they cruise through the atmosphere under continuous power, like an airplane, rather than being shot upward like an intercontinental ballistic missile," the article read. Computers were programmed to guide them around hills or buildings, and the missiles could hug the ground to escape enemy radar and anti-aircraft defenses. The navy called its missile the Tomahawk. Estimated cost was $500,000 each, a relatively low price compared to $10 million for an intercontinental ballistic missile.[31]

Kissinger basically saw the cruise missile as a bargaining chip in his SALT negotiations with the Soviet Union, while Clements was serious about development and didn't want it bargained away. In April 1976, Kissinger had agreed with the Soviets to ban the Tomahawk from submarines and drastically limit them on ships. When President Ford consulted with the National Security Council, he was surprised by the vigorous opposition of Adm. James L. Holloway, who had succeeded Adm. Elmo Zumwalt as chief of naval operations. Holloway was determined not to lose the Tomahawk — as was Clements.[32]

Clements recalled a Kissinger visit to Moscow for the preliminary discussions on SALT negotiations when, without any prior clearance from the NSC, he put the cruise missile program on the table. On hearing of Kissinger's actions, Clements immediately objected to President Ford that Kissinger had no authorization to offer the cruise missile as a bargaining chip and that he "had to be stopped." Within a matter of hours, Clements said, President Ford had Kissinger's plane headed home.[33]

In January 1977, before Clements left the Pentagon, he directed the full-scale development of the GLCM, which would start in 1979. He also created a Navy-Air Force Joint Cruise Missile

Project Office, under the direction of Navy Capt. Walter M. Locke, who eventually retired as an admiral.

According to the Naval War College report issued in 1994, "Presidents facing a crisis are now just as likely to ask 'where are the Tomahawks?' as they are 'where are the carriers?' Conventional Tomahawks are now considered one of the weapons of choice to make political statements against rogue states." In his final report to Congress as director of Defense Research and Engineering, Currie described the cruise missile as "perhaps the most significant weapon system development of the decade." [34]

Clements recalled years later that he received practically no support for the cruise missile from the services or the rest of DOD, with the exception of Currie and his staff, and Locke, who was "swimming upstream" against the navy. "It is awfully easy now for certain people and some agencies to use a well-developed hindsight to talk about what a wonderful weapon the cruise missile is, but that was not the way they talked or acted when we were in the process of getting the program underway," he said in 1995. "It is a wonderful idea from our perspective today, but I guarantee you, in 1974, '75, '76, '77, there were very few believers." [35]

Clements also received resistance when he pushed for development of a new Main Battle Tank. The army wanted to build a conventional tank with a diesel engine. Clements thought new technology should be used, including a jet engine. The army fought the change, contending the idea of a turbojet engine in a tank was absurd, and tried to get the secretary of defense to countermand Clements' decision, but to no avail. Chrysler built the tank, which proved to be superior to any other tank in shootoffs with the French, the English and the German Leopard, then considered the world's finest tank. The Abrams tank, as it was called, was the equivalent of five Russian T-72 tanks. Two decades after Clements began the fight, the Abrams tank was regarded as the pride of the army. [36]

The Aegis cruiser was another innovative new system being developed during Clements' time in the Pentagon. The Aegis weapon system was designed to protect carrier battle groups from saturation missile attacks staged by Soviet aircraft and submarines. The system had the ability to screen and monitor, then track and attack, large numbers of radar contacts simultaneously. The navy resisted the Aegis, saying the system couldn't be placed on the ships they were building. Clements said, "Well, go try." The navy wanted to test the system on a bigger ship but, at Clements' insistence, put it on existing ships. "He pushed them into doing that, and it's a great piece of equipment, on the right ships," Adm. Ken Carr said, years later.[37]

According to Carr, Clements knew more about submarines and shipbuilding than most people in the Pentagon had expected, because SEDCO's semi-submersibles were basically submarine systems. Clements, in fact, was totally comfortable making the shift from semi-submersible drilling rigs to military submarines.

The Schlesinger-Clements years in the Pentagon were productive years in the development of new weapons system, but relations between Secretary Schlesinger and the Ford White House were never smooth.

In September 1974, columnists Evans and Novak wrote that there was little chance Secretaries Kissinger and Schlesinger — called "two smart egomaniacs" — could coexist in the Ford administration into the next summer.[38] Actually, they lasted until the fall of 1975, when President Ford, who never trusted Schlesinger, finally had enough. Schlesinger had become the voice of dissent with Kissinger over SALT and détente; he believed Kissinger's détente diplomacy conceded too much to Moscow. Ford, meanwhile, had become disturbed by the tensions between Kissinger and Schlesinger and thought his presidency was being undermined by their conflict.

Ford wrote in his memoirs that Schlesinger's rivalry with Kissinger made him uncomfortable, but also that "his aloof, frequently arrogant manner put me off. I never could be sure he was leveling with me."[39]

Ford also distrusted Schlesinger because the defense secretary had tried to persuade him to get rid of Clements. Schlesinger kept telling Ford that Clements' involvement with Pentagon matters related to Middle East oil-producing nations could blow up into a scandal. Ford wrote that he "looked into the question and discovered that Schlesinger's assertions lacked substance, which didn't exactly enhance my confidence in him."

Finally, Ford found out that Schlesinger had been the source of newspaper reports that an alert had been ordered during the Nixon-Ford transition to avert any "coup." He regarded such action during a moment of national crisis "inexcusable."[40] On November 2, 1975, Ford fired Schlesinger.

According to Lawrence Eagleburger, "Schlesinger got fired because, among other reasons, he was rude and virtually contemptuous of Jerry Ford, to his face. Ford felt Schlesinger treated him like a child, with contempt and hostility."[41]

According to Clements, Ford told Schlesinger when he fired him, "You have lied to me for the last time."

Ford selected Donald Rumsfeld to succeed Schlesinger as secretary of defense in the shakeup that included replacing CIA Director William Colby with George Bush and forcing Secretary of State Kissinger to give up his dual post as national security adviser. Kissinger's deputy, Brent Scowcroft, resigned his military commission to accept Kissinger's former post at the White House.

Clements' final days in Washington, therefore, were under Secretary Rumsfeld. Rumsfeld had been a colleague of Ford when he was a congressman from Illinois and then held several positions in the Nixon administration. He was NATO ambassador when Ford brought him in to run the White House after Nixon's resignation.

Rumsfeld wanted to bring in his own team to DOD, so Ford tried to shift Clements to another Cabinet position, as secretary of Housing and Urban Development. Clements told the president he didn't want to be secretary of HUD or Commerce or anything else. "That's not what I came up here for, and I don't have any interest in HUD," he said. Clements reiterated that he didn't want to walk away from the commitment he made to the people he recruited. If Ford insisted on moving him, he would just return to Dallas. But he let it be known in no uncertain terms that he would tell the press why he was back home. Ford dropped it. And while Clements' insistence on staying at the Pentagon didn't help his relationship with Rumsfeld, he was able to finish his four-year commitment, and he maintained cordial relations with Ford for the rest of the term and thereafter.[42]

The years that Clements served in the Department of Defense (1973 – 1976) were active years for DOD. They were marked by the Cold War, Soviet buildup, and SALT negotiations. They included the Vietnam pullout, the fall of Saigon, and the capture of the American merchant vessel *Mayaguez* by Cambodians. Occasional pressures surfaced with North Korea. And there were ever-present tensions with the Middle East. When crisis situations emerged, Clements was at command center in the Pentagon, dealing with the chairman of the Joint Chiefs and commanders on the scene. In all of his dealings, whether it had to do with weapons procurement or national security operations, Clements was known for his ability to make a decision and his blunt approach, his outspokenness.

Scowcroft, who went from deputy to national security adviser in the Ford shakeup, found Clements to be "a very bold, brash, frank individual who had strong views and who said what he thought. He was a warm person, but he was not a diplomat. He just said what he thought. That's not always the case in Washington."

Examples could be found in the notes of his daily staff meetings. For example, in an August 1974 staff meeting, in the middle of a discussion on manpower and personnel, Clements said, "The trouble with you guys in the military is that you think you're so god-damned different . . . and you're not!" [43]

Reed, commenting on Clements' management style, said: "What struck us all was that he did not suffer fools gladly. He had an amazing ability when being given a briefing to listen to people and to basically dismiss them once he decided they were telling him what he wanted to hear rather than reality. They would just disappear from his schedule and his life."

Those who worked closely with Clements, such as his top military assistants, Jones and Carr, and his personal secretary, Janie Harris, thought highly of him. Ms. Harris said there was a warm, personal side to Clements, once one got past the tough exterior. "He adored his mother and she adored her Billy," she said. Clements told his secretary that whenever his mother called, she was to get him. She recalled one time he was having a meeting with some admirals and generals and secretaries of the services in the conference room. She related that Clements was "holding court when I went in, and I was standing behind him, waiting for him to pause. He's telling them all about it and he finally says, 'So you just piss on 'em.' At that moment, I tapped him on the shoulder and said, 'Mr. Clements, your mother's on the phone.'"

When Ms. Harris later moved to Dallas as Clements' secretary, she became better acquainted with his mother, and discovered that she was "a strong woman who told you exactly what she thought. He was like her, in that way," Ms. Harris said.

Ms. Harris liked Clements because, among other things, he didn't put on any airs. He would go downstairs to the barber, when others in his position would have the barber come upstairs. He would stand in line in the drug store to make his purchases, just like any clerk in the Pentagon.[44]

While it wasn't always readily apparent, Jones thought that Clements "cared about people." Jones cited as one example how Clements went to bat to get a "career enhancing" reassignment for Chappie James. "It was traditionally difficult for someone in the armed services to get promoted to general officer if their career paths didn't take them through the normal operational employment of the force," Jones said. For an army officer, that meant being a battalion commander or brigade commander, coming up through the tactical or operational chain. "Mr. C took a personal interest in the career opportunities of people who chose materiel acquisition; he took a personal interest in how the services were treating the project managers," Jones said.

Chappie James, who became the first black air force four-star general, had gone to work in the Pentagon as a colonel during Nixon's first administration, after serving as an air force fighter pilot in Vietnam. There were tensions in the country at the time, because many blacks felt that those of their race, unable to elude the draft as many whites were doing, had to bear too much of the burden of the war in Vietnam. General James was brought in as an assistant secretary of defense/public affairs to travel around the country and talk about U.S. policy in Vietnam on behalf of Secretary Melvin Laird. James later was put in charge of a task force of undercover teams to try to locate any trace of missing American servicemen. "He did a tour of duty in a very thankless job," Jones said.

When James came up for reassignment, and Jones heard he was not going to get a good job, he went to Clements with the information. Clements called the secretary of the air force. "He made sure that Gen. James got what was a career-enhancing job," Jones said. James later became head of the North American Air Defense Command (NORAD).

Reed noted that, despite the hostilities between Clements and Schlesinger, Clements was concerned about Schlesinger's wife and large family when the secretary was axed by Ford. "By the end of the game, they detested each other," Reed said, "but when Jim fell, Clements was very concerned about what was going to happen to Schlesinger and his family. He sent me off to look into whether we could organize some consulting" for the fired secretary.

After Schlesinger left the Pentagon, he became affiliated with a think tank at Johns Hopkins University in Baltimore, Maryland, and eventually organized President Carter's energy department. Clements and Schlesinger would, at that point, clash again. Clements said publicly that Carter had surrounded himself with "inexperienced incompetents," starting with the energy secretary, whom Clements called a "bureaucratic opportunist" and an "intellectually dishonest person."[45]

Clements' failure to get along with some folks in Washington extended beyond Schlesinger. His relations with Secretary Rumsfeld, for example, were always tenuous. Not only had Clements refused to vacate the office, but he was thoroughly enmeshed in Pentagon operations, which somewhat stymied Rumsfeld, who had aspirations to be president and wanted to use his DOD job to further that ambition.

During the first half of Clements' tenure, he had differences with Adm. Elmo Zumwalt, chief of naval operations. Zumwalt wrote in his memoirs that his relations with Clements were "never good," that he thought Clements was "too easy on contractors, and seemed anxious to ingratiate himself with the White House." Zumwalt, who distrusted Kissinger, thought Clements worked hard to "keep in close touch with Kissinger after WSAG meetings and by telephone." Clements felt that Zumwalt had his own agenda and that he was not responsive to the civilian leadership in the Pentagon. According to Carr, Zumwalt was a "schemer," and for that reason Clements didn't work well with him. Clements liked people who were open and up-front.

Clements was not without other critics, as well.

"He took a lot of heat from the press in Washington, who said he was abrasive and blunt and lacked tact," Carr said. "The thing they didn't like him for was his bluntness. But if you asked him something, you got an answer."

In April 1975, Clements was criticized in a *New York Times* story as a "conservative Texas oilman whose readiness to make decisions is not always matched by a ready grasp of a problem, in the opinion of many of his subordinates."[46] Try as he might, Clements could not get across the idea to Eastern journalists that there was a difference between being a Texas "oilman" and being a drilling contractor.

In November 1975, shortly after the appointment of Rumsfeld, Joseph Kraft wrote in the *Washington Post* about "The Problem of

William Clements." According to Kraft, Clements lacked any of the background required for understanding the complicated issues connected with achieving a stable arms balance. Kraft suggested that Clements had a deficiency in the area of arms control, and he represented the DOD on the verification panel, the subcommittee of the National Security Council which passed on recommendations for SALT negotiations with Russia. Kraft also said Clements was responsible for abundant arms sales to the oil-exporting countries of the Persian Gulf.[47]

In 1975 and 1976, the DOD was investigating trips taken by some of its people to hunting lodges owned by defense contractors and other trips. Clements was put in charge of the investigation. Then he was branded for going with Howard "Bo" Callaway, on Callaway's last day as secretary of the army, on an extension of a trip to the Air Force Academy, to ski in Colorado. Clements said he paid his own way.[48]

In November 1976, Jimmy Carter defeated Gerald Ford for the presidency, and the Democrats took control of Washington. Clements left Washington, but he would always look upon his service as deputy secretary of defense as a high point in his life. At the end of his tenure, he called his four years at DOD "the most fulfilling of my life."[49]

"The enormity of the job, the associations with all of these people, the leaders of the country at that time — it was an important part of my life. But while it was important to me and I thoroughly enjoyed it, I worked like a dog, from 7:00 A.M. to 7:00 P.M., having lunch at my desk, and under not too good conditions. With people like Schlesinger and Rumsfeld, always watching my backside, that added to the pressure. The international issues, relations with Russia, intelligence gathering, every facet in the international scene comes under your review. You couldn't be up there and not feel a tremendous sense of responsibility," Clements said, in an interview years later.

When it was over, he was ready to return to Dallas and do something else. "He was eager to get out of there and go home," Tom Reed said. "I don't think he had Potomac fever."

Clements went home to Dallas with his new wife, Rita, and tried to get back to normal life. They returned to Clements' roots in Highland Park, buying the Flippen homestead at 4800 Preston

Road, the first large house built in Highland Park. The house was purchased from Sharon Simons, the widow of Pollard Simons. A Texas Historical Commission plaque later was placed on the porch at 4800 Preston, denoting the importance of the house in "attracting Dallas' elite to Highland Park." The plaque says, "Although radically altered externally over the years, the basic Flippen homestead retains significance for its association with the founders of Highland Park and as a reflection of Dallas' early Twentieth Century growth."

The transition back to Dallas was not entirely smooth for Clements with his new bride. He moved back into his old office at SEDCO, but Gill was used to running the company by then, and the company had grown. Clements assumed the title of chairman and chief executive officer, and Gill became president and chief operating officer. "It was unclear what his role was going to be, but obviously if Bill was back, he was going to be in charge," said Steve Mahood, who was then secretary of the corporation. Yet, while Clements was inclined to be the boss, he didn't want to be tied to the daily decision-making. "He was like a fish out of water. It took him about nine months to be convinced he ought to do something else," Mahood said.[50]

After a few months back in Dallas, Clements was both open to a new challenge and eager to utilize the vast experience he had acquired in Washington. His interest in public service in Texas sprang partly from an extreme annoyance with the Carter administration. Spurred by what he thought to be the idiocy of Carter administration energy policies, he was predisposed to take on the challenge of political life if the opportunity presented itself. And it did, when New Mexico Sen. Harrison Schmitt exhorted him to run for governor after the energy panel program at SMU on that November night in 1977.

The 1978 campaign between Clements and Democrat John Hill was a cliffhanger. Some of the news media called the wrong winner.

Ronald Reagan and Gerald Ford, Republican primary opponents in 1976 when Jimmy Carter won the presidency, join Clements on the last day of his trailblazing gubernatorial campaign in 1978.

Part III

Governor

Three decades of Texas governors and their wives include Govs. and Mrs. Shivers, Daniel, Connally, Smith, Briscoe and Clements.

This historic photo taken in 1979 shows three decades of Texas governors including, from left, Allan Shivers, who assumed office in 1949, Price Daniel, John Connally, Preston Smith, Dolph Briscoe and Bill Clements.

Chapter 11

1978 Campaign

"I will not run out of gas in the fourth quarter"

As THE 1978 ELECTION approached, there were two forces driving the Republican Party of Texas. The first goal, as always, was to protect the seat of U.S. Sen. John Tower. Since his first election in 1961, the main thrust of the Texas Republican Party had been to keep Tower in office. The second aim of the party was to take advantage of an unusual occurrence in the Texas congressional delegation. Six veteran members of the U.S. House of Representatives, all Democrats and committee chairmen, were retiring — providing Republicans with unprecedented opportunity.

And, the Reagan movement had begun in Texas.

A record half-million Texans had voted in the Republican Party's presidential primary fight in 1976 between Ronald Reagan and Gerald Ford. Then-President Ford, the choice of Texas' traditional Republicans, had won the nomination. But a new wave of voters known as "Reagan Democrats" had taken advantage of the fact that there was no party registration in Texas. They had invaded the normally tight GOP primary ranks and won the Texas primary for Reagan. So strongly did the Reaganites control the Texas delegation to the 1976 Republican National Convention in Kansas City that they denied Senator Tower a delegate seat, because he had backed Ford.

Against this political backdrop, Lance Tarrance, who had been

187

the Texas Republican Party's first full-time research director in 1964, returned to Texas from Washington to start a political research firm in the summer of 1977. Tarrance was committed to the Republicans' defensive strategy of protecting Tower's seat and to the offensive strategy of going after open congressional seats. But, he said, "I never dreamed we were going to make a real assault on the governorship."[1]

Ray Hutchison was the Republican state chairman at the time, and the presumed gubernatorial candidate. A forty-five-year-old Dallas bond attorney and former state legislator, Hutchison had been working to bring the party back from the ashes of Watergate and Ford's loss to Jimmy Carter. Hutchison had actively sought a candidate for governor in the 1978 election, and even wrote Bill Clements a letter when he was still deputy secretary of defense urging him to run. The letter, according to Hutchison, was never answered. Hutchison believed Gov. Dolph Briscoe was vulnerable and, when no other candidate materialized, basically said, "What the hell, I'll run."[2]

"He was running because he was state chairman, and we didn't have anybody else," Tarrance said. "It clearly was a building year as opposed to a winning year. In terms of winning it, I didn't see it, nor did a lot of other people."

In November 1977, Clements decided to run for governor. He took counsel with no one, except Rita, before making up his mind. It happened after the discussion in his Preston Road home with Sen. Harrison Schmitt of New Mexico, the night he and Schmitt appeared on an energy panel at SMU. The next day, he and Rita went to see Peter O'Donnell, who promised to help. He had, after all, been trying to get Clements on the Republican ballot for years.

But why would Clements now want to take such a gamble? Some suspected he was bored, coming back to business in Dallas after four years on the Washington political scene. Clements denied such was the case. "I have never been bored in my life. The word is hardly in my vocabulary. My business is boring for oil, but it's certainly not boring." Rather, he said, "If I can go to Washington and work fourteen to sixteen hours a day for national security for four years, certainly I can go to Austin and give back something to the state that's been so good to me."[3]

Clements also thought he could win.

The fact that traditional Republican money would be sucked up for Tower's reelection effort did not concern him. He was chairman of the board of a $750-million drilling company which, the year before, reported profits of $43.6 million.[4]

Despite his wealth, Clements had a populistic streak that caused him to believe he could identify with average Texas voters. He had worn overalls and worked in warehouses and driven trucks and started a business from scratch. He didn't ride around in a chauffeur-driven limousine. He could use populistic themes to bridge the gap between the "Wall Street Republicans" and the new, Reagan-based "Main Street Republicans." And, as he and Rita had discussed, the election would depend on his ability to appeal to the traditional Texas ticket-splitter or independent-minded voter. Clements also had a strong sense of Texas history, and felt almost predestined to be a part of that history.

A few days after Bill and Rita decided "let's do it," Rita wrote down a list of pros and cons, as if to reinforce their decision to run. The "pros" included: "taking advantage of opportunities to accomplish goals; winnable; Republican party infusion, state and national; energy issue influence; maintain options; need for challenge — to whom much is given, of him is much required; outstanding candidate — articulate forthright, honest, straight forward, ability to understand issues and present in understandable terms; experience; managerial expertise; ability to pick people — [for] campaign and governing; supporting wife."

The list confirmed that he may have been looking for a new challenge. (One can only guess what "maintain options" meant. Was he thinking in terms of a national position?)

Rita Clements made two lists of "cons." The "personal" drawbacks were: "change of lifestyle, preference for privacy, no longer own boss." The drawbacks to Clements as a candidate were: "dislike of silly questions and small talk; intolerance of extreme positions; divorce; wealth; possibility of bitter primary; lack of interest in certain state issues, inability to remember names — on both our parts."[5]

The pros obviously outweighed the cons. On November 16, 1977, Clements announced at an Austin news conference that he was a candidate for governor. "I am convinced that I can win, and I can assure you that if I didn't feel that way and have good reason to believe that, I wouldn't be declaring and wouldn't be in the race. So, we need to get those ground rules established right quick as far as I am concerned." Under questioning from a press corps unaccustomed to his bluntness, Clements said his objective was to "win, period! If you people have some idea that I'm doing this for experience, you're dreaming. I need to make this race just like a hole in the head. I'm in this thing to win, and if I didn't think I could win, I wouldn't be in it. Any other questions?"

Clements also was convinced that the No. 1 issue in the state was energy, a field he knew something about. He called it absurd that Texas produced half of the oil and gas in the United States "and we have no voice at the policy table where decisions are being made. I think I can supply that voice."[6]

Hutchison had the support of the party machinery — state committee members and many precinct chairmen. It was widely assumed among Republicans, even with Clements in the race, that Hutchison would be the nominee. Clements, however, viewed Hutchison as just another big-city lawyer who had little chance of being elected governor for two reasons: He couldn't raise enough money because of Tower's drain on Republican funds, and he had no special appeal to the ticket-splitter. Clements called Hutchison, who was campaigning in the Rio Grande Valley, and asked him to run for lieutenant governor instead. Hutchison declined. There would be a contested primary.

The Clements strategy quickly became apparent to Hutchison, who said: "He was going to set a new pattern in Texas politics; he was going to spend the wealth without restraint." But, Hutchison said, once they were out on the campaign trail, "the first thing he pulled out of his bag of tricks was that letter from me [asking him to run for governor], waving it around."

Clements needed campaign expertise, and he knew someone who had it. He called his friend Tom Reed in California. Reed had been state chairman in Reagan's second race for governor, was Reagan's director of appointments in Sacramento, and was national Republican committeeman from California. A real estate developer, Reed was a successful California businessman who had worked as an oilfield roustabout in West Texas during college summers. He and Clements had worked together on the 1972 Nixon campaign. Clements had hired Reed to work on his staff in Washington, and Reed had become secretary of the air force. Clements considered Reed a close friend, a man of achievement in business who also was politically brilliant.

"He had decided to run and, in typical Clements fashion, he

had already announced that fact," Reed said. "In other campaigns I've run, you put all the pieces in place and get all the phones ready to ring and then you announce when you have the whole thing orchestrated. Clements announced he was going to run and then started putting the pieces together, which was appalling — the first of many appalls," Reed said.[7] He flew to Dallas to help Clements get organized.

Clements had only minimal knowledge of state government, issues, and campaigns. However, as was his habit when confronted with an unfamiliar subject or situation, he immersed himself in the unknown — seeking information from knowledgeable friends and people in politics. Clements kept handwritten notes on all of those meetings, from the visit with Harrison Schmitt through the end of the year.[8]

He invited Paul Eggers and his wife, Virginia, to dinner. They discussed the importance of the rural vote and, as Clements chronicled, the need to run a "different" campaign. Eggers volunteered to find experts on state issues and to furnish Clements with copies of position papers from his own two races for governor.

Clements' meeting with Dallas County Republican Chairman William A. McKenzie and his wife, Sally, produced a list of thirty-eight do's and don'ts, including: "Must not be overwhelming and come on too strong! Must not talk down to people. Must not 'bulldoze' people." McKenzie thought Clements could win the general election but that the primary would be tough. Even though he had the backing of such big names as Bush, Connally, Armstrong and O'Donnell, they were "too far removed from the grass roots." Clements noted their most elemental suggestions and jotted down names of professionals and party workers he should call. One name was Nancy Brataas, a Minnesota state senator, with the notation "phone banks! the best." Indeed, the Brataas phone banks would turn out to be one of the secrets of Clements' campaign success.

Clements called James A. "Jim" Baker III in Houston for help with Houston people, including Reagan leaders Jimmy Lyons and Ray Barnhart. Barnhart had succeeded Hutchison as state chairman, as part of the Reagan revolution in Texas. In his meeting notes, Clements wrote that Barnhart was a "Reagan man" who believed Clements was too close to Connally and, if elected, would use the governorship to help Connally run for president. Nonetheless, Clements wrote that it was "a very good meeting, no flim flam."

For a short lesson on how state government works, Clements went to Fred Agnich, a Republican state legislator and former Dallas County Republican chairman. Agnich explained the state budget process and talked about state issues. Clements tried to get Agnich to run for lieutenant governor, but Agnich wasn't interested.

These one-on-one meetings produced some basic strategic concepts, including the "I can win" theme. On the issue of energy, Clements wrote, "Relate to every Texan and daily life of every Texan." The meetings also produced the names of the best professionals available and of Texans to work in the campaign.

Tom Pauken, who had worked with Clements on the Nixon campaign, suggested Bill Elliott as Dallas County chairman. Elliott was a young lawyer and president of the Republican Men's Club in Dallas. Clements phoned Elliott, who remembered the conversation. "This is Bill Clements. I'm running for governor, and I want to come to your office to talk," Clements told him.

Clements was little known in lower level Republican circles in those days. "He was known among the Anne Armstrongs, the upper crust Republican establishment, the John Towers of the world," Elliott explained, "but among regular people like me who just voted and work in politics, door-to-door kind of people, he was not known. He was just a name." By contrast, he added, "Everybody knew Ray. Everybody liked Ray. He was exceedingly popular, always picked as one of the best legislators by *Texas Monthly* magazine. He was familiar to Republicans, and he was a terrific state chairman." But, Elliott noted, to work for a candidate, one had to be motivated by that person. Elliott was so motivated by Clements.

"When he came to my office, I thought he was terribly engaging, magnetic, powerful. He dominated the room," he said. Elliott accepted the job of Dallas County chairman. He remembers later getting a call from a Republican woman who told him he would never amount to anything in the Republican Party because he had abandoned Hutchison and signed on with Clements.[9]

In January 1978, the primary campaign team was taking shape. Clements had selected Omar Harvey, a longtime associate in Boy Scout work, as campaign manager. Harvey, a former IBM executive who had been working at First National Bank, was unfamiliar with politics, but he knew how to run an organization. Clements designated Tom B. Rhodes, his trusted SEDCO lawyer and boyhood friend, as campaign treasurer.

Jim Francis, who had been executive director of the Dallas County Republican Party, wrote Clements a letter after he announced, offering to help. Clements had known the Francis family when he was a boy growing up in the Highland Park Methodist Church, though he didn't know young Jim. Francis noted later that, with Clements, "there was no better friend than one he grew up with." Francis became finance director.[10]

Lance Tarrance was hired for polling; Stu Spencer of Newport Beach, California, part of Ford's 1976 team, for strategy; the firm of Ringe-Russo of Boston as media consultants; and Nancy Brataas to run the phone banks.

The campaign organization began working on the mezzanine of the old Baker Hotel in Dallas. Elliott recalled that Peter O'Donnell and Tom Reed were particularly influential in the early organizational days. The young Republican workers were awed by "POD," as they called the Texas GOP guru O'Donnell in private conversations; "POD" was urbane and somewhat aloof, a leader of high reputation with the young foot soldiers as having built the party in Texas. Later, the campaign moved to what had been the location of the Baptist Book Store, a block from the SEDCO headquarters on Akard Street.

Lance Tarrance conducted his first statewide survey for the Clements for Governor Committee in January 1978. His report confirmed what Clements intuited, that voters were concerned about inflation, the energy crisis, and government control over oil and gas supplies. The Carter administration had dipped below 40 percent approval for the first time in the state, largely because of Carter's positions on energy and the Panama Canal "give-away." Incumbent Gov. Dolph Briscoe's approval rating also was around 40 percent and, according to Tarrance, Atty. Gen. John Hill already had passed Briscoe in the Democratic primary. Hutchison had a lead in the GOP primary, but Tarrance believed there was no reason Clements couldn't win the nomination if he had a coherent message and appeared the stronger candidate against either Hill or Briscoe.[11]

On February 1, 1978, in an Austin news conference, Clements talked about campaign plans. He told skeptical reporters he intended to organize in all 254 counties of the state — even though his party had no organization in some counties. He also revealed his main campaign strategy. Of previous Republican gubernatorial candidates, he said, "Every one of them ran out of gas in the fourth quarter . . . I'm not going to fold." In the primary, he intended to concentrate on the twenty counties that would produce most of the Republican primary voters — which he estimated at about 150,000. "If you're going to hunt birds, you have to hunt where the birds are, and in the primary we're talking about 20 counties. In the general election, we're talking about 254 counties," he said.[12]

In February, Clements sought during three meetings in a week's time to enlist George Strake, Jr., an independent oilman in Houston and self-described Goldwater Republican, as his state chairman. Strake had problems with Clements, namely: Clements had voted for LBJ; he believed the U.S. and the Soviet Union were militarily equivalent, and he was for the Panama Canal "give-away." Clements answered Strake's objections. He had thought it was important for a Texan to be in the White House. "I made a mistake," he said. Secondly, he believed that the cruise missile, whose development he had propelled as deputy secretary of defense, put the U.S. on a parity with Russians. Finally, he told Strake, he was withdrawing his support for the Panama Canal treaty, unless the U.S. retained the right to intervene unilaterally if it was in America's self-interest.

Strake finally agreed, and then went home and told his wife, Annette, that "Bill Clements is going to run for governor, and he's going to get elected." She said, "Bill Who?" And he replied, "You don't know who 'Bill Who' is now, but you will know who 'Bill Who' is in November."[13]

Early in the primary campaign, Clements developed his campaign battle cry: "I will not run out of gas in the fourth quarter." Not running out of gas "was the central theme that overshadowed every aspect of the campaign," Elliott said. Clements said it hundreds of times on the campaign trail, and the campaign organizers intended to show that such words were not empty rhetoric. Money was no object, and it was used ostentatiously to illustrate Clements' staying power. "No doubt, the primary was a money-spending machine," Elliott said.

An example was a lunch held at the Baker Hotel's Imperial Club for some fifty men active in the Dallas Republican Men's Club. The menu was lavish. "We wanted to create the impression that this was a different effort; it was going to be real financial power," Elliott said. "We served prime rib that day." Clements wasn't there, but others made the pitch. "Clements is going to win. The theme of this campaign is: we won't run out of gas in the fourth quarter," Elliott said. The young Republican men of Dallas started signing up.

Ann Quirk, campaign staff director in San Antonio, remembered a similar event there, a free lunch for about 200 at a local steakhouse. A meal or entertainment was the draw — not Clements — early in the campaign. "No one turned down a free lunch. Clements spent a lot of money to get people to come to events," she said. "It was difficult to recruit volunteers because the activists were supporting Ray. We had to spend money, so people would at least think Clements was credible." He also had to hire phone bank chairmen. Eventually, volunteers were recruited among the military and retired military in San Antonio. And the crowds began to grow as Clements became more of a curiosity.

Allen B. Clark, Jr., a Dallas banker who had lost both legs in Vietnam, had become active in Republican politics in Dallas and volunteered for the Clements campaign partly because his wife, Jackie, had gone to high school with Gill and Nancy Clements. Jackie Clark had met Bill Clements as a father of schoolmates and chaperone for school activities. Clark went after constituencies he called the "cultural conservatives," where Clements was not known. Clark paved the way for Clements among veterans, retired military people, and former supporters of George Wallace.

Dary Stone, fresh out of law school, was traveling the state as advance team coordinator. Armed with lists of Clements' contacts in the oil industry and Boy Scouts, he was trying to secure houses for events. Once a sponsor was found, all arrangements were made in Dallas. The invitations were hand-addressed, from multiple lists, and flown to the city of the event. There, they were dropped in the mail. The invitations therefore would have a local postmark, and it wouldn't look like the event was orchestrated in Dallas. Scott Bennett, who was a statewide strategist in Dallas, insisted on the local mail drops. Campaign staff members ordered the food, paid the bills, advanced the event, and passed out name tags and literature. They never knew how many people to expect. "Some people might get three invitations. We didn't care. Because the key was to show them we've got power, and we've got the ability to produce, and we're not going to run out of gas in the fourth quarter," Elliott said.

Volunteers from within GOP ranks were hard to recruit, but Elliott was surprised by the number of SEDCO employees who volunteered to work in the Dallas phone banks. "The SEDCO and oil company volunteers just poured out of those downtown office buildings — from Texas Oil and Gas and Delhi Oil. I was struck by that because I was a young guy and Clements was intimidating to me. I thought of him as a big guy who could handle big stuff. I was struck that these people *like* this guy, they genuinely *like* him. There wasn't any intimidation there. They were there because they absolutely wanted to be there," Elliott said.

Meanwhile, enormous tension was developing between Clements and Hutchison on the campaign trail. Hutchison claimed Clements was trying to "shake down" the oil and gas industry in the state for support; that when Clements was deputy secretary of defense he used military aircraft for pleasure trips to a Colorado ski resort; that he was trying to "buy" the nomination with his personal wealth. The issue, said Hutchison, was understanding state government — who could talk in detail about state issues; the state couldn't afford a governor who needed on-the-job training. Clements, meanwhile, would stand up and say, "I'm a businessman-manager. I'm not a lawyer-politician. I'm a Texan from the top of my head to my toenails." On issues, he pledged to cut 25,000 employees from the state bureaucracy — which Hutchison said proved Clements didn't know anything about state government — and to set up a task force to study school financing and education quality. But he also frequently talked about defense spending, atrophy on Capitol Hill, the Panama Canal and other national issues.[14]

Clements was gaining strength. By March, he drew 1,000 people to a reception at the Hilton Inn in Dallas. But he was also developing an image described variously in the press as gruff, arrogant, and abrasive. In March, *D Magazine* printed a story headlined, "The Abrasive Candidacy of Bill Clements: If Nice Guys Finish Last, Clements Should Win It Walking Away."

From the beginning, Rita was part of the policy team and Clements' most trusted adviser. Early in the primary race, having observed her husband on the stump, she wrote on three legal pages a list titled "Constructive Criticism Only!" The list included:

1. Too many I's.
2. Rita shouldn't correct.
3. SMILE
4. Don't talk down to the people.
5. SMILE
6. Be more personal.

7. Too gruff.

8. Learn state issues.

9. "Totally unacceptable to me" . . . Should be totally unacceptable to you — to Texas — to us.

10. Limit speeches to no more than 20 minutes.

11. Not a budget, it's an appropriations bill.

12. Governor appoints all state boards, all boards of regents, all district judges (vacancies), all district clerks (vacancies) etc. and so forth ad infinitum.

13. Answer questions direct instead of talking too long!

14. "You have never read anything like that etc." . . . should say — we have never read anything like this, it hasn't been in the paper because it hasn't happened! Quit talking down to the person asking the question!

15. People don't care how long you have known Abner McCall — i.e. "I have known Abner McCall a long time, when I was on the board at SMU with Dr. Willis Tate etc. etc" . . . Get on the same level with the people. You are asking for their help — not telling them what to do!

16. Again your answers vary from two minutes to as much as five minutes. It is too long in each instance.

17. We together must change the system, etc. Bill Clements as governor ("I want to change the system") can't by himself change the system — it takes the executive branch, the Senate and the Legislature. But the first step is with your help, elect me your nominee.

18. SMILE. You said 29 times "I went to Washington" etc.

19. You are running in a primary — now!

20. No one cares how close you are to the head admiral, the head general etc. Give your answer. You are running, they aren't. . . . don't frown and say, "let me finish."[15]

It was clear from her list that Rita understood politics — and the candidate.

Hutchison had planned a modest primary effort and found himself struggling to keep pace. In early April, according to campaign finance reports, he had $80,000, compared to $1.2 million for Clements, which included $400,000 in loans from friends. Hutchison was arguing that Clements had no broad-based support and wouldn't have any because he was flaunting his wealth. At that point, most of Clements' campaign money was coming from himself and a few close friends and business associates from SEDCO and the oil industry.[16]

By primary election day, May 6, 1978, press reports said Clements had outspent Hutchison 10-to-1. As Jack Rains of Houston, who would become close to Clements in later years, said, "He money-whipped Ray Hutchison."

Clements had become more than a curiosity. He had convinced most of the state's newspaper establishment, led by both home papers in Dallas, to endorse his nomination.

Clements, who had been predicting victory for more than a month, won almost 3-to-1 over Hutchison. His supporters were celebrating at the Baker Hotel's Crystal Ballroom by 8:30 P.M. When it appeared the lopsided trend for Clements was irreversible, Hutchison appeared before 100 grim followers and pledged his support to Clements in the general election. "We were fighting with a little shorter stick than the other fellow," he said. As Clements made his victory statement on TV, giving credit to Rita as his "best weapon," a Hutchison campaign worker muttered, "Yeah, and $2.2 million."[17]

Final reports showed Clements did spend $2.2 million, of which $1.7 million was borrowed, for a primary that attracted just over 158,000 voters.[18] Except for the half-million-vote 1976 presidential primary, the 1978 turnout was the party's heaviest. While Hutchison was campaigning among the usual party activists, drawing only a handful of supporters at events in the Panhandle during the last week of the primary campaign, Clements was trying to bring new voters into the primary. His campaign was specifically going after voters who had moved into Texas since 1970. Tarrance's data showed that 20 percent of the state's voters had moved into Texas as part of the Sun Belt migration of the last ten years. Many were young professionals who settled in the suburbs around Dallas and Houston, where the Clements campaign sent people into the newly developed areas to register voters.

The Republican primary, nonetheless, was still light compared to the Democratic vote, which was 1.8 million. All the other races were still in the Democratic primary. A supporter at Hutchison's election night party admitted to voting for the first time in a Republican primary. "It felt strange," he said. "There wasn't anybody to vote for. There are a million people running for judge in Dallas and they're all Democrats."[19]

In the Democratic primary, incumbent Gov. Dolph Briscoe was ousted by Atty. Gen. John Hill, who won the Democratic nomination with 51.5 percent of the vote against Briscoe's almost 42 percent in a three-way race that included former Gov. Preston Smith.[20]

Uvalde, Briscoe's hometown, was in shock; the street in front of the Briscoe headquarters was blocked off for the celebration that never came. Briscoe, the unassuming millionaire South Texas rancher who frequented the local hotel coffee shop in his ranch clothes and enjoyed hunting with fellow politicians on his vast land, had been elected to a two-year term in 1972 and won reelection to the state's first four-year term in 1974. Hill, who had served as attorney general for six years, claimed Texas voters balked at the idea of allowing a governor to serve ten uninterrupted years. Hill also had promised blanket salary raises for teachers and was endorsed by the Texas State Teachers Association. The support of teachers and the education establishment was instrumental in his upset win over Briscoe.

Tarrance's surveys also showed that while Briscoe was viewed as a solid conservative, he was perceived as a laissez faire governor who was comfortable with the status quo. Voters were ready for a change.

On the Sunday after the primaries, Hill was planning a trip to Washington to meet with congressional leaders on a proposed national energy plan. Having defeated an incumbent governor in the Democratic primary, which was then thought to be tantamount to election, Hill assumed he was the next governor. He told reporters he expected to have an easy time against Clements. Hill said there was no need to resign as attorney general because the fall campaign would be easier than the primary, and he wouldn't have to campaign on a day-to-day basis.[21]

Hill, the heir apparent, was going to Washington for a few days. Clements was headed for the fourth quarter.

Without missing a step, Clements shoved his campaign into another gear. He announced he was moving his headquarters to Austin; Nola Haerle, who had managed the 1972 campaign for Senator Tower, would be his new campaign manager. Omar Harvey would spend the summer organizing rural Texas as head of Project 230, the campaign's effort to organize 230 non-urban counties. Most of the primary staff was fired. They had won the nomination, but they had been profligate. And O'Donnell didn't go for wanton overspending. The staff also had grown like Topsy; it was filled with amateurs. It was time for the pros to take over.

Clements' immediate thrust was to enlist Briscoe backers and to pitch the race to the media as one between an experienced manager-businessman and a "liberal lawyer politician." Even though Hill wasn't worried, Clements told the press, "My opponent is in for a real fracas. If he thinks this is going to be a cakewalk, I can assure him he's got hold of a very hot enchilada." Two days after the primary, the self-assured Clements dropped in on the governor's office to "measure his chair to see if it fits." Asked if he was angling for an endorsement by Briscoe, Clements replied, "Well, sometimes a blind hog picks up an acorn."[22]

Briscoe, however, once he got over the shock of his loss, announced he would stick with the Democratic ticket. "I am a Democrat. I have been a Democrat, and I will die a Democrat. I will support and have always supported — all my life — the Democratic ticket."[23]

But he had not decided how active he would be for Hill. The mild-mannered Briscoe had endured a tough primary campaign, suffered an ignominious defeat, and he believed Hill had been positioning himself for years to run for governor. As early as 1973, newspaper stories were written about Hill's political ambitions. Hill had opened up regional attorney-general offices, and he had been the most active attorney general in years in consumer rights, environmental issues, and criminal justice — one of the areas over which he and the governor's office clashed. Hill had set up a special strike force on organized crime, which the governor's criminal justice division felt constituted illegal dabbling into local police work. While Hill's work drew high marks from supporters, those less charitable said he was meddling, politically ambitious, and a headline-grabber.

At fifty-four, Hill had been a highly successful Houston lawyer. While not as wealthy as either Briscoe or Clements, he was a millionaire from his courtroom practice and from investments in oil and gas and real estate. He had gotten into politics backing John Connally. Governor Connally appointed him secretary of state in 1966, and Hill had made a premature run for governor in 1968 before being elected attorney general in 1972. Hill was a confident, self-made man, and had enough of the right background to offset his big-city image. He had been raised in Kilgore in East Texas, where his family had followed the oil boom. His father was an oilfield worker who eventually owned a prosperous truck line. Hill had been a campus leader at the University of Texas — a cheerleader, fraternity president, and head of the Texas Cowboys service organization. He was described as an intense, mercurial, and ambition-driven workaholic.

Hill was also popular with the Capitol press corps. He trusted the reporters and was informal around them. He sprinkled his conversation with colorful colloquialisms from his East Texas upbringing. A city boy big on country clichés, Hill used phrases such as "that dog won't hunt. . . . there's no meat on that bone . . . don't waste time killing that snake more than once."[24]

But conservative Democrats, and particularly Briscoe associates and friends, were not comfortable with their nominee. Clements acted quickly to capitalize on their unease. His campaign took over what had been the Briscoe headquarters in Austin, and on June 1, he announced that David Dean, who had been Briscoe's general counsel, was joining his campaign as deputy campaign manager and head of Democrats and Independents for Clements. Dean said he received neither encouragement nor discouragement from Briscoe to join the Clements campaign. But after working for Briscoe for six years, he couldn't support Hill, Briscoe's political adversary. With his connections to the Briscoe political network, Dean was a valued asset. As such, he extracted a high campaign position and a seat on Clements' policy council, known within the campaign as the "God Squad."[25]

The "God Squad" consisted of Bill and Rita Clements, Stu Spencer, Peter O'Donnell, David Dean, Nola Haerle, and Tom Reed. Nola Haerle was the nuts-and-bolts campaign manager, but Reed was chairman of the policy committee, which made all of the strategy decisions in weekly meetings. The Advisory Council, which met monthly, included the state campaign chairman, George Strake, Jr., vice-chairman Mrs. Bobbie Biggart of Dallas, Anne Armstrong, Tom Rhodes, and Ashley Priddy. Priddy, longtime mayor of Highland Park, was Clements' finance chairman, and Rhodes was campaign treasurer.

Clements had several Californians with connections to Ronald Reagan working on his campaign. Besides Reed, they included Spencer, Mrs. Haerle (who was then married to California Republican State Chairman Paul Haerle) and George Steffes, who had been Reagan's legislative aide in Sacramento. Spencer worked on strategy and with the advertising firm on the media message. Steffes was over the phone banks and the field organization for Clements. With the exception of Mrs. Haerle, the out-front campaign manager, the rest of the "California mafia" worked hard to be invisible. Until the campaign was over, their influence was largely ignored by the Texas media.

At the beginning of the summer, Clements had an unbelievable amount of ground to make up. Immediately after the May primary, in the first Hill-Clements matchups, polls indicated Hill was ahead by a staggering 52 percent. In one month, Clements moved up five points, while Hill went down nine. But Clements was still a long shot. Only 39 percent of Texans knew who he was in June 1978.[26]

"When I looked at the polling information, I really wondered, can we do this?" Nola Haerle said. But everybody on the Clements campaign team assumed it could be done, including Clements.

The *Austin American-Statesman*'s Jon Ford wrote about the blunt assurance that characterized the Clements campaign: "Bill Clements sneered at John Hill's new poll [showing the Democratic gubernatorial nominee 52 points ahead] and sounded his mirthless and blood-curdling battle cackle. 'You want to know how it's really going to turn out? I am going to wax his ass. I'll beat him about 53 percent to 47 percent.'"[27]

John Connally wasn't active in the campaign, but offered to host a barbecue at his ranch later and to help, however he could, in October. Connally, in a meeting with Bill and Rita, advised the candidate, however, to quit using such phrases as "I'll wax his fanny," and to try to be tolerant, humble and in good humor. He advised Clements to travel the "trails of Texas" — working two trails at a time, with Rita taking one trail and Bill taking another, meeting together every few days for an event.[28]

The "trail" Clements decided to take during the summer months was mapped out in a detailed campaign plan by Reed. Reed figured out that Republican candidates performed well in Texas' urban counties but lost in the smaller counties where there was no Republican grass roots organizations. In general elections, 55 percent of the vote was in the big five counties — Dallas, Harris, Bexar, Tarrant, and Travis. The next quarter of the vote was in 28 counties, and the rest was in 221 less densely populated counties. "It became clear to me," Reed said, "that Republicans would do well in the big five counties. In the next 28 counties they would begin to fall off, and then out here in 221 counties, they'd just vanish off the screen." So Project 230 was devised. Omar Harvey, operating out of a motor home, would try to find a chairman in 230 counties to organize a

Clements committee. At the same time, he tried to reassure local Democratic officials who felt threatened by prospects of a Republican governor. If a Republican loses, Reed wrote in his campaign notebook, it is because of "the hundreds of rural counties, with their Democratic traditions and courthouse crowds." He wisely penned, "This program of organizing rural areas might well be the needed margin for victory on November 7."[29]

"Bill did something no other Republican had the discipline nor the patience to do — to go into the rural counties. It was a brilliant move, to do it in the summer, when the Democratic guard was down and people weren't watching," Tarrance said.

Beginning in mid-June, Bill and Rita Clements spent two and one-half months traveling the backroads of Texas, in separate mobile home caravans. At that time, Republicans controlled only one county courthouse in Texas' 254 counties — Midland County.[30] According to Reed's campaign plan, Clements couldn't physically reach every small community in the state, but the word would get around that he was trying to see and talk to the average Texan and by fall, Clements would be perceived as having talked to people "all over Texas."

George Bayoud, a young aide who had graduated from the University of Texas the preceding December, spent the summer in a motor home, advancing the Clementses' rural schedule and driving them around. He would pick up Clements, and sometimes Rita, at an airport and take them to several small towns, where they would visit the radio station, the newspaper, and appear at an event. Bayoud got to know Clements driving the motor home that summer. In the small towns where he spoke, Clements would talk about his experiences in the area as a young drilling contractor or about the locality's place in Texas history.[31]

Dean was in Austin, enlisting Democrats and independents by telephone. "Every week," he said, "we'd announce another list of Briscoe conservatives who switched over to Bill Clements."

One of Clements' first stops on the rural road was a reception at the First State Bank in Uvalde, which Briscoe owned. Even though Briscoe did not endorse Clements, that event sent a powerful message to Briscoe friends and supporters. John Hill, meanwhile, made little effort to mend fences with the Briscoe Democrats.

Even though Clements was far back in the polls, Reed thought he could win, partly because of Rita. "Clearly she was a major asset.

She could fill the role the vice president does on the national ticket, of keeping the party faithful happy, so that he would not have to spend all this time going to Republican gatherings. She was a good speaker," he said, and she wanted to do it. "It was a decision they made together."

Clements, in fact, was more effective in the rural areas, among ticket-splitters, than he was in Republican events. Reed felt Clements tended to view the hard-core Republicans as "Rita's and Peter's friends." According to Reed, "Doing the Republican thing was not high on his list of likes. That's why Rita played such a great role." Clements, he said, "was just great going to Abilene and Big Spring and Lubbock and talking to the good ol' boys. He understood that for a Republican to win he has to get the last 221 counties up to match his performance in Dallas and Harris and Tarrant. It's what a Republican had to do to win, and the reason a Republican never had," Reed concluded.

"He was the right candidate to be on the cutting edge of history. It was going to happen sooner or later; this was happening all over the South," Reed said, referring to the growing Republican trend. "He was the right candidate to make the case to the court-house crowd. You vote for a Republican for president, surely you don't want to vote for Jimmy Carter's friend for governor."

Clements emphasized the philosophical differences between himself and Hill, linking Hill to Jimmy Carter and portraying the choice as a conservative businessman vs. a "liberal claims-lawyer politician." Over and over, he said, "If you like Jimmy Carter, you're going to love John Hill." He depicted Hill as a big-spending bureaucrat, and seized upon passage of Proposition 13 in California to call for a tax rollback in Texas.

In late June, President Carter came to Texas on a fence-mending trip, which allowed Clements to further tie Hill to the declining popularity of the Democratic president. Hill was not concerned. He appeared with Carter at a fundraiser in Houston, where he said the president would "not be a drag on state Democratic candidates who face Republican opponents."[32]

Clements' boast that he was going to tie Jimmy Carter around John Hill's neck "like a dead chicken" created one of the most celebrated events of the campaign — the rubber chicken incident in Amarillo. Clements and Hill were scheduled to share the platform at a banquet in Amarillo; it was their first joint appearance. Nola

Haerle remembered Clements saying, during a strategy meeting the day before at D/FW airport, that he was "supposed to say something funny" in Amarillo because the event was to be like a "roast." He asked for suggestions. Members of the "God Squad" were flying off to separate destinations and paid no attention to his request for help. Nola Haerle said Clements mentioned he might go to a novelty store to look for "something funny." After the meeting, Clements said he sent his travel aide, Dary Stone, to a novelty shop to pick up a rubber chicken. Stone remembers the incident differently. He claims Clements showed up on the plane to Amarillo with a paper sack, and pulled the make-believe chicken out of the sack with an "evil grin on his face." According to Stone, "Rita gives me this look like, 'you'd better talk him out of this.' We took turns trying to round off his corners."[33] Clements had Stone place the chicken, in the paper sack, behind the podium.

When it came his turn to speak, Clements made some remarks about Jimmy Carter being a dead chicken and he was going to hang that chicken around John Hill's neck. Then, as Austin newspaperman Jon Ford wrote, "As the crowd gasped, Clements suddenly yanked from a paper sack a plucked chicken (it turned out to be plastic, but it looked real enough), and held the thing up by the feet. He tried to hand it off to Mayor Jerry Hodge, but the mayor cringed and would have no part of passing it along to Hill." The chicken landed next to Mrs. Hodge, who placed it between her plate and Mr. Hill's and whispered, "I'm sorry." Hill said, "Don't worry," and threw it under the table.[34]

It was widely reported that Clements threw the chicken in Mrs. Hodge's plate, which Clements said was not true. He was trying to pass it to Hill. He later admitted, however, that he had blown his lines and his attempt at comedy had fallen flat. Stone agreed he misdelivered his lines. "His comedic timing is not terrific, and the audience didn't get it. Nobody laughed," he said. Hill wanted to avoid a photo opportunity with the chicken and got rid of it. Stone said the incident had little impact on the event, but press interpretation — which went on all summer — created the impact. "It was our first joint appearance with John Hill. We'd been struggling with his [Clements'] public persona — that he was rough, insensitive. Little did we know it would be that part of his character that would be the most appealing to the voters," Stone said. The incident, he said, got Clements "tons of name I.D."[35]

Clements later offered an explanation of the incident and his use of the "dead chicken" phrase to George Steffes, one of the Californians working on the campaign. Steffes said, "He told me how farmers in Texas, when a dog got in the chicken coop, would hang a dead chicken around the dog's neck and after a couple of weeks, the dog wouldn't go in the chicken coop anymore and get after the chickens." He recalled Clements saying further, "Now, all you city boys think that rubber chicken incident was a disaster, but every person in rural Texas knows what I'm talking about."[36]

Clements eventually apologized to Mayor Hodge for any embarrassment he may have created and, in the fall, Hodge actively campaigned for Clements.

The chicken incident and a statement made during a campaign trip to the Rio Grande Valley fed Clements' growing image of brashness. Not conceding the Mexican-American vote to the Democrats, Clements was campaigning in South Texas, where he was repeatedly asked about issues of concern to the Mexican-Americans. After lengthy questioning by one reporter, Clements turned away in exasperation. "I'm not running for governor of Mexico, you know."[37] It was a statement that drew considerable attention in the media, and would be repeated for years, as vintage Clements. Jack Germond and Jules Witcover, veteran syndicated columnists, wrote that while Clements' advisers touted his "outspoken charm," he can also be an "unguided missile." They referred to his "not running for governor of Mexico" statement as "true enough, but hardly the politic thing to say."[38]

By the end of the summer, the candidate, his wife, and Omar Harvey had visited more than 200 rural counties and had a county campaign chairman in 244 of 254 counties, which meant Clements was organized in dozens of Texas counties that didn't have enough Republicans to hold a GOP primary the previous May. It was enough to impress *Houston Chronicle* political writer Joe Nolan. "It's time someone admitted that Bill Clements really does have a chance of pulling it off and becoming the first Republican governor of Texas since Reconstruction," he wrote.[39]

Hill, meanwhile, was spending a more relaxed summer, talking to heads of state agencies about the budget, preparing his legislative agenda and saving his campaign fire for the fall. The conventional political wisdom in those days was not to put the campaign into high gear until Labor Day. Hill and his volunteers were worn down from defeating the incumbent and took the summer off. They were convinced there was no way Clements could close the gap.

During the summer, Clements buttressed his appeal to Democrats and independents with a radio advertising campaign which told voters that times had changed — a vote for a Republican wasn't a betrayal of one's ancestry. "I thought at the time it wasn't much of a message," Hill said, "but it was a conditioner for what would come in the later stage of the campaign," Hill said. The later message was that the Democratic Party had gone too liberal. "It was an orchestrated effort that started in the summer, setting the stage for the closing argument," said lawyer Hill.[40]

On Labor Day, Clements staged his fall campaign kickoff at the Clements farm in Forney, where he talked about his roots in Forney — where his muleskinner grandfather settled and his father had farmed. Governors traditionally had come not from the urban centers but from West Texas or South Texas or East Texas. They were men who identified with the soil of Texas, and Clements needed to make that connection.

He also tried to connect philosophically, noting that Labor Day was a holiday to honor "those who produce something useful — with their hands and their backs . . . . I believe in honoring those who produce something useful, not those who talk, complain and regulate. I am for the producers and against the parasitic bureaucrats who live off the producers."

Clements gave an overview of the issues he would develop in the rest of the campaign — the cost of government, energy, education, and immigration. He called for a new national energy plan to provide incentives for exploration and production. "I want a tough-as-nails governor who will not stand for northeastern plundering of our energy assets when the emergency hits. I want a governor who knows enough about energy to show the nation what needs to be done," he said.

Charging that his opponent was the "captive of the teaching establishment," he demanded a "back to basics" approach and the return of control from the educational bureaucracy to local school districts. And he called for a "Taxpayer's Bill of Rights" — constitutional amendments which would provide for the right of initiative and referendum, ban income taxes, require a two-thirds vote of both houses to pass a tax bill, and allow local taxpayers to call an election to ratify or reject tax increases by local governments.[41]

From Labor Day forward, Clements' campaign shifted to the urban areas. Tom Reed began traveling with the candidate, to guard against mistakes and to field-manage the campaign. As Nola Haerle said, "Bill shot from the hip, and sometimes the gun wasn't loaded. With Tom on the plane, that didn't happen." The fall campaign was highly structured. Each week, there was an "issue of the week" to be emphasized in speeches by the candidate and in advertising. The issue for the week of September 11 was national security, designed to play up Clements' service in the Pentagon. Former chairmen of the Joint Chiefs of Staff, Adm. Tom Moorer and Gen. George Brown, came to Texas on September 16 to campaign in military-populated San Antonio and several other cities.[42]

Setting aside the animosities of 1976, former President Ford and former California Governor Reagan campaigned for Clements September 12 at a breakfast in Houston and a dinner in Dallas that raised $1.3 million. Ford called Clements the best manager the Department of Defense had during his twenty-eight years of government service. "We can't rewrite 1976, and we can't leapfrog to 1980," said Ford. "But 1978 can act as a referendum by which the American people endorse or fail to endorse the defense, national security and energy programs of the Carter administration."[43] Ford also was featured at a huge rally on the University of Texas campus, which created excitement on campus despite Ford's problem in mastering the "Hook 'em Horns" sign. George Bayoud, who had been foreman (president) of the Texas Cowboys, got the organization to sponsor the event, and advanced it.[44]

One week, Clements' issue was education. That was Hill's top priority, particularly higher teachers' salaries. In budget considerations, Hill wanted funds allocated first for education. Clements charged that Hill just wanted to throw money at the schools. Hill had locked up the support of the professional education groups, so Clements directed his appeal to parents.

Another week it was energy. The shipment of Texas' clean, low-cost energy to the Northeast was leading to a jobs crisis, a school crisis (because one-third of the state funds spent on public education came directly from oil and gas taxes) and a tax crisis, he said. The week was highlighted by appearances in petrochemical and oilfield areas, from Odessa to Houston to Beaumont, the birthplace of the Texas oil industry with Spindletop. "Oil and natural gas are Texas' heritage," Clements said. "It's our children's schools, our neighbors' jobs and our bulwark against a state income tax." Beaumont was not a Republican area; only 1,000 had voted in Jefferson County in the Republican primary, but 200 showed up to hear Clements speak there.[45]

Clements was particularly effective in playing populistic themes, such as "protecting the Texas way of life." Tarrance defined populism as a common folk assault on the arrogance of the established class. Clements understood and used those kinds of themes largely by instinct.

Hill hit the stump in early September, still operating on the assumption that he would be the next governor. He went around the state making speeches, recognizing local Democratic officials and saying how much he was looking forward to serving with them when he took office. The Hill campaign was described by the opposition as boldly overconfident. Over the summer, Hill backers had been lulled into complacency, even as Clements was picking up momentum. It was difficult for the Hill campaign to kick back into gear. Hill believed the $1.5 million he was spending in the general election campaign, including $600,000 for television advertising, was competitive against Clements' unprecedented $4.3 million budget.[46] But Clements was shoveling money into advertising, eventually spending even more than the $1 million budgeted. The two largest expenditures of the Clements campaign were for paid media and the phone bank, which cost almost half a million dollars.

Because Clements was so little known and had so far to go to catch Hill, he needed to blanket the airwaves with commercials. Don Ringe and Bob Russo created a five-minute TV spot to introduce the Republican candidate to voters and to construct the Clements mystique. Narrated by Clements, it featured photos of the tent city railroad camp at Forney (from the days of his grandfather), and of oilfield derricks and workers, as Clements told how he went to the oilfields during the depression as a roughneck. "I had calluses all over my hands. I have worked sixteen hours a day because I needed the money. When the working man starts talking about how hard he works, I've been there." More photos followed — of Clements from his high school yearbook, of Southeastern Drilling Company's early headquarters, and then of the massive offshore rigs developed by SEDCO — as Clements described how he built a great business "literally on a hope and a prayer and a piece of baling wire." The commercial then flashed to the Pentagon and to photos of Clements with President Ford and Henry Kissinger. "The basic criteria in any management function — be it the Department of Defense or governor of Texas — is to surround yourself with absolutely the best people possible," he said.

Clements produced several spots on energy. One showed him in a hard hat in front of a refinery saying: "Texas is the energy capital of the world, but so far we haven't done much to stop Jimmy Carter from holding back on increased production while siphoning off our precious energy resources. I'm Bill Clements, and I understand the energy problem. As former deputy secretary of defense, I know how to make Washington work for Texas."

John Connally also cut several endorsement commercials. One example: "Some say my friend Bill Clements comes on strong. And I say that's good. Because what we need today is a strong governor — strong enough to ensure that the federal government doesn't dictate every part of our lives."[47]

Clements' television campaign was wrapped in Texas mythology and fostered a larger-than-life image for the Republican candidate. A writer in *Texas Monthly* likened Clements' TV spots to "mini-versions of the Texas epic, *Giant.*"[48] The advertising was professional and effective. And it was omnipresent.

The message was beginning to get through. This was a man of the people, who knew energy and knew his way around Washington, who had raised himself up by the bootstraps. Clements played his background for all it was worth. As Saralee Tiede of the *Dallas Times-Herald* wrote, "Clements' rags to riches story has been sufficiently embellished that his detractors refer to him as 'that poor farm boy from Highland Park.'"[49]

Meanwhile, the Clements telephone campaign was the most massive and sophisticated ever undertaken in Texas. It was masterminded by consultant Nancy Brataas, who had set up phone banks for President Nixon's 1972 reelection effort. The goal was to contact 1.2 million households and reach 2.2 million voters. There were 35 phone centers across the state, calling 17,000 voters a day in 50 targeted counties while some 25,000 home volunteers made calls in smaller towns. Shelma Ahrens, Clements' secretary before his DOD days, headed the phone bank in Dallas County, where volunteers worked at five locations, contacting 250,000 voters.[50]

The elements of the Clements campaign were coming together when Governor Briscoe's wife, Janey, dropped a bombshell that gave Clements added credibility going into the final month of the race. She told Dave Montgomery of the *Dallas Times-Herald* that out of loyalty she would follow her husband's plans to vote Democratic November 7, but she believed Clements was better suited than Hill to be governor. Briscoe, meanwhile, had done nothing to stop his former supporters and even his own children from joining ranks behind Clements. The Briscoe children, Cele, Janey (and her husband Ed Vaughan), and Chip said they were supporting Clements because he was more conservative.[51]

On October 22, 1978, a little more than two weeks before the election, the *Texas Monthly* poll came out showing Hill still in the lead by 11 points. Hill was supported by almost 45 percent to Clements' 34 percent, but 21 percent of the electorate was undecided. On the heels of that poll, Hill asserted, "There is no way I will lose." He was quoted as saying, "It's all over. We think we have enough votes to win regardless of the turnout. The polls show I'm going straight up." Hill told a group of Houston attorneys he had an insurmountable lead and that he would "beyond any doubt" win the election. Clements, meanwhile, claimed his own poll showed he and Hill were in a "dead heat."[52]

On October 24, 1978, Clements and Hill met in debate. Hill emphasized his support of additional funds for education, including teacher pay raises, equalization funding, and more help to school districts on utility and transportation bills. Hill wanted to make education the first priority in the appropriations bill. Clements stressed his back-to-basics approach, bringing discipline back into the classroom. He also accused Hill of increasing the attorney general staff by 300 percent and his own budget by 600 percent from 1973 to 1978. Hill's office had grown from 150 people to 454 and from a budget of $2.6 million to $16.8 million, since he was first elected. Clements, by contrast, wanted to cut 25,000 from the state payroll. When it was over, Clements said: "I wanted the voters to see that we are different. We are not two peas in a pod. We are not on the same vine. We are not even in the same garden."[53]

Hill had a standard pre-election poll conducted, which was released on October 31. It showed Hill was leading 51 to 35 percent. Clements claimed his polls showed the race was a tossup. Clements also was utilizing a sophisticated new polling technique, "tracking polls." Tarrance called 125 persons each night during the "tracking," and the results helped the Clements camp determine day-to-day shifts in voter moods and then plan the appropriate response. When the tracking polls showed Clements faltering in the last week in the Dallas-Fort Worth area, he added a visit to the area and stepped up advertising there. Clements was buoyed by his telephone banks and tracking polls and determined to stay on his game plan. Hill, dashing about the state in the campaign's final days, continued to express confidence.[54] But some things were happening that gave him cause for concern, as he discussed years later in an interview.

The Democrat saw his mother while campaigning in East Texas. She told him that Clements was making him sound like "not just a liberal but a bad, bad ol' liberal."[55] Hill always thought of himself as a moderate, but Clements was tying him not just to Carter but to the "McGovernites, Yarboroughites, Farentholdites and other liberals" whom Clements claimed had control of the Texas Democratic Party. Clements said the liberal and labor leaders were "clustered around my opponent like chicks around a mother hen."[56]

Hill believed Clements was making headway with his promises to cut state government by 25,000 employees and return $1 billion to the voters, while portraying the Democrat as a governor who would keep big spending programs. Clements, running as a conservative businessman, made Hill seem like the incumbent, saying he had been in government too long. "I was the government, and they needed to throw the government out," Hill said.

Hill also thought he was damaged by the *Texas Spectator*, a Clements campaign tabloid which Hill called a "typical dirty tricks type of publication" put together by Clements' out-of-state consultants. Among other things, Hill was portrayed as an ambulance-chasing plaintiff's lawyer who made money out of other people's misfortune. The red-headlined *Texas Spectator* was mailed out to 1.5 million Texans. Even Nola Haerle and Rita objected to the scandal sheet, which depicted Hill, for example, as having made a fortune representing victims of a Braniff plane crash.

Hill believed the Clements campaign got much of the material from "opposition files" kept by then-Comptroller Bob Bullock on public figures he might someday have to run against.

Hill went to San Antonio to cut a television commercial to refute what was in the *Spectator*. But his campaign manager, John Rogers, talked him out of a half-million dollar TV buy to saturate the state with the spot. Stay positive, Rogers told him.

In the final days, despite what the Clements campaign did, Hill stuck to his pledge that he wasn't going to "throw mud or chickens."[57] Hill never responded to the *Spectator* material and, in retrospect, he wished that he had. "When you don't respond, voters assume what is said about you is true," he said.

There was one other aspect of the campaign that Hill, in hindsight, felt was pivotal.

Clements had aligned himself with Corpus Christi radio evangelist Lester Roloff, in his fight against state efforts to regulate his homes for wayward children. As attorney general, Hill represented Texas' claim to the right to license and inspect "Brother" Roloff's private schools, which combined fundamental Christian religious training and strict discipline to deal with problem youths. During the campaign, "Brother" Roloff tried to extract a promise from Hill to exempt his schools from state regulation. Clements had agreed to do so, but Hill refused.[58]

Clements sometimes followed his own basic political instincts. When asked by his strategists why he was embracing "Brother" Roloff, he would just say he believed in what Roloff was doing. Tarrance believed Clements saw the potential impact of a Christian voting bloc even before the Moral Majority came to the fore in the early 1980s.

On the Sunday before the election, followers of "Brother" Roloff distributed pro-Clements literature in church pews and parking lots across the state, primarily in rural areas. In the massive literature drop, Hill was accused of being a liberal and "anti-church and anti-Christian" because he enforced the state law. The Clements campaign financed the flyer.

"It really hit us the Sunday before the election," Hill said. When the religious piece was dropped, even his wife and children became concerned that he might lose the election. In the last three or four days, Hill also had learned what Clements' tracking polls were showing. For the first time, he began to believe he was in trouble.

"Son, you're scared, aren't you? I can see it in your face," Hill's mother said, when he saw her in East Texas in the waning days of the race. Hill replied, "I am, Mama." She told him, "If the Lord doesn't intend for you to win, he'll have something else waiting for you." Those words would later bring consolation to Hill.

Austin political consultant George Christian told Hill he'd

never seen a race close so fast. On election day, Clements' phone banks, which had identified his voters, were going full speed, getting the vote out. Clements had billboards and telephone pole placards throughout the black precincts in Houston. As in other parts of the campaign, Clements had devoted significant resources to a minority outreach program — particularly creating a presence in the predominantly black precincts in Houston and through Hispanic advertising.

Hill's get-out-the-vote effort paled, in comparison. "By the time we realized it was closing so fast, there was not time left to get out the vote," Hill said.

According to Tom Reed, one-third of the voters made up their minds during the last week and 15 percent made up their minds on election day. Clements' phoners contacted 20 percent of the voters on election day, compared to Hill's eight percent.[59]

On election night, the race was too close to call. Some media outlets, nonetheless, prematurely declared Hill the winner. An upbeat Clements appeared before his cheering supporters at midnight at the Sheraton-Crest Hotel to predict that it would be a long night but victory was at hand. Complete returns were not expected until the following day.

After appearing before his supporters, Clements was hungry. He and Rita, George and Annette Strake, and Sen. Walter Mengden went for steak and eggs about 1:00 A.M. at a coffee shop near the university. While they were waiting for their food, recalled Strake, some young men came in and were using foul language. "Bill just pops up out of his chair, stands in front of them like James Cagney and says, 'Hey, my friend, I'm Bill Clements and I'd appreciate it if you wouldn't use that kind of language. There are women in this place.'" Strake said, "The guys looked up and said, 'You're Bill Clements? We voted for you today.' Clements just responded, 'Well, you know, our wives are over here, and I'd really appreciate if you'd kind of hold it down.'"[60] From there, Clements and Rita returned to the hotel and went to bed, still not knowing the results of the election.

Nola Haerle and some of the staff stayed up, getting returns from their workers out in the field. About 2:00 A.M., Clements pulled into the lead, she said. But the Texas Election Bureau (TEB), which tabulated results for the news media, had shut down for the night. The last TEB report, which showed Hill in the lead, was used by some media outlets as definitive and many Texans went to bed believing John Hill would be their next governor.

All night long, the Clements campaign was dispatching lawyers to courthouses around the state, where results had not been reported. Democrats controlled all but one county courthouse, and the Clements campaign wanted to make sure county officials didn't take boxes home in their car trunks before their votes were reported or that ballot boxes didn't turn up missing.

By 6:00 A.M., according to Nola Haerle's count, Clements was 12,000 votes ahead, and she was convinced her candidate had won. She called the Clementses' room and awakened Rita. "May I speak to the governor?" she asked. "That's not funny," Rita replied.

Mrs. Haerle called ABC-TV, which had declared Hill an apparent winner, along with the other networks. She told ABC to get in touch with the Texas Election Bureau, which by then had resumed counting votes. By 7:00 A.M., ABC had announced Clements the winner.

Clements decided to go to the Capitol later that morning to declare victory. In the speaker's committee room, which was jammed with news media (some were standing on the radiators), supporters and well-wishers, he made his victory statement. Jerry Hodge had flown in from Amarillo, hand-carrying a copy of the *Amarillo Globe-News* morning edition which contained a page one headline blaring that Hill had won. The newspaper was passed, hand over head, across the crowded room to Clements, who gleefully held it up. When Clements declared victory, the TEB showed him winning by about 24,000 votes, with 96 percent of the precincts reporting. "My election marks a new day for Texas," Clements declared. "We literally have turned a page in history, and the political scene will never be the same."[61]

Hill's workers were distraught and disbelieving. Tears streamed down their faces as they left the hotel en route to the Capitol Wednesday afternoon, where Hill made his concession statement. Though Hill had been aiming at the governor's office for more than ten years, and for six months had almost assumed the mantle, he said in an interview with the *Dallas Times-Herald*'s Saralee Tiede at his Dripping Springs ranch that the loss was "a disappointment. It was not a shattered dream." The night before he had feared the worst and had told his daughter, Martha, he didn't want his family to fall apart if he lost the election.

Hill did, however, call for a recount. The Clements campaign, leery of Democratic ballot shenanigans from years past, was already into its "ballot security" mode. O'Donnell had insisted that the campaign devise a sophisticated ballot security operation, headed by a lawyer in every region of the state, to make sure Clements' votes stayed intact if there was a recount. A network of volunteers was dispatched to guard the ballot boxes until the recount could be done. The Republicans, according to Nola Haerle, "never had a ballot security program this ready to go." In later years, such a program would not be necessary, but with Republicans fighting Democratic control in courthouses across the state, they feared the Democrats would try to steal the election for their candidate.

After the recount, Clements officially won the race by a margin of 16,909 votes out of 2.2 million cast.[62] It wasn't a huge margin of victory, but it exceeded the margin of Republican standard-bearer John Tower, who defeated his Democratic challenger, Robert Krueger, by only 12,227 votes. Tower had been locked in such a close contest that one Republican activist, after working the phone banks in the final days of the campaign, moaned tearfully that Republicans were finally going to elect a governor but were going to lose their senator.[63] On the morning after the election, Tower called Mrs. Haerle, who previously had worked for him. "Thanks," he said, "for letting me ride in on your coattails."[64]

Charles Deaton, author of the *Texas Government Newsletter*, credited the $7 million expenditure, the most ever spent in a non-presidential political race, with enabling Clements to assemble a team of the "best political brains and trouble shooters in the country." Deaton cited key ingredients in the election: the phone bank, which made a half million phone calls on election day, the "roots" TV spots which softened Clements' "abrasive image," the *Texas Spectator,* which was "full of one-sided stories praising Clements and blasting Hill," and Tarrance's polling data which guided campaign decisions on advertising, scheduling, and phone bank work. Deaton pointed to two tactical errors by Hill: He was overconfident and began "play-acting" governor too early and failed to actively pursue the support of Briscoe backers.[65]

Also key was Project 230. As Reed wrote in his "Post Mortem" on the election: "It worked! A Republican, to win, needs 52 percent in the big five counties with half the vote; needs to break even in the next 28; and cannot lose with less than 46 percent in the remaining

221 counties. Ford got 41 percent in the latter category and lost. We got over 46 percent and won." In the final analysis, Clements won 43 percent of the conservative Democrats and 58 percent of voters classified as "ticket-splitters."

Tom Reed concluded that while the Clements campaign had put a lot of effort into building an organization, the heart of the campaign was the message and the man who delivered it. Post-election survey results determined that the most important issue for Clements was the cost of government, which included the burden of a growing bureaucracy. The second most important issue was education and the third was energy. But underlying all issues was the man. Voters said they wanted a conservative governor, one with experience in business and industry, and one who was tough and forceful.

Haerle gave Clements, the candidate, bottom-line credit for the win.

"Clements really ran the campaign," Mrs. Haerle said. "He had a lot of high-powered people seeing it was done right. We'd all had experience. Rita was really a professional. But he never gave up his way of doing things. He was chairman of the board, he was the taskmaster." Despite entreaties from staff, he wouldn't change his approach. The staff wanted him to lighten up in portraying Hill as a "liberal, claims-lawyer, politician," Mrs. Haerle said, "but he wouldn't do it. He was more comfortable doing it his own way.

"Clements made this happen . . . . That doesn't take away from all the other things — the organization, the campaign, the staff. But he was the main ingredient in his own election . . . . Bill Clements won because he was Bill Clements — a Texan right down to his toenails, and that came across."

William Broyles, in his election analysis in the December issue of *Texas Monthly*, wrote that Clements was a "walking Texas myth, just as, in his own way, Dolph Briscoe was. Briscoe was the archetypal rancher; Clements is the roughneck. Each monopolized one of the state's two most potent symbols: cattle and oil."

Broyles also wrote, "The question now is whether Clements can run the state the same way he ran the campaign, which was one of the most sophisticated in Texas political history."

Chapter 12

First Term

The Governor as CEO

AT HIGH NOON ON January 16, 1979, at the south entrance to the pink-granite, bunting-draped Texas Capitol, William P. Clements, Jr., was inaugurated as the forty-first governor of Texas. Several thousand people massed on the Capitol grounds to watch him become the state's first freely elected Republican governor. Edmund J. Davis had been the only other Republican governor, elected during Reconstruction with the Union Army's bluecoats at his back, when Texans who had supported the Confederacy were denied a vote.

Clements took the oath with his hand fittingly placed on the Sam Houston Bible. Fittingly, because Clements' most admired Texas historical figure was Houston, the former president of the Republic, U.S. senator, and governor. The new governor was, in some ways, like the revered but ornery Houston — independent-minded to a fault and wholly dedicated to the state that was once an independent nation.

For Clements, the inauguration was an occasion of pure delight. He marched to the inaugural stand through the arched sabers of Texas A&M University's Ross Volunteers, with Rita at his side, carrying yellow roses. "Rita is my partner in this endeavor," he declared. When he ended the oath-taking with the words "so help me God," the new governor couldn't suppress a gleeful chuckle, which was duly noted in the newspaper accounts the next day.

218

A barbecue lunch was served on the Capitol grounds for visitors, while family and close friends of Governor and Mrs. Clements, including presidential aspirants George Bush and John Connally, dined at the Governor's Mansion. Inauguration festivities included a prayer breakfast, symphony performance, ice cream party for children, parade, and five different galas, from black tie balls to a public celebration with country-and-western music.

After six years of the rather staid administration of the Briscoes, whose social activities consisted of afternoon coffees and teas, Governor and Mrs. Clements were bringing hoopla back to the Capitol. The new governor and first lady, flanked by other dignitaries, watched the inaugural parade march down Congress Avenue from a reviewing stand. Clements had even suggested — perhaps playfully — during inauguration planning that the parade be led by a special character. "You know the Macy's Thanksgiving Day parade — they have these giant balloons, and I was of a mind that at the head of the parade there would be a giant rubber chicken." Clements' suggestion, made in a meeting with transition director George Steffes, was quickly nixed by Rita.[1]

The Texas inauguration traditionally is a shared activity for the governor and the lieutenant governor. Bill and Diana Hobby were equal participants in the festivities that had been planned by a joint committee headed by two Republicans, H. R. "Bum" Bright of Dallas and Beryl Buckley Milburn of Austin, and Democrat Ann Richards, a county commissioner in Austin. Traveling with Governor and Mrs. Clements from party to party were the Hobbys, George and Barbara Bush, John and Nellie Connally, and Sen. John Tower and his wife, Lilla. At one of the inaugural balls, Connally (by then a Republican) predicted: "This is the start of two-party government. The Republican party could well be firmly established as the principal party in the state by the end of Clements' administration."[2]

At that point, however, it would be a long time in coming. The GOP could claim only 26 of 181 members of the legislature — 22 in the House and four in the Senate. Clements recognized that he had gotten to Austin with the help of conservative Democrats and independents and that he would need Democratic support in the legislature. In the two months between his election and inauguration, Clements worked nonstop from a downtown Austin office, building contacts with legislators in meetings arranged by David Dean, who would become his general counsel. He met with committee chairmen and with more than 100 lawmakers in small groups. A team from the governor-elect's office visited agency heads, reassuring them that Clements didn't intend to throw everybody out but he expected to be kept informed.[3] Clements discouraged Republican members of the Texas House from forming a minority caucus, which would have elevated the level of partisanship.

"He knows the Republican Party's fate may very well be resting upon his shoulders," wrote one Capitol correspondent. "It's taken more than 100 years for a Republican to win the governorship in Texas, and if Clements bungles the job, it might be another hundred years before they get another shot at it."[4]

Clements' first job was to assemble a staff. Republicans hadn't really worked in state government; Clements was starting from scratch. He brought outsiders and a generation of new young conservatives to the State Capitol. His top appointment, secretary of state, went to Houston oilman George Strake, Jr.[5] One of Clements' first hires was decorated Vietnam veteran and Dallas banker Allen B. Clark, who would be in charge of administration in the governor's office.

Clements' idea was to recruit "dollar-a-year" men from the private sector who would work as expense-paid volunteers in government. One was Doug Brown of Dallas, retired chief executive and founder of Owen Laboratories, who became liaison to the state agencies, heading the governor's state affairs office. South Texas rancher Tobin Armstrong, a man of stature with statewide contacts whose wife, Anne, was a prominent Republican, became appointments director. Ed Vetter, a former Texas Instruments executive and undersecretary of commerce when Clements was in Washington, became the governor's energy adviser, a post created by Clements. Tom Rhodes, formerly his SEDCO lawyer, was acting financial director. All were "dollar-a-year" men.

The only "insiders" Clements hired were in the area of legislative and press relations. Veteran Capitol correspondent Jon Ford became press secretary. Jim Kaster, a Democrat and former legislator from El Paso, became legislative director, assisted by another former Democratic legislator, Hilary B. Doran, Jr., of Del Rio. Ray Hutchison, the former Republican legislator Clements beat in the primary, also volunteered to work in the legislative area two or three days a week during the first regular session.

Kaster recalled that, "When I first came on, he [Clements] said,

'Now look. I don't want a bunch of yes men around me. That's what got Nixon in trouble. I expect you to state your position. But once we make up our mind on an issue, I don't want you hiding behind the lick log, bad-mouthing. If you can't support it,' he said, 'I would expect you to resign.'"[6] It was Clements' habit in his staff meetings, on any given subject, to go around the table and ask each staff member to give an opinion. Then he would make a decision which he expected each one to honor.

Janie Harris, Clements' Pentagon secretary who had followed him back to Dallas, moved to Austin as his executive secretary. Sheila Wilkes was his scheduler. George Bayoud became the governor's personal assistant, traveling with him. Omar Harvey headed the Department of Community Affairs, which disbursed federal funds that were routed through the chief executive's office.

Clements was the first governor to set up a separate, full-time political office. The Governor Clements Committee was created to raise funds to repay his $4 milllion campaign debt. It was headed by Jim Francis. Karl Rove became the committee's direct mail expert, and Pat Oles coordinated with the governor's office on appointments.

From the beginning, Clements was different. He had different goals, a unique style and a vision of the job unlike that of previous governors. Coming from a big business background, he saw himself as the chief executive officer, and state government was just another big business. He wanted more oversight of spending and a results-oriented government. He was brash by nature and unashamed to give his views — often in unconventional language. He never lacked for confidence in his own ability to change the course of the ship of state, regardless of barriers or opposition.

George Christian, a veteran Austin consultant and one-time press secretary to Democratic President Lyndon B. Johnson, described Clements as a "businessman governor" who brought a lot of citizen ideas into the office. Other governors had been conservative, but with Clements, he said, "It was not just conservatism; it was more the idea of getting your dollar's worth." Christian watched eight governors over a period of four decades and advised some of them. He thought Clements, in his first term, was an "aggressive, visionary governor. He knew what he wanted and he set out to do it," Christian said.[7]

What Clements wanted to do was refashion state government

— in his own image, some thought. He wanted to cut the bureau-cracy and make it more productive through training and better man-agement techniques. He wanted to utilize the appointments process to bring highly qualified, management-oriented people to the boards and commissions that oversee state agencies. He wanted a sounder economic policy that conserved funds and provided tax re-lief. He wanted to direct national energy policy from Texas and cre-ate a new era in Texas-Mexico relations — two goals that were atypi-cal for a governor. And he wanted to defeat President Jimmy Carter and return a Republican to the White House.

Clements provided a contrast in style to Governor Briscoe. Clements was an activist conservative, where Briscoe had been a passive conservative, not inclined to shake up the system. A former legislator, Briscoe was comfortable with the way things worked in Austin and got along well with the business lobby groups. Clements told the business lobbies to stay away from his office. He neither knew nor was he tied to traditional practices.

Clements had a larger-than-life view of himself unmatched by any previous governor, with the possible exception of John Con-nally. He didn't intend to be a footnote in history; he wanted to make history. Seven days after assuming office, Clements paid a courtesy visit to President José Lopez Portillo in Mexico —a bold stroke for a governor and an indication of the personal diplomacy Clements would pursue with Texas' neighbor to the south.

But his first legislative session was clearly a shakedown period.

In his inaugural address, Clements had laid the cornerstone for his administration. He expected elected officials and other govern-ment leaders to be responsible to taxpayers just as boards of direc-tors and company officials are responsible to stockholders. He pledged to return to the taxpayers $1 billion of the state's surplus, shrink the bureaucracy, improve the quality of education, and give taxpayers the right of initiative and referendum (I&R). "These are not Republican issues or Democrat issues; these are Texas issues," he said. "You will hear voices during my administration expressing doubts about some of my proposals, but, I will persist. We will pre-vail," he said.[8]

Despite the bipartisan overtures, it was the "I will persist; we will prevail" statement that made headlines. Some members of the heavily Democratic legislature reacted with predictable hostility to his proposals for an I&R procedure — whereby citizens could petition to put a proposed law on the ballot, without legislative action, or repeal an unwanted law. Democratic legislators forecast rough sledding for his proposed $1 billion tax cut. Rep. Paul Ragsdale, D-Dallas, led the early opposition. "I think he gets the feeling he's the president of SEDCO and when he gives us an order, we've got to carry it out. He's in for a rude awakening if he thinks that."[9]

Clements was undeterred. He was governor, and that fact both tickled and awed him. He felt a sense of responsibility every time he walked into the Capitol; he enjoyed the sheer exercise of power.

But he quickly found his efforts hampered by the restraint placed on gubernatorial power by the post-Civil War writers of the Texas Constitution. The governor's powers are limited to the right to appoint citizens to the state boards and commissions that oversee some 240 autonomous state agencies; veto bills and appropriations; and call legislators into special session to consider his specified agenda. Otherwise, the governor has the rather nebulous power of persuasion, the bully pulpit. With only twenty-six Republicans in the Texas House and Senate, the "weak governor" system was even weaker for a Republican. Clements' first session was contentious. He believed legislators should submit to his demands, because he had been elected by the entire state, whereas legislators were elected from only a district.

It was a new milieu for the man accustomed to being the boss. Clements was confounded in part because Texas doesn't have a Cabinet form of government; other executive officeholders are elected independently by the people. The governor isn't even in charge of the budget. The constitution gives responsibility for drawing up the budget to the Legislative Budget Board, composed of the lieutenant governor, House speaker, chairmen of the House Appropriations Committee and Senate Finance Committee, and one other senator and House member. The governor's office traditionally submitted a parallel budget to try to influence funding deliberations. John Hill understood the system and had hired a budget expert in the summer of 1978, in the middle of the campaign.

Clements was unprepared to submit a budget, but Comptroller Bob Bullock came to his rescue with an offer to send some of his financial experts to the transition office to help. It was a charitable gesture by the Democratic comptroller. Clements figured former Gov. Preston Smith asked Bullock to do it, and Bullock couldn't say "no" to his mentor. Bullock had worked for Smith and had been his secretary of state. When Clements ran in 1978, Smith was again seeking the Democratic nomination for governor, driving his car around the state without staff or fanfare. His comeback attempt was largely ignored. Clements, however, treated Smith with the dignity deserved by a former governor, and they developed a liking for each other.[10] For Clements and Bullock, both outspoken and forthright men, it was the beginning of a long and cordial relationship, though they were of different parties.

Any incoming governor, but particularly one unacquainted with state government, enters his first session with a legislation gap. Legislative committees, state agencies, and lobby groups devote the year before the session to mapping out legislative positions and lining up support. Clements' agenda was more concept than form, and he was unfamiliar with the subtle applications of legislative pressure. Kaster and his staff identified bills that matched Clements' interests and helped him evolve a legislative program.

Clements established a solid working relationship early with both Lt. Gov. Bill Hobby — who had more real legislative power as presiding officer of the Senate — and House Speaker Billy Clayton. "They cut him a lot of slack, early-on," Christian said.

Clements sensed that he and Hobby were on different philosophical tracks, and he would have to work around that. Eventually, their differences would become more pronounced. But Clayton was a conservative Democrat from West Texas, whose views usually matched those of the Republican governor. During the inaugural activities, Briscoe had pulled Clements aside and told him that Clayton was willing to work with him. "He will be a friend and helpful to you," Clements recalled Briscoe saying.[11] At the time, the legislature was sharply divided along conservative-liberal lines — almost as if there were two parties within the Democratic Party; the small number of Republicans sided with the mostly rural conservative Democrats.

Clements at first relied heavily on Clayton and Hobby concerning legislative matters. "When he first came in, he wasn't aware of what it took to get legislation passed," Clayton said. "But he was a fast learner." Clayton found Clements congenial and frank. He liked his no-nonsense approach. "His attitude was, let's get the job done."[12]

Two issues were paramount in the session. The first was economic — the budget, and the differences between the Legislative Budget Board's proposal and the governor's proposal. The second was political. Three popular Republicans, including two Texans, would be running for the presidential nomination in the Texas Republican primary: Ronald Reagan, John Connally, and George Bush. Conservative Democratic officeholders feared their supporters would defect to the Republican primary to vote in the presidential battle, leaving liberals to dominate the Democratic primary. They rallied behind an effort to separate the presidential primary from the regular state primary. Under the "split primary" concept, voters would be allowed to vote in a Republican presidential primary and later on in the regular state Democratic primary, thus protecting conservative Democrats on the ballot for other offices.

But the first order of business was the budget.

The Sunbelt migration was under way, and Texas was blessed with a robust economy. The state had enjoyed unprecedented economic growth and prosperity during the Briscoe years. No new taxes had been imposed, and income from sales and other taxes had risen with inflation and increased business volume. Although the state's oil and gas production was declining, the price of crude oil had soared with the OPEC embargo on oil exports. The higher prices for oil and gas meant higher tax returns for Texas, which collected a state severance tax at the wellhead.

Times were good, and there was a $2.8 billion surplus in the state treasury. Still, there were challenges. California had passed Proposition 13, forcing its government to grant tax relief, and spawning taxpayer revolts in other states. In the summer of 1978, flushed with Proposition 13 fever and the desire to be remembered as a "tax cutter," then-Governor Briscoe had called the legislature into special session to pass tax-reducing proposals that were approved by voters. That tax relief had to be incorporated into the budget.

Clements and Hobby soon clashed over spending. The Hobby-led Legislative Budget Board had proposed a $20.8 billion budget for the 1980-81 biennium, an increase of about 22 percent over the previous state budget. Clements, who had campaigned against "throwing money at education," insisted the state could get by with $1 billion less by reducing a proposed teacher pay raise and state aid to public education. That would free up $1 billion for a taxpayer rebate. Clements said the taxpayers had first call on the proposed $2.8 billion surplus. He termed the Hobby plan a "letter to Santa Claus" and predicted that Hobby eventually would accept his austerity budget. The governor threatened repeatedly to veto an appropriations bill that did not contain $1 billion in tax relief, and to call a special session at the most inconvenient time for legislators to rewrite the bill.

Hobby was the most vocal critic of the governor's budget. He was joined by Sen. Oscar Mauzy of Dallas, chairman of the Senate Education Committee, and Rep. John Bryant of Dallas, the House's liberal leader, who emerged as an early and permanent adversary of the governor. Professional teacher groups, battling for a 9.8 percent pay hike, were other critics in the budget fight.

The most memorable event of the session, however, was not about the budget. It was over politics — the split primary bill. A dozen senators made national headlines when they hid out for five days to keep the Senate from considering the presidential primary bill. Hobby called them the "Killer Bees," because they buzzed off to break a quorum. Led by Senate liberals, the "Bees" contended that establishing a presidential primary in March in advance of the regular May party primaries would destroy the integrity of the parties and only serve to advance the presidential ambitions of John Connally — no friend of Democrat loyalists after he switched parties.

News coverage of the truant senators increased as the session neared adjournment, especially when the lieutenant governor ordered the Texas Rangers and highway patrolmen to hunt the Bees down. There were reported sightings across the state, but most of the Bees were holed up in an apartment a few miles from the Capitol.

Sen. Bill Meier of Euless immortalized the fugitives in verse. Noting their "S.O." (State Official) automobile license tags, he rhymed:

> ". . . The Texas Rangers hunt for them;
> Bill Hobby issues pleas,
> And says that on their license plates,
> It shows they're S.O. Bees."

Clements was not amused. He said the truant senators were acting like "spoiled children," keeping the Senate from completing its business during five crucial days at the end of the session. He threatened to call a special session to dispose of the buildup of legislation still dangling.[13]

When the Killer Bees finally returned to work, the legislature was barreling toward adjournment, still faced with passage of such major bills as appropriations and tax relief. Much of the governor's program had been sent back to the drawing boards or knocked down, including initiative and referendum. Clements gave the legislature a grade of "F" and promised to call a special session on initiative and referendum. In the final chaotic hours, lawmakers passed the money bills — gobbling up every dime of available funds to the expressed displeasure of the governor.

But they did throw the governor a bone. They passed a somewhat diluted version of his proposal to grant the governor budget execution authority. Clements thought a governor should have, as a basic management tool, the ability to transfer funds between agencies when the legislature wasn't in session and the ability to reduce spending items in the appropriations bill instead of having to veto them. The amendment passed by the legislature would grant the governor the authority to move funds during the off-session, but only with the approval of a committee dominated by legislators. Half a loaf was better than none, however, and Clements worked the Senate floor to gain passage of the bill. But Clements' hard-fought battle for management change failed later to gain approval from Texas voters in a constitutional amendment election.

Clements had problems with some members of the legislature from the outset. "A lot of people thought he was too imperial in dealing with the Legislature," recalled Capitol correspondent Sam Kinch, Jr. "He was just hard-headed as hell. Bill Hobby used to come out of meetings just shaking his head; he couldn't believe how categorical Clements was about everything. Hobby used to complain that instead of talking about how to solve a problem, Clements would talk about how the Legislature ought to change its ways. But that was like turning a battleship."[14]

As the session neared completion, legislators balked over an unexpected veto by Clements and decided it was time to teach this recalcitrant governor a lesson. They drew the line over a seemingly innocuous bill that would exempt Comal County from uniform hunting and fishing regulations. Twenty other counties already had exemptions, and lawmakers thought it their prerogative to adjust bureaucratic regulations, such as those from Parks and Wildlife, to meet local conditions. Clements contended uniform regulations should be just that — uniform. But Democrats castigated the governor for tampering with a "local bill." According to tradition, a bill which affected only one legislator's district was considered that legislator's domain. Rep. Hugo Berlanga enjoined fellow members: "We need to show this governor that we're not going to let local bills get shot down."

Clements wasn't interested in traditions. "You cannot have state government run properly with fragmentation," he said. The legislators won the tussle, handing Clements the first override of a governor's veto since 1941. He responded by calling them "a bunch of idiots."[15]

Clements was equally outspoken in his criticism of opponents of initiative and referendum. The House's maverick liberal leader, John Bryant of Dallas, had offered to help pass I&R if Clements would take a firm stand against the proposed presidential primary bill. Clements told him: "I would take a lot bigger bite out of your hide than that." In the faceoff that ensued, Bryant accused Clements of "blustering," of "naivete" and "hip-shooting." Clements told Bryant to "go jump in a creek."[16]

One of the fears of legislative leaders at the beginning of the session was that Clements would be intransigent, refusing to compromise. That proved not to be the case. He carved out irrefutable positions, presumably in stone, then backed away from some. After threatening to veto any appropriations bill containing more than a 5.1 percent pay hike for Texas teachers, Clements denied he had made such a threat, even though his staff, on demand, produced a tape recording in which he said just that. Another time, the governor proclaimed that he would veto a bill to extend the life of the State Bar of Texas unless certain conditions were met. The legislature met none of the governor's conditions, but he signed it anyway. He also said he would veto any legislation that would raise the interest ceiling on mortgage loans in Texas from 10 to 12 percent, which money-lenders needed to meet a national money crunch. Aides attributed the governor's refusal to extend the usury limit to his basic populistic tendencies; he believed he was protecting the homeowner. Thirty days later, he accepted a compromise for a floating rate which was tied to a national indicator, if home loans could later be refinanced without penalty.[17]

Clements' aide Doug Brown said the governor wasn't wishy-washy, but he wasn't afraid to change his mind, either. "Sometimes when he'd contradict himself, and we would remind him that yesterday you said this and such, and today you're saying something else, he'd say: 'That just proves what a flexible thinker I am.'"

"Clements had a tendency," Brown said, "to swing at anything that came over the plate. Sometimes he hit a foul ball."[18]

At the end of the first regular session, Clements had been unable to make good on his campaign promise to provide an additional $1 billion in tax relief, for which he was roundly criticized by his political opponent, John Hill. "That was his major campaign plank. I couldn't make that promise because I knew I couldn't keep it. He made it and he failed to keep it," Hill said.[19]

Initiative and referendum failed, as did other parts of the governor's proposed Taxpayer's Bill of Rights, including a ban on personal and corporate income taxes and a requirement that a new or increased tax bill must pass by a two-thirds vote of both houses. A proposal to give the governor power to designate the chairmen of state boards and commissions also failed. Clements counted among his biggest disappointments his inability to pass I&R, reduce the size of the state budget, and pass a bill legalizing electronic surveillance in serious drug cases.

In his statement at the end of the 66th session, Clements quoted a story from former President Ford's book, *A Time to Heal*, about an immigrant who was asked on his citizenship exam, "What did President Lincoln do?" The judge administering the exam expected to hear that Lincoln saved the Union or freed the slaves. But the immigrant responded, "He do the best he can."

"If you wanted to say the same thing about my first efforts as governor, I would be satisfied," Clements said in his statement. "Obviously, I did not meet with overwhelming success in my first encounter with the Legislature. But neither, contrary to some reports, was my program ever in shambles." Clements admitted that the session had been a learning process — he learned about the legislature and legislators learned about him. "We got acquainted . . . and we will know better how to get along in the future."[20]

Clements did have some legislative successes, among them the approval of single appraisal districts for each county and the repeal of the ten-cent state property tax for college building. The governor also gained the power to establish conservatorships and name new leaders for troubled state agencies, and to remove his appointees for reason, with approval of the Senate. He obtained a procedure for removal of incorrigible pupils from the classrooms. Among his other credits were consolidation of energy agencies under his leadership, improvement of the Office of State-Federal Relations in Washington, D.C., and the Texas liasion office in Mexico. He also got the legislature to appropriate $1 million for restoration of the Governor's Mansion. The repairs and refurbishing of that historic dwelling would become one of Bill and Rita Clements' lasting legacies to the state.[21]

To the extent that Clements was successful with legislation, it was largely because of his willingness to meet one-on-one with legislators. "Clements, one-on-one, is dynamite," Kaster said. "He's not dynamite making speeches." As the first Republican governor in the century, however, Clements was in big demand for speeches across the state, and he tried to fill as many as he could. George Bayoud, his traveling aide, recalls many evenings where, after a full day of work in the office, Clements would fly off to make a speech somewhere. "There was tremendous demand on him," Kaster said. "He was going all over the state while the Legislature was in session, and we were trying to get him to stay here."

After five months in office, Bill Clements hadn't always prevailed but he had persisted. *Dallas Times-Herald* bureau chief Dave Montgomery wrote that "the cocky former roughneck is garnering popularity as the state's first strong governor since John Connally left office a decade ago" by radiating an intense, can-do personality and assertive leadership — albeit unpredictable and often confrontational. Whatever his legislative failures, Clements was thriving as an administrator. He was making the most of his constitutionally weak executive powers, Montgomery wrote, "by using managerial know-how to improve and reorganize the bureaucratic framework of the governor's office."

Glenn Ivy, of the privately financed Texas Research League, said Clements "knows the tools of management and all the gobble-degook of running a business. We've never had an administrator in this office before and this guy is one."[22]

From a fiscal standpoint, Clements wasn't finished when the legislative session ended. He was determined to make good on at least part of his pledge to pare government spending. He had twenty days in which to use line item vetoes to trim the budget. It was, he said, "just like hunting Easter eggs." Lawmakers had managed to hide pet projects and made it difficult to find fat. But Clements staked out his position: to find cuts amounting to one percent of the budget.

In April of 1979, midway through the legislative session, Clements had hired Paul Wrotenbery as permanent director of the budget and planning office, thus allowing his old SEDCO associate, Tom Rhodes, to return to Dallas. Wrotenbery had recently sold his computer software company and was said to be brilliant, but he had no intimacy with state budgeting. He made the mistake of inviting Hobby in and giving him a lecture on the budget. Hobby responded that he was never going to another meeting "with that Wrotenbery fellow and get preached to."[23]

It became Wrotenbery's job to comb the budget for vetoes. He finally came up with line items totaling $252 million, which Clements pruned with a stroke of his pen. The governor's vetoes, reducing the budget to $19.9 billion, made big news. It was the largest sum ever deleted from a state budget by line item veto.[24]

Most of the cuts were in "bricks and mortar" — funds that would have been used to build government buildings. But Clements also cut what he considered nonessential spending in higher education. According to Wrotenbery, the governor vetoed such "untouchables" as $5.2 million in special items from the $276 million University of Texas budget. Wrotenbery said the governor wanted "to shake up UT and force them to do a little budget discipline." He also vetoed $1.9 million from Texas A&M's $195 million budget and found nonessential items to veto in other college and university budgets.

"At a time when we are asking for a reduction in employment, improved management effectiveness, higher productivity and elimination of unneeded services, our resources should be dedicated to effective service rather than bricks and mortar," Clements said. He had advocated a reduction of 25,000 state employees, and the legislature had endorsed the concept of reducing state employment by five percent per year. Clements said he saw "little need, therefore, for pouring millions of dollars into new office buildings." He believed there was waste in the higher education budgets and said that "universities must also respond to the need for more effective management."[25]

"Bill's way was, don't bother him with the details; just go out and do it," Wrotenbery said. "One political mistake we made, and I made it, was we vetoed prison construction of $30 million. Later, that came back to haunt him." Jim Estelle, called the "boots and tobacco" prison director by Wrotenbery, had stopped the budget director in the hall outside the governor's office and told him the prison system couldn't get around to using the money before the next biennium. "So, if y'all want to take that money, you're not really going to affect the construction of prisons," Estelle told him.

Wrotenbery recommended that the funds be axed. "In rational terms, it was a legitimate veto and didn't have any impact on prison building. But it was a politically naive move on my part, the governor and his staff," Wrotenbery said.[26] Two years later, Clements had to put inmates in tents to alleviate prison overcrowding and answer charges from Atty. Gen. Mark White, who had turned into a political adversary, about the prison construction veto.

Hobby quibbled with Clements' savings claims and said he had no constitutional authority to make some of the cuts, including his veto of a rider directing the Texas Department of Human Resources to build a $46 million state welfare office building — which Clements called a "welfare Taj Mahal." Hobby predicted there would be an attorney general's ruling. Indeed, in time, Attorney General White restored $90 million of the cuts, including some constitutionally dedicated college construction funds and funds for the welfare office building. Clements promised to see the difference through to adjudication in court. "This is not the first time the attorney general has had an opposition view to mine," he said.[27]

Clements and Mark White, in fact, conflicted from the beginning. White had hardly assumed office as attorney general when he began talking to reporters about running for governor. Clements said later that he and White clashed because of White's ambitions and "also because of his mental deficiencies. He was a lightweight."[28] But the two also had different views of White's role. The governor thought the attorney general should be the governor's lawyer; White viewed his job as the state's lawyer, even if it meant crossing the governor.

When the session was over, Clements had a high approval rating from the public. A poll taken by the Democratic consulting firm of Henson, Hopkins & Shipley found his voter approval was over 64 percent, compared to only 29 percent approval for the infamous "Killer Bees." A news release issued by the Austin firm said, "Gov. Clements' abrasive style has not endeared him to the Texas Legislature but it has won him overwhelming approval of Texas voters in the wake of the last legislative session." Clements' own poll by Lance Tarrance showed he had a 55 percent approval rating, well above the legislature, Lieutenant Governor Hobby, and President Carter.[29]

Clements didn't see his job as governor confined to dealing with the Texas legislature. He wanted to spread his influence to the state bureaucracy, and extend his axis northeast to Washington and southwest to Mexico City. He would never be called a do-nothing governor, nor noncontroversial. When he flew to Mexico to meet with the Mexican president, he was accused of upstaging President Carter and trying to create his own foreign policy. He persistently mispronounced the president's name as "Por-til-lio," prompting legislative aide Kaster eventually to write it out for him phonetically as "Por-TEE-o." He had jetted to Washington to meet with the Texas congressional delegation, peeving some members when he berated them over the lack of a national energy policy.

At the governor's first meeting with 400 department heads and top state officials, his plea to hold down state spending and implement a no-hire policy to achieve a reduction in workforce by 25,000 was met with stone-faced silence. "Do we have anyone in disagreement?" he asked. "If we have no disagreement, do we have any agreement?" More silence, "I would say we're not communicating very well. . . . I'll see you in your departments."[30]

Bureaucrats didn't take kindly to his stated intention of paring down the "parasitic bureaucracy" by "attriting" employees. Yet he was commended for beginning a new culture of fiscal responsibility, for having a top-notch staff, an open-door policy with legislators, high-quality appointments, and a new openness with the press.

The combative Capitol press corps posed no threat to Clements. When he went into office, he asked the reporters what kind of access they wanted. They said once-a-week news conferences, and he gladly complied. His press conferences became superb theater. He enjoyed the give-and-take with reporters and invariably supplied entertaining copy with his mixed metaphors and frank, earthy comments. As longtime *Dallas Morning News* bureau chief Richard Morehead recalled, Clements called reporters by their first names and often remembered the answer he had given weeks before to a similar question. He was a master at fielding hostile questions and, if he couldn't answer a question, he didn't mind saying, "I don't know." While his blunt manner failed to convert reporters into Clements admirers, the governor earned some respect for his willingness to make himself more available than his predecessors had. "Clements seemed to enjoy putting reporters down when he deemed they deserved it," Morehead wrote. He proved adept at one-upmanship in his news conferences and in media relations.[31]

"Intimidation was just his style," said reporter Sam Kinch, Jr., then of *The News*. "He likes to be in charge, and one way he expresses it is, he can browbeat people." Clements had a "superiority complex" which he couldn't hide, Kinch said. "I'm not sure he ever wanted to. He wanted everybody to know how he felt."[32]

On one occasion, a reporter confused a vacancy on the U.S. Supreme Court and Texas Supreme Court in a question to the governor. After explaining the difference to the embarrassment of the reporter, Clements sarcastically concluded, "Other than that, there's nothing wrong with your question."

Of the four previous governors — Briscoe, Smith, Connally, and Daniel — not one was as accessible or as routinely quotable as Clements. He had a way of framing his responses like nobody else could. Asked if he were dabbling in foreign affairs with his trip to Mexico City, the governor said, "I think this is a booby trap that has no booby in it." His comments were sprinkled with unusual colloquialisms and bon mots. To the suggestion that he was frustrated with the action of the legislature, Clements portrayed himself as a model of patience. "Your perception is that I was gonna come in and do wonders and eat rotten cucumbers, so to speak, immediately. You've got to realize I didn't get this gray in my hair shootin' marbles with the boys around the corner." On another occasion, he remarked, "I didn't come out of a jelly bean factory."[33]

Jon Ford, his press aide, thought Clements was treated well by the press the first term. "They picked up on his gaffes and tough language, but generally he was treated OK. If he had any difference with a reporter, he told him to his face and avoided contact in the future."[34] Clements drew extensive press coverage because he was "interested in things that had never really occurred in the Texas political establishment before," Ford said.

Clements vigorously pursued his management initiatives. He was convinced that by utilizing new techniques, state government could be leaner and operate better. Wrotenbery helped set up the governor's five-point Management Effectiveness Program. It was designed to restrict the growth of the bureaucracy, encourage agencies to follow management-by-objective (MBO) practices, initiate performance audits of agencies, and provide management training for midlevel managers and training sessions for board members. Clements had been enamored with the MBO management trend while in Washington.

The first task in cutting government employees was to find out how many there actually were. Clements was dismayed to discover nobody knew, and there was no system to find out. Reporter Kinch said he got a call one night from the governor, who was mad as hell. "Do you know that I can't find anybody in state government who can tell me how many people work for the state?" he asked. A few days later at a press conference, Clements declared, "We're going to get to the bottom of this."[35]

It took his office more than a year to get a grip on the number of people on the state payroll. Under the auspices of Comptroller Bullock's office, a system was set up whereby state agencies would use a formula to determine the number of "fulltime equivalent employees" (FTEs). Clements never got close to trimming 25,000 workers, but he did check the growth of government and laid the groundwork for future legislatures and governors to have a base line for the number of state employees. Hilary Doran, who eventually became Clements' chief of staff, considered it one of his major accomplishments in the first term.

"Bill Clements wanted to be a CEO, but in Texas that didn't fit the system," Wrotenbery said. Agency heads don't work for the governor, and there was little interaction between the governor and the agencies. So Clements set up the Management Effectiveness Council to meet periodically with him. It included the heads of the twelve largest state agencies, which accounted for nearly half of the state budget and 71 percent of the workforce excluding higher education. The council enabled the governor to sit, CEO-like, around a table and receive reports from the heads of departments operating the biggest budgets and payrolls. It was his way of forcing more accountability.

Clements' style was to give members of his staff a broad charge, then ask for periodic updates. He wasn't interested in day-to-day implementation of programs. He was interested in appointments and in the broad execution of power.[36]

The appointments process was one way Clements could put his stamp on the state bureaucracy. He sought qualified appointees, of either party. Of some 100 major appointments requiring Senate confirmation, only one was turned down during his first session. Clements wanted the appointed chairs and boards to go beyond policy-making and assume a more active role in the management of the agencies. Their job, he said, was not just to come to Austin and maintain the status quo. He wasn't going to micro-manage the agencies or dictate to board chairpersons, but he did want the chairs and boards to be more involved.

"I want it said years from now that the Texans of the 1980s were the Texans who stopped unreasonable growth in government, the Texans who reversed a trend; and that we were the Texans who started a new trend of efficiency and sound management and better service within state government," Clements told an assemblage of agency officials and members of boards and commissions.[37]

According to George Christian, Clements had "a lot of opportunities for errors and collosal messups, because he was doing things differently. But, he didn't have collosal messups. He had some disappointments. He wanted the chairs of the different departments and agencies to be responsible. I would imagine if Gov. Clements was disappointed in something, it would probably be that a governor can't really get a full handle on state government. There are built-in limitations and it's just too unwieldy."[38]

Wrotenbery felt that being governor may have been the "biggest thing in his [Clements'] life in terms of a titular sense, but in terms of challenge, it wasn't. Building SEDCO was a bigger challenge than being governor — not becoming, but being governor. Because, as governor, you can't do a lot."[39]

At the end of his first two years in office, however, Clements had succeeded in broadening the scope of the governor's office beyond what it had been under previous governors. This was due to his management initiatives and to his interest and expertise in two other areas: energy and Mexico.

Energy was a hot topic in Texas and the nation during Clements' first summer in office; the country was in the midst of a national gasoline shortage. President Carter's approach was conservation. He had asked Americans to reduce their thermostats, and had empowered governors to take emergency steps to control gasoline sales to avoid long service station lines.

Even in Texas, the nation's No. 1 energy-producing state, there wasn't enough gasoline. Clements blamed the shortage on President Carter's wrong-headed energy policy. To deal with the shortages in June 1979, the governor and his energy adviser, Ed Vetter, instituted an odd-even day rationing system pegged to the last digit of a car license for some areas of the state. The governor also proclaimed a "no-coat, no-tie" summer for government offices, encouraging businesses to conserve fuel with higher thermostat settings and a similar dress-down policy.[40]

He went to Washington in February and June, 1979, to meet with members of the Texas congressional delegation. The governor believed Texans in Congress weren't pushing energy legislation as hard as they could and told them so. Of the state's then twenty-four-member delegation, twenty were Democrats. Some resented his message and complained that he had lectured them. One accused him of running for vice-president. There was some belief at the time that Clements' high profile was related, in part, to national ambitions.

But Clements figured he knew his way around Washington, and it made sense for the governor of Texas to try to influence national energy policy because Texas produced one-third of the nation's total energy supply. He believed he was elected to articulate the state's position. The Texas Railroad Commission was responsible for regulating oil and gas production in the state, but there was no arm of government dealing with oil and gas policy. Clements set one up, the Texas Energy and Natural Resources Advisory Council (TENRAC) headed by Ed Vetter. Three existing state energy groups were consolidated by legislation into TENRAC.

Vetter had a mechanical engineering degree from the Massachusetts Institute of Technology and had worked in the California oilfields before becoming president and chairman of the Geophysical Services subsidiary of Texas Instruments. Vetter, with Walt Rostow from the University of Texas, drafted the governor's national energy policy, which Clements then took to meetings of the National Governors Association, Southern Governors Association, and Republican Governors Association. "Clements considered those meetings serious, not just social events, and used them to try to influence national policies," Vetter said.[41]

Clements' plan, presented to the National Governors Association in Washington, was designed to reduce gasoline shortages and the country's reliance on oil from the Middle East. It called for policies that stimulated an all-out production effort in the petroleum industry, the unfettering of the coal industry, removal of barriers to the development of alternative energy sources, freeing up federal lands for energy development, using windfall profits only for development of energy, and seeking petroleum and natural gas from Mexico.[42]

As Vetter pointed out, contrary to popular notion, there were not a lot of J. R. Ewings in Texas at the time — despite the portrayal of J. R. and other Texas oil tycoons on the TV show *Dallas*. Producing oil and gas was tough, risky work, and Clements believed there should be some recognition of that in the national policy.

"Carter's policy was to hunker down and ration what we had," Vetter explained. Clements, in contrast, believed there could be abundant oil and gas. "He argued for an oil import fee, but it was construed as fat-cat Texans trying to feather their nests," Vetter said. "We were trying to get some stability in prices because the ability to drill depended on what banks thought oil would sell for. We also argued that putting Prudhoe Bay in Alaska off-limits didn't make sense. It could be environmentally managed properly and produce elephant oilfields. But it was generally assumed that his was a self-serving attitude toward energy."

As for alternative energy sources, Clements believed it was fine to pursue solar and synthetic fuels but these could only supply a small percentage of the nation's needs, Vetter said, adding, "His attitude was 'don't kid ourselves' that there is some magic bullet that will take the place of oil and gas."[43]

Clements met with some opposition, particularly from Gov. Bruce Babbitt of Arizona, when he took his energy policy before the other governors. "They didn't want some freshman Republican governor coming up with something as momentous as that," his press aide, Jon Ford, said. "The governors finally adopted some form of it. Did it have any permanent effect? I don't know. We still went on to have the Gulf War."[44]

Clements' energy connections produced the biggest controversy of his first year in office. The flap was caused by the Ixtoc I spill that began with a blowout in the Bay of Campeche on June 3, 1979, and eventually dumped 3.3 million barrels of oil into the Gulf of Mexico. Ixtoc I became the world's largest known spill, threatening Texas beaches and Clements' reputation at home as well as in Mexico. Besides the environmental peril to the state, which the governor had to deal with through his Disaster Emergency Services office, the situation for Clements was complicated because the rig involved was owned by SEDCO, although SEDCO had nothing to do with its operation. The rig was under a bareboat charter to a Mexican drilling company which was operating it for PEMEX, Mexico's national petroleum company.

By early August 1979, bad publicity over the likelihood that oil would hit Texas beaches from the Ixtoc spill was scaring away tourists. Clements toured Texas beaches and downplayed reports of oil slicks reaching the Texas coast. At the time, no environmental damage had been found. Clements was quoted in stories across the state saying, "So far, it's not serious. It's a big to-do about nothing. So far, we're really not hurt."[45]

Two weeks after Clements' statement, oil slicks appeared on 90 percent of the beaches from Port Aransas south to the Rio Grande. A Padre Island condominium desk clerk reported that the tar on the beach was so thick it looked like "a one-lane road." Tourist occupancy on the Texas coast was down 50 percent at the peak of the season, and business losses were estimated in the millions of dollars.[46] The ocean currents eventually reversed, taking the oil away from the Texas coast. But the damage continued for Clements.

Ixtoc I provided the opportunity for Atty. Gen. Mark White to get some attention from the media and launch his first big confrontation with the governor. White called a press conference where he criticized Clements for his "big to-do about nothing" statement. He also threatened to sue Mexico for property damage to Texans and to sue SEDCO, if the company run by the governor's son, Gill Clements, was found liable. Clements said it would be "demented" to sue Mexico and accused White of "cheap" politics.[47]

The oil spill quickly became a "big to-do." The governor's office was flooded with negative letters saying his "to-do about nothing" comments were designed to downplay the incident because of his ties to the oil industry and the SEDCO rig. Clements had a hard time convincing people that no slicks had hit Texas beaches when he made the comment, and he was trying to shield the Texas tourism industry. In a *Brownsville Herald* story, the mayor of South Padre Island took the blame for the statement. Mayor Glenn McGehee said he had suggested that the governor "downplay the publicity going out of here" so that tourism could be maintained at least until the beaches had real oil problems. "I feel the governor did respond to our request and I felt that if anyone was at fault, I'm afraid I was the one that initiated that fault."[48]

The rest of the media took little notice of the mayor's mea culpa, and Clements continued to be peppered by questions from the press. He repeatedly explained that the Mexican contractor had full operational and management control of the rig leased from SEDCO, reminding reporters "for the umpteenth time" that he had nothing to do with SEDCO while he was in office. When questioned on a national news show if his SEDCO ties had anything to do with his "staying cool" on the oil spill issue, Clements responded, "That's an improper question. You are impugning my integrity."[49]

Ultimately, Clements assumed the position that "if we remain cool and stop this loud talk of suing our neighboring country, Mexico will be quite willing at the proper time to negotiate a settlement of the damages issues. A possible lawsuit to recover damages should be a last resort and is always an option. If SEDCO is judged guilty in a court of law of negligence, SEDCO should be held accountable."

In November of 1979, Ixtoc I was continuing to spew oil. White sent a telegram to sixteen Texas oil companies and the Clean Gulf Association. He invited them to send representatives to a meeting to discuss what could be done to "bring about more effective action in response to any future oil spills." White said he was "unimpressed with the ability of the existing governmental and commercial structures" to respond to oil spill emergencies.[50]

Clements was livid. He responded with a November 20, 1979, letter, accusing White of impugning the oil spill recovery actions taken by the governor's office, the U.S. Coast Guard, National Oceanic and Atmospheric Administration, Environmental Protection Agency, and six different state departments or agencies. "As you are no doubt aware, your entry into this area is without constitutional or statutory authority," Clements wrote White. "It serves only to confuse and mislead the public and those agencies and officials responsible for crisis management of this nature. Further, your refusal of my personal request to allow my general counsel, David Dean, and Frank Cox, the coordinator of Disaster Emergency Services, to attend the meeting clearly calls into question your motives and intentions in this matter." Clements urged White to "limit your activities to those matters within the purview of your office" and called on White "once again to quit politicizing the oil spill issue."[51]

On March 23, 1980, after it had burned 295 days, Ixtoc I finally was capped by Red Adair's oilwell firefighting company. PEMEX blamed SEDCO and SEDCO blamed PEMEX for the blowout and subsequent oil spill. Raymond Henry, one of the firefighters, said in Adair's biography that "it wasn't SEDCO's fault. It was just their rig that drilled the hole."

The incident, however, made Clements appear insensitive to environmental issues and left the company he founded mired in complicated legal battles. After company officials conferred with engineers and insurance brokers, the rig, insured for $20 million, was declared a total loss and was submerged in July 1979 — an occurrence of particular sentiment inside the company because the SEDCO 135 was SEDCO's first semi-submersible. That SEDCO had scuttled the ruined rig to the bottom of the Gulf led White to charge that the "evidence" for any assessment of negligence had been destroyed. White did sue SEDCO and Permago on behalf of the state of Texas, and the federal government also filed a multi-million-dollar lawsuit against SEDCO. The claims against SEDCO exceeded $371 million and were finally settled by the company in 1983 for $4.1 million.[52]

The oil spill comment wasn't the only Clements remark that created problems for him in his first year in office. He startled a Texas A&M audience when he jokingly said that deep-water diving could be a form of birth control. While being briefed on a sea grant program by an A&M researcher, he was told that dives could result in harm to an unborn child. "They're always looking for birth control. We might say, 'go deep-water diving and exercise birth control,'" Clements said. The remark caused nervous laughter among the gathering of A&M officials and the governor's staff, according to one report. The governor was subsequently criticized by the pro-life movement, and took heat from the press for yet another "insensitive" remark.[53]

Clements' differences with Lt. Gov. Bill Hobby also escalated. In the fall of 1979, in the midst of the Ixtoc hubbub, Clements drew the ire of Hobby by saying higher education had greater waste than any other state agency. He appointed an eight-member committee to look into financial controls for state colleges and universities, headed by former State Sen. Max Sherman of Amarillo, president of West Texas State University. Hobby called Clements ill-informed. "There exists in the Legislature as well a virulent strain of anti-intellectualism that does not reflect well on this state. But it should be the duty of a governor to counteract that sort of thing rather than give it redneck reinforcement," Hobby scolded.[54]

Clements spent considerable time and effort during his first two years in office on his program to improve relations with Mexico. The attention he paid to Mexico seemed almost ironic after his peevish campaign statement, made after a reporter's repeated questions about concerns to Mexican-Americans, that he wasn't running for governor of Mexico. He was the only governor since

John Connally who appeared cognizant of Texas' neighbors to the south. Connally had paid courtesy calls to border state governors in 1964.[55] Clements visited the governors of the border states of Tamaulipas, Nuevo León, Coahuila, and Chihuahua in their capitals in 1979 and invited them to Austin the following year.

Early in his administration, Clements created a division of Mexico and Latin American relations, to strengthen relations with Mexico, especially the Mexican states that bordered Texas, and to coordinate the governor's relationships with the Hispanic community of Texas.

Clements named Richard Rubottom, a retired diplomat with the U.S. Foreign Service who was a vice-president and faculty member at SMU, as his foreign relations adviser. Rubottom, former president of the University of the Americas in Mexico, helped Clements develop a position on immigration, which was presented to the National Governors Association and at meetings of the U.S.-Mexico border governors.

Clements also established the Governor's Office of Regional Development to improve economic conditions and industrial development on the Texas-Mexico border. GORD, as the office commonly was called, provided technical assistance and more efficient delivery of state programs to the forty-eight counties of South Texas and border region. The governor's Mexico and Latin American Relations Division, with assistance from GORD, arranged dignitary visits and border conferences, and developed issues and legislation on such matters as economic development, illegal aliens, immigration, and international bridges.

Clements had long been interested in international affairs, especially as they related to energy and economic issues. He felt his visits with Mexican officials were justified by the proximity of Texas to Mexico and the mutuality of their problems. However, Texan Robert Krueger, who was appointed ambassador at large to Mexico, urged Clements to leave diplomacy between the U.S. and Mexico in the hands of the federal government. Clements refused to coordinate his activities with Krueger, saying Krueger's responsibilities were ill-defined by President Carter. Instead, the governor made periodic reports to the State Department's assistant secretary for inter-American affairs, the post previously held by his foreign affairs adviser, Richard Rubottom.

Visits with Mexican governors from the border states in the

winter and spring of 1980 featured discussions on such issues as undocumented workers and border drug traffic and resulted in informal agreements on a variety of exchange programs. The informal agreements addressed exchanges of agriculture, livestock products, and college students and teachers; improving international bridge connections; and increasing tourism and commerce. Under one program, Department of Public Safety personnel trained Mexican border authorities in identifying and returning stolen vehicles to Texas.[56]

In March 1980, Clements went to Monterrey, where he had his second private conversations with President Lopez Portillo. Afterward, Clements claimed that the Mexican president felt rebuffed in his efforts to be friends with the United States. Clements also elevated aide G. G. Garcia to the newly created post of special assistant for Mexico and Latin American relations, leading critics to ask: When was the last time a Texas governor had his own ambassador to Mexico?[57]

But Clements felt that Mexican-American relations had deteriorated under President Carter, and that he could bring about improved relations, if not between the U.S. and Mexico, at least between Texas and Mexico. In Mexico, Clements was regarded as a distinguished visitor who flattered Mexico by his willingness to pay attention to Mexican concerns and problems.[58]

Some of Clements' philosophy regarding Mexico came out in a press conference in early 1980. "I think it's time that we lower our voices and that we consider our relationship with Mexico on truly a good neighbor basis and properly respect their position, and talk with them on a peer level basis, as equals .... I guess, in the vernacular, what I am saying is, that I think we need to have a simpatico attitude toward Mexico as opposed to one of superiority and of looking down our nose and being super-critical," he said.[59]

Clements joined with the governors of New Mexico, Arizona, and California in meeting with Mexico's border state governors at the first international border governors conference in June 1980, in Ciudad Juarez, Chihuahua. Some 800 people attended, including 200 news media representatives from both sides of the border. Clements presented papers in three areas: tourism, undocumented workers, and energy and commerce. His proposed "guest worker" plan drew some opposition from Arizona Gov. Bruce Babbitt, who feared a return to the old *bracero* program. According to one news report, the meeting set the stage for a lasting relationship that could help revitalize sagging ties between the two nations. Even Babbitt applauded Clements "for his initiative, his dynamism, his drive and his sincerity in promoting international good will."[60]

Clements' work with Mexico did not meet with overwhelming approval. Mrs. B. F. Moore of Montgomery, Texas, sent him a letter in the spring of 1980, attached to a clipping of an article in which Clements had been critical of the Carter administration's handling of several Mexican matters. "You have no right going to Mexico and acting like you are a president," she wrote. "If you are so in love with Mexico, why don't you move there. I am sure we could elect a governor for Texas that would stay in Texas and be for Texans. You would do good if you supported President Carter also. His job is hard enough without governors like you."[61]

Clements wasn't about to move to Mexico or support President Carter. To the contrary, from the spring of 1980 through November, much of Clements' efforts were devoted to presidential politics. He was ready to follow through on his campaign promise to get rid of Jimmy Carter. Clements knew Texas could be instrumental; a Democrat had never been elected president without carrying the Lone Star State.

In early 1979, Clements asked Chet Upham, an independent oil operator from Mineral Wells who had served on the State Republican Executive Committee, to succeed Ray Barnhart, after Barnhart accepted an appointment to the Texas Highway Commission. Clements wanted a state Republican leader who would be neutral in the presidential primary race, who would help organize the small towns and rural areas for the eventual nominee. He told Upham to organize Texas. "If we carry Texas, the United States will elect a Republican," he said. Clements promised Upham a free rein. "I'm Tom Landry, and you're Roger Staubach," Clements said, relating their situation to the coach and quarterback of the Dallas Cowboys. "You call the plays. But if I call one, I want it used." Clements, Upham said, "never sent a play in."[62]

Clements saw the contest between Reagan, Connally, and Bush as an opportunity to attract many more Texans to the Republican primary. The governor himself was being courted by all three Republican presidential candidates. He decided to stay neutral, however — much to the chagrin of his old friend Bush. By the time of the Texas primary, native-son Connally had dropped out, and it was a fight between Reagan and Bush. A Clements endorsement clearly would have been helpful to Bush, but Clements could see the mounting enthusiasm for Reagan. The day after the Texas primary, he endorsed Reagan, the apparent nominee. The ex-movie actor had won a majority of both the popular vote and the delegates in the Texas primary. To Upham's credit, the Texas GOP also had held primary elections in 245 of 254 counties — the most it had ever organized.

Clements now was anxious to jump into the middle of the presidential campaign but, in keeping with his character, if he was to be involved, he wanted to be in charge. Bill Casey, Reagan's national campaign chairman, came to Texas for a meeting and an agreement was struck. Clements had never really been accepted by the die-hard Reagan leaders in Texas, but they agreed he would be chairman of the Reagan for President campaign in Texas, with Ernest Angelo, the Midland mayor and longtime Reaganite, serving as deputy chairman and campaign manager. Angelo had led the Reagan primary effort.

Upham, meanwhile, had stumbled across a little-known provision of the post-Watergate 1976 amendments to the Federal Election Act. It allowed state party operations to set up separate committees to raise money for volunteer activities in presidential elections. The funds were not subject to federal campaign limits. This funding of local party activities would later be known as "soft money" and would become a real bonanza in presidential elections. But Texas Republicans, in 1980, were apparently the first to recognize the extent to which the law could be used.

The 1980 Texas Victory Committee was set up, with Clements people at the top. Karl Rove, who had been working for the Governor Clements Committee, became executive director. Peter O'Donnell, at Clements' insistence, was named finance chairman.

One of Upham's biggest arguments with Clements occurred as the organization was being set up, after the primary. Clements was "hard-headed," according to Upham, and wouldn't agree to all of the people Angelo wanted to name to the committee. "He wasn't going to have the old Reagan group steamroller the process; he wanted balance," Upham said. Clements placed great importance on getting the right people in the right jobs in an organization. During one of the Clements-Angelo organizational meetings, Upham was concerned about bumper stickers, which he thought were extremely important in a campaign. He kept bringing up the subject. "Bubbas," he said, "love bumper stickers." Clements, Upham said, finally turned to him and groused, "I don't give a (blankety-blank) about your goddamn bumper stickers. We've got to get this organization worked out. Just go over there and sit down and shut up about your bumper stickers."

Upham started to resign over the incident but said he loved Clements too much to quit. Months later, Clements asked him, "Why don't we have any bumper stickers?"

"Bill was a tremendous manager, and he was a people person," Upham said. "He'd either get along with the people or he wouldn't, but he liked to have people who were completely organized. Generally, people who are in politics are the front people, the stars; they're not used to putting together a staff."[63] But one of Clements' favorite tasks, as he had shown in Washington and Austin, was putting together an organization.

Clements was part of Reagan's "kitchen cabinet" at the Republican National Convention in Detroit. He was one who counseled against the fleeting notion of putting former President Ford on the ticket as running mate — an idea rejected when "co-presidency" implications surfaced. In meetings of a handful of advisers with Reagan, Clements recommended George Bush as vice-president.

By election day, Texas Republicans had mustered 42,000 volunteers, the largest number of volunteers to participate in any state, and had raised more than $3 million. Clements, Rove said, devoted an enormous amount of energy toward changing Texas politics through the presidential race. There was a massive fundraising dinner in Houston, the Lone Star Tribute, which raised more than $2 million. "We raised and spent more than all the other victory committees in the country combined. We had volunteer phone banks, millions of pieces of mail, and a victory roundup tour with people traveling all over the state to rallies. Clements absolutely turned the afterburners on," Rove said.

Clements also systematically campaigned for Republicans to serve in the Texas legislature. He targeted districts where he thought he could have an impact, and in some of them, Republicans were elected for the first time. Democrats also had begun switching parties; in 1979, one state senator and two state representatives from Dallas County switched from Democrat to Republican. "He deliberately went out in 1980 and did what he could to create political change in Texas," Rove said.[64]

But Clements also had developed a reputation for making remarks which Texas Democrats labeled as "embarrassing" to Texans. Garry Mauro, executive director of the Texas Democratic Party, had sized up the governor. "Bill Clements' biggest asset is also his biggest weakness — he speaks his mind. And he's very aggressive and he says things that a lot of people want to hear, but unfortunately for him, he tends to put his foot in his mouth about two-thirds of the time."[65]

Texas Democrats thought Clements exceeded the bounds of propriety in the presidential election. Clements ridiculed Carter at every opportunity. Carter was a professed "born-again Christian," and when the governor was asked by the media if he had been "born again," he replied, "I've been born once — isn't that enough?"

A remark Clements made less than two weeks before the November 4, 1980, election was the one that really stirred up Democrats. In an editorial board interview with the *Texarkana Gazette*, Clements criticized a claim that President Carter had made that the United States was stronger militarily than it was when he took office. Clements said the president was "lying." But he didn't stop there, according to the October 24, 1980, edition of the *Gazette*. "I just can't say it any stronger. Well, I could say he is a goddamn liar," Clements said.

Clements' advocacy of the military was grounded in his days in the Pentagon. It was perplexing to him that President Carter, who had attended the U.S. Naval Academy and was trained as a nuclear physicist, was not a bigger champion of the military. He found the president, at worst, anti-military or, at best, a-military.

Clements also criticized Carter in the Texarkana interview for not notifying him when the Shah of Iran had been brought to a San Antonio Air Force base to recuperate from cancer surgery. "But in all fairness, I must say this: Mr. Carter understands full well that I am after his ass," Clements said.

Attorney General White was the first to cry foul. In a quickly called press conference, White said Clements had tarred the presidency and tarnished the image of the Texas governorship. "Texans . . . do not like to see the office of the presidency defiled by profanity," White said. Clements confirmed he used the foul language but contended it was a confidential remark, part of a privileged discussion with the editorial board. He refused to apologize.[66]

In various newspaper stories, Clements was criticized by Carter campaign chief Robert Strauss and National Democratic Chairman John White — both Texans — and by Vice-President Walter Mondale, who was campaigning in Austin. But White led in the scolding. He called Clements' behavior the worst by a politician since Republican Congressman Bruce Alger of Dallas "led people in a yelling, spitting and shoving match against U.S. Sen. and Mrs. Johnson in the 60s." To Harris County Republican Co-chairman Hal DeMoss, it seemed the "opening comment of the Mark White campaign for the governorship."[67]

Once again, Governor Clements' mailbag was full. In his response to letter-writers, he contended that President Carter's policies seriously debilitated many of the defense programs which he, as deputy secretary of defense, had worked hard to develop. In one form-letter response, Clements did not apologize for calling Carter a liar but did say he erred "in taking the Lord's name in vain." In some letters, he reassured Texans that he was a Christian. To those letter-writers who supported his remark, he responded: "Your kind words of support are appreciated. While I have received some criticism for these remarks, I have no intention of retracting them. Candor has been my habit from an early age, and it has generally served me well."[68]

The Reagan-Bush ticket won convincingly in Texas with 55 percent of the vote, and carried the election.[69] During the campaign, Clements cemented his own relations with Reagan. He offered Reagan the use of Wexford, his comfortable home in Virginia, as the Californian's East Coast residence during the campaign. After the election, President-elect Reagan asked Clements to be part of his transition team by serving on the sixteen-member Interim Foreign Policy Advisory Board, chaired by William J. Casey, and by preparing a position paper on the Department of Defense.

The Texas impact on the election did not go unnoticed. Texans were invited to Washington for the Reagan-Bush inauguration and they went in droves, creating a notable presence at inaugural activities. The 1980 presidential election had been an awesome triumph for Texas Republicans. Gov. Bill Clements had helped elect a president he believed would be receptive to him as Texas governor on such issues as immigration and energy — one to whom he would have access. And, with that election, the face of Texas politics began to radically change.

Chapter 13

First Term

"What do you want? A bunch of nincompoops and hardly-ables?"

GOVERNOR CLEMENTS FACED HIS second legislative session in January 1981 better prepared and more willing to work with lawmakers. But Clements also was riding high from the successful Reagan election; he felt invincible. The Reagan win had helped to sweep more Republicans into legislative office. The GOP now had forty-two — seven senators and thirty-five members of the House.[1] Clements returned to Austin ready to continue initiatives begun in his first two years, but he also went armed with a specific and well-developed legislative program.

As stubborn as he often was purported to be, Clements proved a willing pupil in the gubernatorial school of hard knocks. He learned from his mistakes. In his first State of the State address, Clements had seen no need to justify his own budget cuts and had challenged lawmakers to justify increases in state spending. In his second State of the State address, he recognized the importance of the legislature and cited veteran members for their service. "He did learn, during the first term, what old politicians knew — you can't do much with force with the Legislature, you have to sweet talk 'em," press aide Jon Ford said.[2]

The governor had laid the groundwork for the 67th legislative session (the session of 1981) by appointing three citizens' task forces. High-profile statewide committees were set up to look at problems in education, drugs, and crime. In these areas, Clements would be highly successful with his legislative program. The most contentious issues of the second session would be legal problems related to state prisons and redistricting — a political matter.

To help develop his legislative program, Clements had persuaded two longtime friends, men widely respected, to head task forces which began work in 1979. Dr. Willis M. Tate, president emeritus of Southern Methodist University, agreed to serve as chairman of the Governor's Advisory Committee on Education. H. Ross Perot, founder of Electronic Data Systems in Dallas, agreed to head up the Texans' War on Drugs. The Anti-Crime Task Force was led by the governor's counsel, David Dean, whom Clements had designated to oversee his criminal justice activities.

Dr. Tate's education advisory committee consisted of twenty education professionals and laypeople. Mrs. Clements was one of the working members. They conducted seven public hearings and had eleven ad hoc committees study issues ranging from student motivation and discipline to curriculum. On June 24, 1980, Dr. Tate's committee issued its report, outlining recommended actions by the legislature and the State Board of Education. Some 8,000 copies of the report were distributed to legislators, educational groups, school administrators, and teachers. The governor's office provided staff support for the committee, and legislative aides turned recommendations into bills with sponsors for the 1981 legislative session.

Out of the Tate task force came the guts of the governor's "Back to Basics" education program that he had promised in the 1978 campaign. Key elements addressed curriculum and student behavior. The task force reported that it had found considerable social engineering in the curriculum. Courses had been added to address "perceived social ills" and myriad special interests. Clements' proposals called for a state basic curriculum and an end to social promotion. Education bills, if enacted, also would enable school districts to establish summer remedial programs and guidance centers to handle discipline problems.[3]

Dr. Tate's task force convinced the governor that teachers needed drastically higher pay. Proposed legislation called for a 22 percent increase, along with a new master teacher's program to reward high-performing teachers with additional pay. It also called for competency testing before teacher certification.

The Texans' War on Drugs, headed by Perot, was equally crucial to Clements' legislative program in 1981. A main target of the eleven-member task force was the torrent of illegal drugs that flowed across the state's borders. At the time of Clements' War on Drugs, two of every three kilos of heroin were coming into the United States through Texas.[4] Perot drew attention to Texas' drug trafficking problem, stimulating grassroots support to pass legislation that was an outgrowth of his committee, and he personally lobbied the legislature.

Clements' top priority was authorization of the use of electronic surveillance in drug cases with a bill that tracked federal law. Other parts of the anti-crime package included: use of oral confessions in criminal cases, stronger laws on sale or distribution of pornographic material to minors, use of shock probation, a statewide system of halfway houses for parolees, and restitution for victims of crime. Legislation also permitted jurors to be informed of parole eligibility during sentence consideration.

Other areas of the governor's legislative program included creation of a State Water Trust Fund and a Department of Commerce that would combine the operations of state agencies involved in economic development, promotion, trade, and commerce. He also went back to the trough on initiative and referendum.[5]

Although upbeat about his legislative program, Clements was concerned about problems on the horizon. In his State of the State address on January 22, 1981, he noted that Texas had undergone two decades of population growth and had experienced its largest population increase ever during the 1970s. According to the 1980 census, Texas had moved up from the sixth most populous state in 1960 to third in population. With three million new residents, its population now was 14 million, with projections of an increase to 21 or 22 million people by the year 2000. Fortunately, the economic output of the state remained strong, the governor noted. If Texas were an independent nation, Clements told legislators, it would have the thirteenth largest economy in the world. No new state taxes had been imposed since 1971, and the state could boast that it had no individual or corporate income tax. Yet, state spending and the number of state employees had been growing faster than the population. Oil and gas production, which accounted for 20 percent of all taxes collected, had declined 21 percent in the 1970s. And now the country was mired in inflation.

"The rapid growth in state government, booming population

growth and eventual decline in our most important tax base, accompanied by a sick national economy with double-digit inflation and double-digit interest rates, demands a better effort of all of us," the governor told lawmakers.[6] He again called for $1 billion in tax relief.

Bruce Gibson, a conservative, business-oriented Democrat, called the second session of Clements' first term "the best session he had in eight years." He had good cooperation with Hobby and Clayton. But, Gibson noted, "It was the beginning of the end of the great period of growth for Texas."[7]

Clements was working closely with Hobby and Clayton to make sure the train stayed on track in the session. Besides meeting frequently with the leaders of both houses, Clements had senators and House members into his office for drinks after 5:00 P.M. and also had frequent luncheons for key legislators. According to legislative aide Kaster, he spent time cultivating the legislators. Hilary Doran, one of his legislative aides, was a beer distributor. On Friday evenings, Doran frequently invited key legislators to "Club Doran," his basement office, for refreshments and schmoozing. Clements didn't expect every legislator to fall in line with him on every issue. "But when somebody would say they'd support him and then vote against him, if they'd tell him one thing and do something else, that would set him on fire," Kaster said.[8]

By his second legislative session, Clements was regarded by fellow Republican Bob McFarland, a legislative leader from Arlington, as being "as good a legislative tactician as I've seen in this state, on a par with [former Governor] Connally." McFarland said Clements was "a very quick study. You can present him with a fairly complex governmental issue and he'll grasp the significance, the pros and cons, almost immediately."[9]

One of the state's mushrooming problems during the 1981 legislative session was created by the *Ruiz v. Estelle* prison suit that had been filed in 1972 by an inmate claiming unconstitutional treatment in Texas prisons. In 1980, U.S. District Judge William Wayne Justice handed down a ruling declaring parts of the Texas prison system unconstitutional. The state had been ordered to relieve overcrowding. During the 1981 session, the governor asked the legislature for $35 million in emergency funds to construct three new prison dormitories.

The request for those funds forced Clements and Prison Director Jim Estelle to justify the governor's veto of $30 million for prisons two years before. The veto had become a major source of contention between Clements and Atty. Gen. Mark White, who said Clements' action had compounded the prison problem. Clements called White's criticism "politically motivated" and "inappropriate." In a hot letter to the attorney general, he explained that Prison Director Estelle had assured him that the $30 million in funds could not have been obligated during the biennium for which they were appropriated and that the funds were for projects that would not impact bed space. "You fail to mention or apparently to understand," Clements wrote, "that I have okayed spending $60.9 million for new construction at the TDC [Texas Department of Corrections] during the 1980-81 biennium which will bring on line an increase of 3,500 in bed space."[10]

Estelle issued a statement early in the 1981 legislative session regarding "confusion" over whether the funds deleted in 1979 caused a prison construction slow-down. Estelle said the veto action "had no impact on prison overcrowding." The money vetoed was for specific construction projects, he said, and could not have been diverted to create more bed space. "To suggest the monies vetoed could have been used for the $35 million project proposed now is a confusion of fact and issues," Estelle said.[11]

The legislature authorized the $35 million in emergency funds for the prison dorms.

The state continued to fight the Ruiz suit, even as Clements sought creative solutions — including the use of army tents — to alleviate the conditions that required inmates to sleep on prison floors. In May 1981, in an effort to get a stay order in the Ruiz lawsuit, Clements announced a conditional parole program. It was designed to get 1,500 of the 3,000 inmates off the prison floors and into work furlough programs through halfway houses or parole. Pending completion of additional permanent housing, Clements also was working through Gen. Willie Scott, adjutant general of the Texas National Guard, to get temporary tent encampments for the other 1,500 prisoners.[12]

Reporters appeared skeptical of the tent idea in a press conference on May 7, 1981. "Are these five-man tents, two-man pup tents . . . ?" one reporter asked. Clements responded, "They are the usual army tent. Have you ever been in an Army tent? Well, you ought to try it sometime." He went on to describe the tents, which would have board floors and cots like those used at Fort Hood by the National Guard. "If they are good enough for our National Guard, I see no reason why they are not good enough for the inmates in our prison," he said.[13]

Meanwhile, Clements was urging Attorney General White to grant the Department of Corrections' request for outside counsel so the state, according to Clements, could muster the "maximum legal talent" in appealing Judge Justice's court order. White, however, had his own political agenda and was not of a mind to work with the governor. The two would continue to have public tiffs for the next year over the prison lawsuit and the other most contentious issue, redistricting.

In the first session after a census, the legislature is required to draw new legislative and congressional districts to reflect population changes. Democrats traditionally tried to protect their members in redistricting, guaranteeing safe districts for Democratic incumbents and diluting Republican strength by packing Republicans into as few districts as possible. In 1981, Republicans were committed to obtaining districts which more clearly reflected their strength in the state. Black Democrats also sought the creation of predominantly minority districts, as required under the Voting Rights Act, that would reflect their strength as a voting bloc. This set up an odd coalition of Republicans and black Democrats, who were trying to change the status quo. More Republican and/or minority districts meant fewer districts for white Democrats. Democratic legislators were walking a fine line in their efforts to appease minority interests and protect incumbents, and could do it only by shortchanging Republicans. Clements brought Karl Rove into his office after the Reagan campaign specifically to handle redistricting.

Clements vetoed the State Senate districting plan because, he said, the two minority districts created didn't have large enough minority populations to insure the election of black senators. At the time, there were none. Clements also thought the plan divided and fragmented communities, combining rural and urban voters so as to destroy communities of interest. He also believed it failed to take into account population trends in the high-growth suburban areas. Clements said the plan treated the 2.5 million residents of the Dallas-area Metroplex badly, dividing them into six senatorial districts.[14]

His veto meant that the Legislative Redistricting Board (LRB),

Bill and Rita Clements followed Dolph and Janey Briscoe as Texas' first couple.

Bill and Rita Clements hit the campaign trail in Lubbock in 1978.

The first Republican governor of Texas in 106 years addresses a joint session of the Texas Legislature in January 1979, with Lt. Gov. Bill Hobby at far left and Speaker Bill Clayton at far right. (AP Wirephoto)

Gov. Clements inspects Texas beaches during the Ixtoc I oil spill scare of 1979.

Comptroller Bob Bullock, Lt. Gov. Bill Hobby, Gov. Clements and Speaker Bill Clayton meet on the porch of the Governor's Mansion in August 1982 to announce the need for a special session. (AP Wirephoto)

Clements discusses using tents to alleviate prison overcrowding in 1981. His weekly news conferences with the Austin press corps were lively but often contentious. (AP Wirephoto)

Gov. Clements, President Reagan and former President Ford enjoy a joke at a political fundraiser in Texas on June 16, 1982.

California Gov. Jerry Brown and New Mexico Gov. Bruce King join Texas Gov. Clements at a conference with governors of Mexican border states during Clements' first administration.

Bill and Rita Clements accept defeat to Mark White on election night, 1982.

The governor is surrounded by House members wearing plaid jackets in honor of his 72nd birthday. Speaker Gib Lewis is at left. (AP Wirephoto)

Supreme Court Justice John Hill, a former political opponent, swears in Gov. Clements, with Rita, in January 1987.

Gov. Clements is welcomed back into office in 1987 during his second inaugural parade. (Dallas Morning News photo)

Gov. and Mrs. Clements are pictured in front of a portrait of Clements' Texian hero, Sam Houston, in the restored Governor's Mansion in Clements' second term.

The annual Easter Egg Hunt on the grounds of the Governor's Mansion features clowns and the Easter bunny with Texas' First Couple in 1987.

During Clements' second term, his grandchildren George Seay, Jr., Bill Clements III and Cathy Clements attended the University of Texas. They are seen here in front of the Governor's Mansion in 1987.

Bill and Rita Clements host their good friends Peter and Edith O'Donnell at their "Rancho Simpatico" near Taos, New Mexico.

Former Texas first ladies join Rita Clements on the grounds of the mansion during Gov. Clements' second term. From left, they are Mrs. Price (Jean) Daniel, Mrs. Preston (Ima) Smith, Mrs. Dolph (Janey) Briscoe, Mrs. Clements, and Mrs. John (Nellie) Connally.

First Lady Barbara Bush greets former Gov. and Mrs. Clements in the White House in May 1991.

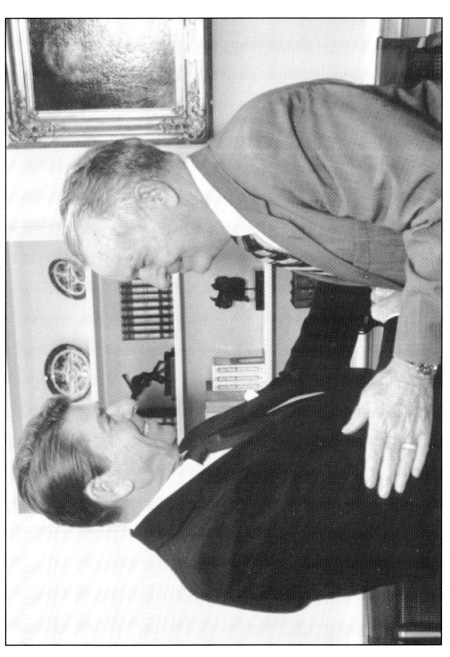

During his first term, Gov. Clements enjoyed a warm relationship with President Reagan, making occasional visits to the White House.

To Bill Clements
With best wishes, from a friend et admirer

G. Bush

Clements enjoys a vist with his old drilling contractor friend George Bush in the White House.

To Bill Clements with best wishes — Great shot!

Gov. Clements joins George Bush on the presidential campaign trail in 1988.

Six Texas governors attend ceremonies dedicating the Capitol after its restoration in April 1995. From left, they are George Bush, Mark White, Dolph Briscoe, Preston Smith, Ann Richards and Bill Clements.

In 1992, former Gov. and Mrs. Clements join President Bush, Mexican President Salinas and Canadian Prime Minister Brian Mulroney at a signing of the NAFTA treaty ceremony in San Antonio.

Ida Clement, a descendant of the founder of the King Ranch, and her husband, Jim Clement, King Ranch board chairman, with the governor.

Bill Clements, longtime supporter of Southern Methodist University, was given SMU's Mustang Award in 1995. Sharing the occasion are, standing, George Seay and Nancy Clements Seay (Clements' daughter) and Pat and Gill Clements (Clements' son).

A hunting trip at Red Nunley's Ranch in South Texas includes David Dean, Clements and Nunley, front, and Gill Clements and Gib Lewis, back.

Clements hunts deer with son Gill and grandson Bill Clements III in East Texas.

The ranch headquarters at Clemgil in Forney.

Dolph Briscoe and Clements hunt deer on the Briscoe Ranch in South Texas, 1986.

Modesta and Clayton Williams, who ran unsuccessfully for governor in 1990, sell cattle at their West Texas ranch to Bill and Rita Clements in 1989.

Clements goes on a 1989 cattle buying expedition to the Clayton Williams Ranch in West Texas with ranch manager Bob Chappell and foreman Larry Shaw.

Bill and Rita Clements enjoy a hunting trip to the King Ranch hosted by their good friends, King Ranch board chairman Jim Clement and Ida Clement, ranch heir. Ida is on Bill Clements' right and Jim is behind her.

which consisted of the lieutenant governor, House speaker, attorney general, comptroller and land commissioner — all Democrats — would have to redraw the lines. Eventually, the Justice Department would reject the LRB's legislative redistricting plans and a three-judge federal panel in Dallas would redraw the districts for the 1982 elections.[15]

The legislature, meanwhile, failed to agree on new boundary lines for U.S. congressional districts. Texas had gained three new districts because of population growth, expanding the Texas delegation from twenty-four to twenty-seven members, but the legislature still couldn't fashion a plan agreeable to all sides. That failure resulted in Clements calling his first special session.

Overall, however, the end of the 1981 regular session was a happier occasion for the governor than the end of the 1979 session had been. Of forty-four items in his legislative program, he passed all but ten, for a 77 percent average. Clements claimed that no session in modern history had passed more potent, far-reaching laws to combat crime and drug traffic. Fourteen of sixteen key elements of his anti-crime program and War on Drugs package were passed, leading the governor to declare that the 67th session would be remembered as the "law enforcement session." Texas passed its first wiretap law, authorizing electronic surveillance by court order in drug cases. Introduction of oral confessions in felony trials would be permitted. Headshops, which dispensed material designed for use by drug users, were outlawed.

In compliance with the federal court order, nearly $160 million was included in the budget for prison construction to relieve overcrowding. Another $20 million was appropriated for a statewide system of halfway houses for parolees, and $6 million for adult probation. Authority was granted the Board of Pardons and Paroles to require restitution to victims of crimes.

In the area of education, Clements got his "back-to-basics" bill passed. It allowed the State Board of Education to provide greater emphasis on basic subject matter. The legislature bumped Clements' proposed 22 percent pay increase for teachers to 26 percent.

The legislature also increased state spending by 20 percent when it passed a $26.6 billion appropriations bill, again eating up all of a $3 billion surplus. Clements noted his disappointment that the appropriations bill was $700 million over his budget proposals, but he did not go through the line-item veto exercise of the previous session. The governor was disappointed that he was unable to get the legislature to create a new Department of Commerce or to pass initiative and referendum.[16]

Shortly after the end of the regular session, Clements issued the call for a special session to begin on July 13, 1981, to deal with congressional redistricting and other matters. In the thirty-day special session which ended in mid-August, the legislature passed a congressional redistricting plan which provided for a new black district and Republican district in the Dallas area. Clements signed the plan, which was expected to pass court muster. It did not. A federal judge later denied the black and GOP seats in the Dallas area, thus gutting the plan, to the benefit of white Democrats. But the fight was not over.

From the end of the regular legislative session in May 1981, through the rest of his term, Clements would fight the courts and Atty. Gen. Mark White over solutions on both redistricting and prisons. But there was much more on his gubernatorial plate.

Among his other pursuits were creating a long-range plan for the state, preparing for the 1986 Sesquicentennial (150th anniversary) celebration of Texas' independence, appointments, and Mexican initiatives.

At one point early in his administration, Governor Clements had asked, "Where's our plan? Our long-term plan for the future?" When he found out there wasn't one (the only existing plan was the state budget that covered a two-year period), he enlisted the support of Lieutenant Governor Hobby and Speaker Clayton in creating Texas 2000, to examine the economic issues that would affect the future of the state.

In the fall of 1979, Clements brought Dr. Vic Arnold from the faculty at the University of Texas' LBJ School of Public Affairs to lay the groundwork for Texas 2000. Arnold had headed a similar study in Minnesota and took the assignments as a nonpartisan professional. Arnold spent nine months gathering statistical data to be used in the forecasting. Then Clements, Hobby, and Clayton agreed on the issues to be examined: population, economy, agriculture, energy, government finance, relations with Mexico, research and development, transportation, and water.

By executive order, the governor created the Texas 2000 Commission. Each of the three top officials then appointed laypeople and legislator-members and, in early 1981, the commission began its year-long effort. Co-chairmen were Clements' appointees, Jack Harbin of Dallas, chairman of Halliburton Oil, and John Armstrong, president of the King Ranch. At the commission's first meeting, Clements gave members a copy of the statistical abstract and forecasts developed by Arnold and his staff and asked them to develop long-range management options on the issues specified. Throughout the process, the governor, lieutenant governor, and speaker sat together as the oversight committee.

Arnold then took the show on the road. He traveled the state, involving business and community groups and special-interest groups ranging from transportation to agriculture to minorities. Local chambers of commerce and institutions of higher education worked with Arnold to set up regional Texas 2000 commissions to contribute to the effort, and hearings were held around the state.

"We were the first to say: 'Look ahead, folks, the minority will be the majority.' We pointed out the rapidly growing Hispanic population. We said we have to think about relations with Mexico, about education . . . about research and development because that's the future of job creation," Arnold said. "The economic history of the state was agriculture and oil and gas. But the world was changing; information technology was critically important to the future of the state, so we had to get serious about research and development. It was extraordinary for government to convince the entire state that our economy was changing, and if we did not get on top of things, we were not going to be a competitive state in the future."[17]

Two issues were covered in Texas 2000 that hadn't previously been among the state's priorities: relations with Mexico and research-and-development and technology as a key to the state's future. Besides forecasting and laying the groundwork for legislation and action by state agencies, Arnold thought Texas 2000 helped to educate the people of Texas to "think about our future. We couldn't just sit back and let it happen."

Arnold found Clements straightforward and the best manager he had ever worked for — once he passed his initial stare-down "test." At his first meeting with Clements, Arnold said he felt someone's eyes on him. "I looked around the table and here was Clements, arms folded, just staring at me, drilling holes right through me. I stared back at him. We must have locked in for a minute and a half, just eyeball to eyeball," Arnold said. When Arnold broke the stare with a smile, Clements grinned back. "He was testing me," Arnold said. The incident told Arnold that "this guy is one strong individual; he's not going to pull any punches.

"He was not the kind of manager that stood looking over your shoulder. He said by his actions, 'I trust you,' do what you need to do, and if you run into problems, don't be reticent to talk to me about them. He took his idea and gave us a long enough tether to expand it," Arnold said.[18]

The commission delivered its report and recommendations on March 26, 1982. Because the lieutenant governor, speaker, and legislators were on the commission, many of the recommendations were turned into legislation for the next session. Louis Beecherl, who served on the Texas 2000 Commission and was chairman of the Texas Water Development Board, began implementing some of the water recommendations, and the importance of transportation was recognized in funding in the next budget.[19]

Clements' emphasis on planning also was critical to the success of the state's Sesquicentennial celebration, which would occur in 1986. State Rep. Chris Semos, a Democrat and the dean of the Dallas delegation, had carried legislation in the House in 1979 to create the Sesquicentennial Commission. The governor had nine appointments to the commission, which included three appointees each from the House and Senate. In February 1980, Clements made the appointment of commission chairman — which Semos considered among the choicest of the governor's administration — to the conservative Democrat from Dallas.

The commission was charged with planning the celebration to be held six years later, working with the Texas State Historical Association, State Fair of Texas, Tourist Development Agency, Texas Historical Commission, Texas Commission on the Arts, Institute of Texan Cultures, Department of Highways and Public Transportation, Texas State Library, and Texas Film Commission.

Clements viewed the Sesquicentennial as a way to promote Texas, attract visitors, increase appreciation for the state's unique history, and create projects of lasting benefit to future Texans. "He wanted a great celebration without spending a lot of money to pay for it," Semos recalled. The only direction Clements gave to Semos was to make sure the celebration was statewide in nature, with festivities planned throughout Texas rather than centered in any one city.

Clements flew home most weekends during the session, and

he frequently invited Semos to join him on the Monday morning flight from Dallas to Austin so they could discuss Sesquicentennial business. One potential project he was interested in was establishing a Texas state art museum in Austin, patterned after the state of Virginia's museum. Clements had talked to some of his wealthy friends about donating artwork, if the state would commit to the facility. The legislature passed a bill to create the museum, but it was never funded.

"Because he had such a great love for Texas history and an appreciation for what the Sesquicentennial could do, he gave me a lot of his time," Semos said.[20]

Clements believed in doing things big. He didn't hesitate to throw out a line to big fish, such as going after noted author James Michener, after David Dean suggested it, to write a book to commemorate the occasion. As Dean said about his former boss, "He's way out there, five years ahead of time. Who's going to come to Texas to write the classic novel? It's got to be somebody big, and who's bigger than Michener?"[21]

The governor arranged a meeting with Michener at the Clements' Wexford home in Virginia to explore the subject. In a June 8, 1981, letter, Clements asked Michener to write the "story of Texas" in anticipation of the Sesquicentennial. The contents of the three-page letter reveals Clements' own passion for his native state.

> Texas is a story — a story so big, so diverse, that its telling must be by an author who works in comfort with the size and scope of such a project. The story of Texas can only be told by someone who has demonstrated that he possesses the vision necessary to comprehend and capture the vastness and openness of the state and is not intimidated by a vast span of time.
>
> Texans, more so than any other state's citizens, feel something special about their state. This may be due to the vast catalogue of her famous sons. I also believe this feeling has its strength in the diverse cultural heritage of our land. I am aware that you are attracted to times in history which depict the comingling of different races and ideologies and Texas was and indeed is today a "melting pot" of various cultures and nationalities. Many characterize Texans as being of one breed — Maverick. Perhaps this assessment is correct.
>
> The story of Texas can be weaved from fabric abundant with adventure, heroic action, and decisive leadership. Texas' strong

foundation has been reinforced over the 150 years by the actions
of powerful leaders and rugged individuals whose foresight knew
no boundaries . . .

Clements' letter spanned the days from Texas' battle for independence to its prominence in the space program, mentioning early
Texas heroes to latter-day powerful politicians, prominent entrepreneurs and artists. He concluded by offering to arrange for Michener's travel to Austin or Dallas to discuss the proposal.

Michener accepted the invitation, visiting Austin on July 30,
1981, where he was offered an office at the University of Texas, the
assistance of graduate students for scholarly research, and the cooperation of university faculty and other resources. Michener spent
thirty months in Texas and the result was his mammoth, thousand-
page work, *Texas*, published by Random House in 1985.[22]

Michener also developed an affinity for Texas, and established
a home in Austin. In 1986 he helped create the Texas Center for
Writers at the University of Texas with a $1 million donation and, in
later years, taught courses there. In 1992 he donated $15 million to
the Texas Center for Writers, now housed in the home of noted
Texas historian J. Frank Dobie.[23]

But nothing, not even Texas history, captured Clements' attention more than the appointments he would make while governor.
Clements devoted careful attention to making, on average, fifteen to
twenty appointments a week. In his first two and a half years in office, he made 2,500 appointments, and would make some 4,000 before the end of his term. "I think if my administration to date has a
hallmark, it's the quality of [my] appointments," Clements said in
May 1981.[24]

Appointments director Tobin Armstrong explained the focus
of Clements' appointments process. "We want people with the capacity to make a leadership contribution — people with some expertise in business organization, manpower, personnel, finance. You
ought to put people on those boards who can bring something to
the table, not just come as a reward for political service to the party
or the state."

While the emphasis was on business and management expertise, there were political considerations. Clements brought new Republicans into government through his appointments, but he also
appointed — to the chagrin of some Republican loyalists — conservative Democrats. Clements felt such appointments were part of his

obligation to the ticket-splitters and Briscoe Democrats who had supported him. Many later switched parties.

Analyses showed Clements used appointments to reward contributors and supporters, to convert conservative Democrats and lure independents into the Republican fold. More than half of his top appointments, according to a 1981 series in the *Fort Worth Star Telegram*, were to people who gave more than $500 to either the Reagan campaign or to the Governor Clements Committee. He used the appointments process to convert Democratic judges into Republicans. After being appointed to vacant judgeships as Democrats, many of Clements' appointees ran in the next election as Republicans.

"My inclination certainly would be to appoint someone who either is now a Republican, or who will declare as a Republican or who can get elected as a Republican. I think that would be a perfectly natural position for me to take, everything else being equal. But on the other hand, I'm sure not going to sacrifice quality for that. Quality comes first," Clements insisted.

In several areas of the state, Republican Party officials and Clements' backers formed screening committees to find prospective appointees. Lawyers were designated in some areas to look for judicial appointees. The Governor Clements Committee solicited suggestions for appointments.

Diversity, however, was not the No. 1 priority. More than two years into his administration, only five percent of his appointments were black or Mexican-American, although those groups comprised 25 percent of the state's population. Though criticized for his level of minority appointments, Clements eventually would appoint more minorities than any of his Democratic predecessors. With eighteen months left to go in Clements' administration, Joe Kirven, director of the governor's Equal Employment Opportunity office, noted that Clements had named fifty-one blacks to various boards, commissions, and advisory groups. Briscoe, by contrast, had appointed forty-four blacks during six years in office.

Clements named the first black member and two Mexican-Americans to the College Coordinating Board. He named former Gov. Preston Smith as head of the College Coordinating Board, a signal to conservatives in the Lubbock area that they could work with Republicans. He also appointed two women to the University of Texas board of regents, including former Governor Briscoe's wife, Janey Briscoe, whose affirmative signal during the campaign had contributed to Clements' election. John Connally's wife, Nellie, was named to the Texas Historical Commission.

Clements named Beryl Buckley Milburn, longtime vice-chairman of the Texas Republican Party, and his loyal SEDCO lawyer Tom B. Rhodes to the UT board of regents — viewed by many as the most coveted appointment. Equally sought-after were appointments to the Texas A&M board. Those appointments went to H. R. "Bum" Bright, Dallas oilman and chairman of the Governor Clements Committee; William A. McKenzie, a Dallas lawyer and former Dallas County Republican chairman; and Joe C. Richardson, Jr., an Amarillo oil operator.

Clements peppered his appointments with acquaintances from the oil industry. To TENRAC, the twenty-one-member Texas Energy and Natural Resources Advisory Council, he named several wealthy oilmen, including Ed Vetter; Dallas oil producer and Clements' Preston Road neighbor Edwin L. Cox; and Houston oil operator Michel Thomas Halbouty.

The governor filled two positions on the powerful three-member Texas Highway and Public Transportation Commission with wealthy contributors: Dallas businessman Robert H. Dedman and Houston oilman John R. Butler. Fort Worth oilman H. E. "Eddie" Chiles was named as a member of the North Texas State University board of regents.

Early in his administration, Saralee Tiede of the *Dallas Times-Herald* wrote that if Briscoe "left a mark on his administration that looked like a branding iron" by appointing cattlemen, Clements assembled men who were "familiar with rigs and royalties." Some Democrats complained. Peyton McKnight of Tyler, chairman of the Senate nominations committee, said Clements was appointing too many millionaires. Rep. John Bryant's gripe was: "Every time I look up, there is another rich guy appointed."[25]

Actually, while Clements sprinkled his boards and commissions with friends from the oil patch, they comprised a small percentage of his overall appointments. He did, however, tend to favor people who had been successful in business and who weren't looking to feather their own, already well-feathered, nests.

Clements made no apologies for his appointments, nor for his reliance on successful businessmen. "My God," he told a reporter, "You're talking about those agencies that in some instances have multibillion-dollar budgets. What do you want? A bunch of nin-compoops and hardly-ables running the deal?"[26]

One of Clements' requisites was that most nominees be willing to devote at least 25 percent of their work time to state business. In response to one letter-writer who complained about his appointing conservative Democrats previously in power or naive campaign contributors, Clements noted that he asked for a "serious time commitment from each prospective board member. Most of these individuals serve without any remuneration, and I believe that the state is fortunate to have successful people volunteering their time and energies." He also wrote, "I am doing everything I can to attract the most talented people available into state government. I have been successful in recruiting outstanding Texans from business, professional fields and academia into my administration and I'm very proud of this accomplishment."[27]

"Gov. Clements brought in a lot of very prestigious business people, people who had never been involved in government but who had been successful in their profession or in running a company. . . . We were interested in minorities and women but that wasn't the main criteria in Clements' first term. He wanted to bring business experience; he wanted the most qualified," said Pat Oles, who moved from the Governor Clements Committee to be a deputy appointments secretary in 1980.

Clements met weekly with his appointments staff to go over pending nominations. Mrs. Clements sat in on those meetings and, according to Oles, made a major contribution. Clements would test staff members to make sure they had done their homework and were confident in their recommendations. "He had great instincts about people," Oles said, but he gave the staff "a lot of rope."[28]

There were many examples of appointees with the kind of experience Clements sought. James B. Adams, associate director of the Federal Bureau of Investigation, put his twenty-seven years of experience in law enforcement to work as head of the Department of Public Safety. H. Moak Rollins, co-founder of Drilco Oil Tools in Midland, who had earned a doctorate in corporate finance after his business career and taught at the University of Texas, was named to the Public Utility Commission.

Clements sought scholarly young lawyers to appoint to the bench. One of his top judicial appointments in his first term was Will Garwood, who had graduated first in his class from the University of Texas Law School. Garwood was tapped to be associate justice on the Texas Supreme Court, where his father had served before him.

Years later, when Clements was asked what difference it made if the governor was a conservative Democrat or a Republican, he said: "Appointments, appointments, appointments." The way a governor controls state government, he said, is through the appointment of people who set the direction of some 240 state agencies, from the highway department to the penal system to higher education. "The single most important thing a governor does," he said, "is make those appointments."

As his appointees began to take control of the boards and commissions of the various agencies and to put their stamp on policy-making, the governor's office was able to initiate performance audits of agency operations and costs. The operational audits utilized volunteers from industry, recruited by the Texas Research League. By the end of 1981, there had been twenty-five operational audits at seven state agencies, using 130 corporate volunteers, many of whom served several months at no expense to state government. Two statewide audits in the areas of personnel and purchasing likewise were conducted.

Also, by the end of 1981, through his Management Effectiveness Program, the governor's office had provided orientation seminars for new board members, plus training for 8,000 state government managers, and had reduced the bureaucracy by 3,000. Clements contended that had the growth patterns of the previous five years prevailed, the state would have had 9,000 more bureaucrats instead of 3,000 less.[29]

With a Republican in the White House, the governor of Texas was comfortable working with members of the administration in Washington. But less than a year after Clements helped Ronald Reagan carry Texas, the governor broke ranks with the president over the issue of immigration policy. In August 1981, Clements harshly attacked the administration's immigration policy in a speech before the American GI Forum, an Hispanic organization. Clements said the administration's guest worker proposal, which was to issue 50,000 temporary work visas, was unrealistic because it failed to deal with the three to six million undocumented aliens in the country who would continue to live underground. He called for changes in procedures that would lead to citizenship for many undocumented workers — essentially a fast-track naturalization process — and in the fines assessed to employers who hired undocumented workers. Clements' proposal would require all employers of illegal aliens to pay a relocation fee to return the workers to their home country.[30]

Clements had been promoting his ideas as chairman of the subcommittee on immigration of the National Governors Association. He had hosted Mexican border state governors during his second legislative session, and he had attended the first international meeting of the U.S.-Mexico border governors in June of 1980, where he pushed his plan to legalize undocumented Mexican workers. The Texas governor served as host to the second international meeting of border governors of both countries in El Paso on October 5-6, 1981. Other U.S. governors attending were Bruce Babbitt of Arizona, Edmund G. "Jerry" Brown, Jr., of California, and Bruce King of New Mexico. Immigration issues were predominant at the meeting, but the only accord the four American and six Mexican governors could reach was to have a binational task force study President Reagan's guest worker proposal before the officials met again in Tijuana in 1982.[31]

The border governors, however, showed their farsightedness in recommending consideration of a North American trade community involving Mexico, Canada, and the United States. This was thirteen years before the North American Free Trade Agreement was passed by the U.S. Congress.

They also recommended joint-venture cooperation, utilizing the twin plant mechanism called *maquiladoras,* to combine Mexico's energy and labor with American technology, management skills, and capital. To increase tourism and commerce, the governors recognized the need for improved transportation facilities for freer flow of goods and people, and the acceptance of the peso by U.S. banks and merchants. During his term, Clements signed legislation to allow the creation of foreign trade zones in Laredo, El Paso, Del Rio, Eagle Pass, and San Antonio.[32]

Before the end of his four-year term, Clements would meet with his Mexican counterparts a total of twenty times in his efforts to improve relations and to better economic conditions along the Texas-Mexico border.

Clements felt he was having such a productive administration that he needn't have to prove it to anybody, certainly not the press. After taking a brief vacation in Taos following the special session in the summer of 1981, he returned in early September to questions regarding his reelection plans. Clements acknowledged that he had every intention of running again. Asked what his "big pluses" were, he replied: "Rita." A reporter answered, "Well, why doesn't she run?" The governor acknowledged that might be a good idea. Then, curtly, he said, "Let's change the subject."[33]

In truth, Rita Clements was a valuable part of the administration. While Janey Briscoe had sat alongside her husband much of the time in the governor's office, Mrs. Clements had her own office in the Sam Houston Building. She maintained her own schedule, making frequent speeches and concentrating on her priorities as first lady: volunteerism, education, and historical preservation. She also participated in the appointments process and was regarded as an important political adviser to her husband.

Mrs. Clements was a full-time first lady, in her office most days by 9:00 A.M. when she wasn't traveling.

There had been in previous administrations a Governor's Office for Volunteer Services, which Mrs. Clements reactivated. The office, managed by Polly Sowell, coordinated with volunteer groups across the state and recognized outstanding volunteers. Mrs. Clements also made numerous speeches promoting volunteer activities. She had been a volunteer herself, serving as president of the Junior League of Dallas, chairman of the Crystal Charity Ball in Dallas, and an active member of various boards, including the United Way and the Hockaday School. She knew the value of the three million Texans who did volunteer work, contributing some 780 million hours each year at an estimated value of $3.6 billion. She praised and encouraged such activity, much of which saved the state money in government services.

But she acknowledged that she would probably be remembered most for the renovation of the Governor's Mansion.[34]

The morning after Clements was elected governor, he and Rita were invited to the Governor's Mansion to have coffee with the Briscoes. Mrs. Clements was surprised at what a "patchwork" the mansion was, including the conglomeration of furniture that various governors had brought and left at the mansion. She and the governor were appalled by the deteriorated physical condition and by some of the alterations made to the original 1856 structure by previous first families.

Briscoe had been the first four-year governor, and Rita was convinced that the reason the mansion was in such deplorable condition was because none of the previous governors — elected to just two years — wanted to give up living in the historic house to enable significant repairs to be made. Shortly before the inauguration, she learned from the Briscoes that a chunk of the double parlor walls had collapsed.[35]

Mrs. Clements was immediately challenged by the idea of renovating the mansion, but the governor had to get the funding for structural improvements from the legislature. She feared the Democratic legislature would never approve the funds while a Republican occupied the mansion. Clements, however, gained approval of the $1 million expenditure. After living only nine months in the mansion, Governor and Mrs. Clements moved into an apartment for the duration of the restoration, which took more than two years.

Clements was familiar with historic preservation from his restoration of the Cumberland School and, because of his appreciation of Texas history, he felt a state treasure was in jeopardy. He knew the mansion's historical significance was second only to the Alamo. Built by Abner Cook and first occupied by Gov. Elisha Pease in 1856, it was one of the finest examples of Greek Revival mansions in Texas. It was where Sam Houston, the hero of San Jacinto who was elected governor in 1859, had met with other prominent anti-secessionists and received word that Texas had voted by state convention to secede from the Union. Among the mansion's hodgepodge of furnishings was Sam Houston's massive canopied bed, made in Seguin.

As the structural improvements were being made, Mrs. Clements took the lead in refurbishing the interior with period furnishings.

In November 1979, under her guidance, the Friends of the Governor's Mansion was established as a nonprofit corporation. It would oversee the acquisition of furnishings and works of art of museum quality for the mansion. Ashley Priddy, former mayor of Highland Park, was chairman and Mrs. Clements was honorary chairman of Friends. The organization raised $3.5 million, to acquire nineteenth-century American and Texas furniture that would complement the mansion's existing furnishings, and to fund the mansion's continued upkeep. The governor's office announced that "under the sponsorship of the Friends, the mansion will continue to be a living home for Texas' first families and will reflect its rich history and proud heritage for all Texans." The 123-year-old home would be returned to its former simple elegance while providing modern conveniences so that the first family could live comfortably and use the mansion for official entertaining.[36]

The Texas Governor's Mansion was the fourth-oldest, continuously occupied gubernatorial residence in the country. Virginia had the oldest and Mississippi the second oldest. Mrs. Clements was committed to restoring the residence with period furnishings as well as repairing it structurally, and she proved to be a valuable resource for the project. She had served on the Department of State Fine Arts Committee when she was in Washington, and knew Clem Conger, the committee's executive director who also was curator of the White House. Conger was invited to Austin for consultation. He recommended setting up a foundation for the permanent upkeep of the mansion.

David Warren of Houston, author of a book on Texas antiques and associate director of the Houston Museum of Fine Arts, was acquisitions adviser. Jed Mace and Tom Sellman of Dallas, who had helped to decorate the Wexford, Taos, and Preston Road homes for the Clementses, were design consultants. Mace and Mrs. Clements made several trips to New York, Philadelphia, Baltimore and Wilmington, Delaware, looking at period furnishings and reproductions. Margot Perot, wife of Ross Perot, headed the acquisitions committee.[37]

Most of the furniture acquired was early nineteenth century — largely American Empire and Federal pieces — although the acquisitions committee also found a few early Texas pieces. The most valuable acquisition, donated by a Houston family, was a painting called the "Fall of the Alamo," which now hangs in the front hall of the mansion. Mrs. Clements found bedroom furniture in the state archives which belonged to descendants of Elisha Pease, the first occupant of the Governor's Mansion. Governor and Mrs. Clements created the Pease bedroom, which included other furniture donated by Pease descendants.[38]

Another area of historic preservation that Mrs. Clements got involved in was the National Main Street Center program. This was a special project of the National Trust for Historic Preservation. It was designed to encourage revitalization through historic preservation in small towns. Texas was chosen in 1980 as one of six states to participate and, in 1981, five Texas towns were designated as Main Street towns — Eagle Pass, Hillsboro, Plainview, Navasota, and Seguin. Seguin was a perfect choice for restoration; its history formed a tapestry of Spanish, Mexican, and German pioneers. Its first building had been constructed on the Guadalupe River during the Spanish mission period. In 1982, five more towns were designated for the project: Gainesville, Georgetown, Kingsville, McKinney, and Marshall.

The project was administered in the state by the Texas Historical Commission, with assistance from the Texas Department of Community Affairs, the governor's office, and more than a dozen state agencies.

Mrs. Clements visited all of the towns and spoke about the restoration of downtown buildings as the basis for economic development of small communities. It was also a way, she stressed, to reflect the pride and craftsmanship of early Texans and the uniqueness of each city. She called on each community to preserve the heritage and beauty of its downtown center of activity.[39]

One newspaper writer compared Mrs. Clements to other famous political wives. "Like Rosalynn Carter, she politically counsels her husband. Like Jackie Kennedy, she is a wealthy socialite. Like Betty Ford, she is outspoken. And like Nancy Reagan, she has personal style and elegance." But, the writer claimed, Mrs. Clements had one-upped those famous first ladies. Another newspaper columnist suggested she might follow her husband some day in statewide elective office. After all, her political savvy and long-time campaign experience were instrumental in getting Clements where he was. No previous Texas first lady was as qualified by her own political experience and community leadership roles.[40]

Mrs. Clements, however, said there were too many things she wanted to do with Bill Clements during their remaining years together to even consider such an idea. And the first one was to get him reelected to a second term.

Chapter 14

1982 Campaign

"The cake's in the oven"

THERE WAS NEVER REALLY any question as to whether Bill Clements would seek reelection. By late 1981, he was immersed in the governorship. He had a string of accomplishments, and he had more task forces working to create more goals for the future. He would complete some projects in 1982, including the restoration of the Governor's Mansion and issuance of the Texas 2000 report, but it would take a second term to implement the report's recommendations. And it would take two years into that second term before he could appoint every member of every state board and commission — thus having total control of the state bureaucracy.

His reelection campaign was launched with a thirteen-city tour of the state, November 16-18, 1981. At every stop, the governor stressed that a businesslike approach to government — accountability, good management and direction, with attention to goals and results — had been his program and would continue to be his emphasis. He boasted that for the first time in thirty years "we have stopped the growth of government dead in its tracks," although he hadn't been able to cut 25,000 employees, as promised. He touted his management effectiveness program, Texas 2000, his appointments, the border governors conferences and improved relations with Mexico, and new laws that came out of his Blue Ribbon Task Force on Education and the Texans' War on Drugs.

The governor already was planning for the 1983 legislative session. By the time he launched his campaign, he had created task forces in thirteen areas: small business, higher education, work-related accidents, foreign investments, aviation, industrial and tourist development, education action groups, equal opportunities for women and minorities, state trust and asset management, agriculture, traffic safety, and undocumented workers.[1]

After the announcement tour, Clements went on with the business of being governor.

By late 1981, there had been some staff changes. Hilary Doran had become chief of staff. George Strake resigned as secretary of state to run for lieutenant governor. A stronger Republican partisan than Clements, Strake felt Texas had a "Bill Clements party, not a Republican party" and that Texas would never be a true two-party state until it elected a second Republican governor or a lieutenant governor. Clements didn't discourage Strake from running but warned him that Bill Hobby would be tough to beat.[2] David Dean replaced Strake as secretary of state, and David Herndon became general counsel. Doug Brown had returned to private life, as had Paul Wrotenbery and Jim Francis. George Bayoud, who had begun his career with Clements driving the motor home in the 1978 campaign and then carried the governor's bags as his travel aide, moved up to head the Governor Clements Committee, the separate political and fundraising arm of the governor's office. Jarvis Miller became budget director. Allen Clark left to accept a federal appointment as deputy administrator of the Veterans Administration, and Polly Sowell became special assistant over administration. Throughout the first term, Jim Kaster was chief legislative aide. Tobin Armstrong remained in charge of appointments for the full four years.

Clark said later he had never been happier than when he worked for Clements. "You knew exactly where you stood all the time," Clark said, and he felt he was involved in important work. Clark recalled that his only disagreement with Clements was over eradicating a pigeon problem on the Capitol grounds. Clements told him, "If you can't take care of this problem, I'll find someone who can." Clark also recalled that Clements once told him, "You're just too Republican." The reference was to Clark's wardrobe. Clark favored dark suits and white shirts, an outgrowth of his West Point and banking background. Clements preferred short-sleeved shirts and plaid sport coats and thought Texans leaned more to his taste in dress.[3]

272   BILL CLEMENTS: Texian to His Toenails

Clements was without opposition in the Republican primary, but the Democratic primary was contested. The Democratic candidates were Land Commissioner Bob Armstrong, a liberal Democrat and a favorite among the Austin press corps; Railroad Commissioner Buddy Temple, a former legislator from Diboll in East Texas and son of Arthur Temple, Jr., the Temple-Eastex timber baron and Time, Inc., vice-chairman; and Atty. Gen. Mark White. White announced on December 16, 1981, making official the race Clements believed the attorney general had been running since both of them had assumed office.

While the three Democrats sparred for their party's nomination, Clements and White continued to conduct their own war over such issues as redistricting and prisons.

The Legislative Redistricting Board's plans for state House and Senate districts had been ruled a violation of the voting rights of minority Texans by the U.S. Department of Justice, a conclusion Governor Clements shared. Nonetheless, Attorney General White had urged a three-judge federal panel, which was considering the lawsuit styled *Terrazas v. Clements*, to adopt the Legislative Redistricting Board's plan for the 1982 elections. Clements was angered by White's representation and wanted outside counsel to represent him in the case. In a February 2, 1982, letter to White, he wrote: "It is clear that you are not representing my interests as governor as a named defendant in the case, nor the state's interests, in providing full voting rights to all its people, including minorities."

The court had indicated its willingness to take suggestions and comments from the parties to the case as to how the Legislative Redistricting Board's plan should be modified. "You are not empowered to tell the court, to the exclusion of the governor, what changes the state wants made," Clements wrote White. "The governor constitutionally is the chief executive officer of the state and, as such, must be allowed to express the interests of the state and its minority citizens through an attorney with no conflict of interest. For you to continue as my attorney in this case when you have not and will not represent my interest as governor is a serious breach of your ethical responsibilities," Clements wrote.[4]

White responded with an equally forceful statement on February 19, 1982, which said: "The state can speak with only one voice. The constitution directs the attorney general to speak for the state on legal matters. The state's position that the plan drafted and approved by the Legislative Redistricting Board is valid, and there is no other state position." White said further that the state should not be asked "to pay the legal costs of representing the personal interest of individual politicians."[5]

When the court approved the plan on March 5, 1982, Clements issued a statement saying the court action "leaves us in a confusing mess." The court had flatly ignored the Justice Department's finding, Clements said, and he suggested that the case might be appealed to the U.S Supreme Court. Clements complained to the media: "Unfortunately, Atty. Gen. Mark White declined to properly represent my interest and Speaker Billy Clayton's interest and refused to permit either of us to have outside counsel. By blocking our request for counsel, Mark White denied the court's hearing the voice of the defendants. He sold us down the river."[6]

Throughout the 1982 primary campaign, White railed as much against Governor Clements as he did against his Democratic opponents. Even the closing of the Governor's Mansion for two years of renovation became fodder for the White campaign. "The first thing we're going to do if I'm elected is walk over there to those padlocks and cut them off and open the mansion to the people," White declared.[7]

The mansion, in fact, became very public after it was reopened on April 1, 1982. Representatives of the news media were welcomed as the first guests to the restored mansion, with Mrs. Clements conducting the guided tour. Public tours resumed three mornings a week. Demand for the tours soon became overwhelming, so that on June 1, 1982, the schedule was extended to Monday through Friday, from 10:00 A.M. to noon.[8]

Despite this increased public access to the "exquisitely refurbished" and "flawlessly authentic" mansion, as it was termed by *Texas Homes* magazine, White found that his statement about cutting the padlock off the mansion gate was resonating; he began using it in a television commercial.

Texas columnist Molly Ivins, a self-professed liberal and usual Democrat apologist, cared little for White. "Biff the Lip," she said, using her usual nickname for Governor Clements, "has a hundred times more personality, even if you don't like it," she wrote.[9] And she didn't, which she attested to many times in her columns.

White, the best-known candidate, was the frontrunner for the Democratic nomination. Buddy Temple was his most serious challenger. A millionaire from his family's timber operation, Temple had borrowed more than $1 million for the primary race. He ran a more aggressive campaign than Bob Armstrong. Temple called White the "Edsel of the attorney generals," the "Pinocchio of Texas politics," and claimed he had "one of the poorest records" of any state official. "Everybody knows what a lousy job he has done," Temple said.[10]

Temple, however, was also trying to show that he would be the toughest opponent for Governor Clements in the fall. At his rallies, Temple said that the more people were exposed to Clements, the less they liked him. "He's always snarling and growling," Temple charged.

Temple liked to cite Clements' controversial remarks. He recalled, for example, how Clements said he would have to travel to New Orleans to eat redfish when the legislature banned commercial catches of redfish in Texas. When it was suggested some Texans couldn't afford trips to New Orleans, Clements said, "Then they'll eat catfish. I like catfish better anyway."

"Clements himself is the issue, his arrogant, contemptuous attitude toward those who have to work for a living. He's a mean-spirited individual, or at least he comes across that way," Temple said.[11]

Texas Monthly magazine called White's record mediocre, noting that he had lost lawsuits involving Texas prisons and bilingual education. In contrast to the hotly contested Briscoe-Hill primary four years earlier, the 1982 race for the Democratic gubernatorial nomination was unimpressive. "It's hard to imagine a better indicator of how much Bill Clements has changed Texas politics than the collective yawn that has greeted this year's Democratic gubernatorial primary. . . . You don't exactly come away from encounters with the three major Democratic candidates . . . convinced that there's a man of destiny among them," the magazine reported.[12]

When the Democratic primary votes were counted, White failed to win the Democratic nomination outright, but led the field with 45 percent of the vote. Temple won 30 percent, and Armstrong ran a poor third. A runoff would be required. Temple, however, realized he would have to spend another $1 million of his own money in a runoff that would leave him or White too crippled to challenge Clements in the fall. He abruptly withdrew, handing the nomination to White.

Some 1.3 million Texans had voted in the Democratic primary, compared to a lackluster 265,000 in the Republican primary. Yet the general election fight for any Democrat would be a tough one against the incumbent Republican, a fact Temple recognized when he withdrew. He attributed his decision in part to the "fundamental change in the Texas political scene. For the first time in 103 years, we have an incumbent Republican governor. In primary campaigns, candidates must now weigh more carefully the effects of their actions on the party's prospects in the general elections, whenever runoffs occur."[13]

Clements' immediate response to the Democratic primary outcome was to declare that he had long been looking forward to running against White. "You might say I've been licking my chops for three years," Clements said.[14]

As soon as he was the Democratic nominee, White resurrected his claim that the governor's veto of prison construction funds in 1979 contributed to delays in prison construction and thus to prison overcrowding. The governor responded that White lied like Hitler. White called the governor's reply "intemperate" and "bizarre." The campaign between the two had been under way for only four days.

Molly Ivins returned to the typewriter with her lance drawn. But her objections to Clements weren't limited to a denouncement of his campaign theatrics; they also were ideological. When not "venting his ill temper on others involved in state government," she wrote, the governor was honing the "wrong-headed ideas" contained in his national energy policy. She called ideas such as pouring more tax money into the nuclear industry, subsidizing synthetic fuels, relaxing air quality standards, and building coal slurry pipe lines "an honor roll of environmental horrors" and suggested that the governor "go tax an oilman." Ivins went on to give this assessment of Clements:[15]

> Bill Clements interests me as an example of the dangers of ignorance. He is a man of considerable force, energy and zest. I like a governor who governs. The last one we had bore a stunning resemblance to a pet rock. I believe Bill Clements is a bright man who is terribly hobbled by his own ignorance. He is a product and a victim of some powerful forces of segregation in our national life. Segregation is not solely a matter of race. Americans are segregated by income level, education, age, even by musical taste. People who love classical music seldom know those who listen only to country . . . .
>
> But it has seemed to me . . . that the rich are just as isolated as the poor. They literally do not know people who are not like

themselves . . . . Oilmen denouncing welfare cheats, doctors con-
demning national health insurance, guys by the pool moaning
about the decline in productivity. I know that sounds like class-
baiting, but it's just as real as sweat. I think Clements is the victim
of that mindset; he thinks people like him are supposed to run
things, [and] when they run things, they're supposed to run
things for the benefit of people like themselves, and they really
believe doing so will benefit everyone.

Aside from that, the Lip just has a bad disposition and bad
manners.

Conservatives and Clements' supporters derided Ivins as a dar-
ling of the liberals not to be taken seriously, but her consistent flailing
away at Clements contributed to the growing image that the governor
was both ill-mannered and an elitist. Cartoonist Ben Sargent of the
Austin American-Statesman also contributed to the image of Clements as a dour aristocrat, given to shooting off his mouth.

In May of 1982, after the primaries were over, Clements called a
special session of the legislature to repeal the state property tax and
provide tax relief. The session reflected the governor's desires, because legislators didn't want to go on record as being opposed to a
tax cut in an election year. However, the prison problem also had
become a political hot potato, and Clements had to add prison construction funds to the agenda. In the five-day session, the legislature
authorized $50 million in emergency funding to speed completion
of new prison facilities. Additional funding was provided to the
Board of Pardons and Paroles and the Texas Adult Probation Commission to hire personnel for increased intensive supervision and
operation of residential treatment centers.[16]

Earlier that month, the Texas Board of Corrections had
shocked the governor by closing the doors of the prisons to incoming inmates. Clements wrote Louis Austin, chairman of the Board
of Corrections, that the "precipitous action" could not be allowed.
He ordered the board to reopen the prisons. The governor also directed the Board of Pardons and Paroles to expedite the release of
eligible TDC inmates to mandatory supervision, specifying that 450
should be released within days of his letter to Austin. "As you are no
doubt aware," he wrote Austin, "some politicians are using the
Board of Corrections' action as a political issue. It is my unequivocal
position that now is the time for cool heads, good judgment and a
rational approach to the problem. We cannot at this time afford po-

litical demagoguery on the issue or any more surprises regarding our prison system."[17]

Clements was beginning to crank up his reelection campaign. By May 1982, his campaign leadership was in place. T. Boone Pickens, Jr., of Amarillo was state chairman of the political division, and H. R. "Bum" Bright of Dallas was state chairman of the financial division. Like Clements, both men had oil patch connections. Pickens was founder and chairman of the board of Mesa Petroleum, and Bright was senior partner in Bright and Company, an oil and gas production firm. Mrs. Bobbie Biggart of Dallas, a longtime Republican volunteer, was the campaign's state vice-chairman. Supervising day-to-day operations as campaign manager was Dary Stone, who had been brought home from Washington where Clements had sent him to head the Texas Office of Federal-State Relations. George Bayoud moved from the fundraising Governor Clements Committee to become finance manager of the campaign.[18]

In June, Clements was endorsed by three former governors, Democrats Allan Shivers and Preston Smith, and Democrat-turned-Republican John Connally. The three were scheduled to join President Ronald Reagan and Vice-President George Bush at a big fundraiser in Houston on June 10, 1982. Walter Mischer of Houston was chairman of the Victory 1982 dinner, and Robert H. Dedman of Dallas was vice-chairman.

The Clements reelection campaign was well-funded and it again utilized some of the winning professionals from 1978, including Lance Tarrance and Associates for polling, Nancy Brataas for the phone banks, and Don Ringe for media.

But the campaign had problems almost from the beginning. Dary Stone, the paid staff campaign manager, and Boone Pickens, the volunteer state campaign chairman, didn't get along. In late July, Jim Francis, thirty-four, who worked for Bum Bright, was brought in as campaign manager, and the thirty-year-old Stone was shifted to coordinator of the traveling campaign.

Pickens said years later that being campaign chairman "was not really something I felt confident with because I didn't know much about what I was trying to do." Pickens thought of himself as a "figurehead" who went to meetings, but otherwise didn't contribute much. The campaign was not his No. 1 priority; his business was. During the time of the campaign, Mesa was involved in a potential buyout by Cities Service.

Part of the campaign's problem was that it wasn't focused on a message. Clements was trying to run again as a businessman and as a governor who had managed state government effectively. He was using his "Roots" commercials again. The basic message was that Governor Clements had done a good job, but from there it splintered into many directions. One campaign memo covered twenty-four unrelated points which ranged from the obvious (education and drug war legislation, efficiency in government) to the obscure. "The campaign was all over the map on issues," said Tony Garrett, the deputy press director who ran the press operation at state headquarters in Austin. "There wasn't an issue we wouldn't address. We may have gone down too many rabbit trails," he said later.

Meanwhile, another factor had slipped into the political equation. The Texas economy had begun to slow down.

Comptroller Bob Bullock delivered a good news-bad news message on July 29, 1982, when he announced a $1.3 billion state surplus. But Bullock pointed to thorns amid the roses. "I hate to be the one who says this, but it is my duty to tell you: The recession has come to Texas."

Bullock noted that 70,000 jobs had disappeared between March and May of 1982. In June, Texas had more people unemployed than ever in its history — 7.7 percent of the workforce. The Texas Employment Commission estimated that the unemployment rate in July would be 8.4 percent. The budget surplus, Bullock said, was the result of good times. But the state was beginning to see significant drops in some major revenue sources. Crude oil was then selling for $31 a barrel, down from a peak of $37.[19]

Clements suggested the economic slowdown was only temporary and promised that the budget surplus would not be drained by careless or foolish spending.

But unemployment continued to rise, threatening the solvency of the state's unemployment trust fund. Benefits paid out of the fund had gone from $26.1 million in February to $55 million in July and were projected to hit $60 million in August. The fund was dangerously low, and if it went broke, an automatic increase in unemployment taxes on businesses would be triggered. Without a quick-fix solution, the fund was expected to run dry by Thanksgiving. After conferring with Lieutenant Governor Hobby, Speaker Clayton and Comptroller Bullock, the governor called a special session of the legislature to convene on September 7, 1982, to keep the state's unemployment compensation fund from running out of money.[20]

While Texas was still better off than much of the nation, some pessimistic news was coming out of Dallas-Fort Worth and Houston, the boom areas of the 1970s. The Dallas-based airline Braniff International had ceased operation in May. Red Ball, Inc., a large trucking firm in Dallas, had shut down. Bell Helicopter Textron, a Fort Worth aircraft manufacturer, had to lay off 10 percent of its workforce. General Motors laid off 900 workers. Mostek Corp., Texas Instruments, and Lone Star Steel also had big layoffs.

In early September, one Texas newspaper wrote about a new voting bloc in Texas: the jobless. But Clements' pollster Lance Tarrance said the unemployed would have a negligible political impact in Texas because the state's economy was healthy compared with the rest of the nation. Clements, in fact, hailed the Texas economy in his speeches, which spurred White to accuse the governor of painting a rosy and inaccurate picture.[21]

In some ways, the 1982 election was turning into a mirror image of 1978. Where Clements had blamed the country's problems on Jimmy Carter in 1978, Texas Democrats were blaming Reaganomics for the economic suffering of 1982.

Clements was unrestrained in his criticism of Mark White. Asked by a television personality why people should vote for him instead of White, Clements responded that "I am competent and he's incompetent."[22]

As the fall campaign got under way, University of Houston political science professor Richard Murray predicted that if Clements was reelected, the Republicans would approach parity with the Democrats, while a loss would push the GOP back to minority party status. Murray also noted that "each time the Republicans have been on the verge of a Texas breakthrough, circumstances have conspired to confirm their minority status." Such was the case with Watergate. In 1982, he contended, there could be a massive rejection of Reaganomics.[23]

Yet, as Clements kicked off his fall campaign with a swing through the Panhandle and North Central Texas — playing up his support from three former governors and four Democratic attorneys general — he drew large and enthusiastic crowds. In Sherman, for example, the crowd was estimated at 1,200. White was so weak that former Attorneys General Will Wilson, John Ben Shepperd,

Waggoner Carr, and Gerald Mann all endorsed Clements — which Clements thought said it all.

Thus the stage was set. Clements was convinced he was doing a good job and was a popular governor, despite his frequent portrayals by the Democrats and the press as mean-spirited and arrogant. The Democrats were determined to link him to Reaganomics and a faltering economy. That was the situation on the outside.

On the inside, the Clements campaign was having problems but not realizing their extent. "I don't think anybody thought Clements could be defeated," said press aide Tony Garrett. "In the summer, we were real confident. We were working hard. We were probably doing too much."[24]

The staff was bloated and filled with a lot of young and inexperienced people, organization director Ann Quirk recalled. There were more than 100 people on the staff in the fall, compared to some thirty who were working for White.[25] Clements had thirteen regional headquarters and fifty phone banks. Garrett's press office included at least twenty people, churning out press releases and radio actualities and schedules and talking to the media. His chief writer was Bill Cryer, a former reporter for the *Austin American-Statesman*, who later went to work for Democrat Ann Richards.[26] Tony Proffitt, a Democrat from Comptroller Bob Bullock's office, worked in the Democrats for Clements operation. He had worked in the primary for Buddy Temple, but said White distorted facts for personal gain and was an "incompetent attorney general."[27] Proffitt was also learning about statewide campaigning, in case Bullock decided to run in the future.

One of the time-consuming activities of Garrett's press staff was putting out releases on various "affinity" groups — Doctors for Clements, Lawyers for Clements, Farmers and Ranchers for Clements, Realtors for Clements, Architects for Clements, Car Dealers for Clements, Veterinarians for Clements, Blacks for Clements, Jewish Leaders for Clements, and the highly touted Democrats for Clements. Endorsements were obtained from people in every conceivable business and professional group; categories were endless.[28] Ridiculed by the press for the obscurity of some of the endorsements, Garrett had a "Reporters for Clements" bumper sticker made up, but could find no takers among the Austin press corps. Garrett believed the press, by then, was universally hostile toward Clements.

Lance Tarrance, the campaign's pollster, thought the campaign had too much money and too little control. There had been a policy in 1978 that no television spot would go out until the policy committee reviewed it. Clements, he said, then was "very coachable," and was more inclined to follow the recommendations of the professionals. "We all worked as a team; we were very careful," he said. But in 1982, Don Ringe worked almost independently with Clements, as a free agent producing commercials. "We had more TV commercials than we had laid out; they just went out and did all these commercials, Clements and Ringe."

Tarrance believed Clements' personality changed during his first term. "He had been very populistic as a candidate. But it was like taking over a company in a hostile takeover. He knew how to get the shareholders, and once he got in, he became a manager's manager." Clements also spent an inordinate amount of time arguing with officials in Washington, and was upset that the Reagan White House wasn't meeting his expectations. Clements had begun to snap at people, Tarrance said. "We were not able to sell him as a man of the people as we were four years earlier. We had to sell him as a man who was doing a good job for Texas. We lost the little guy in 1982."[29]

After the election, campaign officials attributed much of the governor's "snapping" to constant pain he was experiencing from a chronic hip problem, caused by an old handball injury.

In the late summer of 1982, Californian Tom Reed, the mastermind of the 1978 campaign, paid a visit to Texas. Tarrance later recalled sitting in Rita Clements' car when Reed said, "Bill's going to lose this race." Mrs. Clements admitted she was worried, too, Tarrance said. Reed thought Clements was overconfident and unwilling to get on the same level with the common people and ask for their vote again. "Clements' attitude in 1982 was, 'I'm governor. I've done some great things, and if Texas doesn't know it, to hell with it,'" Tarrance said. He remembered Reed saying, "We've got to go back and ask for their vote again, not tell them we're great."[30]

Other campaign officials agreed that the 1982 campaign seemed different from 1978. "The first time, it was like a conquest. The second time, the campaign was competent and well managed but there wasn't the fire in the belly. It was no longer revolutionary," Garrett said. The challenge was gone, plus Clements refused to hear any bad news. Hesitant and intimidated, staff members tried to get Tarrance to bring up problems with Clements, using his research data. Clements, however, saw himself on a roll. He believed he was doing work for Texas that had never been done before and that he was having an impact on the administration in Washington.

"We even thought there was a possiblity for president some day," Tarrance said. There was talk within the campaign's high command that if Reagan didn't do better, maybe Clements would run.

It was not the attitude change, however, that proved fatal to the 1982 Clements campaign. In an ironic turnabout from 1978, the campaign was submerged by "national factors."

"We injected the national anti-Carter, pro-energy themes into the 1978 race. By 1982, the Democrats were saying, we can play the same game," Tarrance said. The nation hit 10 percent unemployment thirty days before the election. And talk of Social Security reform, an issue in the U.S. Senate race between incumbent Lloyd Bentsen and Republican challenger Jim Collins, bled over into the governor's race, notwithstanding its irrelevance as a state issue.

Several other elements affected the outcome of the election, including the use of the campaign's tabloid newspaper, the *Texas Spectator*, to highlight White's brush with the law as a young man; Clements' statement that he didn't know of a housewife qualified to sit on the Public Utility Commission; and Clements' failure to take seriously White's claim that he would save Texans money by cutting out the automatic pass-through charge on utility bills. The governor's personality also became a campaign issue.

Ann Quirk believed the *Texas Spectator* piece was a turning point in the campaign, setting it in a decidedly negative direction. It was a distraction, and it hurt morale among the workers, who wondered if the governor was losing. Otherwise, why stoop to such a low?

The "low" was printing a story in the campaign newspaper, mailed to 1.5 million Texans, that White had been arrested in the East Texas town of Athens when he was a twenty-three-year-old Baylor law school student. White had crashed his Volkswagen into a parked car while drinking. A driving-while-intoxicated charge was later reduced to public intoxication, and White paid a $50 fine. Clements contended that the incident from nineteen years before was part of White's background, and it was not out of place to use it in the campaign.[31]

During a debate in Amarillo on the night of September 24, 1982, White raised a copy of the tabloid and accused Clements of allowing his campaign to take "an ugly turn." White said, "This thing is garbage and that's where the people of Texas are going to throw it." After the debate, White waved the tabloid in Clements' face and said, "I hope you stop the mudslinging, governor." White went on to say, "You won't have any mudslinging in my campaign, like you've seen in his." Clements countered, "Is that a promise? When did you stop? For nine months, you have been saying the most ugly things. Now when the cooking gets a little hot in the kitchen, if you can't stand that heat, you'd better get out of it."[32]

But the incident that generated the most mileage for Mark White was Clements' statement about a housewife sitting on the Public Utility Commission. Clements had gone to Galveston for the unveiling of a restored nineteenth-century sailing ship and for a campaign rally. While there, he agreed to be interviewed by a reporter from a local weekly newspaper. The reporter inquired about an empty slot on the Public Utilities Commission, and asked if he would consider appointing a minority or a housewife to the position. Clements responded that it would not be appropriate to have a housewife on the PUC because "I don't know of any that are qualified in the sense that I am talking about." Clements said he wanted someone who understood bonding and utilities as a business and, he said, "I don't know of any housewife that understands that."[33]

That became an emotional topic for the last two months of the campaign, and was enlarged by the Democrats, who claimed Clements had said he didn't know of a "woman" qualified to sit on the PUC. The statement made him look anti-female and out-of-date. Clements was not concerned because he thought the statement was taken out of context, and he knew he had a good record of appointing women.

Clements would occasionally invite his campaign department heads in for one of his famed "reading group circles," in which he would go around the circle and ask questions. At one such meeting, he asked about the issue of "a woman on the PUC." After hearing the responses from several in the circle, Clements said, "Naw, I don't think it's an issue. I'm not going to let it be an issue. I've got the best record of appointing women of any governor in history."[34]

In an effort to diffuse the "woman" issue, Clements released information on the number of women he had appointed to state boards and commissions. Among them were many "firsts," including the first woman to the Texas Supreme Court, Texas Court of Appeals, Criminal Justice Division Advisory Board, Commission on Law Enforcement Standards and Education, Commission on Jail Standards, Criminal Justice Coordinating Council, Motor Vehicle Commission, Health Facilities Commission, State Board of Public Accountancy, Board of Medical Examiners, State Board of Veterinary Medical Examiners, State Board of Morticians and Board of Tax Assessor-Collectors. He appointed the first woman chairman of the Governor's Flood Control Action Group, and increased the number of women appointed to higher education boards by 33 percent during his administration.

As White sympathized with Texans who had lost jobs, Clements continued to talk about a strong and resilient economy in the state. Though the state's unemployment rate had soared to eight percent and a record number of Texans were now out of work, the governor insisted that what was needed was a little John Wayne-style true grit. He offered his own experience as an example, when he went to the oilfields at age seventeen during the Depression: "I didn't sit up there in Dallas sucking my thumb. I got on a bus and went to South Texas." Clements said there were plenty of jobs in the want ads.[35]

White's most penetrating other campaign shot was to say he would prohibit utilities from being able to automatically pass on to ratepayers increases in the cost of fuel. Clements believed it was a bogus issue; he defended the pass-through charge as necessary for the companies to maintain adequate service.[36] It became the energizing issue for White in the final weeks of the campaign.

Clements' campaign officials acknowledged later that the utility issue was mishandled. Utility rates had gotten out of control, particularly in Houston, and White was turning consumer outrage over high utility rates into a political hammer, claiming Clements was insensitive to the problems of working men and women. Clements' response was to call White a "liar" for saying he could bring the utility rates down.

Tarrance recalled being summoned to a Houston television studio where Clements was cutting a commercial to refute the utility issue. "It was the most defensive, argumentative, defiant, I-know-what's-going-on-you-don't kind of ad," Tarrance said. Clements helped write the ad and didn't want a lot of changes in it. "He was very obstinate and irritable about the whole issue," Tarrance said. "He had his own idea. This was a specious issue. It's wrong for Mark White to grandstand on this issue. He doesn't know what he's talking about, in fact, he's even lying to you on this issue. It was a personal attack."[37]

Some members of the media cast the 1982 election as a referendum on Clements' personality. Albert Hunt of the *Wall Street Journal* wrote that Clements' style and personality were on trial in the Texas election. Hunt wrote:

> It's hard to find a politician as outspoken or eager to brawl. Gov. William Clements bristles when asked if he has made any mistakes or has any regrets. He seems to feel that's the sort of mea culpa that no tough-minded politician would tolerate.
>
> When reminded that President Kennedy's popularity soared when he admitted error following the Bay of Pigs fiasco, Mr. Clements no longer restrains himself. "Well, I don't have any Bay of Pigs," he snaps. "And I didn't drive any girl off a bridge either."
>
> This is vintage Bill Clements: blunt, bull-headed, tactless, tough and mean. This is the way he became Texas's first Republican governor since Reconstruction. This is the way he has behaved for the past four years, and this is the way he is running for re-election.

Hunt concluded that the race was dominated by Clements' controversial and confrontational personality, which he described as abrasive and boorish to opponents and direct and honest to friends.[38]

Clements' personality was an issue. In 1981, Carole Kneeland, who covered the Capitol for Dallas' WFAA-TV, began hosting a monthly statewide show on public television called the "Governor's Report," which featured live call-ins. Texans were accustomed to seeing brief sound bites of Clements, but on the "Governors' Report," they saw him for a full hour. The show was getting call-ins from across the state, from West Texas to East Texas, and Clements was argumentative. He would respond to queries from reporters and viewers alike by saying, "That's a stupid question." Ms. Kneeland said, "He would abuse us [journalists] and he would abuse them [viewers]." The Austin Gridiron Show did a spoof on the program, which it called "The Governor's Retort." Ms. Kneeland said, years later, she thought Clements' performance on the program contributed to his downfall in the 1982 election.[39]

Mark White tried to make Clements the central issue. David Lindsey, White's press spokesman, said: "This is a referendum on Bill Clements . . . not only on policies but also on the substitution of arrogance for leadership." A researcher for the White campaign said, "We tried looking for dirt on Clements, and it was pretty hard to come by. What we found was that there are a lot of people out there who believe that Bill Clements doesn't care about them."[40] White seized every opportunity to reinforce that view.

Meanwhile, the Democrats were running as Democrats and Clements was running as Clements. For the first time since there had been a Republican force in the state, the Democrats were waging a unified campaign. Their top three candidates — Sen. Lloyd Bentsen, Lt. Gov. Bill Hobby, and Mark White — pooled their resources for phone banks and a get-out-the-vote effort, with Bentsen putting in the most money. Clements was outspending White two-to-one. But the "unity campaign" multiplied the Democratic candidate's resources and his effectiveness.

Clements was running solo, avoiding the other Republican statewide candidates. Texas was still awash in ticket-splitters and Clements knew that if he got too partisan, he would lose some of the voters he had attracted in 1978. In addition, he thought the rest of the Republican field was weak. Jim Collins, the conservative Republican congressman from Dallas, had challenged Sen. Lloyd Bentsen, and was attempting to portray Bentsen as a "liberal." Clements respected Bentsen from his days in the Pentagon, and didn't think the Democratic senator was a liberal. He remained virtually neutral in that race.

There was infighting among Republicans, even as the Democrats were unifying. Clements blasted Collins for releasing a poll that showed he was trailing White. "I consider it a breach of good taste and a breach of etiquette for someone to dip into my race," Clements said.[41] Clements wouldn't campaign with Collins, nor would he campaign with his former secretary of state, George Strake, the GOP challenger to Hobby, because Clements expected he would have to work with Hobby in a second term. The Republicans had candidates running against Comptroller Bob Bullock and Agriculture Commissioner Jim Hightower. Clements was willing to say disparaging things only about Hightower; the governor claimed that the liberal Democrat didn't know "any more about agriculture than a hog does about Sunday."

Clements didn't want to be dragged down by other Republicans in his appeal to the ticket-splitters. Press aide Garrett felt Clements was right, that it was too early for Republicans to run as a slate in Texas, though legislative candidates were showing up at his rallies, trying to piggyback on his success.

Strake, however, was incensed that Clements wasn't helping fellow Republicans, including himself. Newspapers reported in late October that Clements was predicting defeat for three fellow Republicans who were running statewide campaigns. Strake's wife, Annette, was angry enough to telephone Clements to complain that the governor had implied Strake couldn't win the lieutenant governorship. Clements hollered for Rita to get on the phone. Then, he said, "Now calm down, Ann-ette, it's not that bad." She responded, "Yes, it is. You have just ruined our campaign." The upshot was that Clements agreed to do a press conference at Hobby Airport days before the election stating he was supporting Strake over Hobby.[42]

On October 23, the day after Clements appeared at the Houston press conference with Strake, Mark White appeared at four black churches in Houston and eight black churches in Dallas, where he slammed Clements' appointments to the Public Utility Commission and attacked high utility rates.[43]

Five days before the election, out on the campaign trail, Clements clearly was peeved by questions on utility rates. When a Houston TV reporter insisted that utility rates were a major issue in the campaign, Clements said, "It is not! It is not!" Instead of agreeing that rising utility rates were a problem, Clements made statements like, "People are just going to have to conserve more. When I grew up, there was no air conditioning and we got along fine."[44]

Jack Rains, Clements' campaign leader in Houston, could see the utility issue growing in importance and reported it to state headquarters. Texans were seeing their utility bills go up; White claimed he could do something about that, and they believed him.

On the Sunday before the election, there was a conference call between the regional chairmen and Governor and Mrs. Clements. Rains remembers being advised beforehand to try not to be negative, to be upbeat. But Houston was a swing area with strong labor and minority blocs. He knew Clements couldn't win without Houston, and told him so. Clements' position, according to Rains, was, "OK, we're losing a little ground, but he [White] can't catch us."[45]

Ann Quirk recalled that the governor was "spouting off poll numbers. It's human nature not to want to rain on the parade — with him more than a lot of people. If you're around him a lot, he almost convinces you of something through sheer will. And he'd been right in 1978 when nobody thought he'd be. The regional chairman felt he wasn't so strong, but they didn't articulate it," she said. "I think the people in the campaign got worn down by his confidence."[46]

Tarrance recalled that in the final days of the campaign, he saw the election growing tighter, but Clements was buoyed when he went to normally Democratic towns and was met by 400 or 500 people. "I'm doing better than you think I'm doing," Clements would tell the pessimists.

On the night before the election, Clements had a final rally in front of the Alamo in San Antonio. Little did he know how symbolic that would be. The Alamo, after all, had been the site of Texas' biggest defeat in the fight for its independence. Clements was pumped by what appeared to be a successful end to a successful campaign — as were his traveling companions and aides. Tarrance's polls that night showed him nine points ahead of Mark White. Tarrance told campaign manager Jim Francis that Clements should win by a margin of 52 to 48 percent, and Francis expressed surprise that the margin would be that close. On the plane from San Antonio to Dallas, Francis exuberantly told the governor, "The cake's in the oven."[47]

The speculation on the plane was not whether he would win, but how big, and who might he bring across the finish line with him. Rita Clements wrote on a notepad the various predictions. She forecast a 53.8 percent win, while Clements predicted 53.7 percent. Dary Stone predicted the closest outcome, giving Clements a scant 50.5 percent win. Other predictions ranged from 51.25 to 55 percent.[48]

It was a miserable election day — foggy, raining or overcast all over the state. In Houston it was raining hard — a "real frog-strangler," according to Jack Rains. Rains knew their campaign was in trouble when he drove the black precincts and found people standing in line, in the rain, to vote. He reported to campaign headquarters in Austin, "These people are motivated. They're mad. We're in deep shit."[49]

Throughout the day, the Austin headquarters kept getting reports of the unbelievable turnout in Houston's minority wards; the polling places were running out of ballots. An atmosphere of fear began to pervade the headquarters. Republicans later complained that massive tie-ups on freeways to the suburbs, with stalled cars blocking exit lanes, kept their voters from getting to polling places after work.

What they didn't know was that, in the waning hours of the campaign, Democrats had made an enormous effort to impart their message by mail and through massive literature drops in minority neighborhoods and other strong Democratic precincts. To connote with urgency that Tuesday was election day, a mock telegram went out under the names of U.S. Sen. Lloyd Bentsen, Lt. Gov. Bill Hobby, and Mark White. In bold capital letters, the "telegram" said: RONALD REAGAN AND HIS RICH FRIENDS ARE BET- TING THAT YOU WON'T VOTE ON TUESDAY. WHY? BECAUSE THEY DON'T BELIEVE YOU CARE ABOUT RECORD-HIGH UNEMPLOYMENT AMONG BLACK AMERICANS, OR THEIR PLANS TO CUT SOCIAL SECUR- ITY. THEY ARE BETTING THAT YOU WON'T REMEMBER OR CARE ABOUT THEIR RECENT EFFORTS TO GIVE FEDERAL MONEY TO SEGREGATED SCHOOLS THAT DISCRIMINATE AGAINST BLACK AMERICANS.

Voters were urged to send Reagan and all Republicans a message on election day by voting the straight Democratic ticket. The names of seven Democrats running for statewide office were listed.[50]

A flyer distributed in the minority precincts listed "Ten Good Reasons to Fight Back!" The list included food stamps, Social Security benefits, AFDC benefits, child nutrition programs, aid for education, housing assistance, CETA jobs, Meals on Wheels, Medicaid/Medicare and Jobs. "Ronald Reagan and his Republican administration have cut hundreds of thousands of our people from these programs and even bigger cuts are planned for next year."

The flyer urged people to vote on November 2. "Need a ride to the polls?" it asked. A telephone number was listed.[51]

Similar tactics were used in Dallas, where minority voters appeared at the polls saying they had to vote "No. 11" — straight ticket Democratic — or lose their Social Security and food stamps.

The Democrats' get-out-the-vote effort also reached out to 60,000 Mexican-Americans in South Texas with a mailgram that screamed: "Breadlines — the sign of Republicans." Block workers and sound trucks prowled the Democratic precincts in San Antonio on election day.[52]

It was the ultimate in scare tactics that produced an overwhelming tide of Democratic voters, and the first Republican governor in the century got caught in the undertow.

In an eerie omen on election day, Brother Lester Roloff, the evangelist who claimed he had delivered 250,000 votes for Clements in the 1978 race, and whose church schools Clements defended repeatedly against legal action by Atty. Gen. Mark White, was killed in a plane crash.

On election night, Clements was still in his office at the Capitol when the early returns began coming in. They weren't encouraging. He told his gubernatorial press aide, Jon Ford: "Aw, it's OK. We're going to have some bad reports out of some of these places, but it's going to turn out OK."[53] Then he headed over to the Sheraton Crest Hotel, where workers and supporters were gathering for the victory party. Less than an hour after the polls closed, CNN and one network already had declared Clements a sure loser. Tony Garrett went to the governor's room at the Sheraton Crest before the 10:00 P.M. newscasts and asked for a statement for the press. Clements refused to concede. He was convinced the early returns were an aberration. "He thought it was going to be a repeat of 1978, that when the final returns came in, he would win," Garrett said.

To the contrary, the final and official returns showed Mark White won easily, with 1,697,870 votes to Clements' 1,465,937, of more than 3.1 million votes cast.[54] White got 53.2 percent of the vote, compared to Clements' almost 46 percent. Two other candidates drew less than one percent.

The night of the election, Tarrance was serving as an analyst for a local CBS station in Houston. At midnight, the commentator turned to Clements' pollster and said, "It's 12 o'clock, Clements is behind by 120,000 votes and most of the other people in the state are calling the election for White. Don't you think it's about time you called it?" Tarrance had to concede that White was the winner.[55]

As head of organization, it was Ann Quirk's job on election night to get the returns from the field staff to Clements. "The shock of the numbers lying to him," she said, referring to the campaign's polling data, "was shattering."[56]

Clements finally appeared about 2:00 A.M. with Rita and told his supporters that "from the looks of the returns and from the present trends, it does seem like our campaign has not been successful." He expressed his gratitude and appreciation for work in the campaign and the dedication of volunteers. But if the trend in returns continued, he said, "we will indeed have a new governor in Texas. And Rita and I wish Mark White success for all Texans. And, you know, there is nothing else to say. That's the way it is. Thank you again. Youall are super."⁵⁷

Clements got almost 300,000 more votes than he did in 1978 but lost the election. George Strake got more votes than Clements did in 1978 and lost his election.⁵⁸ The huge, unexpected turnout of Democratic voters buried the Republicans, making mincemeat of polls that showed Clements leading White up to the final night of the campaign.

Tarrance's post-election polls indicated that the federal issues — unemployment, the economy, Social Security — played a dominant role in getting people to the polls, although the utility issue was also important in the governor's race.

Forty-one percent of Democrats voted a straight ticket, and straight-ticket voting was particularly high in Harris County, where 60 percent of Democratic voters pulled a single lever. The main reason people voted for White, according to Tarrance's analysis, was because he was a Democrat or they didn't like Clements. The other main reason they gave for favoring White was the utility issue. NBC's exit polls showed that women voters turned against Clements, as a result of the housewife-on-the-utility-commission issue.⁵⁹ Turnout was up among Hispanics as well as black voters. Forty percent of eligible Hispanic voters cast ballots. The fact that Clements had named 170 Mexican-Americans to boards and commissions, more than any previous Texas governor, failed to translate into Hispanic voting power on election day.

The Democrats triple-teamed Clements with the combined turnout efforts of Bentsen, Hobby, and White. "If we fell down anywhere, it was in underestimating what we were up against," Garrett said. "We thought we were up against Mark White, who was running a very disorganized campaign. We weren't; we were up against Lloyd Bentsen, Bill Hobby and Mark White." Other Democratic statewide candidates, Jim Mattox running for attorney general, Jim Hightower for agriculture commissioner, and Ann Richards for state treasurer, also had their own personal followings and organization which turned out voters.

The *Texas Government Newsletter*, in analyzing the race, reported that "the Democrats decided to hang together rather than hang separately," even as Clements was trying to distance himself from Republican ultra-conservatives like Jim Collins. Democrats turned their diversity into a source of strength and combined their resources to finance Democrat phone banks. They took the initiative on issues, including Reaganomics and high Texas unemployment. "Motivated by fear and anger, heavily Democratic constituencies such as blacks, Hispanics and blue-collar workers voted in unusually large numbers," according to the newsletter.

Democrats had a clean sweep of statewide offices. Republicans also failed to win any of the three new congressional seats and lost three seats in the Texas Senate. They did manage to hold on to their five seats in Congress and their thirty-six seats in the Texas House of Representatives. The number of Republican county judges went from 10 to 14, and Republican county officeholders grew slightly from 166 to 191. But four of 10 judges that Clements had appointed in Harris County failed to survive the election.[60]

The Republicans were dazed by the turnout. Republican State Chairman Chet Upham observed that it was a "presidential year turnout" by the Democrats.[61]

Tarrance's polls never detected the Democratic tidal wave building. Tarrance had screened his surveys to voters expected to turn out in a state election; those who failed to vote in the previous presidential election were not considered likely voters and therefore not interviewed. "Hell no, we never got the signal," campaign manager Jim Francis said two days after the election. "We didn't expect a 3.2 million turnout. If it had been 2.7 million or 2.8 million, we would have won."[62]

Clements had spent $12 million in the campaign, outspending White two-to-one.

White credited his win to a unified Democratic Party, the active campaigning of Bentsen and Hobby, and to the governor's apparent insensitivity to high utility bills.[63] White's campaign manager, Dwayne Holman, claimed Democrats were spurred to work harder by the prospect that if Clements were reelected, two years into his second term he would have named all members of state boards and commissions. "They could see the end of the two-party system if Clements got another four years to really build and force conversions to the Republican party," Holman said.[64]

The anti-Republican tide in Texas wasn't isolated. Nationwide, a backlash against Reaganomics, double-digit unemployment, and the fear that the Reagan administration was going to reform Social Security led to the defeat of thirteen Republican governors. Even with his attitude problems and the strategy mistakes — which were easier to make in an overconfident campaign — Clements likely would still have won, except for the national influence and the combined effort of the top Democratic candidates in the state. Some said White was dragged to victory by Bentsen and Hobby — and particularly Bentsen, who led the ticket with a muscular 59 percent of the vote.

Years later, Clements said he believed the utility issue cost him the election — that and Tarrance's polls, which gave him a false sense of security.

Tarrance admitted that he failed to pick up on the national trends, and he screened too far down on his surveys. "We were trying to get close to the 50 percent that really vote in an off-year election," he explained. "We did not know that if you take Social Security, unemployment, and special themes that appeal to the lower socio-economic bracket and put a lot of money into getting out the vote, what would happen," he said. Even so, Tarrance said he saw some danger signals along the way, particularly on the utility issue. "Should I have raised more cain about it? Probably, yes," he said, in an interview more than a dozen years later. And, he said, while Clements was consistently ahead in the surveys, there was a large bloc of undecideds. Clements never reached 50 percent in the surveys. In later years, pollsters learned not to take election for granted in off-presidential years if a candidate failed to reach 50 percent in pre-election surveys.

The day after the defeat, a subdued Bill Clements appeared before the press in the Governor's Reception Room and accepted "with good grace" the voters' decision and pledged an orderly transition. "You know, there's nothing nice about losing. But we lost. And we will lose with good grace." He acknowledged that maybe he had called the wrong plays. Asked what they were, he said, "Well, I would have certainly made an audible at the line of scrimmage if I'd known what they were. Obviously, we did something wrong."

Following are excerpts from the press conference transcript, with reporters asking the questions and Clements' responses:[65]

> Q: Did you think that people really bought the idea that you are mean and arrogant?
> A: Well, it could be.
> Q: What effect do you think your defeat and the defeat of the other candidates is going to have on the Republican party?

A: Oh, I wouldn't care to philosophize about that. You know, these things have a strange way of resurrecting themselves and getting new life and new circumstances and, another day, another dollar.

Q: Is this the last we will see of you in politics?

A: Well, you know, I don't intend to just ugly away. I'll be around. I'll be around.

Q: Do you think this is your last race?

A: You used the wrong word. I know it is . . . . I told all of you before that this would be my last campaign, that I would not run for any other office.

Then Clements went with Rita to his headquarters on Brazos Street. As Clements stood inside the building complimenting campaign workers for a "magnificent effort," the governor's limousine was parked in a no-parking zone in front, with the governor's assigned Department of Public Safety officer standing nearby. An Austin policeman rode up on his three-wheeler and took out his ticket pad. The SO1 (State Office No. 1) license plate notwithstanding, the Austin cop was preparing to write out a ticket. After all, this was soon to be the former governor. A heated conversation ensued between the DPS officer in charge of the governor's security detail and the Austin police officer. Finally, the Austin cop folded up his ticket book and left. Inside, Rita Clements was trying to blink back tears as her husband said softly, "As Casey put it, there's no joy in Mudville."[66]

Press aide Jon Ford said there was some grousing among the staff as to who was responsible for the loss, but Clements "wouldn't tolerate that kind of talk," he said. "He just accepted it as matter of factly as he could."

Ford went to work putting together the required Governor's Report to the 68th Legislature, which he later said was completed hurriedly, as staff members were packing up and looking for other jobs. "We had anticipated a second term, at the end of which we'd do a fancy report. We had our sights on what we would be presenting to the Legislature in the way of goals for a second term." The report wasn't slick, but Ford — who had been press secretary to Gov. Price Daniel and had observed several administrations as a Capitol correspondent — felt that even though Clements' programs were cut short, no previous governor had accomplished more. "He had the most positive program and the most positive attitude toward getting it accomplished than any [governor] I knew," Ford said.[67]

As Karl Rove, another one of the governor's staff members, said, the state "spent a lot of money in the 1960s and 1970s from oil and gas revenues, and did not necessarily have a lot to show for it. It would have been easy to go with the flow, but he made some tough actions on the budget and racheted down spending."[68]

On January 4, 1983, shortly before turning over the reins of power, Clements met with members of the press in his Capitol office. He expressed regrets that by not being reelected, his programs would be left in limbo. He wondered what would happen to his vision for the future as presented in the long-range planning effort, Texas 2000. He was concerned about continuation of his management programs, aimed at making government more efficient, and his drive to reduce the bureaucracy. "I doubt that the incoming administration has the inclination — certainly they don't have the background — to continue the program. It has to be on the agenda every day. It'll drop in the cracks."

He had appointed seventeen bipartisan task forces to provide the legislative thrust for the next session. What would happen to their work?

"We have made the highest-quality appointments that have ever been made. Will we have the same kind of mixed appointments — Democrats, independents, Republicans — or will we have a hanky-panky, Mickey Mouse situation where nothing but campaign Democrats are appointed to these very responsible positions, who have no contribution whatsoever to make except the fact that they supported a particular candidate in the last election process?"

Another regret was that his Mexican initiatives might be dropped. "We have made more progress in our relationship with Mexico than any time in our history. Mutual confidence should be a major thrust for any administration. Cross-fertilization on the border is too important to Texas to leave to Washington and Mexico City."[69]

Indeed, University of Texas economics professor William Glade wrote in a letter to the *Austin American-Statesman* in late December, "As Gov. Clements leaves office, it seems appropriate to give him particular praise for fostering improved relations between Texas and Mexico. The considerable energy the governor devoted to establishing and nurturing our state's ties with Latin America in general and Mexico in particular made for a refreshingly innovative contrast with the most habitual disregard of these matters in previous times. It is to be hoped that Governor-elect Mark White will move vigorously to build upon this productive initiative."[70]

Asked his contribution to the Republican Party in this final interview with the press, Clements replied, "Well, I got elected. That's one."

Clements also told reporters about the hip injury that had occurred years before while he was playing for the handball championship at Dallas Athletic Club. It had become a chronic problem that had gotten progressively worse during the campaign. He revealed that he would have a hip replacement operation the last week in January of 1983.

He talked about the possiblity of the SEDCO building becoming home of the Clements Foundation, and said he hoped his personal "liberry" of books would in due course be made available to writers and researchers of Texana.

Despite their often-stormy encounters, Clements said at the end of the interview that he had thoroughly enjoyed his relationship with members of the Capitol press corps. He had never backed away from a scrap with them — nor they with him.

That fact prompted a reporter to respond: "And I think we can all say that it certainly has been an interesting four years."[71]

As the governor prepared to hand over the reins of power, Doug Harlan, a Republican-leaning columnist from San Antonio, wrote of his lasting impression of Clements. It was that of "a bulldog with the seat of someone's pants hanging from his mouth, wagging his tail and looking pleased as punch."[72] Harlan concluded:

> Despite four years in the public eye, Clements is largely misunderstood. He is more than the blunt-talking, aggressive, bulldog personality we have seen. He has an unswerving commitment to do the right thing as he sees it, personal consequences to the contrary.
>
> Clements' performance as governor shows he has been a good trustee of public funds, striving to maximize the buying power of our taxes through business-like management of public affairs. He leaves the state better off than he found it in that regard.
>
> Unfortunately, the accumulation of pants seats makes us forget the bulldog's duty is to guard the house, which he does in the way he knows best.

Chapter 15

SEDCO Sold

The End of a Chapter

FROM THE TIME THAT Bill Clements went to Washington to work in the Nixon administration in 1973 until the end of his first gubernatorial term ten years later, he had almost no involvement in the management of SEDCO, Inc. He was too busy with his public duties to be concerned about private business, and he felt that any business involvement would be a conflict of interest while he was in public office.

B. Gill Clements was president and chief executive officer of the company while his father was in Washington. Steve Mahood, who succeeded Tom Rhodes as the company's general counsel, recalled that "Clements had nothing to do with the company when he was in Washington." Gill had moved into his father's former office, and the elder Clements, he said, "really didn't meddle."[1]

When Clements returned from Washington to Dallas with his new wife in 1977, he assumed the position of chairman of the board and chief executive officer of SEDCO, Inc. But his interests had moved on. Within months of his return, he was campaigning for governor. Gill Clements remained as president and chief operating officer.

Gill had become comfortable in his role as president of SEDCO, a role that at first had frightened him. But the younger Clements had relied on the expertise of the able executives around him. Referring to the company and its success under his supervision, Gill Clements said, "I had a Ferrari to drive. It doesn't take much to beat Chevrolets and Fords if you're driving a Ferrari."

The younger Clements took no interest in his father's political career and wasn't involved in his decision to run for governor. He heard the news on the radio as he was driving home from work that his father was going to be a candidate for governor.

"When he got involved in politics, I didn't like that," Gill said, in an interview years later. "I wasn't comfortable with it. I didn't like all that political foolishness, bowing and scraping, handshaking and baby-kissing and all that stuff. It's just not me." Gill didn't have much admiration for political figures. "I didn't see that as something to assign great value to," he said. In contrast, his father saw it as a challenge and believed that one person could make a difference.[2]

When Clements became governor in 1979, Gill again assumed the title of chief executive officer and continued serving as president of SEDCO, Inc. Tom Rhodes, the company's former senior vice-president and general counsel, became chairman of the board, after working in the campaign and helping the new governor set up his budget office. Throughout Clements' gubernatorial term, Rhodes, by then retired as an officer of the company, was board chairman, and Spencer Taylor, executive vice-president of the company and second in command to Gill Clements, was chairman of the executive committee of SEDCO, Inc. Jerry Cunningham was president of SEDCO's Drilling Division.

While Clements was away, the philosophy of the company continued to recognize the cyclical nature of drilling, the uncertainty of the market, and the long time it took to build the expensive equipment. "The foundation of our philosophy was that we must have a long-term contract that guarantees work for this equipment, so that we know we will get half our money back in the original contract," Gill Clements said. "To have such a philosophy — and I don't know of any other company that had it — you've got to have a premier reputation, customers who believe in you," he said.[3]

During Bill Clements' absence, SEDCO had continued to thrive but had also experienced some difficult times. During the 1974-75 heyday of North Sea exploration, SEDCO increased its earnings over 300 percent. Its stock hit a high of $66 in 1973-74 while Clements was in Washington. But then Norwegians and others brought new semi-submersible capacity into the North Sea in a declining market, and daily rental rates on the expensive drilling units plummeted from $42,500 to a low of $16,000.[4]

According to *Forbes Magazine*, SEDCO was the market leader among drilling contractors near the end of the decade of the '70s. SEDCO had kept its drilling margins up partly through its work in Iran. SEDCO had formed a joint venture company, called SEDI-RAN, while Clements was in Washington. SEDIRAN was 50 percent owned by several Iranian interests, including the ruling family's Pahlavi Foundation. SEDIRAN was under contract to drill for the consortium of Western oil companies that produced 80 percent of the oil in Iran. In 1978, SEDCO's revenues of nearly $390 million included more than $57 million from its contract with the Iran consortium.[5] Gill Clements explained that as the price of oil went up and countries began assuming control of their natural resources, foreign contractors had to work more closely with local interests. Because of the strong nationalistic fervor, he said, "you didn't get the business unless you worked with these local people."[6]

But 1979 was a disastrous year, with the Ixtoc I blowout and its attendant legal problems, and because of the Iranian Revolution.

In December of 1978, as Clements was busy in his transition office preparing to take the reins of government from Dolph Briscoe, the Ayatollah Khomeini and his supporters were in the process of toppling the Shah of Iran. There were huge demonstrations across Iran. Strikes gripped the oilfields, and tensions were high. Many oilmen and their dependents left the country. In the middle of December 1978, Paul Grimm, an operations manager of the consortium (Oil Service Company of Iran) was assassinated in Ahwaz. Grimm, who was on loan from Texaco to the consortium, had been trying to thwart the striking efforts of the Khomeini forces to cut off the oil supply. Thirty-six hours before his death, Grimm had dinner with Carl Thorne, who was running SEDCO's Middle East operations from Dubai.

SEDCO had an enormous presence in South Iran for years, with more than 2,000 employees in the country at its peak. When Grimm was assassinated, Thorne gave the order for the remaining SEDCO employees to evacuate, and helped other oil business expatriates leave the country. By Christmas Day, 1978, Iranian petroleum exports had ceased, and by year's end, the consortium had evacuated its Western employees. In January 1979, the Shah fled his homeland.

Conditions quickly deteriorated in Iran. SEDCO's equipment was expropriated, including sixteen big land rigs, a large spread of pipeline construction equipment and a shipyard, with related camps, inventory, and transportation equipment. The company wrote off its entire investment in Iran, $59 million. Carl Thorne spent the next four years trying to recoup SEDCO's Iranian investment, which exceeded $100 million when lost contract revenue was added to the book value of the equipment. Lawsuits were filed in various jurisdictions and courts in the U.S. and abroad, including the Iranian-American claims tribunal in The Hague, Netherlands.[7]

President Carter had frozen all Iranian assets, about $10 billion, in America. Those funds were later released, except for $2 billion that was put into a fund to pay claims processed through the arbitration system that was set up in The Hague. As money was paid out, Iran had to replenish the fund to keep it at $2 billion.

In April of 1979, then-Governor Clements had an inquiry, through an intermediary, about the Shah of Iran, then exiled in the Bahamas, seeking residency in the U.S. Clements' response was that the U.S. should allow him in, although it would be best to delay it, if possible.[8] The Shah, who was battling cancer, eventually showed up in a San Antonio, Texas, hospital, although Clements had no knowledge beforehand that he was to be given health care in Texas.

While it took years for SEDCO to recover its equipment losses, the overall negative effect of Iran was short-lived. The long-term impact was that the Iranian Revolution created a fervor in the worldwide oil industry to find oil. With the threat that Iranian oil supplies would be shut off, oil companies were scrambling all over the world to buy oil. They foresaw the price of oil going from $18 and $20 a barrel to $60 or $70 a barrel. The oil companies feared there would be huge shortages of equipment and thought they needed to tie up drilling rigs in long-term contracts. That fervor gave rise to federal energy czar James Schlesinger's efforts to keep the oil companies from getting the "windfall" from rising oil prices, resulting in the windfall profits tax passed during the Carter administration.

The Iranian Revolution created the realization by the world oil companies that they needed to develop supply sources outside of nations that were susceptible to revolution. Concerned that revolutions would follow in Saudi Arabia and Kuwait, shutting off their sources, the world oil companies began looking for oil outside of OPEC — in China, Australia, South America, and the North Sea.

As described by Steve Mahood, then executive vice-president and general counsel of SEDCO, the attitude of the oil companies was: "Let's go to the North Sea. Let's drill wells in deep water in England. Let's go to Sweden. Let's go to the deep waters of Western Australia, Northern South America, Brazil. Let's go to places where revolution is not a problem, even if it is more expensive to find the oil. Don't worry, we're going to sell it for $60 to $70 a barrel."

The oil companies didn't care how deep or how rough the water was. They intended to find oil and produce it — no matter how harsh the environment. "The kind of drilling rigs that were used for those kinds of wells were SEDCO rigs. We had the best equipment, the best people. We were the experts in the field. Our services were in huge demand," Mahood recounted.[9]

At that point, SEDCO was entering into joint ventures with oil companies to build and share ownership of the expensive rigs. Other drilling contractors thought SEDCO was foolish to split its equipment ownership with the oil companies. The innovative arrangement, however, would later produce huge dividends for SEDCO, luring a buyer for the company with its modern equipment and low debt.

This was the environment Clements encountered when he moved back into his old office at SEDCO after losing the 1982 election. He resumed the title of chairman of the board of SEDCO, but he had no intention of resuming day-to-day management of the company. He wasn't sure what he wanted to do, other than to devote some time to hunting and fishing.

The former governor told the SEDCO board he would give approximately half of his time to SEDCO and the other half to his outside interests, which included the Boy Scouts, Southern Methodist University, and two national presidential commissions on which he had been asked to serve. One was the President's Commission on Strategic Forces, chaired by Brent Scowcroft. The commission was asked by President Reagan to examine all strategic forces, including the future of the nation's ICBM forces and to recommend basing alternatives. The other was the President's Commission on Central America, which was chaired by Henry Kissinger.

But his first chore was to undergo hip surgery to repair the chronic hip problem that resulted from the handball injury years earlier. After he recuperated from surgery in early 1983, Clements visited the Middle East and the North Sea operations of SEDCO.

"We were the biggest operator in the North Sea," Gill Clements said. His father was amazed at how the business had grown, and surprised at how many of the people in the organization had progressed, accepting greater responsibility.

Bill Clements loved the customer relations and employee relations aspect of the business. "But he'd done that. He'd worn that out before he went to Washington," Gill Clements said. When his father came back from Austin, Gill said, "He decided he didn't want an active role. He took the chairman title back. He was part of the company for that period, but he was just part of the team, rather than the leader. His role had changed in the company."[10]

A new generation of management was running SEDCO. At the corporate level, the company was led by Gill Clements, Spencer Taylor, Steve Mahood and John Milem, vice-president of finance. The Drilling Division was run by Jerry Cunningham, with young vice-presidents such as Dillard Hammett, Charles Purbaugh, Warren Sexton, and Carl Thorne. Some oldtimers were still around — Walter Etherington was a vice-president; W. G. "Bobby" Cox was in charge of the North Sea operations; LeJeune "Rabbit" Wilson was vice-president in charge of personnel; and H. L. "Duke" Zinkgraf was vice-president and equipment manager. Bill Martinovich, the innovative design engineer, was chief operating officer of the Engineering Division, and Bill McDonald was vice-president of engineering for the Drilling Division, responsible for getting the rigs built.

In 1982, SEDCO was in the midst of the largest rig construction program in the company's history. Seven new semi-submersible drilling units were being built at shipyards in South Korea, Japan and Singapore; six had five-year contracts for use upon completion. The units included the SEDCO/BP 711, the SEDCO 710, 712 and 714, and the SEDCO 600, 601 and 602. Cost of the rigs, which were scheduled for delivery through May of 1983, was from $61 million to $168 million each, totaling $680 million. The most expensive was the $168 million SEDCO 710, which was built in partnership with Petro Canada.[11]

Meanwhile, many of SEDCO's competitors were taking on more debt to build rigs on speculation. Other companies in the field at the time included the Hunt brothers' Penrod Drilling Company in Dallas; Reading and Bates; the Western Company of North America (Eddie Chiles' Fort Worth-based company); Santa Fe

Drilling Company; Zapata Corp. in Houston (where George Bush once worked); and Forex, owned by the French giant Schlumberger.

When Clements went to Washington, SEDCO had only two of the huge 700-type rigs in operation, but it had several in the works, the result of his vision for the company. The year he returned from his first gubernatorial term, SEDCO's fleet was at its height with 41 rigs, including the most sophisticated and expensive semi-submersibles ever built.

SEDCO was the largest drilling company in the world. Loffland Brothers, owned by the Cullen Davis family of Fort Worth, had more land rigs. Forex also had a big land-based operation. Global Marine, another competitor, was the biggest operator of drilling ships. But SEDCO had more offshore rigs and was recognized on Wall Street as the most profitable drilling company. It had more dollar investment in drilling equipment, higher gross sales, and larger profits than any other drilling company. In the offshore industry, it was world-renowned. SEDCO was so far ahead of the game in semi-submersibles that Gill Clements didn't figure it had any close competition.

During Bill Clements' absence to serve as governor, SEDCO had gotten involved in exploration both domestically and internationally, in such areas as offshore the Ivory Coast, West Africa. Need for investment capital for the Energy Division resulted in the sale of SEDCO's oilfield Manufacturing Division in 1980 and liquidation of its Construction Division in 1981.

And, while Clements was in Austin in 1980, 1981 and 1982, SEDCO got involved in stock trades, which resulted in big profits for the company. The company realized $50 million from buying and selling stock in Delhi International Oil Corp. Then SEDCO indentified Marathon Oil as a target, became its largest stockholder, and started a bidding war for Marathon. Marathon eventually sold to U.S. Steel, and SEDCO cashed in its chips for a gain of $194 million.[12] SEDCO was making money in new and different ways.

In 1982, Gill went hunting with his dad at Red Nunley's ranch in southwest Texas. Clements, who was still governor, was proud of what SEDCO was doing with Gill at the helm and said so. "He was bragging on us, and I told him we had a serious problem with this success," Gill said. The problem was that "we were a $650 million company, plus we had $450 million in cash. There was a lot of activity in hostile takeovers, a lot of companies were merging. We had to get rid of this liquidity or someone was going to come in and do it for us. Who are we going to go to? The only answer was Schlumberger; it was the only one that made sense," Gill said, referring to the world's largest oil-services company.[13] That was fully two years before the doorbell rang and Schlumberger, Ltd., was standing on the front porch.

SEDCO experienced record-breaking profits in 1982. But in 1983, the boom-and-bust oil cycle was again headed for bust. As Gill Clements wrote in SEDCO's annual report on September 1, 1983: "Contract drilling in general is cyclical and the industry is presently caught in a severe down cycle that was triggered by the 1981-1982 recession, a worldwide surplus of crude oil and speculative over-building of equipment by contractors. Industry utilization of offshore equipment worldwide has fallen to 74 percent, contract day rates have declined as much as 65 percent, and industry profits have dropped sharply." But SEDCO's drilling division was not adversely affected, because of its long-term drilling contracts. Utilization of SEDCO's offshore equipment was 96 percent, and its average day rate was holding at $57,600. Gill wrote that 1984 would be another good year for SEDCO because of its contracts, but beyond that, he couldn't foresee.[14]

Mahood was beginning to think in 1983 that the time was right to sell SEDCO, not only because the price of oil was going down, but also because the major oil companies were buying each other. Mobil bought Superior; Occidental bought Cities Services; Chevron bought Gulf Oil. Some of SEDCO's major customers were being swallowed up. "These large oil companies that we worked for decided they were going to be better off buying oil and gas on Wall Street, rather than going out and drilling for it. They were all borrowing huge sums of money to go out and buy each other," Mahood said. "I could see that drilling budgets were fixing to go to hell in a handbasket. In 1984, it became even more clear to me. I felt like we ought to try to sell the company."[15]

By 1984, Clements had long since stopped licking his wounds from his political defeat. He told a reporter in early 1984 he was pleased to be governor but also happy to be back in Dallas. "Do I miss being in Austin? The answer is no," he said.

Clements explained that he and Rita liked their privacy. He felt he belonged to the people while he was governor. "I had no outside business of any kind . . . and so we gave a hundred percent of our selves to the office and to being governor of the State of Texas. And that, in turn, means that we were literally living in a fishbowl, and we had no privacy."

But he admitted that he wasn't glad he had lost. "I'm afraid that would be contrary to my disposition," Clements said. "When I was growing up, whether playing cops or shooting marbles or playing mumbledypeg or playing football, or what-have-you, I didn't want to lose. I wanted to win."[16]

By early 1984, Clements was heavily involved in the activities of SMU once again as chairman of the board of governors, a role he had resumed in September 1983. The board of governors was focused on such matters as the university's "The Decade Ahead" program — a plan for major improvements in academic programs and supporting facilities which required the raising of more than $170 million.

The university also wanted to build a new student center, and Clements persuaded his old friend and mentor, his high school football coach Charlie Trigg, and his wife, Katharine "Kitty" Hughes Trigg, to fund the center. Trigg was a 1929 graduate of SMU, and his wife had graduated in 1931. After World War II, Trigg opened an automobile dealership in Eldorado, south of San Angelo. His wife owned ranch property which had producing oil wells on it. They had money and no children to leave it to. Trigg recalled that Clements made several trips to San Angelo to talk about funding the new center, telling him about the committee that was visiting student centers around the country. Trigg and his wife donated $10 million to fund the Hughes-Trigg Student Center. They were both given distinguished alumni awards in 1984.[17]

Also in 1984, there were rumblings of more trouble in the football program at SMU. When Clements returned to the board of governors, the SMU football program was finishing up a two-year NCAA probation handed down in 1981. NCAA investigators were back on campus in the spring of 1984 talking to athletes about new allegations. Overzealous, free-wheeling boosters, who did not want to be controlled by the university, were a problem discussed by Clements and Mahood, who was then chairman of SMU's Athletics Development Committee.[18]

But Clements and Mahood also were busy with company matters during that time; overtures had been made to buy SEDCO.

SEDCO had bought an interest in Pogo Production, an oil and

gas company. In April 1984, Mahood was playing in a golf tournament at Preston Trails in Dallas with Stuart Hunt, who was on Pogo's board of directors, and Bill Liedtke, a Pogo executive. Hunt was an oilman and nephew of H.L. Hunt, and Liedtke was the brother of Hugh Liedtke, who later became chairman of Pennzoil. Hunt told Mahood that Bill Liedtke was interested in talking to him. In a locker room conversation, Liedtke passed along to Mahood a tip he had received from one of Pogo's directors who also was a director of Schlumberger. The director, George Jewell, who was managing partner of a large Houston law firm, said Schlumberger was interested in talking to SEDCO about buying four or five big offshore rigs.

Gill Clements didn't react, at first. "We didn't think much about it," he said. "We didn't want to sell any rigs. When we got the message two more times from Bill Liedtke, I thought that something was going on. So I talked to Dad about it, and we decided to put a little bait in the water and see what happened," Gill said.[19]

He called Jewell and told him, "We don't want to talk about selling four or five rigs, but if you want to talk about something bigger, let's get together." Jewell called back with a request for information, which Mahood put together. At that point, the only people who knew something was going on were Gill Clements, Bill Clements, and Steve Mahood. Bill's attitude, according to Mahood, was that "nothing would ever happen."

But Jewell indicated that the Schlumberger board chairman, Jean Riboud, was interested and wanted SEDCO to reveal all of its day rates. This was a critical point, because Schlumberger was asking for some very sensitive information. It was time to fish or cut bait, Mahood said. "If we're going to call it off, it was time to call it off," he said.

Bill Clements at first said, "No, let's steer our own ship." By the next day, however, he had changed his mind. "Go ahead," he said. Mahood believed that, along with the other factors, the fact that Bill's friend Ross Perot had made a deal with General Motors to sell his company, Electronic Data Systems, for a big price had some influence on Clements' decision.[20]

Gill Clements was surprised that his dad agreed to go forward with the discussions. When he did, Gill and Mahood and John Milem, SEDCO's vice-president of finance, accumulated the figures and all the critical information and proceeded.

The tentative negotiations began in June 1984 and continued through July. Gill Clements met with Arthur Lindenauer, Schlumberger's executive vice-president, in Chicago in July and later at Schlumberger's U.S. corporate headquarters in New York City, when Schlumberger officials proposed a merger with SEDCO. Several SEDCO directors and managers, along with legal counsel, went to New York to consider the proposal. SEDCO's fiscal year had ended June 30 with a net profit of $121.7 million on revenues of $517.2 million, down 9 percent from fiscal 1983 and down 53 percent from the record year of 1982.[21] Rig utilization stood at 89.9 percent in comparison to 96.9 percent in 1983 and 100 percent in 1982. This was still above the industry norm of 76 percent.

But the worldwide glut of oil was in its second year, and with it, the drilling industry was turning down. Oil prices had fallen from their 1981 highs of around $40 a barrel to the $28 range. SEDCO had fared far better than its competitors during the downturn, and although 23 of the 41 SEDCO rigs were either going to be idle or were coming to the end of their present contracts between September 1984 and September 1985, management's position was cautious optimism for the future.[22] SEDCO had practically no debt, and no equipment under construction.

Gill Clements met with Michel Vaillud, Schlumberger president and chief operating officer, in Paris in early September, and took exception to what he perceived to be a condescending attitude. "Vaillud was acting as if SEDCO approached Schlumberger," Clements said. He then went to London, where he had dinner with Riboud, the CEO. They talked price. The price per share finally agreed to was $48. On September 14, 1984, SEDCO directors accepted the takeover offer, which was estimated at more than $1 billion. Members of the Clements family and other insiders, who owned 21 percent of SEDCO's stock, agreed to the selling price and granted Schlumberger the option to buy outstanding stock in the open market so that Schlumberger would have approximately 45 percent of SEDCO's common shares. SEDCO's price per share on the New York Stock Exchange in the 1984 calendar third quarter reached a high of 46 and a low of $27\frac{1}{8}$.[23] At $48 a share, the sale was a great deal for the shareholders.

Even as SEDCO officials were in the process of negotiating the merger, they had reached out to capture other opportunities, as demonstrated by the Ocean Drilling Program, funded by the federal government and managed by Texas A&M University, to probe the earth's deep-ocean geology. The SEDCO/BP 471, a dynamically positioned drill ship owned jointly by SEDCO and British Petroleum, was being readied for the contract that would take fifty international scientists around the world collecting scientific data below the ocean floor in water depths ranging to more than 20,000 feet. The operation, an effort of the National Science Foundation and Joint Oceanographic Institutions, was scheduled to begin in 1985 and continue for four years, with an option to continue until the year 2000.[24]

At the time the merger was agreed on, SEDCO's fleet of forty-one offshore drilling units, including the world's only dynamically stationed semi-submersibles able to work at 6,000-foot depths (the 709 and 710), was the most modern of any drilling contrator. SEDCO employed approximately 4,300 people; two-thirds were nationals in the countries where they worked, and twenty-seven nationalities were represented in the workforce.

Schlumberger, Ltd., was a French firm that, in its early days, had identified oil-bearing formations and drilled for oil. For years, Schlumberger's main business was electrical logging of the formation inside the hole of an oil well. Two French engineers who invented the electrical logging tool, and for many years held the only patents, had founded Schlumberger. The company later diversified and became the giant of the oil service industry, operating in more than 100 countries with approximately 69,000 employees, encompassing seventy-five nationalities. Forex Neptune, Schlumberger's drilling firm, consisted of sixty-seven land rigs and eighteen offshore units, four of which were semi-submersibles.[25]

Forex Neptune was primarily an on-shore drilling contractor, and Gill Clements thought Schlumberger would honor its commitment of allowing SEDCO to emerge as the dominant company once it merged with Forex.[26]

Carl Thorne was scheduled to take over as president of the SEDCO Drilling Division, succeeding Jerry Cunningham, who was moving up to chairman. Thorne had moved back to Dallas in the summer of 1984, just prior to the merger, to assume that position.

The deal was closed on December 24, 1984, Christmas Eve. It was a big transaction in the oilfield service business. Bill Clements was to serve on the executive committee and the board, and Gill Clements was to be an executive vice-president over a group of

Schlumberger companies in the oilfield sector, operating out of Dallas. Thorne was to stay on as president of the combined drilling companies, SEDCO/Forex.

Thorne had a mixed reaction to the sale. He was a SEDCO director and was in favor of the sale because he knew it was best for the stockholders. But he quickly saw that where SEDCO had been a family-type company, Schlumberger was an enormous bureaucracy.[27]

"The SEDCO bunch was unusual. They were a lot of strong-willed, maverick-type people. But we got along well together because we respected each other," Gill Clements said. "But as soon as we sold out to Schlumberger, there was a big culture clash. We worked hard to preserve the feeling of a family. To some degree, I let our people down, because the cultural merger never took." The merger, he said, "was a great deal for our shareholders. It was a reasonably good deal for our customers. But I'm afraid not a very good deal for our employees."

Nonetheless, Gill Clements believes it was the right decision, because of the long bust period in the petroleum industry. "We were healthier than any of our competitors, and no doubt we would've survived. But it would've been unpleasant. We would've had to let a lot of people go. I'm glad I didn't have to oversee that," he said.[28]

It didn't take long for the cultures to clash. Carl Thorne was in Calgary and was scheduled to have breakfast with Warren Sexton on the morning of February 22, 1985. About 7:15 A.M., he said, the phone rang in his hotel room, and it was Michel Vaillud, president of Schlumberger, who asked him to come to New York. "I think [Gill] Clements has resigned," he told Thorne.

"What the hell are you talking about? Either he has or he hasn't resigned," Thorne replied.

"Well, he has resigned," Vaillud responded.

Thorne got on a plane to New York, stopping in Toronto, where he called Gill Clements and said he would resign too. Clements told him to hold off until they could discuss the situation. Thorne finally agreed to stay on as president of SEDCO-Forex for two years to protect the interests of the SEDCO employees.[29]

Gill Clements had been asked to relocate to New York, a move he never even considered. New York was not his style. His family had moved to Forney, where they lived on some acreage and raised horses. He saw that it simply was not going to work. The philosophies of the two companies were too far apart. Forex decided to break the back of SEDCO management and impose its own style of operation. Gill Clements would have no part of it.

"It was the end of the chapter, a major chapter in Bill's life, the company he had started and his son had taken over thirteen years before," Mahood said. Even though the company had been built into an even larger organization, Mahood said, "Bill was still our guiding light, our leader, even though in abstentia. What made SEDCO was the incredible amount of loyalty he commanded. There are not many people I've known in my life who have the ability to command respect like this guy," said Mahood. "None of our competitors had the respect or reputation this guy had. He's the glue that kept the whole thing together, even after he left. Our customers kept up with him. He was a folk hero — the only guy who came out of the drilling industry and got into the inner sanctum of the highest levels of government."

In the final analysis, Mahood also believed the decision to sell was the right decision. It preserved Bill Clements' wealth. "We would have been a survivor in the industry because we had a large asset base and we didn't have any debt. But it would have been a completely different picture for Bill. He wouldn't have had all that money to give away," Mahood said.[30]

After the sale, the oil industry didn't decline, it collapsed — starting in 1985 and continuing into 1986 and 1987. Oil prices fell steadily from about $30 per barrel in September 1984, when the merger agreement was reached, to $8 per barrel in April 1986. Rig utilization fell to about 50 percent. Had SEDCO remained independent, its share prices would have certainly fallen, as did other contractors', when energy stocks tumbled in 1986 by as much as 50 percent.[31]

The friendly acquisition turned out to be just the opposite. Though Schlumberger got new equipment, it wasted the people and expertise that made the equipment work. Schlumberger ignored SEDCO's "people philosophy" and tried to operate the company on a strict financial basis. Few of the SEDCO executives and managers — with the exception of Jerry Cunningham, who remained a consultant even after retirement — stayed with the new company for any length of time. Carl Thorne stayed until Schlumberger agreed to honor its commitment to pay retirement benefits to SEDCO personnel. The result of the merger was that shareholders benefited financially, and SEDCO executives made personal fortunes. But the energy industry lost an excellent drilling contractor, and many SEDCO employees lost their company and their careers.[32]

Dillard Hammett, who was a vice-president and member of the board of SEDCO at the time of the merger, resigned in 1987 out of frustration over what he felt Schlumberger was doing to the "finest drilling contractor in the world."

"Middle managers, who had positions of responsibility at SEDCO, were turned into messengers and checkers," Hammett said. Schlumberger discriminated against former SEDCO employees and, at the time Hammett resigned, not one American was in a senior line management position. "Schlumberger, without regard to the international image it attempts to portray, is French, and French it will remain," he said. "Schlumberger bought a fine company made up of equipment, people and reputation. The equipment is deteriorating due to fiscal restraints and maintenance practices, most of the key people are gone, and the reputation or goodwill is practically worthless," Hammett said, when he resigned in 1987. "Historically in the oilfields, one's word has been his bond, but with Schlumberger it means nothing."[33]

What made SEDCO special, according to Carl Thorne, was the strength and integrity of Bill Clements and his son, Gill. "They're so similar, and yet they're so different," he said. "Bill's strength is overt. Bill intimidates with his strength. I've seen Bill Clements make mistakes, but I've seen the strength of his character make them turn out right. That's what built SEDCO, the strength of character, that sense of purpose. It was a company where the strong survived; nobody had time for politics. Politics weren't tolerated; we had a strong person at the helm of SEDCO at all times.

"Gill was much more reserved. He was good for the company at a different point in time. He took over the company under very difficult cirumstances, from his father, a person who had built an empire through the strength of his character," Thorne said. "I'm not sure Gill could've started the company like Bill did, but he did every bit as good a job, maybe even better during those years of expanding the company, than Bill would have. That ramrod steel bar, that rawhide, is every bit in one as much as the other."[34]

In 1987, Thorne formed Energy Service Co., Inc. (ENSCO), an offshore company fashioned after SEDCO, which employed several SEDCO managers. It subsequently acquired the Hunt brothers'

Penrod operations and by 1993 was the world's largest publicly traded offshore drilling contractor.

Bill Clements retired from the Schlumberger board of directors and executive committee in May 1986. After SEDCO was sold, he never looked back. Was it the right move? "Oh, hell, yes," he said later.[35]

Chapter 16

1986 Campaign

"Gee, I Miss Gov. Clements"

ONCE OUT OF OFFICE, Bill Clements had been adamant about not running again. Then, in the fall of 1984, he was invited to a weekend deer hunt, a reunion of some former gubernatorial staff members, at Hilary Doran's ranch in the southwest Texas brush country not far from the Mexican border. Tentative agreement had been reached to sell SEDCO to Schlumberger in September, and Clements was looking forward to consummation of the deal in December when he went to Doran's ranch for the deer hunt. On hand were Doran, George Bayoud, Jim Kaster, David Dean, Pat Oles, Tony Garrett, and a few others. As the hunters sat around the fireplace playing "Texas Trivia" on Saturday night, talk turned to the governor's race. They went around the circle, giving their opinions on various potential candidates. Someone even suggested Rita. Clements listened intently, and, when it came his turn, said he hadn't found a candidate to personally support. "What about you?" asked Garrett, raising the question of another Clements campaign.

Clements' response was undeniably vague, but he left the implication that the door wasn't closed. Bayoud and Doran thought he reflected a clear change in attitude — from an obdurate "no" to a more elastic "maybe." The conversation made enough of an impression on Doran that he later agreed to support Congressman Tom

Loeffler's bid for the Republican nomination with the proviso that if Clements decided to run, he would switch his allegiance.[1]

Other Republicans and former backers, however, took Clements at his public word. They went after someone they thought could be a winner and a party-building candidate — Kent Hance. Hance had been a Democratic congressman from Lubbock, a "good ole boy" who had served in the Texas Senate. Hance was one of the conservative Southern "Boll Weevil" members of Congress who often voted in a coalition with Republicans to back Reagan programs; he had been a Democratic sponsor of the Reagan tax cut. In 1984 he lost the Democratic nomination for U.S. Senate to liberal State Sen. Lloyd Doggett, an outcome indicative of the narrowing philosophical bent of the Texas Democratic primary. Hance was ripe for a party change. Phil Gramm had switched parties in 1983 and, as a Republican, beat Doggett in the 1984 general election. Republicans recognized the new support Gramm brought to the party from his congressional area in Central Texas and Texas A&M University, where he had taught. Now there was a chance to bring West Texans into the fold with Hance. Among those who worked with Gramm to persuade Hance to switch parties and then run for governor were Jim Francis, Clements' 1982 campaign manager, and Lance Tarrance, Clements' pollster in 1978 and 1982.

In early 1985, the two congressmen, Loeffler and Hance, were lining up backers and financial supporters in anticipation of declaring their candidacies. Both were fairly young lawyers who had spent much of their adult lives in politics.

Clements previously had encouraged Boone Pickens of Amarillo, head of Mesa Petroleum, to run for governor that year. Part of Clements' reason for naming Pickens his state campaign chairman in 1982 was to provide Pickens with some campaign experience.

In February 1985, Clements invited Boone and his wife, Bea, to be overnight guests at 4800 Preston on their way to Washington on business. Pickens recalled Clements asked him if he intended to run in 1986, and Pickens responded that he couldn't take the time away from Mesa Petroleum, the company he had founded and ran as chairman of the board. The oil business was in its worst depression, one that had begun in 1982 with the glut of foreign oil on the world market. No, Pickens said, he wouldn't be running.

The next morning, en route to the airport, Bea Pickens remarked to her husband, "I think Bill's going to run again." Boone responded, "No way."[2]

In March 1985, Karl Rove, who had handled Clements' direct mail in the 1982 campaign, was asked by Hance to be his campaign adviser. Rove went to Dallas to test the temperature of the ex-governor. "You go sign up with whoever you want," Clements told him. "I ain't running." Even though Clements sounded explicit, Rove accepted the job with the Hance campaign with the caveat that he couldn't stay if Clements ran.

Clements still appeared disinclined to run when Martha Weisend, the Reagan grassroots organizer and Clements' Dallas County chairman in 1982, paid him a visit at his office in the Cumberland School Building in the spring of 1985. "There's a great sense that if you want to be governor, finish what you started, that office is yours," she said, telling him of calls she had received from around the state.

"Not interested," he replied.

Several days later, however, Clements called Ms. Weisend and asked her to return to his office for another meeting. He said he had been thinking about their previous conversation, and he wasn't sure whether people really wanted him to run again. Obviously, he didn't want to run if public sentiment was stacked against him. "Why don't we do this," he suggested. "Why don't you run a poll of 10,000 people and see what the thinking is." Ms. Weisend said a normal poll of 800 to 1,000 people would be adequate. Clements insisted on 10,000.

"Do you have any ideas as to how we do this?" Ms. Weisend asked.

"You'll figure it out," Clements responded.

Martha Weisend went to work, using her network of regional Reagan chairmen and phone bank volunteers, recruiting people across the state to survey voter reaction from identifiable Reagan voters to potential GOP gubernatorial candidates. When the results were tallied, Ms. Weisend presented the findings to Rita, Bill and Peter O'Donnell in the board room at the SEDCO building. Clements had garnered 53 percent in the trial heat. After looking at the geographical analysis, O'Donnell concluded that the primary belonged to Clements — but he challenged him to be sure he wanted the job again.[3]

Clements was encouraged and scheduled another meeting.

Meantime, another effort was about to get under way which would also encourage the former governor.

In May 1985, three young Dallas Republicans who had helped Clements in 1978 were having lunch. When Bill Elliott, Gary Griffith and Ken Nelson got together, the conversation usually turned to politics. They believed Gov. Mark White had been a disaster as governor and could be defeated, yet none of the three was excited about the apparent gubernatorial field. Elliott said, "Why don't we draft Clements, bring him out of retirement?"

"That's not a bad idea," Griffith answered. "Hell of an idea, in fact."

The three picked up two other allies, Jay Patterson and James Huffines, and paid a visit on Clements at his Dallas office. They had asked others, but were turned down. Hance and Loeffler were already locking up supporters, and there was speculation another substantive candidate might get in the race, possibly Jack Rains, a Houston civic-political leader and businessman-lawyer.

"Governor, we're here to tell you we're forming a Draft Clements Committee," Elliott, the spokesman, said. The group did not ask Clements' permission; they merely told him what they intended to do. They believed there was widespread support for Clements and didn't believe Loeffler or Hance could beat White.[4]

Elliott talked about the popularity of a bumper sticker seen on cars around the state which said, "Gee I Miss Gov. Clements." Chet Upham of Mineral Wells, former state Republican chairman, had originated the sticker and had some 15,000 printed — white lettering on red background — more than a year before. They had caught on.

Clements told the draft committee, "I don't want to encourage you or discourage you. I don't think I'm going to think about it 'til the fall. Maybe in the fall, Rita and I will reconsider." Clements explained that his summer calendar was already full, and it included a month-long fishing trip to Alaska. "If you guys want to carry forward, be my guest. But if you don't, be my guest, too," he said. "But let's talk about what it's going to take to win."

Clements then pulled out a legal pad and began writing numbers on it. According to his calculations, to win in 1986 would require exceeding the historical Democratic vote of 2 million. He recalled that in 1978, 2.2 million Texans voted and he got 1.1 million votes, roughly half. In 1980, Democratic presidential candidate Jimmy Carter drew 1.8 million votes in Texas while Republican can-

didate Reagan got 2.4 million. Two years later, in the 1982 gubernatorial year, the Democrats turned out 1.8 million again — the
equivalent of their turnout in the previous presidential year. Meanwhile, Clements got only 1.4 million, one million less than Reagan.
According to Clements' calculations, the Democrats had proved
their ability to turn out the same number of voters in an off-year as
in a presidential year. Since a record two million Democrats voted
for the Mondale-Ferraro presidential ticket in 1984 (Reagan-Bush
got 3.4 million votes) Clements assumed Democrats could produce
two million voters again in 1986.

Elliott figured this exercise showed that Clements had been
thinking about running. Clements commented, "Well, I like politics, so I think about what it takes to win." The truth was that those
numbers were permanently imbedded in Clements' brain, because
they told the story of his defeat in 1982. In analyzing his losing race
for the press back in 1982, he had pointed to the fact that Democrats
were able to repeat their presidential voter turnout in a nonpresidential year. "Once burned, twice leery," was one of his favorite
phrases.

The campaign emissaries left and went to work. They wrote
letters and made phone calls; they raised $50,000. A surrogate began
showing up at every Republican meeting in the Dallas-Fort Worth-
North Texas area. That surrogate was usually a twenty-five-year-old
stockbroker named Scott Jones, who explained the formation of the
Draft Clements Committee and distributed support cards.

The goals of the committee were listed on a one-page memo
from Gary Griffith to Bill Elliott on June 11, 1985: Distribute 5,000
"Draft Gov. Bill" bumper stickers, arrange for 20,000 letters and
preprinted postcards to be mailed to Clements at home, culminating
with an announcement rally in Dallas on September 15. The memo
also listed some "assumptions" for Clements: that he would "stop
being abrasive/corporate fat cat," that he would run a campaign appealing to the working man and woman, not the elitist, and that
there would be a revival of the "spirit of 78" shirt sleeve campaign.

On June 13, 1985, Clements wrote a letter to Elliott saying he
was grateful for the interest in his candidacy. The visit, he said, "gave
me a very warm feeling of 'being wanted' and I guess fundamentally
all of us like to feel that we are wanted and needed." Clements also
said that if any of the candidates "emerges as a viable statewide credible candidate — wonderful, but if one of them does not and there

has not been an emergence by late September; then Rita and I will have to reconsider the situation."⁵

As it turned out, they didn't wait until September.

Press reports on the Draft Clements Committee heightened speculation of Clements' reemergence. A June 26, 1985, cartoon by Bob Jackson in the *Dallas Times-Herald* showed Clements in an army uniform and smoking a corncob pipe, a la Gen. Douglas MacArthur, walking on oil-slickened water to a beach, with the caption: "I may return!"

In mid-to-late July, Clements met a couple of times with some of his close political associates, which included Rita, Peter O'Donnell, Martha Weisend, George Bayoud, David Dean and Dary Stone. Bayoud, Dean, and Stone wanted him to decide about the race before he went away on his extended summer vacation. If he was going to run, they reasoned, he needed to announce and not wait until the fall. Clements scheduled a series of campaign apppearances in East Texas on behalf of Republican congressional candidate Edd Hargett. In addition to helping Hargett, it would be a good opportunity to test the waters for his own comeback. Clements was buoyed by the welcome he received on the East Texas swing.

In the men's room at a small airport during the swing, Clements encountered Sam Attlesey, political writer for *The Dallas Morning News*. As they stood at the urinal, Attlesey asked the former governor flat-out, "Are you going to run for governor again?" Clements reponded, "Yeah, I think I am. Rita and I were talking about it last night." At a press conference in Marshall, he said, "Rita and I are seriously considering whether we should make this race. It's pillow talk," he said, adding, "We're pretty far down that road." He told Attlesey he was "95 percent certain."⁶ Attlesey wrote the story.

That night, when Clements returned to Dallas, the decision was made to announce the next day. Among those at 4800 Preston with Bill and Rita were Stone, Bayoud, and Dean. The East Texas trip had iced the decision, and his remarks to Attlesey triggered the need to make that decision public. Martha Weisend got a call in Washington, D.C., where she was scheduled to have dinner at the White House, that Clements would announce the next day. Clements had already asked Ms. Weisend to be campaign co-chair, if he ran. The next morning, he called Jack Rains to be his other co-chair.

On July 26, 1985, at a hastily called press conference at Dallas'

Union Station, Clements became the first Republican candidate to officially enter the race. Elliott was invited to join Clements at the podium, to cut off the "Draft" part of the "Draft Clements" bumper sticker.

"With Clements, expect the unexpected," Arnold Hamilton wrote in the *Dallas Times-Herald* on July 27, 1985. "In a single stroke, the former governor on Friday dramatically altered the 1986 political equation in Texas by announcing he would be a candidate for the GOP nomination."

Jim Francis, for one, was skeptical about the "unexpectedness" of the announcement. "He intended to run from day one," said Francis. "This [maneuvering] has all been a charade," Francis told the *Times-Herald*.

Clements made several phone calls the day he announced. One was to Hance, who told the former governor he wasn't getting out of the race. The day before Clements' announcement, Hance had unveiled a 450-member Dallas County steering committee. (Bayoud later tried to get Hance to run for attorney general, to no avail.) Clements also called Bum Bright, a previous supporter whom he had appointed to the Texas A&M board of regents. Bright had signed on as Hance's finance chairman and Francis, who worked for Bright, was running Hance's campaign.

Clements managed to locate Karl Rove at a conference center west of Austin, where he was conducting a business planning retreat for his company, and got him on the phone. "Karl, it's Bill. I got Rita here with me. We've just come from announcing I'm running for governor. I need you to be my strategist, my consultant," Clements said.

Bright and Francis refused to change horses in midstream, but Rove did, telling Hance that he had no choice. If Clements ran, he said, he either had to be involved with Clements or not be involved at all. It was Clements who had enabled Rove to create his own business, and Rove could not turn his back on his mentor. When Clements had asked Rove to work in his 1982 campaign, Rove said he wanted to be an entrepreneur — like Clements — and create his own company to do the work. Clements had given his blessing, becoming Rove's first direct mail client in 1982. After Rove's explanation, Hance responded with his usual droll humor, "Well, you remind me of my sixth grade girl friend. She didn't know if she liked me or my friend Bobby Joe." But Hance released Rove.[7]

Clements also called Lance Tarrance, his 1978 and 1982 pollster. During a heated conversation, Tarrance told Clements he was too deeply involved with Hance to switch. Tarrance had helped to recruit Hance, and he was convinced that Hance's party switch and subsequent run for governor was part of a national political realignment. "Texas was the lead horse to show what was happening," Tarrance said. He couldn't abandon ship. Clements looked at it differently. Hance was a Democrat, and Tarrance shouldn't be working for a Democrat. "I don't know why you're making such a big deal about that," Tarrance responded. "You supported Lyndon Johnson in 1964 when all the Republicans were for Goldwater." That ended the conversation — and their relationship.

"I loved Bill Clements and still do," Tarrance said, in a 1995 interview. "But I felt in 1986 he was not right for governor. He'd already run against Mark White and got beat. We had these Democrats switching to the Republican Party. There was momentum from Reagan winning in 1984, and White hadn't kept his promises. I felt like we were putting another piece of the puzzle in place with a former Democrat. We were making the state Republican party a populist, conservative, New Wave, next generation party — as opposed to a national, Wall Street, Republican party that wins occasionally in the state."[8]

Among other past supporters who failed to jump back on the Clements bandwagon was Tobin Armstrong, who had supervised the former governor's appointments in the first term. Armstrong was quoted in the course of the primary campaign as saying Clements "had a lot going for him and he blew it."[9]

Following his announcement, Clements promptly left for his long-planned Alaskan vacation.

He had not named a campaign manager or finance director. His supporters were left with no bandwagon to board. Out of necessity, Dary Stone assumed the temporary job of campaign manager.

Meanwhile, controversy swirled within partisan circles over Clements' reemergence. Some members of the State Republican Executive Committee, which met August 3, 1985, in Amarillo, remained angry over what they considered "arrogance" by Clements in his unsuccessful 1982 reelection bid. Clements had disregarded any suggestions made by state committee members then and had not attempted to contact any of them about running again in 1986. They wanted to present a resolution asking him to reconsider.

State GOP Chairman George Strake, Clements' state campaign

chairman in 1978 and his first secretary of state, smoothed the ruffled feathers. Strake said the intraparty squabbling represented
"growing pains" in a maturing party that's unaccustomed to having a
wealth of candidates to challenge the long-dominant Texas Democrats. "We've never had anybody who wanted the nomination before. At least now we have something that somebody wants," he
said. The resolution was withdrawn.[10]

Years later, however, Strake said he was against Clements' running again. When he heard the former governor was thinking about
it, he called him and questioned his motives. Strake thought Clements was running for the wrong reason — that he was mad about
being beaten by White in 1982, and he wanted to whip White in a
rematch more than he actually wanted to serve another four years.
"Nobody had ever beaten him at anything," Strake noted.[11] And,
Strake admitted, he wasn't positive that Clements could win again.

Nor did Sen. Phil Gramm appear enthusiastic about Clements'
candidacy. While professing to be neutral in the primary contest,
Gramm said publicly that he believed Hance, not Clements, had the
best chance of beating White. Either Hance or Loeffler, he said,
would "bring new strength" to the party. And Hance, because of his
party switch, "can continue to broaden the base of the Republican
party," he said.[12]

Clements and Gramm were never chummy, and were even less
close after the 1986 race. While Clements and Strake remained
friends through the years, they had their differences over state policy when Clements resumed office.

Bayoud, who had developed almost a son-to-father relationship with Clements over the years, defended Clements when criticism followed him out of office that he had run only to gain vengeance. "Foremost, he wanted to beat Mark White, and he didn't
think Loeffler or Hance could do it. He didn't think White was the
kind of person who ought to be governor. Call it being vindictive or
whatever, but he just felt that White should not be that person sitting in that office and making appointments and making those
[judgment] calls, and he felt he was the only one out there who
could go heads-up with a sitting governor," Bayoud said.[13]

By the time Clements returned from his Alaskan vacation,
trouble was brewing at SMU. When he thought he might run again
for governor, Clements had wanted to resign as chairman of the
SMU board of governors. He recommended William "Bill" Hutch-

ison, chairman of Texas Oil and Gas Company, to be his successor. But Ed Cox, chairman of the board of trustees, and President Donald Shields prevailed upon him to stay because SMU was going through a difficult period.

In May 1985, SMU had been found guilty of football recruiting violations again by the NCAA. The board of governors meeting on June 6, 1985, considered its options: to accept the findings, appeal, or sue the NCAA. The SMU leadership believed that other Southwest Conference schools also had recruitment violations, and that SMU had been targeted for "selective enforcement." Since 1983, they had suspected a conspiracy among the supporters of the University of Texas, Texas A&M, other universities, and the NCAA enforcement officials to "get" SMU. Clements expressed that sentiment in a note to his son, Gill, asking for Gill's advice. Gill doubted that allegations of selective enforcement could be proved; he suggested accepting the penalties and turning over information on the other schools to the NCAA. The board decided to appeal the findings. But on August 16, 1985, with all appeals exhausted, the NCAA issued the SMU football program a three-year probation which included severe sanctions, including a reduction of scholarships, a two-year ban on bowl games, one year without televised games, and a ban on any athletic recruiting activity by anyone outside of the university. When the board met on August 19, 1985, some members thought that the athletic department should be reorganized and that Coach Bobby Collins and Athletic Director Bob Hitch should be fired. Clements, however, suggested that the problems within the athletic department were not going to be cleared up overnight. Hitch and Collins stayed on and, outside of public knowledge, SMU proceeded to "phase out" its illegal recruiting program.[14]

In the fall of 1985, Clements' campaign was taking shape.

Martha Weisend and Jack Rains would co-chair the campaign. Robert Stewart was state finance chairman. Ed Cassidy, a professional political operative from Washington, was hired to manage the primary campaign. George Bayoud was state finance vice-chairman during the primary and then assumed the role of campaign manager in the general election, renting an Austin apartment with a view of the Capitol to remind him every day of the goal. John Deardourff, Washington media consultant, was hired to create the television commercials that would depict a kinder, gentler Clements and compare his record to Mark White's. Richard Wirthlin, who had been

Ronald Reagan's pollster, did the polling. Nancy Brataas was hired again to run the phone bank operation. And Karl Rove, campaign strategist, charted where the campaign was and where it was going, utilizing graphs and bar charts and bell curves. Clements fancied charts and numbers, one campaign aide said, and thought Rove a guru.

As Bill Elliott of the "Draft" movement said, after the race started, the "pros" took over. Elliott felt there was always a struggle in Clements' campaigns between the grassroots and the pros. Clements was a corporate man who was used to the best. He was more comfortable when surrounded by people he knew were professionals, so he was intent on getting the best professionals available in 1986. As for the grassroots, Martha Weisend had earned her stripes in the Reagan campaigns; she knew how to get the grassroots. Although a volunteer, Ms. Weisend was professional in knowledge and approach, and she was tenacious and forthright — traits Clements appreciated.

An important hire for Clements was Reggie Bashur, who became press secretary. Bashur was Washington press aide for Sen. Gordon Humphrey of New Hampshire, and he had campaign experience. Bashur wanted to move to Dallas, the home of his fianceé, and secured an interview for a campaign staff position. Bashur vividly recalled his first meeting with Clements, which took place in the old SEDCO board room with Clements, Jack Rains, and a half dozen others. The scene, as he described it, was eight-against-one and all of them Texans against a native New Yorker. "I'm looking at these guys and thinking, this is not going to happen. So I just got very relaxed and let it fly," Bashur said. As it turned out, that's the kind of attitude Clements liked.

Facing Bashur across the conference table, Clements looked first at Bashur's résumé and then locked a gaze directly at him. "What are you? What are you?" he asked.

Bashur wondered to himself, was that a philosophical question? No, he thought, he must be asking about his ethnic background. "Lebanese. If you're asking me what my ethnic background is, it's Lebanese," Bashur replied. Score one. Clements liked Lebanese people from his drilling contracting work in the Middle East.

Clements asked Bashur what he thought his chances were in the primary. Bashur had an insider view from Washington and presumed Hance and Loeffler were in the frontrunner positions; he thought Clements would have a hard time after his 1982 defeat.

Clements, in a typical gesture, waved his hands back and forth as if to dismiss Bashur's assumption, "I'm not going to have any problem in the primary. And, I'll beat Mark White," Clements told him.

Clements said the group would confer and give Bashur a call in Washington. Bashur decided to go for broke. "Look, if all of your people are here, why don't you just make up your minds right now, and tell me yes or tell me no." Clements, he said later, liked that. "He likes directness." They sent him out of the room for five minutes, called him back in and hired him — effective immediately.[15]

Bashur's first impression of Clements was reinforced during the campaign. While he found Clements to be a complicated person with many sides, he was always very direct, confident, and tended to be optimistic. "He likes to deal in directness. He's open about what he thinks. I was on the campaign trail with him in 1986 every day. I got to see Clements morning, noon and night. He's very focused. He has a goal and he works for it. And during the campaign, he had a tremendous amount of energy and enthusiasm. He's very confident and optimistic. He's a positive thinker," Bashur said. There were certain parts of the public activity Clements didn't relish. He didn't like being on display all of the time. He didn't relish plunging into crowds and shaking every hand, but one-on-one, he was a "people person." And he didn't relish answering the same questions day after day from the press. But he had learned from past experience that he had to do that, and he had to act like he was enjoying it. It was part of the winning strategy, and Rita insisted on it. Asked during his announcement press conference what he was going to do differently in 1986, he responded, "I'll smile more."[16]

When Karl Rove came to Dallas for early strategy meetings with Clements, he found that "Rita had already worked him over pretty good about the need to smile." This campaign had to have a different attitude from 1982. The image of Clements as arrogant and mean-spirited had to be dispelled. Clements couldn't fall back into old patterns of style — as Rove described, "this aggressive attitude that comes across as nasty and bullheaded — especially when it came to the Capitol press corps."[17] That was part of the consideration taken in the hiring of the media firm and the press secretary. John Deardourff was good at taking the edges off tough personalities in his TV commercials. Basher had dealt with Sen. Gordon Humphrey, a difficult personality who had a hard time getting along with the press.

A March 17, 1986, campaign memo to executive committee members detailed goals for the primary campaign. (The executive committee included Bill and Rita Clements, Jack Rains, Martha Weisend, Peter O'Donnell, Bob Stewart, Ed Cassidy, Reggie Bashur, George Bayoud, Dary Stone, David Dean, Richard Wirthlin, Karl Rove, and John Deardourff.) The first order was to keep the race focused on Mark White. Clements should ignore as much as possible his primary opponents; rather than responding to them, he should attack White's credibility, his broken promises and lack of leadership. A concurrent goal was to stress Clements' business background as evidence he could help create jobs and get the economy moving, that he could do a better job of running the state and be counted on to tell the truth.

Clements was to use the primary to rebuild the public perception of the job he did as governor and dispel the 1982 image that he was mean and arrogant. "Developing a public perception that Clements is looking to Texas' future will diminish the view that this is a grudge match," the memo stated. "At all costs, avoid appearing as if we think Clements *deserves* re-election."

The memo also noted that the candidate is "most likely to make mistakes or mis-statement when he is tired." As a result, he was to be scheduled no more than five days a week, never on Sunday, and never in more than two [media] markets a day. Wear and tear on the candidate was to be kept at a minimum, with plenty of "down time" before an evening event. Other than that, the first rule of scheduling was to "go where the votes are." Consequently, Clements spent much of the last two months of the primary campaign in Harris, Dallas, Tarrant, and Bexar counties.[18]

Loeffler's challenge was to get his name known outside his southwest Texas congressional district, using television ads to introduce his family and even his horse, "Liberty," to the voters. Since he had worked in Washington for fourteen years, he was vague about state issues. He talked about bringing the Reagan revolution to Texas and leading the state into a new era. "If there are any doubters about our future, I'm going to say . . . . Look, we're Texas. Don't tell us it can't be done."[19] One of his favorite campaign declarations was: "Texas will always be Texas." At one joint appearance after Loeffler made that pronouncement, Clements leaned over to Hance to say, "What the hell does that mean?" His microphone happened to be on, blaring the comment to the audience.

Loeffler also tried to run against Mark White in the primary, as in this ad: "In Texas . . . what we have is a leadership crisis and, listen, Mark White's flunked the test and if he can't pass, he shouldn't play." It was clear by this time that the no-pass, no-play provision of White's educational reforms — which sidelined for six weeks any student athlete who was failing a course — was unpopular, particularly in the small towns and rural areas. Clements wanted to reduce the no-play penalty to three weeks.

Hance's hope of winning was to draw conservative Democrats into the primary to vote for him, and to discredit Clements, mainly by casting him as too old to serve again. In one TV spot he referred to his opponents: "One has no experience in state government and the other is sixty-eight years old." Hance, however, with Clements in the race, was having trouble raising the money he needed to saturate the air waves. And he had a problem with old-line Republicans, who questioned his true-blueness as a Republican. Clements campaigners noted that Hance publicly supported Democratic presidential nominee Walter Mondale, though in the campaign he said he secretly voted for Reagan.

Loeffler tried to depict himself as the only candidate without baggage, whereas Clements was saddled with a negative image and Hance with being a recent convert to Republicanism.

Campaign co-chair Jack Rains blamed Clements' unpleasantness during his last months in office and the 1982 election campaign on a painful hip joint, which he had repaired once he was out of office in 1983. Clements should have had the surgery before, Rains said, "but he kept putting it off. He was living with a lot of physical pain. But he was from the grin-and-bear-it school, so he grinned and beared it and growled a lot."[20]

Clements' ads were designed to remind voters what they liked about him before. He was shown in childhood photos in his Eagle Scout uniform and football jersey and, as a young man, turning to the oil business in the hard times of the 1930s. Other ads compared his record with Mark White's, noting there had been plenty of jobs when he was governor and a $1 billion surplus.

By March 18, 1986, when the *Houston Chronicle* released its joint poll with KTRK-TV in Houston, Clements was clearly dominating the Republican gubernatorial primary. At that point, Clements had the support of 53 percent of voters surveyed, compared to Loeffler's 19 percent and Hance's 16 percent; he was winning without a runoff. Clements, who the summer before had said that the Draft Clements movement gave him a "warm feeling," used the same words in reacting to the poll numbers. "It gives you a great, warm feeling to have those kinds of numbers come up when it's been three years since you've been in office." Clements was staying in his warm and fuzzy mode.

Clements had the muscle, both financially and politically, to cut the other Republicans off at the knees. Francis said later that Hance "made the best of it he could, but he didn't have a chance" once Clements got into the race. Francis paid the price for sticking with Hance after his former boss got into the race, suffering a bitter breach with Clements that wasn't repaired for many years.

But the Clements campaign also was benefiting from other factors. Doug Harlan wrote in his *Dallas Morning News* column on March 15, 1986, that the state's financial crisis was working in Clements' behalf, because the budget crisis put a priority on management skills. Teacher dissatisfaction with teacher competency testing, mandated during the White administration, was also helping the Clements campaign. The more unhappy teachers became with White, the easier it was for Clements to portray White's shortcomings, contrasting their two records, and the more severe the state's financial crisis, the easier it was for Clements to portray his own strengths as a businessman-manager, Harlan wrote.

For the most part, Clements stuck to his script, refusing to respond to allegations from the other primary candidates. He held his fire for Mark White.

But while he had put on a happy face, he didn't undergo a personality transplant. He was still the same outspoken guy who was going to call it like he saw it. Scott Jones, who had gone from being the Draft Clements Committee surrogate to Dallas field representative for the campaign, recalled driving Clements to Collin County during the primary to meet a county official he described as "religious." Driving down the road with Clements and the county official in the car, they encountered a series of Kent Hance signs and began discussing a Hance vote in Congress. Clements' position was that Hance couldn't be trusted. "He said he wasn't going to change his vote," Clements said, "and I'll kiss your ass at sunrise if the next day he didn't." Jones had seen Clements in situations where he could be offensive and "here he was with a deacon of the church and saying, 'I'll kiss your ass at sunrise . . .'" But, Jones added, that was just his manner of speech.[21]

On May 3, 1986, Clements overwhelmingly won the Republican nomination. A half-million Texans participated in the GOP primary, and Clements garnered 58 percent of the vote. With the help of the military community in San Antonio, he even carried Loeffler's home base.

He now had his chance for the repeat bout with his old enemy, Mark White.

Governor White had come to power at the worst moment in modern Texas history. The sun had started to set on the Sun Belt. The oil boom was over, and the state's revenue stream had dried up. Besides the faltering economy, over which White had no control, his education reforms had played havoc with one of the state's sacred cows — high school football. White wanted to be remembered as the governor who brought academic excellence to Texas; instead, he was blamed for the no-pass, no-play rule. Coaches were so enraged that they formed a lobbying group to oppose White's reelection, which became known as FlunkPAC. Teacher groups which had backed him in 1982 had now filed suit to stop mandatory teacher tests.

White also had developed a reputation for indecisiveness and an inability to lead. Political writers said he had a greater propensity for campaigning than for governing. "It is hard to look up to a leader whose ear is to the ground," Paul Burka wrote in *Texas Monthly* magazine, and White's ear was always to the ground.[22]

During the primary campaign, Clements repeatedly referred to his Republican opponents as "lawyers." What the state needed was a businessman, he said. He would use the same tactic in the general election against White — depicting himself as a businessman running against a lawyer and "professional politician." He would cast himself as a "workhorse, not a showhorse," building on White's reputation as one who governed by polls, "Media Mark" — the perpetual campaigner.

Martha Weisend had never seen a candidate more focused, more determined to win, than Bill Clements in 1986. This time around, he was willing to take direction from his staff. He was both disciplined and easy to manage.

As the campaign went forward, the state's economic difficulties worsened. The national recession had finally reached Texas. The state's major industries were troubled — banking, savings and loans, oil and gas, real estate, and even high technology.

Crude oil prices bottomed out at just under $10 a barrel on April Fool's Day of 1986, after peaking in January at $26.57 a barrel.[23] The U.S. oil rig count was down to an all-time low of 663 in July of 1986. Unemployment peaked in Texas in June 1986, at 10.5 percent. Real estate values tumbled, leaving Houston and Dallas to vie for the dubious distinction of having the most vacant office space in the country. The state's business climate was plagued by bankruptcies. LTV, which was $4 billion in debt, became the second-largest bankruptcy in United States history in July 1986. By the end of the first nine months of the year, there had been nearly 1,200 bankruptcies in Houston alone.[24]

Unstable returns from oil and gas taxes played havoc with state government revenue estimates, finally forcing White to call special sessions in August and September of election year to deal with the budget shortfall. That shortfall diverted attention from the campaign to the state's problems and resulted in a tax increase only weeks before the election. The legislature was forced to raise the state sales tax from 4⅛ to 5¼ cents on White's watch and increase the gasoline tax temporarily from a nickle to fifteen cents a gallon.[25] Clements' response was to call White the "Governor of Taxes."

Clements capitalized on the economic climate by projecting himself as a governor who could get the state back on its feet. His message: Texas has to create jobs, jobs, job. In speeches and appearances, Clements had talked about the need to scrub the budget, to "cut the cloth to fit the pattern" on the state budget, i.e., spend according to the revenues that were available. He repeatedly called on Governor White to sell his $3.1 million Japanese jet to help reduce the budget shortfall. But, above all, he emphasized, he knew how to create jobs, jobs, jobs. He never mentioned the word "jobs" that he didn't say it three times. In meetings of the kitchen cabinet, if the focus occasionally strayed, Peter O'Donnell would bring it back. "Jobs, jobs, jobs," he would say. When pressed on how he would solve the state government's budget problem, Clements would say only that he had a "secret plan" which he would reveal when he was back in office.

Clements also focused on White's broken promises to voters and constantly repeated the "litany of broken promises." White had promised not to raise taxes, but taxes and fees had increased by $5.5

billion. White had promised not to raise tuition, but tuition had increased 300 percent. White had promised to lower utility rates, but electric rates per household had increased substantially.[26]

Campaign strategists wanted to portray White as a liar but without making Clements seem mean-spirited. The answer was the "Pre-var-i-cate" ad. The commercial began with a narrator defining "prevaricate" as "to stray from the truth." Then the narrator asked: "Is that what Mark White did when he promised not to raise taxes and then tried to raise them every year he's been in office?" Four unidentified Clements supporters said so.

Another memorable commercial was called "What's Up." The narrator began with, "Say, what's up with Mark White?" Against a backdrop of White's smiling face, he proceeded. "Well, sales taxes are up, property taxes are up, gasoline taxes are up, franchise taxes are up, crime is up, tuition is up . . . utility bills are up, state spending is up, the budget deficit is up, unemployment is up, small business failures are up . . ." After each item, there was the "ding" sound of a cash register. "We dinged him to death," Rains said.

White, however, got credit for the funniest ad in the otherwise acrimonious campaign. It featured old-time movie cowboys riding the range in search of Clements' "secret plan" to balance the budget. "Do you think you can find it?" asked one. "If that secret plan is out there, we'll find it," said another, as the posse rode off.[27]

White's big battle cry to Clements was: "Didn't you know, or didn't you care?" White would bring up problems ranging from economics to falling student test scores and then ask the question. "Bill, why didn't you work to improve education during your four years as governor? Why didn't you better prepare us for our current economic problems? Didn't you know . . . or didn't you care?"[28]

From Labor Day until Election Day, Clements' efforts were concentrated in the major media markets, particularly Houston, Dallas-Fort Worth and San Antonio. Rains insisted, "I wanted him rested at the end. We didn't want any questions about his temperament or his health. And he was the best candidate he ever was — vastly improved from four years before."[29]

Clements even bantered with members of the traveling press, nicknaming them the "wise owls" and then the "strange Hindu wise owls."

During the campaign, high school football coaches put stick-on red dots on their watches to remind them of the no pass-no play rule. On a campaign stop in San Antonio, one coach showed his watch to Clements and gave him a strip of red dots. When he emerged after a reception, members of the press corps had each stuck a red dot in the center of their foreheads. Clements cracked up laughing. "You all look like a bunch of strange Hindu wise owls," he said.

At a later stop, before 1,000 or so people at a Corpus Christi fish fry, Clements was delivering his basic stump speech, during which he asked a series of questions designed to point out White's broken promises, such as: "How many of you know your utility bills have gone up, not down? How many of you know the state budget has increased in the last four years, not decreased?" Every time he asked a question, the reporters would raise their hands. Finally, Clements looked over at them, laughed, and told a befuddled audience, "Pay no attention to the strange Hindu wise owls."

A few times, his impatience emerged. On a visit to McKinney, where he worked the courthouse square area, Clements encountered several visitors from outside the state. Frustrated because he wasn't meeting any voters, he walked up to a woman in a coffee shop and said, "Where are you from, Timbuktu?" She had no idea what he was talking about.[30]

Clements walked a fine line between joke and insult. On the McKinney stop, for example, he went up to one hefty fellow in overalls and said, "I don't think you're getting enough to eat." That was just Clements' way, a campaign aide would explain.

Driving stories about Clements were legend. He was known to order drivers to go down one-way streets the wrong way, if the coast was clear. "Go, go, go — nobody's coming," he'd say, as others covered their heads. If he was driving, he would zigzag through Highland Park to miss two signal lights. He initiated one new travel aide by cutting across four lanes of traffic to go where he wanted to go. The aide was a bundle of nerves in the front passenger seat, and Clements just slapped him across the chest and said, "Goddamit, Jim, you don't need to drive. Just sit there and remain tranquil."[31]

On another occasion, he didn't like the way his travel aide was driving, so he got behind the wheel, headed down Central Expressway in Dallas. The next morning, he accosted members of the press corps, who had gathered on the driveway of his house. "All right, which one of you wrote the story about me driving 80 miles per hour without a seat belt down Central?" When the culprit was determined, he said, "Well, you got me in trouble with Rita."[32]

Rita was extremely important to the 1986 win, according to key players in the campaign. First of all, she insisted that he change his demeanor. Secondly, she had excellent political judgment and reactions and was often the most important adviser to her husband. And she worked hard. Organizational director Ann Quirk said, "Rita knew every county chairman, every phone bank chairman. She took over a lot of the small and middle sized counties, traveling to them. She was tightly scheduled."[33]

Martha Weisend could not overestimate the role played by Rita Clements. "She knew the issues, she was articulate, she believes in Bill Clements and she worked untiringly." She described Mrs. Clements as a "professional woman and a very professional wife. There was a place for her in the campaign and then, when we were off the clock, she became a wife and a helpmate to the governor. Never did she get in the way of the campaign leadership."[34]

Occasionally, however, if there was a sensitive matter to be dealt with in the campaign or with the governor, campaign members relied on Rita to carry the message or to nix a bad idea.

"He and Mrs. Clements, I think they thought through that campaign a lot," press aide Bashur said. "He knew he needed to be patient and take questions and answer questions, to participate in the interaction with the press." Toward the end of the campaign, Bashur sensed his boss was tiring of that process. He compared Clements to Ronald Reagan who, if asked a question a hundred times, would give the same answer a hundred times. Clements' mind was "more active," Bashur said. "He got tired of the same question. Sometimes his answer would vary. He could show some impatience. Part of it was his personality. He's a very competitive guy and he likes the combat. If somebody pushes him verbally with a question or challenges him, he doesn't think twice about pushing back or challenging back. That's out of the norm for a politician," Bashur said.[35]

Clements was rested enough to avoid the kind of fiery exchanges with his opponent that had occurred in 1982, such as the one after the Amarillo debate when Clements accused White of saying "the most ugly things" after White had claimed there wouldn't be any mud-slinging in his campaign.

The memorable debate moment for 1986 was far different. In preparation for the fall debates, the Clements campaign had used Kent Hance as a stand-in for White. Clements had practiced the line against Hance, which was a take-off on the then-popular *Dallas* television show. Bobby Ewing, one of the show's characters, had been "killed" in the previous season. In the new season premier, Ewing returned. He hadn't died, according to the story line; his wife, Pam, merely had a bad dream. So, at an appropriate place in the debate, Clements turned to White and said, "You remind me of Pam Ewing. It's all a bad dream." The line, credited to consultants Ken and Lisa LeMaster years later, sucked the wind out of White's sails.[36]

In the last two weeks of the campaign, members of the traveling press were surprised at both the pace of the campaign and Clements' good humor. Most days they were out by 9:00 and back to Dallas by 5:00. Anne Marie Kilday, who was writing for the *Houston Chronicle*, said later that it was like the press was being taken for "little outings." The campaign entourage went to Fort Worth, where it wandered through the Amon Carter Museum with Clements asking a guard questions about the value of some Russells and Remingtons. He scrapped an opportunity for two hours of free air time on a San Antonio radio station so he could stay in Fort Worth and eat at a favorite Mexican restaurant. The next day, he showed off his prize Longhorns at an event at his farm in Forney. "He was in constant good humor, laid back, mellow, he was a happy camper," reporter Kilday said. "The staff would make sure he got a rest or an ice cream in the afternoon," she said. "It wasn't a campaign, it was a field trip — to the art museum, the farm, a golf tournament at the Woodlands."[37]

It was, in fact, a textbook campaign. The incumbent was down in the polls. The challenger was sticking to his script ("jobs, jobs, jobs"). Most of the race was being waged on TV. The strategy was not to make a mistake, because Clements was ahead and would win if he didn't make a mistake in the final days.

The Saturday before the election, Clements didn't want to campaign; he wanted to go to the SMU football game. It was homecoming, and he and Rita had ridden in the homecoming parade around the campus. The staff convinced him he would appear overconfident if he went to the game, so he didn't. Reporters following the candidate were consumed by the release of the latest polling information and paid little attention to the less-than-exuberant response Clements, then chairman of the SMU board of governors, received on campus. They later surmised the tepid reception may have been prompted by the sanctions levied against the football program and what turned out to be continuing problems in the athletic program.

The campaign had narrowed in the final days. Polls had shown Clements with a lead up until the end. The last weekend, however, Clements' internal polls showed him dipping below White. On Monday night, according to Bayoud, the race was neck and neck. On Tuesday morning, Bayoud and Martha Weisend went to a little church at the corner of Brazos and 10th Street in Austin. There was nothing else to do but pray.

Their prayers were answered. On election night, all three networks called the race for Clements shortly after the polls closed. He won with 52.7 percent of the vote, 1.8 million votes to White's 1.5 million.[38] Clements didn't have to reach the Democrats' historic high of 2 million votes. The turnout this time didn't match that of the previous presidential election, as it had in 1982 with Sen. Lloyd Bentsen at the top of the Democratic ticket and the Democratic unity campaign scaring voters to the polls. The high turnout of 1982, when Clements was ousted, therefore appeared more abberation than a new pattern.

Miriam A. "Ma" Ferguson had been the first Texas governor to win a comeback bid for office. She did it in 1933.[39] William P. Clements, Jr., became the second, repeating the feat more than fifty years later.

Despite a faltering economy in Texas, the governor's race was the costliest ever, with $25 million spent between the two candidates — $12 million by White and $13 million by Clements.

Clements had little time for celebration over his win. Nine days after the election, a news story broke that presaged trouble for Clements' return to the public arena. On November 13, 1986, WFAA-TV, Channel 8, in Dallas, aired a special report in which David Stanley, a former lineman for the SMU Mustangs, declared that he and his family had received cash payments from SMU's recruiting coordinator, Henry Lee Parker, even after the latest probation period had been imposed. The report included an interview with Parker, Athletic Director Bob Hitch and Coach Bobby Collins, in which they appeared caught totally by surprise by evidence presented on camera that players had been paid.

Channel 8 producer John Sparks and sportscaster Dale Hansen had been on campus on October 27, 1986, several days before the November 4 election, to interview Parker, Hitch, and Collins. There was speculation in subsequent years that Channel 8 held the story until after the election, so as not to embarrass Clements. Sparks, however, said two factors delayed the broadcast. First, he wanted Stanley to take a polygraph test, which wasn't arranged until November 2, and the story was still being checked out by the station's lawyers. Sparks didn't want any loose ends that would destroy the credibility of the story, nor any repercussions based on false presentation. "We were dealing with a hometown school that was about to lose its football program [if the interview was aired], and we wanted it nailed down," he said. "We wanted to make sure we dotted all the 'i's' and crossed all the 't's.'" At the time, he said, Clements' knowledge and/or involvement as chairman of SMU's board of governors was "kind of ancillary" to the story. Secondly, even as the SMU story was being prepared, Sparks was in charge of the station's political unit, which meant he was supervising the crews that were covering the elections, and involved in three days of election rehearsals beginning the day the SMU interview was taped.[40]

The Channel 8 story had immediate repercussions. Donald Shields, who had been on a thirty-day medical leave, announced his resignation as president of SMU, citing health reasons. After an emergency meeting of the board of governors on November 25, 1986, Clements announced the end of special admissions policies for football players. He also called for formation of a committee to study the long-range future of athletics at SMU and pledged a speedy investigation into the latest allegations. Saying he was tired of "this monkey business, this Mickey Mouse business" in the football program, the board of governors chairman said the football program could be abolished completely, should the probe warrant such action.

By January 1987, the athletic director, head coach, and recruiting coordinator had resigned. The in-house probe was under way, as SMU sought to avoid even tougher sanctions from the NCAA — the so-called "death penalty" that threatened to shut down its football program. Bill Clements resigned from SMU's governing board, citing achievements including a growth in the endowment from $13 million in 1962, when he first went on the board, to just under $300 million, and an increase in endowed chairs from three to fifty in the same period.

With the SMU scandal aside, Clements had other things to think about. He would soon be sworn in for his second term as governor of Texas.[41]

Chapter 17

Second Term

"Ponygate" and Budget Problems

IF BILL CLEMENTS ASSUMED office the first time with a giggle, the second time around it was more like a growl. The environment was completely different. The Texas economy was in deep trouble. Legislative leaders, faced with a budget shortfall and a governor vowing to veto any tax increase, were bracing for a monumental battle over how to make the state's dollars stretch.

On the day of his second inauguration, January 20, 1987, Clements still hadn't buried the hatchet with Mark White. His contempt remained unconcealed for the man who had unceremoniously removed him from office. The outgoing governor traditionally has a reception in the governor's office and then takes his leave inconspicuously by the north entrance to the Capitol, before the new governor's swearing-in at the south entrance. White, however, was intent on forcing Clements to shake his hand and, trailed by reporters, went looking for the governor-elect. Striding up to Clements in the Capitol rotunda, White extended his hand with a "Congratulations, governor." Clements shook it without comment and turned away. News reports said he "snubbed" the former governor. Clements simply had no use for Mark White, either before or after his reelection.

Ironically, Clements was administered the oath of office by John Hill, the Democrat he had defeated in 1978, who had become

336

chief justice of the Supreme Court. In contrast to the Clements-White breach, Clements and Hill developed a mutual respect and enjoyed a cordial relationship during Clements' second term.

The novelty was gone when Clements returned to Austin for his second administration. He knew how the process worked; only some of the players had changed. It was an easier transition than before, and he was able to quickly get down to work.

The governor selected his staff, relying largely on people with whom he had previously worked. His campaign co-chairman, Jack Rains of Houston, was named secretary of state. Hilary Doran, legislative aide in his first administration, now was chief of staff. George Bayoud, the governor's personal aide early in his first administration and his 1986 campaign manager, was executive assistant. Reggie Bashur was press secretary. James Huffines, a thirty-six-year-old Dallas banker and co-chairman of Clements' Dallas County campaign, was appointments director. Jim Kaster returned as legislative liaison. Bob Davis, a veteran House member who had chaired the tax-writing Ways and Means Committee, was brought in as budget director. Rider Scott, who had been chief prosecutor for Dallas district attorney Henry Wade, was appointed general counsel and would oversee the criminal justice division.[1]

Clements furnished his office with Texas antiques, including the massive "partners' desk" made nearly a century before by two Waxahachie cotton brokers, oak chairs borrowed from the University of Texas, a bronze longhorn donated by former Gov. Dolph Briscoe, a chair of leather and steer horns rescued from a fire in the original Capitol, a Western scene painted by Tom Lea, and a painting of the Alamo. When he returned to office, Clements missed the bronze longhorn donated by Briscoe. His staff found it in the Houston office of former Governor White, and had it returned to the Capitol.[2]

Clements was comfortable in his surroundings, but the return to office was more difficult than even he anticipated. He had settled an old score with Mark White by winning the 1986 election, but the reality of assuming office as governor during the state's worst fiscal crisis since the Depression diluted some of the sweetness of that revenge.

The global collapse of oil prices had broken the back of the state's petroleum industry, leaving a train of joblessness, business losses, and bankruptcies. Only 296 rotary rigs were working in

Texas at the end of 1986, half as many as a year before. Offshore, the situation was no better. Pennzoil, Amoco and Tenneco, all major Texas employers, had cut workers. Atlantic Richfield (ARCO) had cut 1,000 jobs in Dallas, the largest layoff of white-collar workers ever in the city's energy industry. Texas oil prices were controlled by the Organization of Petroleum Exporting Countries; while OPEC had set a price target of $18 a barrel as 1987 began, it was not enough to project much improvement in the Texas economy.

At least twenty-six Texas banks had failed, more than in any other state, largely because of over-reliance on energy and agriculture loans. Bankruptcies were at record levels. The most celebrated bankruptcy was declared by the Hunt brothers — Lamar, William Herbert, and Nelson Bunker Hunt — sons of oil magnate H. L. Hunt, who were sued by twenty-two banks for $1.28 billion. Texas unemployment, which had peaked in June of 1986 at 10.5 percent, remained at 9.5 percent as Clements took office. More than 800,000 Texans were out of work, the most in the state's history, and Texas had lost 230,000 energy-related jobs since 1982.

The oil and gas crisis dominated attention because it was considered the main cause of the state's high unemployment and state government's projected budget deficit. The taxes oil and gas brought to state coffers had enabled the state to avoid an income tax. In the 1981 fiscal year, oil and gas had accounted for 28 percent of state government budget revenues. But that figure now was down to 15 percent in the 1986 fiscal year, and Comptroller Bob Bullock was estimating that oil and gas taxes would account for only 10.3 percent of the budget for the upcoming 1988-89 biennium. Energy-related industries — everything from oil and gas extraction and processing to rigs, pipe and drilling mud — which had accounted for 30 percent of the state's economy in 1981, were down to less than 20 percent as Clements started his second term.

Texas had had its cattle, cotton, and timber heydays. But since the discovery at Spindletop in 1901 and the vast East Texas field in 1930, oil had been the lifeblood of the Texas economy. Now oil was in a steady decline, from its peak in 1972. The petroleum industry, in which Bill Clements had made his millions and his mark, had become Texas' version of the collapses in other states of automotive and steel industries.

Texas' largest banks also were troubled. A merger was planned by InterFirst Corp. and Republic Bank Corp., and Texas Commerce

Bancshares Inc. was being acquired by Chemical Bank of New York. High hopes for high technology had been tempered by plant closings and layoffs in response to worldwide overcapacity in semiconductors, personal computers, and other segments of the electronics industry.[3]

As Clements saw it, the restructuring of Texas' industrial base, diversification of the economy, and creation of jobs was his biggest challenge. When he resumed office, he intended to be the state's business cheerleader in attracting plant relocations and corporate headquarters.

But first there was the matter of passing a budget in a time of declining revenues. Should the legislature raise taxes by $5.8 billion to support a budget at current service levels, or should it cut services to meet revenues? Clements advocated no new tax increases, while Lt. Gov. Bill Hobby was committed to raising revenue to meet the expenses of a "current services" budget.

Republican strength in the Texas House had increased to a record 56 members of 150, and the 31-member State Senate had six Republicans. Clements had enough support in the House of Representatives to sustain a veto (which required a two-thirds vote to override), but the deck remained stacked against him in the Texas Senate, which was controlled by a strong majority of progressive Democrats, led by Sen. Carl Parker of Port Arthur. Parker could normally be counted on to swing sixteen to eighteen votes. The House, under the leadership of Speaker Gib Lewis, was more conservative.[4] As the session progressed, it was apparent that Clements got along better with the House leader, Lewis, than the Senate leader, Hobby.

Besides the budget, the next most controversial issue of the session was tort reform. Legislators, trial lawyers, consumer groups, and the insurance industry were preparing for a bloody fight over liability insurance and tort reform. As Texans faced skyrocketing premiums and shrinking coverage, the insurance industry blamed the civil justice system, claiming multimillion-dollar jury verdicts, frivolous lawsuits, and attorneys working for contingency fees were driving the problem. An automobile bumper sticker was emblematic of the times: "Go ahead — hit me. I need the money."[5]

The state's prison problems also were mounting. In early January, U.S. District Judge William Wayne Justice issued a contempt order against TDC for falling short of his reform orders in the momentous Ruiz lawsuit. Judge Justice had found the Texas prison system unconstitutional as a result of the suit filed in 1972. The state had made agreements in 1980 to improve inmate living conditions and staffing in Texas' 38,000-inmate prison, but Judge Justice believed the state was dragging its feet. Part of the Ruiz settlement mandated the release of prisoners once the prison population reached 95 percent, and prison overcrowding was a constant problem. Judge Justice now gave the state only until March 31, 1987, to comply with orders that included single-celling certain inmates, providing better medical care, recreation facilities and more guards, or be hit with stiff fines. One of Clements' first acts as governor-elect was to gain a face-to-face meeting with Judge Justice in Tyler to discuss the Ruiz settlement.[6]

During the campaign, Clements had convinced Dallas insurance man Charles Terrell to head up a Texas Criminal Justice Task Force; it became the governor's task force after the election. Terrell said Clements was convinced he was going to win and wanted to "hit the ground running" on criminal justice. The state previously had assumed an adversarial role in fighting Ruiz. Clements believed the suit, then twenty years old, had gone on too long; that Mark White had made agreements which he had not kept, and that the federal judge "had the hammer."

"He decided early-on that we were not going to be enemies of the court," Terrell said. Clements told Judge Justice in Tyler on January 9, 1987, "I may not agree, but a deal's a deal."[7]

Rider Scott, who became head of the governor's criminal justice program, called Clements' meeting with Judge Justice "unprecedented." Sometimes it takes two years to get on a federal docket; yet, Scott had been able to arrange the meeting between Clements and the federal judge in less than two weeks. "That meeting was the beginning of the last chapter of Ruiz," Scott said. With the judge and the governor in the meeting were Scott, Atty. Gen. Jim Mattox, special master Vince Nathan, and plaintiff's lawyer William Bennett Turner. "It was probably the only time that Justice ever sat with the major litigants in the suit," Scott said, who described the meeting as cordial. "Justice could not have been more gracious. We had coffee. It was probably the only time that Mattox and Clements ever shared coffee." Mattox acknowledged the governor's leadership, and it was clear he was going to comply with the consent decrees, Scott said.[8] Justice later dismissed the contempt citation.

Clements had invited other state leaders, including the lieutenant governor and Attorney General Mattox, to his office in Dallas to discuss the settlement before the legislative session began. At that point, it appeared the governor and lieutenant governor were off to a good working relationship. But it didn't last long.

In late January Clements met with Hobby and several senators in the lieutenant governor's office. Clements drew Hobby's ire when he referred to the prison situation as "our" problem. Hobby bluntly laid responsibility for the state's prison dilemma on Clements because of his 1979 veto of $30 million in prison construction funds and his no-new-taxes campaign promises. A few days thereafter, the governor returned to the Senate chambers to discuss an education measure with Hobby. The lieutenant governor pulled Clements aside and, according to Clements, insulted him. That was the last time Clements would pay a friendly visit on the presiding officer of the Texas Senate. From that point forward, if Hobby wanted to talk to the governor, he had to call and make an appointment to see him in the governor's office.[9]

Hobby remembered the start of their rocky relationship that session a little differently. Clements had a proposal to discuss, and Hobby suggested he talk to the Senate committee chairmen about it. Most of the discussion at the meeting was about prisons, and Senators Parker, Ted Lyon of Mesquite and Ray Farabee of Wichita Falls, according to Hobby, "piled on" Clements. Clements became angry at Hobby because he thought Hobby had set him up by orchestrating the meeting.

But it was also obvious from the beginning of the session that Hobby and Clements were at opposite poles on the budget and taxes. Hobby thought Clements was too "doctrinaire" about not increasing taxes. Clements, he said, "wanted to be tough on crime and improve education, but he didn't want to pay for it."[10] Hobby and the Democratic Senate majority were concerned about how the state was going to fund public schools, higher education, mental health, mental retardation, and other social services programs, while increasing spending for prisons — all without a tax increase.

Some of Clements' detractors claimed that the governor went into office the second time with no real agenda, other than a desire to boot Mark White out of office. An aide to Democrat Comptroller Bob Bullock, who had worked for Clements in his 1982 gubernatorial campaign, observed that Clements was looking for ways to change state government in his first term instead of assuming things couldn't be changed; but in his second term, he had accomplished 90 percent of his goals when he defeated Mark White.[11] Yet, Clements had made it abundantly clear throughout the campaign what was foremost on his agenda: problems in the state's economy, which he believed needed his expertise as a businessman to solve. "You don't run for an office like this without having some kind of agenda," his press aide, Reggie Bashur, said later. "He's a businessman, and the state had almost 10 percent unemployment, so economic development was his No. 1 priority." Criminal justice was his second priority, followed by public education, Bashur said, particularly undoing some of the centralization of public school policy in Austin that had occurred on Mark White's watch. But there was a rancorous atmosphere, coming off the negative gubernatorial campaign of 1986. "It was just a very difficult time," Bashur recalled. "The dominant issue was the economy, energy, and whether Texas was going to be able to move forward and diversify its economy. The state had never gone through anything like that. It had gone from such a high, where people didn't think there were any limits, to such a low, where people were really afraid."[12]

In his February 4, 1987, State of the State address to a joint session of the legislature, two weeks after taking office, Clements said he was not looking for confrontation nor trying to be contentious. But, he said, "we are in a time of economic distress, and I will veto a $5.8 billion tax hike." He listed as his No. 1 priority "jobs, jobs, and more jobs. We can't tax and spend our way to a healthy economy." At the same time, however, he recommended spending $520 million for the Department of Corrections to build more prison space. His other priorities included tort reform, the reduction of the no pass-no play penalty for student athletes from six to three weeks, and education legislation to return authority and responsibility to local school boards. He called for a restructuring of the state's criminal justice system according to proposals to be submitted later by his Criminal Justice Task Force, headed by Charles Terrell. He also pledged to seek support in Washington for an oil import fee, and to reestablish relations he previously had promoted with Mexico, an initiative that had faded under Governor White.[13]

It wasn't the agenda that seemed lacking, but rather a definitive roadmap for achieving the goals. It seemed clear where Governor Clements wanted to go. But he still hadn't come up with his "secret plan" — touted during the campaign — for balancing the budget. *Austin American-Statesman* cartoonist Ben Sargent depicted Clements in a chef's hat slumped in a kitchen and surrounded by cookbooks as a waiter at the kitchen door asked, "C'mon, ain't that 'chef's surprise' ready yet?" The monthly special was listed as "Budget Plan a la Clements."

The governor was only five weeks into his second administration when storm clouds arose that would rain relentlessly on the rest of the five-month legislative session and threaten to dampen his entire second term. The issue had nothing to do with state affairs; it was over a football recruiting scandal at Southern Methodist University that became known as "Ponygate."

Clements, who was chairman of SMU's board of governors before going to Washington in 1973, had been vigorously recruited to return to the post in 1983. For five months, board of governors chairman Robert Stewart, board of trustees chairman Edwin Cox and SMU President Donald Shields talked to Clements about succeeeding Stewart, who wanted to step down. Reluctantly, Clements finally agreed. He served from September 1983 until just before his inauguration in January 1987 as chairman of the board of governors, which acted as the executive committee of the larger board of trustees.

Much had transpired at SMU during Clements' ten-year absence. The private, liberal arts school had developed a high-powered football program that had sent its teams to bowl games four times from 1980 to 1984 and twice earned rankings in the Top Ten. The school also had been cited by the National Collegiate Athletic Association for illegal recruiting in 1981 and was under investigation again when Clements returned to the board of governors.

In August 1985, the NCAA slapped another probation on SMU for continued violations and ordered the university to make efforts to ensure that outside representatives of the university's athletic interest were not engaged in recruiting.

Finally, on February 25, 1987, after Clements had resigned from the board and been sworn in as governor, the NCAA awarded SMU the "death penalty," the most severe sanction ever imposed in collegiate sports. The NCAA banned SMU's football program for 1987 and imposed other sanctions because of infractions which included paying $61,000 to thirteen players since 1984. At a press conference that day, SMU's acting president, William Stallcup, denied that the university's in-house investigation showed any involvement by Clements in the pay-for-play scheme.[14]

As the story over the controversy unraveled, Clements insisted he had been brought back on the board without being told that some members of the SMU Mustang team were being paid from a slush fund provided by athletic boosters.

After returning, he became aware that there was a recruiting problem in the athletic department. President Shields and the board of governors hired John McElhaney, an attorney with a prominent Dallas firm, to investigate. Clements did not know the scope of the problem until that investigation was made.

The full extent of the problem became evident at a meeting at the SEDCO building on March 26, 1985, of Clements, McElhaney, former Dallas Mayor Robert Folsom, Athletic Director Bob Hitch, and others, with three key boosters, Sherwood Blount, George Owen, and Bill Stevens. At the meeting, Clements ordered the boosters to get out of recruiting "for the good of the university." Blount replied that he would do that, but the group had a problem to face up to, and that was the outstanding payments that still had to be made to players. He gave some details and said, "You have a payroll to meet. Maybe you should consider adding a line item in the university budget." Clements' response was that this was not the time or place to talk about that.[15]

In May 1985, Clements and others reached agreement with the principal boosters that no new payment commitments to new players would be made, but that commitments already in place would be honored — in essence, agreeing to "wind down" the system of illegal payments.

When the death penalty was handed down, Clements was in Washington for the winter meeting of the National Governors Association and other meetings with members of Congress and the Reagan administration. Robert Riggs, a reporter for WFAA-TV, the ABC affiliate in Dallas, tracked him down on the sidewalk outside the White House. Riggs told Clements that SMU officials had met during the August 1985 NCAA investigation and decided to keep making the payments to the athletes. "Were you aware of that meeting?" Riggs asked.

Clements responded, "I'm not sure that that's correct and I don't know where they get their information and exactly what officials they're talking about. Who's making the payments? Certainly the school's not."

Riggs: "The alumni. Were you aware that there was a decision for the alumni to keep making the payments?"

Clements: "No, I don't have any recollection of that sort of thing, and I just question whether that's really correct or not."

The meeting to which Riggs referred, later detailed in a report prepared by a special committee of bishops of the United Methodist Church, revisited the issue of continuing the payments to the upperclassmen players, since the stakes had been raised by NCAA enactment of the "death penalty" legislation. The meeting was held in President Shields' office and included Shields, Clements, board of trustees chairman Cox and Athletic Director Bob Hitch. Clements, who was on inactive status as board of governors chairman because he was campaigning for state office, agreed to attend the meeting and offer his advice, but said it was their decision to make.

At the meeting, Clements and Hitch advocated continuing the payments; Cox and Shields took the other side. Clements argued that the season would begin in two weeks, and that three of the players were All-Southwest Conference. The players receiving payments were the stars. If the payments stopped, those players were sure to leave and announce to the world why. There were no new commitments; they would be finished at the end of the 1987 season. There was "light at the end of the tunnel," he said. If they continued the payments, there was a risk it would all blow up at some time in the future; but if the payments were stopped, it was sure to blow up immediately. When Clements left the meeting, nothing had been decided.[16] In an interview years later, Clements said, "How they resolved it, I had no idea."[17]

Asked by a *Dallas Morning News* reporter in Washington on the same day that he encountered Riggs if he had ever authorized payments to any SMU athletes, Clements snapped: "Hell, no. Absolutely not. I have never in my life recruited a single athlete for SMU — never."[18]

Within days after the death penalty was invoked, Dallas investigative journalists were developing stories from secondhand sources about the knowledge Clements and others had of the illegal recruiting scheme. On the morning of March 2, 1987, *Dallas Morning News* editor and publisher Burl Osborne stopped in the office of editorial writer Scott Bennett, who had good relations with the governor's office, and suggested Bennett might be able to arrange an interview for *The News* with Governor Clements. Bennett called Dary Stone, who called George Bayoud — passing along the information that it was only a matter of time until the stories broke. That afternoon, Bennett got a call back; he and Osborne were invited to dinner with the governor that night at the Governor's Mansion. Clements was willing to meet, but only if it was CEO to CEO — the governor and the publisher. Osborne and Bennett caught a 4:00 P.M. flight to Austin.[19]

Over drinks and dinner at the Governor's Mansion, Clements described the recruiting system as one that had been put into place by Ron Meyer and Russ Potts and continued by Bob Hitch and Bobby Collins, two sets of athletic directors-coaches. He said he had "inherited" their policies when he returned as chairman of the board of governors. In a long and rambling conversation, Clements explained that the system was being racheted down. "We were well on our way to cleaning up our problems at SMU . . . after really agonizing over what we should do, and I want to emphasize we — under no circumstances should anyone ever consider that this was a unilateral decision by Bill Clements as the chairman of the board of governors at SMU." While there was never any formal action by the board, Clements suggested that several people were involved in the decision to finish out commitments that had been made to players while prohibiting any future violations.

"In our own funny way, we swapped a bad deal and I knew it was a bad deal. It's totally contrary to any of my nature. I've never participated in anything like this. And, you know, I walked into a first-class, A-number one mess, which I had nothing whatsoever to do with. It was not of my creation, and so, I was the person, the designated person. And we said, well, OK, let's clean it up. And we've tried to clean it up," Clements said.[20]

Osborne and Bennett took the last flight back to Dallas from Austin that night, arriving after 10:00 P.M., and decided to meet with reporters and editors the next morning to determine what to do with the information. The next day, March 3, 1987, was the day of the governor's regular weekly press conference. WFAA-TV's Austin bureau reporter Carole Kneeland, at the suggestion of Channel 8 producer John Sparks in Dallas, who had long worked on the recruiting story, asked Clements if he knew about the payments to

SMU football players and if he had agreed to honor them. He answered that he had.[21]

Clements' response exploded in the news media. That SMU's illegal payments to football players had been condoned by the now-governor of Texas made it a national news story. Plus, SMU provided an example of a pervasive problem in college football. ABC-TV's *Nightline* did a segment. *The New York Times*, in a front-page story, quoted former Gov. Mark White as saying the continued payments constituted "hush money" to keep the players from squawking during the gubernatorial campaign.

Questions were raised by the media about whether Clements' credibility with the legislature would be affected. George Christian, a Democratic lobbyist, said he doubted that the scandal would spread to legislative politics. "The budget problem is so severe that everybody's mind is on that," he said. House Speaker Gib Lewis, a Democrat, downplayed the importance of the story in the state capital, saying, "That's between him and SMU. That doesn't have anything to do with state business." Yet, under Texas' weak governor system, the only power Clements had over the budget, besides the veto, was persuasion. Dr. Richard Murray, a political scientist at the University of Houston, said, "The only question is how much damage. In a state where the governor has relatively weak formal powers, his public standing is important . . . . If you lose credibility, you suffer."[22]

The public was flooded with television and newspaper stories and commentary. A wire service sportswriter told how troubled the Southwest Conference was; all but one Texas school in the SWC, dubbed as "Sure We Cheat," were either under NCAA investigation or sanctions, or in-house investigations. Only Rice University, never a gridiron power in a football-crazed state, had escaped suspicion.[23]

The political writers went after Clements. Here was a governor who had blasted the incumbent out of office by calling him a "pre-var-i-ca-tor." "There is a certain twisted logic about having a moral obligation to continue an immoral contract," Austin columnist Dave McNeely wrote. Columnist Molly Ivins wrote, "No one minds a sinner much, we've all been there, but few folks care for a hypocrite. Even people who don't like Bill Clements always figured him for a straight-shooter." The editorialists also weighed in, with the *Fort Worth Star-Telegram* calling Clements' involvement a "black mark on [the] governor."²⁴ A March 6, 1987, *Houston Post* cartoon showed Clements sitting at the governor's desk with a football on it labeled SMU. On the sign, "The buck stops here," the word "stops" was crossed out and replaced with "phased out."

At SMU, 400 students demonstrated on campus, carrying signs that said "Impeach Gov. Clements" and "Rename Clements Hall." The deans and vice-presidents issued a statement calling for resignations of any member of the board or administration who participated in or had knowledge of the payments. The university community was indignant over the fact that SMU faculty member Lonnie Kliever had been placed in charge of the university's joint investigation with the NCAA and knowledge of any involvement by members of the board had been denied to him.²⁵ Board members scrambled for cover, with all but one denying any knowledge of the continued payments.

On March 10, 1987, at his weekly news conference, Clements read a statement in which he apologized for condoning the continued payments, admitted it was wrong, and tried to put the whole affair into historical context. After he returned to the board, he said, he and several members of the board and SMU administration found out boosters were making payments to twenty-six athletes. "Shocked that such practices were occurring, appalled to find out through investigation that such a system had been established and was on-going since the middle 1970s, we were determined to put an end to it and return to a system of full compliance and integrity," he read. "After much discussion and much agonizing, we chose a phase-out system. We did it reluctantly and uncomfortably, but feeling that this approach would be in the best interest of SMU, the Dallas community, the players and their families. It is clear now that we made the wrong decision. Periodically, members of the Board and Administration met with the Athletic Department to monitor the phased-down program, and by December 1986, three players remained."

Clements went on to say that he was "saddened by what has happened. SMU has been a part of my life for many, many years." In hindsight, he said, "It was clear we were wrong." The system should have been stopped immediately, he said, but "we decided to phase the system out. To those rightfully upset and angry about the decision, I am truly sorry." Clements said he had three options when he learned of the infractions: he could blow the whistle on the whole affair, he could resign from the board and walk away, or he could try to find a solution and move forward. He chose the latter.

Questioned about whether he lied to the NCAA, Clements responded: "I said, 'We are cleaning up the program.' Now everyone of you are writers, and you know that that is in the present and future tense. It's not that we have accomplished our purpose, we are working on it. And, I've never told the NCAA anything but that."

Asked by Dave McNeely of the *Austin American-Statesman* if he had given the "whole truth and nothing but the truth," Clements finally made one of those unforgettable, quintessential Clements statements. "Well, you know, we weren't operating like inaugural day, with a Bible, Dave, and there wasn't ever a Bible present."[26] The following week, at the March 17 press conference, reporter Sam Kinch, Jr., showed up carrying a Bible and placed it beside the tape recorders on the governor's lectern. Clements, never one to miss an opportunity to gig the press, could still joke, "I know that none of you were capable of bringing Bibles, so whose is it?" he asked. When reporters laughed, Clements said, "I'm glad y'all haven't lost your sense of humor."[27]

Clements had refused to identify the other lay leaders and administrators who had been involved, asking that they identify themselves. With the exception of former board of governors chairman Robert H. Stewart III, his friends failed to come forward and admit their own knowledge and/or participation. Stewart, who had been chairman when the "slush fund" was begun, issued a public statement supporting Clements' position that he had told the board in "approximately April 1985" that he was dedicated to cleaning up the athletic program but that it would take some unwinding and that the NCAA "clearly understood this."[28]

Ron Calhoun, a columnist for the *Dallas Times-Herald*, wrote that Clements often tried to convey the impression that he was supported in his views and actions by others of stature, by using phrases such as "without question" and "under no circumstances" and somebody else "clearly understood this" to punctuate his points.[29]

On March 12, 1987, the Special Committee of Bishops of the South Central Jurisdiction of the United Methodist Church began its three-month investigation of SMU. On March 20, 1987, the SMU board of trustees voted to abolish the board of governors, a move that was followed by sweeping reforms of the board of trustees.

Back in Austin, life in the middle of a legislative session was grinding on. The SMU crisis was only one of Clements' problems.

Early in the administration, the legislature had passed and the governor had signed an emergency funding bill which authorized early parole for several hundred inmates. This had helped persuade Judge Justice to lift the threat of nearly $1 million in fines against the state for failing to comply with prison reform agreements. After criticizing White for his early release of prison inmates, Clements had begun approving the early transfer of inmates to halfway houses as a method of easing prison overcrowding. That overcrowding was forcing the nation's second-largest prison system (after California) to open and close weekly, and emergency good time was being given to nonviolent inmates to trigger the early releases, all in accord with Judge Justice's ruling.[30]

Meanwhile, Clements had said he would approve a permanent extension of the increase in the gasoline tax to fifteen cents a gallon, and the sales tax to 5.25 cents on the dollar, to raise an additional $2.9 billion in the next biennium. Beyond that, Clements had established a bottom budget line of $36.9 billion, from which he wouldn't yield. His budget was some $3 billion less than the budgets being prepared in both the House and Senate. Hobby thought the budget figures coming from the governor's office, prepared by budget director Bob Davis, were faulty.

Three months into the session, the legislature was deadlocked over where to find the additional $3 billion — the difference between the $5.8 billion shortfall and the $2.9 billion provided by extending the temporary sales and gasoline tax increases. Higher education leaders were demanding that their funding, which had been cut the previous year, be restored to its 1985 level. Hobby was frustrated by the governor's refusal to budge on the tax issue, and Democratic state senators and the governor were at serious odds. Senate Education Committee Chairman Carl Parker predicted that "we are charting the course for disaster in our higher and public education." Hobby thought that Clements was "just hostile to education, in general." Speaker Gib Lewis called it "the roughest session I've ever gone through."[31]

Clements took on the critical senators. In a wire service interview, he likened the liberal Democrat senators to "prairie chickens thumping the ground," saying they had turned the debate over state finances into a partisan brawl despite his willingness to compromise (by agreeing to make the temporary taxes permanent to raise $2.9 billion). In the Associated Press story used across the state, Clements explained that prairie chickens, during the breeding season, have a "genetic compulsion" to thump the ground. "It's a historical, genetic dance that they do. And so, I think, these Democrats have been going through a thumping period that they felt compelled to do. Now, hopefully, we'll get down to serious business." Clements repeated the line in an interview with reporter Anne Marie Kilday of the *Houston Chronicle*. She reported that over breakfast at the Governor's Mansion, Clements clasped his hands and flapped his elbows, demonstrating how legislators acted like prairie chickens. "They're just doing their little dance. Thumping. Like prairie chickens. Thumping. They'll settle down."[32]

Hobby and several other senators were off on a trail ride, hosted by Sen. John Montford of Lubbock, when Clements referred to the senators as prairie chickens. They returned to Austin prepared to retaliate. T-shirts were printed with the picture of a prairie chicken over the state seal and the words, "Proud to be a Prairie Chicken." A resolution was drafted and senators delivered personal privilege speeches on the Senate floor.

Senator Parker said he'd rather be compared to a prideful prairie chicken than to a rattlesnake trying to rob the nest of vital state services. "I'm told a prairie chicken would kill a rattlesnake if he tried to get its eggs. We'll just let the people judge who the prairie chickens are who are guarding the nest and the eggs, and who the rattlesnake is trying to get them." Senator Montford said he would rather be called a prairie chicken than "an ostrich with his head in the sand."

A resolution expressing "heartfelt and sincere gratitude for the contributions of the prairie chickens of Texas" was passed by the Senate on April 15, 1987, designating the prairie chicken as the "official state grouse." The resolution authored by Sen. Ray Farabee also noted that the Senate preferred "the thumping of prairie chickens to the throwing about of rubber chickens," referring to Clements' rubber chicken incident in his 1978 campaign with John Hill. Hobby called for a vote on the resolution. "All in favor, signify by thumping. Those opposed thump twice. The single thumpers have it; the resolution is adopted."[33]

During that same period, recognizing the problems various Southwest Conference schools were having with illegal recruiting by boosters, the Texas Senate passed a bill giving universities in the conference greater power to sue boosters who were getting schools in trouble by violating NCAA rules. Senator Montford, sponsor of the bill, noted that Texas universities had no legal recourse against boosters whose violations of NCAA rules resulted in sanctions against the schools. At that time, four Southwest Conference schools were on probation for violations.[34]

The governor's staff members and close friends said they felt the wind went out of the governor's sails during the SMU crisis, that the legislative session became a struggle just to endure. Clements, however, would never adopt a defeatist attitude. Some staff members sunk to levels of depression, but not Clements. What was done was done; he kept moving on. One day he walked into the governor's office and admonished his executive assistant, George Bayoud: "I'm sick and tired of seeing you down in the doldrums." Clements' outlook, Bayoud learned, was that there would be a lot of sunny days but there would also be some rainy ones. Clements believed that how you comport yourself on those rainy days is the measure of a person, Bayoud said.[35]

As the session plodded on, Clements never seemed to lose his confidence. But members of the Capitol press corps complained that he became more ornery with each passing day. Clements felt he had inherited a mess and had tried to clean it up. He felt used by his friends, who had lured him back to the board without telling him of the enormity of the problem and, when the chips were down, failed to stand by him. And he felt the Capitol press wasn't giving him a fair shake; they just wouldn't turn loose of the story. The SMU situation soured the relationship between Clements and the Capitol press and diminished his normal enthusiasm. It was the job of the press to deal with the governor; he couldn't escape them because they were there. But the environment was like two armed camps. Associates of the governor said it took the fun out of the job for him.

Carole Kneeland of WFAA-TV, who had asked the fateful question about SMU at the March 3 press conference, complained that she had been cut off; the governor refused to recognize her for questions in subsequent press conferences. She finally went to press secretary Reggie Bashur and asked for a meeting with the governor. They had a frank discussion during which Clements told her he had a problem with the way she asked questions; he felt she was deliberately trying to make him look bad. She agreed to ask the questions more diplomatically, and he agreed not to cut her out. Thereafter, she would frequently begin a question by saying, "Governor, I'm sure you had a good reason for doing this, but would you explain . . ." They would both smile, she said, and he would usually answer the question.[36]

Clements' relations with the press continued to deteriorate. After his March 5 apology, he refused to entertain any more questions about SMU and threatened to end his weekly news conference if reporters persisted. Because he was irritable and cranky with members of the press corps, many of them felt he didn't really want to be in Austin. The truth was that the SMU controversy had soured him on the press. They were no longer the strange hindu wise owls; they were the enemy.

The SMU controversy caused the staff in the governor's office to batten down the hatches. It was as if they were operating from a bunker, chief of staff Hilary Doran said. "It was something the governor had to work through, himself. All we could do was try to do our jobs and take as much of the load off of him as possible. But it had an effect on all of us," Doran said.

"It was a firefight the first six months. All we did was fend off the press corps, national as well as state," Bashur acknowledged.[37]

In late April, however, Clements decided to go on the offensive and take his no-new-taxes message to the people on a seventeen-city tour of the state. According to associates, Clements showed for the first time his old exuberance during the tour. He appeared energized by the tour, as he explained the stalemate between his proposed $36.9 billion budget, the Senate's $40 billion and the House's $39.4 billion proposal.[38]

Other forces, meanwhile, had entered the budget battle, including his old friends Peter O'Donnell and Ross Perot. Philanthropist O'Donnell was concerned about higher education funding. Computer magnate Perot, who had headed Gov. Mark White's Select Committee on Public Education which launched sweeping reforms of public education, was concerned about public school funding. Perot had been persuasive during the White administration in getting the largest tax increase in state history passed to finance improvements in public schools, including preschool for disadvantaged four-year-olds and smaller classes in the early grades.

The spotlight already was on education when State District Judge Harley Clark ruled on April 29, 1987, that the state's system of funding its public schools was unconstitutional. A coalition of poor school districts and the Mexican American Legal Defense Fund (MALDEF) had brought the suit, contending that the wide disparity in spending between the richest and poorest systems violated the state constitution. State officials said they would appeal. While the ruling had no immediate effect on the appropriations bill, it was an issue that would grow over time.[39]

The education establishment had joined the budget fray and on May 6, 1987, an Austin rally spearheaded by University of Texas Board of Regents Chairman Jess Hay, a Dallas mortgage banker, drew some 2,000 supporters. Speakers included Perot and San Antonio Mayor Henry Cisneros. They argued that education funding should be increased at least $1.1 billion and that taxes should be raised to pay for it. Representatives of public schools, junior colleges, public and private universities, chambers of commerce and community organizations attended. Also declaring support for more revenues for education were the mayors of major cities, plus John Connally, Lady Bird Johnson, former Congresswoman Barbara Jordan, and another old Clements friend, retired SMU Chancellor Willis Tate. Even as Clements was winding up his seventeen-city tour, O'Donnell and Perot were acting as behind-the-scenes catalysts to get him to agree to a budget summit with Lieutenant Governor Hobby, Speaker Lewis, and Comptroller Bob Bullock.[40]

Clements agreed to consider an expansion of the sales tax base, which produced a furor among Republicans and a field day in the press. On May 7, 1987, the state's newspapers reported that Clements had made a 180-degree turn and abandoned his pledge to veto new taxes. Angry Republican legislators said that he had broken his most important campaign promise. "It's a betrayal of the citizens of this state," said Rep. Randy Pennington, a Houston Republican. Rep. Mike Toomey, another Houston Republican and one of Clements' legislative lieutenants, tried to analyze the shift. Clements had the votes to block a tax bill in the House, but he didn't have the votes to pass his other legislation, which included a new Department of Commerce and reorganization of the criminal justice agencies into one department. If he was to accomplish anything else the rest of his term, he had to win back the hearts and minds of the other elected officials, Toomey said, by being part of the solution. Toomey also noted that Peter O'Donnell and Ross Perot were the governor's peers. If they believed a tax hike was essential to protect the state's education system and other services, he said, Clements had to believe there was something to it. But the newspapers were unforgiving. The *Houston Post* headlined: "Clements in U-Turn on Tax Pledge."[41]

Among the angriest Republicans was State GOP Chairman George Strake, who called Clements' office and demanded to see the governor. The governor was busy all day, but his secretary, Janie Harris, finally called Strake back at Republican headquarters and told him Clements was having a 5:00 P.M. reception at the mansion, after which they could meet. Strake wanted to catch a flight to Houston and was about to leave the outdoor reception, when Clements' executive assistant, George Bayoud, drew the governor inside. Sitting down with Strake, Bayoud, Rita, and the state GOP's executive director, John Weaver, Clements barked, "What do you want?"

Strake pulled out the *Houston Post* and said, "This headline is what I came to talk about."

"I don't read that paper. What does it say?" answered Clements.

"You might want to pick up your *Dallas Morning News* or *Fort Worth Star-Telegram* or El Paso paper or Amarillo paper. They're all the same," Strake replied. Arguing that Clements was reneging on his no-new-taxes promise, Strake said, "Right now, I don't see any difference between you and Mark White." Whereupon, according to Strake, a chill came over the room.

Clements countered that he was elected by the people of Texas and not just the Republicans, while Strake contended, "We have the Legislature about to break, and you're giving in, right here at the end. I know they're threatening to open the prisons and close the schools and quit building roads, but this is when you get something done. You have all the Republicans in the Legislature hanging on at the end of the limb and you're sawing it off for them." Strake and Clements were both in a huff as Strake left.[42]

The next morning, Republican legislators had breakfast with the governor and told him the same thing. In that meeting and throughout the day to reporters, Clements explained that no deals had been made. He was showing some "flexibility" in his new stand that would enable the consideration of increases to the revenue stream by revamping the tax system, largely by expanding the sales tax base and by redrawing the corporate franchise tax. Representative Toomey, who was one of Clements' ad hoc budget advisers, wanted Clements to hold the line, but admitted Clements was in a box on whether to ease his position against additional taxes. "If he doesn't do that, he's branded as an inflexible old codger. And he's branded as abandoning his position if he does."[43]

A day later, Clements said that expansion of the tax base was no longer an option. Besieged by protests from his own party and angry at the way his position had been portrayed in the media, Clements said, "I think the press and the media has not done itself justice by jumping to some conclusions about my changed position, my flip-flop, 180 degree [turn], and all the other wonderful terms you've used. That's not true. What I've said is that we were going to consider, and we should consider, all of the various alternatives and options." However, he said, there was insufficient time remaining in the session to undertake a complex revamping of the tax base. "We're not going to expand the tax base. I want to make that very clear. It was something we were considering as an option. It is no longer an option. I am opposed to it." Clearly peeved at the press, he said, "You all are in some kind of never-never land."[44]

A week later, press aide Reggie Bashur announced that Clements was dropping his regular weekly news conference, saying the governor needed the time to work with the legislature. Besides his annoyance with the Capitol press corps, Clements' candor at his news conferences, plus occasional forgetfulness, had begun creating problems for Republican legislators and for members of the governor's staff. Sen. O. H. "Ike" Harris acknowledged that the governor's statements gave Democrats "something to get sideways about." Harris said, "Yes, we've got a governor that is available and is candid with the media. He's going to give you an answer to any question you ask . . . . And it's creating problems." By then, Republicans had become a body of power in the legislature.

Reggie Bashur was urging the governor to be less accessible to the press, though he defended his boss' candor. "He's a blunt-speaking man. He tells you what's on his mind. Strictly from a PR standpoint, there is a distinct disadvantage to a Clements press conference. But I think that a lot of the public, a lot of people, respect the fact that he is candid."[45]

According to a Texas Poll released May 10, 1987, however, Clements' popularity had taken a nose dive, which was partly ascribed to his linkage to the SMU football scandal. James Dyer, director of the poll conducted at Texas A&M University for Harte-Hanks Communications, said it had cut into Clements' basic appeal of rugged honesty. His negative rating rose 11 points in two months — from 45 percent in February to 56 percent, which was near Mark White's record disapproval rate of 60 percent in August 1986. Only one in four Texans said they thought Clements was performing well in office, while more than half said he was doing a poor or a fair job. Clements responded that efforts to reach accord on the budget and tax questions were consuming his thoughts, not polls.[46]

As the session headed toward adjournment, the legislature remained deadlocked on the budget. The situation between the governor and the Senate had deteriorated and, in the session's final days, Clements was communicating only with the House. The session ended without an appropriations bill, and without the civil justice and insurance reforms that Clements had demanded. The legislature did, however, agree in the final hours to consolidate all of the state's economic development efforts into a new Texas Department of Commerce. Clements lauded the action as among the top achievements of the session.[47]

The governor announced he would call the legislature back into session on June 22, 1987, to write a budget bill. But first he would call an immediate special session to complete work on tort reform, since the two houses were close to agreement on a compromise package of civil justice and insurance reforms. In the two-day special session, sweeping changes were approved that included caps on punitive damages, sanctions for filing frivolous lawsuits, and limits on the liability of cities and defendants in multiparty suits.[48]

Clements' first five months back in office had been an unpleasant time. The governor and his wife had enjoyed returning to the historic Governor's Mansion, so different from the rundown house they had encountered in 1979. There was a sense of pride in the restoration and refurbishing, for which they could properly take credit, and they enjoyed inviting old friends or associates to dine or meet there. But there had been little pleasure, otherwise, to be taken from the first regular session of that second term. In the last three months of that contentious session, some observers felt the governor had decided to occupy the office, do the job as best he could, be there from Monday to Friday, and then get out of town — to Dallas, his East Texas Hollyglen house, or to his *casa* in Taos.

On Friday, June 19, 1987, the Bishops' Committee Report on SMU was released. As members of the press gathered in the governor's reception room, where the governor was signing proclamations, he tried to joke, telling a visiting youngster to go kick one of the reporters in the shins.[49]

The Bishops' Committee reported that members of the board of governors who knew about the unauthorized payment scheme included former board of governors chairman Robert Stewart, chairman of the board of trustees Edwin Cox, Paul Corley, former Dallas Mayor Robert Folsom, SMU President Donald Shields and Athletic Director Bob Hitch. Clements, Cox, Corley and William Hutchison, who replaced Clements as chairman of the board of governors, were singled out for trying to conceal the decision to continue the payments.

The report also noted that at least as early as 1981, Stewart and Cox were aware of payments to players: "Shields was told on October 9, 1980, shortly after he had been selected as president, that payments were being made to athletes at SMU in violation of the NCAA rules. Mike Harvey, the SMU faculty representative to the NCAA, gave this information to Shields in clear, unmistakable terms." Shields, according to the report, conducted his own investigation, and passed the findings along to Cox and Stewart.[50]

Clements was the only member of the board of governors or senior administration to testify under oath to the Bishops' Committee. He later took exception with some of the information in the report, which was obtained by interviews with people who were not testifying under oath — including athletic director Hitch. Clements denied vigorously allegations that he had "ordered" the continuation of payments after that August 1985 meeting in Shields' office. Hitch worked for Shields, Clements said, and it was their decision to make.[51]

What Clements may have not understood is that once he expressed his opinion or desire, the sheer force of his personality — unless he ran up against someone of equal presence, and there weren't many — often created action by others, whether or not he ordered it.

With all the blame-laying, the withholding of information, denials and changed stories during the course of the SMU controversy, plus the passage of time and selective memory by some of the principals, it's unlikely that the complete truth will ever be known. One point appears incontrovertible: Bill Clements had no part in creating or administering the slush fund under which boosters and the SMU athletic department began to pay players. He always believed that those who created the problem should have gotten more of the blame.

Lonnie Kliever, the religious studies faculty member who headed the university's cooperative investigation with the NCAA, said in an interview eight years after the Bishops' Report that "human beings are finite and they make decisions based on information and sometimes they make tough decisions that turn out to be the wrong ones. That's what I felt about Gov. Clements. I didn't see it as some vast conspiracy to protect the governor's future. It was just one of those situations where decisions are made in incremental steps, none of which are decisive but all of which collectively are later seen to be wrong."

The scandal, he said, would have been "peripheral" had it not been for the fact that people at the highest level of leadership knew about the continuance of payments and gave tacit approval and that a governor was involved. The integrity of the academic program of the university was never involved, and university money was not used. After the scandal, admissions were not affected, and faculty members and financial support were not lost. "In a sports town where the sports world is the real world, this was a great story and a huge tragedy, but the university was not that seriously affected once we worked through the public embarrassment of it," Kliever said.[52]

In a 1995 interview, Stewart called Clements a "victim of circumstances." Since he had persuaded Clements to replace him as board of governors chairman, Stewart said, "I guess you could blame me for getting him into that mess."[53]

Clements said eight years after the Bishops' Report was issued that he felt "used" by those who had long known about the illegal program and that he became the scapegoat because he was the governor. "If there was anything in my life I could do over it would be to say absolutely 'No' to rejoining the board of governors; I should never have agreed to do that. There are not many things I can look back on in my life and say that was a mistake. But that was a mistake . . . . In everyone's life a little rain has to fall. I got sprinkled."[54]

The Bishops' Report came out on a Friday. On Monday, June 22, 1987, the legislature reconvened for its second special session, to try to resolve its budget impasse. It was the first time since 1961 that the Texas legislature had failed during the regular 140-day session to write a budget for the biennium that would begin September 1. Since the regular session had adjourned three weeks earlier, State Comptroller Bob Bullock had raised his projected budget deficit for the biennium to $6.5 billion. Lieutenant Governor Hobby had told some of the state's most prominent business and civic leaders that "if we cannot adopt a budget by August 31, our schools won't open and our prisons will." The lieutenant governor was continuing to insist on additional revenues to enhance the state's colleges and universities and to protect funding for health and welfare as caseloads increased due to the sagging economy.

There was momentary talk among a few legislators of impeaching Governor Clements for his role in allowing illicit payments to be made to SMU football players. Atty. Gen. Jim Mattox, meanwhile, had initiated an inquiry to determine if any criminal or civil laws had been broken. Speaker Lewis said, "I'm here to solve the budget problem and nothing else." The impeachment idea soon faded, and Lewis came in with a budget that took the middle ground between the lieutenant governor's much-higher-taxes posture and the governor's hold-the-line stance.[55]

The pressure stayed on. Former Gov. John Connally and San Antonio Mayor Henry Cisneros made a bipartisan appeal in San Antonio, Austin, and Dallas for increased education funding, discussing the link between education and economic vitality. Connally also took the message to five West Texas towns. At a rally on the Capitol grounds on the last day of June, Hobby reminded that lawmakers three years before had enacted consequential public school reforms. "That was a commitment regardless of the price of oil, regardless of the price of real estate, and that's a promise that we've got to keep," he said. Chairman Strake, meanwhile, continued to call for the governor to stick to his campaign pledge of "cutting the cloth to fit the pattern."[56]

As the thirty-day special session neared the end, Clements agreed to accept a compromise $38.3 billion budget bill with companion tax measures to raise $5.7 billion, again angering Republicans. However, Clements had been informed by Rep. Tom Craddick, Republican caucus chairman, that several Repbulican votes were wavering, and another veto probably could not be sustained.

Democrats attempted to force Republican holdouts into accepting the tax package by denying increased funding to colleges and universities in Republican districts. The compromise taxes would extend the sales tax to a wide range of services which previously had been exempted, and increase the gasoline and corporate franchise taxes. Legislators continued to bicker until the bitter end. Finally, some conservative Democrats and Republicans agreed to support the package only after a complicated set of parliamentary maneuvers was designed to allow them to escape blame for the tax increase.[57]

The Republican legislators were meeting weekly with Governor Clements, and their chairman, Rep. Tom Craddick of Midland, almost daily. Craddick tried to talk Clements out of signing the tax measure. "But he felt like he had to do something, that the state was going to be at a standstill if we didn't get something done," Craddick said later.[58]

Jim Kaster, the governor's legislative aide, took the bill over to the Governor's Mansion late one evening, and Clements, in his pajamas, signed it. Kaster and Hilary Doran, the governor's chief of staff, both of whom had been Democrats and became Republicans after going to work for Clements, advised the governor to sign the bill. Because of the bloody fights and bruised egos already suffered in the long budget battle, Doran felt there was little chance of getting any more reductions after a veto.

It had been a bitter and highly partisan battle. When it was over, Clements' hometown newspaper editorialized that while the governor had signed the largest tax bill in the history of the state, it would have been even larger had he not been in office. The Senate started out demanding a $40 billion budget that would have required a $7.5 billion tax bill. Clements' consistent threats to veto the budget helped reduce that amount by $1.8 billion. Clements said he had no apologies for how he had handled the budget issue, claiming taxpayers were saved almost $2 billion. "I think that is a significant accomplishment," he said.[59]

Bashur said he thought Clements "fought the good fight for as long as he could. The Republicans in the Legislature wanted him to stand his ground, if it took ten special sessions. But the situation was very divisive, and without a budget, you get to the end of August and programs close, nursing homes close. He wasn't going to create a crisis," Bashur said. "One of his characteristics is that he's a manager. He manages things. 'Create solutions' is one of his favorite phrases. He's not trying to blow things up. He pushed his arguments as far as he could, and while it was a large tax increase that was ultimately signed, it was still significantly less than it might otherwise have been."

Gib Lewis called the signing of the tax bill one of Clements' "strongest moments in government." In an interview years after that contentious session, Lewis said, "It takes a lot of courage to make a hard decision. It's easy to vote 'no' and duck tail and run. It's difficult to do some unpopular things. But that's part of leadership. We had scrubbed it [the budget] down, done everything we could," he said. "He was opposed to a tax increase. So was I opposed. But there comes a time and place to keep government services functioning, that you have to bite the bullet."[60]

Kaster said, "He did what he thought was right, and then he would never look back. When he made his mind up, right or wrong, he would never go back and say, what if I'd done this or what if I'd done that. When the decision was made, he stuck with it and went right to bed and never thought again about it," Kaster said. "He took heat on that one but to not have done it would have been more disastrous."

Doran said later he could remember the accomplishments of Clements' first administration better than the first session of the second administration. "I think it was because it was so bitter on that budget battle and the tax bill."[61]

The rancorous budget-and-tax battle and the SMU controversy had taken its toll on Bill Clements' popularity as governor of Texas. The summer 1987 Texas Poll, taken the last week of July and first week of August, gave Clements a disapproval rating of 68 percent. It was the highest disapproval rating of any governor in a ten-year history of quarterly surveys made by the Texas Poll.[62]

Chapter 18

Second Term

"Jobs, jobs, jobs"

THE PARADOX THAT WAS Bill Clements emerged again in the last half of his second gubernatorial term. As legislators gathered in Austin in January 1989 for the 71st session, the meanness that had characterized the previous regular session seemed to have evaporated. The governor talked characteristically tough, but there now was a conciliatory manner about him. The crabbiness was gone. The man who could be both stubborn and flexible showed he could be as amiable as he had been unpleasant.

Clements began by saying the session was going to be kinder and gentler than the one two years before. Acknowledging that the 1987 session may have been the most acrimonious in recent history, Clements conceded that "maybe a good lesson has been learned by all."[1] The governor spoke about a new spirit of cooperation and understanding between the House and Senate and the governor's office.

By early 1989, the climate was changing, economically and politically. Since the legislature had last met, George Bush had been elected president, succeeding Ronald Reagan. Clements had served as co-chairman of the successful Bush campaign in Texas.

Clements also had placed a high priority on the 1988 race for Texas Supreme Court waged by his appointee, Tom Phillips. There was a growing perception that justice could be bought in Texas, through campaign contributions to Supreme Court candidates.

Phillips had won his race, as had Clements' appointee to the Texas
Railroad Commission, Kent Hance. The two had become the first
Republicans of the century to win Texas statewide elections in races
other than for U.S. Senate and governor.

Meanwhile, the future political ambitions of Lt. Gov. Bill
Hobby were no longer a factor, and that helped shape Clements'
new approach. In the summer of 1987, after the special sessions were
over, Hobby had announced that he would not be a candidate for
office in 1990; he would neither run for governor nor for another
term as lieutenant governor. Until then, Hobby had been considered the Democratic frontrunner to succeed Clements and, during
the difficult 1987 session, Clements had blamed many of Hobby's
actions on his political aspirations. As the 1989 session got under
way, however, both were lame ducks, and each wanted to go out of
office on a positive note.

There also may have been medical reasons for Clements' kinder
and gentler approach. In the summer of 1988, the governor suffered
a slight stroke. As Jesse Jackson was delivering his speech to the
Democratic National Convention in Atlanta, a message scrolled
across the television screen that Governor Clements had been hos-
pitalized with a possible stroke. Clements had been working in his
office in Austin when he became ill. His secretary, Janie Harris, and
aide George Bayoud insisted he go to the hospital. He was released
after a few days and announced that the problem was not serious.[2]
But it served as a warning to the seventy-one-year-old governor that
it was no longer in his best interest to let his blood boil.

There were other changes, as well, in early 1989. The SMU controversy had receded. And the Texas economy had begun to rebound. Although a large number of savings and loans in the state
had defaulted, and the problem was continuing, overall economic
conditions were improving. Clements was beginning to get credit
for luring new business and industry to the state. And Texas had
been chosen by Congress as the site for the U.S. Department of
Energy's coveted $4.4 billion atomic research facility known as the
Superconducting Super Collider — an economic boon Clements
had been determined to secure for the state. There now were
329,000 more Texans working than two years before, and the unemployment rate was at 6.2 percent, the lowest level in four years. Oil
prices had risen to $18 a barrel. As Clements said in his State of the
State address, "the enormous engines of the Texas economy are

fired up once again." The budget situation was far different from two years before: Comptroller Bob Bullock certified that the state had more than $1.6 billion in additional general revenue to begin the new biennium, which Clements felt would negate any need for a tax increase.[3]

Entering that last regular legislative session, Clements would be taking his final turn at bat in a political career marked, according to one article, by strikeouts as well as home runs. He needed a strong finish, to leave a positive legacy. He started by making changes in his staff and in his personal style.

Recognizing that the governor had had a rocky first session, Bayoud, who had become chief of staff, suggested that Clements bring in a new team. Two well-regarded legislators were persuaded to give up their House seats to work for the governor — Republican Mike Toomey of Houston and Cliff Johnson, a conservative Democrat from East Texas. Toomey, a respected Republican leader in the House, who always preferred policy to politics, was agreeable to giving up his seat to work full-time on policy for real wages. Johnson, a good-old-boy from Palestine, was well-liked; he would help smooth relations with legislators. Toomey became deputy chief of staff, in charge of legislative policy development in several areas. Janie Harris remained the governor's secretary and unofficial "gatekeeper"; she controlled the flow of traffic into and out of his office. Reggie Bashur, the unofficial crisis manager, stayed as press secretary. Bashur was not afraid to speak his mind to Clements, but the staff usually looked to Bayoud, who had a special kinship with the governor, to tell Clements when he was off track. Bayoud had an instantaneous feel for issues and, Cliff Johnson said, "better political instincts for a man who had never held public office than anybody I'd ever met."[4]

Convinced by staff members that he could accomplish more in peace than at war with the legislature, Clements adopted a more agreeable style. Legislators were surprised when they were invited to a cocktail buffet at the Governor's Mansion on opening day. He began having weekly breakfasts at the mansion, called "eggs-and-policy summits," with Speaker Gib Lewis and Lt. Gov. Bill Hobby. The difference in his demeanor was like night and day, Austin political consultant George Christian said. "By what he does in the next few months, he can write the history of his administration," Christian predicted.

Aides said Clements had good reason to be conciliatory. "He's not going to run again, so this is it. This session is extremely critical for him to finish the work he needs to do," said Toomey. Bayoud noted, "When the governor leaves office, he wants people to say he definitely put something back in the pot. And he took us through a time when we were down." Clements wanted to be remembered as the governor who had guided the state into economic recovery and reformed ineffective institutions such as workers' compensation, judicial selection, budget accounting, and prisons. One example of the governor's new diplomacy was to adopt the Legislative Budget Board's budget proposal as his own, rather than presenting an alternative budget.[5]

His standing was on the rise. One Dallas newspaper, in a story headlined "Clements shifts gears in style of governing," reported: "Clements, whose blunt talk has angered most major constitutent groups from preachers to teachers, lawyers to minorities, is in the midst of a dramatic career comeback." Allies and adversaries alike were saying Clements' reputation had been restored by his role in the state's successful effort to land the Super Collider. Dallas County Republican Party Chairman Tom James said, "Two years ago, because of the public furor, he was in trouble and that resulted in the party being in trouble. Now it's the opposite. He is on a crest and that is good for the party." James said that Clements was proving again that he was a "better manager than politician. He does a good job if you don't listen to him."[6]

Not only was Clements trying to get along better with legislators, he also adopted a somewhat friendlier attitude toward the press — although he discontinued regular appearances on "The Governor's Report" television program. Carole Kneeland, the show's moderator, explained, "It seemed like on program after program he would say something that he could spend weeks recovering from."[7] Being his usual outspoken self would not help his new effort to be more diplomatic with the legislature. He resumed referring to the Capitol press corps as the "wise owls" — as in a press release saying he would enter a Dallas hospital for stroke-related tests. The tests would be routine, he said, and "probably the wise owls don't give a hoot." But he knew better than to try to keep something quiet around the Capitol.

While Clements had mellowed, he nevertheless continued to conduct business in his usual no-nonsense manner. His attitude was: "We've got a job; let's get the job done," aide Cliff Johnson said. "Janie would line his work out for him, and he would stay in his office and do his work. Then he would go back over to the mansion, and he'd go home to Dallas on weekends. He was kind of an 8-to-5 guy. He was here, stayed in his office and did his work. He wasn't a glad-hander, out in the halls," Johnson said.

And he was still blunt and outspoken. As Johnson said, "He would challenge you in a heartbeat." The aide added that he stopped wearing blue shirts to meetings because the governor "would be so abrupt and blunt, which is so uncommon in the political arena — just in-your-face frank — that I would pop little beads of sweat through the front of my shirt. I had to start wearing white shirts."

In the governor's dealings with legislators, it didn't matter if they were Republicans or Democrats. "He wanted direct, abrupt, what-do-you-want, what-do-you-want-me-to-do, this-is-what-I-believe, kind of talk," Johnson said. "If you asked him a question, you got an answer. There was no fuzziness. If you liked it or didn't like it was not his concern. His concern was making sure you understood what he said," Johnson said.[8]

Of course, it would have been contrary to Bill Clements' nature to avoid getting into scrapes altogether. For example, he got into one with Agriculture Commissioner Jim Hightower, a Democrat. Clements thought Hightower was using his state position to build a populist political network. The governor tried to eliminate Hightower's job as a statewide elective office — a battle he eventually lost.[9]

Another scuffle involved a constitutional amendment that had been proposed to raise legislator pay from $600 a month. The governor, who opposed the measure, and Speaker Gib Lewis, who supported it, squabbled over the issue at a luncheon held by the Dallas and Fort Worth Chambers of Commerce. Asked if he supported the pay raise, Clements replied curtly: "No. Got any more questions?" When Lewis reminded Clements of the disparity between the governor's annual salary, $91,600, and that of legislators, $7,200, Clements' response was, "And I hope that gap gets wider." Lewis attributed Clements' remark to "an attempt to be cute and funny," and said, "The only thing that upset me is that it could be taken as a slap toward the legislative body." Legislators took it as that, and slapped back. Rep. Keith Oakley, a Terrell Democrat, introduced a bill to cut the governor's pay to $7,200.

The staff told the governor he had offended the speaker. To try to make it right, Clements picked up the telephone and called the speaker. "Gib," he said, "They tell me I need to come rub some salve on you, and I'm headed that way." His apology to Lewis was: "It's like Rita told me: 'Bill, you're not funny. So don't try to be.'"[10]

Later in the session, however, legislators had some fun with Clements. They held a wardrobe-imitation birthday party for him on the House floor, with members vying to see who could wear the most outrageous plaid sport coat. Those in plaid formed an honor guard to escort the governor into the House, where he was proclaimed, at seventy-two, the oldest governor in Texas history. "That's not exactly a title I would seek, but it's better than others I could think of," responded Clements, attired in a blue-and-gray plaid coat. When Lieutenant Governor Hobby said he didn't have a plaid coat, Clements couldn't resist taking a shot: "It's nice to know that you have been deprived of something." (Clements always thought Hobby, who was born into a wealthy and politically prominent Houston publishing family, had been given his station in life rather than having to work for it.[11]

The members engaged in good-natured banter at the birthday party. Keith Oakley, who had criticized the governor earlier over the pay raise issue, joked that he went to Goodwill but couldn't find a jacket "near as ugly as the governor's." Rep. Ron Wilson, D-Houston, affixed beige packing tape to his white sport coat, and was mistaken by one colleague for a UPS package. Rep. Steve Wolens, D-Dallas, wanted to know "how many polyesters had to be killed" to produce all the plaid coats on the house floor. Harold Dutton, D-Houston, wrapped it up with his comment: "This is why Austin doesn't have a zoo. People can just come here."[12]

Clements never minded the ribbing he took over his plaid jackets. He liked them, and that was what was important to him. In one incident, Secretary of State Jack Rains picked up one of Clements' loud sport coats and offered it for sale in a Houston fundraising auction. Clements wasn't happy; it happened to be one of his favorites. He found out who bought it at the auction and bought it back. "That's Clements," said Johnson, his aide. "He liked what he liked and he wasn't hung up on fashion."[13]

Clements' top priorities for the last two years of his administration included reforming the state's workers' compensation laws, prison expansion, and economic development. The governor's agenda also included restoring local control to public school districts and reducing state regulation of schools. He wanted to offer financial incentives for school districts that showed improvement. His agenda further included merit selection for judges, uniform accounting and payroll procedures in state agencies, and the renovation of the Capitol.[14]

Reform of workers' compensation headed the governor's legislative list because Texas' system for compensating on-the-job injuries was considered a disincentive for attracting and expanding business. Texas businesses were paying among the highest premiums in the country, and seriously injured workers were receiving among the lowest benefits. Denoting its importance, the workers' comp bill was designated House Bill 1.

The governor's prison program was equally as important, as federal court monitoring of the prison system was phasing down. Clements' program called for 11,000 new beds in nine new prisons at an initial cost of $350 million. In the previous session, 13,000 new prison beds had been authorized. At the end of Clements' four years, Texas would have 24,000 new beds if he was successful in this session. Clements proposed that new prison construction be bonded to free up general revenue. "Why take tax dollars from current programs to pay for capital structures that will be used for fifty years?" he asked. He also recommended, as alternatives to incarceration, 2,000 community-based boot camp facilities.

The governor's criminal justice package included mandatory flat prison time for repeat felony offenders, mandatory drug testing and drug treatment as a condition of parole, asset forfeiture for drug dealers, a uniform crime information gathering system, and an increased penalty for aggravated assault with a deadly weapon on a peace officer.

Clements also was proposing the consolidation of all criminal justice agencies into a new Texas Department of Criminal Justice, and a new Texas Department of Transportation that would combine all transportation agencies.

Clements now was spending a lot of time on prisons and criminal justice matters. He met regularly with Rider Scott, his general counsel and criminal justice director, and Dallas insurance man Charles Terrell, who had become chairman of the Texas Department of Corrections (TDC) board.

Groundwork had been laid in the 1987 session, Terrell said, so it became easier to get criminal justice legislation carried and adopted in the 1989 session. Terrell had spent considerable time in the 1987 session just gaining the trust of members of the legislature. That strategy paid off in 1989, when Speaker Lewis and key members of the House helped to push for criminal justice legislation. By the third week of March, the legislature had sent to Clements a $324 million prison bill that included his 11,000 new beds.[15]

Terrell recalled, "We passed 29 pieces of anti-crime legislation that set the tone for the future. We set into movement the largest prison construction program in the history of the world. By our group, or the governor, alone? Hell, no. You have to have key people in leadership positions; the public's got to support it with votes on bond issues. But he [Clements] set it into motion and it has carried forward," Terrell said. "He inherited a terrible revolving door situation. Now, we're keeping the worst of the lot in a lot longer," he said, in a 1995 interview.[16]

Clements, in fact, had been roundly criticized during the 1988 presidential campaign for the revolving-door prison situation. Clements had accused Democratic presidential nominee Michael Dukakis of presiding over the "most liberal furlough program in America" as governor of Massachusetts. In turn, Texas Democrats had lambasted Clements for twice signing legislation liberalizing Texas' prison furlough program. Clements blamed bureaucrats for giving weeklong passes to thousands of inmates, including murderers and rapists, and promised to repair the situation with legislation in the 1989 session.[17]

Terrell met with Clements monthly, and talked between meetings, about construction and other issues, such as tracking the educational level of inmates. "There was never a time he wasn't absolutely up to date," he said. Terrell, who considered himself a conservative Democrat, disputed the theory that Clements was disengaged in the second term. "He was as engaged as any governor could be. Never did I catch him unprepared, so I knew I better damn well be prepared. One thing Bill Clements doesn't do to your time is waste it."[18]

Convinced that the criminal justice system was about to implode, Clements put the issue on center stage. "In addition to sounding the alarm bell, he gave the state a blueprint to follow for the next decade," Rider Scott said. He recalled that Clements had gone on bended knee to the legislature in 1987 for funds to create the heavy-duty, 2,250-bed Michel unit in Palestine. That unit became the design model, and it was replicated throughout the state. By 1995, when the state had excess prison space for the first time since the *Ruiz* suit began, there were twelve such prison units. The blueprint also included building trustee barracks outside the major prisons to gain cell capacity inside for hardcore prisoners. Clements also authorized the largest experiment in the nation in private prison building: four 500-bed facilities. The private prisons could be built faster than the public prisons, and the state didn't have to put up the capital.

One of the big changes that occurred under Clements was to move the prisons outside of the traditional East Texas corridor, which ran from Palestine to Huntsville. The governor went to local communities and chambers of commerce around the state and explained what a Michel unit could mean for the community. It represented a $20 million-a-year operation, with a 600-employee payroll, besides providing short-term construction jobs. Once sites were regarded as economic development opportunities, the TDC board came under considerable pressure to select certain sites for the prisons. Clements, Terrell noted, never interfered in the site selection process.

To facilitate the massive prison construction program, the governor hired a supervisor for construction managers. The state had a history of losing money on change orders during construction, and Clements' directive was that the prisons would be built on time and on budget. "He brought business management to the prison system," Scott said.[19]

The final part of the prison construction blueprint was to gain legislative and then voter approval to use general obligation bonds, which would be amortized over the life of the institution. Operational money was provided in the appropriations bill. It took eighteen to twenty-four months to build each of the new prisons after ground was broken, so many of those authorized during Clements' administration came on line during the following administration of Gov. Ann Richards.

Terrell said in an interview after Clements left office that he was surprised by the cordiality of his relationship with the governor. "I had heard for ten years that he was a mean S.O.B. or a rough S.O.B. There was always 'S.O.B.' on the end of it. I saw him kick butts out of that room and yell at people who worked for him. But with people on an equal level, who were doing work for the government for free, he always treated them with respect."[20]

Rider Scott, who was involved daily with the governor on prisons and criminal justice issues, said Clements was "highly engaged," and kept an active schedule. "He met with agency heads personally and was a hands-on management individual. He didn't discuss the weather. He came in with an agenda, and you got down to business or the governor would usher you out pretty quickly," Scott explained. "Did he lay down after he beat Mark White? No. Clements was hands-on involved," he said.

Toomey agreed, noting that Clements took personal responsibility for performing certain actions himself. His modus operandi was to keep a yellow legal pad on his desk with his "to-do" list. "He'd pick up the phone and make his own phone calls, then go back and cross it off his legal pad. He didn't delegate some of it, he just did it himself. I think it was his way of making sure he wasn't insulated," Toomey said.

Toomey also noted that Clements often did his own preparation for meetings, not relying on staff briefings. "He'd do some checking himself, so he would know what was going on when people came in to see him."[21]

Scott recalled that early in Clements' second administration, he got a call from Chief Justice John Hill. Clements wanted to meet with Hill about judicial selection issues. Scott set it up and accompanied Clements to the meeting in the Supreme Court Building. "It was the chief of the executive branch and the chief of the judicial branch, former political opponents in 1978. I was holding my breath," Scott said. Hill began the meeting by thanking Clements for allowing him to make history. "What do you mean?" Clements asked. "By your winning in 1978," Hill replied, "I became the first to hold the office of secretary of state, attorney general and chief justice of the Texas Supreme Court. I couldn't have done it without your help." The three men chuckled, and the meeting began on a cordial note. Clements agreed to study the possibility of trying to change the partisan election of state judges to some kind of merit selection system. He eventually endorsed the idea of merit selection, and met several times with Hill and with members of the Senate, and included merit selection as part of his legislative agenda.

Chief Justice Hill resigned in January 1988, so he could devote more time to trying to reform the state's judicial system. Afterward,

Clements invited Hill to a meeting at the mansion, where he asked for Hill's suggestion for a replacement. Hill wrote down one name on a piece of paper — Tom Phillips, a Republican. Hill assumed Clements would appoint a Republican, and he considered Phillips a brilliant Houston lawyer and a distinguished young district judge. Clements, in fact, had appointed Phillips to a state district bench. Hill believed the state would be well served by a younger judge. As for himself, he said, "I'd become so determined to remove the excessive partisanship and political influence from the court that it had become almost an obsession."[22] The governor's appointments staff did its checking and came back with a Phillips recommendation.

Again, in his second administration, Clements placed a great importance on his appointments. And, again, Rita Clements was highly involved in the appointments process. Clements valued her professional advice. She sat in on the appointments meetings, along with Bayoud. But there was some change in the process the second time around. Clements' appointees were more Republican than they had been in his first term, and they were younger. James Huffines, his appointments secretary, was younger than former appointments secretary Tobin Armstrong. He also had different connections and a different style. A young Dallas banker whose family was in the car business, Huffines probed his own network of young business leaders to find appointees. And he spent a lot of time courting favor with the senators to get appointees confirmed. Of 3,970 appointments, 2,400 had to be confirmed by the Senate.

The governor had several long talks with Huffines to make sure they were in agreement on the mission. "He wanted to bring in more younger people, between thirty-five and fifty-five, to give them experience, exposure and training to serve the state long after he was gone," Huffines said. "He thought one of the biggest legacies he could leave was his appointments. He referred to individuals Gov. Connally had appointed, who were still working for the state fifteen years later." Clements also wanted diversity, and he wanted business people who had experience in the private sector. Huffines thought Clements also was more interested in building the Republican Party during his second administration. He knew he wouldn't be running again, so he didn't have to placate conservative Democrats.[23]

In the first half of his second administration, Clements got to rearrange the Texas Supreme Court. Two other justices quit after John Hill resigned from the court, and Clements appointed Republicans Eugene Cook and Barbara Culver. When Clements was elected in 1986, there wasn't a Republican on the appellate court. Within two years, there were three Republicans. And, after four years, when Clements left office, there would be four Republicans on the nine-person court. Of some 4,000 appointments Clements made during his second administration, more than 100 were judicial appointments.

To State Republican Chairman George Strake, the biggest improvement of Clements' second administration was that he was appointing more Republicans to office.[24]

Clements appointed the first two women ever to serve on the Supreme Court. He also appointed Texas' first black statewide officeholder in 100 years when he named Lewis Sturns of Fort Worth to the Court of Criminal Appeals.

During his first term, Clements suffered a number of rejected appointments from the Senate. In the second administration, he had fewer "busts." But he nonetheless had some significant fights over his appointees. One, which occurred early in his second term, was over the filling of three vacancies to the University of Texas board of regents. He tapped former Congressman Tom Loeffler, whom Clements had defeated for the gubernatorial nomination, former GOP State Chairman Chester Upham, Jr., and Robert Cruikshank of Houston. The appointment of three white men to this prestigious board drew immediate opposition. Sen. Carlos Truan, D-Corpus Christi, cricitized Clements for making the board a group of "rich, politically powerful and well-connected Anglo males. He has left us with a board of regents which has no Hispanic members."[25]

Responding to criticism, Clements said, "I have literally named hundreds of minority people to boards and to positions within state government." In the wake of the outcry, Clements named the first black female, Houston lawyer Mamie Moore Proctor, to the State Board of Corrections. He also named a black woman to the Texas Housing Agency. Finally, with Clements under increasing pressure to remove one of his white appointees to the UT board, Upham's name was withdrawn, allowing the governor to nominate Mario Ramirez of Rio Grande City. Craig Washington, a black state senator, commented: "The governor has an excellent record on the appointment of minorities and women, except for the UT board of regents. Now it appears he is going to cure that oversight."[26]

Clements' minority appointments nearly doubled those of his

first administration, and were running at an even pace with Gov. Mark White's minority appointments at midterm. In four years, Governor White named 160 blacks to state boards and commissions, while in the first two years of his second administration, Clements had named 79. While White appointed 290 Hispanics and 550 women in four years, Clements in two years had named 149 Hispanics and 355 women. At that point in time, he was ahead of White's record on women and minority appointees.[27]

Clements also had to fight to gain his two appointments to the Public Utility Commission, Marta Greytok and William Cassin. There were seven Republicans in the thirty-one-member Senate, and it only took eleven senators to block an appointment. Senators used opposition to appointments as a way to get the governor's attention — often on some other subject.

According to Huffines, "The governor's philosophy was to get quality people and then delegate." He didn't try to micro-manage the boards. "Mostly, he told the appointee to do what he [the appointee] thought was right," Huffines said.[28]

At least one appointee, in fact, thought Clements wasn't involved enough in the boards and commissions. He had named Paul Wrotenbery, who had been his budget director in his first term, to the State Board of Insurance. The board had been controlled by the insurance lobby, and Wrotenbery agreed to take the job only if Clements was serious about reform. Clements said he was. But Wrotenbery felt that, after he went on the board, Clements assumed everything was all right and forgot about the insurance board. The governor later named another board member whom Wrotenbery believed was a friend of the insurance lobby. Wrotenbery resigned before his term was up and, in the next election, supported Democrat Ann Richards because he believed she was committed to insurance reform.[29]

Among Clements' appointments during the second term were former Speaker Billy Clayton to the Texas A&M board, and Jerry Hodge (the former Amarillo mayor who had supported Clements after the infamous rubber chicken incident) to the prison board. Among the mistakes that would come back later to haunt him was the appointment of former Lubbock Mayor James H. "Jim" Granberry, the Republican nominee for governor in 1974, to the Board of Pardons and Paroles. After resigning from the board in 1991, Granberry pleaded guilty to a perjury charge for lying to a federal hearing about how many inmates he represented as a parole consultant. Granberry was rebuked in the media for helping some violent offenders obtain parole. According to Huffines, Granberry was guilty of bad judgment after he completed his service on the board. But he added that, "If you make a mistake on appointments, it's hard to remove them."

In the midst of all the political maneuverings of being governor, Clements also played a key role in the restoration of the Capitol, just as he had in the renovation of the Governor's Mansion. A 1983 fire in the Capitol, when Mark White was governor, actually had spurred the renovation. A faulty television set in what was then the lieutenant governor's apartment, behind the Senate chambers, had sparked an almost catastrophic blaze. Governor White and Lieutenant Governor Hobby watched the fire from the Capitol lawn and later vowed to make the Capitol safe for posterity. White had a staff member research how to set up a State Preservation Board, and Speaker Lewis along with Lieutenant Governor Hobby shepherded legislation through both houses which created the board, authorized $6 million to repair fire damage, and called for a master plan for a full-scale restoration of the Capitol. Because of the economic downturn, however, the total restoration was put on hold. As White said later, "It was just not something I wanted to go raise taxes for, frankly."[30]

Clements, however, returned to office with a personal goal of restoring the 1888 pink granite, Italian renaissance structure to its original grandeur. He appointed Dealey Decherd Herndon to the State Preservation Board. Mrs. Herndon had been curator for the Governor's Mansion during that restoration. She later became administrator and then president of Friends of the Governor's Mansion. Her husband, David Herndon, had been assistant secretary of state in the first Clements administration and later became general counsel to the governor.

Mrs. Herndon recalled that "Mark White made a big deal about cutting the lock off the mansion gate in 1983, when he came in as governor — which was a ridiculous issue, because Clements had let through about 45,000 people in the six months after it was finished. It was probably the most visible public time of the whole building," she said. But Mark and Linda Gale White appreciated what had been done to the Governor's Mansion, she said, and thought if the mansion could be renovated, why not the Capitol. While it was White's initiative to restore the Capitol, very little had actually happened until Clements returned to office.

The State Preservation Board had met only a few times when Mrs. Herndon was appointed. She went to the governor, who was chairman of the board, and asked him how committed he was to the restoration. "One hundred percent," he said. "I want this to happen." She then went to the speaker and the lieutenant governor, who were vice-chairmen, and found them also committed.

What Clements brought to the project, Dealey Herndon said, was: "He understood preservation, and he was a business manager, so he knew how to get the job done. The statute called for a master plan, but no one knew how to create a master plan." Clements oversaw development of a master plan, and then spearheaded the funding, along with Hobby and Lewis.[31]

Clements had toured almost every statehouse in the nation, and knew the Texas Capitol was special. "There isn't any other state Capitol that even comes close to comparing to our Capitol — in architectural design, in just plain old mass, m-a-s-s," he said. But the wiring and plumbing systems were faulty and outdated, and offices were so jammed-packed with workers and equipment that officials limited the amount of furniture in some offices for fear that floors might collapse.

"We had 1,300 people in a building that holds 750," Mrs. Herndon said. Once-grand rooms with twenty-foot ceilings had been double-decked with offices, "a rat's nest of little cubicles," as Governor Clements described the haphazard, make-do remodeling over the years. "The challenge was what do we do with all these people," Mrs. Herndon said. Architect Allen McCree came up with the idea of building an underground extension to the north to house some members of the legislature and their staffs. But the design had to be compatible with the Capitol. It had to have the same sense of space and light, she said. Otherwise, legislators and their staffs weren't going to agree to move into a "basement."[32]

McCree, an architect for the University of Texas System who was hired in September 1988, believed the Capitol was "Texas' secular cathedral." He explained it as being "different from any other state, the way Texans feel about their history, their background and their heritage . . . . This unique building symbolizes that." MeCree's deadline was to obtain the plans, find the money and begin construction by 1991, when Clements' term would end — because nobody knew if Clements' successor would be as committed to the project.[33]

At one point, McCree told the governor that he wanted an Army Corps of Engineers-type guy who was "the meanest man you've ever met" to oversee the restoration. Clements replied, "Sorry, I'm not available."[34]

According to Mrs. Herndon, the restoration project was "an amazing collaboration between owner and architect. The three top board members were the three top leaders of the state, all of whom had a very clear picture of Texas and the Capitol, and what they wanted to see." What they wanted was "a new building complementing the old building, the same sense of Texas, the same sense of space, of public openness, the same sense of strength." Mrs. Herndon recalled that, at one point, the architects came up with something that looked like a Texas Louvre, with a glass dome. Clements said, "That's not what we want." Clements told designers of the extension, "If there's any question about what this building ought to look like, I'll tell you where the example is. You just walk back over to the Capitol. That's the way it ought to be."[35]

During the 1987 legislative session, $45 million in funding was approved for Capitol restoration. But, Mrs. Herndon said, "without a master plan, nobody knew what it would be used for." Once the master plan was developed, the primary goals were to restore the Capitol to its 1880 architecture while making it the functional seat of government. The plan called for using compatible materials, and making the total structure a one-stop government, by providing auxiliary rooms in the extension, such as hearing rooms, a cafeteria, and an auditorium.

The legislative session of 1989 funded the project with $161 million, which was the architect's estimate of what it would cost to do everything. In May 1990, excavation began on the sixty-foot-deep chasm that would house the extension. At that point, it was a gamble. While the funds had been authorized, the building had not been bid. But the decision was made to commit to the project by digging what would be called the biggest hole in Central Texas.[36]

In December of 1990, only weeks before Clements was scheduled to go out of office, the bids came in. The bids on the extension were below estimate, while the bids to restore the Capitol were 50 percent over estimate, producing a crisis situation over what to do next. "He [Clements] really wanted to get it all tied up before he left office," Mrs. Herndon said. "Our goal was to restore the Capitol, and here we were ending up with a new building [the extension] but we couldn't do the restoration. She got in touch with Clements. "It took him about five minutes to figure out his position, once the issues were out there," she said. His decision was to go back to the architects and ask them to redesign the Capitol, and move forward with the extension.

"When we hit a crisis, he just handled it like a business decision and kept it moving," she said. If the Capitol was ever going to be done, it was necessary to go ahead with the extension. In January 1991, the board voted to let the contract on the extension and to redesign the Capitol — just prior to the inauguration of Gov. Ann Richards, the Democrat who would succeed Clements.[37]

Under Governor Richards, the legislature authorized another $29 million for the project, which was finished with almost equal usable square footage in the original Capitol and in the extension. Of the 150 House members, 99 moved their offices into the extension.

Bill and Rita Clements later served as honorary chairs of a $5 million capital campaign for interiors and endowment. They gave the lead gift of $100,000 to restore the interior of the original governor's office.

On January 11, 1993, the underground building was dedicated. Buried so as not to block the view of the historic Capitol, the extension covered roughly four blocks. Skylights ensured that most offices in the subterranean showplace had daylight. Doors, columns, hallways, stairway railings, and flooring all had the look and feel of the original Capitol. Its new nickname became "the Taj-Ma-Hole."[38]

"The single thing Clements brought was how to get it done. You can want something forever, but if you don't know how to get it done, how to bring people together, solidify things, it doesn't get done," Mrs. Herndon said. He also had that basic Texas history orientation — that Texas had treasures to be appreciated, whether it was land, or people or buildings, she said, and they should be preserved. "But the how-to-get-it-done part is what he was best at."

"When we were selling $161 million to the public and to the Legislature, it was quite a push. He was clearly the leader, but he had a partnership with Gib Lewis and Bill Hobby; there were moments when each of the three of them truly saved the project. There was teamwork there, but no question, Clements was the leader. When he came in, he made it happen," Mrs. Herndon said.[39]

While Clements had his hand in many pies during his second administration, his No. 1 priority was always the economy. Clements said years later he decided to run for governor again because he was convinced Mark White had no idea how to help the state rebound after the oil decline, nor did the two congressmen — Tom Loeffler and Kent Hance — who were seeking the Republican nomination. They both were lawyers who had been in politics. Clements felt they knew nothing about entrepreneurship and industry and creating jobs. "So how are they going to cure this sick patient?" he asked. "If you're sick and you need a doctor, you call somebody who knows something about what's ailing you. In my case, I felt like I was needed and knew what to do, and I knew how to do it," Clements said. "And, we did it," he added.[40]

Immediately after being elected to his second term, Clements created a task force on business development and jobs creation comprising Texas business and industry leaders. One of the key recommendations from the task force was to restructure the various agencies associated with economic development into one agency. The governor led the drive to create the Texas Department of Commerce, which opened in September 1987. The agency was designed to be a single point of contact for businesses assessing start-up, expansion, or relocation opportunities in Texas. Clements appointed his old Dallas friend, Ed Vetter, to the commission overseeing the Commerce Department. The commission also included such recognized business leaders as John V. Roach of Tandy Corporation in Fort Worth and James R. Lesch of Hughes Tool in Houston.

Vetter later recalled that Clements remained true to his promise to produce "jobs, jobs, jobs." He personally recruited industries, by telephone and in person, meeting with corporate leaders and visiting their plants. He championed the state as a good place to do business. "One thing he could do was get on the phone with these CEOs and tell them why they ought to be in Texas," said Rosanna Salazar, who was one of Clements' press aides.[41]

Clements opened trade offices in Tokyo and Frankfurt, met with automotive industry leaders in Detroit and Chicago, and recruited in England and France. He promoted Texas as a no-income-tax, right-to-work state.

He understood that the state needed to diversify and move away from its dependence on the petroleum industry to a more sophisticated type of industrial development. So part of the push was for high-technology jobs. In January 1988, the governor announced that the innovative semiconductor manufacturing consortium Sematech was locating in Texas, and would act as a lure for other high-tech industry.

The roll call of economic relocations was impressive. Companies that moved their headquarters to Texas included such industry giants as Exxon Corp., J.C. Penney Co., and GTE Telephone Operations. Other major industrial locations came from Fujitsu, Formosa Plastics, Mitsubishi Metals Corp., Fruit of the Loom, Bausch and Lomb, and American Airlines. These companies brought manufacturing, processing plants, maintenance facilities, and offices to Texas.[42]

Texas landed the Superconducting Super Collider in November 1988, after a concerted effort and the help of Energy Secretary John Harrington and President Reagan. Later abandoned by the federal government, the $8 billion research facility in Ellis County would have been the world's largest scientific instrument, establishing Texas as a global leader in particle accelerator research.

Clements went after the collider with a vengeance, setting up the Texas National Research Laboratory Commission to help win the project. Clements asked Morton H. Meyerson, the former president and CEO of Ross Perot's Electronic Data Systems to come out of retirement to replace Dr. Peter Flawn as commission chairman when Flawn became president of the University of Texas. Meyerson considered himself apolitical and knew Clements, who had been a member of the EDS board of directors. But Clements convinced him of the importance of the project. Meyerson told the governor he would "give it a try." To that, Clements responded, "You're not listening to me. I want to win this!"

Meyerson said later that what impressed him most was the brain trust that Clements had assembled for the commission — Republicans and Democrats and nonpartisans. "I was just amazed at how talented and smart and conscientious these people were. It was the most talented, hardest working pro bono team I had ever worked with," he said. Clements told Meyerson: "I'll help you in any way you want, but it will be your job [to win the bid]. I'm not going to tell you how to do it," he said. Meyerson found out that working with Clements was much like working with Perot. "He would help you but he wouldn't get in your hair. I had as much of Clements as I needed. I didn't have any of Clements that was obstructive or bothersome."[43]

Meyerson spent half of his time for a couple of years on the project. With political muscle provided by key members of the Texas congressional delegation, Texas landed the project. Unfortunately for the state, after land was bought, state contributions were made, and several years of construction, Congress totally withdrew funding for the project. Texas was left with a giant hole in the ground and little else to show for its effort, except some construction jobs and the short-term relocation to Texas of some high-caliber scientific talent.

Meyerson went away from the project with respect for Bill Clements and an impression far different from what he had seen portrayed in the media. "My friends would ask, how in the world could you work with him?" Meyerson said. From reading about Clements, they envisioned a domineering egomaniac. Meyerson found Clements extremely professional and easy to get along with. "I never had a harsh word with him. I found him to be deep as a person, and good at socializing with the scientists and the selection committee. The picture I have of Bill Clements in my mind is quite different from what I have seen him painted in the press."[44]

During Bill Clements' second administration, efforts also were stepped up to promote tourism in Texas, as a way of producing more jobs in the labor-intensive hotel and hospitality industry. Mrs. Clements became chairman of the Texas Tourism Advisory Council, under the Commerce Department, which launched an advertising campaign that attracted attention nationwide. The campaign theme was "Texas. It's like a whole other country." The campaign was funded by the governor's decision to dedicate a half cent of the hotel tax to tourism promotion. In her last few months as first lady, Mrs. Clements also launched "Rediscover Texas," a media campaign to urge Texans to travel their home state. Visiting cities in every corner of Texas, she drew attention to the importance of tourism to the state's economy.[45]

She promoted the Main Street program, which combined historical preservation and economic development in the downtowns of communities across the state. Mrs. Clements also worked on the Heritage Tourism program. Under the auspices of the National

Trust for Historic Preservation, the effort was aimed at merging preservation with the travel industry. Governor and Mrs. Clements assembled an interagency task force to identify unique Texas historic locations, which resulted in Texas receiving assistance from the National Trust to develop Heritage Tourism attractions. These included the LBJ Heartland, Cotton Industry region, Galveston Bay region, and the Missions of El Paso.[46]

Clements also continued efforts begun during his first term to improve relations with Mexico. He met with Mexico's President Carlos de Gortari and with border governors to promote industrial development along the border — particularly expansion of the *maquiladora* (twin plant) manufacturing industry and the *maquiladora* supplier industry. The Texas Commerce Department addressed border infrastructure financing issues, to assist in the growth of the twin plant industry. From November 1987 to November 1989, the number of twin plants located on the border of Mexico with Texas increased from 545 to 742. When it became evident that growth in international commerce was hampered by congested ports of entry on the border, Clements worked with Mexican and U.S. officials to get new crossing points. The Zaragoza international bridge in El Paso was constructed during Clements' second term, and three other points of entry were authorized — a bridge to connect Laredo to Nuevo León, another north of Laredo, and a third port of entry near Harlingen.

The governor also had a multifaceted legislative program that addressed economic development. Several initiatives were combined in the Texas Jobs and Opportunity Blueprint (JOBS), a package of new laws to enhance Texas' high technology base, provide greater tax incentives for job creation, bolster rural development, offer customized job training, and expand international trade. Part of the effort was designed to enhance Texas' food and fiber industry and encourage development of new products.

But the centerpoint of the legislative agenda was the workers' compensation law reform. And it was the biggest failure of the regular legislative session. Negotiators for labor, business, and trial lawyers struggled in vain to reach agreement on revamping the state's system for compensating on-the-job injuries. Legislation passed in both the House and the Senate, but differences between the two chambers could not be settled by the end of the session. Clements promptly announced he would call lawmakers back into special session three weeks after adjournment.

Among other major issues that failed in the regular session were merit selection for judges, passage of a lottery, and product liability reductions.

But the session coasted, sometimes serenely, to settlement on a number of complex issues, including a historic $643 million criminal justice reform package and an extra $450 million to help equalize state funding between rich and poor school districts. Budget-writers produced a $47.4 billion, two-year spending plan that increased funding for education and prisons and provided a pay raise for state employees and university faculty, without a tax increase. To balance the budget, legislators relied on a series of one-time accounting manuevers and the sale of bonds to finance new state prisons.[47]

After the regular session, however, it took two special sessions, one in June and another in November and December, to gain passage of the $3 billion workers' compensation system. It was finally passed less than two weeks before Christmas 1989 — shortly before insurance rates were scheduled to go up 22 percent in January 1990. Texas employers already had suffered a 148-percent increase in their workers' comp premiums since 1985. Senate holdouts objected to the last that the bill was evil and that it would create a huge government bureaucracy, which would be the "lapdog" of the insurance industry, and deny benefits to injured workers.

The comp debate pitted House against Senate and business against organized labor and the Texas Trial Lawyers Association. On this issue Lieutenant Governor Hobby was in agreement with the governor and speaker that changes had to be made; they backed his plan. Even so, there was a family fight within the Senate, with the liberals claiming that injured workers and the trial lawyers were being "sold out."

The bill changed the Industrial Accident Board to a six-member Texas Workers' Compensation Commission, with far greater staffing and oversight powers, and included other reforms aimed at shrinking the swollen Assigned Risk Pool for employers who couldn't buy insurance on the open market. The bill also permitted self-insurance, and allowed deductible policies and group insurance as alternatives for small employers. It increased weekly benefits for injured workers and set up cost controls for medical providers. The new law was designed to lessen attorney involvement as one way of cutting costs.

Proponents believed the system would deliver benefits more efficiently and fairly, lessening the need for costly litigation.

"Let there be no mistake," Clements declared, after passage, "the black eye on our business environment has just been lifted. No longer will jobs and new investment go to other states because of our workers' compensation laws." Liberty Mutual Company, the largest writer of workers' comp in Texas, had threatened to withdraw from the Texas market if a reform bill didn't pass.[48]

Mike Toomey, Clements' deputy chief of staff who was heavily involved in the issue, thought the governor's workers' compensation initiative was one of his most successful legislative endeavors. "It was the strongest comp bill in the country. It cut the lawyers out of the process and made it an administration matter. It made it objective, tied to AMA [American Medical Association] guidelines, instead of being subjective, where you just harangue the insurance company to get as much as you can out of it. It has brought down rates 10 to 30 percent," Toomey said in 1995. But it was a brutal battle. Clements, he said, "held their feet to the fire until there was a good bill."[49]

Rosanna Salazar, Clements' deputy press secretary who became top press aide after Bashur left late in the administration, considered the massive overhaul of workers' compensation legislation the most significant piece of legislation to pass during Clements' time in office. Cliff Johnson thought Clements had a very "pro-business" session, with the establishment of several business incubator programs. But the most important pro-business element was passage of the new workers' comp law.

Throughout his second term, Clements enjoyed a special relationship with House Speaker Gib Lewis. They had a lot in common. Their philosophy was similar. Both were conservatives, but both were problem solvers. They also enjoyed the same hobbies — hunting and fishing, and sometimes went together. Lewis was comfortable with Clements and with his forthrightness. "He was a very direct type of individual; he didn't sit there and try to play politics," Lewis said.

Clements was more focused on business issues than most governors, and Lewis also was business-oriented. The speaker, who owned a small business in Fort Worth, shared the governor's concern that the "absurd cost of workers' comp" was driving business out of the state. "We had to stop the hemorrhaging and stabilize the businesses in the state," he said. Businesses were declaring bankruptcy because they couldn't afford worker compensation premiums. "It drove more businesses into bankruptcy than any other factor since the Depression," Lewis said.

To pass new worker compensation laws, he said, "we had to wrestle the power away from the trial lawyers." Clements, he said, kept the pressure on, and made the public aware of the issue. "When the general public realized what was going on, we broke the back of the trial lawyers," Lewis said.

During Clements' second administration, Lewis said, the state was "more successful in stopping the bleeding, bringing in new business, changing some bad laws, and reversing the anti-business climate through acts of the Legislature."

He credited Clements' success to having good staff people, his pro-business attitude, and having the courage to pursue innovative approaches to solve the state's economic problems. "He was the turning point for economic conditions, because he understood business, and understood government and business have to work together," Lewis said. "Every governor contributes in his own way. Clements was the right person for the time."[50]

While all three leaders were together on workers' comp, Hobby was never converted to the importance of Clements' other business initiatives, such as establishing the Department of Commerce. "I don't think those things make that much difference," he said in an interview several years after both he and Clements left office. "I'm not at all sure that anybody agrees to build a plant in Texas because of us [in state government]. I think the local chambers do a better job on things like that."[51]

Saralee Tiede, Hobby's chief aide, noted that there was a concerted effort at the staff level, both in the governor's office and lieutenant governor's office, "to bring a lot of things together" in the last session for the two leaders. There were "real philosophical differences" between Clements and Hobby, she said. Hobby thought the state had special problems because of its diverse population and was not putting enough money into education, health, and human services. Clements, on the other hand, was forever trying to find ways to reduce government expenditures. "But they found things to work together on. There were good feelings after that 1989 session," she said.[52]

Even after the two special sessions to pass the workers' compensation bill, however, the work of the 71st Legislature wasn't finished. Clements was forced to call the legislature back into session in late February of 1990 to try to fix the school finance system that the Texas Supreme Court had ruled, in *Edgewood v. Kirby*, was discriminatory against poor districts. The high court had directed the legislature to devise a new system that would send more money to poor schools. Three more special sessions on school funding followed, keeping the legislature in session almost continuously to June 1990. As a result of this seemingly intractable school funding issue, Governor Clements had the dubious distinction of calling more special sessions in one biennium than any other Texas governor.

Clements wanted to raise more money for the poor districts through a series of budget cuts and fund transfers, including a reduction in contributions to the Teacher Retirement System. He insisted that money was not the only answer to problems in education, and called for more local control and less state regulation of public schools. Clements urged the legislature to pass reforms that would "free our schools of the stranglehold of state government mandates." In late April 1990, the legislature passed a $555-million school reform package that would be financed with budget shifts and a half-cent increase in the state sales tax. Clements, calling it a "no-good bill," vetoed it as promised.[53] The sixty Republicans in the 150-member House were able to block an override of the governor's veto.

As the fourth special session convened in June, however, Clements finally agreed to end the three-month stalemate by signing a compromise bill which would boost state education aid by $528 million and include reforms to raise achievement levels in schools, including testing according to nationwide standards, and bolster local control. The compromise package which increased funding for poor districts required a quarter-cent increase in the sales tax and a fifteen-cents-a-pack increase in the cigarette tax, making Texas' cigarette tax the highest in the nation at forty-one cents a pack. Clements managed to save taxpayers a quarter-cent in sales taxes by his standoff. But the most important concession was granting to the governor the right to appoint the top education official, the commissioner of education, who previously had been appointed by the State Board of Education.[54]

The increase of the state sales tax from six cents per $1 to 6.25 cents made Texas' sales tax the third highest in the country, behind

Connecticut and Washington, and Texas' reliance on consumption to fund state government was growing. The sales tax, which accounted for less than 40 percent of Texas' overall state revenue in 1980, was expected to account for 50 percent of all state revenues in 1990.[55] Texas, however, still had no income tax.

The courts were not satisfied with the remedy, however, and school funding would be a persistent problem, even after Clements left office.

In his final report to the 72nd Legislature at the conclusion of his second administration, Clements counted economic diversification and the building of a new economic foundation for the state as his greatest contribution. "The creation of a strong and diversified business climate capable of generating and retaining thousands of permanent and well-paying jobs is the single most important achievement of my second term," he wrote in January 1991. Oil rigs and cattle still dot the Texas landscape, he said, but they had been joined by innovative research facilities, as Texas extended its reach to the cutting edge world of high technology, biomedical research and telecommunications. Business and industry had brought their employees and payrolls to the state. Texas exports were at an all-time high, and the Texas economy once again was outperforming the nation's.[56]

When Bill Clements began his second administration, the Texas mainstays of energy and agriculture could no longer fuel the state's economy. When he left, they no longer had to.

Chapter 19

After Governor

"We're preserving a way of life . . ."

ON THE MORNING OF his last day in office, January 16, 1991, William P. Clements, Jr., attended the traditional reception for former governors in the Capitol. Then he and Rita, George Bayoud, and Rider Scott rode the elevator down from the governor's office for the last time. The inauguration of Governor-elect Ann Richards was about to begin on the south steps, and they could see the flanks of the waiting press. As they exited the elevator, Clements gave directions: "Rita, turn right, keep walking and don't look back." Gov. and Mrs. Clements walked out the Capitol's north entrance, got into their station wagon, and drove to Dallas.[1]

They never looked back; life went forward for the state's former first couple. They moved on to a very pleasant, private life, with only an occasional dalliance by either Bill or Rita into politics.

When Clements had run for governor the third time, after selling SEDCO, he listed his occupation as "farmer." Rita thought he could at least have called himself a rancher, which had a little more panache. Indeed, Clements had become a gentleman rancher, and life after being governor included working his cow-calf operation on ranch property near Forney and Kaufman. The Clementses also began doing more traveling, spending summers at their "Casa Simpática" near Rancho de Taos, and weekends and holidays at Hollyglen, the lakehouse near Athens which they share with Clements' son,

Gill, and his wife, Pat. Bill and Rita dusted off their golf clubs. When in Dallas, Clements routinely would go twice a week to his office in the old Cumberland Hill School building, where he kept his Texas library.

But two or three days a week, he would head out to the Clemgil Farm at Forney or to the Cartwright Ranch at Kaufman. After being an oil drilling contractor, a federal appointee and governor, he was pursuing a fourth career in the cattle business.

Clements had bought his first piece of property in Forney in 1950. By 1995, Clements had acquired 2,600 acres at Clemgil near Forney. The farm-to-market road alongside his property, FM 460, had been named Clements Drive. He had another 2,600 acres at the Cartwright Ranch near Kaufman. Clements was running 450 Brangus cows on each ranch, building toward a herd of 1,000 mother cows. It was nothing like Dolph Briscoe's cattle operation, which had 20,000 mother cows, or the King Ranch in South Texas. Four hands could run each place for Clements, but it was a quality operation.

"He [Clements] loves to see good cattle, and he likes to have a nice place," said Bob Chappell, Clements' ranch manager for thirty years, who transformed bottom land of sunflowers and weeds into fields of maize. In 1995, Clements had 1,000 acres in cultivation at Forney, with oats, coastal bermuda, maize and hay, and about 800 acres at Kaufman in similar cultivation.

In 1995, when this author visited with Clements at Clemgil, the setting appeared peaceful, pastoral — and prosperous. Black Brangus bulls grazed in pastures dotted with clusters of Texas pecan trees along the fence lines. A few longhorns could be seen in the field. The longhorns are only a minor part of the operation — thirty-five mama cows and a few steers and bulls. Raising longhorns, Clements said, "has a lot of romance to it." The first longhorn cattle were brought to Texas by Spanish conquistadors in the late 1600s. Millions were driven to slaughter in the big cattle drives after the Civil War, and they were becoming extinct when Sid Richardson of Fort Worth began putting them in a reserve in the 1920s. Now they're coming back. Clements said the longhorns were an indulgence for him. "They relate to what Texas is all about. It's a nostalgic thing that I thoroughly enjoy, a reminder of the old Texas," he said.

But Clements' basic cattle operation is Brangus, a mix of Brahman and Angus, and the most popular breed in Texas in 1995.

He sells both registered and commercial (nonregistered) bulls and bred heifers. He breeds the mother cows, and then sells calves at weaning time, as yearlings and as two-year-olds. He and ranch manager Chappell and the hands frequently cull the calves that are not up to quality. The registered cattle are sold to other registered cattle owners throughout the Southwest and in Mexico; the commercial cattle to farmers and ranchers nearby who want to upgrade herds that are not registered. The culls go to the slaughterhouse. "Our market is not the meat market; we take our culls to the auction sales," Clements explained. "The rest of the cattle we sell by private treaty. They bring a premium price."

"We've built up a reputation," Clements said. "People know I won't tolerate anything but good cattle."[2] As his one-time legislative aide Jim Kaster once remarked, "Anything he does, he does well — deputy secretary of defense, SEDCO, even his mother cow operation in Forney."[3]

The Forney ranch is only thirty minutes from the Clements' Highland Park home. It is an easy trip to move from the urban comforts to culling cattle, making sure a water tank is being built properly, overseeing the growing of the feed and the sale of the animals. "There's nothing fancy about this deal. It's a working ranch. I've never spent a night here," Clements explained. "It's not a weekend place."

But it could be. Or it could be called the unofficial William P. Clements, Jr., Museum.

The ranch headquarters is located in a picturesque limestone house that Clements built after his first term in office. The limestone came from fields around Fredericksburg, giving the house a look of the Texas Hill Country. Cut into the side of a hill, it looks like a cottage from the front, but actually is a spacious three-story house. Visitors walk into a large living-dining area, which is the second story. Upstairs are bedrooms; on the bottom floor is the ranch office. Bathrooms have towels with the same C Bar brand that the cattle carry. The back porch, with its natural-wood rocking chairs, looks out on well-kept pastures.

Everywhere inside the house is memorabilia. Framed photographs show Governor Clements with President Bush in front of a seal of Texas; Deputy Secretary of Defense Clements making a speech in front of the Lincoln Memorial; Clements and Rita on a winning election night; Clements and Rita in front of a picture of Clements' hero, Sam Houston; Clements, President Ford, and Rita.

There's a historic photo of Clements with five other governors — Allan Shivers, Price Daniel, John Connally, Preston Smith and Dolph Briscoe — signed by each; autographed photos of the Joint Chiefs of Staff; the SEDCO management team photographed inside the Governor's Mansion. There are architectural drawings of Wexford, the Virginia home Clements bought in 1974 and sold in 1993.

Also on display are artifacts of Texas history, the branding iron from Crocker (Rita's parents') Ranch, and a poem by a cowboy poet, "Springtime at Crocker's." There are presentation saddles, including one made by a Texas prison inmate and another given to Governor Clements by the governor of Nuevo León, Mexico. There is a state of Texas chair, a Clements for governor poster, a "Gee I Miss Bill Clements" bumper sticker.

Old family photos show Clements as a child with his bird-dog Joe, who followed him to Armstrong School each day and waited in the school yard until it was time to walk home; Billy with his mother and sister at their Maplewood home; Billy at about age three, fishing with his dad; a wall of photos of ancestors. There are more recent family pictures, including Bill hunting and fishing with Gill and on safari with Gill and Rita.

The trophy room includes animal heads from African safaris, the head of a deer killed at Dolph Briscoe's ranch, and a red drum redfish above the fireplace. As governor, Clements took pleasure in helping to pass legislation to return the redfish, which had been decimated by commercial fishermen, to game fish status. A plaque denotes his work in the enhancement of natural resources.

All of the important aspects of Bill Clements' life are represented at the ranch headquarters — roots, family, work, public service, the land. But the ranch is one area of his life that Rita is not particularly interested in. She had enough of ranching as a young girl.

Part of the Forney property abuts Lake Ray Hubbard, which was built by the City of Dallas after Clements purchased his property. Construction of the lake was followed by the construction of expensive new waterfront homes in the old farm area. The lakesites on the Clements property someday will be valuable homesites, but the property is in his grandchildren's trust, and will not be vested until the youngest of his great-grandchildren is twenty-one. Although the former governor recognizes there is an economic factor to the appreciation of the land, he maintains it for now for his own enjoyment. "In time, but not in my lifetime, it will be divided up and there will be houses on it. Meantime, we're preserving a way of life out here. I don't intend to ever sell a foot of it," he said.

To the east, over near Kaufman, Clements acquired in 1989 the remnants of the original 4,300 acres in the Cartwright league of land deeded by the State of Texas in 1848 to one of the state's original landowners, Matthew Cartwright. The ranch was about to be foreclosed when Clements bought it from Jim Cartwright, a cousin of his first wife, Pauline. Pauline's grandmother was a Cartwright. Clements didn't want to see the land divided any further, and he wanted it kept in the family because his children and grandchildren are Cartwright descendants. Through the Cartwright line, his great-grandchildren are ninth-generation Texans.

The men who run the ranches, ranch manager Bob Chappell and cattle manager Larry Shaw, are like Clements' old SEDCO employees — long-term and loyal. Chappell was born on the Cartwright Ranch. At eighty, he has never known any other life but ranching. Shaw, who lives on the Cartwright Ranch, joined Clements in 1981, after working on Bunker Hunt's ranch. Another hand worked thirty-five years on the Cartwright Ranch; now his three sons, who were raised on the ranch, work there. "These hands sort of define the place," Clements said. "You don't have a lot of hands coming and going and turnover that represents dissatisfaction. These people are reliable, responsible, hard working, and they're compatible."

Clements is a good neighbor in Forney. He allows his land to be used for a local chili cookoff and donates calves to community events. When visiting the ranch, he eats at a local cafe. His cowboys form a team to compete in local rodeos.

Ranching is completely different from being an oil drilling contractor. "This is a long-term situation; you don't think about profit and loss for this year. A rancher has a totally different outlook economically. It's much slower paced; it's not anything like as competitive [as drilling contracting]. This is more like a way of life. There's a pace to the way you go about your business, there's a community to it; there are work cycles."[4]

Clements likes the way everything is done in a planned cycle, from plowing and planting, to putting the cattle in the field and breeding them at the right time. It fits in with his philosophy of life: "To everything there is a season . . ."

On a spring day in 1995, this author was present when Clements met his hands on the Cartwright Ranch to wean the calves and separate the culls that would be sent to market. The mother cows were brought down a chute and examined by a veterinarian to see if they were carrying calves. Then the hands brought the calves into the pen, two or three at a time, for Clements to look over. They wrote down the ear tag numbers of the ones he wanted registered.

The work was done with Chappell, Shaw, and four hands. The hand who opened the gate to let the calves in looked like old Texas — his worn Wrangler jeans stuffed into his cowboy boots, spurs, and a rolled and sweat-stained cowboy hat. The cowboys gently used cattle prods or their arms or feet to wave the cows into the designated pens. They were comfortable in their work. Nobody was in a hurry.

Clements stood with Chappell on a two-by-four platform that extended down one side of the pen, so he could get a better view of the animals. "They're both keepers. Get their numbers," he ordered. Of the next three, Clements sent two to the "keeper" pen and the other one off to be sold. "She lacks bone. She'll never develop into a big cow," he explained to an observer uneducated in the cattle business. Shaw walked over about that time and remarked about the cull, "She don't carry no bone."

Shaw, the ranch foreman, walked around the pen in worn Wranglers, work boots, and a bill cap. He knew the animals by sight. "That calf lost its mama; the boys fed her on the bottle," he said about one.

In an adjacent pen, the cattle were bawling. Clements explained what all the bawling was about — the different sounds, from low pitch to high pitch. "We're pulling calves from their mama. It may all sound the same to you, but the mama knows the bawl of her calf, and the calf knows the bawl of its mama," he said.

Two more were let in the pen. "Move 'em around," Clements said. "Let 'em go, both of them." Clements sized up the animals and made his decisions, swifly and cleanly. "Those are OK. Sell that one." Two hours later, the work was done, and Clements was off in his Suburban to another endeavor. The hands were left to finish the job and put the cattle back out to pasture on horseback.[5]

Clements has an affinity for the land and for the people of East Texas. A little farther to the east, in Henderson County, he owns another 1,100 acres, where he built a 226-acre lake and a lakehouse. The property, called Hollyglen, is adjacent to the exclusive Koon Kreek Klub, which Clements joined in 1953. The Clementses' house there, a cottage originally built in 1930, is now used by his grandson, Bill Clements III.

The newer house at Hollyglen is a copy of a San Augustine dog-run house built in 1854 that is included in the National Register of Historic Houses. "It's a true, early Texas house," Clements said of the two-story, beige structure, trimmed in hunter green, with wide, circular porch. The house is furnished with authentic early Texas pieces and country-style furniture. The pine floors came out of an 1850s cotton gin. The woodwork is East Texas cypress. Longhorn skins made into rugs are scattered on the floors.

The interior decor combines a Lone Star motif with fish and ducks and other wildlife featured in tiles, paintings, and photographs. The house is the hunting and fishing headquarters for Clements and his son, Gill. There are boats and a boathouse, pens for the hunting dogs, and a nearby warehouse full of hunting and fishing equipment. In the "mud room" of the house are frog gigging helmets and the mounted head of a wild hog. Other hunting trophies adorn the walls. They include the head of a mule deer shot on the West Texas ranch of 1990 Republican gubernatorial nominee Clayton Williams, an Alaskan caribou, and an Alaskan moose with an eighty-inch span of antlers, mounted over the fireplace.

Photos provide a reminder of Clements' gubernatorial days. An upstairs sitting room contains the Clements political cartoon collection. Of all his memorabilia, Clements says he cherishes more than anything else the original cartoons, which depict different aspects of his gubernatorial career. In a typical one, by Bob Taylor of the *Dallas Times-Herald*, Clements is portrayed as a Texas cowboy. The caption says, "Wake up, everybody. Quick-Draw is Back!"

Hollyglen is located in the middle of a general conservation, game-controlled area of more than 50,000 acres in East Texas. Along with Hollyglen, the area includes a state game reserve, other privately owned property, and the Clements Scout reservation. There are coyotes, deer, armadillo, wild hog, wild turkey, and ducks on the property. Clements planted 30,000 pine trees, five different kinds, when he developed the property. He and Gill named it Hollyglen because of three huge holly trees.

"This is a special place," Clements said. It is special to him because of his longtime ties to the area, from fishing expeditions with his father to his early oil drilling days, because of his love for the land and the wildlife, but also for political reasons. Henderson County is the birthplace of Ralph W. Yarborough, Texas' liberal Democrat U.S. senator of the 1960s. In recent years, the area has been repopulated by more Republicans from the Dallas area, who have built vacation and retirement homes around Cedar Creek Lake. Clements helped to make it and other parts of East Texas more Republican. "I turned Henderson County around. I flipped it," he boasted.[6]

Cliff Johnson, the conservative Democrat from East Texas who worked on Clements' staff, said East Texans "thought a lot of Bill Clements. He had a kind of East Texas mentality." That area of the state had always been more Southern than Western in its social and political traditions, and Johnson could draw upon his own background as he summed up Bill Clements' personal and political style. Johnson's family had lived in Anderson County since the 1850s. He described East Texans as conservative, tenacious, independent, proud people with a frontier spirit which included pride in taking care of themselves and pursuing a task to completion. Clements, he noted, cared about the same fundamental, conservative attitudes and values as the people who lived in East Texas. "Farmers, businessmen, cattlemen in East Texas, he talked their kind of talk. They liked to listen to him. They liked the gruffness. They respected him," Johnson said.

Johnson found Clements fierce and tireless, as a campaigner and in pursuit of a goal as governor. "He was almost like a hunter stalking something — whatever it took, however long I have to wait in this trail, no matter how wet I get, how cold I get, I'm going to wait until it comes by. He was probably like that in everything he did in his business life. I know some old oil and gas guys in East Texas who are that way. They don't deviate from their task. They do the best job at that thing, whatever it is." He recalled that when Clements was governor, he would say, "I drilled oil wells by the foot, and I did the best job you could do at it."

"It's like the single-mindedness of a mule plowing a field. I'm going to pull this row, and I'm going to do the best job I can do at it. These guys that were old Texas just set their mind to the task, and they were relentless until they accomplished it," Johnson said. They did not take kindly to defeat; it was just unacceptable, Johnson said. Clements reflected that spirit when he ran against White a second time. He focused, because he wasn't going to be whipped — twice.

Johnson said he doubted Clements had the same intense fire after the election of 1986, when he returned to office, that he had before the election. But he had an agenda. "Clements' agenda was Texas. Clements had a deep sense of respect and love for the state. Clements never wavered from what he wanted for Texas. There was something deep inside of him; he wanted to be part of Texas history."

While Clements had a lot in common with other Texans that Cliff Johnson knew, there was also a uniqueness about him — his mannerisms, his speech patterns, and the unexpectedness of what he might say or do. Johnson recalled a dinner party at the mansion during the time that Clements was building his lake near Athens. Several staff members and senators were there, and Clements was talking about the lake, and looking forward to duck hunting at Hollyglen. Johnson was a duck hunter, and knew that a good duck call is a brass reed duck call made in Louisiana. He asked Clements if he had some good duck calls. Clements replied, "Heck, I can call a duck with my hand to my mouth." Johnson responded that he had lived in the swamps in East Texas and hunted ducks all his life, and he didn't believe anybody could call a duck with his hand to his mouth.

Clements just pushed his chair back, Johnson said, put his hand to his mouth, and commenced to call ducks. *"Quaack, quaack, quaaaaack, quack, quack, quack."* Everyone at the table looked at the governor in stunned silence. They had never heard a man call ducks like that — at least not at the dinner table. George Bayoud broke the ice, bursting into laughter, and the others followed.[7]

Clements understood the importance of changing the Democratic domination of East Texas if Republicans were ever going to get majority control in the state. Despite Republican growth in other parts of the state, there remained a yellow dog Democrat tradition in East Texas that had seeped over from the South in post-Civil War days. Clements helped to change that tendency to vote according to tradition and, in East Texas, paved the way for the election of the second Republican governor, George W. Bush.

Bush, the oldest son of President Bush, sought Clements' counsel in September 1993, early in his gubernatorial campaign. Bush recalled that the visit lasted four hours. "I remember him saying: 'It's all East Texas, it's all East Texas.' It's never all East Texas. If I'd lost Harris County or Dallas County, it would've been all metropolitan. But part of the strategy we developed was a rural strategy. I spent a lot of time in rural Texas very early, and a lot of time in East Texas very early." After that meeting, whenever George W. Bush would see Clements, he would report on his last trip to East Texas.

In the 1994 gubernatorial election, Bush switched 100,000 East Texas votes that had been Democratic in 1990 to Republican; he carried East Texas with 53 percent of the vote. He said later he believed that was one reason he won. "A lot of that was Bill Clements," he said. East Texans, he added, felt comfortable voting for a Republican based upon philosophy, but not upon party. But having voted first for a conservative, no-nonsense, straightforward person like Bill Clements, they were receptive to George W. Bush. Though Bush had a different personality, he reflected the same values and a similar conservative philosophy.

"He [Clements] broke the ice for a Republican being elected. He showed Texas that a Republican could bring to the governor's office a philosophy that was acceptable to most Texans. He began the change at the state level for conservative Democrats to vote Republican for governor. That's a huge legacy," Governor Bush said.[8]

In his inaugural address in January 1995, Governor Bush paid public tribute to his GOP predecessor. "I would not be standing here without the trailblazing efforts of Governor Clements," he said.[9]

Chapter 20

Legacies

"He broke the mold"

BILL CLEMENTS WILL BE remembered foremost as the first Republican governor of Texas since Reconstruction. But there are other legacies.

When he left office in January 1991, he had served longer as governor than anyone else. He was the first to serve two four-year terms. Prior governors who won reelection served only two-year terms.

He was one of only two governors, along with Miriam "Ma" Ferguson, to have been voted out of office and returned to win it a second time.

Clements won by the closest margin of any two-party Texas gubernatorial election when he defeated John Hill by fewer than 17,000 votes in almost 2.4 million cast in 1978. He drew the largest number of Republican votes in Texas in a nonpresidential election (1,813,779) when he turned Mark White out of office in 1986. That number was superseded by Clayton Williams in a losing race to Democrat Ann Richards in 1990.

Clements' first race against Ray Hutchison in 1978 attracted a record number of voters to the Republican primary (158,403). Although small in comparison to the Democratic primary of 1.8 million that year, the Republican gubernatorial primary would grow to a half-million when Clements was nominated in 1986 to 855,231 in 1990, a record to that time in a nonpresidential GOP primary.[1]

Clements was also the oldest governor, 69.8 years, when he began his second term. Sam Houston had previously been the oldest at 66.8 years.[2]

Journalist and author Sam Kinch, Jr., a thirty-five-year observer of the Austin political scene, said, Clements' "firsts, his multiple firsts," were his most important legacy. "It is the firstness of him that is the enduring quality. Few will recall anything he did, but most people will recall that he was the first Republican governor in 100 years."[3]

By being the first Republican governor, and proving that Republicans could govern successfully, Clements set in motion a chain of political events that helped bring the Republican Party to parity with the long-dominant Democratic Party in Texas.

Democratic consultant and pollster George Shipley of Austin said, "Clements will be judged as one of a handful of Texas' most important governors, not only because he broke the mold and was the first Republican governor, but because he brought a generation of young Republican activists to the scene. Clements made it respectable to admit you're a Republican. He brought a lot of excited young people to Austin who hadn't been involved in politics."

Clements' ability to deal successfully with conservative Democrats created the environment that made conservative Democrats comfortable in changing parties, Shipley said. "He was probably the catalyst that hastened the emergence of Republicans as a viable party down now to the courthouses," he said.

Shipley began polling hardcore partisans in Texas in 1988. In 1993, for the first time, he found that more Texans thought of themselves as Republicans. The nature of party identification had changed. In 1995, Texans who identified themselves as strong Republicans exceeded, by 10 percent, those who called themselves strong Democrats. "Whether that's a permanent realignment or a momentary romance, time will tell," Shipley said.[4]

According to the Texas Poll, the percentage of Texans who called themselves Democrats declined from 50 percent in 1974 to 29 percent in 1994, while the percentage of Texans who identified themselves as Republicans increased from 16 percent in 1974 to 25 percent in 1994.[5]

When the New York firm of Blum and Weprin polled according to party identification in January 1996 for *The Dallas Morning News/Houston Chronicle Poll*, it found 33 percent of Texans called themselves Republicans and 26 percent called themselves Democrats.[6]

Clements should be credited with institutionalizing the partisan shift in elections, by getting conservative Democrats to vote for a Republican for governor, not once but twice.

"Clements' election in 1978 marked the first time that the Connally-Shivercrat wing of the Democratic party shifted to the GOP. It could have been an anomaly. But when it was repeated in 1986, it institutionalized the structure. It created a deep line of demarcation, creating a two-party institution," said Clements' last chief of staff, Rider Scott.[7]

In the years prior to the 1961 election of Republican U.S. Sen. John Tower, the parameters of Texas politics had been the two factions of the Democratic Party, the liberal and the conservative wings — almost two different parties under the same partisan umbrella. By the time Bill Clements ran for office, Texas, like other states in the South, had begun its partisan realignment by rejecting Democratic presidential candidates such as Adlai Stevenson and George McGovern.

The extent of the partisan realignment became apparent in 1994, sixteen years after Clements' first election as governor. Texas elected its second Republican governor, George W. Bush, and Republicans captured almost half of all statewide offices, including a majority of the Texas Supreme Court, Texas Railroad Commission, and the State Board of Education. For the first time, Republicans held the Texas governor's office and both U.S. Senate seats. Republicans had won three of the last six gubernatorial elections and carried the state in five of the last seven presidential elections.[8]

The 1994 election year was the year that Texas shed its post-Reconstruction Democratic skin. No longer were Texans willing to vote for a "yellow dog" over a Republican. Even Democrats acknowledged the change in the Texas political climate. The liberal *Texas Observer* described the once venerable "yellow dog" Democrat in Texas as one "sick puppy." A *Dallas Morning News* columnist said it was the year the "yellow dog" died in Texas. National political analyst Bob Beckel, who managed the Walter Mondale presidential campaign in Texas in 1984, commented that the defeat of a popular

Democrat governor like Ann Richards in Texas meant the political shift was "deep, and it is permanent."⁹

The statistics over a twenty-year period attest to the change.

After the 1994 election, Republicans held thirteen statewide offices; twenty years earlier, they had held none. Instead of the paltry 19 of 181 members of the State House and Senate the GOP held in 1975, it had 76 members in 1995. And the change at the county level was enormous; from 1975 to 1995, Republicans went from holding 63 county offices to 733. Clements was the breakthrough. Texas had not only become a competitive two-party state, political scientists agreed that it was headed toward becoming a majority Republican state unless Democrats found a way to reverse or slow the growing Republican tide.¹⁰

By June 1995, political analysts and partisans were debating the possibility of Republicans gaining a majority in the 1996 elections in the Texas Senate, still Democratic by a 17-to-14 margin, and in the Texas House of Representatives, which remained Democratic by an 88-to-62 margin.¹¹

In 1996, Republican primaries would occur for the first time in all 254 counties, with King County, the home of the 6666 Ranch in northwest Texas, agreeing to hold a GOP primary. King, with 224 registered voters, and the adjacent Cottle County, were the last Texas counties to agree to conduct Republican primaries.¹²

Several measurements may be used to confirm the change in Texas politically since Clements was first elected. They include the increase in the percentage of people voting in the Republican primary, the number of Republican candidates elected statewide, the increase in Republicans in the legislature and in county offices. "We have had a change unparalleled by any state in the country with maybe the exception of South Carolina and Florida," said Republican consultant Karl Rove, who attributed the change to the elections of Reagan-Bush and Phil Gramm as senator, as well as to Clements.¹³

Political scientists generally classify an election into three types: 1) as a maintaining election, where a coalition continues; 2) as a deviating election, which deviates from the norm; or 3) as a realigning election, in which significant change occurs. Clements' election in 1978, according to political scientist Lance Tarrance, probably would be classified as a deviating election, since the next election was won by a Democrat. In later years, however, when political historians look at 1978, they may determine that it was the beginning of the realigning elections that would reshape the Texas voting universe.

As Tarrance noted, John Tower connected Texas Republicans to the national Republican Party and provided a point of identification for Texas Republicans. But Tower's election to the U.S. Senate failed to translate into other Republican gains in the state. "There's a big difference between running a government and sending people to Washington to express your values," Tarrance said. Clements showed that Republicans could govern.[14]

Governor and Mrs. Clements left other footprints. Their greatest legacies together are restoration of the Governor's Mansion and the Capitol.

"What he and Rita did was to say, 'This is important. It's part of our heritage. This is something Texans can be proud of,'" Dealey Herndon said. "It was that physical expression that we're special in Texas, that we should appreciate together where we came from, that we have these historic treasures."[15]

"When people look back at the Clements administrations, they may not remember a lot of particulars about things he did. He was greatly interested in management, and that was his strong suit," said Democrat consultant George Christian. But Clements "put his stamp on the two central institutions of government more than anybody else has ever done or ever will do," Christian added. "When people look back, it's going to register with them that Clements is the Capitol and he's the mansion."[16]

Beyond that, did it make a difference that he was governor? Each governor leaves an imprint, and Clements' imprint can be found in the quality of his appointments, the expertise he brought into state government, and the Republican "farm club" he founded with his appointments. Many became candidates or continued to work in government. One of his greatest fortes was persuading prominent Texans to serve the state. "He could get people to do things. I was amazed at some of the appointments he was able to get," said Rep. Tom Craddick, who formed the Republican legislative caucus during Clements' second term.[17]

During the transition meeting between Clements and Governor-elect Richards, the outgoing governor gave Ms. Richards a list of his appointees he felt had not measured up. He told her, "If you can get these people out, get them out. I made a mistake with them." He also told her, "The greatest power you have and the most serious responsibility is appointments." Among the 4,000 appointments that a governor makes in four years are the people who really run the government under Texas' agency form of government.[18]

Clements also paid constant attention to the bottom line, arrested the growth of government, though he didn't stop it, and brought management techniques into state government, such as the use of task forces and long-range planning. Clements' studies of agency operations and costs evolved into the Texas Performance Review under Democrat Comptroller John Sharp, during the Richards administration, when the practice became known as "reinventing government." Clements established the principle of the performance reviews in his first administration. Bob Bullock, as comptroller, had continued them under Gov. Mark White. Bullock, as lieutenant governor, later obtained statutory authority for the performance reviews, giving Sharp the legal authority to do what Clements had started informally. Sharp's reviews resulted in recommendations for structural changes in Texas government.

History will view Bill Clements as a businessman who brought a business management style to state government.

"If we had a bad financial picture in the mid-1980s, it would have been considerably worse had Clements not been tighter with the dollar than other governors might have been," consultant Karl Rove said. "We spent a lot of money in the 1960s and 1970s from oil and gas revenues and did not necesssarily have a lot to show for it. At a time when it would've been easy to go with the flow, he made some tough actions on the budget and racheted down spending.

"He worked systematically in his first term and then by habit in his second term to change Texas politically," Rove said. "He changed Texas very much his first term policy-wise and, in the second term, by habit, continued that process of change. A lot of things that happened in Texas happened because of things Bill Clements was part of or set in motion."[19]

From a public policy standpoint, what difference does it make whether the governor is Republican or Democrat?

Governor Bush sees the difference as being more one of philosophy. It makes a difference, he said, whether the state has a conservative governor or a liberal governor. The problem for Democrats is that, for years, they played a "philosophical accordion," varying from conservative to liberal officeholders with no consistency. "Would there have been any difference between Gov. Allan

Shivers, Democrat, and Gov. George Bush, Republican, philosophically? Probably not." But it may be that Shivers, who was governor in the 1950s, would have been a Republican today, he said. In Clements' first race in 1978, in fact, Shivers supported Clements, as did former Democratic governors Preston Smith and John Connally.

Governor Bush also noted the effect of the change in the political environments between his administration and the administrations of Clements. "There is a time for politics and a time for policy, and I think Clements had to deal with that much more so than me. I've got fourteen Republican senators (only three shy of a majority) to help." Clements, who had fewer, "had to forgo party to get something done. The body's more conservative for me," Bush said. "Gov. Clements didn't have the luxury of people who were anxious to work with him, people who were of the same party."[20]

From a policy standpoint, Clements is given credit for taking a leadership role in economic development and for establishing new relations with Mexico. But Democrats faulted him for not understanding the complexities of the budget process, and for his lack of ardor for settling the Edgewood school suit and mental health legal issues.[21]

When many Texans think of Bill Clements, they tend to think not so much of what he did as governor, but what he was like as a person. George Bayoud, who progressed from driving the motor home in the first gubernatorial campaign to being the last secretary of state under Clements, commented, "I'm not sure people are going to sit back and remember Clements and [his initatives with] Mexico. People are going to remember him more for his personality. He's one of the few people in public office who really would speak his mind. I still hear people say, 'I didn't always agree with Bill Clements, but I sure miss the way he used to say it.'"[22]

Clements' favorite Texas historical figure was Sam Houston, perhaps because Houston was one of the most powerful personalities in the state's history, one of the most outspoken, and one with whom he shared some character traits. Houston is regarded as the governor with the tartest tongue. Once in criticizing a political opponent, Houston said the man had all the characteristics of a dog — except fidelity.[23] Houston was vain and egotistical, but also a man of the people; he held remarkable power over others. He also was a controversial figure, both loved and hated. And he had an immense love of Texas. His dying words were, "Margaret, Margaret. Texas, Texas." Clements regarded Houston as a "Texian" in the true tradition, an independent, elder statesman of the Texas Revolution and Civil War period, to be admired and emulated.

Certainly, Bill Clements could lay claim to being distinctive.

Jim Francis, who worked in Clements' first administration and then fell out of favor for several years before finally getting back together with his former boss, assessed Clements' strengths and his weaknesses. Strengths: high I.Q., great energy level, focused, extremely determined, strong willed, brave, and "not afraid of the devil himself." Francis said he never saw him be afraid of anybody or anything. Weaknesses: "bullheaded to a fault, doesn't have great political skills, can be a bully, can be too cocky, too self-assured, and an absolute know-it-all."

As his aide Cliff Johnson noted, Clements became legendary in Austin for two peculiarities: his wild driving habits and his easy movement between the seats of high power and the common man. Clements would dump his Department of Public Safety drivers and insist on driving his own car. He was a man who liked to be in command of his destiny, and his destination. He also picked a car that fit his personality. "He'd take that land yacht, that big station wagon, and we'd go eat at Austin Country Club or go get a hamburger at Dirty's. He loved hamburgers," Johnson said. "He was not a good driver, and a lot of times I wish I'd had a helmet. The station wagon was intimidating, so usually people would get out of the way. He loved that big old station wagon."

Mike Toomey, the governor's deputy and then chief of staff during his term, had similar recollections. The staff didn't like for him to drive, because he would start talking and forget to watch the road. But Clements would insist. "Give me the keys," he would growl. Toomey recalled one incident, driving along the highway to Austin Country Club, when Clements observed a woman driving with her door partially open. "He drove up close to her, honking his horn," Toomey said. "Here was the governor of the state, trying to flag this woman down and tell her that her door was open. He was weaving in and out, trying to watch her and watch the road and yell at her."

If he didn't have much time for lunch, the governor liked to go to a hamburger joint near the Capitol called "Dirty's," where he sat at a regular stool and would watch as the short-order cook threw a wad of hamburger meat onto the grill and then smashed it flat with one whap of his spatula. "All these 'bubba' guys would come in and say, 'Hi, governor.' He'd just sit there, eating his hamburger and french fries, not like a governor at all. I like that. He didn't act like he was something special," Toomey said.[24]

Even in Washington, Clements moved easily from meetings with other governors and administration officials, from his elegant Wexford home where he often entertained other dignitaries, to eating unnoticed at a local hamburger place. Reggie Bashur, the governor's press aide during his second term, was in Washington with Clements for a National Governors Association meeting when Clements would go out for a hamburger instead of eating in the hotel dining room. Bashur recalled going to a place on Capitol Hill called the "Tune-In." He said, "There weren't any tables available, so we sat at the bar. He [Clements] got up on a barstool and ordered a hamburger and a beer. Here he is, this seventy-year-old guy in a checkered jacket — he looked like somebody's grandpa taking a tour of the Capitol."

The bartender asked Clements, "What do you do?"

Clements responded, "I'm from Texas."

"Well, what do you do down there in Texas?" the bartender asked.

"I'm in government," Clements responded.

The bartender persisted. "And what do you do in government down in Texas?"

"Aw, I'm the governor," Clements said.

Despite frequent exhibitions of bravado, Clements had humility, Basher said.[25]

Rudy Cisneros, owner of Cisco's Bakery, a longtime political hangout that serves homestyle Tex-Mex breakfast and lunch in Austin, considered Clements the most interesting governor he has known, going back to the 1950s, because he was so "down to earth."

At Cisco's, anybody can go in and sit at the "Liar's Table," a big table where they can eat and "tell lies," Cisneros said. Clements, he said, would come in and sit down at the Liar's Table. Or he and Rita would come in for a late Sunday breakfast, have a beer and a breakfast of huevos rancheros, migas, or chorizo, picking a table in the midst of Cisneros' full house. Clements would go into the kitchen and lift the covers off the food and say, "I want some of this and some of that."

Other people in the small cafe frequently would want to meet the governor; Cisneros would ask him if he minded saying hello, and he always complied. "He wasn't uppity," Cisneros said. And he didn't bring his Department of Public Safety security officers in with him, as other governors did.

Cisneros once introduced Clements to a lawyer who started the conversation by saying, "You know what, governor, I never did like you." Clements, said Cisneros, "got uptight and red in the neck." Then the man went on, "until I heard you make that speech at the Cattlemen's Association. I've liked you ever since."

Cisco's walls feature autographed photos of politicians such as former President Lyndon Johnson, Sen. Kay Bailey Hutchison, President Bush, and former Governor Connally. Cisco paid $500 for a portrait of Clements painted by a prisoner at Huntsville. Clements complained that it didn't look like him. "He said it was too mean-looking," Cisneros recalled.[26]

Clements' favorite hamburger place in Dallas was Goff's on Lovers Lane. Goff's was a Dallas institution, in business for more than forty years. The proprietor, Harvey Goff, had a reputation for being even more gruff than the governor; he would insult customers, new and old alike. Clements had driven himself to Goff's and was eating a hamburger alone in the fall of 1989 when a robber walked in, waving a gun, and held up the place. The robber held the gun to an employee's head, forcing him to empty the cash register, and then fired several shots as he ran away. Clements finished eating his hamburger and went home. If the police wanted to question him as a witness, he said, they knew where to find him. "He was unflappable. He'd sit through an armed robbery and eat a cheeseburger," said his aide, Rider Scott. "There was very little in terms of political or life crises that would unnerve him.[27]

As a politician, Clements wasn't a casual conversationalist. Yet, he was an engaging conversationalist when he met another person of accomplishment. He had an inquiring mind, and was highly interested in the achievements of others. But he never really considered himself a politician. In fact, he seemed to have a basic distaste for politics, particularly in his second administration. Despite entreaties from staff, he refused to cut the cake with this or that group, or have his picture made, or court the press. He could be charming when he wanted to be, but more often than not, he didn't want to be. "The public would have had a better perception of him if he'd done some of the nice things," Toomey said. "But he didn't care about that."²⁸ He wouldn't put up with the pettiness of some of the House members — that somebody's vote would depend on getting the queen of the Tomato Festival's picture made with the governor.

As George Christian said, "Clements was good at a lot of things, but I don't think he was ever good at politics."

Besides seeing himself as a businessman and not a politician, Clements also saw himself as a catalyst for change. He once told James Huffines, his appointments director in the second term, "James, I'm kind of like the little boy with a garden hose who sprays the wasp nest and then runs like hell." According to Huffines, Clements "would spray and then step back and watch everything buzz around."²⁹

Eschewing the niceties of personal interactions was part of Clements' paradoxical nature as a public figure. While he engendered a high degree of loyalty and respect from his staff and many who worked with him, he also strained some relationships and shattered others. Ed Vetter, who worked in the first administration on energy matters and the second on commerce, admitted he could "love and hate Bill Clements, all in the same twenty-four hours." George Strake, a Clements campaign chairman, secretary of state and Republican state chairman, acknowledged a "love-hate relationship" with the governor. In later years, Clements became totally estranged from Anne Armstrong, the counselor to the president who had been a special friend during his Department of Defense days and whose husband, Tobin, had been his first appointments secretary. An acquaintance of both explained that Clements sometimes could not contain his male chauvinism, which resulted in some cross words between him and Mrs. Armstrong.

Ray Hutchison, Clements' opponent in the 1978 Republican race and his first political opponent, believes Clements has an "unfortunate trait" that resulted from not understanding the political process. "He becomes a man of many and easy hates, myself among them. He seethes around people he doesn't like. You can feel it and you can sense it."

Clements, in the opinion of both Hutchison and Strake, was not an overt Republican Party builder. That aspect of service was important to Hutchison and Strake, who had each served as chairman of the Texas Republican Party. "It made a difference obviously to have elected a Republican governor," Hutchison said. "But

Clements as that governor was not a party builder. It was not a part of his agenda. He was basically Clements, dedicated to his agenda. I think it is a proper duty of an officeholder of stature to give a piece of your time to the party that 'brung ya,'" Hutchison said.

Strake expressed similar sentiments. In his five years as state Republican chairman, from 1983 to 1988, fifty-four officeholders or former officeholders switched parties. "If I would hear of anyone thinking of switching, I'd go see them," Strake said. He would also get Sen. Phil Gramm or Vice-President Bush to call potential party-switchers — but not Bill Clements.

However, he added, "Bill Clements was a party builder just by winning and being there. He proved people were not going to break out in a terminal rash if they voted Republican, and the more you win, the more people want to be with you. So, instead of having to recruit Daniel Boones, we started to get the Eagle Scouts."

But Clements was not inclined to give party-rallying speeches, or campaign as part of a ticket, or make phone calls to try to persuade Democrats to become Republicans — though he worked hard to put Republicans in the White House. He worked for individual state candidates, such as Tom Phillips for Texas Supreme Court or Roy Barrera, Jr., for attorney general, to remove liberal Democrats he didn't like, or because of personal interest. As governor, he was conservative, but he also was more managerial than ideological. He was more interested in making the trains run on time than in building the Republican Party for the sake of party-building. He was also, always, a bit of a maverick.

Still, Republican Party-building was a natural byproduct of his election because of the appointments power. He brought Republicans into state government, into the boards and commissions, where they had never been. He appointed judges who the next time ran as Republicans. Legislators and judges switched parties. As a result of Clements being governor, the election of Ronald Reagan in 1980, and the cajoling of such leaders as Dallas County Republican Chairman Fred Meyer, Democratic officeholders began to switch parties prior to the 1982 election. Even as Clements was losing in 1982, fifty of fifty-nine judges elected in Dallas County were Republicans, including nineteen former Democrats who switched and filed as Republicans, as the GOP gained control of the Dallas County courthouse.

Fred Meyer, a later state Republican chairman, characterized

Clements as a "power player. What he accomplished was through power." Clements approached politics and government with this thought in mind: "What do I need to do to get the ball across the goal line." Clements, he said, wasn't concerned with the "warm fuzzies. Power is his style. He understands power, and the people around him understand he's a power player."[30]

After Clements left office, he was only peripherally involved in politics. After being asked late in President Bush's reelection campaign in 1992 for help in East Texas, he did a ten-day swing, visiting such towns as Nacogdoches, San Augustine, Longview, and Tyler. Bush carried East Texas. Clements also supported Tom Pauken, whose association with the former governor went back to the 1972 Nixon campaign, in his race among fellow Republicans to become state chairman over the handpicked candidate of Sen. Phil Gramm and outgoing chairman Fred Meyer. In the 1994 state elections, Clements advised George W. Bush in his gubernatorial race. And he helped Charles Matthews win a seat on the Texas Railroad Commission, by raising money, making calls and advising Matthews, who had been his appointee to the Texas Turnpike Authority.

In the race for the GOP presidential nomination of 1996, Clements bucked most of the rest of the state's Republican political establishment when he failed to join Phil Gramm's presidential bid. Instead, he helped to persuade California Gov. Pete Wilson to seek the nomination and became Wilson's Midwest finance director. Wilson, however, made an early withdrawal from the race.

Clements said he thought Wilson's executive experience as governor of a large state made him more qualified to be president. He also had little respect for Gramm's ability to recruit good personnel to work in the executive branch. "Gramm is not well suited to be president. He is not broad-gauged enough; his views are too parochial," Clements said, after Gramm entered the race. "I like Gramm right where he is, in the Senate. He votes right," Clements said. As for Sen. Bob Dole's presidential candidacy, he said, "Dole is a great patriot, a great American. He's given his adult life to this country. But he's too old. Being seventy-eight, I know one when I see one," Clements said.

In a reflective mood in a 1995 interview, Clements also commented on four presidents that he had known intimately.

Richard Nixon, he said, was a workaholic. "As far as personality, he was removed. I never knew anyone who had a solid friendship or personal relationship with Nixon. He was work-oriented. He was fascinated with international relations. He was an historian; he understood U.S. history and U.S. relations with the world. He was an extremely capable person, but he was not a people person."

Gerald Ford, he said, was an extremely likable congressman from Michigan who never lost his congeniality. Clements came to know him well when Ford became vice-president. "We had a mutual interest in national security. He was a leader in the national Republican party and in Congress. I respected and liked him. He had played football at Michigan, and was on one of their outstanding teams. He was an Eagle Scout. We related to each other," Clements said. "When he became president, we continued that relationship. It was not unusual for me to meet with him in the White House or for him to call the Department of Defense. I attended all of the National Security Council meetings, and was on all the subcommittees. He was one of the nicest people I've ever known — considerate, gregarious. He had a great personality. He knows the Congress and the way Congress operates, backward and forward."

Ronald Reagan and Bill Clements hit it off from the beginning. Clements liked and admired Reagan. After the Texas primary of 1980, in which Clements tried as governor to remain neutral, he campaigned for Reagan and traveled with him. When Reagan was elected, he asked Clements to serve on his transition committee and to write a transition paper recommending Reagan's positions on the Department of Defense and national security. "I was close to Reagan. I saw him fairly often and talked to him fairly often. I admired him. I thought he was a good president. He listened extremely well; that's a great attribute. The thing he probably took the most pride in was the outcome of his policies with respect to Russia," Clements said.

Of the four presidents, Clements knew George Bush the longest and the best, having been in joint drilling ventures with him. "George is an extremely nice person. I'm not sure that goes well with the presidential territory. My observation is that to be president, you have to be about half mean. I don't think there is a mean streak in George Bush. In my judgment, he was not well served by some of the people he appointed," he said. "I don't suppose there has been a president of the United States that's had as many international friends and close relationships with heads of state of other countries as George Bush. It goes back to that basic personality — a very nice person."[31]

Clements was not reluctant to pass judgment on other politicians. Mark White, to him, was a "show horse, not a workhorse," who aspired to be vice-president. Ann Richards, he believed, devoted too much time and energy to being a political and media star. Her appointments were viewed by Clements as being too liberal and a "disaster" for Texas, although Democrats thought them more reflective of the population of Texas as a whole.

Clements viewed himself as a "people person." He attributed his SEDCO success to his ability to work with people, both in his company and with the customers. And he thought he had a talent for getting good people to work with him. He maintained that the transition from the private sector to the political arena was not that difficult. Management techniques are the same, he would say, whether you're running a big drilling company, which had 8,000 employees at its peak, or state government with 180,000 employees, or the Defense Department, which had 2.2 million employees. "Good management is good management. It has primarily to do with people relationships," he said.[32]

Picking people for positions of responsibility was, for Clements, the most enjoyable part of being governor. He also enjoyed editorial board interviews and the campaign debates — most likely because he enjoyed the process of matching wits. He didn't particularly relish campaigning, but making contacts and building a campaign organization came easy. And, while he took pleasure in his achievements as governor, he found part of the job "distasteful and onerous." For example, "You have to associate with some people you don't like personally or don't like what they believe in. As a free-enterprising drilling contractor, you don't have to put up with those things," he said. In business, there are certain norms of behavior, and things are negotiated in a contractual way. He found those elements not to be present in the legislature.

Being governor was a "mixed bag," he said. "Half of it is pure hard work — dealing with the legislature, for example." The intense budget battle of 1987, the economic and prison initiatives of 1989, workers' comp, and all of those special sessions had been sheer, hard work. But, he added, "I enjoyed getting things done."[33]

He found most of the relationships in Austin, however, to be superficial. "You have working relationships, not friendships, because it's an artificial environment. It's a passing relationship, here today, gone tomorrow," Clements said. He valued the relationships he had with House Speakers Billy Clayton and Gib Lewis. They were good "working friends," Clements said. "I feel about them like I do about my drilling managers. We've gone through good and bad times and solved problems together," he said. Clements also established a lasting relationship with former Gov. Dolph Briscoe.[34]

Lewis understood Clements' competitive nature from hunting with him. "He was driven to make sure he got the biggest deer. Then he delighted in bragging about it," Lewis said. Clements also invariably surprised Lewis with his broad and unexpected knowledge, gained from his life experiences. Lewis told of one time he mentioned the name of an obscure Pakistani villege he had visited on a hunting trip. To his amazement, Clements began to provide him with a detailed history of the region.[35]

Lewis, although a Democrat, considered Clements "a great governor. He was the right person at the right time. He was controversial, but anybody who is going to stand up and have some backbone is going to be controverisal. In that job [governor], you've got to have somebody who stands for what they believe in and lets the public know." Lewis credited Clements with keeping the cost of government down — by his leadership, his presence, and his threat of the veto. "He kept that budget down and well scrubbed."[36]

In contrast, Lt. Gov. Bill Hobby thought other governors were more successful at legislative consensus than was Clements. Hobby also thought that Clements' electoral success was only symptomatic of the growing Republican strength in Texas and throughout the South; he didn't cause it.[37]

After Clements left office, his best friends and most enduring relationships were still his SEDCO associates and old school buddies. While he called himself a people person, Clements didn't aspire to having a multitude of friends. He once said that "too many relationships distract you from doing constructive things. It's better to have a few good friends than a lot of superficial friends."[38]

Hilary Doran, one of Clements' chiefs of staff, thought Clements was a "good people person. I would tell that to a lot of folks and they would just kind of shake their heads. Most people just saw the gruff side, the give-and-take with the press."[39]

It never really bothered Bill Clements that some people found him abrasive. If he thought he had to be unpleasant to get a job done, he went for the job over being pleasant. Rita, however, and some of Clements' gubernatorial staff, thought his true personality was largely misunderstood — that he was quite soft-hearted with those he considered his real, as opposed to superficial, friends.

Rita was very protective of the governor. Besides maintaining her own full-time schedule as first lady, she attended many functions with her husband. She generally went with him when he was being interviewed on "Capitol Report," the statewide TV show hosted by Carole Kneeland, which succeeded the "Governor's Report." Ms. Kneeland's husband, Dave McNeely, a writer for the *Austin American-Statesman*, frequently was one of the reporters asking questions, and they usually were tough questions.

After one show, Mrs. Clements approached Carole Kneeland and said, "You know, we have more in common than you might think."

Ms. Kneeland asked the governor's wife what she meant.

Rita said, "A lot of people think our husbands are jerks."

Ms. Kneeland responded, "I don't think McNeely's a jerk."

Whereupon Rita Clements said, "And I don't think Bill is."[40]

Besides remembering his distinctive personality, people frequently associate Bill Clements with the SMU athletic scandal, and invariably blame him for the demise of SMU's football program. Clements, however, wasn't responsible for the corruption, commercialization, and increasing professionalism of what once was amateur college football. He did not create the problem at SMU, though he can be criticized for not insisting on the immediate dismantling of the pay-for-play system rather than a phase-out. His reaction may be regarded as contrary to his Eagle Scout upbringing, but what he did was in character, part of his nature after twenty-five years as a drilling contractor. To Clements, a deal was a deal; the commitments should be honored.

Years later, Clements would say: "It was wrong. SMU should carry the burden that it was wrong, but SMU had a contract with those boys. SMU made an agreement with those boys, and SMU had an obligation to perform under their agreement," Clements said. "It's not to say that SMU shouldn't have been penalized. They had violated the rules, but they shouldn't have penalized the boys. People may not agree, but that's the way I felt about it."[41]

His role in the SMU controversy also was in character for a risk-taker. The risk was that SMU — and Bill Clements — would be stung later if the phase-out was uncovered, against the certainty that SMU would immediately lose its football program if the payments were abruptly stopped. It was one gamble he lost. When Clements was younger, his sister Betty liked to say that he seemed especially blessed; he seemed to go through life with an angel on his shoulder. The SMU controversy proved to be an exception to her rule.

In later years, Clements was reunited with SMU. In 1992, SMU President Kenneth Pye invited Clements back into the life of the university community to serve on his new President's Leadership Council, which was organized to identify financial resources for academic uses at the school. The appointment provided redemption for Clements, but caused a minor flap with some alumni and students who objected. Dr. Pye defended his actions in public and by letter, saying Clements was not responsible "for the fall of the SMU Athletic Department."[42]

In one letter, Dr. Pye said that there was no evidence suggesting that Clements ever made a payment to any athlete. "I am convinced that he had no knowledge that payments were being made at the time he accepted the chairmanship of the Board of Governors. The fat was in the fire when he learned of what had been transpiring," Dr. Pye said. Clements, he said, "hoped to avoid the death penalty by phasing down the improper program as fast as possible. It is not my role to defend his conduct, but I think that the primary responsibility should rest on the people who began and continued the payments and not the person that directed that the program be limited and stopped."[43]

In the fall of 1994, Clements made a gift to SMU which combined his affection for the institution with his appreciation of Texas history. Clements donated $10 million to SMU to endow its history department and create an interdisciplinary Center for Southwest Studies. The gift would enable SMU to develop a doctoral program in history, with an emphasis on the American Southwest. The university responded by naming its history department and the Center for Southwest Studies after Clements.

Through the gift, Clements said, he wanted to make it possible "for others to learn more about our unique history of the Southwest and to train educators who will pass along this knowledge to young people who will be the future leaders of this region."

Clements was a part of that unique history. He was in many ways symbolic of the old Texas even as, ironically, he brought Texas into a new era, an era of increased trade and high technology. When he left office at the end of 1990, Texas economic growth exceeded

U.S. growth for the first time since 1985. A year after he left office, energy had declined to 13 percent of the state's economy. Energy-based industry had accounted for 27 percent of the Texas economy in 1981.[44]

"To understand Bill Clements, you need to understand he was a self-made man, a man who faced enormous adversity in life. He literally came up from the bootstraps, and then gave of himself to public service, and did so without sacrificing his essential nature. He was a do-it, get-it-done, focus-on-the-problem, solve-it, kind of guy," Republican consultant Karl Rove said.[45]

His old friend Peter O'Donnell was asked if Clements was a "dying breed" of Texan.

"No, he's a different breed. I think we have a strong entrepreneurial tradition in Texas; we've got a lot of self-starters. It's just that they ain't gonna make it in the oil and gas business. There are people around here who are very entrepreneurial and very capable. They're not going to be drilling contractors or cattlemen."[46]

When Clements left office in 1991, in his official report to the 72nd Legislature, he wrote that "being governor of the State of Texas for eight years, longer than any of my predecessors, has been the highlight of my life. To the people of Texas, let me say how grateful, deeply grateful, I am for this honor."

In the same report, Texas historian and author T. R. Fehrenbach observed that Clements "led an era of incisive improvement in governance, of diversification of the traditional economy, of the making of new jobs where none had been before . . . . He marked, and in a large way caused, the emergence of a modern, two-party state."

And, he added: "Bill Clements pushed at new frontiers; he left the state better than he found it. And he may go at peace."

The SEDCO 445, which completed its first well in 1972, was the first full scale oil exploration drilling ship equipped for dynamic stationing.

Chronology

SEDCO, Inc.

January 1, 1947: Southeastern Drilling Company formed with two used drilling rigs by William P. Clements, Jr., and Ike LaRue, with backing by Toddie Lee Wynne.

1949: Eight land rigs bought from Creole Petroleum in Venezuela and moved to West Texas and New Mexico, increasing number of rigs from four to twelve.

1950: Headquarters of Southeastern Drilling relocated from Jackson, Mississippi, to Dallas; becomes first tenant in the Employer's Insurance Bldg.

1950: Clements buys out Toddie Lee Wynne for $83,000.

1952: Southeastern Drilling moves into shallow-water offshore drilling in Texas and Louisiana.

1954: Southeastern Drilling Company's first foreign venture with post type barge in Trinidad.

1955: Three-rig operation for Stanvac begins in India, West Pakistan, and East Pakistan in a partnership with Turnbull and Zoch.

1955: Clements buys out Ike LaRue for $1.2 million.

1958: Iran Oil Company contract awarded to Southeastern to operate two rigs in Iran.

1959: Work begins for the Iranian Oil Exploration & Producing Company, the consortium of the world's largest oil producing companies in Iran. Work begins for Japan's Arabian Oil Company Ltd. in the Neutral Zone between Saudi Arabia and Kuwait.

419

1960: Work begins in Argentina on the largest drilling contract ever awarded, to drill 1,000 wells on land for the government oil company, Y.P.F.

1963: Work completed in Argentina.

May 1965: Southeastern Drilling becomes publicly owned and is listed in the national over-the-counter market. SEDCO 135 christened. Decision made to specialize in deep water drilling.

1966: Two joint venture companies formed: SEDNETH with Dutch partners in the Netherlands to drill in the North Sea and ALFOR with the Algerian government to drill in the Sahara Desert.

1967: Baylor Company, a Houston company specializing in sophisticated electrical equipment for offshore drilling, is acquired.

1968: Earl and Wright, a San Francisco engineering firm, is acquired. Seven units in the 135 series at work or under construction. SEDNETH II begins work in the North Sea. B. Gill Clements joins Southeastern Drilling.

1969: Name of Southeastern Drilling changing to SEDCO Inc. Trading begins on the New York Stock Exchange. Houston Contracting Company, the largest cross-country pipeline company, is acquired.

1970: Contract received from Royal Dutch Shell for the design and operation of a dynamically positioned, self-propelled drill ship, after three years of research.

1971: SEDCO, Inc., moves its corporate headquarters to the restored Cumberland Hill School building. Contract signed with Royal Dutch Shell to build the first in the 700 series of semi-submersible rigs, followed by four more contracts for 700s.

1972: First drill ship without anchors, the SEDCO 445, drills its first well offshore Brunei. Training center opened in Aberdeen, Scotland.

1973: William P. Clements, Jr., becomes deputy secretary of defense and B. Gill Clements becomes president and chief executive officer of SEDCO. Four in the 700 series of semi-submersibles delivered. SEDIRAN, a joint venture with the Pahlavi Foundation and the Bazargani Bank, formed to provide drilling services in Iran. SEDCO/REDCO joint venture formed with oilfield fire fighter Red Adair to develop a semi-submersible fire fighting barge.

1974: The SEDCO 445 drills in 2,150 feet of water off the coast of Gabon, West Africa, the deepest water challenged to date in offshore drilling.

1975: Phillips Petroleum Company Norway signs a five-year contract for use of the $45 million Phillips SS semi-submersible oilfield service/firefighting unit developed with Red Adair. The SEDCO 445 drills to another record depth, in 2,295 feet of water offshore Gabon, West Africa. SEDCO joins an international consortium to recover manganese nodules from the ocean floor in water depths to 20,000 feet.

1976:   The SEDCO 702 becomes the first drilling rig to drill a well successfully in the high current area offshore Brazil near the mouth of the Amazon River. The SEDCO 706 and SEDCO 707 completed and delivered.

1977:   The SEDCO 707, the first dynamically stationed semi-submersible able to maintain location without anchors, is constructed. The SEDCO/Phillips SS arrives in the North Sea to work in the Ekofisk Field offshore Norway for Phillips Petroleum. The SEDCO 703, working for British Petroleum, drills the first discovery well in the North Sea area west of the Shetland Islands. The SEDCO 707, working offshore western Ireland in the Celtic Sea for Shell U.K., drills in 1,550 feet, the deepest water location ever drilled by a SEDCO semi-submersible. Outside the Gulf of Mexico and the North Sea, Brazil is the most active offshore area in the world; SEDCO has three rigs in Brazil.

1978:   The ocean mining consortium, after three years of design and development engineering, is successful in collecting a stream of manganese nodules aboard the SEDCO 445 from the ocean floor in 17,300 feet of water.

1979:   Revolution in Iran; SEDCO assets are nationalized, including sixteen land rigs, a shipyard and affiliated equipment. The SEDCO 135, SEDCO's first semi-submersible, is lost after a blowout and fire, while under charter to a Mexican drilling contractor operating the Ixtoc I for Pemex. SEDCO has twenty-seven drilling and production units operating offshore with two support units and eighteen land rigs, excluding equipment in Iran.

1980:   Contract signed for $75,000 day rates in the North Sea. Manufacturing Division sold; international segment of the Construction Division liquidated. Complex litigation begins as a result of Iranian and Ixtoc I losses.

1981:   Largest rig construction program in SEDCO's history under way, a gross value of $892 million. Investment position acquired in two other energy companies, Delhi International Oil Corp. and Marathon Oil Company.

1982:   Economic environment for energy companies has turned quickly from boom to bust. Energy consumption drops in the wake of

1981-82 recession. Some rigs are idle and Engineering Division begins reducing personnel. Position in Delhi International and Marathon sell for $316 million profit.

1983: William P. Clements, Jr., rejoins SEDCO as chairman of the board of directors. SEDCO's average day rates on offshore equipment is $57,600. SEDCO 710, most expensive rig built by SEDCO, delivered at an estimated cost of $168 million. SEDCO 712 and 714 delivered at costs of $100 million each.

1984: SEDCO/BP 471, dynamically positioned drill ship, contracted to Texas A&M Research Foundation for an ocean drilling program to explore the ocean basins and study how the earth was formed and developed; program funded by the National Science Foundation and nine foreign countries.

December 1984: SEDCO sold to Schlumberger Limited for $1.2 billion.

Personal and Political Chronology: William P. Clements, Jr.

April 13, 1917:   William P. Clements, Jr., born in Dallas.
1934:   Graduates from Highland Park High School.
1934-35:   Works on geophysical crew in South Texas oilfields.
1935-36:   Attends Southern Methodist University.
1936-37:   Attends University of Texas.
1937-38:   Works as a roughneck for Trinity Drilling Company in South Texas oilfields.
1938-1946:   Works for Oil Well Supply Company in Houston; Jennings, La.; Jackson, Miss.; Dallas; Tulsa, Okla.; Pampa, Texas; Canada; San Antonio.
April 6, 1940:   Marries Pauline Allen Gill in Temple, Texas.
October 13, 1941:   B. Gill Clements born in Dallas.
December 30, 1942:   Nancy Clements born in Dallas.
1950:   Begins buying farm and ranch land in Forney with purchase of 168-acre Carter Farm; renamed Clemgil Farm.
1951:   Clements family moves to 4622 Meadowood in Dallas.
1964:   State Republican Chairman Peter O'Donnell asks Bill Clements to run for U.S. Senate. Clements recruits George Bush and serves as Bush's state finance chairman. WPC's first political involvement.
1965-73:   Chairman of the SMU Board of Governors.
1968:   Raises money in Texas for Richard Nixon's presidential campaign.
1969:   Appointed by President Nixon to Blue Ribbon Defense Panel.
1972:   Serves as co-chairman of the Texas Committee to Re-Elect the President.
1973-77:   Serves as deputy secretary of defense.
June 2, 1974:   Separates from Pauline Gill Clements.

February 5, 1975:   Divorced from Pauline Gill Clements.

March 8, 1975:   Marries Rita Crocker Bass.

November 1977:   Becomes a candidate for governor of Texas.

May 1978:   Wins Republican primary to become party's gubernatorial nominee.

November 1978:   Elected first Republican governor of Texas since Reconstruction.

1979-1983:   First Clements term.

November 1982:   Loses reelection to Democrat Mark White.

November 1986:   Defeats Democrat Mark White to gain second gubernatorial term.

1987-1991:   Second Clements term.

Notes

Introduction

1. 1989 Press Club of Dallas Roast videotape produced by Weekly/Gray/McKinney Inc.

2. *Los Angeles Times,* March 7, 1979.

3. Clifton McCleskey, Allan K. Butcher, Daniel E. Farlow, J. Pat Stephens, *The Government and Politics of Texas,* 96.

4. Tom Reed interview, March 15, 1995.

5. George Bush interview, November 15, 1994.

6. *Ibid.*

7. The *Dallas Morning News,* August 23, 1984.

8. Select Committee on Tax Equity, *Rethinking Texas Taxes: Final Report of the Select Committee on Tax Equity,* and Texas Comptroller of Public Accounts, Legislative Budget Board, *Fiscal Size Up: 1994–1995 Biennium.*

9. Daniel Yergin, *The Prize,* 402–403, 719.

10. McCleskey et al, *Government and Politics of Texas,* 169.

11. George Strake interview, June 8, 1995.

12. *Update,* a newsletter for SEDCO employees, No. 6, 1978. (Clements often used this phrase in speeches, although journalists, failing to grasp the nuance, usually reported it as "Texan to his toenails.")

13. Walter P. Webb, *The Handbook of Texas,* 1952 edition.

Chapter 1: "Let's Do It"

1. *SMU Campus,* November 1, 1977.

2. SEDCO, Inc. 1977 Annual Report.

3. Felix McKnight column, *Dallas Times-Herald,* October 23, 1977.

4. Harrison Schmitt interview, September 20, 1994.

5. *SMU Campus,* November 4, 1977.

425

6. *Texas Almanac,* 1968–69.

7. *Ibid.*

8. James R. Soukup, Clifton McCleskey and Harry Holloway, *Party and Factional Division in Texas,* 21–23, 173.

9. "A Mustang in the Mansion," *The Mustang,* SMU Alumni Association magazine, Winter 1979. A review of these elections can also be found in Victoria Loe, "Governor's races cutting it closer than they once did," The *Dallas Morning News,* November 8, 1994.

10. *Dallas Times-Herald,* November 14, 1977.

11. William P. Clements, Jr., interview, Taos, N.M., August 26-28, 1994.

12. John R. Knaggs, *Two-Party Texas,* 120.

13. Peter O'Donnell interview, August 15, 1994.

14. O'Donnell interview, WPC interview, Taos.

15. O'Donnell interview.

16. John Connally, *In History's Shadow: An American Odyssey,* 231.

17. Mike Kingston, Sam Attlesey, and Mary G. Crawford, *Political History of Texas,* 91, 95.

18. O'Donnell interview.

19. Robert Allyn, "How Dallas Switched Parties," unpublished master's thesis, SMU, 1983.

20. O'Donnell interview.

21. Rita Clements interview, May 25, 1994; *Dallas Times-Herald,* October 22, 1978.

22. Bush interview.

Chapter 2: Roots
1. WPC interviews, Taos. (Unless otherwise noted, all information on Clements' ancestry comes from the Taos interviews and the William P. Clements, Jr., private genealogical files.)

2. *Forney Messenger,* Centennial edition, 1974.

3. *Texas Almanac,* 1986.

4. *Forney Messenger,* Centennial edition.

5. WPC interview, September 27, 1994, Forney.

6. Philip Lindsley, *A History of Greater Dallas and Vicinity,* 153.

7. WPC genealogical files; information on Dallas from Sam Acheson, *Dallas Yesterday,* 50.

8. William L. McDonald, *Dallas Rediscovered: A Photographic Chronicle of Urban Expansion 1870–1925,* 65–68.

9. Lindsley, *A History of Greater Dallas and Vicinity,* 307-308.

10. Acheson, *Dallas Yesterday,* 360.

11. Mike Kingston, *A Concise History of Texas,* 177; Jane Wolfe, *The Murchisons: The Rise and Fall of a Texas Dynasty,* 26.

12. Walter Rundel, Jr., *Early Texas Oil,* 34-38, 93-94.

13. Acheson, *Dallas Yesterday,* 52-55.

14. Galloway, *The Park Cities: A Photo History.*

15. Diane Galloway and Kathy Matthews, *The Park Cities: A Walker's Guide and Brief History,* 244.

16. Galloway, *The Park Cities: A Photo History*, 2, 41; *On Location*, SEDCO Inc. employee magazine, Winter 1979, 17.

17. *Dallas Morning News*, October 30, 1978; WPC interviews. Unless otherwise noted, information on Clements' childhood comes from the Taos interviews.

18. William Solomon interview, June 5, 1995.

19. Boy Scout information from WPC interviews, Taos, and Dallas, December 8, 1994.

20. An account of Clements' first speech is in the September 1930 Circle 10 Boy Scout Newsletter, WPC Personal Papers, Texas A&M.

21. Tom Rhodes interview, September 19, 1994.

22. Highland Park H.S. *Highlander*, 1934.

23. Charlie Trigg interview, September 12, 1994.

24. *Dallas Morning News*, August 23, 1984.

25. *Highlander*, 1934.

26. HPHS Spring Follies of 1933 and Negro Minstrel program, WPC Personal Papers, TAMU.

27. Joint interview with high school friends, Betty Skillern Baird, Randolph McCall, Mary Jane Chambers Honea, Helen Davis Lindsley, Tom Rose, Philip Lindsley and Jerry Cunningham, October 26, 1994.

28. *Ibid.*

29. Mary Ann Thomasson Todd interview, September 29, 1994.

30. Betty Skillern Baird, joint interview, October 26, 1994.

31. Tom Rose, joint interview, October 26, 1994.

32. Rundell, *Early Texas Oil*, 223-225; Kingston, *A Concise History of Texas*, 180.

33. Tom Rose, Philip Lindsley, joint interview.

34. WPC interviews, Taos; HPHS commencement program, 1934, WPC Personal Papers, TAMU.

Chapter 3: "Can't Do, Can't Stay"

1. Lon Tinkle, *Mr. De: A Biography of Everette Lee DeGolyer*, 159-169, 190.

2. WPC interviews, Taos, August 26-28.

3. *Ibid.*

4. Clements interview, Dallas, December 8, 1994.

5. Randolph McCall, from author's joint interview with Clements' high school friends, October 26, 1994.

6. WPC interview, Taos.

7. Jack Stoltz, *Terrell, Texas*, 49, 88-89; WPC interview, January 12, 1995.

8. Nancy Clements Seay interview, December 15, 1994.

9. *Sea Power Magazine*, November 1973.

10. WPC interview, January 12, 1995.

11. Unless otherwise noted, all information on Clements' life as a roughneck for Trinity Drilling came from the Taos interviews.

12. Gerald Lynch, *Roughnecks, Drillers, and Tool Pushers*, 23.

13. Bobby Weaver, introduction to Lynch, *Roughnecks*, xii, x.

14. WPC interview, Taos.

15. Unless otherwise noted, information on Clements' early days at Oil Well Supply come from the Taos interviews.

16. Mary Ann Thomasson Todd interview, September 29, 1994; WPC interview, January 12, 1995.

17. Seay interview.

18. WPC interview, Taos. (Unless otherwise noted, all information on Clements during the war years comes from the Taos interviews.)

19. Kenton Chickering interview, January 5, 1995.

Chapter 4: Betting on the Jockey

1. WPC interview, Taos. (The conversation between Clements and LaRue is Clements' recollection.)

2. Wolfe, *The Murchisons*, 87.

3. *Ibid.*, 88-127, 228. (Information on Toddie Lee Wynne comes from Wolfe unless otherwise noted.)

4. Information on the founding and early days of Southeastern Drilling comes from the Clements' Taos interviews unless otherwise noted.

5. Nancy Sayer, "History of SEDCO," *Connection*, August 1992.

6. *Dallas Times-Herald,* October 22, 1978.

7. Nancy Clements Seay interview.

8. Robert Nash and Peggy Nichols Nash, *Mr. McCamey, Claude W. Brown: The Life of a Texas Oilman*, 40.

9. Otis Conatser interview, January 6, 1995.

10. Sayer, "History of SEDCO."

11. The story of the Creole deal comes from WPC interviews, Taos.

12. Sayer, "History of SEDCO."

13. *Ibid.*

14. SEDCO company magazine, Summer 1973, 20.

15. Spencer Taylor interviews, May 20 and 27, 1994.

16. B. Gill Clements interview, September 1, 1994.

17. WPC interview, Taos; Taylor interviews.

18. W. G. "Bobby" Cox interview, February 27, 1995. SEDCO company magazine, Summer 1973. *On Location*, Fall 1978. (The conversation is Cox' recollection.)

19. Sayer, "History of SEDCO."

20. Cox interview.

21. W. E. "Bill" Armentrout interview, February 2, 1995.

22. *On Location,* Summer, 1975, 32; *Update,* No. 1, 1977.

23. John Rhea, Jr., interview, August 11, 1994.

24. WPC interview, Taos.

25. Sayer, "History of SEDCO."

26. Jerry Cunningham interview, August 31, 1994.

27. Chickering interview.

28. Cox interview.

29. Cunningham interview.

30. H. W. Solsbery interview, January 5, 1995.

31. Cunningham interview.

32. Sayer, "History of SEDCO."

33. Solsbery interview.

34. Sayer, "History of SEDCO."

35. Armentrout interview.

36. WPC interview, January 19, 1995; *Austin American-Statesman,* October 29, 1978.

37. Taylor interview, May 20, 1994; Sayer, "History of SEDCO."

Chapter 5:   Growing a Company

1. B. Gill Clements interview, September 1, 1994.

2. T. Boone Pickens, Jr., *Boone,* 38.

3. The story of Southeastern Drilling's first foreign venture comes from the Clements interviews, Taos.

4. *On Location,* Winter 1983–84, 15, and Fall 1978, 18.

5. Rhea interview.

6. WPC interview, Taos.

7. Yergen, *The Prize,* 455, 470, 476-477.

8. WPC interview, Taos.

9. Rhea interview.

10. Spencer Taylor interview, January 30, 1995.

11. SEDCO Inc. Annual Report, 1965.

12. Bobby Cox interview.

13. WPC interview, Taos.

14. Cox interview.

15. Taylor interviews.

16. Sayer, "History of SEDCO."

17. *On Location,* Spring 1974; Carl Thorne interview, February 22, 1995.

18. *William N. Dillin v Commissioner of Internal Revenue,* U.S. Tax Court reports, September 3, 1971. WPC Personal Papers, 16-3, TAMU.

19. WPC interview, Taos.

20. *Dillin v IRS* suit; WPC interview, Taos; Rhea interview.

21. James Presley, *Never in Doubt: A History of Delta Drilling Co.,* 306.

22. Tom Rhodes interview, September 19, 1994.

23. WPC interview, Taos.

24. Edwin J. "Jack" Smith, Jr., interview, February 13, 1995.

25. WPC interview, Taos.

26. Rhodes interview.

27. Interviews with Clements, Taylor and Rhea; Tom B. Rhodes letter, December 19, 1979, WPC Personal Papers, 12-11, TAMU.

28. *Dillin v IRS* suit and Rhodes letter. WPC Personal Papers, 12-11 and 16-3, TAMU.

29. Presley, *Never in Doubt,* 306. (The quote is from J. M. "Mark" Gardner, head of Delta Gulf.)

30. Nancy Clements Seay interview, December 15, 1994.

31. B. Gill Clements interview.

32. Seay interview.

33. B. Gill Clements interview.

34. WPC interview, December 8, 1994.

35. Seay interview.

36. Steve Mahood interview, February 20, 1995.

37. B. Gill Clements interview.

38. Seay interview.

Chapter 6: Offshore and Overseas
1. Rhodes interview.
2. J. E. Brantly, *History of Oil Well Drilling*, 1383–1386; John S. Ezell, *Innovations in Energy: The Story of Kerr-McGee*, 169; Yergin, *The Prize*, 429.
3. *On Location*, Fall 1979; Philip Singerman, *An American Hero: The Red Adair Story*, 129.
4. O'Donnell interview.
5. *On Location*, Fall 1979.
6. Sayer, "History of SEDCO"; Rhodes interview.
7. SEDCO, Inc. Annual Report, 1965.
8. Spencer Taylor interviews, May 20 and May 27, 1994.
9. SEDCO, Inc. Annual Report, 1965; *On Location*, SEDCO, Inc., Winter 1974.
10. Sayer, "History of SEDCO"; Taylor interviews.
11. WPC interview, Taos.
12. Bill Martinovich interview, March 17, 1995.
13. SEDCO, Inc. Annual Reports, 1965 and 1967; Sayer, "History of SEDCO"; *On Location*, Spring 1974.
14. SEDCO, Inc. Annual Report, 1969; Jerry Cunningham interview, February 3, 1995.
15. Cunningham interview; *On Location*, Fall 1979.
16. Yergin, *The Prize*, 525-527; Singerman, *An American Hero*, 24, 40; Sayer, "History of SEDCO."
17. *On Location*, Fall 1973, and Winter 1975; Cox interview.
18. Rhodes interview; Carl Thorne interview, February 22, 1995.
19. *On Location*, Fall 1973.
20. Yergin, *The Prize*, 668-669; Jack Smith interview.
21. Martinovich interview.
22. Cox interview.
23. *On Location*, Spring 1974.
24. Cox interview.
25. SEDCO, Inc. Annual Report, 1967; Gilda Stanbery, "Duke Zinkgraf," SEDCO-FOREX *Connection* (from Dillard Hammett files).
26. SEDCO, Inc. Annual Report, 1967; Clements interview, Taos.
27. Martinovich interview.
28. SEDCO, Inc. Annual Report, 1967 and 1968; Martinovich interview; Dillard Hammett interview, February 7, 1995.
29. Martinovich interview.
30. SEDCO, Inc. 1968 Annual Report.
31. Gill Clements interview.
32. SEDCO, Inc. Annual Report, 1969 and 1971; Sayer, "History of SEDCO."
33. SEDCO, Inc. Annual Report, 1969.
34. SEDCO, Inc. Annual Report, 1970.
35. SEDCO, Inc. Annual Report, 1970 and 1971.
36. SEDCO, Inc. 1970 Annual Report.

37. Southeastern Drilling Co., Inc., Brief Historical and Operational Guide, circa 1968.

38. *Marine Science Affairs*, National Council on Marine Resources and Engineering Development. (U.S. Government Printing Office, Washington, D.C.), SEDCO, Inc. Annual Report, 1971.

39. Hammett interview; SEDCO, Inc. Annual Report, 1971.

40. Sayer, "History of SEDCO"; *On Location*, Winter 1974.

41. Hammett interview.

42. Rhodes interview.

43. WPC interview, Taos; Rhodes interview.

44. SEDCO, Inc. Annual Reports, 1972, 1973.

45. WPC interview, Taos.

46. SEDCO, Inc. Annual Report, 1971; Martinovich interview.

47. Edwin L. Cox interview, February 6, 1995; Singerman,*An American Hero*, 127.

48. WPC interview, January 30, 1995; Cox interview.

49. Hammett interview.

50. Rhodes interview.

51. Margaret Hunt Hill, *H. L. and Lyda*, 251.

52. *Austin American-Statesman*, October 29, 1978.

53. Armentrout interview; Rhodes interview.

54. Cox interview.

55. Thorne interview.

56. *Update*, employee newsletter, No. 1, 1978; Steve Mahood interview, February 20, 1995.

57. WPC interview, Taos.

58. Yergin, *The Prize*, 500, 589.

59. SEDCO, Inc. Annual Report, 1972.

60. SEDCO Company Magazine, Summer 1973.

61. Taylor interview.

Chapter 7: Boss Talk

1. Shelma Ahrens interview, February 1, 1995.

2. WPC Personal Papers, 12-29, TAMU.

3. Rhodes interview.

4. WPC Personal Papers, 12-29, TAMU.

5. "Power in Dallas: Who holds the cards?," *D Magazine*, October 1974.

6. *Ibid.*

7. WPC interview, December 8, 1994.

8. Jackson Donahue, *Wildcatter: The Story of Michel T. Halbouty and the Search for Oil*, 170.

9. Robert H. Stewart interview, February 8, 1995.

10. "Power in Dallas," *D Magazine*, October 1974.

11. WPC interview, December 8, 1994; Harry Hurt, *Texas Rich*, 247.

12. Ahrens interview.

13. Thorne interview.

14. Stewart interview.

15. Jim Tarr interview, November 23, 1994.

16. WPC Personal Papers, 57-4, TAMU; *Dallas Morning News*, May 5, 1974.
17. Tarr interview.
18. Hammett interview; WPC Personal Papers, 12-22, TAMU.
19. Tarr interview.
20. WPC Personal Papers, 57-17, TAMU.
21. Edwin L. Cox interview, February 6, 1995.
22. WPC Personal Papers, 12-29, TAMU.
23. Cox and Stewart interviews. WPC Personal Papers, 77-20, TAMU.
24. SEDCO Annual Report, 1967.
25. *On Location*, SEDCO Inc. employee magazine, Winter 1979.
26. Dr. James E. "Jim" Brooks interview, September 23, 1994.
27. WPC interview, Taos; WPC Personal Papers, 77-12, TAMU.
28. WPC interview, Taos.
29. WPC interview, Taos; Cox interview.
30. WPC Personal Papers, 77-10, TAMU.
31. SMU Office of News and Information, press release, October 28, 1994.
32. *Dallas Morning News*, March 23, 1970.
33. John Merwin, "The Abrasive Candidacy of Bill Clements," *D Magazine*, March 1978.
34. WPC interview, March 20, 1995.
35. Merwin, "The Abrasive Candidacy."
36. *Dallas Morning News*, March 23, 1970.
37. SEDCO Inc., Summer 1973 company magazine; Ahrens interview.
38. WPC interview, College Station, February 17, 1995.
39. WPC interview, Taos; Ahrens interview.
40. WPC Personal Papers, 48-1, TAMU.
41. Ahrens interview.
42. WPC interview, December 8, 1994.
43. Richard Morehead, *50 Years in Texas Politics*, 101-105; John Connally, *In History's Shadow*, 143; Mike Kingston, Sam Attlesey and Mary G. Crawford, *The Texas Almanac's Political History of Texas;* WPC interview, December 8, 1994. (The most extensive explanation of the Tidelands issue and Shivers' role in the 1952 presidential election may be found in Sam Kinch and Stuart Long, *Allan Shivers: Pied Piper of Texas Politics.*)
44. Bush interview.
45. Knaggs, *Two-Party Texas*, 1-31.
46. Robert Allyn, "How Dallas Switched Parties."
47. "Nov. 22: Twenty Years Later," a commemorative section in *The Dallas Morning News*, November 20, 1983; Knaggs, *Two-Party Texas*, 38.
48. WPC interview, December 8, 1994.
49. Knaggs, *Two-Party Texas*, 55.
50. Doug Wead, *George Bush Man of Integrity*, 18.
51. O'Donnell interview; Morehead, *50 Years in Texas Politics*, 200.
52. Ahrens interview.
53. Ron Calhoun, *Dallas Times-Herald*, as quoted in Knaggs, *Two-Party Texas*, 164; WPC Personal Papers, 36-15, TAMU.
54. O'Donnell interview.
55. WPC Personal Papers, 12-29, TAMU.

56. O'Donnell interview.

57. WPC Personal Papers, 36-36, 36-37, TAMU.

58. Linda Montgomery interview, February 14, 1995.

59. *Ibid.*

60. Tom Pauken interview, March 3, 1995.

61. Scott Caven interview, March 6, 1995.

62. Morehead, *50 Years in Texas Politics*, 241-245; Connally, *In History's Shadow*, 262.

63. Caven interview.

64. Carolyn Barta, *Dallas Morning News*, October 22, 1972.

65. WPC Personal Papers, 37-12, Texas A&M. (No author is listed on the evaluation form but it likely was Peter O'Donnell or Tom Reed.)

Chapter 8:   DOD 1

1. SEDCO, Inc. company magazine, Summer 1973.

2. Dave McNeely, *Dallas Morning News*, December 3, 1972, December 13, 1972.

3. *Dallas Morning News*, December 13, 1972.

4. Congressional Record, Senate proceedings, January 23, 1973; *Business Week*, January 27, 1973.

5. WPC interview, December 11, 1995.

6. Supplemental Statement to Report of Blue Ribbon Defense Panel on "The Shifting Balance of Military Power," September 30, 1970.

7. *Dallas Morning News*, December 13, 1972.

8. Evans and Novak column, *Washington Post*, November 30, 1972.

9. Eleanora W. Schoenebaum, *Profiles of an Era: The Nixon-Ford Years*, 352.

10. WPC memo on November 22, 1972, Camp David discussion with President Nixon and Bob Haldeman, dated November 30, 1972. WPC personal papers, DOD files, TAMU.

11. *Ibid.*

12. WPC interview, September 27, 1994; WPC Personal Papers, Box 66, TAMU.

13. WPC memo of November 30, 1972, on Camp David meeting.

14. WPC handwritten notes, meeting with Elliot Richardson, November 30, 1972, DOD files, TAMU.

15. *Dallas Morning News, Dallas Times-Herald*, December 18, 1972.

16. *New York Times*, December 18, 1972.

17. *Washington Post, Dallas Morning News*, December 19, 1972.

18. *Dallas Times-Herald*, January 12, 1973, January 17, 1973; *Dallas Morning News*, January 17, 1973.

19. *Business Week*, January 27, 1973.

20. *Congressional Record*, Senate proceedings, January 23, 1973.

21. *Ibid.* (In one of life's paradoxes, Tower was able to help Clements, an outsider, get the No. 2 job at the Pentagon when, many years later, he was unable to gain confirmation for himself, an insider, to be secretary of defense when nominated by President Bush.)

22. *Dallas Morning News, Dallas Times-Herald*, January 24, 1973.

23. Jonathan Aitken, *Nixon, A Life*, 457; SEDCO, Inc. company magazine, Summer 1973.

24. WPC handwritten notes, WPC Personal Papers, Box 72, TAMU.

25. SEDCO news release, WPC Personal Papers, Box 1, TAMU.

26. SEDCO, Inc. company magazine, summer 1973.

27. February 6, 1973, letter to Willis M. Tate, WPC Personal Papers, 1-38, TAMU.

28. Letter from David Oscar Elkin, WPC Personal Papers, 1-9, TAMU.

29. Heather David, *Sea Power Magazine,* official publication of the Navy League, November 1973.

30. WPC Deputy Secretary diary (appointments schedule), February 1973-January 1977; DOD Box 67, TAMU.

31. WPC interview, September 27, 1994.

32. O'Donnell interview.

33. Frederic V. Malek, "Mr. Executive Goes to Washington," *Harvard Business Review,* September–October 1972.

34. John Jones interview, November 3, 1994.

35. WPC appointments diary, DOD Box 67, WPC Personal Papers, TAMU.

36. Ken Carr interview, October 31, 1994; *Business Week,* January 27, 1973.

37. Carr interview.

38. Jones interview.

39. Janie Harris Hollingsworth interview, January 9, 1995.

40. Jack Hammack interview, February 8, 1995.

41. Ed Vetter interview, June 27, 1995.

42. Carr interview.

43. Lawrence Eagleburger interview, November 3, 1994.

44. Kissinger became secretary of state September 22, 1973. (Eagleburger became acting secretary of state under President Bush in August 1992, and secretary of state December 8, 1992.)

45. *Los Angeles Times, Washington Star & News,* March 27, 1973.

46. Carolyn Barta, "Clements Warns Against Letup," *Dallas Morning News,* April 14, 1973.

47. Rotary Club of Houston speech, April 12, 1973, WPC Personal Papers, DOD Box 70, TAMU.

48. Dallas Council on World Affairs speech, April 13, 1973, WPC Personal Papers, Box 1, TAMU.

49. Salute to Vietnam Veterans speech, WPC Personal Papers, DOD Box 70, TAMU.

50. WPC press remarks, June 5, 1973, WPC Personal Papers, DOD Box 70, TAMU.

51. Aitken, *Nixon,* 502; Schoenbaum, *Profiles of an Era,* xv.

52. WPC interview, September 27, 1994.

53. WPC speech, Keel Laying of the USS *Texas,* Newport News, VA, August 18, 1973, DOD Box 70, TAMU.

54. November 23, 1973 DepSecDef staff meeting minutes, WPC private files.

Chapter 9: DOD 2

1. Adm. Thomas Moorer interview, November 2, 1994.

2. See Walter Isaacson, *Kissinger,* 512-524, for discussion of various accounts.

3. Sources on the Middle East war include various press reports and Aitken,

Nixon, A Life, 503-505; Marvin and Bernard Kalb, *Kissinger*, 465-478; and Henry Kissinger, *Years of Upheaval*, 316, 450-544.

4. WPC interview, November 2, 1995.

5. News clippings, June 1973-March 1978, DOD files, TAMU.

6. Eagleburger interview.

7. WPC diary, personal papers, DOD Box 67, TAMU.

8. Aitken, *Nixon*, 505. (Ford was sworn in December 6, 1973.)

9. Henry Kissinger, *Years of Upheaval*, 871-873, 885.

10. Tom Reed interview, November 17, 1994.

11. Janie Harris interview.

12. Carr interview.

13. WPC interview, December 11, 1995.

14. 1973 *New York Times* story by Richard J. Levine, "New Questions About Holdings of the No. 2 Man at Pentagon Are Raised by Energy Crisis." (WPC personal papers, Box 1, 1973 correspondence, TAMU.)

15. WPC DepSec staff notebooks, December 19, 1973, press conference briefing. WPC interview, November 2, 1995.

16. Correspondence, WPC Personal Papers, DOD Box 2, TAMU.

17. Bob Woodward and Carl Bernstein, *The Final Days*, 514.

18. NYT story in *Houston Post*, August 25, 1974, and *Dallas Morning News*, August 25, 1974. *Washington Star-News*, August 30, 1974.

19. News clippings from June 1973-March 1978, DOD, TAMU.

20. Reed interview.

21. WPC interview, September 27, 1994.

22. Correspondence, WPC Personal Papers, DOD Box 2, TAMU.

23. Gerald Ford, *A Time to Heal*, 142-145, 325.

24. *Los Angeles Times*, September 26, 1974.

25. Karen Elliott, "Life is very different in the capital," *Dallas Morning News*, January 20, 1974.

26. *Dallas Morning News*, July 26, 1974, July 28, 1974. WPC appointments diary, Personal Papers, DOD Box 67, TAMU.

27. *Dallas Morning News*, July 28, 1974.

28. Correspondence, WPC Personal Papers, DOD Box 2, TAMU.

29. *Ibid.*

30. *Ibid.* (George Bush announced in a November 16, 1973, statement on Republican National Committee letterhead that he would not be a candidate for governor of Texas in 1974, though being governor had enormous appeal and he believed a Republican could win. "But our political system is under fire and I have an overriding sense of responsibility that compels me to remain in my present job. I am confident that full disclosure on Watergate will vindicate the President," he said. Bush acknowledged the Republican Party had been through some traumatic times but disbelieved polls that indicated problems for Republican candidates in 1974. "All in all, I continue in this job with confidence, feeling proud to go on serving our party — yet hating to turn down the chance to become governor of my great state of Texas.")

31. Nicki Finke Greenberg, Rita Clements High Profile, *Dallas Morning News*, February 14, 1982.

32. *Ibid.*

33. Gill Clements interview.

34. WPC Personal Papers, Box 2, TAMU.

35. *Ibid.*

36. *Ibid.*

37. Correspondence, WPC Personal Papers, Box 77, TAMU.

38. *Dallas Morning News,* March 7, 1975. WPC Personal Papers, Box 46, and state papers, Box 3, TAMU.

39. Rita Clements High Profile, *Dallas Morning News.*

Chapter 10:   DOD 3

1. Tom Reed interview, November 17, 1994.

2. Nick Thimmesch, "Professor in the Pentagon," *Washington Post,* October 6, 1974; Tad Szulc, "Pentagon Cool," October 1974 *Washingtonian;* Schoenbaum, *Profiles of an Era,* 573-574.

3. Jones interview.

4. Carr interview.

5. Brent Scowcroft interview, November 3, 1994.

6. Carr interview.

7. Adm. Thomas Moorer interview, November 2, 1994.

8. Eagleburger interview.

9. Henry Kissinger interview, February 22, 1995.

10. Jones interview.

11. Reed interview.

12. WPC interview, November 2, 1995.

13. WPC interview, September 27, 1994.

14. Jones interview.

15. DOD meeting notes, October 1973-March 1974, WPC personal files.

16. *Ibid.*

17. DOD meeting notes, April-May 1974, WPC personal files.

18. DOD meeting notes, April-May 1975, WPC personal files; *Washington Post,* May 21, 1975.

19. Carr interview.

20. Reed interview.

21. Jones interview.

22. Carr interview.

23. *U.S. News and World Report,* July 15, 1974; *New York Times,* October 4, 1974. A discussion of the F-14 problems can be found in Zumwalt, *On Watch.*

24. Hammack interview.

25. *U.S. News and World Report,* July 15, 1974; Reed interview.

26. Carr interview.

27. WPC interview, September 27, 1994.

28. WPC interview transcript with Gerald Green for *Electronic, Electro-Optic and Infrared COUNTERMEASURES,* Santa Clara, California, January 1977, DOD Box 68, TAMU.

29. WPC interview, September 27, 1994; WPC letter to Lee Willett, Chiswick, London, England, October 26, 1995, WPC private files.

30. "The Politics of Naval Innovation," Strategic Research Department Research Report 4-94, U.S. Naval War College, August 1, 1994.

31. *Washington Star,* November 22, 1975; *Newsweek,* November 24, 1975.

32. "The Politics of Naval Innovation."

33. WPC interview, November 2, 1995.

34. "The Politics of Naval Innovation."

35. WPC letter to Lee Willett.

36. WPC interviews, September 27, 1994, November 2, 1995; Jones interview.

37. "The Politics of Naval Innovation"; Carr interview.

38. Evans and Novak, *Washington Post,* September 1974.

39. Ford, *A Time to Heal,* 320-324.

40. *Ibid.*

41. Eagleburger interview.

42. WPC interviews, September 27, 1994, November 2, 1995.

43. DOD meeting notes, June-August 1974, WPC personal files.

44. Janie Harris Hollingsworth interview.

45. *Dallas Times-Herald,* October 23, 1977.

46. John Finney, "The Pentagon, Without a War to Fight," *New York Times,* April 27, 1975.

47. Joseph Kraft, "The Problem of William Clements," *Washington Post,* November 1975.

48. January 1976, DOD clipping files, TAMU.

49. *Electronic, Electro-Optic and Infrared COUNTERMEASURES,* January 1977.

50. WPC, Mahood interviews.

Chapter 11: 1978 Campaign

1. 1978 gubernatorial campaign files, Voter Attitude Surveys Box, TAMU. Lance Tarrance interview, April 13, 1995.

2. Ray Hutchison interview, April 24, 1995.

3. *Austin American-Statesman,* October 29, 1978; *San Antonio Express-News,* October 22, 1978.

4. *Austin American-Statesman,* October 29, 1978.

5. November 8, 1977, notes by Rita Clements, WPC Personal Papers, 59-24, TAMU.

6. November 16, 1977, announcement press conference transcript. First Term, Press Relations, 40-3, TAMU.

7. Tom Reed interview, March 15, 1995.

8. WPC's handwritten notes on November-December 1977, meetings in preparation for the 1978 campaign are in WPC Personal Papers, 59-14, TAMU.

9. Bill Elliott interview, March 27, 1995.

10. Jim Francis interview, January 6, 1995.

11. WPC Personal Papers, box labeled "Surveys of Political Attitudes in Texas, January, June, September, 1978," TAMU.

12. February 1, 1978, press conference transcript. First Term, Press Relations, 40-3, TAMU.

13. George Strake interview, June 8, 1995.

14. Coverage of the primary campaign from various Texas newspapers, file box labeled 1978 Campaign Clips, February-December, in the Clements Collection, TAMU.

15. WPC Personal Papers, 1978 Campaign, 59-24, TAMU.

16. *Dallas Morning News,* April 21, 1978; *Houston Chronicle,* April 24, 1978; *Dallas Times-Herald,* April 26, 1978; *Texas Observer,* April 28, 1978.

17. Election night coverage in the *Dallas Morning News,* May 7, 1978; *Dallas Times-Herald,* May 7, 1978; *Corpus Christi Caller Times,* May 8, 1978.

18. Clements won 115,345 votes, Hutchison 38,268, and 4,790 went to a third candidate, according to election results in *Governors of Texas,* published in 1992 by the *Texas Almanac.*

19. *Dallas Times-Herald,* May 7, 1978.

20. Hill won 932,345 votes; Briscoe 753,309 votes (41.7 percent) and Smith 92,202 votes, *Governors of Texas.*

21. Associated Press, May 8, 1978.

22. *Houston Post, Houston Chronicle, Dallas Times-Herald,* May 10, 1978.

23. *Houston Post,* May 12, 1978.

24. Background on Hill from *Dallas Times-Herald,* October 22, 1978; *Austin American-Statesman,* October 22, 1978; *Houston Chronicle,* March 18, 1978, August 30, 1976, April 10, 1977; *Houston Post,* May 17, 1978; *Dallas Morning News,* May 16, 1978. (1978 Campaign Clips, Hill Research, Clements Collection, TAMU.)

25. Interviews with David Dean, April 4, 1995, and Nola Haerle Gee Fowler, March 31, 1995.

26. Tom Reed's campaign notebook; 1978 press clips, Clements Collection, TAMU.

27. *Austin American-Statesman,* June 18, 1978.

28. WPC notes on May 15, 1978, meeting with Connally, WPC Personal Papers, 1978 Campaign Files, 59-24, TAMU.

29. Reed interview, Reed campaign files, Healsburg, California.

30. *Dallas Times-Herald,* June 18, 1978.

31. George Bayoud interview, April 7, 1995.

32. *Austin American-Statesman,* June 24, 1978; *Houston Post,* June 23, 1978.

33. Dary Stone interview, April 5, 1995.

34. *Austin American-Statesman,* July 2, 1978.

35. Stone interview.

36. George Steffes interview, March 15, 1978.

37. *Dallas Morning News,* August 28, 1978.

38. *Dallas Times-Herald,* September 20, 1978.

39. *Houston Chronicle,* September 24, 1978.

40. John Hill interview, June 21, 1995.

41. Clements' Policy Statements, Tom Reed campaign files.

42. Tom Reed's campaign notebook.

43. *Dallas Morning News,* September 13, 1978.

44. *Austin American-Statesman,* September 13, 1978. Bayoud interview.

45. *Houston Chronicle,* October 26, 1978; *Dallas Times-Herald,* October 26, 1978. Tom Reed's campaign notebook details the issue of the week in the fall campaign.

46. *Austin American-Statesman,* October 22, 1978.

47. Videotapes of commercials, 1978 campaign files, Clements Collection, TAMU.

48. William Broyles, *Texas Monthly*, December 1978.

49. *Dallas Times-Herald*, October 22, 1978. (There are repeated references in the press coverage of the 1978 campaign about Clements' father going broke on the family farm in Forney during the depression. These accounts are incorrect. Perry Clements was working in Dallas when he lost his job during the depression. William P. Clements, Jr., began acquiring property in Forney in the 1950s.)

50. *Dallas Times-Herald*, September 28, 1978; *Dallas Morning News*, October 16, 1978.

51. *Dallas Times-Herald*, September 28, 1978.

52. *Dallas Morning News, Dallas Times-Herald, Austin American-Statesman*, October 22, 1978, *Houston Chronicle*, October 24, 1978.

53. *Austin American-Statesman*, October 25, 1978; *Fort Worth Star-Telegram*, October 29, 1978.

54. *Austin American-Statesman*, October 29, 1978; *Dallas Morning News*, October 31, 1978. Charles Deaton, "How Clements Did It," in William Earl Maxwell et al, *Texas Politics Today*, 2nd ed., 255-256.

55. Hill interview.

56. *Houston Post*, October 27, 1978. (George McGovern was the 1972 Democratic presidential nominee; Ralph Yarborough a former U.S. senator from Texas; and Frances Farenthold ran for the Democratic gubernatorial nomination against Dolph Briscoe in 1972.) *Dallas Morning News*, October 29, 1978.

57. *Dallas Morning News*, October 29, 1978.

58. *Houston Chronicle*, October 27, 1978; *Dallas Times-Herald*, November 8, 1978. Hill interview.

59. Tom Reed's "Post Mortem" on the 1978 election, Reed files.

60. Strake interview.

61. Knaggs, *Two-Party Texas*, 229.

62. Official election results are Clements, 1,183,828, Hill 1,166,919, according to Kingston et al, *A Political History of Texas*.

63. Knaggs, *Two-Party Texas*, 225.

64. Nola Haerle Gee Fowler interview.

65. Deaton, "How Clements Did It," in Maxwell et al, *Texas Politics Today*. (According to Deaton, David Janison of Los Angeles helped produce the *Texas Spectator*.)

Chapter 12:   First Term

1. Steffes interview.

2. Inauguration details from the *Washington Star, Austin American-Statesman*, January 17, 1979; the *Dallas Morning News*, January 17, 1979, January 21, 1979.

3. David Dean interview, April 4, 1995.

4. George Kuempel, *Dallas Morning News*, January 8, 1979.

5. Strake edged out James A. "Jim" Baker III, unsuccessful candidate for state attorney general in 1978. Baker went on to become U.S. secretary of state.

6. Jim Kaster interview, May 8, 1995.

7. George Christian interview, July 12, 1995.

8. WPC inaugural address, 1979, Press Relations, First Term, Box 30, TAMU.

9. *Austin American-Statesman, Fort Worth Star-Telegram*, January 17, 1979.

10. WPC interview, April 24, 1995.

11. *Ibid.*

12. Billy Clayton interview, September 13, 1994.

13. Various press clippings, May 19-25, 1979; Governor's office press release, May 22, 1979; Kent Biffle, "Legislators Live Down to Reputation," *Dallas Morning News*, June 17, 1990.

14. Sam Kinch, Jr., interview, September 13, 1994.

15. *Houston Chronicle*, January 12, 1987, May 16, 1979; Scott Bennett, "Clements' First 200 Days," *Texas Business*, August 1979.

16. May 23, 1979, statement by John Bryant, Governor's Press Office files, 14-64, TAMU.

17. Bennett, "Clements' First 200 days"; Governor's office press releases, April 16, 1979, May 13, 1979, PR 17-82, TAMU.

18. Doug Brown interview, May 5, 1995.

19. Bennett, "Clements' First 200 Days"; *Dallas Morning News*, June 1979.

20. Governor's office press release, May 28, 1979, PR files, TAMU.

21. Legislative accomplishments, failures from the *Dallas Morning News*, May 28, 1979; *Houston Chronicle*, May 29, 1979; *Texas Business*, August 1979; Staff memo from Jim Kaster files, Legis. 9-1, TAMU.

22. *Dallas Times-Herald*, May 20, 1979.

23. Kaster interview.

24. In 1969, Gov. Smith vetoed the entire second year of the biennial budget and called lawmakers back to write reduced appropriations for the second year.

25. *San Antonio Express-News, Fort Worth Star-Telegram*, June 16, 1979.

26. Paul Wrotenbery interview, May 8, 1995.

27. *Dallas Morning News*, June 23, 1979, September 1, 1979.

28. WPC interview, April 24, 1995.

29. July 17, 1979, press release by Henson, Hopkins & Shipley of Austin, PR 16-139; May 7, 1979, Thomas C. Reed remarks, PR 16-140, TAMU.

30. George Rodrigue, "Clements Plays for High Stakes," *D Magazine*, November 1982.

31. Morehead, *50 Years in Texas Politics*, 213, 278-279.

32. Kinch interview.

33. *Dallas Morning News*, April 13, 1978, April 15, 1979.

34. Jon Ford interview, September 13, 1994.

35. Kinch interview.

36. Wrotenbery interview.

37. Governor's Report on the Texas State Government Effectiveness Program, December 17, 1980.

38. Christian interview.

39. Wrotenbery interview.

40. *Austin American-Statesman*, June 19, 1979.

41. Ed Vetter interview, June 27, 1995.

42. *Dallas Morning News*, February 28, 1979.

43. Vetter interview.

44. Ford interview.

45. *Austin American-Statesman, Dallas Morning News, Houston Post, San Antonio Express-News*, August 11, 1979.

46. *Dallas Morning News, Houston Post,* August 20, 1979; Allen B. Clark memo, August 24, 1979, WPC state papers, Administration 4-41, TAMU.

47. *Dallas Morning News,* August 22, 1979.

48. *Brownsville Herald,* September 6, 1979.

49. *Dallas Morning News,* August 28, 1979, September 1, 1979, September, 28, 1979.

50. Associated Press, August 21, 1979.

51. Ixtoc correspondence, WPC state papers, Admin. 13-15 and 23-9, TAMU.

52. Singerman, *An American Hero: The Red Adair Story,* 262-263; *Dallas Morning News,* May 26, 1981; *On Location,* Fall 1979; SEDCO Annual Report, 1983.

53. *Dallas Morning News,* August 31, 1979, September 1, 1979.

54. *Dallas Morning News,* October 20, 1979, November 1, 1979.

55. E. V. Niemeyer, Jr., "Texas Discovers Its Mexican Neighbors," *Rio Bravo.*

56. Governor's Mexican-American and Latin American Relations office memo on Accomplishments in International Affairs, WPC state papers, MALAR 12-8, TAMU.

57. *Austin American-Statesman,* April 3, 1980.

58. *Houston Chronicle,* March 23, 1980.

59. January 3, 1980, press conference transcript, MALAR 13-6, TAMU.

60. *Dallas Times-Herald,* June 28, 1980.

61. March 19, 1980, letter, MALAR 14-1, TAMU.

62. Chet Upham interview, June 2, 1995.

63. *Ibid.*

64. Rove interview, May 18, 1995.

65. *Dallas Morning News,* December 16, 1979.

66. *Dallas Morning News,* October 25, 1980.

67. *Houston Chronicle,* October 26, 1980.

68. WPC state papers, Admin. 1-8, TAMU.

69. Reagan, 2,510,705; Carter, 1,881,147. (John Anderson, Independent, 111,613; Ed Clark, Libertarian, 37,643.) *Texas Almanac,* 1982-1983.

Chapter 13: First Term
1. *Texas Almanac,* 1982-83.

2. Jon Ford interview, September 13, 1994.

3. Governor's Advisory Committee on Education Report, June 1980.

4. WPC State of the State Address, January 22, 1981, WPC state papers, Legislative 8-25, TAMU.

5. Staff memo from Jim Kaster files, Legislative 9-1, TAMU.

6. State of State address, January 22, 1981.

7. Bruce Gibson interview, June 9, 1993.

8. Kaster interview.

9. *Fort Worth Star-Telegram,* October 24, 1982.

10. WPC letter to Mark White, February 22, 1980, WPC state papers, Press Relations 16-48, TAMU.

11. Jim Estelle statement, February 19, 1981, PR 16-148, TAMU.

12. Governor's office press release, May 7, 1981, PR 16-131, TAMU.

13. May 7, 1981, press conference transcript, PR Box 29, TAMU.

14. Governor's veto proclamations for 1981 regular session, PR 17-88; June 18, 1981, press conference transcript, PR 29-9, TAMU.

15. Governor's Report, January 18, 1982, PR 29-65, TAMU.

16. Kaster memo on legislative achievements, Legis. 9-1; June 1, 1981, press statement, PR 16-48, TAMU.

17. Vic Arnold interview, June 1, 1995.

18. *Ibid.*

19. Texas 2000 files, PR 30, TAMU.

20. Chris Semos interview, June 19, 1995.

21. Dean interview.

22. WPC press conference, July 30, 1981, PR 29-13, TAMU.

23. *Dallas Morning News,* October 29, 1989, August 14, 1992.

24. *Fort Worth Star-Telegram,* May 3, 1981.

25. *Dallas Times-Herald,* September 16, 1979.

26. *Fort Worth Star-Telegram* series on appointments, May 3-5, 1981, Appointments and Personnel series, 13-45, TAMU.

27. June 25, 1982, WPC letter to Tom Culbertson, San Antonio, AP series, TAMU.

28. Pat Oles interview, May 8, 1995.

29. December 9, 1981, Governor's Report on the Texas State Government Effectiveness Program, PR 30, TAMU.

30. *Washington Post,* August 30, 1981; PR 16-6, TAMU.

31. *Dallas Times-Herald,* October 7, 1981; MALAR 16-4, TAMU.

32. WPC accomplishments in international affairs, MALAR 12-8, TAMU.

33. WPC press conference, September 4, 1981, PR 29-18, TAMU.

34. Rita Clements interview, May 31, 1995.

35. Notes prepared for Mrs. Clements for press tour of the Governor's Mansion, April 23, 1982.

36. Governor's office press release, March 11, 1980, PR 16-64, TAMU.

37. Rita Clements interview; Friends of the Governor's Mansion press release, March 11, 1980, PR 16-64, TAMU.

38. Rita Clements interview.

39. Main Street project files, PR 16, TAMU.

40. RCC "High Profile," *Dallas Morning News,* February 14, 1982.

Chapter 14:   1982 Campaign

1. November 16, 1981, announcement statement, State Papers, Administration 20-14, TAMU.

2. George Strake interview, June 7, 1995.

3. Allen Clark interview, April 4, 1995.

4. February 2, 1982, letter to White, State Papers, PR 16-172, TAMU.

5. February 19, 1982, White statement, PR 16-169, TAMU.

6. WPC statement March 5, 1982, PR 16-171, TAMU.

7. Spring 1982 statement by White to Mexican-American audience in Arlington, RCC files.

8. Press release, PR 15-128, TAMU.

9. *Dallas Times-Herald,* April 15, 1982.

10. "Off and Limping," *Texas Monthly,* April 1982.

11. *Dallas Times-Herald*, April 11, 1982.

12. "Off and Limping."

13. *Houston Chronicle*, May 7, 1982.

14. *Dallas Times-Herald*, May 8, 1982.

15. *Dallas Times-Herald*, May 16, 1982.

16. *Dallas Times-Herald*, May 30, 1982.

17. WPC letter to T. L. Austin, May 12, 1982, PR 16-148, TAMU.

18. Gov. Clements Committee COMMENTS, April-May, 1982, AP 13-25, TAMU.

19. Press release, PR 15-30, TAMU.

20. *Fort Worth Star-Telegram*, August 27, 1982.

21. *Fort Worth Star-Telegram, Sherman Democrat*, September 1982.

22. *D Magazine*, November 1982.

23. *Dallas Times-Herald,* September 5, 1982.

24. Tony Garrett interview, July 10, 1995.

25. *Fort Worth Star-Telegram*, October 10, 1982.

26. After the election Cryer went to work for State Treasurer Ann Richards and then become press secretary to Ms. Richards during her four-year term as governor, beginning in 1990.

27. *Texas Spectator*, September 1982.

28. *Third Coast*, January 1983.

29. Lance Tarrance interview, April 13, 1995.

30. *Ibid.*

31. *Fort Worth Star-Telegram*, September 24, 1982.

32. *Austin American-Statesman*, September 25, 1982; videotape, Amarillo debate, TAMU.

33. *Dallas Morning News*, November 7, 1982; *D Magazine*, November 1982.

34. Garrett interview.

35. *Fort Worth Star-Telegram*, October 10, 1982.

36. *Houston Chronicle*, October 12, 1982.

37. Tarrance interview.

38. *Wall Street Journal*, October 18, 1982.

39. Carole Kneeland interview, September 12, 1994.

40. *D Magazine*, November 1982.

41. *San Antonio Express News*, September 5, 1982.

42. *Houston Post*, October 23, 1982; George Strake interview, June 8, 1995.

43. *Austin American-Statesman*, October 24, 1982; *Houston Chronicle*, October 25, 1982.

44. *Dallas Morning News*, November 7, 1982.

45. Jack Rains interview, June 7, 1995.

46. Ann Quirk interview, June 6, 1995.

47. Francis interview.

48. RCC campaign files, APP 27-1, TAMU.

49. Rains interview.

50. RCC campaign files, APP. 27-1, TAMU.

51. *Ibid*

52. *San Antonio Express,* November 7, 1982.

53. Ford interview.

54. Texas Almanac's *Governors of Texas,* 1992 edition.

55. Tarrance interview.

56. Quirk interview.

57. Election night statement, November 2, 1981, PR 29-59, TAMU.

58. *Dallas Morning News,* November 9, 1982.

59. Post-election Tarrance analysis, RCC files 27-1, TAMU; *Fort Worth Star-Telegram,* November 12, 1982.

60. *Dallas Morning News,* November 5, 1992, November 9, 1992.

61. *Austin American-Statesman,* November 5, 1982.

62. *Dallas Times-Herald,* November 5, 1982.

63. *Austin American-Statesman,* November 3, 1982.

64. *Dallas Morning News,* November 5, 1982.

65. Press conference transcript, November 3, 1982, PR files, TAMU.

66. Garrett interview; *Third Coast,* January 1983.

67. Ford interview.

68. Rove interview.

69. January 4, 1983, press interview transcript, PR 29-63, TAMU; *Fort Worth Star-Telegram,* January 5, 1983.

70. *Austin American-Statesman,* December 26, 1982.

71. January 4, 1983, press interview, PR files, TAMU.

72. *Dallas Morning News,* January 1, 1983.

Chapter 15:   SEDCO Sold

1. Steve Mahood interview, February 20, 1995.

2. B. Gill Clements interview, September 1, 1994.

3. *Ibid.*

4. James Flanigan, "Why SEDCO is keeping its stiff upper lip closed," *Forbes,* September 17, 1979.

5. *Ibid.; Dallas Times-Herald,* January 7, 1978.

6. Gill Clements interview.

7. Carl Thorne interview, February 22, 1995; SEDCO, Inc. Annual Report, 1979; Yergin, *The Prize,* 681.

8. WPC Personal Papers, Box 24, TAMU.

9. Mahood interview.

10. Gill Clements interview.

11. SEDCO, Inc. Annual Report, 1982.

12. *Ibid.;* Mahood interview.

13. Gill Clements interview.

14. SEDCO, Inc. Annual Report, 1983.

15. Mahood interview.

16. Transcript of Dave McNeely interview with WPC, January 30, 1994, McNeely personal files.

17. WPC Personal Papers, Box 76. TAMU; Trigg interview.

18. WPC Personal Papers, Box 76, TAMU.

19. Gill Clements interview. Information about the original overture came from Mahood, G. Clements and WPC.

20. Mahood interview.

21. Schlumberger Limited and SEDCO, Inc. 1984. *Prospectus/Proxy Statement,* 27.

22. *Ibid.,* 59-60.

23. *Ibid.,* 27; *Dallas Morning News,* September 15, 1984.

24. SEDCO, Inc. Annual Report, 1984.

25. Bryan N. Fox, "Schlumberger Limited and SEDCO, Inc. 1984 Merger Agreement," *New Mexico Business Forum,* 29-30; *Sedco Forex Connection,* August 1992.

26. *Ibid.,* 32.

27. Thorne interview.

28. Gill Clements interview.

29. Thorne interview.

30. Mahood interview.

31. Fox, "Merger Agreement," 32.

32. *Ibid.,* 32-34.

33. Dillard Hammett statement on Schlumberger/SEDCO merger, 1987, D. Hammett personal files.

34. Thorne interview.

35. WPC Personal Papers, Box 76. TAMU; WPC interview.

Chapter 16:   1986 Campaign

1. Bayoud, Doran, Garrett interviews.

2. Boone Pickens interview, June 9, 1995.

3. Martha Weisend interview, May 18, 1995.

4. Bill Elliott interview, March 27, 1995.

5. Elliott interview, Elliott's personal Draft Clements Committee files.

6. Sam Attlesey interview, June 1, 1995.

7. Karl Rove interview, May 18, 1995.

8. Tarrance interview.

9. *Fort Worth Star-Telegram,* March 2, 1986.

10. *Dallas Times-Herald,* August 4, 1985.

11. Strake interview.

12. *Dallas Times-Herald,* August 3, 1985.

13. Bayoud interview.

14. Whitford, *A Payroll to Meet,* 145-153; *Dallas Morning News,* February 26, 1987; *Bishops' Committee Report on SMU;* WPC Personal Papers, Box 76, TAMU.

15. Reggie Bashur interview, May 8, 1995.

16. *Dallas Morning News,* July 27, 1985.

17. Rove interview.

18. 1986 campaign files, TAMU.

19. *Austin American-Statesman,* February 23, 1986.

20. *Fort Worth Star-Telegram,* March 2, 1986.

21. Scott Jones interview, May 19, 1995.

22. *Texas Monthly,* October 1986.

23. Governor's Report to the 72nd Legislature, January 1991. *Dallas Morning News,* December 31, 1986.

24. *Dallas Morning News,* December 15, 1986; *Fort Worth Star-Telegram,* January 10, 1987.

25. *San Antonio Express-News,* December 28, 1986.

26. Clements campaign press release, June 11, 1986, C.Barta files.

27. Videotapes of Clements and White commercials, 1986 campaign, TAMU.

28. *Texas Business,* August 1986.

29. Rains interview.

30. Anne Marie Kilday interview, June 1, 1995.

31. Jones interview.

32. Kilday interview.

33. Quirk interview.

34. Weisend interview.

35. Bashur interview.

36. Jones interview.

37. Kilday interview.

38. Kingston et al, *Political History of Texas,* lists official results as Clements, 1,813,779, and White, 1,584,515.

39. Texas Almanac, *Governors of Texas.*

40. John Sparks interview, November 14, 1995.

41. Whitford, *A Payroll to Meet,* 175-194; *Dallas Morning News,* January 9, 1987, February 26, 1987.

Chapter 17:   Second Term

1. *Austin American-Statesman,* January 18, 1987.

2. *Houston Chronicle,* April 12, 1987; WPC interview.

3. Various news sources, particularly the *San Antonio Express News,* December 28, 1986; *Dallas Morning News,* December 14, 15, and 31, 1986, and January 2, 1987; *Houston Post,* January 2, 1987; *Fort Worth Star-Telegram,* January 10 and 16, 1987.

4. *Houston Chronicle,* January 12, 1987; *Dallas Times-Herald,* January 18, 1987. Bill Hobby interview, June 14, 1995.

5. *Dallas Morning News,* December 30, 1986.

6. January 6, 1987 *Dallas Morning News, Austin American-Statesman, Houston Chronicle, Dallas Times-Herald.*

7. Charles Terrell interview, June 23, 1995.

8. Rider Scott interview, July 11, 1995.

9. *Houston Post,* January 29, 1987; WPC interview, April 24, 1995.

10. Hobby interview.

11. Tony Proffitt interview, September 13, 1994.

12. Reggie Bashur interview, May 8, 1995.

13. State of the State address, February 4, 1987.

14. *New York Times,* March 6, 1987; *Dallas Morning News,* February 26, 1987.

15. *Bishops' Committee Report on SMU,* 20.

16. *Ibid.,* 25-26.

17. WPC interview, May 22, 1995.

18. Transcript of Robert Riggs report, WFAA-TV, Dallas, February 25, 1987; *Dallas Morning News,* February 26, 1987.

19. Scott Bennett interview, May 16, 1995.

20. "Transcript of Clements' interview on SMU football," *Dallas Morning News,* April 1, 1987.

21. Transcript of March 3, 1987, press conference.

22. *The New York Times,* March 6, 1987; AP story, March 5, 1987.

23. Scott McCartney, Associated Press, March 8, 1987.

24. *Austin American-Statesman, Fort Worth Star-Telegram*, March 5, 1987.

25. *Houston Post*, March 10, 1987; Whitford, *A Payroll to Meet*, 210.

26. Transcript, March 10, 1986, press conference, Austin.

27. Dave McNeely, *Editor and Publisher*, March 1987; Kinch interview.

28. *Dallas Morning News*, March 5, 1987.

29. *Dallas Times-Herald*, March 9, 1987.

30. Associated Press, March 5, 1987; *Dallas Morning News*, April 7, 1987, June 2, 1987.

31. *Houston Chronicle*, April 5, 1987, April 12, 1987; *Austin American-Statesman*, April 10, 1987; *Fort Worth Star-Telegram*, April 5, 1987; Hobby interview.

32. Michael Holmes, AP, April 12, 1987; *Houston Chronicle*, April 12, 1987.

33. *Houston Chronicle*, April 14, 1987; Associated Press, April 15, 1987, *Houston Post*, April 15, 1987.

34. *Houston Chronicle*, April 14, 1987.

35. George Bayoud interview, April 7, 1995.

36. Carole Kneeland interview, September 13, 1994.

37. Hilary Doran interview, May 8, 1995; Bashur interview.

38. *Dallas Morning News*, April 26, 1987, May 2, 1987.

39. *Dallas Times-Herald*, April 23, 1987, May 5, 1987; *Austin American-Statesman, Dallas Morning News*, May 6, 1987.

40. *Dallas Times-Herald*, April 23, 1987, May 5, 1987; *Austin American-Statesman, Dallas Morning News*, May 6, 1987.

41. *Houston Post, Dallas Morning News, Austin American-Statesman*, May 7, 1987.

42. George Strake interview, June 8, 1995.

43. *Dallas Morning News*, May 8, 1987.

44. *Austin American-Statesman, Dallas Morning News*, May 9, 1987.

45. *Houston Chronicle*, May 12, 1987; *Dallas Times-Herald*, April 20, 1987.

46. *Dallas Morning News*, May 10, 1987.

47. *Dallas Morning News*, May 31, 1987, June 4, 1987.

48. *Dallas Morning News*, June 3, 1987.

49. Kilday interview.

50. *Dallas Morning News*, June 24, 1987; *Bishops' Committee Report on SMU*.

51. WPC interview, May 22, 1995.

52. Lonnie Kliever interview, May 22, 1995.

53. Stewart interview.

54. WPC interview, May 22, 1995.

55. *Dallas Morning News*, June 21-25, 1987.

56. *Dallas Morning News*, June 24, 1987, July 1, 1987.

57. *Dallas Morning News*, July 19-22, 1987.

58. Tom Craddick interview, December 1, 1995.

59. *Dallas Morning News*, July 22-23, 1987.

60. Gib Lewis interview, June 12, 1995.

61. Bashur, Kaster, Doran interviews.

62. Texas Poll archives, February 8, 1995, Austin. The Texas Poll was conducted for Harte-Hanks Communications by Public Policy Resources Laboratory of Texas A&M University, 1984 through Spring 1994, and the Office of Survey

Research, College of Communications, University of Texas beginning in Summer 1994.

Chapter 18:   Second Term
1. *Fort Worth Star-Telegram,* January 11, 1989.
2. *Dallas Morning News,* July 20, 1988.
3. Governor's State of the State Address, January 31, 1989.
4. Cliff Johnson interview, May 18, 1995. (Clements named Bayoud secretary of state before the end of his second term, and Toomey became chief of staff.)
5. *Dallas Times-Herald,* January 12, 1989, January 30, 1989; *Dallas Morning News,* January 18-19, 1989; *Austin American-Statesman,* January 24, 1989, January 20, 1989.
6. *Dallas Times-Herald,* January 30, 1989.
7. *Fort Worth Star-Telegram,* February 3, 1989.
8. Johnson interview.
9. *Austin American-Statesman,* April 30, 1989.
10. Johnson interview; *Dallas Morning News,* February 15, 1989.
11. WPC interview, April 28, 1995. (Hobby's father, William P. Hobby, served as governor of Texas and his mother, Oveta Culp Hobby, headed the Womens' Army Corps.)
12. *Dallas Times-Herald,* April 14, 1989.
13. Johnson interview.
14. Governor's State of the State Address, January 31, 1989.
15. *Austin American-Statesman,* March 21, 1989.
16. Charles Terrell interview, June 23, 1995.
17. *Dallas Morning News,* October 20-22, 1988.
18. Terrell interview.
19. Rider Scott interview, July 11, 1995.
20. Terrell interview.
21. Scott interview; Mike Toomey interview, June 1, 1995.
22. Hill interview.
23. James Huffines interview, June 6, 1995.
24. *Austin American-Statesman,* January 30, 1989.
25. *Houston Chronicle,* January 18, 1989; *San Antonio Light,* January 20, 1989.
26. *Dallas Morning News,* February 8-9, 1989.
27. Carolyn Barta and Scott Bennett, "Clements' minority appointment record is equal to White's," *Dallas Morning News*, January 29, 1989.
28. Huffines interview.
29. Wrotenbery interview.
30. *Austin American-Statesman, The Capitol of Texas: A Legend is Reborn.*
31. Dealey Decherd Herndon interview, June 1, 1995.
32. *Ibid.*
33. *The Capitol of Texas: A Legend is Reborn.*
34. *Dallas Morning News,* April 19, 1989.
35. Herndon interview; *The Capitol of Texas.*
36. *The Capitol of Texas.*
37. Herndon interview.
38. *The Capitol of Texas.*

39. Herndon interview.

40. WPC interview, April 28, 1995.

41. Vetter interview; Rosanna Salazar interview, June 21, 1995.

42. Governor's State of the State Address; Governor's Office Report on Economic Development, TAMU.

43. Mort Meyerson interview, August 8, 1995.

44. Meyerson interview.

45. Governor's Report to the 72nd Legislature, January 1991.

46. *Ibid.*

47. *Dallas Morning News,* May 30, 1989.

48. *Dallas Morning News,* December 13, 1989, December 17, 1989.

49. Toomey interview.

50. Gib Lewis interview, June 12, 1995.

51. Bill Hobby interview, June 14, 1995.

52. Saralee Tiede interview, June 14, 1995.

53. *Dallas Morning News,* April 27, 1990, April 28, 1990.

54. *Dallas Morning News,* June 4, 1990, June 8, 1990.

55. *Dallas Morning News,* July 1, 1990.

56. Governor's Report to the 72nd Legislature, January 1991.

Chapter 19:   After Governor

1. Rider Scott interview, July 11, 1995.

2. WPC interview, September 27, 1994; Bob Chappell interview, September 27, 1994;

3. Kaster interview.

4. WPC interview, September 27, 1994.

5. WPC interview, May 24, 1995.

6. *Ibid.*

7. Cliff Johnson interview, May 18, 1995.

8. George W. Bush interview, May 8, 1995.

9. *Dallas Morning News,* January 17, 1995.

Chapter 20:   Legacies

1. Election figures are from *Governors of Texas, 1992 Edition,* prepared by the *Texas Almanac.*

2. *Ibid.*

3. Kinch interview.

4. George Shipley interview, July 13, 1995.

5. *Dallas Morning News,* January 10, 1995.

6. *Dallas Morning News,* January 12, 1996, January 14, 1996; *Houston Chronicle,* January 14, 1996.

7. Scott interview.

8. *Dallas Morning News,* November 10, 1994, January 10, 1995.

9. Carolyn Barta, "Yellow dog finally dies," *Dallas Morning News,* November 13, 1994; Sam Attlesey, "Where's the party?" *Dallas Morning News,* January 10, 1995.

10. *Ibid.*

11. *Dallas Morning News,* June 2, 1995.

12. *Dallas Morning News*, November 30, 1995.

13. Rove interview.

14. Tarrance interview.

15. Herndon interview.

16. Christian interview.

17. Craddick interview.

18. Bashur interview.

19. Rove interview.

20. Bush interview.

21. *Dallas Morning News*, October 14, 1990; *Austin American-Statesman*, December 23, 1990.

22. Bayoud interview.

23. *Governors of Texas.*

24. Mike Toomey interview, June 1, 1995.

25. Reggie Bashur interview, May 8, 1995.

26. Rudy Cisneros interview, September 14, 1994.

27. *Dallas Morning News*, October 14, 1989; Rider Scott interview, July 11, 1995.

28. Toomey interview; Johnson interview.

29. Huffines interview.

30. Fred Meyer interview, January 30, 1995.

31. WPC interview, April 28, 1995.

32. Sayer, "History of SEDCO."

33. WPC interview, April 28, 1995.

34. *Ibid.*

35. Scott Bennett, "Clements will be missed," *Dallas Morning News*, January 10, 1991.

36. Lewis interview.

37. Hobby interview.

38. WPC interview, April 28, 1995.

39. Doran interview.

40. Anne Marie Kilday interview, June 1, 1995.

41. WPC interview, April 28, 1995.

42. Kenneth A. Pye letter to Donald N. Williams, February 25, 1992; SMU correspondence files.

43. Letter from A. Kenneth Pye to Ann Graeber, February 28, 1992, SMU correspondence files.

44. *Dallas Morning News*, March 17, 1996.

45. Rove interview.

46. O'Donnell interview.

Bibliography

BOOKS

Acheson, Sam. *Dallas Yesterday*. Dallas: Southern Methodist University Press, 1977.

Aitken, Jonathan. *Nixon, A Life*. Washington, D.C.: Regnery Publishing, Inc., 1993.

Austin American-Statesman, The Capitol of Texas: A Legend is Reborn. Atlanta, Ga: Longstreet Press Inc., 1995.

Banks, Jimmy. *Gavels, Grit & Glory*. Burnet, Texas: Eakin Press, 1982.

———. *Money, Marbles and Chalk*. Austin: Texas Publishing Company, Inc., 1971.

Brantly, J. E. *History of Oil Well Drilling*. Houston: Gulf Publishing Co., 1971.

Clark, Allen. *Oh, God, I'm Dead*. Austin: Texas Publishers Co., 1986.

Connally, John, with Mickey Herskowitz. *In History's Shadow: An American Odyssey*. New York: Hyperion, 1993.

Dealey, Ted. *Diaper Days of Dallas*. Nashville: Abingdon Press, Nashville, 1966.

Donahue, Jackson. *Wildcatter: The Story of Michel T. Halbouty and the Search for Oil*. New York: McGraw-Hill Book Company, 1979.

Ezell, John S. *Innovations in Energy: The Story of Kerr-McGee*. Norman, Okla.: University of Oklahoma Press, 1979.

Ford, Gerald. *A Time to Heal: The Autobiography of Gerald R. Ford*. New York: Harper & Row, Publishers, 1979.

Galloway, Diane. *The Park Cities: A Photo History*. Dallas: Mercury Printing, 1989.

Galloway, Diane, and Kathy Matthews. *The Park Cities: A Walker's Guide and Brief History*. Dallas: SMU Press, 1988.

Green, George Norris. *The Establishment in Texas Politics*. Westport, Conn.: Greenwood Press, 1979.

Highlander, Highland Park High School annual, 1934.

Hill, Margaret Hunt. *H. L. and Lyda*. Little Rock, Ark.: August House Publishers Inc., 1994.

Hodel, Donald P., and Robert Deitz. *Crisis in the Oil Patch*. Washington, D.C.: Regnery Publishing, Inc., 1994.

Hurt, Harry III. *Texas Rich: The Hunt Dynasty from the early Oil Days through the Silver Crash*. New York: W. W. Norton & Co., 1982.

Isaacson, Walter. *Kissinger: A Biography*. New York: Simon & Schuster, 1992.

Jones, Eugene W., and Joe E. Ericson, Lyle C. Brown and Robert S. Trotter Jr. *Practicing Texas Politics, 7th Ed.* Boston: Houghton Mifflin Company, 1989.

Kalb, Marvin, and Bernard Kalb. *Kissinger*. Boston-Toronto: Little, Brown and Co., 1974.

Kinch, Sam, and Stuart Long. *Allan Shivers: The Pied Piper of Texas Politics*. Austin: Shoal Creek Publishers, Inc., 1973.

Kingston, Mike. *A Concise History of Texas*. Houston: Gulf Publishing Co., 1988.

Kingston, Mike, Sam Attlesey, and Mary G. Crawford. *The Texas Almanac's Political History of Texas*. Austin, Texas: Eakin Press, 1992.

Kissinger, Henry. *Years of Upheaval*. Boston-Toronto: Little, Brown and Co., 1982.

Knaggs, John. *Two-Party Texas: The John Tower Era 1961-1984*. Austin, Texas: Eakin Press 1986.

LaRue, Frank. *Have I Told You This One?* Athens, Texas: n.p., 1980.

Lindsley, Philip. *A History of Greater Dallas and Vicinity*. Vol. I. Chicago: The Lewis Publishing Co., 1909.

Lynch, Gerald. *Roughnecks, Drillers, and Tool Pushers: Thirty-three Years in the Oil Fields*. Austin, Texas: University of Texas Press, 1987.

Maxwell, William Earl. *Texas Politics Today*. St. Paul, Minn.: West Publishing Company, 1981.

McCleskey, Clifton, Allan K. Butcher, Daniel E. Farlow, and J. Pat Stephens. *The Government and Politics of Texas*. 7th ed. Boston: Little, Brown and Company, 1982.

McDonald, William Lloyd. *Dallas Rediscovered: A Photographic Chronicle of Urban Expansion 1870-1925*. Dallas: The Dallas Historical Society, 1978.

Michener, James A. *The Eagle and the Raven*. Austin: State House Press, 1990.

Morehead, Richard. *50 Years in Texas Politics*. Austin, Texas: Eakin Press, 1982.

Nash, Robert, and Peggy Nichols Nash. *"Mr. McCamey": Claude W. Brown, The Life of a Texas Oilman*. Austin, Texas: Eakin Press, 1994.

Payne, Darwin. *Big D: Triumphs and Troubles of an American Supercity in the 20th Century*. Dallas: Three Forks Press, 1994.

Pickens, T. Boone, Jr. *Boone*. Boston: Houghton Mifflin Company, 1987.

Presley, James. *Never In Doubt: A History of Delta Drilling Company*. Houston: Gulf Publishing Co., 1981.

Rundell, Walter, Jr. *Early Texas Oil: A Photographic History, 1866-1936*. College Station, Texas: Texas A&M University Press, 1977.

Schoenebaum, Eleanora W. *Profiles of An Era, The Nixon-Ford Years*. New York: Harcourt Brace Jovanovich, 1979.

Shropshire, Mike, and Frank Schaefer. *The Thorny Rose of Texas*. New York: Birch Lane Press, Carol Publishing Group, 1994.

Singerman, Philip. *An American Hero: The Red Adair Story*. Boston: Little, Brown and Company, 1990.

Soukup, James R., Clifton McCleskey, and Harry Holloway. *Party and Factional Division in Texas*. Austin, Texas: University of Texas Press, 1964.

Stoltz, Jack. *Terrell, Texas 1873-1973: From Open Country to Modern City*. San Antonio, Texas: The Naylor Company, 1973.

Swansbrough, Robert H., and David M. Brodsky. *The South's New Politics: Realignment and Dealignment*. Columbia, S.C.: University of South Carolina Press, 1988.

Texas Almanac, (volumes) 1968-69 (through) 1994-95. Dallas: A.H. Belo Corp.

Tinkle, Lon. *Mr. D: A Biography of Everette Lee DeGolyer*. Boston: Little, Brown and Company, 1970.

Van Buren, Ernestine Orrick. *Clint: Clinton Williams Murchison, a Biography*. Austin, Texas: Eakin Press, 1986.

Wead, Doug. *George Bush Man of Integrity*. Eugene, Ore.: Harvest House Publishers, 1988.

Webb, Walter P., et al, eds. *The Handbook of Texas.* Austin: Texas State Historial Association, 1952.

Whitford, David. *A Payroll to Meet*. New York: Macmillan Publishing Co., 1989.

Wills, Garry. *Certain Trumpets: The Call of Leaders*. New York: Simon & Schuster, 1994.

Wolfe, Jane. *The Murchisons: The Rise and Fall of a Texas Dynasty*. New York: St. Martin's Press, 1989.

Woodward, Bob, and Carl Bernstein. *The Final Days*. New York: Avon Books, 1976.

Yergin, Daniel. *The Prize: The Epic Quest For Oil, Money and Power*. New York: Touchstone, Simon & Schuster Inc., 1991, 1992.

Zumwalt, Elmo R., Jr. *On Watch*. New York: Quadrangle/The New York Times Book Co., Inc., 1976.

MAGAZINE ARTICLES, NOTEWORTHY NEWSPAPER ARTICLES

"A Mustang in the Mansion." *The Mustang*, SMU Alumni Association Magazine, Winter 1979.

Bennett, Scott. "Clements' First 200 Days." *Texas Business*, August 1979.

Berry, Laurie. "The Final Days." *Third Coast* (Austin: Third Coast Media), January 1983 (Vol. 2, No. 6).

Blow, Steve. "The Ultras." *Dallas Morning News* commemorative section, "November 22: Twenty Years Later," November 20, 1983.

Calhoun, Ron. "Clements' decision to run." *Dallas Times-Herald*, November 14, 1977, p. 2-C.

Cox, Louis. "Highlanders Seek Initial Victory in Friday Night Game." *Dallas Times-Herald*.

Elliott, Karen. "Life is very different in the capital." *Dallas Morning News*, January 20, 1974.

Erwin, Dorothie. "Victorian Flavor: Old Cumberland School to Be Office," *The Dallas Morning News*, May 23, 1970, p. 1-AA.

Flanigan, James. "Why SEDCO is keeping its stiff upper lip closed." *Forbes Magazine*, September 17, 1979.

Ford, Jon. "Clements pursues new goal with enthusiasm, dedication." *Austin American-Statesman*, October 29, 1978.

Greenberg, Nicki Finke. Rita Clements High Profile. *Dallas Morning News*, February 14, 1982.

Loe, Victoria. "Governor's races cutting it closer than they once did." *Dallas Morning News*, November 8, 1994, p. 13-A.

McNeely, Dave. "A Man of Promises." *Houston City Magazine*, September 1982.

Merwin, John. "The Abrasive Candidacy of Bill Clements." *D Magazine*, March 1978, pp. 106-109, 154-155.

"Off and Limping." *Texas Monthly*, April 1982.

"Power in Dallas: Who holds the cards?" *D Magazine*, October 1974, Vol. 1, No. 1, pp. 47-55.

Rodrique, George. "Clements Plays for High Stakes." *D Magazine*, November 1982.

Sayer, Nancy. "History of SEDCO." *Connection*, a magazine for Sedco Forex employees, Special Anniversary Issue, Cedex, France, August 1992.

Tomsho, Robert. "Bill Clements." *The Dallas Morning News*, High Profile, August 23, 1984, p. 1-G.

NEWSPAPERS

Austin American-Statesman
Dallas Morning News
Dallas Times-Herald
Forney Messenger
Fort Worth Star-Telegram
Houston Chronicle
Houston Post
Los Angeles Times
New York Times
San Antonio Express-News
San Antonio Light
SMU Campus
Washington Post
Washington Star & News

PUBLICATIONS

Allyn, Robert. "How Dallas Switched Parties." Master's thesis, Southern Methodist University, December 7, 1983.

The Bishops' Committee Report on SMU. Report to the Board of Trustees of Southern Methodist University from the Special Commitee of Bishops of the South Central Jurisdiction of the United Methodist Church, June 19, 1987.

Congressional Record. Senate proceedings, January 23, 1973.

David, Heather. *Sea Power Magazine*, the offical publication of the Navy League, November 1973.

Fox, Bryan N. "Schlumberger Limited and SEDCO Inc. 1984 Merger Agreement," *New Mexico Business Forum*, the Journal of the College of Business Administration & Economics, Volume 8:1, Spring 1990, published by New Mexico State University, Las Cruces, N.M.

Hayes, Capt. Bradd C., and Cmdr. Douglas V. Smith, eds. (Dr. Thomas C. Hone, Cmdr. Gregory A. Engle, Cmdr. Roger C. Easton, Jr., contributors). "The Politics of Naval Innovation," Strategic Research Department Research Report 4-94, U.S. Naval War College, Newport, R.I., August 1, 1994.

Malek, Frederic V. "Mr. Executive Goes to Washington." *Harvard Business Review*, September-October 1972.

Marine Science Affairs, National Council on Marine Resources and Engineering Development, U.S. Printing Office, Washington, D.C.

Niemeyer, E. V., Jr. "Texas Discovers Its Mexican Neighbors: Border-State Governmental Relations, 1978-1991." *Rio Bravo,* A Journal of Research and Issues, Volume II:1, Fall 1992, published by the Center for International Studies at the University of Texas-Pan American, Edinburg.

On Location. SEDCO, Inc. employee magazine, published quarterly, Fall 1973-Fall 1984.

SEDCO Co. magazine, Summer 1973.

SEDCO, Inc. Annual Reports, 1967-1984.

Select Committee on Tax Equity. *Rethinking Texas Taxes: Final Report of the Select Committee on Tax Equity.*

Southeastern Drilling Company, Inc. *Brief Historical and Operational Guide,* circa 1968.

Supplemental Statement to Report of Blue Ribbon Defense Panel, submitted to the President and the Secretary of Defense on "The Shifting Balance of Military Power," September 30, 1970.

Texas Comptroller of Public Accounts, Legislative Budget Board. *Fiscal Size Up: 1994–1995 Biennium.*

Update, newsletter for SEDCO employees, No. 3, 1977-September 1984.

CLEMENTS COLLECTION, TEXAS A&M UNIVERSITY LIBRARY

PERSONAL PAPERS, William P. Clements, Jr. (includes correspondence, SEDCO, Department of Defense, divorce, wedding, biographical materials, travel, Argentina, William Dillin, Iran, early political activities, real estate, safaris, Boy Scouts, Cumberland Hill School building, Southern Methodist University.)

PERSONAL PAPERS, William P. Clements, Jr., uncatalogued boxes on 1978 gubernatorial campaign: Surveys of Political Attitudes in Texas, January-June, September 1978; Press Clips, February-December 1978. Videotapes, 1978 campaign.

GUBERNATORIAL PAPERS, FIRST TERM. (Series titled Administration, Advisory Committee on Education, Appointments and Personnel, General Counsel, Governor's Budget and Planning Office, Governor's Handicapped, Legislative, Mexico and Latin American Relations, Press Office, Refugee Resettlement, Scheduling, Staff Services, Task Forces and Volunteer Services.)

GUBERNATORIAL PAPERS, SECOND TERM. (Series titled Appointees, Central Administrative Services, General Counsel, Legislative, Press Office, Scheduling Office, State Development.)

PERSONAL PAPERS, Rita Crocker Clements.

OTHER PERSONAL FILES
Dillard Hammett personal files.
Dave McNeely personal files.
William P. Clements, Jr., personal files, minutes of Deputy Secretary of Defense meetings.
Tom Reed personal files, 1978 campaign.

SPEECHES
Clements, William P., Jr. Highland Park High School commencement, May 31, 1984, Personal Papers, Box 23-File 28, Texas A&M University Library.
———. Rotary Club of Houston, April 12, 1973, Personal Papers, DOD Box 70, Texas A&M University Library.
———. Dallas Council on World Affairs, Personal Papers, Box 1, Texas A&M University Library.
———. Keel Laying of the USS Texas, Newport News, Va., August 18, 1973, DOD Box 70, Texas A&M University Library.
———. Salute to Vietnam Veterans Speech, DOD Box 70, Texas A&M University Library.

VIDEOTAPES
Press Club of Dallas Roast, 1989, produced for the Press Club of Dallas by Weekly/Gray/McKinney Inc.
Campaign commercials, 1978, 1982, 1986, Clements Collection, Texas A&M University.

INTERVIEWS
(All interviews were conducted in Dallas unless otherwise noted)

William P. Clements, Jr., April 8, 1984, College Station; August 26-28, 1994, Taos, N.M.; September 27, 1994, Forney; October 26, 1994, Dallas; December 8, 1994, Dallas; January 19, 1995, Dallas; January 30, 1995, Dallas; February 17, 1995, College Station; April 24, 1995, Dallas; April 28, 1995, Dallas; May 22, 1995, Dallas; May 23, 1995, Kaufman and Athens; September 25, 1995, Dallas; November 2, 1995, Dallas.
George Bayoud, April 19, 1994, April 7, 1995.
Spencer Taylor, May 20, 1994, May 27, 1994, January 30, 1995.
Jim Oberwetter, May 24, 1994.
Rita Clements, May 25, 1994, May 31, 1995.
John Rhea, Jr., August 11, 1994.
Peter O'Donnell, August 15, 1994.
Paul Eggers, August 16, 1994.
Jerry Cunningham, August 31, 1994, February 3, 1995.
Gill Clements, September 1, 1994.
Charles Trigg, September 12, 1994, San Angelo, Texas.
Dave McNeely, September 12-14, 1994, Austin.
Carole Kneeland, September 12-14, 1994, Austin.
Jon Ford, September 13, 1994, Austin.
John Knaggs, September 13, 1994, Austin.
Billy Clayton, September 13, 1994, Austin.

Sam Kinch, Jr., September 13, 1994, Austin.
Tony Proffitt, September 13, 1994, Austin.
Rudy Cisneros, September 14, 1994, Austin.
Bill Miller, September 14, 1994, Austin.
Tom Rhodes, September 19, 1994.
Harrison Schmitt, September 20, 1994, telephone interview, Albuquerque, N.M.
Dr. James Brooks, September 23, 1994, telephone interview.
Bob Chappell and Larry Shaw, September 27, 1994, Forney.
Mary Ann Thomasson Todd, September 29, 1994.
Mary Jane Chambers Honea, October 20, 1994.
Mary Jane Chambers Honea, Philip Lindsley, Helen Davis Lindsley, Tom Rose, Betty Skillern Baird, Randolph McCall, Jerry Cunningham, joint interview, October 26, 1994
Kenneth Carr, October 31, 1994, Washington D.C.
Lloyd Bentsen, November 1, 1994, Washington D.C.
G. Robert Hillman, November 1, 1994, Washington D.C.
Thomas Moorer, November 2, 1994, Washington D.C.
John Jones, November 3, 1994, Washington D.C.
Brent Scowcroft, November 3, 1994, Washington D.C.
Lawrence Eagleburger, November 3, 1994, Washington D.C.
George Bush, November 15, 1994, Houston.
Tom Reed, November 17, 1994, telephone interview, San Francisco, Calif.
Scott Bennett, November 22, 1994.
Jim Tarr, November 23, 1994.
Nancy Clements Seay, December 15, 1994.
Kenton Chickering, January 5, 1995, telephone interview.
H. W. Solsbery, January 5, 1995, telephone interview, San Antonio.
Otis Conatser, January 6, 1995, telephone interview.
Jim Francis, January 6, 1995.
Janie Harris Hollingsworth, January 9, 1995, San Antonio.
Fred Meyer, January 30, 1995.
Shelma Ahrens, February 1, 1995.
Bill Armentrout, February 2, 1995, telephone interview.
Edwin L. Cox, February 6, 1995.
Dillard Hammett, February 7, 1995.
Robert Stewart, February 8, 1995.
Jack Hammack, February 8, 1995.
Edwin J. "Jack" Smith, February 13, 1995.
Linda Montgomery, February 14, 1995, telephone interview, Fort Worth.
Steve Mahood, February 20, 1995.
Carl Thorne, February 22, 1995.
William G. "Bobby" Cox, February 27, 1995.
Tom Pauken, March 3, 1995, telephone interview.
Scott Caven, March 6, 1995, telephone interview, Houston.
Tom Reed, March 15, 1995, Healdsburg, Calif.
George Steffes, March 15, 1995, Healdsburg, Calif.
William M. "Bill" Martinovich, March 17, 1995, Auburn, Calif.
Bill Elliott, March 27, 1995.

Nola Haerle Fowler, March 31, 1995, Austin.
Allen Clark, April 4, 1995.
David Dean, April 4, 1995.
Dary Stone, April 5, 1995.
Lance Tarrance, College Station, April 13, 1995.
Ray Hutchison, April 24, 1995.
Doug Brown, May 5, 1995.
Reggie Bashur, May 8, 1995, Austin.
Gov. George W. Bush, May 8, 1995, Austin.
Jim Kaster, May 8, 1995, Austin.
Paul Wrotenbery, May 8, 1995, Austin.
Pat Oles, May 8, 1995, Austin.
Hilary Doran, May 8, 1995, Austin.
Cliff Johnson, May 18, 1995, Austin.
Karl Rove, May 18, 1995, Austin.
Scott Jones, May 19, 1995.
Martha Weisend, May 19, 1995.
Lonnie Kliever, May 22, 1995.
Dr. Vic Arnold, June 1, 1995, Austin.
Dealey Herndon, June 1, 1995, Austin.
Mike Toomey, June 1, 1995, Austin.
Sam Attlesey, June 1, 1995, Austin.
Anne Marie Kilday, June 1, 1995, Austin.
Chet Upham, June 2, 1995, Mineral Wells.
William Solomon, June 5, 1995.
Ann Quirk, June 6, 1995, Austin.
James Huffines, June 5, 1995, Austin.
Jack Rains, June 7, 1995, Houston.
George Strake, Jr., June 7, 1995, Houston.
Boone Pickens, June 8, 1995.
Gib Lewis, June 12, 1995, Fort Worth.
Margaret Solomon, June 12, 1995.
Bill Hobby, June 14, 1995, Austin.
Saralee Tiede, June 14, 1995, Austin.
Chris Semos, June 19, 1995.
Kent Hance, June 21, 1995, Austin.
John Hill, June 21, 1995, Austin.
Rosanna Salazar, June 21, 1995, Austin.
Charles Terrell, June 23, 1995.
Ed Vetter, June 27, 1995.
Tony Garrett, July 10, 1995.
Rider Scott, July 11, 1995.
Richard Rubottom, July 11, 1995.
George Christian, July 12, 1995, Austin.
George Shipley, July 13, 1995, Austin.
Mort Myerson, August 8, 1995.
John Sparks, November 14, 1995.
Tom Craddick, Midland, telephone interview, December 1, 1995.

Index

Navy-Air Force Joint Cruise Missile
    Project Office, 175-176
NBC, 291
NCAA, 305, 322, 335, 343-349, 352,
    358, 359
Nelson, Gaylord, 133
    Ken, 316
Netherlands Offshore Company
    (OFFNETH), 86
Neutral Zone, 66, 68
New Kent County, Virginia, 17
New York Times, 129, 131, 154, 181,
    347
Nightline, 347
"96" rigs, 51-52, 56-57
Nixon, Richard, 9, 101, 115, 117-121,
    125, 128-130, 133, 136, 145, 148,
    150, 151, 153-156, 160, 165, 166,
    169, 210, 221, 411-412
Nolan, Joe, 206
no-pass, no-play, 326, 328, 330-331,
    342
Norman Wells field, 42
North American Air Defense Com-
    mand (NORAD), 180
North American Free Trade Agree-
    ment, 265
North Dallas, 19
North Korea, 178
Northrop Corporation, 173
North Sea, 85-88, 94, 95, 96, 298, 300
North Texas State University, 262
Northwood Country Club, 77
Nova Scotia, 84
Nuevo Leon, Mexico, 383
Nunley, Red, 303

O
Oak Cliff, 19
Oak Lawn, 19
Oakley, Keith, 367, 368
Occidental, 100, 304
Ocean Drilling Program, 307-308
October War of 1973, 148-150
Odeco, 87, 96, 98
Odessa, Texas, 208
O'Donnell, Edith, 163
    Peter, 8-9, 10-11, 81, 108, 115, 116-
    117, 118, 136, 139, 141, 161, 163,

188, 191, 193, 199, 201, 216, 245,
    315, 318, 325, 329, 353, 354, 417
O'Donnell Foundation, 163
offshore drilling, 56, 57, 60, 63, 80-
    100, 304, 308, 312
oil crisis, 4, 338
oil embargo, 4, 62, 151-153, 225
Oil Exchange, 19
oil prices, 151-153, 278, 299, 300, 304,
    307, 310, 329, 337, 338, 364
oil production in: Argentina, 69-74;
    Borneo, 83; Brunei, 93; free
    world, 99, 144; Iran, 65, 299-300;
    Kuwait, 9, 68, 300; Libya, 97;
    Middle East, xiv; Nigeria, 96;
    Saudi Arabia, 63, 90, 149, 151-
    153; Texas, xiv, 18, 45, 225, 237-
    238, 251; Trinidad, 57-58, 61, 63;
    Tunisia, 68; U.S., 42, 99
Oil Service Company of Iran, 299
oil spill emergencies, 237-241
Oil Well Supply, 37, 39, 46, 47, 49, 50,
    51-52, 54-55, 60, 65
Okotoks, Alberta, 42
Oles, Pat, 221, 263, 313
Oman, sultan of, 152
O'Neall, Charles F., 69, 73
OPEC, 62, 151-153, 338
Operation Desert Storm, 171
Organization of Petroleum Exporting
    Countries, (OPEC), xiv
Oriental Hotel, 17
Osborne, Burl, 345-346
Owen, George, 344
Owen Laboratories, 220

P
Padre Island, 239
Pahlavi, Reza, 65, 152, 153, 172, 247,
    299, 300
Pahlavi Foundation, 299
Palestine, Texas, 49, 371
Palm Desert, California, 158
Pampa, Texas, 40
Panama Canal, 193, 194, 196
Pan American International Oil
    Company, 68
Parker, Carl, 339, 341, 350
    Henry Lee, 334